MONEY, TRADE, AND POWER

The Carolina Lowcountry and the Atlantic World

Sponsored by the Carolina Lowcountry and Atlantic World Program of the College of Charleston

MONEY, TRADE, AND POWER

The Evolution of Colonial South Carolina's Plantation Society

Edited by
Jack P. Greene, Rosemary Brana-Shute, and
Randy J. Sparks

UNIVERSITY OF SOUTH CAROLINA PRESS

UNIVERSITY OF SOUTH CAROLINA **BICENTENNIAL**

© 2001 University of South Carolina

Published in Columbia, South Carolina, by the
University of South Carolina Press

Manufactured in the United States of America

05 04 03 02 01   5 4 3 2 1

Library of Congress Cataloging-in-Publication Data

Money, trade, and power : the evolution of colonial South Carolina's
  plantation society / edited by Jack P. Greene, Rosemary Brana-Shute,
  and Randy J. Sparks.
    p. cm. — (The Carolina lowcountry and the Atlantic world)
  Includes bibliographical references and index.
  ISBN 1-57003-374-9
  1. South Carolina—Economic conditions. 2. South Carolina—Social
conditions. 3. Plantation life—South Carolina. 4. South Carolina—
History—Colonial period, ca. 1600–1775. I. Greene, Jack P. II. Brana-
Shute, Rosemary, 1944– III. Sparks, Randy J. IV. Series.
HC107.S7 M56 2001
306.3'49—dc21   00-012601

Contents

Colonial South Carolina
An Introduction
JACK P. GREENE

The past generation has witnessed a profound revolution in the study of colonial British American history. From a low point in the 1940s and 1950s, it began in the 1960s to attract widespread interest among younger scholars. Inspired by new developments in early modern historical studies, especially in France and Great Britain, an increasing number of scholars in the United States and elsewhere turned their attention to colonial studies. Focusing first on intellectual and political and then on social, economic, and cultural history, they produced an enormous and proliferating body of literature that significantly enhanced and transformed historical understanding of the early modern overseas Anglophone world.

In particular, they identified six discrete regions, each with its own patterns of socioeconomic and cultural life: the Chesapeake, composed of Virginia, Maryland, and northern North Carolina; New England, consisting of Massachusetts, Connecticut, Rhode Island, New Hampshire, and Nova Scotia; the West Indies, including Barbados, the Leeward Island colonies of Antigua, Montserrat, Nevis, and St. Kitts, Jamaica, the Windward Island colonies of the Dominica, Granada, St. Vincent, Tobago, and the Virgin Islands; the Atlantic islands, composed of Bermuda and the Bahamas; the Middle Colonies, consisting of New York, New Jersey, Pennsylvania, and Delaware; and the Lower South, including South Carolina, southern North Carolina, Georgia, East Florida and West Florida.

Beginning first with New England, where the older historiography was most dense and the intellectual history particularly rich, historians soon developed an interest in the Chesapeake, where they quickly learned to put existing records to the service of the new social history. Already by the mid-1970s, the historiography of these two regions, the oldest of the continental regions of colonial British America, had achieved a high degree of analytical density and intellectual sophistication, and scholars were beginning to turn their attention to the West Indies and to newer areas of settlement on the continent. By the early 1980s when a group of historians assembled at a conference in Oxford to produce an assessment of the bewildering variety of new literature on colonial British American history, the Middle Colonies had already attracted considerable scholarly attention.

Despite the fact that it was, by the middle decades of the eighteenth century, one of the most dynamic areas of demographic, economic, and territorial growth in the whole of colonial British America, the Lower South attracted far less interest. Several important books had begun to chart the social history of the region. These included Harry Roy Merrens's comprehensive *Colonial North Carolina in the Eighteenth Century: A Study in Historical Geography*,[1] Converse D. Clowse's careful reconstruction of the *Economic Beginnings in Colonial South Carolina, 1670–1730*,[2] Peter H. Wood's pioneering discussion of the African foundations of South Carolina in *Black Majority: Negroes in Colonial South Carolina from 1670 through the Stono Rebellion*,[3] and Daniel C. Littlefield's imaginative *Rice and Slaves: Ethnicity and the Slave Trade in Colonial South Carolina*.[4] In 1983, Robert M. Weir produced a superb synthesis of existing monographic and periodical literature, *Colonial South Carolina: A History*.[5]

Yet, in comparison with other regions, the study of the Lower South elicited little interest. Important dissertations by, among others, Richard Waterhouse,[6] Philip D. Morgan,[7] Diane Sydenham,[8] and George D. Terry[9] remained unpublished. In *Colonial British America: Essays in the New History of the Early Modern Era*, the volume of essays that emanated from the Oxford conference, even the West Indian colonies received more attention than the Lower South. Only the small Atlantic island colonies of Bermuda and the Bahamas received less.[10] Of four synthetic works published on colonial British America during the late 1980s, only my *Pursuits of Happiness: The Social Development of Early Modern British Colonies and the Formation of American Culture*[11] tried to present a comprehensive discussion of the Lower South while Bernard Bailyn, *The Peopling of British North America: An Introduction*,[12] and D. W. Meining, *Atlantic America, 1492–1800*,[13] treated it only cursorily, and David Hackett Fischer, *Albion's Seed: Four British Folkways in America*,[14] ignored it altogether.

Since the late 1980s, this situation has improved dramatically. In particular, South Carolina, the economic and cultural center of the Lower Southern region, has been the subject of impressive monographs that have explored with sophistication and in detail many aspects of its colonial history. These include Richard Waterhouse's analysis of the formation of an elite class,[15] Peter A. Coclanis's exploration of the structure of the lowcountry economy and society,[16] James H. Merrell's study of the adaptation of the Catawba Indians to the intrusion of Europeans,[17] Rachel M. Klein's examination of the extension of African slavery into the backcountry,[18] Joyce Chaplin's study of the dynamic and innovative character of colonial lowcountry agriculture,[19] Philip D. Morgan's detailed analysis of slave culture,[20] and Robert Olwell's examination of the impact of slavery upon social and political life.[21]

These studies, all of which are outgrowths of doctoral dissertations, both represent and have helped to stimulate the development of a significant expansion of interest in the colonial Lower Southern colonies, particularly in colonial South Carolina. Over the past fifteen to twenty years, more than a score of other scholars from a wide variety of institutions, including Duke, Emory, Johns Hopkins, Maryland, Minnesota, North Carolina, Princeton, Rice, the Sorbonne, South Carolina, Tulane, William and Mary, and Wisconsin have also written doctoral dissertations on aspects of colonial South Carolina history. The intention of this volume is to highlight some of the more important findings and arguments of this growing volume of work. Together, the fifteen chapters it includes provide both a rich sample of this work and a useful introduction to many of the main themes that are emerging from it.

The first three chapters treat aspects of the formative decades in South Carolina history, from the founding of the colony in 1670 through the 1730s. In chapter 1, "Creating a Plantation Province: Proprietary Land Policies and Early Settlement Patterns," Meaghan N. Duff takes a careful and penetrating look at the shifting land policies of the Carolina proprietors. Demonstrating how the proprietors effectively used their major resource, land, to attract European immigrants and promote the establishment of a European-style social and cultural landscape in the lowcountry, she also points to the critical role of the settlers themselves in determining the character of that landscape. Bertrand Van Ruymbeke examines the early fortunes of one of the most conspicuous groups of those settlers in chapter 2, "The Huguenots of Proprietary South Carolina: Patterns of Migration and Integration." Based on a careful prosopographical analysis, his essay explores the geographic and socioeconomic origins of the Huguenot emigrants who comprised just under a fifth of first-generation settlers and shows how, with many of them migrating in family groups, they were able successfully to create in their new homes Huguenot-centered kinship networks and to construct distinctively Huguenot modes of integrating with the emerging lowcountry society. In chapter 3, "The State in the Planters' Service: Politics and the Emergence of a Plantation Economy in South Carolina," Gary L. Hewitt persuasively shows how settler and planter interests quickly came to dominate the South Carolina polity and to use state power to promote agricultural expansion, expand the money supply, and otherwise manipulate the economy in their interests.

The next three chapters deal with other aspects of the colonial South Carolina economy. In chapter 4, "The Organization of Trade and Finance in the Atlantic Economy: Britain and South Carolina, 1670–1775," R. C. Nash provides a broad overview of the South Carolina export economy, analyzing the organization of overseas trade and stressing the interdependence of trade and agriculture in the colony's economic life. Stephen G. Hardy takes a closer look at South Carolina's principal export, rice, in chapter 5, "Colonial South Carolina's Rice Industry and the Atlantic Economy: Patterns of Trade, Shipping, and Growth, 1715–1775." Challenging existing historiographical theories that explain colonial economic growth in terms of improvements in trade organization and shipping, Hardy finds that, although such changes were important before 1738, a burgeoning slave population, more intensive and productive agriculture, and an expanding market for rice among West Indian slaves and poor Europeans largely accounted for the rapid growth of the lowcountry rice industry between 1740 and 1775. In chapter 6, "Indian Traders, Charles Town, and London's Vital Links to the Interior of North America, 1717–1755," Eirlys M. Barker provides a detailed history of the Indian trade, a significant component of the colonial South Carolina economy until after the middle of the eighteenth century. She both analyzes the structure of the trade and shows how the trade changed over the four decades covered by her essay.

Five chapters cover aspects of slavery, the primary source of labor for South Carolina for most of the colonial era. In chapter 7, "'All & Singular the Slaves': A Demographic Profile of Indian Slavery in Colonial South Carolina," William L. Ramsay uses wills and estate inventories to estimate the extent of Indian slavery. Although Indians may have accounted for as much as a quarter of South Carolina's enslaved labor force during the first decade of the eighteenth century, he finds that their numbers declined rapidly after 1715 until by 1730 few estates any longer had Indian slaves. Ramsay links this decline to a combination of the Yamassee Indian War in 1715, dwindling sources of supply in the interior, and the increasing availability of slaves from Africa. In chapter 8, "This is Mines": Slavery and Reproduction in Colonial Barbados and South Carolina," Jennifer Lyle Morgan examines the function of women in the formation of the slave systems that, developing first in Barbados, settlers brought from the West Indies to South Carolina. She suggestively explores the relationship between the language of slave ownership and slave owners' attempts to exploit the reproductive potential of slave women and the tensions between those attempts and the determination of slave women to retain control over their own bodies. In chapter 9, "Affiliation without Affinity: Skilled Slaves in Eighteenth-Century South Carolina," S. Max Edelson imaginatively uses runaway advertisements, plantation records, and other documents to explore the social parameters of the lives of the growing body of skilled slaves in the colony. At the same time that their skills increased their productive capacities and their value to their masters, Edelson argues, they also expanded their scope for individual autonomy and, by enlisting them in the plantation enterprises that lay at the heart of the colony's socioeconomic system, brought them into a far closer affiliation with white society than unskilled slaves ever experienced.

Chapter 10, "'Practical Justice': The Justice of the Peace, the Slave Court, and Local Authority in Mid-Eighteenth-Century South Carolina," by Robert Olwell and chapter 11, "'Melancholy and Fatal Calamiti[es]': Disaster and Society in Eighteenth-Century South Carolina," by Matthew Mulcahy examine still other aspects of the slave regime. In his analysis, Olwell shows how South Carolina public officials adapted the office of justice of the peace, a traditional institution in English local governance, to the needs of a slave society. Presiding over local slave courts, South Carolina justices exerted broad powers of social control over slaves and thereby functioned as the principal public instrument for the assertion of settler authority over the majority slave population. Examining the social consequences of two mid-eighteenth-century lowcountry disasters, the Charleston fire of 1740 and the hurricane of 1752, Mulcahy shows both how such calamities could exacerbate the omnipresent problem of slave control and how varying socioeconomic conditions produced sharply different responses to such events on the part of both masters and slaves.

The last four chapters cover aspects of colonial South Carolina's social and cultural development. In chapter 12, "'Planters Full of Money': The Self-Fashioning of the Eighteenth-Century South Carolina Elite," Edward Pearson uses a wide variety of literary evidence to describe the process by which the colony's emergent elite sought to assert and to exhibit its new status. In chapter 13, "Economic Power among Eighteenth-Century Women of the Carolina Lowcountry: Four Generations of Middleton Women, 1678–1800," G. Winston Lane uses legal wills and estate inventories among four generations of women in one of the most prominent and wealthy South Carolina colonial families to consider the question of the economic power of widows, a common social category in a society with high mortality. He finds that the first three generations of widows successfully sought economic independence while the fourth, all beneficiaries of handsome inheritances, showed far less interest in pursuing economic goals. In chapter 14, "Investing Widows: Autonomy in a Nascent Capitalist Society," Elizabeth M. Pruden also uses estate inventories to explore a hitherto unnoticed phenomenon: the significant participation of women with surplus capital in the brisk mortgage market that developed in the lowcountry during the middle decades of the eighteenth century. Women, in far higher proportions than men, she shows, used this market as a strategy for producing income and adding to their estates. By this behavior, they thereby played a major role in the colony's rapid economic development. In chapter 15, "'Adding to the Church Such As Shall be Saved': The Growth in Influence of Evangelicalism in Colonial South Carolina, 1740–1775," Thomas J. Little charts the process by which South Carolina, nominally Anglican but always with a significant proportion of religious dissenters, became ever more religiously diverse and religiously oriented after the mid-1740s, as, under the aegis of a group of energetic and powerful preachers, evangelical religion spread rapidly through the colony.

Impressive as they are, these fifteen essays do little more than contribute to the further opening up of the rich history of colonial South Carolina and of the Lower South region of which it formed the principal part. As the authors of these essays continue their work, as other, still younger scholars also begin to do research in the area, and as scholars begin to devote similar levels of energy and sophistication to the study of southern North Carolina, Georgia, and East and West Florida, we may expect over the next few decades the sort of illumination about the Lower South that made New England in the 1960s and the Chesapeake in the 1970s the principal foci of attention in colonial British studies. Only then will we have a more comprehensive picture of the many social strands that comprised the history of early modern colonial British America.

Notes

1. Harry Roy Merrens, *Colonial North Carolina in the Eighteenth Century: A Study in Historical Geography* (Chapel Hill: University of North Carolina Press, 1964).

2. Converse D. Clowse, *Economic Beginnings in Colonial South Carolina, 1670–1730* (Columbia: published for the University of South Carolina Tricentennial Commission by the University of South Carolina Press, 1971).

3. Peter H. Wood, *Black Majority: Negroes in Colonial South Carolina from 1670 through the Stono Rebellion* (New York: Knopf, 1974).

4. Daniel C. Littlefield, *Rice and Slaves: Ethnicity and the Slave Trade in Colonial South Carolina* (Baton Rouge: Louisiana State University Press, 1981).

5. Robert M. Weir, *Colonial South Carolina: A History* (Millwood, N.Y.: KTO Press, 1983; reprint Columbia: Unversity of South Carolina Press, 1997).

6. Richard Waterhouse, "The Colonial Elite of South Carolina: A Study in Social Structure and Political Culture in a Southern Colony, 1670–1766" (Ph.D. diss., Johns Hopkins University, 1973).

7. Philip D. Morgan, "The Development of Slave Culture in Eighteenth Century Plantation America" (Ph.D. diss, University College, London, 1977).

8. Diane Meredith Sydenham, "Practitioner and Patient: The Practice of Medicine in Eighteenth-Century South Carolina" (Ph.D. diss., Johns Hopkins University, 1970).

9. George D. Terry, "'Champaign Country': A Social History of an Eighteenth Century Lowcountry Parish in South Carolina, St. Johns Berkeley County" (Ph.D. diss, University of South Carolina, 1981).

10. Jack P. Greene and J. R. Pole, eds., *Colonial British America: Essays in the New History of the Early Modern Era* (Baltimore: Johns Hopkins University Press, 1984).

11. Jack P. Greene, *Pursuits of Happiness: The Social Development of Early Modern British Colonies and the Formation of American Culture* (Chapel Hill: University of North Carolina Press, 1988).

12. Bernard Bailyn, *The Peopling of British North America: An Introduction* (New York: Knopf, 1986).

13. D. W. Meining, *The Shaping of America: A Geographical Perspective on 500 Years*

of History, vol. 1, *Atlantic America, 1492–1800* (New Haven: Yale University Press, 1986).

14. David Hackett Fischer, *Albion's Seed: Four British Folkways in America* (New York: Oxford University Press, 1989).

15. Richard Waterhouse, *A New World Gentry: The Making of a Merchant and Planter Class in South Carolina, 1670–1770* (New York: Garland Publishing, 1989).

16. Peter A. Coclanis, *The Shadow of a Dream: Economic Life and Death in the South Carolina Low Country* (New York: Oxford University Press, 1989).

17. James H. Merrell, *The Indians' New World: Catawbas and Their Neighbors from European Contact through the Age of Removal* (Chapel Hill: University of North Carolina Press, 1989).

18. Rachel M. Klein, *Unification of a Slave Society: The Rise of the Planter Class in the South Carolina Backcountry* (Chapel Hill: University of North Carolina Press, 1990).

19. Joyce Chaplin, *An Anxious Pursuit: Agricultural Innovation and Modernity in the Lower South, 1730–1815* (Chapel Hill: University of North Carolina Press, 1993).

20. Philip D. Morgan, *Slave Counterpoint: Black Culture in the Eighteenth-Century Chesapeake and Lowcountry* (Chapel Hill: University of North Carolina Press, 1998).

21. Robert Olwell, *Masters, Slaves and Subjects: The Culture of Power in a Colonial Slave Society: The South Carolina Lowcountry, 1740–1790* (Ithaca, N.Y.: Cornell University Press, 1998).

MONEY, TRADE, AND POWER

I

Creating a Plantation Province

Proprietary Land Policies and Early Settlement Patterns

MEAGHAN N. DUFF

Upon regaining the English throne in 1660, Charles II rewarded eight of his loyal noblemen with a vast tract of land in southeastern North America. Named "Carolina" in his honor, the territory granted by charter in 1663 and 1665 included all the land lying between the latitudes 36°30' and 29° North, stretching from the Atlantic coast to the Pacific shore. Proclaiming the recipients the "true and absolute proprietors" of this province, the king collectively bestowed on the region's new rulers the responsibility and right to populate, govern, and profit from settlement on the southern frontier of England's continental colonial empire. The language of the charters clearly indicates that the crown envisioned the creation of a colony distinctly feudal in character. The Lords Proprietors held their land from the king "in free and common socage," enjoyed the power to grant lands by "rents, services and customs" in fee simple or entailed, and received the authority to appoint a provincial aristocracy by conferring "marks of honor and favors." The governing privileges extended by the charters far exceeded those permitted palatine or sovereign lords in England. Moreover, the form of provincial government outlined by the Lords Proprietors in the Fundamental Constitutions maximized the feudal nature of their administration of the colony. While the tenets and revisions of this governing document were never implemented fully, its spirit and scope dramatically shaped the land policies and settlement patterns in early Carolina.[1]

More than any other incentive to migrate, liberal land policies lured settlers to England's southernmost mainland colony. While colonial promoters widely advertised the vast acreage available in Carolina, the Lords Proprietors desired strict control over distribution of land in the region. By issuing an explicit program for settlement, appointing land agents, instituting a headright system, and collecting quitrents, the proprietors expected to create a compact colony with nucleated towns. The dispersed plantation province that ultimately developed resulted from administrative difficulties, environmental circumstances, and the individual and collective refusal of settlers to adhere to the letter and spirit of proprietary land policies. An examination of the evidence surviving from the colony's beginning in the 1670s to the assumption of royal control in the 1720s suggests how the planters and proprietors each responded to and shaped the procedures for obtaining and distributing land, the pattern of settlement, and thus the contest for control over the character of South Carolina's geographic and human landscapes. Legal mandates concerning property acquisition, correspondence of the lords with colonial officials regarding land allocation, statistical records of land warrants and grants, and documents revealing the responsibilities and practices of contemporary surveyors and land grantees all illustrate how the proprietors and planters negotiated the occupation of Carolina. As colonists staked claims to property and shaped individual land parcels, they directed or subverted policy and shaped collective land patterns. When, where, and how settlement occurred resulted from struggles waged between opposing interests in law, letters, land patents, and lines drawn on surveyors' plats.

In the Fundamental Constitutions of 1669 and Temporary Agrarian Laws issued in 1671–1672, the Lords Proprietors articulated their vision of a provincial society founded upon land tenure. "Since the whole foundation of the Government is setled upon a right and equall distribution of Land," they argued, "the orderly takeing of it up is of great moment to the welfare of the Province." However, their motives and methods for constructing a colony based primarily on property holding were not original to this or any American plantation enterprise. The practice of seizing lands and granting lordships possessed a centuries-long history in England's oldest colony across the Irish Sea. In particular, the sixteenth-century Munster plantation in southwestern Ireland attempted to reorganize escheated lands into feudal colonies. George Calvert, the first Lord Baltimore, gained his title and a seignorial grant in Ireland in the early 1620s. In 1632 he received the first proprietary grant in North America, land that became the settlement of Maryland. Yet without the unitary leadership characteristic of its Chesapeake counterpart, the Carolina patent holders designed a land system considerably more complex than that proposed in Maryland. The Fundamental Constitutions mandated that land in Carolina be rigidly divided into *counties* of 480,000 acres. Each county would contain eight *seignories* of 12,000 acres belonging to the eight proprietors, eight *baronies* of 12,000 acres granted to a hereditary nobility, and four *precincts* (each with six 12,000-acre *colonies*) to be planted by freemen. Thus, within the 750 square miles of an idealized county, the proprietors held 96,000 acres, 3 noblemen (1 landgrave and 2 cassiques) also held 96,000 total acres, and the common settlers owned 288,000 acres collectively. By design, the proprietors and aristocrats would each control one-fifth of the land in Carolina while freemen would occupy the remaining three-fifths.[2]

The Lords Proprietors clearly understood that provincial governors could not immediately implement this elaborate plantation program. In order to prevent the "takeing up [of] great Tracts of land sooner than they

TABLE 1.1

LAND SYSTEM OUTLINED IN THE FUNDAMENTAL CONSTITUTIONS

Unit	Acres/Unit	Owner	Total Acres
County	480,000	8 seignories, 8 baronies, 4 precincts	
Seignory	12,000	1 per proprietor per county	96,000
Barony	12,000	4 per landgrave and 2 per cassique per county	96,000
Precinct	72,000	All for common planters, 4 per county	288,000

SOURCE: "First Set of the Constitutions for the Government of Carolina," in *The Shaftsbury Papers* (Charleston, S.C.: Tempus Publishing, 2000; originally published in 1897), 94.

ILLUSTRATION 1.1

IDEALIZED PROPRIETARY COUNTIES

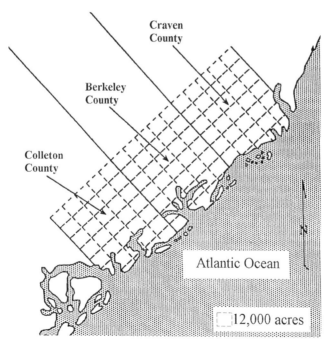

SOURCE: Adapted from the WPA Historical Records Survey, Collections of the South Carolina Department of Archives and History, Columbia, S.C.

can be planted . . . and exposeing the safety of the whole by stragling and distant Habitations," they suspended or modified property laws and plantation instructions in the first years of settlement. These changes effectively limited the amount of land anyone could claim upon arrival. Not "till by the increase of the Inhabitants," or the migration of enough common settlers, when sufficient land "shall be possessed by the people," would it be time "for every one to take up the proportion of Land due to his dignity." Provincial noblemen were instructed to settle their granted lands with at least a minimum number of colonists. While the landgrave or cassique "who first makes his demand, and plants on it" could choose the location of his estate, he "shall not choose a second Barrony till he hath one hundred inhabitants upon his first." The lords similarly restricted their own ability to claim specific tracts of land. Recognizing that the challenges of peopling a frontier colony required some flexibility in the beginning, the proprietors pragmatically amended their original plantation program. However, they remained adamant that the "land is ours and we shall not part with it but on our own terms."[3]

The terms set by the Lords Proprietors for securing land changed frequently, and often in direct response to the disregard with which the colonists received them. The conflict over where colonists should settle and who selected the land's location generated the most controversy and thus correspondence. The proprietors feared that their colony might falter if they granted tracts of land too large for immediate cultivation, too distant from the provincial capital for effective governance, and too isolated on the frontier for adequate defense. The language in their letters to Carolina's colonial leaders reinforced the content of their instructions: "Wee haveing noe other Aime in the frameing of our Laws but to make . . . us a quiet equall and lasting Government wherein every mans Right Property and Welfare may be soe fenc'd in and secured that the preservation of the Government may be in every ones Interest." In the minds of the proprietors, only fenced property—or a well-designed system of landownership—would secure public welfare, undergird a stable government, and create a prosperous colonial society pleasing to planters and proprietors alike. Toward that end, the Lords Proprietors instructed the governor and council as early as 1669 "to order ye people to plant in Townes," and to create "one Towne at least in each Collony" in a manner "most Convenient & profitable for ye people yᵗ are to inhabitt them." Acutely aware of the settlement experiences in other colonies, Sir Anthony Ashley Cooper, the proprietor most active in Carolina affairs, argued that this approach to settlement was "the Cheife thing that hath given New England soe much the advantage over Virginia and advanced that Plantation in so short a time to the height it is now." Lord

Ashley recognized that, despite "requiring that all the Inhabitants of every Colony should set there houses together in one Place," the selection of said "Place wee leave to the choice of the Inhabitants themselves."[4] This practice of indiscriminate location, of allowing individual settlers to choose the site and shape of their property, consistently undermined the proprietors' plantation objectives.

The array of provincial agents contracted to carry out these objectives, coupled with a cumbersome appointment system and delays in executing proprietary instructions issued across the Atlantic, further limited the implementation of the land program. The Fundamental Constitutions created seven administrative offices within the proprietorship—chief justice, chancellor, constable, high steward, treasurer, chamberlain, and admiral—to be held exclusively by the lords depending on their seniority and rank. The chief justice designated the colony's register of the province while the high steward typically selected the surveyor general. By requiring that planters register their lands and have them surveyed by an official in the colonial administration, the proprietors exceeded practices common in contemporary England. On June 24, 1672, Lord Ashley commissioned Joseph West "register for the Province of Carolina" and ordered him to record "not onely the Titles of the Lords Proprietors but of all Deeds amongst yourselves." Accentuating the importance of West's new office, Lord Ashley observed "noe Deed being good that is not registered." Although the Fundamental Constitutions called for the appointment of registers in every county, and despite the commission of Andrew Percival as "Register of Berkeley County & the Parts adjoyneing" in 1675, multiple offices were never created. Conflicting instructions from England and a considerable overlap between the offices of the secretary and register of the province created great confusion within the colony. Although the secretary eventually assumed most of the register's responsibilities, frequent changes in the former office impeded the land allocation process. Before the turn of the eighteenth century, no fewer than ten secretaries and eight deputy secretaries had administered the affairs of Carolina.[5]

The efforts of the Lords Proprietors to appoint capable surveyors to carve counties out of the Carolina landscape were even less effective. At a meeting in April 1672 the Grand Council called "for the laying out of three Colonies or Squares of twelve thousand acres" near Charleston, James Town, and Oyster Point. No land surveys survive from the proprietary era, and it is unlikely that agents surveyed much, if any, property in the 1670s besides laying out town lots in the colonial capital. The Lords Proprietors removed Florence O'Sullivan, an Irish mercenary who became the first resident surveyor general, from office once the colonists complained of his abusive behavior and poor skills. O'Sullivan's "absurd language" and "base dealings" notwithstanding, most upsetting to the settlers were that "the lands that he hath pretended to lay and run out is verie irregular" and he knew not "how to give us sattisfaction in things of plaine cases."[6]

Much more capable than O'Sullivan, Carolina's next surveyor general, John Culpeper, quickly set about platting the lands of three proprietors (Lord Ashley, Sir George Carteret, and Sir Peter Colleton) near Charleston and creating an overall map of plantations in the region. Culpeper's short tenure as surveyor ended in the summer of 1673 when he and several members of the Grand Council rebelled and fled to the Albemarle colony in North Carolina. The proprietors then appointed Stephen Bull, John Yeamans, and Stephen Wheelwright as the collective surveyors of the colony. Not until April 1677 did Maurice Mathews, a man with considerable scientific, artistic, and managerial talents, assume the office of surveyor general. In the spring of 1682, more than a decade after the colony's founding and five years after Mathews's appointment, the Lords Proprietors reiterated the necessity of surveying county boundaries, namely Berkeley, Craven, and Colleton, in squares of 12,000 acres. Despite their promise to pay Mathews £150 for his services, once again there is no evidence that the surveyor general staked out any county. When these county names began appearing on maps and in grants in 1683, they merely indicated general areas and not defined territories. Yet, as these same maps and land grants reveal, the failure to complete county surveys in no way hindered the pace of settlement.[7]

The proprietors, in particular, took up property without following their own procedural guidelines. Before his appointment as surveyor general and in his role as Lord Ashley's agent or deputy, Mathews "marked 12000 acres of land for my Lord Ashley on the first bluff bank upon the first Indian plantacon on the right hand in the Westerne branch of the North [Cooper] river." The Grand Council reserved this land for Lord Ashley in March 1673, but it was never officially granted to him. In 1679 Lord Proprietor Sir Peter Colleton added the property to his own sizable holdings adjacent to the north at a place he called Fair Lawn Barony. Without first obtaining a warrant, the legally required order for survey, Lord Ashley secured a formal grant for another seignory in March 1675. It was located, appropriately, along the Ashley River, and he named it St. Giles Plantation. This behavior—staking out and reserving lands, receiving grants without warrants—sent a twofold message. First, the Lords Proprietors approached land settlement and the implementation of their program with considerable flexibility, at least in the beginning and where their own seignorial lands were concerned. Second, it signaled the ease with which all colonists could disregard the proprietary land policies set forth in the Fundamental Constitutions and Temporary Agrarian Laws.[8]

Land could be acquired legally in Carolina in five main ways: feudal grants to provincial noblemen, headright grants, compensation grants, gifts, and outright purchase. From the records it is impossible to determine with certainty the type of grant received in most cases. The size of a grant sometimes suggests its type, and occasionally other sources indicate if land was given or sold to the grantee. In order to obtain a legal patent, a settler initially petitioned the governor and council for land. He then received a warrant instructing the surveyor general to prepare a plat of the property. The potential grantee next took a certified survey of the land to the secretary of the province and acquired a sealed grant. Once signed by the governor and council, the register of the province recorded the official land grant. This was not a simple process even, or perhaps especially, in a nascent colony with a small population.[9]

During the first two decades of settlement, the proprietors modified the language, terms, and procedures for recording warrants and grants (later called indentures). Legitimate and logical reasons drove these constitutional amendments and administrative changes. In addition to establishing an orderly and effective process for land distribution, the Lords Proprietors wanted to prevent property engrossment and speculation, curtail abuse of loopholes in the original system, and, most important, reap financial rewards from their investment in Carolina. Hence, they gradually reduced the size of headright grants from 150 acres to 50 acres, depending upon an individual's sex, social status, and arrival date. The largest tracts went to colonists who migrated in the first years of settlement and thus assumed the greatest risks.

As the plantation began to prosper and landowners imported slaves in increasing numbers, the proprietors reduced the headright grants for servants to impede the formation of large estates. To minimize fraud they also ordered the secretary of the province to record in the warrants the names of all household members claiming a headright grant. Free men and women always received headrights in equal proportion; male servants earned larger grants than did their female counterparts or minors. After 1709, settlers seeking grants of land larger than of 500 acres required a warrant issued directly from the proprietors.[10] In their eagerness to profit from the province, the proprietors attempted to secure monies and goods for granted lands. In 1682 they changed the commencement date of quitrent, the annual land dues, from 1689 to just two years after the register sealed the grant. When the first deadline approached in 1684, the proprietors offered to remit and abolish the quitrents, which the settlers found loathsome, in exchange for one-time cash payments of twelve pence per acre. They also sold land outright—at variable rates of £25 for 500 acres, or one shilling per acre—with explicit instructions to the provincial governor that revenue from each sale be returned to the proprietors in London instead of filling the administrators'

TABLE 1.2
SIZE OF HEADRIGHT GRANTS OVER TIME

Status of Emigrant	Arrival before 1671	Arrival before 1672	Arrival after 1680	Arrival after 1682
All free persons above 16 yrs	150 acres	100 acres	70 acres	50 acres
Male servants above 16 yrs	150 acres	100 acres	70 acres	50 acres
Female servants/servants under 16 yrs	100 acres	70 acres	50 acres	50 acres
All servants with completed indenture	100 acres	70 acres	60 acres	50 acres
Unmarried female servant	n/a	n/a	n/a	40 acres

coffers in Carolina. Finally, the Lords Proprietors threatened to seize or sue for the personal property of grantees in default.[11]

The Lords Proprietors' efforts to shape early settlement patterns toward their own ends met with qualified success, and this suited many colonists. In the contest for Carolina the objectives of the settlers and the proprietors did not always or necessarily conflict. Despite their frequently tense relations and terse exchanges, the members of both groups desired a secure, populated, and prosperous province. However, not all colonists—noblemen, freeholders, or servants—shared the same outlook on plantation policy. There were significant differences in the experiences of large land magnates like Jonathan Amory, who accumulated at least twenty-one grants of land totaling more than 7,850 acres, and the likes of Hannah Smith, who received a single 50-acre headright grant. In the end, the value of statistical evidence derived from the catalogs of proprietary land records is limited by the quality and quantity of extant sources. Fortunately, of all the literary materials surviving from seventeenth- and early-eighteenth-century South Carolina, the official land record of warrants and grants are among the most complete.

The land warrants contain instructions from the provincial governor (addressed to the surveyor general and recorded by the secretary) regarding the allocation of land in the colony to specific individuals. These early warrants contain invaluable biographical and demographical information about potential grantees, but the descriptive quality of these records varies over time and declines markedly in the late 1690s with changes in the secretary's office. Nevertheless, the warrants are the best surviving source for understanding proprietary efforts to control land distribution and settlement in the first few decades of lowcountry colonization. The land grants, by contrast, detail when, how, and often where actual grantees took possession of real property.[12]

The number of warrants issued in the first four decades of settlement varied dramatically from year to year. In 1672 the secretary wrote 113 permits to acquire land while the very next year he signed only fifteen such documents. More warrants were issued the last year of extant record-keeping than in any previous year. However, this increase was not dramatic when compared with the total number of warrants signed in several previous years. The range varied from as few as three warrants issued in both 1690 and 1691 to as many as 252 signed in 1711. Changing rates of immigration do not explain these fluctuations in the number of warrants recorded annually in the secretary's office. Census statistics for proprietary South Carolina are notoriously difficult to attain because few contemporaries took time to estimate the size of the colonial population, whether free, servant, or slave. This paucity of data notwithstanding, there is no correlation between the number of warrants issued and the best estimates of the number of white settlers

TABLE 1.3
LAND WARRANTS, 1671–1711

Number of warrants	3,656
Number of persons receiving warrants	1,641
Mean warrants per person	2.2
Mean warrant size in acres	355
Median warrant size in acres	200
Total acres warranted	1,298,794

TABLE 1.4
LAND GRANTS, 1670–1722

Number of grants	1,327
Number of persons receiving grants	580
Mean grants per person	2.3
Mean grant size in acres	539
Median grant size in acres	212
Total acres granted	714,838.875

living in the province. When the colony expanded most rapidly, between the mid-1680s and early 1690s, the number of warrants fell to the lowest recorded levels.[13]

Politics, not population, thwarted land allocation in Carolina. The proprietors dismissed secretary John Moore in 1685 for poor performance, and they replaced his successor Robert Quary in 1687 amidst allegations that he "misbehaved himselfe." In addition to the many charges leveled at the secretaries (both men held multiple offices in the colonial administration), the lords specifically criticized their management of land records and complained that they failed to send copies of the documents to England as required. The number of warrants issued during the tenures of Moore and Quary declined dramatically from 184 in 1684 to 4 in 1687. This trend reversed in the next two years when a more faithful administrator named Paul Grimball assumed the office. He remained secretary until a coup d'état led by Seth Sothell (and supported by Moore and Quary) temporarily unseated the established government. After Grimball's release from prison and return to office in 1692, the number of warrants issued to settlers soared and remained high until his death in 1697. Thereafter, secretaries recorded only abstracted warrants, which typically noted just the date, acreage amount, and recipient's name.[14]

FIGURE 1.1
FREQUENCY OF WARRANTS BY YEAR

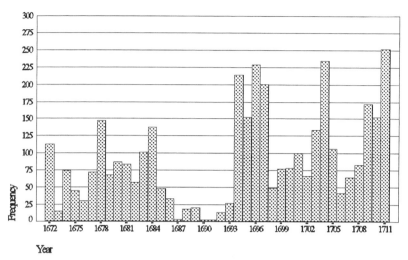

Beginning in the 1680s, the Lords Proprietors vigorously promoted their colonial enterprise both in England and abroad in the hope of recruiting more emigrants. Shipping lists and detailed correspondence do not survive to indicate whether the influx of settlers met their expectations in quality or quantity. Since the number of warrants correlate with changes in the secretary's office, not changes in total population, they do not reveal the frequency of requests for land among new migrants or earlier settlers. Yet over time, the warrants, better than any other extant source, demonstrate the proprietors' practical efforts to apportion property and power among free white Carolinians. They further reflect the provincial governors' attempts to implement proprietary policy and to direct the colony's development geographically and socially. Thus, analysis of land-warranting patterns reveals the proprietors' actions and effectiveness apart from the desires and demands of colonists.

The number of warrants issued annually fluctuated wildly, peaking in 1694, 1696, 1704, and 1711. Perhaps because of sailing schedules or the planting and harvest seasons, the secretary recorded almost one-third more warrants in March and April than during September and October. The governor and council ordered warrants issued in any size, small or large, tending toward round figures. Robert Gibbes, for example, received three warrants for marsh lands in increments as small as half an acre in 1694 and 1703. By contrast, the Lords Proprietors had a warrant for 48,000 acres of land "in or about Coleton County" in May 1711. More than half of the warrants allocated land in multiples of 100 acres. On the average, a person received 2.3 permits for lands totaling 355 acres. The median warrant size was 200 acres. In 603 cases the secretaries indicated no precise amount of land. Instead, they issued permits for unspecified acreage often lying between established properties or other natural boundaries. In sum, the secretaries ordered surveys of more than 1,298,794 acres—over 2,000 square miles—in nearly forty years. Yet the warrants rarely indicated where in the province settlers should take up land. In only one-quarter of the cases did the proprietors or governor assign land in a specific county. The dynamics of warranting land did little to ensure that colonists settled in compact communities or defensible locations. Instead, the proprietors permitted surveys of more land than could possibly be cultivated by the number of residents in the province, and they allowed individuals to choose the site of their land with little restriction.[15]

Although the land-warranting process thoroughly failed to guide the geographical settlement of Carolina along the lines articulated by the Lords Proprietors, it enjoyed somewhat more success in shaping the social development of the colony. Of the 44 recipients of an individual warrant for 1,500 acres of land or more, 12 can be identified as provincial nobles and another 11 were proprietors or their deputies. Similarly, among the 50 people receiving warrants for the most land, at least 11 were provincial aristocrats and 13 were proprietors or their deputies. In keeping with the spirit of the original land scheme described in the Fundamental Constitutions, one-half of the recipients of the largest warrants were colonial aristocrats, proprietors, or their agents. Together, the proprietors and the provincial nobility, although fewer than 2 percent of the people receiving warrants, claimed more than one-fifth of the total acres warranted. The land-warranting process implemented in the province did not allocate property in strict accordance with the proprietors' instructions. Yet, had the settlers occupied all the lands for which the secretaries ordered surveys in the first four decades of settlement, the highly stratified society described in the colony's founding documents would have materialized in South Carolina. The proprietors' settlement program, which rooted social rank and privilege in property holding, effectively allocated land in a manner capable of creating the colony they imagined. Though feudal in character, their vision of Carolina was neither naive nor impractical. The plan faltered when too few immigrants arrived in the colony, and those who did come settled without much regard for proprietary land policies. Much more than the land-warranting process, the procedures for and patterns of land granting demonstrate what actually occurred in Carolina, and the roles played by both the proprietors and the provincials in shaping the region's geographical and social landscapes.[16]

FIGURE 1.2
FREQUENCY OF WARRANTS BY MONTH

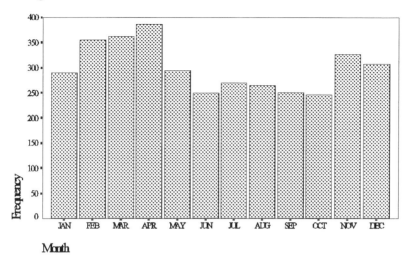

TABLE 1.5
ACRES WARRANTED BY COUNTY

County	No. of Warrants	Acres Warranted
Unspecified	2,728	844,416
Berkeley County	406	173,389
Colleton County	355	214,237
Craven County	125	466,122
Granville County	42	20,140
Total	3,656	1,298,794

From the 1670 advent of English settlement in South Carolina to the third decade of the eighteenth century, the proprietors and their agents granted almost 715,000 acres of land lying between the Santee and Savannah rivers. Interestingly, this sum does not equal the size of just two idealized counties envisioned by the Lords Proprietors in their Fundamental Constitution. In 1,327 separate grants, 580 individuals received lands by headright, purchase, gift, and/or for services rendered to the colony. The colonists averaged 2.3 grants per person during the first three decades of lowcountry colonization. The mean, or arithmetic average, of all grants equaled 539 acres, with plots ranging in size from the minimum of one-eighth acre to the maximum of 48,000 acres retained by individual proprietors. The median grant was 212 acres. Half of the total acres granted were located along the early settlement's primary waterways—the Ashley, Cooper, Edisto, Santee, and Stono rivers, or their tributaries. One-eighth of the total grants were designated as whole or partial town lots typically dispersed in half-acre increments. Forty-two percent of the grants ordered settlement in a specific county, with almost one-third of these indentures lying in Berkeley and Colleton, the counties closest to Charleston. Thus, in keeping with the proprietors' wishes, most colonists possessed at least a small parcel of land in town. A majority, perhaps, also settled along the province's main transportation arteries or near the colonial capital in accessible, if not always contained and easily guarded, locations.[17]

As with the land warrants, the frequency of land grants could vary dramatically from year to year. Grants to settlers peaked in 1684, 1694–1696, and in 1711. The increase in the amount of land taken up by the colonists correlates roughly with changes in the population and political administration of the province. Partly a positive response to a promotional campaign begun by the proprietors in the early 1680s, the population of Carolina doubled from 1,000 to 2,000 inhabitants in the first few years of that decade. The register of the province recorded 126 grants between 1680 and 1683. In the following ten years, as promotion of the colony waned and as more provincials refused to comply with the proprietors' changing land policies, he registered only thirty such indentures.[18]

The next surge in land grants resulted from the arrival of Governor John Archdale and the settlers' assumption of greater control over land distribution in the colony. In 1693 the provincial assembly sent a list of grievances to the governor and the proprietors' deputies. Chief among the fourteen complaints was "that the Right Honorable the Lords proprietors have not all agreed to the same forme for conveyancing of Land, and that the latest forme agreed to by some of them [is] not satisfactory to the people." In response, the Lords Proprietors dissolved the assembly, appointed Archdale governor, and empowered him to bring order to the land system. Mediating between the demands of the proprietors and the wishes of the settlers, the governor approved, and the new assembly passed, a series of acts (later called Archdale's Laws) in March 1696. The most sweeping of these acts forgave all arrears in rents for legally granted land. Henceforth, headright grants carried quitrents of one penny per acre, payable in currency or commodities. Purchased lands sold at a minimum of £20 per 1,000 acres and carried quitrents of twelve pence per hundred acres. The proprietors also abolished the rents on all new grants for five years; thereafter, those who failed to pay arrears would forfeit their land. Finally, the lords agreed not to

TABLE 1.6
ACRES GRANTED BY COUNTY

County	No. of Grants	Acres Granted
Unspecified	769	451,022
Berkeley or Colleton	1	1,000
Berkeley or Craven	2	1,300
Berkeley County	267	147,663
Colleton County	173	68,115
Craven County	65	25,414
Granville County	50	20,325
Total	1,327	714,839

FIGURE 1.3
FREQUENCY OF WARRANTS BY YEAR

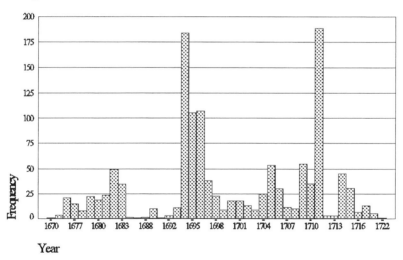

alter further the terms for granting land without one year's notice. Although intended to encourage immigration, these laws were designed primarily to compel settlers to confirm their title to lands held only by warrant, survey, or mere occupation, and to begin paying rents. Only then would Carolina turn a profit for its proprietors. In direct response to these policy changes, the colonists certified their land grants in unprecedented numbers, recording 458 indentures for 108,705 acres of land from 1694 to 1698. The final spike in proprietary grants came in 1711 and coincided with the passage of an assembly act validating the title of all lands held for seven consecutive years regardless of an owner's past failure to pay quitrents. The Lords Proprietors consented. By the turn of the eighteenth century, they no longer set the terms for parting with their lands.[19]

Despite obtaining land grants, the settlers in South Carolina seldom paid rents on their property sufficient to satisfy the proprietors. The failure of provincial agents to keep a regular rent roll suggests that tax collectors rarely knocked on the colonists' doors. Though frustrated in their effort to turn a profit on Carolina lands, the proprietors did not lose complete control over the system of property distribution or, by extension, the character of the colony's physical and social topography. The land policies instituted in Carolina, while increasingly a product of negotiation with the provincials, often reflected the intentions of the proprietors. For example, when the assembly suggested in February 1699 that preventing "no greater quantities than one thousand acres of Land" to be granted would "much strengthen this Settlement," the proprietors concurred. The following October they ordered "that where no settlement is designed no great shares of land ought to go to one person by which means the growth of the settlement may be prevented." While far from groundless, the concerns of contemporaries about land aggrandizement may well have been exaggerated by the large acreages apportioned to aristocrats in the Fundamental Constitutions, and by the contentiousness of subsequent debates over land policy. The land system successfully limited the engrossing of property. Ninety-three percent of grants were for plats smaller than 1,000 acres. Forty percent of the land grants were in the precise amount of various headright sizes or in simple multiples thereof (specifically 50, 70, 100, 140, 150, 200, 210, 280, 300, 400, and 500 acres). In other words, the headright was the most common type of land grant. As the only form of indenture directly linked to the size of the expanding colonial population, the headright more effectively controlled the acreage-to-settler ratio in Carolina than could any open sale of lands.[20]

The idea of offering free land as an incentive for settlers to migrate to America had coincided with the earliest English effort to plant a colony in the New World. In 1588, Thomas Hariot praised Sir Walter Ralegh's "large giving and graunting lande" to the Roanoke voyagers and noted that the "least that hee hath graunted hath beene five hundred acres to a man onely for the adventure of his person." These first headright grants well exceeded later allowances, but the idea took firm root. All the southern colonies offered some form of headright as a primary means for settlers to obtain land. In theory and often in practice, this system distributed property in some proportion to the number of settlers able to work the land or in need of the fruits of this labor. When combined with the practice of indiscriminate location (allowing individual site selection), such reliance on the head-right system in Carolina could have created circumstances conducive to rapid and chaotic settlement, not the planned and orderly growth so favored by the proprietors and provincials alike. That it did not resulted from the constraints of proprietary land policies and the manipulating tactics survey-ors and settlers used to maneuver within that system.[21]

In addition to frequently modifying land-warranting and land-granting policies, the proprietors also restructured the official procedures for con-ducting, certifying, and recording property surveys. They issued and reis-sued instructions with precise measurements to govern the size and shape of granted lands. Yet individual site preference and intended use of the prop-erty, not colonial policy, ultimately determined where an immigrant settled. Since waterways served as the basic routes for colonial transportation and commerce, the proprietors limited the amount of river frontage allowed per tract. In theory, no planter, whether nobleman or freeholder, could monop-olize the most valuable properties in his community, and all settlers would enjoy some access to the region's transportation network. The land warrants routinely ordered the surveyor that, if property "happen upon any naviga-ble River or any River capable of being made navigable, you are to allow only one fifth part of the depth thereof by the water side." For example, a tract fifty acres long could have only ten acres fronting a navigable river. In prac-tice, colonial surveyors derived much of their authority from the responsi-bility for certifying a river's navigability. Grantees often circumvented this policy and maximized frontage along the rivers by exploiting natural bends or selecting land at an angle to the waterway. Though agents of the propri-etors, colonial surveyors were also settlers. They could not always be relied upon to implement official land policies, particularly at the expense of their neighbors' property. By the mid-1680s, no provincial leader could ignore that where colonists chose to settle, along the rivers and marshes, conflicted with the proprietors' expressed intention that "people shall plant in Townes which are to be laid out into large, straight & regular streets." However, the proprietors came to understand that mandating where freemen settled might alienate potential emigrants to Carolina and risk the survival of the province. Secretary Joseph Dalton informed his lords as early as 1671 that as "more people are come, we find that if they be not suffered to choose their own conveniencyes, it may prove a great retarding of a speedy peopling this Country; for non omnibus arbusta juvant [not all plantations are pleas-ing]; some delighting to be near the sea, and others from it, the denyall of which we find to have been fatall."[22]

Although unsuccessful in their attempts to control the allocation and distribution of land in Carolina by setting policy, the proprietors shaped set-

tlement patterns in more subtle ways. The proprietors influenced by example where other colonists chose to plant when selecting their personal lands.
Lord Ashley established St. Giles Seignory along the banks of the Ashley
River in 1675. Later that same year his agent Andrew Percival settled on
2,000 acres a few miles north of the earl's estate. Jacob Waight received a
grant for 764 acres immediately to the south of the St. Giles plantation, and
John and Robert Smith obtained grants for 2,400 acres on the opposite side
of the Ashley River. The proprietors also eventually ordered the surveyor
general to return certified plats directly to the secretary of the province
rather than to the prospective grantee. This measure further prevented settlers from claiming lands without signing an indenture, assuming responsibility for quitrents, and receiving a sealed land grant. Finally, the
two-dimensional surveys and plats, unlike the topography they depicted,
usually formed the rectilinear shapes prescribed in the Fundamental Constitutions.[23]

The experiences of two grantees and their families illustrate the variety
and complexity of land acquisition patterns in the province. John Ashby, a
London merchant and investor in several overseas adventures, received his
first warrant for 2,000 acres in Carolina on November 17, 1680. Just five
months later, on April 25, 1681, the proprietors granted the gentleman
"2000 acres on the Southernmost side of the Eastern branch of Cooper
River." Not a headright or purchase, this land grant most likely reflected a
noble claim or the proprietors' gratitude for favors rendered the colony. The
following year Ashby became a cassique, and a letter to the governor and
council instructed that "M[r] John Ashby who has done us much good service in procuring seeds wishes to enlarge his plantation. Permit his agent to
take up not more than three thousand acres." Whether John Ashby ever visited the colony remains unclear. The Charleston town lot warranted in
October 1681 was not granted until two decades later, suggesting that the
provincial nobleman may have administered his lands in absentia and built no
house in town.[24] Ashby's son, his namesake and agent, appears to have emigrated to Carolina or visited on more than one occasion and to have acquired
grants for his father. Seven warrants for land dated between January 1696 and
October 1704 correspond with grants received in the same period. Given
their size, the grants appear to be headrights. In this instance, the number of
acres warranted to Ashby equaled the total amount of land granted. But this
was not typical of most property distribution in the province. In the first two
decades of settlement, the number of acres warranted to an individual
exceeded the number granted more than 75 percent of the time. In only 10
percent of 1,641 cases did granted acres precisely equal warranted acres.

Thus, Ashby's experience was not representative of most grantees' land

TABLE 1.7
JOHN ASHBY'S LAND ACQUISITIONS

Warrant Date	Warranted Acres	Grant Date	Granted Acres	Time Elapsed
17 Nov. 1680	2000	25 April 1681	2000	5 months
06 Oct. 1681	town lot	28 Aug. 1701	town lot #18	20 years
17 Jan. 1696	250	09 Sept. 1696	250	9 months
01 April 1697	140			5 months
01 April 1697	280	01 Sept. 1697	490	5 months
01 April 1697	70			5 months
24 Oct. 1704	200	12 Jan. 1705	200	2.5 months
24 Oct. 1704	200	12 Jan. 1705	200	2.5 months
24 Oct. 1704	500	12 Jan. 1705	500	2.5 months
Total	**3,640**		**3,640**	

TABLE 1.8
COMPARISON OF ACRES WARRANTED AND ACRES
GRANTED, 1670–1722

Acres warranted < Acres granted	219 cases	13.3%
Acres warranted = Acres granted	161 cases	9.8%
Acres warranted > Acres granted	1,261 cases	76.8%
Total	**1,641 cases**	**100%**

FIGURE 1.4
COMPARISON OF ACRES WARRANTED AND ACRES GRANTED,
1670–1722

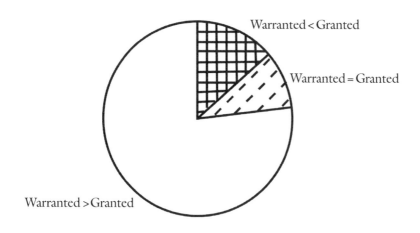

acquisition patterns. Many settlers staked a land claim with only a warrant or plat in hand. The proprietors exacerbated this situation by warranting more lands than could reasonably be cultivated and by recognizing the squatters' claims in their demand for quitrents from individuals without sealed grants. In 1696 the Commons House of Assembly ordered that "all Lands Possest by any Persons by their running out the same and sitting downe thereon by warrants" were responsible for quitrent dues since they "hinder[ed] others from settling thereon." Other planters bypassed the warranting process completely. After Ashby's death in 1699, his son received a 1,500-acre grant in January 1705 without previously securing a warrant.[25]

Even the men most familiar with the dictates of proprietary land policy, the colonial agents, circumvented and often ignored the warrant-plat-grant system. Stephen Bull, who served as both register of the province and surveyor general, claimed at least two tracts of land equaling 270 acres without obtaining official grants. Instead he relied upon warrants (and perhaps surveyed plats, though they do not survive) to certify his ownership. The language of the early grants stated that the proprietors would not begin collecting quitrents until September 1689. In effect, this policy allowed the settlers years to complete the land acquisition process and to obtain sealed grants, all while avoiding their rent burden. Many planters, like Bull, never secured grants. More often, years and even decades lapsed between the issue of a warrant and the recording of a corresponding grant. In Bull's case, 400 acres of land warranted in May 1672 were not officially granted until October 1676, more than four years later. The proprietors attempted to correct this problem by stipulating in the warrants that prospective grantees "Signe the Counterpart of the Indented Deed with[in] ninety days after the said Land is admeasured" or surveyed on threat of forfeiture. Their effort failed to alter this colonial practice significantly. The duplication of warrants and erratic record-keeping further confused the land distribution process. Three warrants issued to Bull in 1672 reappeared in the records of the register in 1674. In each case, the language was so similar that the second warrants even repeated the names of the servants in his indenture. In general, it is more difficult to distinguish new warrants for additional lands from duplicate patents.[26]

The pattern of seventeenth-century land warrants and grants reveals that the changes made in proprietary policies did not disrupt or hinder, and may even have encouraged, migration to the province. The vast majority of land grants occurred in the early 1680s and mid-1690s, both times when revisions of the procedures for allocating land occurred and the population increased. The simple correspondence of these events does not provide enough evidence for reaching definitive conclusions. Still needed is a thorough analysis of the changes in land grant numbers, acreages, and locations over time, as

TABLE 1.9
STEPHEN BULL'S LAND ACQUISITIONS

Warrant Date	Warranted Acres	Grant Date	Granted Acres	Approximate Time Elapsed
21 May 1672	170	none	0	n/a
21 May 1672	400	31 Oct. 1676	400	4.5 years
21 May 1672	100	none	0	n/a
18 April 1674	duplicate 170	none	0	n/a
18 April 1674	duplicate 400	none	0	n/a
18 April 1674	duplicate 100	none	0	n/a
10 Nov. 1674	100	16 Dec. 1676	97	2 years
22 June 1680	70	1699	70	19 years
10 Nov. 1680	town lot	18 Nov. 1680	town lot #17	1 week
6 Oct. 1681	not stated	22 Oct. 1681	190	2 weeks
22 Nov. 1694	100	Jan. 1695	100	2 months
17 Nov. 1704	200	15 Sept. 1705	110	10 months
no source	no source	4 Jan. 1714	town lot #276	n/a
no source	no source	not stated	town lot #277	n/a
Total	1810		967	

well as an examination of the nature of grants to emigrants of varying social status. However, these findings suggest that the Lords Proprietors and their land policies had a greater effect on the settlement patterns of early Carolina than contemporaries and historians have acknowledged. In 1808 historian David Ramsay observed that the proprietary governors "were either ill qualified for their office, or the instructions given them were injudicious." The "weak, unstable, and little respected" government "did not excite a sufficient interest for its own support." He criticized the creation of a landed aristocracy as particularly damaging to the process of settlement. "The title of landgraves were more burthensome than profitable," he wrote, "especially as they were only joined with large tracts of land, which, from the want of laborers, lay uncultivated." Certainly, the Lords Proprietors recognized what historian Converse Clowse called "the erosion of their brand of feudalism by the South

Carolina governments." But Clowse's assertion that they tried "in vain . . . to keep the pattern of land development under their own control," overlooks the influence their guiding vision, policy changes, and personal examples exerted in shaping the early settlement of the colony.[27]

This does not diminish the importance of the planters' individual and collective control over the character of the settled and social landscape in the colony's pioneer years. By petitioning governors and deputies for redress of their grievances, choosing the location of their lands, influencing the shape and surveys of plats, and agreeing or refusing to pay quitrents, emigrants to South Carolina played as pivotal a role in creating a plantation province as did the Lords Proprietors who governed this enterprise. As most historians have recognized, "controversies concerning the land policies had much to do with the ultimate failure of the proprietary regime." In the geographical and social contest for Carolina, land was the penultimate spoil. Only profit surpassed property in the desires of settlers.[28]

Notes

1. In America, "free and common socage" implied that the land grantee owed fealty and rent to the land grantor on penalty of escheat or forfeiture. This was the typical form of landholding throughout the colonial period. Land possessed in fee simple provided the owner and inheritor the unqualified power to dispose of the property. Entailed land was limited in its transmission or bequest to a particular class of owners and heirs. The proprietors generally granted Carolina land in fee simple not fee tail. Mattie Erma Edwards Parker, ed., *North Carolina Charters and Constitutions, 1578–1698*, The Colonial Records of North Carolina, 2d ser., vol. 1 (Raleigh: Carolina Charter Tercentenary Commission, 1963), 74–104. The thirteenth-century English statute of *Quia Emptores* prohibited subinfeudation (creation of new fiefs and vassals) by the nobility. However, the Carolina charters specifically exempted the colony from this law, thus allowing the proprietors to create their own landed aristocracy in the province. Robert K. Ackerman, *South Carolina Colonial Land Policies* (Columbia: University of South Carolina Press, 1977), 6–10.

2. William J. Rivers, *A Sketch of the History of South Carolina* (Charleston, S.C.: McCarter & Co., 1856), 355; Michael MacCarthy-Morrogh, *The Munster Plantation: English Migration to Southern Ireland 1583–1641* (Oxford: Clarendon Press, 1986), 30; Russell R. Menard and Lois Green Carr, "The Lords Baltimore and the Colonization of Maryland," in *Early Maryland in a Wider World*, ed. David B. Quinn (Detroit: Wayne State University Press, 1982), 176–215; "First Set of the Constitutions for the Government of Carolina," in *The Shaftesbury Papers* (Charleston, S.C.: Tempus Publishing, 2000), originally published as Langdon Cheves, ed., "The Shaftesbury Papers and Other Records Relating to Carolina and the First Settlement on Ashley River Prior to the Year 1676," *Collections of the South Carolina Historical Society* (hereafter cited as *CSCHS*) (1897), 94; Rivers, *A Sketch of the History of South Carolina*, 83–84; Ackerman, *South Carolina Colonial Land Policies*, 15–16.

3. Rivers, *A Sketch of the History of South Carolina*, 351–59; A. S. Salley, ed., *Commissions and Instructions from the Lords Proprietors of Carolina to Public Officials of South Carolina, 1685–1715* (Columbia: Historical Commission of South Carolina, 1916), 71.

4. Rivers, *A Sketch of the History of South Carolina*, 349–50; R. Nicholas Olsberg, intro-

duction to *Warrants for Lands in South Carolina, 1672–1711*, ed. A. S. Salley, (Columbia: University of South Carolina Press, 1973), ix–xii; "To Sir Jno: Yeamans," *CSCHS*, 5:314–15; "Coppy of Instruccons Annexed to ye Comission for ye Govern.r & Councell," *CSCHS*, 5:121; Edward T. Price, *Dividing the Land: Early American Beginnings of Our Private Property Mosaic* (Chicago: University of Chicago Press, 1995), 14.

5. "First Set of the Constitutions," *CSCHS*, 5:94; Charles H. Lesser, *South Carolina Begins: The Records of a Proprietary Colony, 1663–1721* (Columbia: South Carolina Department of Archives and History, 1995), 428; "To Mr Joseph West," *CSCHS*, 5:405–6; Records of the Register, Conveyances, vol. 2, South Carolina Department of Archives and History, Columbia (hereafter cited as SCDAH), 1; Lesser, *South Carolina Begins*, 155–57.

6. "The Council Journals," *CSCHS*, 5:391; "Henry Brayne to Lord Ashley," ibid., 215.

7. Lesser, *South Carolina Begins*, 436–37; Records of the Register, Conveyances, vol. 2, SCDAH, 54; Proprietors to Maurice Mathews, in *Records in the British Public Record Office Relating to South Carolina* (hereafter cited as *BPRO*), ed. A. S. Salley, 5 vols. (Columbia: Historical Commission of South Carolina, 1928–1947), 1:130–37. For maps and plats detailing settlement in the colony's first years see Culpeper's *Draught of Ashley* (1671), *CSCHS*, vol. 5, frontispiece; Culpeper's *Plot of the Lords Prop* (1672/3), Public Record Office, London; and Joel Gascoyne's *A New Map of the Country of Carolina* (1682), in William P. Cumming, *The Southeast in Early Maps* (Chapel Hill: University of North Carolina Press, 1962), pl. 39.

8. A. S. Salley, ed., *Journal of the Grand Council, August 25, 1671–June 24, 1680* (Columbia: Historical Commission of South Carolina, 1907), 55; Records of the Register, Conveyances, vol. 2, SCDAH; Henry A. M. Smith, *The Historical Writings of Henry A. M. Smith*, 3 vols. (Spartanburg, S.C.: Reprint Company, Publishers, 1988), 1:2–28.

9. The proprietors distributed the vast majority of land in Carolina through headright grants. Grantees received property in exchange for paying the passage of themselves and other emigrants. The amounts of land granted varied over time and ranged from 150 to 50 acres per person. Feudal grants to the indigenous aristocracy were much larger, usually 12,000 acres. The proprietors and their provincial magistrates occasionally compensated settlers for services rendered to the colony with sizable land grants. For example, in 1677 Lord Ashley ordered the governor to give the explorer Dr. Henry Woodward 2,000 acres for his efforts on behalf of Carolina (*BPRO*, 1:50). Other potential emigrants received gifts of land for promising to transport settlers to the province. The open sale of Carolina land in England and the colony began in the 1680s; however, purchased property never constituted a significant proportion of the total land granted in the proprietary era. Rivers, *A Sketch of the History of South Carolina*, 349–50; R. Nicholas Olsberg, introduction to *Warrants for Lands*, ed. Salley, ix–xii.

10. Proprietors to governor and council, *BPRO*, 1:82–83; proprietors to deputies and council, ibid., 3:271–74.

11. Instructions for governor, ibid., 1:150; format for indenture, ibid., 1:228–32; proprietors to governor, ibid., 1:291–92; proprietors to trustees, ibid., 2:296; proprietors to governor, ibid., 3:84–98.

12. The database assembled for this study contains 3,656 land warrants issued between 1672 and 1711, and 1,327 land grants registered from 1670 to 1722 (tables 3 and 4). Each record contains all extant information concerning grantee names, recordation dates, acreages, geographic locations of granted properties, household members, and neighbors. The land warrants are printed in Salley, ed., *Warrants for Lands*, a literal transcription of

two manuscript volumes. The original warrant and grant records are located in the SCDAH. Ten of the eleven proprietary conveyances volumes kept by the register of the province are available on microfilm in the Library of Congress's Early State Records Project and the collections of the Genealogical Society of Utah. Vol. C has been microfilmed by the SCDAH.

13. The best estimates for the size and character of the colonial population in South Carolina's early years of settlement are found in Converse Clowse, *Economic Beginnings in Colonial South Carolina 1670–1730* (Columbia: University of South Carolina Press, 1971), 251–52.

14. Lesser, *South Carolina Begins*, 136–43, 426–27.

15. Of those warrants that did indicate where colonists should settle, more named Berkeley County (406) as the location for future landholdings, than Colleton (355), Craven (125), or Granville (42) counties. However, the secretaries warranted more acres in Colleton County (214,237) than in Berkeley (173,389) or the other two proprietary counties (table 5).

16. Salley, ed., *Warrants for Lands*, 460, 606, 667; Agnes Leland Baldwin, *First Settlers of South Carolina 1670–1700* (Easley, S.C.: Southern Historical Press, 1985), 267; Lesser; *South Carolina Begins*, 513, Salley, ed., *Warrants for Lands*, 683, 700. The proprietors and the local aristocracy received almost 5 percent of the total warrants issued with an average permit of 1,664 acres, an amount almost five times greater than the mean warrant size for the total population.

17. My aggregate figures differ from Converse Clowse's statistics in table 2 of the appendix in *Economic Beginnings*. He uses contemporary indices, which he acknowledges are incomplete, to estimate the lands granted annually. He finds that between 1670 and 1719 the proprietors disbursed 552,361 acres in 1,062 separate grants. I believe that there is a conveyance volume containing grants from the 1680s and 1690s that no longer survives from the colonial period. I expect that my further research in an "Abstract of Grants" compiled in 1765 for the Board of Trade and sent to London (CO 5/398, Public Record Office; British Manuscript Project, roll D460) will reveal a sizable number of missing land grants.

18. Clowse, *Economic Beginnings*, 98, 251.

19. Rivers, *A Sketch of the History of South Carolina*, 433–34, 439; instructions for Archdale, *BPRO*, 3:140–42; Ackerman, *South Carolina Colonial Land Policies*, 38–40. The negligence of provincial agents in keeping a regular rent roll, despite the near constant demands of the proprietors, suggests that tax collectors knocked infrequently on the colonists' doors. Even those settlers with perfected titles to their lands seldom paid sufficient quitrents.

20. Nathaniel Sayle to proprietors, *BPRO*, 5:300–303; Rivers, *A Sketch of the History of South Carolina*, 442; proprietors to Governor Blake, *BPRO*, 4:111–14.

21. Thomas Hariot, *A briefe and true report of the new found land of Virginia* (1588), in *The Roanoke Voyages, 1584–1590*, ed. David Beers Quinn (New York: Dover Publications, 1991), 385; Price, *Dividing the Land*, 14, 334–35. In her study *Surveyors and Statesmen: Land Measuring in Colonial Virginia* (Richmond: Virginia Surveyors Foundation and Virginia Association of Surveyors, 1979), Sarah Hughes argues that once established, the practice of indiscriminate location promoted rapid economic development at the expense of more orderly expansion.

22. Ackerman, *South Carolina Colonial Land Policies*, 30–31; Salley, ed., *Warrants for Lands*, 4; Linda M. Pett-Conklin, "Cadastral Surveying in Colonial South Carolina: A

Historical Geography" (Ph.D. diss., Louisiana State University, 1986), 87, 111–14; Rivers, *A Sketch of the History of South Carolina*, 358; Dalton to proprietors, *CSCHS*, 5:284–85.

23. Smith, *Historical Writings*, 1:10–11; proprietors to governor, *BPRO*, 2:93–94; Olsberg, xi; Pett-Conklin, "Cadastral Surveying in Colonial South Carolina," 104–16.

24. Ashby was a member of the Royal African Company along with Proprietors Ashley Cooper, Craven, Berkeley, Carteret, and Colleton. Smith, *Historical Writings*, 1:149; Salley, ed., *Warrants for Lands*, 236–37, 260, 531, 572–73, 622; Records of the Register, Conveyances, vol. 2, SCDAH.

25. Records of the Register, Conveyances, vol. C, vol. G, SCDAH; A. S. Salley, ed., *Journal of the Commons House of Assembly of South Carolina, January 30–March 17, 1696* (Columbia: Historical Commission of South Carolina, 1908), 31–41.

26. Lesser, *South Carolina Begins*, 430, 440; Ackerman, *South Carolina Colonial Land Policies*, 34; Salley, ed., *Warrants for Lands*, 5–6, 70, 91, 226, 235, 264, 490, 624; Records of the Register, Conveyances, vol. 2, vol. F, vol. K, SCDAH; Smith, *Historical Writings*, 2:226, 3:75.

27. David Ramsay, *History of South Carolina from Its First Settlement in 1670 to the Year 1808* (Newberry, S.C.: W. J. Duffie, 1858), 23; Clowse, *Economic Beginnings*, 102–3.

28. Ackerman, *South Carolina Colonial Land Policies*, 38.

II

The Huguenots of Proprietary South Carolina

Patterns of Migration and Integration

BERTRAND VAN RUYMBEKE

Isaac Mazyck was born in June 1661 to a mercantile family established in the small port town of Saint-Martin on the northern coast of Ile-de-Ré, an island off La Rochelle.[1] His parents, Paul Mazyck and Elisabeth van Vick, were both Walloons who had moved from Maastricht, the Netherlands, to Saint-Martin by 1642.[2] In November 1685, a few weeks after the revocation of the Edict of Nantes which deprived French Protestants of their religious and civil rights, Isaac left Saint-Martin with his brother Etienne [Stephen]'s wife, Sara Ayrauld, and a nephew.[3] "Coming out of France and escaping the cruel persecution carried on there against the Protestants," and following well-traveled trade routes between Ile-de-Ré and the Netherlands, Isaac and Sara settled in Rotterdam where they joined Stephen.[4] Sometime in 1686, they all left for England and were "denizened" there in April 1687.[5] Whereas Stephen and Sara chose to remain in England, Isaac decided to continue on to South Carolina where documents record his presence as early as August 1689.[6]

In June 1693 Isaac obtained a warrant for a town lot in Charleston. The following October he married Elisabeth LeSerrurier, daughter of Charleston merchant Jacques LeSerrurier and his wife, Elisabeth Léger, both Huguenots from Saint-Quentin, Picardy.[7] Isaac established a successful trading business in Charleston based partly on his Huguenot connections, relatives and fellow refugees settled in the British Isles and South Carolina.[8] In 1697 Isaac was naturalized by the South Carolina Assembly.[9] After a long and materially successful life, Isaac died in 1736 at the age of 75. According to his will, at his death he owned a house, a shop, and a few lots in Charleston as well as several plantations and an island that totaled more than 4,000 acres. Additionally, he bequeathed nearly 32,000 Carolina pounds (4,600 pounds sterling) to his children, grandchildren, and several Charleston congregations.[10]

In many ways, Isaac Mazycq's story is representative of the overall South Carolina Huguenot experience. Aged twenty-four when he left France and twenty-seven when he reached Charleston, Isaac's emigration as a young adult mirrored that of most of his fellow refugees. Also like the majority of them, he hailed from the French Atlantic seaboard. Isaac was a merchant and came from a port town of average size. Among the lowcountry Huguenots, merchants were the second largest occupational group, after the artisans, and a large section of them came from towns like Saint-Martin de Ré. Even though Isaac crossed the Atlantic alone, he had fled to the Netherlands and then to England in the company of close relatives, as had most Carolina Huguenots. Isaac married within his social milieu, the urban mercantile gentry, and married his children to Huguenots of similar wealth and background.[11] Finally, though his marriage was performed by an Anglican minister and he bequeathed money to "the episcopal church," Isaac remained deeply attached to the Calvinist faith in which he had grown up and had raised his children and for the preservation of which he had left France.[12] If he, by and large, quickly and successfully integrated into the nascent Anglo-American Carolina host society, he nonetheless retained a diffuse yet distinct identity based on regional and social affiliations. In this essay, I will first determine how many Huguenots emigrated to proprietary South Carolina and what their geographic and socioeconomic origins were. Then, I will show how their preservation of kinship networks and common social milieus determined three distinct patterns of settlement and integration in the lowcountry.

Estimates of the South Carolina Huguenot Population

Unfortunately, for lack of adequate records, the exact number of Huguenot refugees who settled in South Carolina will never be known. Because only three Huguenot passenger lists are still extant (for the *Richmond* [1680], the *Margaret* [1685] and the *Loyal Jamaica* [1692]) and because arrivals were not systematically recorded, historians have to reconstruct the refugee population from postmigratory records.[13] These consist of specific Huguenot records such as the 1697 naturalization documents and the 1699 census, as well as the more general land, court, probate, and miscellaneous records.

The 1697 naturalization list, known as *"Liste des François et des Suisses,"* names 356 refugees (200 adults and 156 children) to whom twelve adults mentioned in the Act of Naturalization but not in the *Liste* must be added.[14] The 1697 *Liste* enumerates the refugees by name with information about their parents and, if applicable, their spouses and children. The act gives the occupation of each beneficiary. However, because these two sources were compiled in 1697, seventeen years after the arrival of the first Carolina Huguenots, they do not include those who died or left the colony before that year or those who arrived subsequently to 1697. Neither do these sources mention Huguenots who happened to be absent from the colony when the

FIGURE 2.1

NUMBER OF HUGENOTS IN SOUTH CAROLINA BY FIVE YEAR
INTERVALS

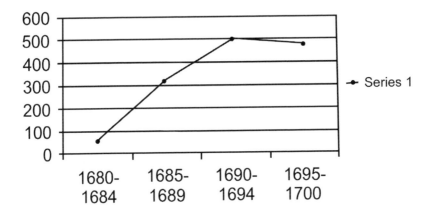

act was passed.[15] Finally, for reasons that are unclear, a few Huguenots whose presence in Carolina at that time is documented elsewhere were not listed either.[16] Therefore, a demographic reconstruction based solely on the 1697 naturalization documents can only produce inaccurate results. Additional names must be gleaned from all types of proprietary records to estimate the total number of Carolina Huguenots. A systematic examination of these records to 1710 yields the names of 135 other refugees.[17] Adding these names to the 212 adults drawn from the naturalization documents results in a total of 347 adult Huguenot migrants present in the colony from 1680 to 1710.[18]

Any attempt to reconstruct the South Carolina Huguenot population and describe its evolution from 1680 to 1710 is seriously complicated by the absence of baptismal, marriage, and burial records. This means that any estimate of the refugee population can only be obtained through hypothetical statistical calculations based on the 1697 *Liste,* which is the only document that gives us precise and reliable demographic information on the Huguenot community at a given time. Since the children are not included in my list, by applying the adult-child ratio found in the 1697 *Liste* to the number of list of 347 adult migrants it is possible to make a fairly accurate estimate of the total number of Huguenots who migrated to South Carolina. This calculation yields a total of 642 individuals.[19]

This number represents only a hypothetical estimate of the Huguenots who were living in South Carolina at one point or another between 1680 and 1710. To determine the evolution of the refugee population this ratio must be applied to the number of adult Huguenots known to be in the province at given times. Following a five-year-interval periodization from 1680 to 1700, from the arrival of the first French settlers to the numerical decline of the Huguenot community, the Carolina Huguenot population evolved thus: between 60 and 80 from 1680 to 1685; 330 and 350 from 1685 to 1690; 480 and 500 from 1690 to 1695; 460 and 480 from 1695 to 1700.[20] Rough as they may be, these figures compare favorably with available contemporary estimates. A Carolina pamphlet written in French in 1685 mentions "a hundred French people" settled in Carolina.[21] In a 1687 letter to the Marquis de Seigneulay, French secretary of the navy, the intendant of La Rochelle wrote that sailors coming from Saint Domingue reported a figure of approximately 400 Huguenots living in Carolina.[22] Finally, the 1697 *Liste* mentions 396 individuals, and the 1699 census 438.[23] In proportion to the colony's white population, the Huguenots represented, respectively, 7 (56/800) in 1680, 20 (497/2,400) in 1690, and 14.5 percent (474/3,260) in 1700, which constitutes an average of 14 percent for the 1680–1700 period.[24]

The Geographic Origins of the Refugees

The geographic origins of the South Carolina Huguenots are quite varied, as no less than fifteen different French provinces are represented.[25] However, this diversity masks the importance of the western regions in general and the La Rochelle area in particular. The five western provinces of Aunis, Saintonge, Poitou, Normandie, and Bretagne make up nearly 60 percent (146/242) of the refugees, with the three provinces of Aunis, which includes La Rochelle, Saintonge, and Poitou accounting for more than 45 percent (109/242).[26]

The predominance of Aunis, Saintonge, and Poitou is explained by the strong economic role La Rochelle played in trade with the Americas. In the decade that preceded the 1685 revocation of the Edict of Nantes, La Rochelle concentrated on colonial trade, which the local intendant called its "great and principal commerce."[27] Whereas in 1664 La Rochelle had only eighteen 100-ton ships, the number had risen to 50 by 1682 and to 93 by 1686. Similarly, from 1664 to 1682 the number of shipowners increased from 37 to 60.[28] Trade with the Americas, especially the West Indies whose traffic grew from ten ships a year in 1642 to fifty-five in 1686, was the reason for this spectacular increase.[29] In the 1670s and 1680s, La Rochelle served as a port of embarkation for its hinterland of Aunis, Saintonge, and Poitou, and a western center for news about the Americas. This role as a regional center and point of contact with North America and the Caribbean became crucial when Huguenots living in the area began to flee the king-

FIGURE 2.2
MAP OF THE PROVINCES OF FRANCE IN 1700

SOURCE: Jacques Carpentier and François Lebrun, eds., *Histoire de France* (Paris: Seuil, 1987), map 10, p. 403.

Huguenots in the sample were from the provinces as listed, with percentages in parentheses. France accounted for 97% of the Huguenots; another 2.5% of the sample were born in Switzerland, and 0.5% were born in London or Amsterdam.

2. Artois (0.4%)
3. Picardy (3.3%)
4. Normandy (10.7%)
5. Ile de France (7.3%)
9. Brittany (4.5%)
11. Orléanais (0.8%)
15. Touraine (6.6%)
16. Berry (3.7%)
18. Poitou (11%)
21. Aunis (22%)
22. Saintonge (10.7%)
25. Lyonnais (0.4%)
26. Dauphiny (4.9%)
27. Guyenne (5.2%)
28. Languedoc (5.5%)

FIGURE 2.3
URBAN ORIGINS OF SOUTH CAROLINA HUGUENOTS

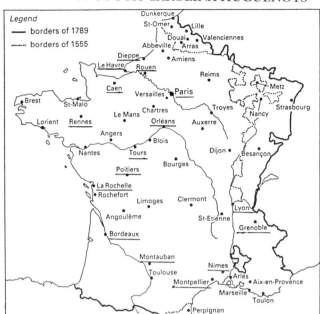

SOURCE: Philip Benedict, ed., *Cities and Social Change in Early Modern France* (London: Unwin Hyman, 1989) 6.

Cities and towns where Huguenots were from are underlined.

dom in the early 1680s. Jean Migault, a schoolteacher from Poitou who settled in England, explained in his memoirs that many Huguenots from Poitou went to La Rochelle and "having found there foreign vessels . . . some fled to Holland, others to England, Ireland and a few to Carolina."[30]

The prominence of this area in the recruitment of refugees for Carolina is also found in the French Protestant emigration to the Caribbean and Québec (New France). The studies of Gérard Lafleur for the French West Indies, as well as of Leslie Choquette and Marc-André Bédard for New France, show that, respectively, 49 percent and 65 percent of Huguenot emigrants came from the three provinces of Aunis, Saintonge, and Poitou.[31] By emphasizing the role of La Rochelle and its Atlantic trade connections, these figures clearly establish that the recruitment of the Carolina Huguenots largely followed pre-revocation transatlantic migratory patterns.

However, the presence of significant numbers of Carolina refugees from areas of France that were *not* involved in the colonial Atlantic economy illustrates that the post-revocation Huguenot exodus was still "a migration of extraordinary nature."[32] More than 14 percent of the Carolina Huguenots came from Dauphiné, a mountainous area in southeastern France, and nearly 20 percent were from Ile-de-France (Paris basin) and the Loire Valley. In contrast, in her study of the New France population, Choquette found only two Huguenots from Touraine and Ile-de-France and one from Dauphiné.[33] Similarly, out of 177 Huguenots established in the French Antilles for whom Lafleur has determined the geographic origins, only five came from Ile-de-France and Touraine.[34] These figures show that, if involvement in or exposure to the transatlantic economy exerted a determining influence on the recruitment of the Carolina Huguenots, other factors, such as promotional literature, local persecution, and simply chance also drew French Protestants from areas having little or no contact with the colonial world to Carolina.

More than 65 percent of the Carolina refugees came from urban areas, of whom 55 percent were from cities, 31 percent from large towns, and 13.5 percent from market towns.[35] Nearly one-third of these Huguenots came from the four maritime ports of Dieppe, Le Havre, La Rochelle, and Bordeaux, which had long been involved in the colonial Atlantic trade. In comparison, Lafleur found that 44 percent of the French Antilles Huguenots came from La Rochelle and 17 percent from Dieppe, for a combined representation of 61 percent.[36] Nonetheless, the migration to South Carolina departs significantly from colonial transatlantic migratory patterns as more than one-third of the Huguenots were from villages. This is a relatively high proportion considering that these refugees were less informed about the colonies and less likely to travel long distances than their urban coreligionists.[37] In contrast, Choquette found that only 14 percent of the New France Huguenots came from rural communities.[38]

Occupations and Status of the Migrants

Of the number of Huguenots whose occupations or status could be identified, artisans made up the largest group with 30 percent (53/175), followed by merchants with nearly 25 percent (39), yeomen and indentured servants with 14 percent each (25), the gentry[39] with 11 percent (20) and professionals[40] with 7.5 percent (13).[41]

Artisans

The large and seemingly homogeneous group of artisans contains important disparities. Artisans who worked wood or metal are the best represented at 22 percent (38/53). The large majority of them were coopers, followed by joiners and different types of smiths. This proportion is largely explained by the fact that Charleston was then a small coastal community that exported lumber and provisions to the Caribbean. In the series of questions and answers

FIGURE 2.4
OCCUPATIONAL DISTRIBUTION OF THE SOUTH CAROLINA
HUGUENOTS

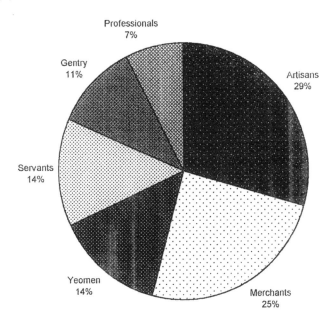

inserted in the pamphlet *Suite de la description de la Carolline*, the answer to
the question "What kind of artisans are the most necessary there [in South
Carolina]?" was "smiths, carpenters, [and] all those who work in the building trades." Similarly, the author of *Plan pour Former un Establissement en
Caroline* advised investors to recruit metal and wood workers, all regarded as
"absolutely necessary."[42] Much less in demand in the nascent South Carolina
economy, the artisans (15 out of 53) working in the textile industry formed
a very homogeneous subgroup. Most of them were weavers (12 out of 15)
and many came from the same areas in France. Unlike the tanners and
shammy-dressers[43] sought by the Indian traders, weavers most likely did not
practice their trades and instead rapidly acquired land to raise livestock, keeping weaving as a secondary activity. A good example is Jean Pétineau, a weaver
who at his death owned a farm of a hundred acres, six slaves, fourteen head
of cattle, two geldings, eleven sheep, and an "old weaver loom."[44]

Other artisans worked in either the luxury or maritime trades. The former, usually goldsmiths, were particularly successful, as the career of Nicolas
de Longuemare, Jr., illustrates. Born in Dieppe in the 1670s, Nicolas arrived
in South Carolina in 1685 with his father, also a goldsmith.[45] His account
ledger for the years 1703–1711 shows that not only did he furnish the

Charleston elite with watches, mourning rings, clocks, silver spoons, and other precious articles, but he also received orders from the colonial government to fashion official seals.[46] Conversely, maritime artisans, most of them marine carpenters, were singularly unsuccessful, as in the case of Pierre and Isaac Dugué, originally from Berry, who left for Jamaica soon after their arrival in the colony.[47]

Merchants

Merchants were the second largest group among the South Carolina Huguenots. They were either local merchants or retailers mixing mercantile activity with agriculture or, especially at turn of the eighteenth century, factors for large London-based companies. The former, by far the most numerous, were either refugees who succeeded in transferring funds to England before leaving France and who thus were able to engage in Caribbean trade shortly after their arrival, or farmer-retailers who sold their production locally, usually silk, wine, and meat. Josias Dupré, for example, was already actively exporting luxury items to Antigua barely three years after his arrival in the colony.[48] La Rochelle refugee Pierre Manigault is also a good example of the farmer-planters who engaged in a multitude of activities besides trade. Upon his arrival in the colony, Pierre first worked as a cooper. He then acquired 400 acres and moved out of Charleston. A few years later, he sold his land, moved back to Charleston, opened a distillery and began to export whisky and rum to England.[49] Likewise, Jean Guerrard, who appeared in the 1697 Naturalization Act as a weaver, cofounded a trading company with fellow refugees ten years later.[50] These merchants usually did not own ships but sold their merchandise to English importers, who were often themselves Huguenot or of recent Huguenot origin. Others leased space on ships, like Isaac Mazycq who bought "one fifth of the hull of the 200-hundred-ton ship called Rebecca and Mary" for 350 Carolina pounds in 1711.[51]

At the turn of the eighteenth century, when trade in Carolina commodities soared, Huguenot factors representing the interests of English companies arrived in Charleston. A generation younger than their predecessors, they first worked for London-based and sometimes Huguenot-owned companies and after a few years, went out on their own, made their fortune, and settled permanently in the colony.[52] One of them, Benjamin Godin, was particularly successful in both politics and economics. Originally from Le Havre, Normandie, he arrived in South Carolina in 1707 as a factor for a British company. He soon became associated with fellow Huguenot refugees Benjamin de la Conseillère and Jean Guerrard in a successful mercantile enterprise. He also entered politics, was twice elected to the South Carolina Assembly, and appointed to the South Carolina Council.[53] At his death, Benjamin Godin possessed an estate of over 11,000 acres, 30,000 Carolina pounds, a plantation in Goose Creek, a house in Charleston, and several hundred slaves.[54]

The geographic origins of the Carolina Huguenot merchants played a crucial role in their decision to migrate to North America. Out of twenty-seven merchants whose place of origin is known, seventeen came from Aunis, Poitou, or Normandie, and fifteen from maritime ports, and seven were from La Rochelle itself.[55] The predominance of Aunis and La Rochelle, even more pronounced for the merchants than for the entire Carolina Huguenot community, is explained by the Huguenot control of the La Rochelle trade and the involvement of Huguenot merchants in transatlantic routes. In the 1680s, when La Rochelle's colonial commerce was growing at a fast pace, twenty-one of the twenty-five wealthiest shipowners in La Rochelle were Huguenot.[56] Several members of these families, such as the Manigaults, the Belins, and the Perdriaus, eventually migrated to South Carolina. In the case of the Manigaults, Bosher has shown that they had traded with Newfoundland and the French West Indies before the revocation of 1685.[57]

Landed Gentry

Along with the merchants, the landed gentry formed an integral part of the South Carolina Huguenot socioeconomic elite. Bearing the titles of *écuyers* or esquires, these Huguenots were *gentilhommes*,[58] that is, members of the French lower provincial nobility, such as the Ravenels, the Bruneaux, the Chasteigners, or the Legrands.[59] The proprietors advertised with some success in promotional pamphlets published in French the possibility of acquiring manorial estates with judicial privileges, at a very low price or as an outright gift. These manors turned out to be an efficient promotional device probably because the Huguenots were familiar with the seigniorial system that was prevalent in Québec at the time. Granting manors to Huguenots was a subtle way to attract the wealthiest of them without relinquishing much power, as Carolina manorial lords were not members of the colony's infant aristocracy as they did not sit in the council.[60] With or without manorial privileges, the promise of owning large estates remained attractive to wealthy Huguenots. This is illustrated by the extant land warrants of fifteen of these refugees, which indicate that collectively they acquired 24,000 acres, for an individual average of 1,600 acres, and that six of them bought or received 3,000 acres each.[61]

Yeomen

Nearly 15 percent of the South Carolina Huguenots referred to themselves as planters. This term is very confusing to a modern reader as the seventeenth-century South Carolina planters were all but rich landowners. In fact they were yeomen. Unlike the term esquire, the word planter refers to an occupation, not a status. The 1697 Naturalization Act, which lists recipients along with their occupations in parentheses, contains no esquires and indicates that the Huguenot planters were at best modest farmers, some of them actually owning no land at all. Extant land sources show that, of the twelve Huguenots referred to as planters in the act, ten had not yet acquired land and the other two owned only 150 acres each, the minimum granted to a family of three.[62] The majority of these farmers settled on land owned by close relatives, like Pierre Poitevin, who settled with his father Antoine, or Louis and René Juin, who worked on their brother George's farm, or were hired by other Huguenots.[63] Landless or not, these farmers were generally of modest socioeconomic extraction, usually former artisans, who were free or indentured at the time of their migration.[64] These refugees thus were not peasants who emigrated, but artisans who were unable to practice their trades and had to work land for a living.

Indentured Servants

Although they represent a significant proportion of the migrants, Huguenot indentured servants either have been underestimated or ignored by historians, probably because none of them are mentioned in extant inventories and no contract of indenture survives.[65] Huguenot servants appear only in the passenger lists of the *Richmond* and the *Margaret* and in a few wills and land warrants. These servants totaled thirty-seven, of whom twenty-five are mentioned by name, and twelve are referred to anonymously.[66] These twenty-five identified servants represent 14 percent of the Carolina Huguenots whose status or occupation is known. This percentage is corroborated by the passenger list of the *Margaret,* which contains nine servants out of fifty-four free migrants or 16 percent.[67] Huguenot servants were especially numerous in the first years of the migration, more than 90 percent (28) of them arriving in South Carolina before 1687 and 38 percent (14) before 1685, a time when there were few slaves in the colony and when proprietary land policies made importing servants profitable. The occupations of the Huguenot indentured servants is difficult to determine because they appear in the sources either as *engagés* or servants.[68] Of the five male servants whose trades can be identified, four were artisans (two coopers, a weaver, and a saddler), and one was a planter.[69] A total of fourteen Huguenots arrived in Carolina with thirty-seven servants, for an average of slightly less than three servants per master, with a range between one and six. The Huguenots who owned servants were mainly merchants. Of nine masters whose occupation or status is known, five were merchants, two were large landowners (esquires), one was an artisan (gunsmith), and one a pastor.

Others

The eleven other Huguenots whose occupations have been determined were in the medical (6), pastoral (4), and legal (1) professions. Of the first six, five appear in the sources with the title of doctor, which like that of esquire, was often loosely used.[70] Except perhaps for Jean Thomas, whose medical expertise was emphatically recognized by Anglican commissary Gideon Johnston, in all likelihood most of them were surgeon-barbers and none of them, including Thomas, practiced their trade on a regular basis.[71] Conversely, the four Huguenot pastors were assuredly doctors of theology and ministered congregations throughout their lives. Finally, one refugee was recorded as a lawyer although it is doubtful that he ever practiced law in Carolina.[72]

Social Networks and Patterns of Settlement

One of the letters compiled in the Carolina promotional pamphlet *Suite de la Description de la Carolline* recommended that "to decide to go to America, one must travel among several families because otherwise . . . one has to spend his life with people who do not always turn out to be honest.[73] The Huguenots heeded this recommendation, and the preservation of kinship ties proved to be a determining factor in their migration to South Carolina. Of the 347 migrants identified, more than 40 percent emigrated with one or several family members other than their spouse and their children.[74] For nearly half, the relative was a sibling; close to a third of these refugees arrived with at least one parent.[75] A study of the passenger lists of the *Richmond* and *Margaret* corroborates these findings. Thirteen out of the twenty-two Huguenots on board the *Richmond* were registered with their families, and the fifty-two French passengers of the *Margaret* made up a group of just eight families. Family sizes on both ships varied from two to eight members, but the majority of them included more than four people.[76]

A significant proportion of Carolina Huguenots also emigrated in clusters of families. Some, usually from the same area in France, met in London and decided to continue on to Carolina from there. In other cases, related families from the same town and socioeconomic milieu migrated together to Carolina from France via England. The pattern appeared at both ends of the social spectrum: with the gentry families of Ravenel, DuBourdieu, Saint-Julien and De Farcy from Vitré in Bretagne and with the weavers Poitevin, Trézévant and Dutartre who were from contiguous parishes in Beauce. These refugees, who arrived in Carolina either together or within a few years of each other, were all related by marriage, and in the case of the gentry families, had been so for generations.[77] Unlike the gentry and the weavers, who migrated in established family networks, families from urban mercantile communities of western France emigrated separately. They often left behind relatives in France, England, or Holland and formed marital alliances and/or business partnerships based on common regional and social origins once in South Carolina. These merchant families may or may not have known each other before the migration—though some most likely did—and did not migrate together, but a strong sense of communal identity later cemented their unions in the colony. The Guérards, Manigaults, Pasquereaus, Godins, and Mazycks are illustrative of this type of regrouping.

Once in South Carolina, the transfer of these networks to different areas of the lowcountry illustrates three distinct patterns of integration: urban mercantile and artisanal in Charleston, rural gentry in Santee, and rural artisanal in Orange Quarter. The Huguenots who settled in Charleston before 1700 were almost exclusively urban merchants and artisans.[78] More than half of them were from French towns of more than 10,000 inhabitants, and many of them acquired contiguous lots in Charleston, thus forming "French quarters." The Huguenot community of Santee, some forty miles north of Charleston, was predominantly composed of members of the lower gentry. Acquiring large estates, sometimes with manorial privileges, they established a local landed elite following premigratory patterns. Not surprisingly, five of the six Craven (Santee) County representatives elected to the 1692 South Carolina assembly belonged to the Chasteigner, Ravenel, Bruneau, Saint-Julien, and Lebas families. Two of them, the Ravenels and Saint-Juliens, were even related by marriage before the migration.[79] The community of Orange Quarter, a few miles up the Cooper River, offers a third type of settlement pattern with the weavers-turned-yeomen from Ile-de-France and Beauce who belonged to a few related families such as the Dutartres, Trézévants, Poitevins, and Bochets.[80]

Therefore, by 1700 three distinct Huguenot communities were established in the lowcountry, all predominantly based on an often preexisting network of a few related families who shared common social and geographic origins. The Charleston community, composed of urban mercantile and artisanal families from western France were wealthy, educated, and thoroughly anglicized. The merchants especially possessed extensive trade and familial connections across the Atlantic, which were reinforced and enlarged with the arrival of the younger Huguenot factors at the turn of the eighteenth century. The semi-isolated settlement of Santee, which was controlled by an equally wealthy although perhaps more provincial elite, kept in close contact with the Charleston Huguenot mercantile community. Finally, the isolated Orange Quarter, where no wealthy merchants or manorial lords settled, was without a French elite that could represent their specific interests. Not surprisingly, the process of integration of the Carolina Huguenot population,

measured by the two indices of exogamous marriages and Anglican conformity, occurred at an unequal pace and in different circumstances in these
three distinct communities.[81]

Patterns of Integration: Marital Unions and Anglican Conformity

Before 1700 very few Carolina Huguenots had married outside the group,
and those who did were predominantly merchants residing in Charleston.[82]
This is due to the fact that the Huguenot mercantile community lived in a
somewhat cosmopolitan environment and needed to establish contacts
throughout the English-speaking world. Yet, these were exceptions until
1700, as even in Charleston most Huguenots had a French spouse, like Isaac
Mazycq who married Elisabeth LeSerrurier.

In Santee, the Huguenot gentry families intermarried almost exclusively
among themselves or with Charleston merchant Huguenot families. The
Saint-Juliens intermarried with the Ravenels, as they had done in their
hometown of Vitré, and the Dubourdieus with the Dugués, a Charleston
merchant family. These unions served to consolidate estates, to strengthen
the political control that these families had over the county, and after 1706,
parish institutions, and were the expression of an esprit de corps.

In the first decades of the eighteenth century, however, these
Huguenots began to intermarry with English settlers. For them, the preservation of estates and status became more important than their French identity. Viewed from a broad perspective this trend can be interpreted as a sign
of an overall integration. From a local perspective, however, these exogamous unions represented more the merging of Huguenot and English
landed and mercantile families. In the Orange Quarter settlement, one finds
the same endogamous marriage trend among Huguenots of equal status as
long as the local French matrimonial market made it possible. Ten out of the
eighteen individuals listed under the Orange Quarter entry in the 1697 *Liste*
belonged to the three related artisan families of Poitevin-Trézévant-
Dutartre.[83] As in the other Huguenot communities, the Orange Quarter
Huguenots progressively intermarried with English settlers. Jon Butler's
study of the parish records of St. Denis and St. Thomas[84] shows that out of
five unions celebrated between 1701 and 1710, three were exogamous, with
the proportion reaching six out of seven for the period 1711–1720 and five
out of six for the years 1721–1730.[85] These figures clearly demonstrate that
after 1710 with the Carolina-born generation coming of age, the majority
of marital unions were made outside the group.

The three Huguenot communities of Charleston, Santee, and Orange
Quarter also reacted differently to the problem of conforming to the Angli-

can church after it became the official, or established, religion in the colony in 1706. In Charleston, while the French Calvinist church resisted conformity and remained active until the 1790s, most Huguenots, especially the merchants, maintained what Butler has called "a dual affiliation."[86] Thus, for example, while signing documents as an elder of the French church, the merchant Benjamin de la Conseillère was at the same time an Anglican church commissioner in the Act of Establishment of 1706.[87] Patterns of testamentary bequests among Charleston Huguenot merchants also indicate a dual affiliation, as the wealthiest of them gave funds to both the Anglican parish of St.Philip's and the French church for the ministers and for the relief of the poor. Isaac Mazyck, for example, bequeathed twenty-five pounds for the poor of the Anglican and Presbyterian churches, respectively, and fifty pounds for those of the Huguenot church.[88] This dual affiliation represents an effort to integrate into the urban socioeconomic structure of the colony while attempting to preserve an ancestral identity.

In the rural parish of St. James Santee, the wealthy Huguenot landowning families quickly took control of the vestry. René Ravenel and Phillipe Gendron were appointed commissioners for Santee in the 1706 Act of Establishment.[89] Yet, in a 1708 document, the same individuals used the French Calvinist term *ancien* (elder) to designate themselves.[90] This shows that the Santee Huguenots managed to preserve a French Calvinist structure within an Anglican parish, what Amy Friedlander calls "a cultural residue within an English superstructure,"[91] and confirms the fact that a few prominent families controlled both the religious and political life of the Santee community. These families served as a sort of "cultural buffer" between the Carolina Anglo-Anglican elite and the Santee refugees, and as such played a crucial role in facilitating their integration.

In Orange Quarter, where no such landed or mercantile elite emerged, the religious integration of the Huguenot community within the Anglican fold proved to be long and tumultuous. Unlike the Santee community, the Orange Quarter Huguenots did not manage to obtain their own parish when the Anglican church was established in 1706. Therefore they knew that their congregation, temporarily named St. Denis parish, would at some point be absorbed by the larger English parish of St. Thomas of which it was a part.[92] As a result, when dissension appeared within the St. Denis community in the early 1710s, as it did in all South Carolina Huguenot congregations that were divided over the conduct of the services, the nonconformist[93] faction took over the congregation, fired their conformist minister, and seceded from the colony's Anglican parish network. They first asked the Charleston Huguenot pastor, Paul L'Escot, to serve their congregation, and after being refused, they turned to the London Huguenot church of Threadneedle Street, which sent them a Calvinist pastor. The newly appointed minister, Pierre Stouppe, eventually conformed to Anglicanism and moved to New Rochelle, New York, as a missionary of the Society for the Propagation of the Gospel in Foreign Parts.[94]

In 1722, a few years after the isolated Orange Quarter congregation had been more or less spiritually left to its own devices, they welcomed back the original St. Denis conformist pastor, Jean LaPierre. The following year, three Orange Quarter Huguenot families fell victim to religious fanaticism predicting "the destruction of mankind a Second Time from off the face of the earth."[95] Religious fanaticism led to civil disobedience as they refused to serve in the county militia or to help maintain the parish highways. The affair turned bloody with the murder of a Huguenot justice of the peace who had come to place them under arrest.[96] Interestingly enough, two of the three Huguenot families involved in resisting Anglican conformity during the "St. Denis revolt" and the "Dutartre affair" were among the original Orange Quarter families of artisans from Ile-de-France, the Dutartres, and the Bochets.[97] In this community, families of lower social extraction lived in isolation and resented the domination of an Anglo-Anglican elite, even though it was as tolerant as it could be. Their attempt to preserve their French Calvinist identity turned violent precisely because of the absence of a "cultural buffer" similar to the one provided by the Huguenot gentry families in Santee.

About six hundred Huguenots emigrated to South Carolina between 1680 and 1710. During this period, they never represented more than 20 percent of the colony's white population, with their proportion reaching a peak in the early 1690s. Although they came from more than sixteen French provinces, close to half of them were from the western seaboard, especially the provinces of Aunis, Saintonge, and Poitou. Predominantly of urban origin, most of the Carolina Huguenots were artisans and merchants. The vast majority of them emigrated in families or groups of related families and successfully transferred their premigratory kinship and social networks, which determined their pattern of settlement. Through the proprietary period, these transplanted networks played a crucial role in their integration into the Carolina Anglo-American society. While being absorbed by the dominant cultural and religious model, they managed to preserve an identity that was neither Calvinist nor French but familial and social. Finally, with the emergence of the second generation, the French networks expanded and merged with English networks and allowed the Huguenots to exert a subtle but nonetheless significant influence in shaping Carolina colonial society.

Notes

1. "Extracts from the Register of Saint-Martin de l'Ile-de-Re," in "Notes on the Mazyck Family," comp. and ed. Katherine B. Mazyck, *Transactions of the Huguenot Society of South Carolina* 37 (1932): 47.

2. Archives Nationales, série TT, fol. 263 A, "Registre Consistoire/Ile-de-Ré,

1628–1677," pièce 401. Genealogists have Paul Mazyck in Saint-Martin "sometime before 1648" because the church register resumed in 1648, after the church had been closed for two decades, and Paul Mazyck appeared in it that year. However, the above-cited document in the Archives Nationales mentions the birth of Paul's eldest son, Paul, in 1642 in Saint-Martin. The name Mazyck comes from the town of Maaseyek, on the Maas River, located in the bishopric of Liège, in present-day southeastern Belgium. Mazyck, "Notes on the Mazyck family," 43. Once in France both names, Mazyck and Van Vyck, were made more French by replacing the "k" with either "cq" or "cque." Thus, they were spelled Mazycq and Van Evycq in the French records. Interestingly enough, in South Carolina Isaac Mazyck spelled his name Mazycq but his Carolina-born children reverted to the Walloon spelling. Isaac Mazyck, along with the Boyds, Jacques, Jean, and Gabriel, are Carolina examples of Huguenots of recent foreign (non-French) origins described in John-Francis Bosher's article "Huguenot Merchants and the Protestant International in the Seventeenth Century," *William and Mary Quarterly*, 3d ser., 52 (1995): 77–102.

3. "A Literal Translation taken from My Grand father Stephen Mazyck's Registry kept and wrote by himself in an old French Bible by me his Grand Son Peter Hamon in the year 1786," Huguenot Society of South Carolina Library, Charleston, S.C., Mazyck folder, 2.

4. Ibid.

5. William A. Shaw, ed., *Letters of Denization and Acts of Naturalization for Aliens in England and Ireland, 1603–1700*, Huguenot Society of London Publications, quarto series, vol. 18 (Lymington, England, 1911), 188–89. Denization was granted by the crown, as opposed to naturalization, which was the exclusive prerogative of Parliament, and conferred only limited rights. Daniel Statt, "The Birthright of an Englishman: The Practice of Naturalization and Denization under the Later Stuarts and Early Hanoverians," *Proceedings of the Huguenot Society of Great Britain and Ireland* 25 (1989): 61–74.

6. Miscellaneous Records (conveyance book), vol. 1682–1690, South Carolina Department of Archives and History (hereafter cited as SCDAH), 335–36.

7. A. S. Salley, and R. Nicholas Olsberg, eds., *Warrants for Lands in South Carolina, 1672–1711* (Columbia: University of South Carolina Press, 1973), 435 and 631. Isaac Mazyck's marriage license was mistakenly filed with the land warrants. Settlers first received warrants, and after having their properties surveyed, they were given grants. Mazyck received his grant in October 1696. Colonial Land Grants (copy series), vol. 38, SCDAH, 208. On the LeSerruriers see Daniel Ravenel, ed., *"Liste des François et des Suisses" from an old manuscript list of French and Swiss Protestants settled in Charleston, on the Santee and at the Orange Quarter in Carolina who desired naturalization prepared probably about 1695–6* (Charleston, 1868; reprint, Baltimore: Clearfield Company Reprints and Remainders, 1990), 45.

8. In London, he had his father-in-law, Jacques LeSerrurier, as well as his brother Etienne. In South Carolina, he married his daughter to Benjamin Godin, a wealthy Huguenot merchant. He also had connections in the Caribbean where he traveled in 1689.

9. Thomas Cooper and David J. McCord, eds., *Statutes at Large of South Carolina*, 10 vols. (Columbia, A.S. Johnston, 1836–1841), 2:131–32.

10. Will of Isaac Mazyck (10 Jan. 1736), South Carolina Court of Probate, vol. KK, SCDAH, 338–42.

11. For example, his daughters married into the Godin and Gendron families. Ibid.

12. In his will, Isaac mentioned his escape from "la nouvelle babylonne" and warned his children "never to abandon our good and holy religion in which they were born and raised" ("de ne jamais abandoner notre bonne et sainte religion den laquelle ils sont né & eslevé"). Will of Isaac Mazyck, 341.

13. The existence of these passenger lists is not just coincidental but is due to specific contemporary circumstances prevailing at the time of their recording. The list of the *Richmond* was duly recorded and filed in the Admiralty papers because the *Richmond* was an HMS frigate and her voyage was financed by the crown. The *Margaret* left England after the Monmouth rebellion at a time when ship captains were required to report the names of their passengers. As for the *Loyal Jamaica*, it is not strictly speaking a passenger list that is extant but a list of passengers who disembarked in Charleston and for whom some Carolina settlers posted bond because the *Loyal Jamaica* was believed to be a "privateer or a Pyratt ship." For the *Richmond* see Orders in Council, 1679–1688, Admiralty Papers (ADM) 1/5139, Public Record Office, London (hereafter cited as PRO), 162; E. H. Fairbrother, comp., "Foreign Protestants for Carolina in 1679," *Proceedings of the Huguenot Society of London* 10 (1912):187–89; and St. Julien R. Childs, "The Petit-Guérard Colony," *South Carolina Historical and Genealogical Magazine* 43 (1942):1–17 and 88–97. For the *Margaret*, see State Papers (SP) 44/336, PRO, 163; "The Passenger List of the *Margaret*," *Transactions of the Huguenot Society of South Carolina* 93 (1988): 32–34; and Charles H. Lesser, *South Carolina Begins: The Records of a Proprietary Colony, 1663–1721* (Columbia, South Carolina Department of Archives and History, 1995), 78. For the *Loyal Jamaica*, see the appendix to *Journal of the Grand Council of South Carolina, August 25, 1671–June 24, 1680*, ed. Alexander S. Salley (Columbia, The historical Commission of South Carolina, 1907), 61; Salley, ed., *Journals of the Grand Council, April 11, 1692–September 26, 1692* (Columbia, 1907), 16–19; and Lesser, *South Carolina Begins*, 219 n. 102. A third ship was recorded in June 1685 planning to leave England Carolina-bound with "about two hundred French people" on board but no passenger list has survived. Privy Council (PC) 2/71, PRO, 99. I would like to thank Thomas O. Lawton for informing me of the existence of this fourth ship.

14. Daniel Ravenel, ed., *Liste*. The 1697 Naturalization Act is in *Statutes at Large*, ed. Thomas Cooper and McCord, vol. 2 (1682–1716): 131–32. The original is no longer extant but a contemporary copy can be found in the John Archdale Papers, Library of Congress (microfilm copy at the SCDAH), 140–42.

15. Barthelemy Gaillard, for example, returned to France in 1697 to sell his parents' house and is therefore not included in the *Liste* or the Naturalization Act. Jeanne Skalsky-Coignard, "Une famille languedocienne en Caroline du Sud: les Gaillard," *Cahiers du Centre de Généalogie Protestante* 19 (1994): 9–13.

16. Their absence from the 1697 naturalization records could be due to their unwillingness to be naturalized, the unawareness of the existence of the *Liste*, or simply the fact that parts of the original *Liste* may be missing.

17. These records are Miscellaneous Records (Proprietary Series), Conveyance Books, Records of the Court of the Common Pleas; and the volumes of land grants, all deposited at the SCDAH, as well as Salley and Olsberg, eds., *Warrants for Lands*.

18. This figure corresponds to the number of adult refugees who *migrated* to South Carolina and does not differentiate between the Huguenots who stayed and those who left. For a description of the methods used to identify Huguenots in the records see Bertrand van Ruymbeke, "L'émigration huguenote en Caroline du Sud sous le régime des Seigneurs Propriétaires: Etudes d'une communauté du Refuge dans une province britannique d'Amérique du Nord, 1680–1720," (Thèse de doctorat, La Sorbonne-Nouvelle, 1995), 1:283–90. The 347 adult refugees represent more than two and a half times the number included in Friedlander's list (136), almost exclusively based on the 1697 naturalization records. Amy E. Friedlander, "Carolina Huguenots: A Study in Cultural Pluralism in the Low Country, 1679–1768" (Ph.D. diss., Emory University, 1979), 86–88 and 322–25.

19. The adult-child ratio in the 1697 *Liste* is 0.85 (182 adults for 156 children). Not all the *Liste* could be used for determining this ratio as section three (Orange Quarter)

does not list the children. Therefore the number of adults is smaller by 18 (182 instead of 200). We applied this ratio to our list of 347 adults to determine a number of children and then added this number to the 347 (347 x 0.85 = 295; 347 + 295 = 642). Unfortunately, this method has two problems. First, it takes the 1697 adult-child ratio as a set parameter, whereas it necessarily evolved through time. Second, it does not differentiate between the children born in Carolina after the migration and those born overseas.

20. After 1700 this method of calculation becomes less reliable because of the emergence of the second generation refugees, as those who were children in the 1680s start to form families.

21. "*Une centaine de François,*" "Questions et Responses faites au sujet de la Caroline," 54. Bibliothèque Municipale de La Rochelle, Recueil de documents divers, n. 1909.

22. "*Environ 400 François,*" "Lettre au Marquis de Seigneulay" (14 June 1687), MS Naf., Arnoul 21334, Bibliothèque Nationale, 194. This figure is to be interpreted as a minimum since, as a rule, royal officials wished to play down the number of Huguenots who managed to escape France.

23. Ravenel, ed., *Liste;* and CO 5/1258 (1699), PRO.

24. For estimates of the white population of South Carolina see Peter Coclanis, *The Shadow of a Dream: The Economic Life and Death of the South Carolina Low Country* (New York: Oxford University Press, 1989), table 3.1, 64.

25. The geographic origins could be determined for 242 refugees, that is, nearly 70 percent of my list.

26. The breakdown by province is Aunis (55 refugees/22%), Poitou (28/11%), Normandie (26/10.7%), Saintonge (26/10.7%) and Bretagne (11/4.5%).

27. Quoted in Marcel Delafosse et al., ed., *Histoire de La Rochelle* (Toulouse: Privat, 1985), 163.

28. John G. Clark, *La Rochelle and the Atlantic Economy during the Eighteenth Century* (Baltimore: Johns Hopkins University Press, 1981), 26 and 27. Jean Delumeau, "Le commerce extérieur français au XVIIe siècle," *XVIIeme Siecle* 70 (1966): 94–95. La Rochelle also actively traded with Quebec, Boston, and New York. Bosher, "Huguenots Merchants," 80–83.

29. Delafosse et al., *Histoire de La Rochelle,* 167. Clark, *La Rochelle and the Atlantic,* 26–27.

30. *Journal de Jean Migault ou malheurs d' une famille protestante du Poitou victime de la révocation de l' édit de Nantes (1682-1689),* Yves Krumenacker, ed., (Paris: Editions de Paris, 1995), 37. For an English version of Migault's account, see *Jean Migault or the Trials of a French Protestant Family during the Period of the Revocation of the Edict of Nantes,* William Anderson, ed., (Edinburgh: Johnstone and Hunter, 1852).

31. For Lafleur 38/77; for Choquette, 90/137 just for Aunis and Saintonge; and for Bédard, 103/156. Gérard Lafleur, *Les protestants aux Antilles françaises du Vent sous l'ancien régime* (Basse-Terre, Guadeloupe: Société de l' histoire de la Guadeloupe, 1988), 38. Leslie Choquette, *Frenchmen into Peasants: Modernity and Tradition in the Peopling of French Canada* (Cambridge, Mass.: Harvard University Press, 1997), 133–34. Marc-Andre Bédard, "Les protestants en Nouvelle-France," *Cahiers d'Histoire de la Société Historique de Québec* 31 (1978): 43.

32. Following the classification of French historical demographer, Jean-Pierre Poussou, who distinguishes between traditional or customary migrations, colonial migrations, migrations of an exceptional nature, and migration without settlement. Jean-Pierre Poussou, "Les mouvements migratoires en France et à partir de la France de la fin du XVe siècle au début du XIXe siècle: Approches pour une synthèse," *Annales de Démographie Historique,* vol. 7 (1970): 22.

33. Choquette, *Frenchmen into Peasants,* 134. Bédard's figures differ slightly as he found 12 Huguenots from "Ile-de-France" and none from Dauphiné. Bédard, "Les protestants en Nouvelle-France," 43.

34. Lafleur, *Les protestants aux Antilles,* 38.

35. A city (*une grande* or *très grande* [+ 30,000] *ville*) has more than 10,000 inhabitants, a town (*ville moyenne*) between 5,000 and 10,000, and a market town (*une petite ville*) between 2,000 and 5,000. Although population is only one of the criteria that differentiate a city or a town from a village, along with the presence of walls, military and/or financial autonomy, the location of a court or a see, and economic structure, this is the one that has been retained for statistical purposes. The term "urban" has to be understood only in contrast to rural. My representation rate is somewhat lower that the rate I recorded for the geographic origin because many refugees gave their province of origin without naming a place of residence and because I was not always able to find the seventeenth-century population of the communities of origin mentioned by the refugees, and finally because I did not include the Swiss. Benoît Garnot, *Les villes en France aux XVIe, XVIIe et XVIIIe siècles* (Paris: Ophrys, 1989); Jean Meyer et Jean-Pierre Poussou, *Etudes sur les villes françaises: Milieu du XVIIe siècle à la veille de la révolution française* (Paris: SEDES, 1995). Philip Benedict, "La population réformée française de 1600 a 1685," *Annales E.S.C.* (Nov.–Dec. 1987): 1440; *The Huguenot Population of France, 1600–1682: The Demographic Fate and Customs of a Religious Minority, Transactions of the American Philosophical Society* 81 (Philadelphia, 1991): 28–68.

36. Lafleur, *Les protestants aux Antilles,* 41–42.

37. Exactly 34.6 percent (51/147).

38. Choquette, *Frenchmen into Peasants,* 134.

39. The term "gentry" refers to Huguenot large landowners who bore the titles of *écuyer* (esquire) or *sieur de* and for whom no occupation was recorded (see also n. 41).

40. Professional is a loose term used to denote refugees employed either in medicine, religion, or law.

41. It was possible to determine the status or occupations of 168 out of the 245 men and also 7 female indentured servants for a total of 175 individuals. This is a representation rate of 68.5%. Being more interested in occupation than status when I had both, as in the case of a "merchant-esquire," I recorded merchant.

42. *Suite de la Description de la Carolline* (Geneva: Jacques de Tournes, 1685), 16; *Plan pour Former un Establissement en Caroline* (The Hague: Meindert Uytwerg, 1686), 16.

43. A dresser finishes leather after tanning. Shammy, which comes from the French *chamois* (mountain goat), refers to the deer hide.

44. Inventory of Jean Pétineau (21 Nov. 1722), Miscellaneous Records (Proprietary series), 1722–1724, SCDAH, 21–23.

45. Ravenel, ed., *Liste,* 61; "Passenger List," 34.

46. Samuel G. Stoney, ed., "Nicholas de Longuemare: Huguenot Goldsmith and Silk Dealer in Colonial South Carolina," *Transactions of the Huguenot Society of South Carolina* 55 (1950): 59. Alexander S. Salley, ed., *Journal of the Commons House of Assembly, 1707* (Columbia: The Historical Commission of South Carolina, 1940), 14–15, and Salley, ed., *Journal of the Commons House of Assembly, 1707–1708* (Columbia: The Historical Commission of South Carolina, 1941), 20. See also E. Milby Burton, *South Carolina Silversmiths, 1690–1860* (1942; new edition revised by Warren Ripley, Charleston: Contributions from the Charleston Museum, 1991). Let us note that like the weavers, early Carolina goldsmiths had to find other sources of revenues. De Longuemare, for example, sold silk along with his silver and gold artifacts.

47. Records of the Secretary of the Province, 1727–1729, SCDAH, 84.

48. St. Julien R. Childs, "Exports from Charles Town, 1690," *Transactions of the Huguenot Society of South Carolina* 54 (1949): 30–34.

49. Maurice A. Crouse, "The Manigault Family of South Carolina, 1685–1783" (Ph.D. diss., Northwestern University, 1964), 5–15.

50. Will of Jean Guérard (20 June 1714), Miscellaneous Records (Proprietary series), 1711–1719, SCDAH, 46–49. Cooper et al., eds., *Statutes at Large*, 2:132. R. C. Nash, "Trade and Business in Eighteenth-Century South Carolina," *South Carolina Historical Magazine* 96 (1995): 8–9.

51. Miscellaneous Records (Proprietary series), 1711–1717, SCDAH, 9.

52. R. C. Nash, "Cosmopolitan Influences in the Development of the Atlantic Economy: The South Carolina and European Huguenots and the Growth of the South Carolina Economy, 1680–1775" (paper presented at the 1997 Charleston Huguenot Conference, "Out of Babylon: The Huguenots and Their Diaspora"), 14–15.

53. Walter B. Edgar and Louise Bailey, eds., *Biographical Directory of the South Carolina House of Representatives*, (Columbia: University of South Carolina Press, 1977), vol. 2, *The Commons House of Assembly, 1692–1776*, 296.

54. This an estimate made from his will dated 26 Dec. 1747. Charleston County Wills, WPA (Work Progress Administration) Transcripts, vol. 6 (1747–1752), 85–88; Jon Butler, *The Huguenots in America: A Refugee People in New World Society* (Cambridge, Mass.: Harvard University Press, 1983), 122.

55. The others are 3 from Bordeaux, 1 from Dieppe, 1 from Le Havre, and 3 from Saint-Martin-de-Ré like Isaac Mazyck.

56. Louis Perouas, *Le diocèse de La Rochelle de 1648 a 1724: Sociologie et pastorale* (Paris: S.E.V.P.E.N., 1964), 137. See also Clark's study, which shows that in 1685, the year of the revocation, of the 16 most important La Rochelle merchant families 14 were Huguenot. Clark, *La Rochelle and the Atlantic*, 45.

57. Bosher, "Huguenot Merchants," 82–85. Bosher, *Men and Ships in the Canada Trade, 1660–1760* (Ottawa: Canada Communication Group, 1992), 93. The same can be said of the Boyds who were from Bordeaux. Ibid., 93.

58. Historians of late seventeenth-century France distinguish three strata within the nobility: the *ducs et pairs de France,* who were very few and who, most of the time, were related to the monarch, the members of the *noblesse seconde,* who occupied high administrative and military positions, and the *gentilhommes,* who controlled much smaller revenues, lived on their estates and exerted little influence beyond their communities. Jean-Marie Constant, *La société française aux XVIe-XVIIe-XVIIIe siècles* (Paris, Ophrys, 1994), 29–31. Only the Huguenot Jacques Martel Goulard de Vervant, who bore the title of "chevalier baronet," seemed to have been of a higher status than *gentilhomme.*

59. By landed gentry I mean Huguenots who lived off large estates and for whom no occupation is recorded. The often inflated title of esquire is not of course distinctive in itself as merchants and "doctors" often bore it too. Also, it is clear that some merchants could stop practicing their trade and then become part of the landed gentry.

60. As explained in *Suite de la Description de la Carolline* (34), "those who own 3,000 acres do not have more powers in the Lower House than those who own 500 acres."

61. Salley and Olsberg, eds., *Warrants for Lands;* Salley, ed., *Records in the British Public Record Office Relating to South Carolina [1663-1710],* 5 vols. (Columbia: The Historical Commission of South Carolina, 1928-1947).

62. Cooper and McCord, eds., *Statutes at Large,* 2:132. Salley and Olsberg, eds., *Warrants for Lands.* Van Ruymbeke, "L'émigration huguenote en Caroline du Sud," 1:313–15.

63. Ravenel, ed., *Liste,* 59.

64. For example, before becoming planters, Antoine Poitevin was a weaver, Charles

Fromaget an indentured servant, and Louis Lansac a merchant. Ravenel, ed., *Liste,* 59. Salley and Olsberg, eds., *Warrants for Lands,* 245; Conveyance books, v. 1707–1711, SCDAH, 28–29.

65. Hirsch briefly touches on the subject but does not differentiate between servants and apprentices. Butler mentions them only in passing. Only Friedlander includes them in her study with 5 percent of the migrants. Arthur H. Hirsch, *The Huguenots of Colonial South Carolina* (Columbia: University of South Carolina Press, 1999 [1928]), 179–80; Butler, *The Huguenots in America,* 101; Friedlander, "Carolina Huguenots," 94.

66. Duplicates were avoided by comparing the masters' names. None of the masters of the 25 identified servants were Thibou, de la Plaine, and Bruneau, the three Huguenots who arrived with unidentified servants.

67. "Passenger List," 33–34.

68. When occupation is mentioned, it is only when the indentured servants appear in the records as free settlers, which excludes those who died before the expiration of their terms and those who left the colony once freed.

69. Cooper and McCord, eds., *Statutes at Large,* 2:132. Female servants whose occupation is mentioned worked as maids. "The Will of François Macaire" (2 Dec. 1687), in "South Carolina Gleanings in England," ed. Lothrop Withington, *South Carolina Historical and Genealogical Magazine* 5 (1904): 225; will of Cézar Mozé (20 June 1687), Miscellaneous Records (Proprietary series), 1675–1695, SCDAH, 283.

70. The sixth, Joseph de la Brosse Marbeuf, was an apothecary. Cooper and McCord, eds., *Statutes at Large,* 2:132. As South Carolina historian St.Julien R. Childs writes, "Distinctions between physicians, surgeons and apothecaries . . . received scant recognition in South Carolina. Popular usage granted to all the courtesy title of 'doctor.'" *Malaria and Colonization in the Carolina Low-Country, 1526–1696* (Baltimore: The Johns Hopkins University Press, 1940), 254.

71. In July 1710 Gideon Johnston wrote to the secretary of the Society for the Propagation of the Gospel in Foreign Parts (SPG), "John Thomas, a frenchman, the only person that deserves the name of a Physician in this Place." Frank. J. Klingberg, ed., *Carolina Chronicle: The Papers of Commissary Gideon Johnston, 1707–1716* (Berkeley: University of California Press, 1946), 41. Ironically, Jean Thomas sometimes appears as "chirurgeon" in the records, but he seems to have been a doctor.

72. Pierre Villepontoux migrated to South Carolina via New Rochelle, New York, where he lived until 1702. He appears in the South Carolina records as a "planter." Charles W. Baird, *History of the Huguenot Migration to America,* 2 vols. (Baltimore: Genealogical Publishing Company, 1991 [1885]), 2:141 n. 1. Records of the Court of Common Pleas, SCDAH, box 2, folder 713.

73. "Letter of February 1685," *Suite de la Description de la Carolline,* 8 n. 3.

74. Exactly 43 percent (152/347).

75. Exactly 45 percent (69/152), brother (49), sister (13), both (7).

76. "*Richmond,*" ADM 1/5139, PRO 162; "Passenger List," 32–34.

77. Van Ruymbeke, "L'émigration huguenote," 1:346–48 nn. 202–7.

78. Out of 28 Charleston Huguenot heads of household whose occupation has been determined, 15 were artisans and 10 merchants. The other 3 were 2 pastors and a surgeon. Van Ruymbeke, "L'émigration huguenote," 2:664 n. 376.

79. Edgar and Bailey, eds., *Biographical Directory,* 2:21.

80. Ravenel, ed., *Liste,* 62–64; Cooper and McCord, eds., *Statutes at Large,* 2:132.

81. The settlement of Goose Creek, where a few Huguenot families resided at the turn of the eighteenth century is not included in this study because Goose Creek never was a distinctively Huguenot settlement.

82. Spouses are not easy to identify because they are often mentioned only by their first names and these can be either anglicized by the clerk (e.g., Marth*a* instead of Marth*e* or Eli*z*abeth instead of Eli*s*abeth) or identical in both languages (like Anne), which make the source unreliable from this viewpoint. Nonetheless, only five of our list of male refugees had English spouses by 1700. Of these five, four were merchants and one was an artisan and all resided in Charleston. Van Ruymbeke, "L'emigration huguenote," 1:355–57 and 355 n. 241. In her study Friedlander also found that 95 percent of the first generation Huguenots that she identified had married within the group and that the 5 percent of exogamous unions involved exclusively Charleston residents. "Carolina Huguenots," 262–64.

83. Ravenel, ed., *Liste*, 62–64. This concentration of families was so well known in South Carolina that the SPG pastor Francis LeJau, in a 1708 letter, referred to the Orange Quarter as the "Poitwin [Poitevin] Quarter." Frank Klingberg, ed., *The Carolina Chronicle of Dr. Francis LeJau, 1706–1717* (Berkeley: University of California Press, 1946), 39.

84. Following the passage of the 1706 act that established the Anglican Church in South Carolina, Orange Quarter became the parish of St. Denis, but the act stipulated that it was included in the larger English parish of St. Thomas, and that its existence was dependent on the need to have Anglican services in French. Cooper and McCord, eds., *Statutes at Large*, 2:283.

85. Butler, *The Huguenots in America*, 133. However, it must be stressed that many marital unions, most likely endogamous, do not appear in these records, which were kept by the English (Anglican) minister of St. Thomas, at a time when a Huguenot faction hired nonconformist Calvinist ministers whose records have been lost and also because Orange Quarter Huguenots could celebrate their marriages in the nonconformist Huguenot church in Charleston.

86. Butler, *The Huguenots in America*, 138.

87. Ibid., 140.

88. Will of Isaac Mazyck, 338–42.

89. Cooper and McCord, eds., *Statutes at Large*, 2:288.

90. Henry deSaussure, "Huguenots on the Santee River," *Transactions of the Huguenot Society of South Carolina* 3 (1907): 24.

91. Friedlander, "Carolina Huguenots," 199.

92. Cooper and McCord, *Statutes at Large*, 2:283.

93. In British and American Huguenot history, the conformists are the refugees who conformed to the Church of England by using a French version of the Book of Common Prayer, recognizing the authority of the bishops, and having their pastors ordained. The nonconformist Huguenots are those who refused to conform and remained French Calvinists.

94. Van Ruymbeke, "L'émigration huguenote," 2:440–41.

95. Alexander Garden, *A Brief Account of the Deluded Dutartres* (New Haven: James Parker and Company, 1762), [1].

96. For more detailed accounts of this case see Butler, *The Huguenots in America*, 117–120, and Van Ruymbeke, "L'émigration huguenote," 2:436–50.

97. In a letter to the influential Huguenot conformist minister Claude Grotète de la Mothe, the St. Denis minister Jean LaPierre mentions "master Bochet" (Abel Bochet) as one of the ringleaders. "Letter to rev. Grotète de la Mothe" (14 Aug. 1714), *The Aufrere Papers*, Huguenot Society of Great Britain and Ireland Publications, quarto series, 40 (Frome, England, 1940), 211–12.

III

The State in the Planters' Service
*Politics and the Emergence of a Plantation Economy
in South Carolina*

GARY L. HEWITT

After 1700 South Carolina experienced rapid economic, demographic, and territorial expansion. Previously dominated by the Indian trade and supported by mixed agriculture, the colony was transformed into a plantation economy devoted to the production of rice and naval stores by slave labor. Although South Carolina was politically turbulent during this period of expansion and transformation, with three major political crises in 1706, 1719, and 1728, the next generation of Carolinians enjoyed remarkable political stability. In fact, South Carolina politics remained calm from the arrival of royal governor Robert Johnson in 1730 until the Stamp Act Crisis of 1765.[1]

Historians have generally believed that South Carolina's plantation economy itself was responsible for political stability, that prosperity brought by plantations made political harmony possible. Yet this explanation ignores the intense political instability caused by South Carolina's transformation to a plantation economy. For the most part, in fact, political historians have neglected the influence of economic change on the colony's politics. Planters and merchants appear intermittently in their histories as factions in the political struggles between 1702 and 1731, but the economic goals of these parties, beyond the narrowest calculation of economic "interest," are far less clear. Instead, historians have viewed politics largely in constitutional terms, identifying the governor and assembly as chief participants in the colony's struggle, and political power itself as the struggle's object.[2]

Economic historians, on the other hand, have ignored the political forces at work in South Carolina's transformation and have almost entirely omitted politics, government, and the state from their explanations for the colony's economic development. They have seen the emergence of a plantation economy and the dependence of plantations on slave labor as the product of various economic forces: the providential appearance of profitable staple crops, the maturing of colonial society, the imperfections of international capital markets, the changing circumstances of an Atlantic commercial world, and the accumulation of local capital from earlier economic enterprises. Neglecting the role of the state seems a mistake; after all, the early eighteenth century was an age of "political economy," which

expected governmental intervention in finance, immigration, labor procure-
ment, and land markets. In spite of the prominence of mercantilist economic
thought during this period, economic histories of South Carolina have generally restricted the role of the state to that of bumbling promoter of ill-fated
exotic commodities like olives, silk, and wine.[3]

Neither economic nor political historians have recognized the close
intertwining of the South Carolina's structural economic changes and political action during the colony's eighteenth-century transformation. Economics shaped politics, and politics dictated new economic realities. At the
beginning of the eighteenth century, South Carolina's economy was
expanding so rapidly that the colony was in danger of falling prey to its own
success. Impressive plantation development after 1690 pushed the zone of
colonial settlement far beyond its seventeenth-century boundaries at the
same time as a booming Indian trade brought Europeans into the midst of
Indian settlements. The colony's encroachment on its indigenous neighbors
by traders and plantations created tensions and intensified conflicts between
colonists and native peoples. Carolina politics worked to protect the most
profitable sectors of the economy by attempting to reduce friction with
neighboring Indians.

Although the needs of the expanding plantation economy and the needs
of the expanding Indian trade were already diverging, most white Carolinians before 1715 saw no necessary conflict between plantation development
and a flourishing Indian trade supplemented by the conquest and enslavement of Indian enemies. Instead, they had confidence that military conquest
would clear the way for the expansion of the plantation zone. Carolinians
believed that conquest, trade, and plantation agriculture were complementary; they also believed that all three could be promoted by the state with
the same policies. For instance, the colony's paper currency both financed
conquest and relieved landowners of the burden of paying for it while providing them with easy credit for purchasing land and slaves. Similarly, the
enslavement of Indians provided both a labor force for plantations and a
profitable commodity for South Carolina's traders. The colonial state's inter-
ventions in South Carolina's economy advanced an expansive vision of the
colony's future, in which trade, conquest, and plantations coexisted in a
diverse political economy. Before 1715, assembly politics supported this
diverse system.[4]

After the disastrous Yamasee War of 1715, however, the easy combination of trade, conquest, and plantations no longer seemed possible. For
planters, the Indian trade with its diplomatic instability had become incompatible with the security of plantations. Almost immediately, the planter-
dominated assembly stepped in to subordinate Indian trade to the needs of

a plantation economy. More than a rise to power, the assembly's actions were part of a deliberate effort by the planters who controlled it to safeguard plantation agriculture. By elevating the plantation economy into a "public" interest, the assembly was able to enact a series of policies that overrode the interests of traders and upheld the interests of planters. The regulation of the Indian trade and the issue of paper money were the two most striking examples of policies that began as attempts to preserve a diverse system of trade, conquest, and plantations but ended by putting the state into the planters' service.

Two economic developments led to demands for the regulation of the Indian trade: the development of the South Carolina plantation economy and the expansion of the Indian trade itself. Staple crop production on plantations emerged as a significant and rapidly growing sector of the colonial economy after 1690. While deerskins remained a significant colonial export through 1715, the combined value of exports of rice and naval stores (pitch, turpentine, and tar) passed that of deerskins early in the eighteenth century, marking a watershed in the development of the economy. Enslaved plantation workers—of Native American and African descent—became the majority of South Carolina's population by 1708, and Africans themselves outnumbered Europeans and Indians in the European-settled part of the colony a year later. The new staple crop economy also helped to stimulate the development of subsidiary enterprises like provision farming, barrel making, and house building, allowing the colonial economy to develop a sizable internal market.[5]

The introduction of plantation agriculture also made land more precious. Before rice emerged as a significant crop, land was cheap, but rice plantations carefully cleared and ditched by slave labor represented a far greater investment. The improvement of land, combined with the general scarcity of good rice lands, drove up real estate prices and made plantations even more valuable. The high prices and land speculation characteristic of South Carolina's vibrant land market drove poorer white Carolinians to the frontier, dispersing settlement, increasing encroachment on Indian territories, and ironically making plantations more vulnerable to attack. To protect the plantations, good relations with Indians seemed more urgent, as well as more difficult to achieve.[6]

While the plantation economy took root near the coast, transformations in the trade between colonists and Indians made Carolina's relations on the colony's frontier even more unstable. From the beginning of colonial settlement in 1670, South Carolina's trade with its Indian neighbors had been the most dynamic sector of the colonial economy and a central part of the colony's diplomatic relationships with its neighbors. A series of changes in the circumstances of Indian trade, along with the French colonization of Louisiana after 1697 and England's cycle of wars with France after 1689, helped to accelerate the growth of the trade while transforming both the trade itself and its diplomatic functions. When imperial struggle emerged on a grand scale in the southeast with renewed Anglo-French hostilities in 1702, Carolinians became more directly involved in Indian warfare than before. Indians and Carolinians joined forces in a series of expeditions against Spanish- and French-allied Indians across the southeast. In late 1702, for example, Governor James Moore led 500 Carolinians, slave and free, and 300 Savannah warriors in an attack on the Spanish settlement at St. Augustine. Moore and his men sacked the town and returned with perhaps 350 newly enslaved Indians. Two years later, Moore led another force of Indian and Carolina warriors against the Spanish-allied villages at Apalachee, and attacked Apalachee again in 1706. For the next several years, South Carolina—in a shifting set of alliances with the Savannahs, Yamasees, and Creeks—triumphed across the southeast. Victory required strong alliances between Carolina and its neighbors, alliances solidified by an ever increasing trade in guns, textiles, and animal skins.[7]

The invasion of South Carolina's war-making regime into the southeastern backcountry was accompanied by the simultaneous penetration of its trade regime into Indian village life. While Indians of the colonial southeast had used European trade goods for well over a century before 1700, the physical act of trading, in which Europeans gave guns and textiles for Indian skins and furs, traditionally took place not in Indian towns, but in European settlements. The locus of the trade limited the extent to which European traders affected Indian societies. These constraints would deteriorate, however, as coastal Indians declined in number and power, as imperial stakes escalated, and as merchants reinvested their profits in larger-scale trading ventures. Eighteenth-century English traders began to travel further into the backcountry in search of skins, and intruded more and more into native villages as disease carriers, war makers, enslavers, and traders. Traders began living among, and often like, Indians, taking Indian wives, fathering mixed-blood children, socializing with Indians, and exploiting them. Living far beyond the reach of colonial authority, traders were yet not quite within the realm of indigenous authority.[8]

Uncontrolled trader behavior was disturbing to Indian, colonial, and imperial authorities alike. Traders were arrogant and often violent men, yet they held a great deal of influence within Indian communities. They spoke Indian languages, formed bonds of marriage and friendship, and possessed items of critical importance to Indian life. They displaced older forms of political power and distribution of goods, bypassing headmen in contracting with individual warriors for skins. The traders brought alcohol not only as an item of trade but as a tool of socializing and negotiation, fomenting drunkenness and violence and further disrupting Indian societies. Eager to acquire Indian slaves, who brought lucrative profits in the lowcountry, traders overturned subtle native notions of prisoner, slave, and adopted fictive kin by enslaving anyone they could get their hands on.[9] Traders were necessary for maintaining Indian alliances and keeping Indian allies armed in the struggle against French- and Spanish-allied Indians, but the disruptive intrusions of traders into indigenous societies could threaten alliances—causing the Savannahs to abandon their alliance with South Carolina in 1707, for instance—and endanger the colony.

Trade regulation was intended to alleviate the problems of uncontrolled trader behavior while ensuring that the diplomatic and financial benefits of trade would continue. Although South Carolina's governors had attempted to regulate the Indian trade several times before, so that they could monopolize the trade and gather its profits to themselves, the issue became more urgent after war broke out in 1702.[10] The war reminded assembly members that the colony's safety and the trade's own existence depended on the Indians' continued good will. Accordingly, the assembly resolved in January 1703 to bring the Indian trade into a "Publick Stock," returning all profits from the trade to the public treasury, not to the governor's pockets. In the assembly's trade bill, no unlicensed person would be permitted to trade: approved traders would instead be employees of the "public," receive a salary, and be required to post a bond for their good behavior. The assembly's proposed public monopoly would allow assembly members to favor particular traders by making them the official, public traders, and to exclude others. Since traders' salaries and trade revenues would flow through the public treasury, the assembly would control nearly all aspects of the Indian trade. By taking control, the assembly hoped to ensure that the trade would serve the colony's diplomatic needs and would continue to profit the colony in general.

However, South Carolina's governor, James Moore, feared that a public monopoly would give the assembly too much power over the colony's governors, and he refused to approve the bill. An Indian trader who had unsuccessfully attempted to establish a personal monopoly over the trade in 1701, Moore stood to lose money as well as control if the bill became law.[11] Although Moore's successor, Sir Nathaniel Johnson, importuned each legislative session to enact a law regulating the Indian trade, the assembly and the governor could not agree on the specifics of regulation. Religious issues distracted the assembly from the issue of trade regulation from 1704 through 1706, but when these struggles ended, Governor Johnson again recommended regulatory legislation to both sessions of the assembly and assured it that, unlike his predecessor Moore, he had no "particular interest" in the trade to sway his judgment.[12] A combined French-Spanish invasion that fall had once again reminded the assembly that immediate measures were necessary to keep the Indians on their side, and they were ready to act quickly.

Realizing that abolishing the private trade altogether might antagonize both the governor and influential traders, the assembly took a more moderate approach to regulating the Indian trade in 1706. Instead of abolishing the private trade, the assembly's bill of December 1706 placed regulatory power in the hands of an assembly-appointed board of commissioners. According to the proposed law, no trader would be allowed to work within South Carolina without receiving a license from the commissioners, at a cost of £8. Traders would also be subject to strict rules regarding their general deportment, the extension of credit to Indians, and the provision of rum. The commissioners would be given the power to punish offenders by fine or imprisonment and seizure of their trade goods.[13] The law would also forbid the governor from receiving Indian presents and would replace them instead with an annual gift of £200 from licensing fees.

Johnson agreed with the general purpose of the regulation bill but balked at the restriction on presents, which he claimed was more "to restrain your Governr. th[a]n the Traders." He insisted that £200 would not compensate for the presents he currently received.[14] Johnson also objected to the assembly's control over the board of commissioners. While the governor would sit on the Board by virtue of his office, he was only one of ten, with no greater voice than the others. Therefore, he returned the bill to the assembly without his approval, asking for a new law "safe to the Countrey Honourable and proffitable to my self and no way Chargeable to the publick." Johnson reminded the assembly that he would not accept any bill that took all control of Indian regulation out of his hands.[15] After a six-month adjournment, the assembly sent up a bill, but Johnson did not approve it because he refused to consider a bill on the same subject twice in one session.[16] In November 1707, however, he approved a fundamentally similar bill, perhaps because the assembly refused to act on the fortification of Charles Town (clearly an urgent matter) if he opposed it. To ensure the bill's passage, the assembly eased the governor's pecuniary fears by increasing the annual gift in lieu of Indian presents to £300 and paying Johnson an additional £400 outright for his support in securing proprietary approval of the bill—that is, a bribe.[17]

The regulation law was intended primarily to defuse potential conflicts between Indians and colonists while ensuring that the assembly maintained its power over the trade. Under the law, the Commissioners of the Indian Trade were charged to free improperly enslaved Indians, annul illegally contracted debts from Indians to traders, and enforce prohibitions on rum trading. The Indian agent, also created by the law, was to serve as the commissioners' eyes and ears in the Indian villages. The agent was directed to live in Indian villages for at least ten months of every year, collect information, and adjudicate disputes among traders, between traders and Indians, and even among Indians. This reformation of the Indian trade was anything but complete, because both the commissioners and the agent had only limited powers.[18] Still, the Indian agent represented an effort on the part of the assembly to project its power into the backcountry, to bring the Indian traders and the Indians themselves under the political jurisdiction of the British colony. Thomas Nairne, the colony's first Indian agent, estimated in 1710 that "subject" Indians outnumbered the white and enslaved black colonists of South Carolina by two to one. This demographic analysis was part fantasy, as the South Carolina government could not possibly claim sovereignty over 20,000 Indians, but it was at least a rhetorical attempt to establish Carolina's dominion over the backcountry, in the words of the regulation law, "by putting entirely in the power of the Representatives of the Colony the management of all affairs with the Indians."[19]

The regulation of the Indian trade was designed to promote, not restrict, the expansion of South Carolina's trade regime into the interior. In 1708, as his first action as agent, Nairne took an extensive voyage with Thomas Welch, an Indian trader, into the South Carolina interior, nearly reaching the Mississippi River. Nairne sent back ethnographic and military information about the Ochese, Tallapoosa, Choctaw, Yazoo, and Chickasaw settlements of present-day Alabama and Mississippi. In a letter to the British secretary of state, Lord Sunderland, he also charted a plan for British expansion into the Gulf of Mexico to counter the French. South Carolina, according to Nairne, could conquer the southeast for Great Britain, enslave any Indians who resisted, and then build a plantation economy worked by African and Indian slaves on the ruins of Indian villages. Nairne combined trade, conquest, and plantations in an expansive vision of South Carolina. His 1708 expedition might best be considered as a strategy to win diplomatic alliances with the powerful Indian nations who dwelled near the French, to establish trade relationships with those nations, and finally, to ensure that Carolina political authority, in the person of the assembly's Indian agent, was in the vanguard of this process, not trailing behind.[20]

The day-to-day activities of the Indian agent and Indian commissioners centered chiefly on easing the potentially explosive tensions that emerged between Indians and colonials. The Commission spent much of its time redressing Indians' grievances against the traders in their midst. Indians suffered beatings, extortion of labor, and enslavement at the hands of traders. Improper enslavement of Indians was the most urgent problem, and the commissioners tried to control it by creating specific regulations for traders' purchase of Indian slaves and by calling traders to account for their violations of these rules. The nature of Indian debts was another pressing matter. Traders were wont to make deals with intoxicated Indians, who on sobering up would find themselves in debt far beyond the value of the goods they had received, not to mention their means of payment. The commissioners attempted to forbid traders to sell rum on credit or to provide any credit to an intoxicated Indian.[21] By restraining the worst abuses of traders, the assembly hoped to protect the colony's system of trade and conquest.

In addition to regulating the Indian trade, the assembly took other measures for managing contacts between Indians and colonists. In 1706, at the height of fears of a French or Spanish invasion, the assembly passed a law authorizing Governor Nathaniel Johnson to prohibit "offensive" white colonists from going into Indian villages. Although the law expired after six months, plans to separate colonists from Indians revived in 1707. The assembly passed a second law reserving a large tract of land on the southern edge of the colony for the Yamasee Indians, who had recently replaced the now-dispersed Savannahs as South Carolina's closest ally. While the colony had tried before to ensure that particular territories were secured for friendly Indian villages, the new law went much further in establishing Yamasee rights to land. The law not only forbade colonists from encroaching on Yamasee lands, but also ejected any that had already settled on the reservation, offering them reimbursement for any costs incurred. It also protected Yamasee livestock from Carolinian poachers. This law was followed by other reservations of territory for friendly nations.[22]

The establishment of a Yamasee reservation and the regulation of the Indian trade together comprised an effort on the part of the Carolina Assembly to put the colony's Indian relations on a more rational, orderly footing. The Indian Act closely regulated contacts between white settlers and Indians, prohibiting any unlicensed colonist from even entering Indian settlements. The reservation was designed to create a new wall of separation between Indians and colonists, drawing a protective line between areas of European settlement and areas of Indian habitation. At the same time, the rationalization of South Carolina's Indian policy attempted to maintain Indian alliances vital to the colony's military security. Reserving Indian lands was a way to ensure that the expansion of agricultural settlement would not undermine these alliances. It was a small price for planters to pay, since the amounts of land reserved for the Yamasee and other Indian peoples were not significant. At the same time, the reservation law provided for the eventual conquest of the Yamasees, who were to forfeit their land if they ever turned against South Carolina. The Yamasees now seemed to hold their land by Carolina title.

The Carolina Assembly's policies did not effectively restrain traders. Traders did not obey the law, and the commissioners had difficulty enforcing any of their rules. Traders could easily ignore the Commission altogether while the agent was out of earshot. The presence of unlicensed traders in South Carolina's Indian villages was also a persistent problem. Even in 1714, the Commission's secretary told the board that "almost all the Traders were without Licenses." Some of these unlicensed traders were Carolinians, but many were Virginians, who not only were unlicensed but carried their goods overland to their own colony, avoiding Carolina's import and export duties. As the law stood, therefore, trade regulation was generally ineffective, even if it marked the beginning of a grand attempt to project colonial power into the backcountry.[23] At the same time, the expansion of plantation agriculture impinged upon Indian lands regardless of the existence of reservations. Ecological crisis loomed for South Carolina's Yamasee allies, who were no longer agriculturalists on a large scale and had become dependent on the colonial trade for their subsistence.[24]

The combined attack of Yamasee, Catawba, and Creek warriors against South Carolina in April 1715 demonstrated in no uncertain terms how tenuous South Carolina's position was. After a decade of trader abuse and enslavement in the southeastern woodlands, even their strongest Indian allies hated the colonists. Perhaps nothing better symbolized the failure of South Carolina's trade regulation and the system it was designed to protect, than the fate of Thomas Nairne, the colony's Indian agent. More than anyone, Nairne believed that the Indian trade, if properly regulated, could coexist with and even support an expanding system of plantation agriculture. His political career—as author of promotional pamphlets, legislation, and as Indian agent—had been devoted to the expansion of South Carolina. He was one of the first victims of the Yamasee invasion and a particular object of the Yamasees' hatred, suffering a three days torture at the hands of his captors before being killed.[25]

Nairne's vision of an expansive Carolina perished with him at the stake. Even before the Carolina forces and their allies had won the war, Carolinians began looking for the reasons why the Yamasees and Creeks, the staunch allies of Carolina for nearly a decade, had turned so violently against the colony. For the assembly, the most obvious answer was the abusive behavior of the Indian traders, who had been the first targets of Yamasee violence in April 1715. The mistreatment Indians had suffered at the hands of traders, including the enslavement of allies, exploitation, and casual violence, had continued in spite of the 1707 law. Finally, these abuses had provoked the wrath of nearly every surrounding Indian nation against the colony.[26]

The solution, for the assembly, was no longer to manage private Indian-colonial contacts, but to eliminate them as much as possible. The assembly quickly revived its 1703 plan for bringing the Indian trade under the complete control of the public, in order to "prevent for the future the practices of evil minded persons to bring upon us an Indian war. . . ."[27] With little difficulty, in 1716 the planter-dominated assembly passed "An Act for the better Regulation of the Indian Trade, by impowering the commissioners therein named, to manage the same for the sole use, benefit and behoof of the publick." The act made private trade with Indians illegal. All traders were to be employed by the assembly and would be required to provide bonds for their good behavior. All profits accruing from the trade would go into the public treasury, pay for the salaries of traders and commissioners, and perhaps help to lighten the load of taxes levied for the colony's defense. The act also provided that Indian-white trading would take place in three specified trading forts at Savannah Town, the Congarees, and Wineau, to be built and maintained at public expense. This provision would not keep the traders entirely out of the Indian towns, for trade goods would still have to be carried to the villages, but the intention was to reverse the trend of the preceding years by centralizing and regulating the arena of Indian-white trade contact. The new regulatory law abandoned Nairne's expansionist vision, consolidating and restricting the trade even more dramatically than the proposed public monopoly of 1703.[28]

The phrase "for the . . . benefit . . . of the publick," embedded in the title of the law, carried powerful implications. The assembly asserted that the Indian trade, as it had previously been conducted, did not serve the public good, but served instead the private interests of traders and their merchant partners. Traders' untrammeled pursuit of profits, along with their exploitative and abusive treatment of Indians, had caused the Yamasee War, endangering the welfare and even the continued existence of the colony. Plantations were destroyed, Carolinians and their slaves were killed, and high taxes were levied to pay for defending the province. Therefore, trader interests had to be forcibly subordinated to the interests of the public—that is, of planters and their plantations. The passage of the 1716 act was a grand assertion of the assembly's power over the colony's economic affairs. The assembly assumed the right to restrict one of the primary sectors of the Carolina economy for the security of plantation agriculture.

In addition to the regulation of the Indian trade, the South Carolina Assembly's assertion of state power included a series of financial innovations concerning the colony's emissions of paper currency, as well as comprising tax policy, import and export duties, and the government's role in the province's credit markets. At first, paper money was an expedient for financing South Carolina's expensive wars of conquest, allowing the colonial government to borrow large amounts of money. The Carolina Assembly made paper money not only the financial vehicle of conquest but also a medium of trade supported by import and export duties that weighed heavily on merchants. It even made paper money an alternative source of capital for landowners and slaveholders, funding agricultural expansion. Like trade regulation, paper money policies began by supporting the colony's diverse economy, but eventually the planters in the assembly used paper money policies as the foundation for an economy dominated by plantations.

In the seventeenth century, South Carolina had no paper money, and virtually no specie of English coinage circulated in the colony. Most circulating money was in the form of foreign coins. To attract more foreign coinage into the colony and keep it there, the South Carolina Assembly followed other colonies in raising the legal value of foreign coins and English pounds sterling, beginning as early as 1685. Thus, a Spanish silver dollar worth four shillings sterling in England was declared to be worth six shillings in Carolina. This overvaluation, the assembly hoped, would help to bring money into the colony and to retard its export. By 1700, a quantity of foreign-coined silver worth £100 sterling in England carried a legal value of £161 in South Carolina, one of the highest rates in British North America. The assembly also overvalued the commodities that formed the bulk of colonial produce and functioned as a medium of trade—"commodity money"— in many domestic transactions. In 1687 it established prices for corn, peas, pork, beef, tobacco, and tar and made these commodities legal tender to settle public and private debts. The intention was to guarantee a sufficient supply of money—silver or commodity—for colonists to pay their debts.[29]

Without printing or coining a single shilling, the assembly effectively invented an imaginary "current money" composed of foreign coins and agricultural produce. Even before South Carolina emitted any paper money, it had what amounted to a currency, although its uses were limited. South Carolina's imports, which increasingly came from England, had to be paid for in English sterling money, sterling bills of exchange, or foreign silver, not in an invented current money. Merchants and government officials were reluctant to accept the imaginary currency, which lost a third of its nominal value as soon as it arrived in London. The values of sterling money and current money diverged as merchants began to demand more current money for sterling bills of exchange drawn in London.[30] Thus, even before the first paper issue of 1703, South Carolina's "current money of the people" had depreciated compared to British sterling.[31]

Still, the colony's pre-paper currency system was an expedient for creating a circulating medium of trade in a specie-scarce corner of the Atlantic economy. Since the currency was nominally metallic (except for commodity money), easily transportable, and readily interchangeable across the Atlantic and in other colonies, it was not particularly controversial. Moreover, the role of the colonial government in this pre-paper currency system was minor, since the colony neither minted coins nor printed money. The state was not yet intimately involved with the financial affairs of South Carolina's colonists, except in tax collection, the payment of governmental expenses, and court cases over debt.

Paper money in South Carolina was superimposed upon this earlier monetary system but did not descend directly from it. As in other English colonies, South Carolina first stamped paper money to defray the debts incurred in an expensive military venture, Governor Moore's 1702 expedition against St. Augustine.[32] The cost of that expedition had far outstripped the assembly's appropriations, leaving the treasury indebted for some £4,000 sterling. To discharge these debts, the assembly ordered £6,000 of paper money, called "Country bills," stamped in a range of denominations from £20 down to 50 shillings. The large denominations were useful for paying off the colony's sizable debts, and the bills paid 12 percent interest to their holders to make them "val[u]able among the people." Insofar as these bills replaced the provincial treasury's IOUs, they were like general-obligation bonds, promises to pay the holders of currency out of future tax revenues. As such, the bills were receivable for all colonial taxes, excluding quitrents.[33]

Moreover, the 1703 issue was accompanied by a tax to raise £4,000 over two years, which, combined with the proceeds of the colonial import and export duties, would be sufficient to retire the entire currency in that time and pay the interest on the outstanding paper. As the public treasurer received the bills in payment of tax, they were to be collected and subsequently destroyed, thus extinguishing both the public debt and paper money at the same time. Alternatively, if the public treasurer had specie on hand from taxes or duties paid in gold or silver, he could redeem outstanding bills of credit with this cash, saving the redeemed bills for destruction. The orderly redemption of the public debt, the assembly believed, would help to maintain the value of the bills of credit.[34]

The new paper money took the value of South Carolina's current money, and its exchange rate was the same: £150 currency was worth approximately £100 sterling. Contrary to many assertions by both contemporaries and historians, the bills never circulated at par with sterling, since they were never intended to stand for sterling money.[35] However, there was a series of significant differences between paper money and the earlier, imaginary colonial currency. Paper money was neither readily transportable beyond the colony's borders nor convertible into other currencies. Since it could not be redeemed for specie anywhere and was legal tender only in South Carolina, there was little or no market for South Carolina bills outside the colony.[36] Since foreign silver had what contemporaries would call "intrinsic value," and could be used as money nearly anywhere in the Atlantic world, its price had no particular tendency to drop; in fact, the assembly had to lower its sterling price artificially by setting statutory exchange rates. In contrast, an unredeemable paper money—fiat money— was worth only what people thought its future value might be: in the payment of future taxes, as an interest-bearing investment, or in its ready acceptance in private transactions. The very name of the paper money, "bills of credit," and the concern the assembly gave to the "public credit" when deliberating paper money policy illustrate not only that this paper money was, in fact, a loan but also that its value was a matter of creditability—that is, belief—and not simply a function of the quantity of currency in circulation.[37]

Therefore, the value of South Carolina's paper money was potentially volatile, depending on the political decisions of the assembly that issued it. If the assembly chose to levy taxes to retire the currency, then the currency would seem to have value, at least to pay those future taxes. If the assembly failed to levy these taxes, or if the colony's future seemed in danger, then the currency would seem to have much less value. The question was whether paper money was a worthless IOU or an obligation the assembly was firmly committed to discharging. Compounding these problems was South Carolina's persistent balance of payments deficit, its exports being continually less than its imports. Either foreign silver or British sterling was necessary to buy overseas commodities, slaves, and trade goods. If a planter or trader had paper money, how would he acquire the necessary hard money? Merchants who had sterling money could demand more and more currency, which would tend to drive the value of currency even lower relative to sterling.

Despite these difficulties, the Carolina currency maintained its value admirably well for its first eight years, at a fairly constant 150:100 ratio relative to pounds sterling (a sterling exchange of 150). Neither the shifting legal-tender status of the various emissions of currency, the cessation of interest payments after 1707, the repeated proclivity of the assembly to reissue rather than retire bills of credit, nor emissions of currency entirely unsecured by the promise of any future tax managed to drive down the rate of exchange. Historians have not succeeded very well in explaining this fact, usually because they have erroneously believed that the currency was depreciating during this period.[38] However, there are several probable reasons why the rate of exchange did, in fact, remain reasonably stable. First, the assembly was fairly rigorous in maintaining at least the appearance of public credit. It consistently proclaimed the absolute importance of funding the redemption of the bills of credit, promising repeatedly to devote all tax and duty revenues to paying for the debt even while simultaneously issuing more money. Second, the Carolinians were winning their wars. Even the 1706 combined French-Spanish invasion of Charles Town turned out spectacularly well for the English colony, and Carolina, Yamasee, and Creek men at arms across the southeastern woodlands were triumphant against Spanish, French, and allied Indian forces until 1715.

These expansionist victories seemed to guarantee further successes for the colony's plantations and the Indian trade alike. A high confidence in the colony's future was demonstrated by a round of expansionist pamphlets extolling the wonderful opportunities to be found in South Carolina and by the arrival of waves of immigrants on the colony's shores. Production of naval stores and rice was rising, and an influx of slaves promised even further increases in the production and export of these commodities. The new town of Beaufort was established in the southern portion of the colony to serve the growing staple crop production. An expanding currency was commensurate with an expanding colony; while South Carolina continued to prosper, its currency was unassailable. Paper money underlay an expansionist system of conquest, Indian trade, and plantation development.[39]

By 1712, the currency had proven itself to be admirably successful, but at the same time two problems remained. First, the property taxes levied to retire the currency were beginning to become a burden on the colony's landowners. Carolinians had paid few taxes before 1702, when the assembly first levied a property tax to pay for Governor Moore's campaign against St. Augustine, but new taxes piled rapidly on one another during the next decade of warfare.[40] Second, the success of the currency in maintaining its value was predicated on its speedy retirement or, at least, the belief in its retirement. The utility of paper currency, however, had drifted away from its original purpose. While it had originally been an expedient way for South Carolina to pay for its wars of conquest, it had quickly become medium of trade in a place where hard money was scarce. Paper money was more like the fictitious "current money" than a government bond—a point reinforced when the assembly abandoned interest payments on outstanding currency and declared paper money legal tender in 1707. For Carolina planters accustomed to using paper to pay their debts and taxes, the currency had become necessary for the health of the plantation economy. Retiring the currency accordingly seemed disastrous to planters, especially since they would have to pay the very taxes that retired it. The outstanding currency in 1712 already amounted to £20,000, a sum that would take years to extinguish, even at high tax rates.[41]

The assembly of 1712 solved the problem of retirement by creating British North America's first so-called land bank. The assembly ordered that £52,000—more than twice the outstanding currency—be stamped. Of this sum, £16,000 was to replace all the older issues of currency (except the £4,000 in money issued in 1711 for the Tuscarora War) in order to bring all of the colony's currency onto the same basis. Another £4,000 was to be appropriated for the colonial treasury for contingent expenses of the government. The remaining £32,000 was to be lent over the course of five years to the colonists, in amounts ranging from £100 to £300. These loans were to be secured by mortgages on land or slaves amounting to twice the value of the loans and repaid over a twelve-year period. As repayment and taxes were received, a proportion of the amounts repaid would be loaned out again until all money in circulation was effectively supported by mortgaged real property.[42]

Instead of borrowing money from the colony, the assembly would lend money to the colony's planters and earn interest on its investment to help to defray the costs of government. Since the currency was based on mortgaged real property of twice the currency's value, its value would not decline, at least in the dreams of the law's planners, because lands and slaves lent an "intrinsic" value to the money. The merchants would not suffer from receiving payments of dubious value, interest earned from the loans would ease the colonists' tax burdens, and the government could continue to finance military ventures. By supporting the value of the currency, the land bank was intended to protect the colony's diverse and expansive economy of trade, conquest, and plantation development.

Most significantly, the land bank would foster the continued growth of the plantation economy. The provincial loan office promised to infuse an extraordinary amount of capital into the South Carolina economy, public capital raised against the promise of twelve years' future plantation growth and provided on extraordinarily easy terms. The loan office served as a liberal source of credit for the colony's planters and provided them with much-needed capital to pay for further importations of slaves; even the smallest possible loan amount, £100 currency, would purchase one or two slaves. In addition, the effective interest rate was extraordinarily low: approximately 6.9 percent, far below the colony's customary rate of at least 10 percent.[43] And the repayment term, twelve years, was far longer than the average 13.8-month term of private mortgages during that decade. While no records of the bank's commissioners survive, it is known that all of the £32,000 was loaned, compared to approximately £7,000 in private mortgages recorded by the secretary of the province during the 1710s.[44] Colonial planters took this opportunity well in hand, more than quadrupling their annual slave importations between 1712 and 1714. The first £32,000 loaned under the

Bank Act was more than enough to pay for the 578 slaves imported between the passage of the act and the Yamasee War.[45]

With the land bank, the assembly completed the transformation of the province's paper money from an expedient for financing military adventures into a vehicle for plantation development. The act's preamble stated that there were "no hopes or probability" for the colony's debts to be "discharged in any tolerable time," forcing that debt—the currency, really—to be placed on another, more permanent footing. The new currency would not only ease the "streights and exigencies" of the colonial government's finances, but also "answer the ends of money," giving a "quick circulation and encouragement to trade and commerce." To the planters who dominated the assembly, paper money had become more than an easy way to finance governmental expenses; it was a necessity for their day-to-day economic well-being. For the planters' sake or, as the assembly put it, the "public good," the currency would be perpetuated for more than a decade, and the colonial loan office would become an impressive source of credit for the colony's plantation economy. Only land and African slaves (the law specified "negroes"), the pillars of plantation agriculture, were acceptable as security for the loans that were the basis of the new paper currency. The assembly had placed the health of its currency on the foundations of agricultural expansion and enslaved African labor.[46]

The large emission of currency in 1712 combined with the financial disruptions of the Yamasee War began a process of depreciation that drove a political wedge between merchants and planters. While the large currency emission of 1712 pushed down the value of South Carolina's currency only slightly, the war forced the assembly to turn once again to its usual expedient of stamping bills of credit to defray military expenditures. Legitimate fears for the colony's future accordingly drove down the value of South Carolina's currency. By the end of the war, over £50,000 had been emitted, and the sterling exchange dropped to 500 by 1720.[47] This rapid deterioration in the value of paper was not due only to the large amount of currency printed. Depreciation occurred because the assembly no longer seemed concerned with retiring the currency at all, and rather seemed committed to the perpetuity of paper currency: it kept printing more money and failed to retire outstanding issues.

More importantly, the colony's future, both economic and political, seemed perilous. The province's southern settlements were devastated by Indian warriors, the Indian trade was effectively put to a stop, ranching ended as a viable economic enterprise, and—to add insult to injury—the French embarked on an extraordinary period of colonization in Louisiana, sending some 7,000 settlers and slaves to that colony between 1718 and

1721. This ambitious effort showed that European rivals would remain a thorn in Carolina's side for the immediate future. An assembly not particularly committed to redemption of its currency, a contracting economy, and a questionable future for the entire colony together conspired to make investment in South Carolina or its currency a risky undertaking. The short-term economic consequences of the war assisted depreciation: the disruption of the Indian trade and of ranching, along with the destruction of some rice plantations, severely reduced the colony's exports, causing a severe disturbance in the colonial balance of payments. Sterling money was simply harder to come by, as Carolinians had less produce to sell. This shortage drove exchange rates even higher, but when the short-term disruption of trade flows had ended, there was little reason for exchange rates to return to former levels.[48]

The rapid decline of the currency continued to exacerbate political divisions between the assembly and the proprietors, and between planters and merchants. Merchants saw the value of their currency-based assets (mostly debts owed them by the colony's planters and the colonial government) decline by an average of nearly 20 percent every year between 1714 and 1720. The same £150 in currency that was worth £100 sterling in 1712 was only worth £30 sterling by 1720.[49] The assembly turned to its 1712 formula and passed a bill in 1716 that created a second land bank. Like its predecessor, the new bank would refinance the wartime currency issues with a new paper money backed by mortgages on land and slaves. Continuing depreciation, however, rallied the merchants against any form of paper money, especially because the postwar assembly was increasingly inclined to retire the currency through import and export duties in addition to taxes on land. Paper money, which had begun by supporting merchants and planters alike, became instead the single strongest symbol of the divergence of planters' and merchants' interests.

While the assembly, in general, blamed the Indian traders for causing the Yamasee War, the war also forced the assembly to reconsider the consequences of the colony's transformation to a plantation economy. Was South Carolina militarily weak because of its large number of slaves? Many slaves had fought bravely for the colony, but it seemed possible that the patterns of scattered settlement characteristic of plantation agriculture had made the colony vulnerable. The assembly in 1717 passed an import duty on slaves so high as to make their cost prohibitive in order to restrain the growth of the plantations and to help secure the colony. The assembly's plans for the lands confiscated in 1717 from the Yamasees (according to the 1707 reservation law) illustrate how much planters had become convinced that uncontrolled development endangered the entire colony. Due to "a great neglect" in the granting of lands, settlers had taken up land "without any restriction." Consequently, only a small number of white South Carolinians were spread out across the frontier. The assembly hoped that the Yamasee lands would become a zone of small family farms compactly settled for better defense. In fact, they attempted to prevent plantation development on the Yamasee lands by limiting the size of land grants, requiring that an adult male live on each farm, and restricting the sale, partition, and mortgage of the land. They hoped to limit the new settlers' access both to mortgage-based credit and to land, effectively ensuring that few slaves would inhabit the confiscated territories.[50]

Despite these measures, the Carolina Assembly wanted to protect, not repudiate, the plantation economy: for example, it passed a law providing for the state-sponsored importation of white servants to work in the colony's plantations.[51] The assembly had, however, retreated from its older expansionist dreams. The purpose of the new land policies was to turn South Carolina away from its dangerous dependence on Indian alliances and the conquest of Indian enemies. It was not enough to regulate the Indian trade; instead, the trade had to be placed completely in the hands of the government. The old aggressive system of expansion and conquest could no longer be maintained; instead, the assembly adopted a new, largely defensive stance, in which free white settlers, royal troops, and a string of garrisoned forts would serve as the colony's protective barrier against Indian incursions.[52] By 1717, the assembly had enacted a series of policies that would make South Carolina safe for plantation agriculture: abolishing the private Indian trade in favor of a public monopoly, temporarily halting slave importation, developing a new strategy to protect the colony's frontiers, and creating a new land bank to bolster the colony's paper currency.

Each time the assembly projected its power over the colony's economy, it tried to support the plantation economy and to elevate the interests of planters into a "public" interest. The creation of a public Indian trading company, the distribution of the confiscated Yamasee lands, the restriction of the importation of slaves from Africa, and the perpetuation of the paper currency were all profound exertions of state authority on the planters' behalf. The colony's proprietors, however, viewed each of these policies as a direct assault on their authority within the colony, which had steadily eroded from the colony's first settlement in 1670. The proprietors were also heavily influenced by Carolina's merchants, who had a far more significant presence in London than the planters and were deeply opposed to the planters' import and export duties, paper money policies, and abolition of the still-profitable private Indian trade. Not surprisingly, therefore, the proprietors in 1717 and 1718 repealed each and every one of the assembly's assertions of state power on behalf of the plantation economy. Furthermore, the proprietors rescinded their plan to distribute the Yamasee lands (which initially was nearly identical to the assembly's plan) and granted the lands to themselves instead. They closed their Carolina land office altogether in September 1718, making it nearly impossible for Carolinians to obtain title to more land. They even gave all their land between the Savannah and Altamaha rivers to a Scottish baronet, who planned to establish a new colony politically independent from the South Carolina Assembly.[53]

The assembly, which had been petitioning for royal government since the Yamasee War, struck back in late 1719, and removed Governor Robert Johnson from office in a bloodless coup.[54] Once in power, the assembly enacted a series of laws designed to solidify planters' control over the colony. Its only notable failure was not being able to continue the public monopoly on the Indian trade, which expired sometime after 1723. On the other hand, the assembly emitted large amounts of paper money in 1720, 1721, and 1723, and when the last was repealed by the Privy Council, the assembly succeeded in slowing its retirement to a glacial pace. In an attempt to weaken the political power of the Charles Town merchants, who were the most vocal opponents of paper money, the assembly incorporated Charles Town as a city and designated a self-perpetuating board of commissioners selected from men more friendly to the assembly's goals.[55] The assembly also pursued the interests of debtors, most of whom were planters. It established a system of county courts, moving debt cases out of Charles Town and into plantation districts, where juries presumably would be more friendly to defendants.[56] In 1726, the assembly even altered the form of serving notices of actions for debt to benefit planters: from the summons, which could be left at the debtor's residence, to a writ of capias, which had to be handed to the debtor in person. A merchant later argued that this change allowed planters to terrorize officials by ordering their slaves to attack the marshal serving the writ.[57]

The merchant's argument was a vivid example of how planters' and merchants' interests had diverged. According to the merchant, the writ of capias also demonstrated in microcosm the political power that planters derived from slave owning itself. Having put the government into the planters' service, slave owners had lost all restraint. In the merchant's view, the colonial state had made planters insolent and ungovernable by validating their self-interest. In fact, some planters in the assembly were ready to shut down the government if their demands were not met. After ejecting the proprietary governor in 1719, the assembly eventually brought the colony's government to a standstill in 1728 when the acting royal governor refused its paper money demands.[58]

The political chaos of the 1720s ended abruptly with the return of Robert Johnson, this time with a royal commission as governor, although tensions between traders and planters remained. The Indian trade continued to be a highly profitable venture, and trade regulation still occupied the assembly, as Indian alliances remained crucial to the colony's security. The £100,000 of paper money outstanding in 1728 remained legal tender for the entire colonial period and was even supplemented by a series of non-legal-tender issues. Yet neither trade regulation nor paper money issues caused political crisis after 1730. South Carolina's planters had cleared a path for agricultural expansion in the first decades of the eighteenth century, first by exerting state power to help Indian trade, conquest, and plantation development coexist and then by enlisting the state to subordinate trade and conquest to the needs of the plantation economy. That work was largely done by 1730, when South Carolinians began an extraordinary decade of expansion, importing large numbers of African slaves and dramatically increasing the production of rice.

As Carolina planters continued to prosper, political conflict was replaced by political stasis, noninvolvement, or highly esoteric disputes over the proper constitutional relationships among governor, council, and assembly. Members of the elite began to give up their privilege of serving in the assembly at an unprecedented rate, withdrawing from public life into the private pursuit of prosperity. The victory of the planters and the plantation economy was so complete that Carolinians convinced themselves that plantation development had occurred by a natural and inevitable process, rather than the direct intervention of the state. Historians should not be fooled.[59]

Notes

1. Robert Weir, "'The Harmony We Were Famous For': An Interpretation of Pre-Revolutionary South Carolina Politics," *William and Mary Quarterly*, 3d ser., 26 (1969): 473–501; Richard Waterhouse, "Merchants, Planters, and Lawyers: Political Leadership in South Carolina, 1721–1775," in *Power and Status: Officeholding in Colonial America*, ed. Bruce C. Daniels (Middletown, Conn.: Wesleyan University Press, 1986).

2. Jack P. Greene, *The Quest for Power: The Lower Houses of Assembly in the Southern Royal Colonies, 1689–1776* (Chapel Hill: University of North Carolina Press, 1963); Clarence L. Ver Steeg, *Origins of a Southern Mosaic: Studies of Early Carolina and Georgia* (Athens: University of Georgia Press, 1975); M. Eugene Sirmans, *Colonial South Carolina: A Political History, 1663–1763* (Chapel Hill: University of North Carolina Press, 1966).

3. Peter A. Coclanis, *The Shadow of a Dream: Economic Life and Death in the South Carolina Low Country* (New York: Oxford University Press, 1989); R. C. Nash, "South Carolina and the Atlantic Economy in the Late Seventeenth and Eighteenth Centuries," *Economic History Review* 45 (1992): 677–702; Converse A. Clowse, *Economic Beginnings in South Carolina* (Chapel Hill: University of North Carolina Press, 1973); David L. Coon, "The Emergence of Market Agriculture in South Carolina" (Ph.D. diss., University of Illinois, 1972).

4. See Gary L. Hewitt, "Expansion and Improvement: Land, People, and Politics in South Carolina and Georgia, 1690–1745" (Ph.D. diss., Princeton University, 1996), 25–71.

5. Russell R. Menard, "Financing the Lowcountry Export Boom: Capital and Growth in Early South Carolina," *William and Mary Quarterly*, 3d ser., 51 (1994), 660; Coclanis, *Shadow of a Dream*, 5, 66; Peter H. Wood, *Black Majority: Negroes in Colonial South Carolina from 1670 through the Stono Rebellion* (New York: W. W. Norton, 1974), 131–66. One-quarter of enslaved Carolinians in 1708 were Indians; see Governor Nathaniel Johnson and council to the Board of Trade, 17 Sept. 1708, *Records in the British Public Record Office Relating to South Carolina* (Columbia: Historical Commission of South Carolina, 1928–1947), 3:205 (also known as the "Sainsbury Transcripts"; hereafter cited as *BPRO*); Peter H. Wood, "The Changing Population of the Colonial South: An Overview by Race and Region, 1685–1790," in *Powhatan's Mantle: Indians in the Colonial Southeast*, ed. Wood et al. (Lincoln: University of Nebraska Press, 1989), 35–103, esp. 38–39.

6. Coclanis, *Shadow of a Dream*, 48–75; Aaron M. Shatzman, *Servants into Planters: The Origins of an American Image: Land Acquisition and Status Mobility in Seventeenth-Century South Carolina* (New York: Garland Press, 1989); Richard L. Waterhouse, *A New World Gentry: The Making of a Merchant and Planter Class in South Carolina, 1670–1770* (New York: Garland Press, 1989).

7. Sirmans, *Colonial South Carolina*, 84–86; Crane, *Southern Frontier*, 71–77, 158–61; Kathryn E. Holland Braund, *Deerskins and Duffels: The Creek Indian Trade with Anglo-America, 1685–1815* (Lincoln: University of Nebraska Press, 1993), 32–33.

8. Braund, *Deerskins and Duffels*, 28; Richard White, *The Roots of Dependency: Subsistence, Environment, and Social Change among the Choctaws, Pawnees, and Navajos* (Lincoln: University of Nebraska Press, 1983), 34–68; James Merrell, *The Indians' New World: The Catawbas and Their Neighbors from European Contact through the Era of Removal* (Chapel Hill: University of North Carolina Press, 1989), 49–91; Merrell, "'Our Bond of Peace': Patterns of Intercultural Exchange in the Carolina Piedmont, 1650–1750," in *Powhatan's Mantle*, ed. Wood et al., 196–222.

9. Merrell, *Indians' New World*, 92–133, e.g.

10. Sirmans, *Colonial South Carolina*, 49–67, 82–83; Verner W. Crane, *The Southern Frontier: 1670–1732* (1928; reprint, New York: W. W. Norton, 1981), 22–46.

11. *Journal of the Commons House of Assembly* (Columbia: Historical Commission of South Carolina, 1946–), 20 Jan. 1703 (hereafter cited as *JCHA*). Sirmans, *Colonial South Carolina*, 83, notes that the original of the bill is not to be found, but claims that it provided for a licensed private trade. The assembly's resolution of a "Publick Stock" seems to indicate a public monopoly, rather than a continuation of a private trade. In the context of Governor Moore's open avowals of self-interest in a governor-controlled monopoly, the assembly might have been more likely to have taken the public monopoly route, if the profits could be routed through the assembly-controlled treasury. See Crane, *Southern Frontier*, 144.

12. *JCHA*, 7 Mar. 1705/6. The religious issue at stake was the establishment of the Church of England and the accompanying disqualification from political office of all Dissenting Carolinians—who formed the most coherent faction in opposition to Governor Johnson. A "rump" assembly had passed the law in the absence of Dissenter members (who lived further from Charles Town). In the end, the Church of England remained established, but Carolina's Test Act was repealed by the order of the House of Lords. Dissenters were allowed to serve in the assembly and even as vestrymen in parishes where Dissenters were a majority. See Sirmans, *Colonial South Carolina*, 86–89.

13. Crane, *Southern Frontier*, 146–48; Sirmans, *Colonial South Carolina*, 90–91.

14. *JCHA*, 31 Jan. 1706/7.

15. Message of Nathaniel Johnson to Commons House of Assembly, *JCHA*, 31 Jan. 1706/7.

16. *JCHA*, 6 June 1707, 26 June 1707, 7 July 1707. The first bill the assembly offered in July apparently returned to the 1703 formula of a public trade. Governor Johnson and the council rejected that option, but the assembly quickly retreated to the 1706 model of a regulated private trade. See Sirmans, *Colonial South Carolina*, 90–91.

17. These sums are in South Carolina currency, worth about two-thirds their nominal value in sterling money. *JCHA*, July 1707, passim. See also Crane, *Southern Frontier*, 148–51; and Sirmans, *Colonial South Carolina*, 90–93; the act is in Thomas Cooper and David J. McCord, eds., *The Statutes at Large of South Carolina, Edited, under Authority of the Legislature* (Columbia, S.C., A.S. Johnson, 1837), no. 269, 2:309–17.

18. W. L. McDowell, ed., *The Colonial Records of South Carolina: Journals of the Commissioners of the Indian Trade, 1710–1718* (Columbia, S.C.: A. S. Johnson, 1955); and Crane, *Southern Frontier*, 150–53.

19. Cooper and McCord, eds., *Statutes at Large*, 2:677–80; and Thomas Nairne, *A Letter from South Carolina* (London, 1710), in *Selling a New World: Two South Carolina Promotional Pamphlets*, ed. Jack P. Greene (Columbia: University of South Carolina Press, 1989), 60. Other early demographic estimates made no such claim. Compare Governor Johnson and council to Board of Trade, 17 Sept. 1708, *BPRO*, 5:205.

20. Nairne's biography is best detailed in Alexander Moore's introduction to *Nairne's Muskhogean Journals: The 1708 Expedition to the Mississippi River* (Jackson: University of Mississippi Press, 1988), 3–31. Nairne's letter to the Earl of Sunderland is reprinted in ibid., 73–79; see Hewitt, "Expansion and Improvement," 72–130. For the controversy between Nairne and Governor Johnson, see Sirmans, *Colonial South Carolina*, 92–94. See also *Nairne's Muskhogean Journals*, 32–36, 56–57, 62–64. Nairne was something of an ethnographer, and he sent his thoughts and observations about social and sexual behavior and material culture, as well as descriptions of the region's geography, along with his political analyses. See ibid., passim. For a further indication of Nairne's enthusiasm for plantation agriculture, see his *Letter from South Carolina*.

21. McDowell, ed., *Journals of the Commissioners of the Indian Trade*, passim.; *Nairne's Muskhogean Journals*, passim.

22. Cooper, ed., *Statutes at Large*, no. 251, 2:274; no. 271, 2:317–18.

23. Quotation in McDowell, ed., *Journals of the Commissioners of the Indian Trade*, 59; see also 5–6, 14–15, 22, 24, 38, 43–44, 56. For Virginia competition more generally, see James Merrell, *Indians' New World*; M. Thomas Hatley, *The Dividing Paths: Cherokees and South Carolinians through the Era of Revolution* (New York: Oxford University Press, 1993); and Crane, *Southern Frontier*, 154–57.

24. Richard L. Haan, "The 'Trade Do's Not Flourish As Formerly': The Ecological Origins of the Yamassee War of 1715," *Ethnohistory* 28 (1981): 341–58.

25. For the war, see Braund, *Deerskins and Duffels*, chap. 1; Crane, *Southern Frontier*, 162–86.

26. For attributions of the Yamasee War to the traders, see Board of Trade minutes, 10 July 1715, *BPRO*, 6:137–39.

27. *JCHA*, 13 Apr. 1717, quoted in Sirmans, *Colonial South Carolina*, 115.

28. Most of the act is reprinted in Cooper, ed., *Statutes at Large*, no. 360, vol. 2, 677–80. Compare Marc Egnal, *A Mighty Empire: The Origins of the American Revolution* (Ithaca, N.Y.: Cornell University Press, 1988), 102–22, which argues that the planter-dominated assembly was thoroughly expansionist.

29. Curtis P. Nettels, *The Money Supply of the American Colonies before 1720* (Madi-

son: University of Wisconsin Press, 1934); Cooper, ed., *Statutes at Large*, no. 45, 2:37 (for prices of commodities); ibid., no. 150, 2:127 (for rates of exchange; the bill's title was not printed). See also [William Bull?], "An Account of the rise and progress of the Paper Bills of Credit in South Carolina," in ibid., 9:770–80.

30. Nettels, *Money Supply of the American Colonies.* I call the currency "fictitious" because it was not coined, emitted, or regulated by any government: there was no tangible thing called "Carolina" currency before 1703, nor any "proclamation money" ever.

31. Alexander Moore, "Daniel Axtell's Account Book and the Economy of Early South Carolina," *South Carolina Historical Magazine* 95 (1994): 284 n. 7.

32. The first paper money in British North America was printed by Massachusetts after that colony's expedition of 1690, to pay angry volunteers. See Leslie Van Horn Brock, *The Currency of the American Colonies, 1700–1764: A Study in Colonial Finance and Imperial Relations* (New York: Arno Press, 1975). The South Carolina Assembly did not precisely print money, since there is no indication of there being a printing press in South Carolina before 1732. According to Eric P. Newman, *The Early Paper Money of America* (Racine, Wis.: Western Publishing Company, 1967), 299, the 1703 bills were engraved, probably on copper, by Joseph Massey. The bills issued in 1715 appear to have been engraved as well. Colonial officials almost always referred to the process of producing paper currency with the verb "to stamp."

33. Cooper, ed., *Statutes at Large*, no. 205, 2:206–11.

34. Ibid.

35. This point is important: the value of South Carolina current money did not immediately drop when the first paper money was emitted. In fact, since foreign coin was overvalued by law at a ratio of 161:100, the paper currency may be seen to have appreciated in value, to a ratio of 150:100 relative to pounds sterling, and to have held this value for nearly a decade. The handsome 12-percent interest paid on the country bills probably assisted this process; they were in high enough demand to cause reports of hoarding and lead the assembly to drop interest payments after 1707. See Cooper, ed., *Statutes at Large*, no. 262, 2:302–7.

36. Compare Thomas L. Purvis, *Proprietors, Patronage, and Paper Money: Legislative Politics in New Jersey* (New Brunswick, N.J.: Rutgers University Press, 1986), 144–75. New Jersey's paper money found a ready market in both Pennsylvania and New York, and was even preferred over those colonies' own currencies. Theoretically, South Carolina's major colonial trading partners—the West Indian islands—might have developed a taste for Carolina bills for their own purposes. The nature of South Carolina's trade with the islands and the overwhelming disparity in the size of the Carolinian and West Indian economies, however, seem to have prevented this from happening.

37. Quantity theory, which supposes at bottom that price levels—the value of a currency—depend linearly on the amount of circulating medium, fails to take into account the role of either trade flows or "faith," and so is ultimately inadequate as an explanatory principle for exchange rates. For a critique of quantity theory, see Joseph Albert Ernst, *Money and Politics in America, 1755–1775: A Study in the Currency Act of 1764 and the Political Economy of Revolution* (Chapel Hill: University of North Carolina Press, 1973), chap. 1.

38. Most appraisals have stressed a lockstep relationship between currency issues and depreciation of the currency, following the arguments of paper currency's contemporary opponents. See the discussion in Ernst, *Money and Politics in America*, 3–10; see also Richard M. Jellison, "Paper Currency in South Carolina, 1703–1764" (Ph.D. diss., Indiana University, 1953); and Brock, *Currency of the American Colonies;* for exchange rates,

see John J. McCusker, *Money and Exchange in Europe and America, 1600–1775: A Handbook* (Chapel Hill: University of North Carolina Press, 1978), 222, 315.

39. See Coclanis, *Shadow of a Dream*, 102–3.

40. Cooper, ed., *Statutes at Large*, no. 198, 2:188; no. 205, 2:206; no. 277, 2:324; and no. 297, 2:352.

41. For a recapitulation of the currency issues from 1702 to 1712, see Brock, *Currency of the American Colonies*, 116–17.

42. "An Act for raising the sume of Fifty-Two Thousand Pounds, by the stamping and establishing new Bills of Creditt, and putting the same out to interest, in order to call in and sink the former Bills of Credit, and thereby give a farther encouragement to Trade and Commerce," in Cooper, ed., *Statutes at Large*, 9:759–66. The act is not reprinted in its proper chronological order in Cooper's collection.

43. Ibid., 760. Assuming straight-line amortization of the loan over twelve years, with an annual payment of 12.5 percent of the original principal balance, the interest rate calculates to 6.87 percent. For private-market interest rates, see Menard, "Financing the Lowcountry Export Boom," 669. Menard notes that the legal ceiling of 10 percent was often crossed through the use of complex loan instruments, implying that this limit was too low to attract capital from outside the colony.

44. Menard, "Financing the Lowcountry Export Boom," 668. The figure is derived by multiplying his average loan by the number of loans, and adjusting the loan amount back into South Carolina currency. The shifting exchange rates after 1715 make this last step tenuous.

45. For slave imports, see Menard, "Financing the Lowcountry Export Boom," 662.

46. Cooper, ed., *Statutes at Large*, 9:759.

47. McCusker, *Money and Exchange in Europe and America*, 222, 315.

48. For Louisiana, see Daniel T. Usner, *Indians, Settlers, and Slaves in a Frontier Exchange Economy: The Lower Mississippi Valley before 1783* (Chapel Hill: University of North Carolina Press, 1992), 32. For exchange rates, see Brock, *The Currency of the American Colonies*, 116–18; and [Bull?], "An Account of the rise and progress of the Paper Bills of Credit in South Carolina," in Cooper and McCord, eds., *Statutes at Large*, 9:770–80.

49. McCusker, *Money and Exchange in Europe and America*, 222, 315.

50. Cooper and McCord, eds., *Statutes at Large*, no. 357, 2:641–46; Hewitt, "Expansion and Improvement," 110–12.

51. That the assembly hoped to attract white laborers bound to a term of service while simultaneously subsidizing free white settlement on the Yamasee lands demonstrates the assembly's ambivalent and sometimes contradictory ideas about the expansion of the colony. For a theoretical perspective on this conundrum, see Barbara L. Solow, "Slavery and Colonization," in *Slavery and the Rise of the Atlantic System*, ed. Solow (Cambridge: Cambridge University Press, 1991), 21–42.

52. For this transformation, see Hewitt, "Expansion and Improvement," 106–11. The major histories of South Carolina see this process as fundamentally an expansionist one; e.g., Egnal, *A Mighty Empire*, 102–22; Crane, *Southern Frontier;* W. Stitt Robinson, *The Southern Colonial Frontier, 1607–1763* (Albuquerque: University of New Mexico Press, 1979); and Sirmans, *Colonial South Carolina.*

53. Hewitt, "Expansion and Improvement," 168–70.

54. Commons House of Assembly to the king, Nov. 1716, *BPRO*, 6:258–60, presented at St. James's, 25 Jan. 1716/7, ibid. 7:5–8; "Humble Address of the Representatives and Inhabitants of South Carolina to King George," 26 Feb. 1717/8, ibid., 88–97

(names of signatories), 128–30 (petition); memorial of Joseph Boone to Board of Trade, 13 May 1718, ibid., 126–27; Sirmans, *Colonial South Carolina*, 125–28; Richard P. Sherman, *Robert Johnson: Proprietary and Royal Governor of South Carolina* (Columbia: University of South Carolina Press, 1962).

55. Bruce T. McCully, ed., "The Charleston Government Act of 1722: A Neglected Document," *South Carolina Historical Magazine* 83 (1982): 303–19.

56. Sirmans, *Colonial South Carolina*, 129–44; Hewitt, "Expansion and Improvement," 170–77.

57. Thomas Lowndes to Board of Trade, 14 Dec. 1731, *BPRO*, 11:134–35.

58. Sirmans, *Colonial South Carolina*, 157–59; Arthur Middleton to Duke of Newcastle, 17 May 1728, *BPRO*, 13:44–47; South Carolina Council to Newcastle, 19 Dec. 1728, ibid., 13:230–35.

59. Waterhouse, "Merchants, Planters, and Lawyers"; Weir, "Harmony We Were Famous For"; Sirmans, *Colonial South Carolina;* Robert L. Meriwether, *The Expansion of South Carolina, 1729–1765* (Kingsport, Tenn.: Southern Publishers, 1940). Compare Hewitt, "Expansion and Improvement," 313–23.

IV

The Organization of Trade and Finance in the Atlantic Economy

Britain and South Carolina, 1670–1775

R. C. NASH

Recent research on the organization of trade in the eighteenth-century British Atlantic economy has contrasted the thriving and indigenous commercial capitalism that emerged in the northern mainland colonies with the entrepreneurial backwardness that marked mercantile life in the southern plantation regions.[1] In the north, overseas trade was controlled by large, native-born merchant communities that succeeded in establishing what Jacob M. Price has called the "entrepreneurial headquarters" of their respective colony's trade, first in Boston in the latter seventeenth century and then in New York and Philadelphia in the early eighteenth century.[2] These merchants controlled the export of the principal northern staples—grain, fish, and timber—as well as the major import trades in manufactures from Britain and in tropical produce from the West Indies. The northern merchants self-financed their intercolonial trade, but in their trade with Britain they drew heavily on British capital, which was channeled to them by the correspondents who supplied them with manufactured goods on credit.[3]

The southern slave-based plantation colonies, by contrast, adopted three different methods of trade organization: the commission and stores system and the "cargo" trade. In the first method the sugar planters of the West Indies and the wealthier tobacco planters of Virginia and Maryland, who produced the higher-quality grades of tobacco, embraced the commission system of trade. Under this system the planters marketed their crops on their own account and risk by shipping them to British ports, where they were sold by British commission agents at the planters' direction. In the second method, the lesser tobacco planters, who produced the bulk of tobacco, sold their crops to networks of rural stores, which were operated in the Chesapeake by English and Scottish merchants. Both of these southern systems of trade tended to squeeze out local merchants. Planters also became indebted to British merchants, either to their commission agents in Britain or to British-owned stores in the Chesapeake.[4] This domination of the plantation colonies' trade by the commission and stores systems both constricted local mercantile development and contributed to the plantation zone's notable lack of urban development.[5] However, the most recent research has shown, at least for the Chesapeake, that indigenous merchants were not entirely eliminated by British competition. Beginning in the 1750s, a third system of trade arose as groups of local, independent traders began to import manufactured goods into Virginia and Maryland on their own account and risk, goods that were supplied on credit by British merchants in the "cargo" trade.[6]

The accepted orthodoxy of South Carolina's mercantile development is that it, too, lagged behind that of the northern colonies, and that its trade was dominated by British, rather than indigenous, merchants. As Jacob Price, the leading authority on colonial trade, has commented, "on the eve of the Revolution, we find some big firms in Charleston that are in effect branches of houses in London or Liverpool under the management of a local resident planter. There were of course locally based organizations as well but they never succeeded in dominating trade as indigenous firms did in the northern ports."[7]

There are two main problems with Price's view. First, our evidence for the Anglo–South Carolina trade is scanty compared with that available for the other major regions. The relative importance of the commission and stores systems and the cargo trade remains unknown. Likewise, our knowledge of the role of British merchants and capital in the South Carolina trade is very limited. Second, the view that indigenous merchant capitalism was largely absent from South Carolina sits somewhat uneasily with the existence of Charleston, the only large city in the plantation South, and one whose rapid eighteenth-century growth was based on the expansion of trade.[8]

Taking these problems with the current orthodoxy as its starting point, this essay seeks to provide a fuller study of the organization of South Carolina's trade than is presently available. The essay raises three major questions. First, what modes of trade organization were employed in South Carolina, and to what degree did they parallel those found in the other colonial regions? Second, what was the commercial and financial role of British merchants in the South Carolina trade? Finally, how did commercial developments in the Anglo–South Carolina trade compare with the general trends that occurred in the commercial organization of the wider eighteenth-century Atlantic economy?

The history of South Carolina's overseas trade in the colonial period falls into two halves.

In the first fifty years, from the settlement of the colony in 1670 to c. 1720, trade grew slowly; even by the latter date South Carolina's exports made up only 12 percent of the mainland's total export trade.[9] In the next fifty years trade grew much more rapidly, with exports increasing eight-fold by 1768–1772, when they comprised 30 percent of exports from the mainland. Two slave-produced staples were responsible for this growth: rice and

TABLE 4.1
SOUTH CAROLINA'S MAJOR IMPORT AND EXPORT TRADES,
1718–1722 AND 1768–1772
(Annual Averages: £000s)

EXPORTS

Years	Rice	Indigo	Deerskins	Grains and Provision	Naval Stores	Total
1718–1722	19	—	17	2	16	54
1768–1772	284	119	15	12	5	435

IMPORTS

Years	From Britain	Slave Imports	From Caribbean	Total
1718–1722	18	11	6	35
1768–1772	293	100	39	432

SOURCE: Nash, "Urbanization in the Colonial South: Charleston, South Carolina, As a Case Study," *Journal of Urban History*, 19 (1992): 7. There were four main export staples: deerskins and provisions, the colony's earliest exports; and rice and naval stores, which came into prominence after 1700. The data for rice and indigo exports and for imports from Britain are for South Carolina. Other data are for Charleston; however, as explained in the text, by far the greater part of South Carolina's trade was routed through Charleston.

from the late 1740s, indigo. By contrast, exports of deerskins and naval stores declined while the export of provisions increased very slowly. The major imports to South Carolina throughout the colonial period were, in order of value, manufactured goods and other imports from Britain (dry goods); slaves from Africa and the West Indies; and rum and sugar from the West Indies.

The great bulk of trade was channeled through Charleston, which handled in excess of 90 percent of both imports and exports and which was as dominating a force in the trade of South Carolina as the ports of Philadelphia or New York were in the trades of their colonies.[10] The pace of the city's growth reflected the development of its commercial economy: that is, slow until 1720, when Charleston was a medium-sized colonial town with a population of 3,000, and more rapid in the period from 1720 to the Revolution, when Charleston's population more than quadrupled to 12,800, making it the fourth-largest town in colonial America.[11]

What business methods were employed in Charleston to organize the region's rapidly growing overseas trade? This question can best be answered by first considering the commercial organization of Charleston's leading export trades in rice, indigo, and naval stores and, second, the city's principal import trades in dry goods and slaves.

The Export Trades in Rice, Indigo, and Naval Stores

In the other plantation colonies the sugar planters and the richer tobacco planters marketed their crops in Britain via the commission system while the poorer tobacco planters sold them locally to rural stores operated by British or colonial merchants. Given that South Carolina's planters were on average much wealthier than the tobacco planters, one might predict that the commission system would have predominated in South Carolina's overseas trade. In fact, the commission system was hardly used in the rice trade and was only of limited significance in the indigo trade. Why did the South Carolina planters not adopt the commission system on a wider scale? The rice planters were discouraged from marketing their own crops partly because the fragmented nature of rice's overseas markets, and the high costs of its shipment relative to its value, required a greater knowledge about freight and commodity markets than rice planters were likely to possess or wished to acquire. Moreover, there were far fewer variations in quality in rice than in tobacco and sugar, which meant that the rice planters, unlike those in sugar and tobacco, had few opportunities to earn premium prices for the higher grades by consigning their rice for sale in British markets. Therefore the rice planters marketed their crops in America rather than in Europe. As they produced on a large scale, for the most part, they chose not to deal with local, rural stores, like those that dominated the internal economy of the Chesapeake. Rather, they preferred to sell their rice in the large, central market of Charleston.[12]

The commission system played a greater part in the indigo trade because commercial conditions for indigo were similar to those found in the sugar and the higher-quality tobacco trades. First, virtually all indigo exports were shipped to a single market, London. Second, freight costs for indigo were low because the staple had a high value-to-bulk ratio. Therefore planters marketed their own crops without the need for any great commercial expertise in the international commodity and freight markets. Third, like sugar and tobacco, indigo was marked by great variations in quality. Quality grades were much more likely to fetch premium prices in British than in colonial markets. This incentive further encouraged the richer indigo planters to market their own crops in Britain on their own account and risk.[13] The lesser planters, who produced a high proportion of South Carolina's indigo, also consigned part of their crops to Britain via Charleston merchants, who acted as brokers for groups of small-scale producers.[14]

By about 1700 South Carolina's trade was centralized in Charleston. When rice first began to be exported in quantity, a professional, local merchant community had already emerged from the streams of migrants reaching the colony in the late seventeenth century. The majority of these merchants were British, but they also included a high proportion of Huguenot migrants, as well as immigrant traders from the British colonies, particularly the West Indies.[15] Until the 1720s the Charleston merchants generally acted as the factors or agents of British merchants from whom they received consignments of dry goods, which they sold to local shopkeepers and rice planters. The shopkeepers paid for their dry goods in cash or in rice and other goods, which they obtained from their customers and valued at market prices. The rice planters, the most important purchasers, usually contracted to make future payments for their purchases of dry goods in "merchantable" rice when their crops were harvested.[16] The Charleston merchants then remitted the rice they received from shopkeepers and planters to their British correspondents, usually in ships that the British merchants supplied.

From the 1720s the planters, for the most part, ceased to contract to deliver their rice to particular Charleston merchants in payment for goods received. Instead, they began to sell their rice on the open market in Charleston, receiving payment in cash or paper money, which they used to discharge their debts to the merchants.[17] This change suited both parties in the trade, although for different reasons. With their scale of production increasing in the 1720s and 1730s, the planters could now attempt, if they wished, to manipulate the market by holding back their crops until prices rose.[18] The Charleston merchants found that they could trade much more flexibly if they purchased rice for cash in the open market than by the cumbersome method of contracting with individual planters for future deliveries of rice. These merchants needed this flexibility to buy rice in advance of the arrival of ships from Britain, which were consigned to their care, to turn these ships around as quickly as possible.[19] In general, these ships continued to be owned by the British merchants for whom the Charleston merchants acted as agents and on whose behalf the Charleston merchants bought and shipped the rice. The Charleston merchants, or the export merchants as they can be conveniently termed, then reimbursed themselves for their rice purchases by drawing bills of exchange on their merchant-correspondents in England, bills which were sold in Charleston or, more usually, remitted for payment in England.[20]

In King George's War (1739–1748) the basic method of marketing rice in South Carolina underwent a further fundamental change. In the war, the rice market collapsed and the planters, in an attempt to boost prices, which had fallen to disastrously low levels, ceased to sell their rice themselves in Charleston and instead began to employ agents in the city, known as the "country" or "rice factors," who sold the planters' rice on commission to the Charleston export merchants.[21] The first advertisements offering the services of the country factors were placed in the *South Carolina Gazette* in 1741, heralding the appearance of a business group that marketed most of the rice in Charleston for the rest of the colonial period and beyond.[22] In the ten-year period 1742–1751, 15 factors advertised in the *Gazette;* the number increased to 28 in 1752–1761 and to 40 in 1762–1771. The factors invariably owned or leased wharfs and warehouses in Charleston to which the planters sent their rice, either in their own boats or in those owned by the factors.[23] The origins of the factors varied, but the majority came from one of two backgrounds. Some were Charleston merchants who specialized as "country factors." These included the South Carolina revolutionary leader Christopher Gadsden and his half-brother Thomas Gadsden and John Poyas, who had come out to join the Purrysburg settlement in about 1737 and who later established a factorage business in Charleston, in which he was succeeded by his son James Poyas. The other main group consisted of planters, or the sons of planters, who moved to Charleston and used their rural connections to launch themselves into business. These included the brothers Edward and Maurice Simmons, descendants of a planting family established in the area above French Water Creek (Parish of St. Thomas) in the 1690s, who moved to Charleston to become factors about 1763.[24]

Soon the commercial interests of the country factors and of the export merchants became antithetical, and the scene was set for a continuous struggle between these two most important factions in the Charleston business community. The country factors, whose interests coincided with those of the planters, wanted high rice prices and low freight rates while the export merchants wanted low prices and because they also handled the shipping sent out by their English correspondents, high freight rates. The factors formed cartels to keep up the price of rice and secondarily to push down freight rates, by periodically instructing their clients to "stop their boats," that is, not to send rice to Charleston until the export merchants agreed to their terms.[25] These tactics achieved some success because the country factors, who acted in a remarkably cohesive fashion, had a strong bargaining position. This was especially true when the Charleston harbor was full of British ships. In such times the export merchants were under pressure to agree to the rice factors' terms in order to save their English correspondents the heavy costs incurred when ships remained in port for long periods.[26] The planters and factors also spread commercial disinformation, as in 1763, when they greatly exaggerated the quantity of rice left in the country, thereby attracting an excess of shipping to Charleston late in the season. This tactic forced up prices to artificially high levels.[27] The general effect of the country factors' manipulations was to push up the price of rice in Charleston rather than in Europe, thus eating into the profit margins of the Charleston export merchants and their British correspondents.

The bulk of rice was exported to Europe on the account and risk of British merchants throughout the colonial period.[28] In 1762–1763 and 1766 (the latest years for which we have data) 15 percent of rice exported from Charleston was shipped in Charleston-based vessels, 60 percent was exported in British-based ships, and 25 percent in ships owned in other ports.[29] Charleston merchants did undertake a limited trade on their own account, sometimes in partnership with British merchants for whom they more usually acted as agents.[30] On the other hand Charleston merchants acted with the greatest degree of mercantile independence from the British in the rice-export trade to the West Indies. This was a major change from the early eighteenth century, when merchants resident in the West Indies almost entirely controlled this trade and the return cargoes of sugar and rum. From c. 1740, when the market grew very rapidly, Charleston merchants played a greater, although by no means dominant, part in the business.[31] Thus, in 1762–1763 and 1766, 29 percent of shipping clearing Charleston for the Caribbean was Charleston based, and 46 percent West Indies based.[32] Charleston merchants also increased their share of the expanding rice trade to southern Europe, although they handled the greater part of exports to this area on behalf of British merchants.[33]

Naval stores' exports grew rapidly from 1700 to the late 1720s, at which date they equaled rice exports in value; thereafter, the trade went into a rapid absolute and relative decline. The commission system, by which producers marketed their own crops in Europe, was little suited to this business, which dealt in a cheap, bulk staple, although it was not unknown for an enterprising group of producers to consign a shipload of tar or pitch for sale on commission in Britain.[34] Naval stores' exports to Britain, the major market, were nearly all shipped on the account and risk of British merchants, with only a minor part of the business being conducted on the account of Charleston merchants.[35] As with rice, in the early eighteenth century Charleston export merchants usually contracted with producers for future deliveries of naval stores.[36] Indeed, this method of trade persisted throughout the colonial era, and an open market for naval stores in Charleston never evolved to the same extent as it did in rice. The failure of a more general market to develop reflected both the small size of aggregate exports of naval stores and the great bulk of the staple in relation to its value, as it made little sense to incur the high costs of warehousing naval stores in Charleston while negotiating for their sale.[37] Export merchants more economically contracted in advance for naval stores to be delivered either to Charleston or later in the eighteenth century, to Georgetown, the colony's northern port, which was closer to the most important centers of production.[38]

The Import Trades in Dry Goods and in Slaves

From 1700 to the Revolution, South Carolina's dry goods imports from England rose more than twenty-fold, increasing the region's share of total imports into the American colonies from 3 to 11 percent.[39] How was this trade organized, and in particular, what was the relative importance of the British and colonial merchants? Until 1700, before a professional Charleston merchant class had fully emerged, a variety of traders imported dry goods into South Carolina: resident planters, shopkeepers and merchants, as well as transient traders, such as the captains and supercargoes of visiting trading vessels. The bulk of the business was conducted on the account of British merchants, although it was also common in the late seventeenth century for dry goods to be reexported from the Caribbean to Charleston on the account of West Indian merchants.[40] From c. 1700, however, the main group of professional Charleston traders, the export merchants, handled the dry goods trade. They acted as factors for British exporters, on whose behalf they sold the dry goods to planters and others on credit.[41]

More significantly, from the 1720s if not before, a high proportion of the first generation of major Charleston export merchants commenced an extensive *independent* trade in dry goods, which supplemented or even

replaced their commission business. These merchants, who sometimes operated in partnerships with British merchants, included a number of the early
colony's leading commercial figures, such as Alexander Parris and the firms
of Samuel and Joseph Wragg and of Andrew Allen and William Gibbon.[42]
The number of export merchants importing dry goods in this fashion continued to grow in the late colonial period, when it even became common for
minor merchants to import small parcels of dry goods on credit.[43] The number of independent importers was further increased from the 1740s, when the
country factors began to import dry goods on their own account.[44] Country
factors then retailed these goods to their planter-clients and also sold them on
a wholesale basis to Charleston traders and country shopkeepers.[45]

Thus, by the end of the colonial period Charleston rather than English
merchants conducted most of the dry goods trade. This is shown most
clearly by the detailed evidence contained in the claims made by English
merchants after the American Revolution for their prewar South Carolina
debts, which unlike the Charleston evidence, provides a comprehensive
overview of the organization of the English export trade in dry goods. It
shows that the chief business of *all* the British mercantile houses for which
evidence survives, including the great majority of the leading London firms
trading with South Carolina, was to act as agents for Charleston merchants
to whom they supplied dry goods on the latters' account and risk.[46] In this
way, the South Carolina trade in dry goods came to be organized in a manner similar to that identified by Price in the Chesapeake "cargo" trade. As in
the Chesapeake trade, British correspondents always supplied dry goods on
credit to independent Charleston importers. From c. 1750 British merchants provided free credit for six to twelve months from the date of the
British invoice, after which they charged interest at 5 percent per annum.[47]
Along with the credit made available by British merchants in the slave trade,
these credit advances for dry goods formed the core of the financial relations
linking Britain and South Carolina.

The increase in the number of importers of dry goods, particularly those
who traded independently, mirrored trends in the northern ports, which also
saw a proliferation of importers trading on British credit in the late colonial
period. The profusion of traders and credit led to a persistent saturation of
the market for dry goods in all the major colonial cities.[48] Certainly, the frequency with which Charleston's merchants complained that the market was
glutted suggests that overtrading in dry goods in the city, as in New York or
Philadelphia, was a structural problem in South Carolina's trade.[49] The cause
of the problem lay both in the variety of Charleston's merchant groups, each
of which provided a channel by which dry goods could enter the city and,
most importantly, in the ease with which independent importers could

expand their business on the basis of credit advances from British merchants. As Henry Laurens wrote to a Bristol merchant in October 1768, "our place is so well supplied with every Article of Merchandize by Merchants who import . . . upon their Accounts & retail for a very moderate Profit at 12 Months Credit, that there is very seldom an Opportunity of making even a saving Sale of Goods in the track that we pursue. . . ."[50] As early as 1732–1737, when imports from Britain averaged £84,000 per year, there were 74 traders advertising the sale of dry and miscellaneous goods in Charleston. By 1762–1767, the number advertising had nearly doubled to 130 while average imports had increased over threefold to £271,000 per annum.[51]

If dry goods constituted the major import into South Carolina, the second major import was enslaved Africans. Slaves had originally been brought to the colony by settlers from the Caribbean, and they continued to be imported both from the West Indies and more particularly from Africa during the rest of the colonial period. Until 1720 slave imports were modest, rarely numbering more than 200 per year. However, with the expansion of rice, naval stores, and later, indigo production using slave labor, imports increased to 2,000 to 3,000 per year, making Charleston by far the most important slave market in the mainland colonies.[52]

What roles did British and Charleston merchants perform in this trade? Slaves were mainly supplied by British merchants, with London, Bristol, and Liverpool successively dominating the trade, and the participation of Charleston merchants in the *direct* importation of slaves, especially from Africa, was always very restricted.[53] Charleston merchants known as the slave factors took delivery of slave cargoes arranged for their sale at auction and for the remittance of the proceeds to Britain. The trade was concentrated in the hands of a few Charleston slave factors. The excellent data on imports show that while in the period 1735–1775 hundreds of Charleston merchants handled slaves, an inner group of ten merchants participated in a series of overlapping firms, which imported 57 percent of cargoes in these years.[54] Through this concentration these merchants benefitted from dealing on a large scale in the slave trade. They lowered their considerable overheads on incoming cargoes and reduced the high risks both of slave mortality and defaulting customers.[55] Nearly all of the elite slave factors belonged to the ranks of the export merchants, the very traders who bought and sold rice and dry goods on commission. These included such well-known Charleston merchants as Henry Laurens, Miles Brewton, and John Guerard. A small number of country factors also dealt in slaves, although the great majority of the country factors apparently had little or no connection with the trade.[56]

Slave factors were the most eminent merchants in Charleston and possessed sizable trading capital. For example, Laurens claimed in 1755 that his "small business" was often "in Advance more than 10,000 Sterling."[57] Moreover, the capital required for this trade tended to increase during the colonial period due to the growing obligations that were placed upon slave factors by British slave merchants. In the early eighteenth century, the factors acted like any other commission agents and were held responsible neither for the debts incurred by their planter-customers to whom they sold the slaves nor required to make remittances to the English slave merchants within a specified period. However, as the English slave merchants needed greater liquidity and security in a trade where large sums of capital were locked-up for long periods of time, they imposed much greater demands on their Charleston factors who received the substantial commission of 10 percent of the gross value of business.

Beginning in the early 1730s the British slave merchants required the factors to provide good financial securities in England and made them legally liable for all debts incurred in the sale of slaves to planters. In addition, they fundamentally changed the method by which the Charleston factors paid for the slaves. Until c. 1750 the British merchants required the factors to remit the proceeds of slave sales only as these came in from the planters to whom the slaves had been sold.[58] From the 1750s the British required the Charlestonians to pay for slaves immediately after they were auctioned. The factors paid the English slave merchants, who were now mainly of Liverpool, in sets of long-dated bills of exchange, due for payment in six months or a year. The Charleston factors returned the bills in the vessels that had imported the slaves, and drew the bills on a number of leading London merchants trading to South Carolina, who acted as the factors' guarantors.[59] Before the bills matured, that is, before the British slave merchants presented them to the London merchants for payment, the factors sold the slaves to the planters on credit and then collected the planters' payments. The factors then remitted these payments to the London merchants in goods, cash, and short-dated bills of exchange. In this way the London merchants were supposed to receive the proceeds of the slave sales, which they used to discharge the long-dated bills drawn upon them, before the latter were presented for payment. In practice, however, the factors invariably failed to remit the full proceeds of slave sales from Charleston before the long-dated bills became due in London because they were unable to collect a high proportion of the debts owed to them by the planters. This meant that the Charleston factors built up long-term debts to their London correspondents. In periods when the slave trade was expanding rapidly, such as the years 1764–1775, these debts increased at a rapid rate. For example, the firm of Middleton, Liston and Hope imported about 1,600 slaves in 1764–1765, about one-sixth of the slaves imported into South Carolina in those years. By late 1767 the firm was owed over £25,000 sterling by South Carolina planters on account of these slaves and itself owed at least £32,000 to its main correspondents, the London firms of Sarah Nickleson and Issac King and Arthur and Benjamin Heyward. Similarly, the Charleston firm of Powell, Hopton and Co. imported about 4,300 slaves in 1771–1774, about a fifth of the slaves imported in those years. By 1775 the firm was owed £44,000 by South Carolina planters for slaves and several years later still owed its London merchant-backers at least £35,000.[60] Thus, the debts owed by Charleston slave factors to British merchants increased substantially and, added to the capital advanced in the dry goods trade, comprised the chief element in the financial network that linked South Carolina to Britain.

In sum, what can be concluded about the relative importance in the South Carolina trade of the basic modes of commercial organization that were employed in trade to the other American regions? The West Indian sugar and Chesapeake tobacco planters marketed their export staples and obtained their manufactured goods either through the commission system or through networks of rural stores, both modes of trade circumventing the need for centralized colonial markets and urban development. In South Carolina these systems were only of secondary importance. Here, commission dealing was only common in the indigo trade from c. 1750 while rural stores handled only a fraction of the trade of the Charleston firms, of which they were often subsidiaries. Instead, South Carolina's trade, as in the northern colonies, was heavily centralized in a *single* market, Charleston. In Charleston three groups of local merchants achieved a high degree of commercial autonomy, especially in the import trades, whose structure fostered the growth of specialized merchant groups. These included, first, the rice factors, a trading group for which no parallel can be found in the other plantation colonies, who, as well as selling the planters' rice and indigo, became major importers of dry goods; second, many other independent importers of dry goods; and, finally, the slave factors, who were also independent players in a major colonial business. The control of trade by indigenous merchants, however, was less complete in Charleston than in Philadelphia or New York, as the role of the Charleston merchants in the transatlantic *export* trades in rice and naval stores was primarily, although not exclusively, restricted to that of commission agents trading in Charleston on behalf of British principals.

British Merchants in the South Carolina Trade

Having considered the nature of business organization in South Carolina, it is necessary to examine which British ports and merchants were involved in the trade and what role they played in the financing and organization of

TABLE 4.2

THE DISTRIBUTION OF ENGLISH TRADE TO CAROLINA BETWEEN LONDON AND THE OUTPORTS, 1700–1774

(Annual averages: 000s £s: Rice Imports = 000s cwts[a])

	(A) Exports				(B) Imports				(C) Rice Imports			
			%S				%S				%S	
Years	L	OPs	L	OPs	L	OPs	L	OPs	L	OPs	L	OPs
1700–1709	8	4	67%	33%	11	4	73%	27%	3	2	60%	40%
1710–1719	12	9	57%	43%	21	14	60%	40%	11	8	58%	42%
1720–1729	22	14	61%	39%	48	37	56%	44%	38	31	55%	45%
1730–1739	59	23	72%	28%	83	84	50%	50%	64	79	45%	55%
1740–1749	95	36	73%	27%	84	85	50%	50%	77	85	48%	52%
1750–1759	145	32	82%	18%	93	131	42%	58%	61	114	35%	65%
1760–1769	234	36	87%	13%	129	190	40%	60%	76	176	30%	70%
1770–1774	295	51	85%	15%	160	195	45%	55%	98	246	8%	72%

SOURCE: Customs 3, vols. 4–74, PRO.

NOTE: There are no data for 1705, 1712, 1728. "Carolina" includes both North and South Carolina, although the great bulk of trade was with the latter; see, Coclanis, *Shadow of a Dream*, 76, 248–49.

NOTE: [a]Cwts. In the English records, from which the data are taken, the cwt=a hundredweight of 112 lbs. In the South Carolina records the cwt=a hundredweight of 100 lbs.

commerce. Until c. 1720 London dominated Britain's trade with South Carolina, which, as in the early days of British trade to the West Indies and the Chesapeake, tended to overshadow the contribution made by the English outports, that is all English ports other than London. In the period 1700–1720, London handled 61 percent of total exports to Carolina and 66 percent of total imports from the region, including 58 percent of rice imports. From c. 1720 London's significance in the *import* trade declined. By the 1730s, the proportion of rice imported into London fell to 45 percent of the English total, and by the 1760s London's share was only 30 percent.[61]

Clearly the main trend in the organization of South Carolina trade at the English end was thus the shift of the rice trade from London to the leading outports of the south and southwest, whose growing participation in the Carolina trade reflected the advantages they offered in the marketing of rice in Europe. Northern Europeans, not Britons, consumed the great bulk of South Carolina's rice exports although rice, as an enumerated commodity, had to be cleared through a British port on its way to a European market.[62] In Europe, rice competed with cheap, locally produced grain stuffs, which meant that there was an absolute necessity to keep transport costs to the minimum.[63] Until the 1720s London was the major port used for transshipping rice to Europe. Thereafter, England's expanding reexport trade in rice centered on a number of south-coast ports, such as Cowes, because their location and their low costs provided the most economical means to reexport rice to Europe.

As John Guerard commented on the rice trade in 1752, "I have done little or nothing there [London] for a long time, [as] the monstrous Charges attending adventures to that Markett are discouraging."[64] British ships departing from Charleston therefore usually cleared for south-coast ports. British merchants, who had access to the latest commercial intelligence, sent information to their ships' captains specifying which continental port would provide the best market for their cargo of rice.[65] For this reason British ships in Charleston usually took freight not for a specific European port, but for "Cowes and a market," meaning a market in Holland, Germany or Scandinavia.

Bristol and a number of otherwise minor south-coast ports, including Cowes, Poole, Gosport, and Portsmouth, led the rise of England's southern ports in the trade. Bristol, as the leading provincial port in the American trades, established commercial ties with South Carolina from the colony's foundation, and in the early eighteenth century maintained a broad participation in the colony's import and export trades. The lesser south-coast ports originally played a sizable role in tobacco importing in the late seventeenth century, but had lost this important foothold in the Atlantic trade in the

TABLE 4.3

RICE EXPORTED FROM CHARLESTON TO GREAT BRITAIN, 1717–1766

(Annual Averages: 000s Lbs.)[a]

Years	London	Bristol	Cowes	Other South-Coast Ports	Scotland	Other[b]
1717-1720	5,940	590	791	1,303	0	31
1731-1731	15,900	4,736	3,729	6,626	0	1,389
1734-1738	12,338	3,869	9,632	2,852	0	986
1756, 1758–1760	10,276	5,717	5,548	2,358	4,219	5,533
1762–1764, 1766	11,602	3,334	21,549	7,699	1,765	4,085

SOURCE: Clowse, *Charleston's Overseas Commerce*, 59; *South Carolina Gazette*, July 29th 1756, Nov 5th 1764.
NOTE: [a] The source gives figures in barrels which have been converted into lbs using the formula suggested in *Historical Statistics of the United States*, 2, 1163–64. [b] Includes some Scottish and south-coast ports not specified separately in the source.

Nine Years and Spanish Succession Wars (1689–1697, 1702–1713) when the scattered trade of the south coast proved impossible to defend against French privateers.[66] From c. 1720 these ports needed a new function in transatlantic trade and were well positioned to shift into rice, because their location gave them considerable cost advantages in the reexport trade to Europe. Merchants from Bristol also began to make extensive use of south-coast entrepôts in rice reexporting from the 1720s, and by the 1730s more than twice as much Bristol-owned shipping cleared through Cowes as did London shipping, the next major participant in the trade.[67] In the 1750s and 1760s Liverpool and a number of Scottish ports also began to import and reexport rice. Liverpool's participation in rice importing flowed from its involvement in the Charleston slave business. The entry of Scottish ports into the trade reflected the widening of that country's commercial horizons in colonial trade after 1750 and more particularly the advantages of shipping to Europe via north Scottish routes in the war years 1756–1763, when the south coast of England was once again vulnerable to French privateering attacks.[68]

Despite the relative decline of London in the rice trade, its participation in the major *export* trade to South Carolina, that in dry goods, increased in the eighteenth century, and after 1750 London came to exercise an almost complete control of the trade. Thus, while London *imported* only 30 percent of rice from 1760 to 1774, it provided 85 to 90 percent of English *exports* to Carolina. This dominance reflected the need to provide export credits in the dry goods trade, as London's financial resources and its merchants' ability to tap the credit supplied by tradesmen and warehousemen appears to have been significant. London's dominance also reflected its superior access to textile imports from Asia and Europe, reexports of which made up a growing part of total English exports to Carolina. In the other major export trade to Charleston, that in slaves, London's early dominance, as in the British slave trade generally, gave way to Bristol which ceded its position to Liverpool after 1760.[69] However, although her role in shipping slaves declined, London's role in financing the slave trade remained fundamental, as the Charleston slave factors invariably depended on the credit and guarantees supplied by London, not by provincial merchants.

Thus, although a large number of British ports shared the trade between Britain and South Carolina and distributed it more widely than the trades to the Chesapeake and to the West Indies, there remained clear lines of specialization. First, from the 1720s there was a high degree of separation between the bulk-import trades, handled by the outports, and the export trade in manufactures, which was controlled by London. Second, London played the key role in financing business by supplying credit in both the slave and the dry goods trades.

These changes in the roles of British merchants in the South Carolina trade inevitably had a significant influence on the organization and financing of business in Charleston. In Charleston, the country factors and others who imported dry goods relied on London merchants not only to supply these goods but, more importantly, to provide them on long-term credit. Similarly, the elite Charleston slave importers looked to London merchants to back the long-dated bills that they used to buy cargoes of slaves from outport merchants, without which their business as slave factors would have been impossible, but which drew them into large debts to London merchants.

On the other hand, the Charleston export merchants, who bought rice and other staples on commission found it increasingly difficult to tap into English capital. Until c. 1720 they acquired rice and other staple commodities through the sale of dry goods, supplied to them by their merchant correspondents, who were mainly in London. But after c. 1720 the export-staple and dry goods trades became increasingly separated, as the outports took over the staple trades and London specialized in dry goods. As a result, the Charleston export merchants had to pay cash for commodities or more rarely bought them on short-term credit. The funds required to finance trade in Charleston, then, were supplied *not* by the English outport merchants but by their Charleston agents, who had to draw on their own resources when striking deals with planters and country factors.[70] In addition, those agents advanced monies to meet the heavy port charges of the outport ships that entered Charleston and were consigned to their care. To recoup these expenses on commodities and ships, the Charleston merchants drew bills of exchange on their outport correspondents, bills, however, that could not be presented for payment in England until some weeks or months had elapsed. Consequently, the Charleston export merchants drew bills much more on the outports than on London. As Laurens wrote to a London merchant in August 1756, "you will please to Accept of Bills on Bristol, Liverpool, or Other Trading Towns. . . . We shall prefer Bills on London when they are to be had but the *Trading men* [of Charleston] *draw much more on Bristol than on your City.*"[71]

That the capital advanced to South Carolina was overwhelmingly made available by London rather than by outport merchants is confirmed by the evidence of the claims made by English merchants for debts owing to them from South Carolina in 1775, debts that were repudiated during the American Revolution.

Of the debts still outstanding in 1790, 87 percent were owed to London merchants. Furthermore, such debts were heavily concentrated within London itself, where five merchant houses held 73 percent of London's debts.[72]

TABLE 4.4
PRE-1776 DEBTS DUE FROM SOUTH CAROLINA TO BRITISH MERCHANTS STILL OWED IN 1790, INTEREST DEDUCTED (000s £s)

London	Bristol	Glasgow	Chester	TOTAL	% London
370	5	7	42	424	87%

SOURCE: Chatham Papers, PRO 30/8/343/167-69, PRO.
NOTES: Interest has been deducted according to the formula suggested by Jacob M. Price, see his *Capital and Credit in British Overseas Trade: The View from the Chesapeake, 1700-1776* (Cambridge: Havard University Press, 1980), 9.
    For South Carolina there are some arithmetical errors in the original source which have been corrected.

The detailed claims made by London firms show that the debts represented credit advanced to Charleston importers of dry goods and to a lesser extent, to Charleston slave factors. The major outport claims for prewar debts were also related to the dry goods rather than to the rice trade.[73] No comprehensive picture of the financial structure of the South Carolina trade exists for the period before 1775, but the considerable, if fragmentary, evidence shows that the bulk of credit in the trade was, as on the eve of the Revolution, supplied by London firms to Charleston importers of dry goods and slaves.[74]

Who were the London merchants dealing with South Carolina? In the late seventeenth and early eighteenth centuries they were mainly merchants active in other branches of colonial trade, or Huguenot merchants who had family or other connections with their coreligionists in South Carolina.[75] However, after c. 1720, when the trade entered its most rapid period of growth, London merchants trading to Charleston comprised two main groups. The first and most important were British merchants who had spent long periods in Charleston as export merchants or slave factors and had returned to London to set themselves up as merchants. For instance, Samuel Wragg, unquestionably the most eminent trader in Charleston in the early eighteenth century, returned to London in 1718, where for twenty years afterwards he was the leading merchant in the trade.[76] Wragg's premier position in London was assumed by the Scot James Crokatt, one of Charleston's major merchants in the 1720s and 1730s, before moving to London in 1737, where he also acted as South Carolina's agent.[77] Similarly, John Beswicke migrated to Charleston from London soon after 1734 and became a major trader until 1747 when he returned to London, where his firm was second only to that of Crokatt. After Beswicke's death in 1764 his London junior partners, nephew William Higginson and William Greenwood, took over his business. On the eve of the Revolution their house was by far the largest in the trade.[78] The continuing strength of London firms founded by former expatriates from Charleston is shown by the fact that five such firms claimed 63 percent of the prerevolutionary debt owed from South Carolina to London merchants.[79]

The second group of London merchants, those who traded to Charleston but who had never been resident there, was a miscellaneous group. First, they included merchants who had never been to South Carolina, but had close family or business relations with those who had. These included John Nutt, a leading London merchant of the late colonial era, who married James Crokatt's daughter and whose brother, Joseph, represented the family's business in South Carolina for many years, and the major firm of Richard Grubb and Alexander Watson, who had formerly been Crokatt's partners.[80] Second, there were a number of London merchants trading to Africa and the West Indies, like Richard Oswald, who had wide connections in the transatlantic trade. Third, was a circle of London warehousemen, linen and woollen drapers, and ironmongers, types of businessmen who, as Price has shown, played a very significant part in financing the export trades to British America, many of whom were active in the dry goods trade to the northern colonies as well as to Charleston.[81]

South Carolina Trade in the Eighteenth-Century Atlantic Economy

Finally, to what degree did business developments in the Anglo–South Carolina trade correspond with broader changes in the commercial organization of the Atlantic economy in the eighteenth century? The most important change in the organization of British Atlantic commerce in this period was the rise of the commission system of trade. In c. 1700 English merchants conducted nearly all of England's transatlantic trade on their own account and risk and employed colonial residents as their agents and factors. In the eighteenth century, in the trade with the northern colonies, the West Indies and in part of the trade with the Chesapeake, the whole system of trade was changed. The English merchants, mainly of London, ceased to be entrepreneurs who traded on their own accounts and risks and became agents who sold consignments of goods received from America on commission and in return paid bills of exchange and sent out cargoes of manufactured goods to colonial merchants and planters.[82]

The outports controlled the remaining English export and import trades with the colonies, trades in which entrepreneurial control remained firmly in English rather than colonial hands. These export trades included slaves from Africa and provisions from Ireland. The import trades included the cheaper grades of tobacco produced in the Chesapeake, but mainly reexported to Europe, and fish from Newfoundland reexported to southern Europe. The Atlantic trades of the English outports thus form an heterogeneous group, but had two things in common. First, they were *not* organized on a commission basis but on the account and risk of the outport merchants. Second, they were long-distance and in part multilateral bulk trades in which port and shipping charges, which were lower in the outports than in London, made up a high proportion of total costs.[83]

To what extent did the methods of organizing Anglo-South Carolina trade conform with those employed in the wider Atlantic economy? The commission system played a much smaller part in the South Carolina staple-export trades than it did in the trades of the West Indies and the Chesapeake. In this respect the organization of the South Carolina trade differed quite markedly from that found in the other plantation economies. Initially London handled the greater flow of imports from Charleston, but from the 1720s control of the import and reexport trades in rice and naval stores shifted to the outports. This shift conformed to the general pattern in British colonial trade, by which the bulk, *noncommission* trades came to be controlled by the outports. In fact, London held the lion's share of only one import trade, that in indigo.[84] The organization of the export trades to South Carolina also in part conformed to and in part diverged from the wider pattern of Atlantic business organization. First, in the slave trade from Africa to Charleston, as in the slave trade to the other plantation colonies, the outports supplanted London. Second, the export trade in manufactures came to be almost completely concentrated in London. However, the manufactures supplied by London commission agents were exported to South Carolina on the account of Charleston merchants, not on the account of the planters as in the trades to the West Indies and the Chesapeake.

How did the methods of financing Anglo–South Carolina trade compare with those used more widely in the Atlantic economy? In the West Indies and the Chesapeake, the eighteenth-century growth of production depended on direct capital advances from English merchants to colonial planters. In South Carolina, however, planters had few direct commercial dealings with English merchants and hence did not receive *direct* advances of capital and credit from British traders. There was a flow of credit from England to South Carolina, but through the Charleston business community to the planters. In particular, the planters bought their imported slaves and manufactured goods on extensive credit from Charleston merchants. In this way, the planters tapped only indirectly into English credit, or rather

London credit, as London capital almost entirely funded the slave and dry goods trades. In contrast, the English outport merchants who controlled the colony's staple-export trades did not advance capital to the South Carolina plantation economy. The outport merchants invested heavily in shipping and in inventories of commodities in Europe; they did not wish, in addition, to advance credit to South Carolina. They therefore required their Charleston agents to bear the financial burden of buying staples in Charleston.

How did the evolution of business organization in South Carolina compare with developments in the other colonial regions? Recent research suggests that South Carolina's level of commercial development in the colonial period was analogous to that achieved in the other plantation regions: backward compared with that attained in the northern colonial cities. This view needs to be qualified in two major respects. First, the commercial expansion of Charleston had no parallel in the other plantation colonies. For example, in the Chesapeake tobacco regions, urban and mercantile development was very restricted.[85] Charleston also evolved a sophisticated mortgage market, which financed a large part of the economic growth of its hinterland and which again had no counterpart in the other plantation colonies.[86] Second, the view that Charleston's commercial development lagged behind that of the northern ports is to some extent misguided. Charleston's expansion was accompanied by the growth of a large and specialized merchant community, one that gained a degree of entrepreneurial independence comparable to that attained by merchants in the north. This was most marked in the *import* trades, where a number of groups of Charleston merchants traded independently on a large scale. These included the slave factors, the "country factors," and other independent importers of dry goods. Nevertheless, Charleston's position as the "entrepreneurial headquarters" of the region's overseas trades remained incomplete, as the Charleston merchants only partially controlled the region's major *export* trades in rice and other staples, trades that continued to be largely conducted on the account of British traders.

Why did Charleston merchants fail to achieve an hegemony in the staple-export trades in the manner achieved by their northern counterparts? This was partly because these trades were mainly focused on the British market and therefore naturally attracted the attention of British merchants. However, even in those trades where Charleston's exports were shipped not to Britain but to the West Indies and Southern Europe, the bulk of business was done on foreign rather than Charleston account. In contrast, the merchants of the northern cities took control both of their export trades to Britain and to the Caribbean and southern Europe. Charleston merchants, then, were only prepared to trade on their own account in the import trades—in slaves and dry goods—where British finance heavily supplemented their capital resources and where little investment in shipping was required. In the export trades in rice and other staples, where Charleston merchants had little access to British capital and where the control of trade required a heavy investment in shipping, their participation was mainly limited to the role of commission agents.[87] Yet given the great wealth accumulated by Charleston merchants in the eighteenth century, it seems implausible that their failure to invest in the staple-export trades was the result of any absolute, local shortage of capital. Rather, in the long run, the Charleston merchants preferred to follow a strategy of investing in nontrading activities. Above all, the lure of investment in the region's slave-plantation economy proved a much stronger attraction than the impulse to concentrate their resources in the foreign trade sector.[88]

The first group of South Carolina traders was not wealthy enough to adopt a strategy of investing in plantations. Thus, the great majority of the so-called merchants of the 1680s and 1690s were in fact mere shopkeepers, men of very limited resources, who possessed very few slaves and little land. These included the Huguenot Alexander Pepin and the English migrant Samuel Osborne, who traded in the colony in the 1680s.[89] The early eighteenth century, however, saw the appearance of the first generation of true overseas merchants, the majority of whom invested in land and slaves. For example, at least 60 percent of the major merchants identified in Stuart Stumpf's important study owned plantations.[90] Once this pattern was established it tended to be maintained and even intensified so that the merchants of the second and third generations who organized Charleston's trade in the period up to the Revolution usually combined trade with planting. This can be ascertained most clearly from Walter B. Edgar and N. Louise Bailey's directory of the South Carolina House of Representatives, which shows that, of the 156 merchants elected to the House from 1692 to 1775, at least 119 (nearly 80 percent) owned plantations.[91] Such merchants were among the most enterprising investors in the expansion of South Carolina's plantation system. For example, in the 1740s and 1750s a number of leading Charleston traders invested in rice and indigo estates in the southern (Beaufort) districts of South Carolina, one of the fastest-growing sectors of the plantation economy in that era.[92] Merchants also made very substantial *indirect* investments in agriculture by lending money to planters on mortgage.[93]

It should be emphasized that, in general, merchants became planters rather than the other way around. This was true of migrants from Britain such as George Austin, Benjamin Godin, and John McQueen, as well as of the native-born such as Henry Laurens, Gabriel Manigault, and John Guerard, all of who established themselves as leading export merchants before they became great planters.[94] Thus, examples of planters or the sons of planters becoming merchants are far outnumbered by the movement in the opposite direction. Of the 119 merchant-planters who served in the House of Representatives, 96 (81 percent) were merchants before they were planters while only 13 (11 percent) were planters before they were merchants, with another 10 (8 percent) apparently having entered trade and planting concurrently.[95] Planters did contribute to the financing of trade through passive investments in merchant-led trading ventures or shipowning groups, or by lending money to merchants. However, it was much more common for planters to be indebted to merchants and most trade debts were held between merchants, that is, within the commercial community, rather than outside it.[96] In general, then, it was trade that lent assistance to planting rather than planting that financed trade.

Finally, how did the investment behavior of Charleston merchants, and hence their impact on the wider regional economy, compare with that pursued by merchants elsewhere in colonial America? For Baltimore County, Maryland, Steffen argued that a large, new merchant class dominated trade after c. 1750, one that involved itself far less in agriculture and slaveholding than the small number of "gentry merchants" who had organized trade in Baltimore County before that date.[97] Steffen's picture of a growing separation between old planters and new traders fits well with the long-held view that the Chesapeake plantocracy was becoming an increasingly closed caste in the late colonial period. For Philadelphia, Thomas Doerflinger demonstrated that few merchants before the Revolution owned nonurban property, and the overwhelming majority, even among the very richest, owned only one or two slaves. After 1776 Philadelphia merchants, in response to the adverse conditions that blighted their activities in the revolutionary and postrevolutionary years, mounted a powerful diversification into new trade areas, as well as into land and manufacturing. Doerflinger contrasts this "entrepreneurial efflorescence" with the fossilized business culture of the South. In the South the domination of a hereditary, risk-avoiding planter class, and the lack of towns to act as the forcing-houses of entrepreneurship, stifled the growth of trade and manufacturing.[98]

South Carolina followed a different route from either that pursued by Maryland merchants or that suggested by Doerflinger as being typical of the South. Trade and planting did not become more separate, as in Maryland, but less so. Nothing seems clearer than the growing interpenetration of the two sectors in the colonial period. Second, the business culture of South Carolina did not become moribund in the eighteenth century. The merchant class, unlike that of the Chesapeake, was not widely scattered, but concentrated in a single city where it fashioned important changes in business organization. At the same time, of course, Charleston merchants poured money into plantations, not as a response to adversity, but as a strategy pursued energetically by every generation of merchants from c. 1700 onwards. This diversification into planting was not a symptom of entrepreneurial backwardness, but a rational investment in a booming and profitable agricultural sector.[99] Of course, as Steffen has recently emphasized, southern merchants also invested in land and slaves for noneconomic reasons, to enhance their claims to gentility and patriarchal authority.[100] Nevertheless, whatever the causes of the diversion of capital from trading to planting, it is hard to escape the conclusion that while this investment made a significant contribution to the development of South Carolina's plantation economy, it also slowed the rate of capital investment in commerce. This was a major reason why the merchants of Charleston achieved less commercial autonomy than that enjoyed by the merchants of Philadelphia or New York. The diversion of capital from trade to planting explains, at least in part, why Charleston merchants did not take over their colony's export trades and why they therefore failed to establish Charleston more completely as the "entrepreneurial headquarters" of South Carolina's overseas trade.

Notes

The research in South Carolina, upon which this paper is mainly based, was made possible by a grant from the Economic and Social Research Council, England. The author expresses his gratitude for this research support. He would also like to thank his good friend Hilary Wood for her excellent research assistance and his colleague Steve Rigby for his valuable criticisms of earlier drafts of the paper.

1. See, amongst a large literature, Richard Pares, *Merchants and Planters, Economic History Review*, supp. 4 (Cambridge: Cambridge University Press, 1960), 32–37; Jacob M. Price, "Economic Function and the Growth of American Port Towns in the Eighteenth Century," *Perspectives in American History* 8 (1974): 121–86; Thomas M. Doerflinger, *A Vigorous Spirit of Enterprise: Merchants and Economic Development in Revolutionary Philadelphia* (Chapel Hill: University of North Carolina Press, 1986), esp. 344–64.

2. Price, "Economic Function and the Growth of American Port Towns," 138–60; the quotation is from p. 173.

3. Richard Pares, *Yankees and Creoles: The Trade between North America and the West Indies before the American Revolution* (London: Longmans, Green, 1956); Virginia D. Harrington, *The New York Merchant on the Eve of the Revolution* (New York: Columbia University Press, 1935); John W. Tyler, *Smugglers and Patriots: Boston Merchants and the Advent of the American Revolution* (Boston: Northeastern University Press, 1986); Doerflinger, *Vigorous Spirit of Enterprise*.

4. For summaries, see Pares, *Merchants and Planters*, 32–33; Price, "Credit in the Slave Trade and Plantation Economies," in *Slavery and the Rise of the Atlantic System*, ed. Barbara L. Solow (Cambridge: Cambridge University Press, 1991), 325.

5. For a summary, see Pares, *Merchants and Planters*, 33.

6. Price, "Economic Function and the Growth of American Port Towns," 163–69;

Price, "Buchanan and Simson, 1759–1763: A Different Kind of Glasgow Firm Trading to the Chesapeake," *William and Mary Quarterly*, 3d ser., 40 (1983): esp. 22–29; Charles G. Steffen, "The Rise of the Independent Merchant in the Chesapeake: Baltimore County, Maryland, 1660–1769," *Journal of American History* 76 (1989): 9–33. Pares had earlier identified the growing independent role of Caribbean merchants in the late colonial period, both in what he called the "cargo business" and in slave importing; see his *A West-India Fortune* (London: Longmans, Green, 1950), 240–41; and "A London West-India Merchant House, 1740–1769," in Pares, *The Historian's Business and Other Essays* (Oxford: Oxford University Press, 1961), 221–25.

7. Price, "Economic Function and the Growth of American Port Towns," 162–63. On Charleston's relative backwardness see also David A. Smith, "Dependent Urbanization in Colonial America: The Case of Charleston, South Carolina," *Social Forces*, vol. 66, (1987): 1–28.

8. As John J. McCusker and Russell R. Menard, *The Economy of British America, 1607–1789* (Chapel Hill: University of North Carolina Press, 1985), 185, comment: "The sources of Charleston's growth are but poorly understood; indeed, it is the least studied of the principal colonial ports." See, however, Leila Sellers, *Charleston Business on the Eve of the American Revolution* (Chapel Hill: University of North Carolina Press, 1934); George C. Rogers, *Charleston in the Age of the Pinckneys* (Columbia: University of South Carolina Press, 1980), esp. 3–25; Stuart O. Stumpf, "The Merchants of Colonial Charleston, 1680–1756" (Ph.D. diss., State University of Michigan, 1971); Peter A. Coclanis, "The Hydra Head of Merchant Capital: Markets and Merchants in Early South Carolina," in *The Meaning of South Carolina History: Essays in Honor of George C. Rogers, Jr.*, ed. David R. Chesnutt and Clyde N. Wilson (Columbia: University of South Carolina Press, 1991), 1–18; R. C. Nash, "Urbanization in the Colonial South: Charleston, South Carolina, as a Case Study," *Journal of Urban History* 19 (1992): 3–29.

9. For the region's general economic history, see Converse D. Clowse, *Economic Beginnings in Colonial South Carolina, 1670–1730* (Columbia, University of South Carolina Press, 1971); Robert M. Weir, *Colonial South Carolina: A History* (New York: KTO Press, 1983), 141–72; McCusker and Menard, *Economy of British America*, 169–88; Coclanis, *The Shadow of a Dream: Economic Life and Death in the South Carolina Low Country, 1670–1920* (New York: Oxford University Press, 1989), 63–110; the percentage figures are of exports to England, and are taken from Coclanis, *Shadow of a Dream*, 72.

10. It has been estimated, for example, that 95 percent of South Carolina's rice exports and 92 percent of indigo were shipped through Charleston in the late colonial period, see U.S. Bureau of the Census, *Historical Statistics of the United States: Colonial Times to 1970*, 2 vols. (Washington, D.C.: Government Printing Office, 1975), 2:1161, 1164.

11. For Charleston's population, see Coclanis, *Shadow of a Dream*, 114.

12. Nash, "Urbanization in the South," 14–16; Kenneth Morgan, "The Organization of the Colonial American Rice Trade," *William and Mary Quarterly*, 3d ser., 52 (1995): 443. The relative importance of city and rural traders can be judged from the fact that in the sample years 1756–1761, 210 traders and firms advertised goods for sale in Charleston (see J. A. Calhoun, M. A. Zierdan, and E. A. Paysinger, "The Geographic Spread of Charleston's Merchant Community, 1732–1767," *South Carolina Historical Magazine* 86 [1985]: 203–7) while in the same years only 17 advertisements or other notices appeared in the *South Carolina Gazette* concerning rural stores. In any case, the majority of these were subsidiaries of Charleston firms.

13. Nash, "Urbanization in the Colonial South," 12–14. For the adoption of the com-

mission system by the indigo planters, see transcripts of the Commission of Enquiry into Losses of American Loyalists amongst the Audit Office Records, claim of Mrs. Orde, vol. 52, New York Public Library (hereafter cited as Loyalist Transcripts), 28–30; claim of Thomas Boone, Loyalist Transcripts, vol. 53, New York Public Library, 457; Wills, Inventories, and Miscellaneous Records, vol. 87B, Charleston Public Library, Charleston, 479–82; inventory of Culcheth Golightly, Inventories of Estates, 1736–1776, Records of the Secretary of State (hereafter cited as Inventories), vol. V (1761–1763), South Carolina Department of Archives and History (hereafter cited as SCDAH), 446–56; Court of Chancery, bundle 1761–1762, SCDAH, 2–42–47; Philip M. Hamer et al., eds., *The Papers of Henry Laurens*, vols. 1–12 (Columbia: University of South Carolina Press, 1968–1990), 1:320; 2:18, 52–53, 68, 72, 120, 215, 341, 412–13; 3:15, 21, 44, 222; 4:150 (hereafter cited as Hamer et al., eds., *Henry Laurens*).

14. However, much, probably most, indigo was sold in Charleston, although the nature of the evidence makes it difficult to be certain whether the Charleston or the British market was the more important. For the Charleston market, see Inventories, vols. R (2) (1753–1756), S (1756–1758), T (1758–1761), V (1761–1763), W (1763–1767), SCDAH; John Guerard to William Jolliffe, 17 Jan. 1754, 31 Jan. 1754, [John Guerard] letterbook (hereafter cited as Guerard letterbook), 7 Mar. 1752–17 June 1754, South Carolina Historical Society, Charleston (hereafter cited as SCHS), 34–321; merchant's daybook [James Poyas], 1764–1766, SCHS, 34–325; Hamer et al., eds., *Henry Laurens*, 1:66–67, 114, 200, 269, 337; 2:13, 21, 329; 3:131, 498; 4:44, 78, 81, 88, 577–78; 5:571.

15. Stumpf, "Merchants of Colonial Charleston," table 1, 75, lists 37 major South Carolina merchants of the early eighteenth century. Of the 26 merchants whose origins I can establish, 18 came from Britain and Ireland, including 9 Huguenots; 5 from other colonies, including 1 Huguenot; and 3 were born in South Carolina.

16. The rice was valued at an agreed advance price or at the market price prevailing when the debts became due, although very often debts were expressed simply in rice quantities. See daybooks of merchants [John Blackwood and Alexander Nisbett] in Charles Town, South Carolina, G.D. 237/10/4/1–2, Scottish Record Office, Edinburgh (hereafter cited as Scottish RO); account book of Alexander Baily and Nathanial Lewis, 1711–1712, MS 11,096, Guildhall Library, London; Records of the South Carolina Court of Common Pleas, Judgment Rolls, 1703–1790 (hereafter cited as Judgment Rolls), 1720, SCDAH, 5–A-3, 13–A-3; inventory of Captain Albert Muller, Records of the Secretary of the Province, vol. E (1726–1727), 423–29, Records of the Secretary of the State, Miscellaneous Records, main series (hereafter cited as Records of the Sec.).

17. Walter B. Edgar, ed., *The Letterbook of Robert Pringle, 1737–1745*, 2 vols. (Columbia: University of South Carolina Press, 1972), 1:30, 52, 337, 422; 2:530, who noted, with some exaggeration, that rice could only be bought in Charleston for cash; Graffin Prankard to Jenys and Baker, 7 Oct. 1732, 5 July 1733, 31 Oct. 1733, Graffin Prankard letterbooks, DD/DN 425, Dickinson Papers, Somerset Record Office, Taunton (hereafter cited as Dickinson Papers). Jenys and Baker were prominent merchants in Charleston; J. H. Bettey, "Graffin Prankard, An Eighteenth-Century British Merchant," *Southern History* 12 (1990): 34–47.

18. For the planters' tactics, see Edgar, ed., *Letterbook of Robert Pringle*, 1:53, 62, 322; 2:530, 564.

19. Nash, "Urbanization in the South," 16–18.

20. Edgar, ed., *Letterbook of Robert Pringle*, 1:238, 269, 281, 337–38; Graffin Prankard to Jenys and Baker, 7 Oct. 1732, 8 July 1734, DD/DN 424, 426, Dickinson

Papers. In December 1767 Laurens described the standard procedure in Charleston: "The method of doing business here is to load or Ship Goods & for the amount of Costs & Charges to draw [bills of exchange] as soon as the Bills of Loading [Lading] are sign'd upon some Person in England," Hamer et al., eds., *Henry Laurens*, 5:528.

21. For commercial conditions in the 1740s see Stumpf, "Implications of King George's War for the Charleston Mercantile Community," *South Carolina Historical Magazine* 77 (1976): 161–88.

22. The "country factors" have been largely ignored in the recent literature; for example, the valuable study by Morgan, "The Organization of the Colonial American Rice Trade," scarcely mentions them.

23. From c. 1750 it became customary for the country factors to extend to their planter-clients the vital guarantee that they would make good any bad debts they encountered in their dealings with the export merchants.

24. E. Stanley Godbold, Jr., and Robert H. Woody, *Christopher Gadsden and the American Revolution* (Knoxville: University of Tennessee Press, 1982), 11–13, 73–75; inventory of Thomas Gadsden, Inventories, vol. Y (1769–1771), SCDAH, 255–63; merchant's daybook [James Poyas], 1761–1764, Charleston Museum Archives, Charleston; merchant's daybook [James Poyas], 1764–1766, SCHS, 34–325; Katherine A. Kellock, "London Merchants and the Pre-1776 American Debts," *Guildhall Studies in London History* 1 (1974): 143; *South Carolina Gazette,* 15 Oct. 1764. Hamer et al., eds., *Henry Laurens,* 4:385 n.

25. For the country factors, who also sold indigo and other goods for the planters, see Hamer et al., eds., *Henry Laurens,* 2:200; 3:247; 4:239, 244–45; 5:243, 499–500, 648–49; 6:396–97, 401; John Guerard to William Jolliffe, 3 Jan. 1754, 23 May 1754, Guerard letterbook, SCHS. Merchant's daybook [James Poyas], 1764–1766, SCHS, 34–325.

26. See, for example, Hamer et al., eds., *Henry Laurens,* 3:247.

27. See the disapproving discussion of these tactics in the *South Carolina Gazette,* 4 July, 9 July, 23 July, 30 July, 1 Aug., 6 Aug., 1763. For the sharp rise in prices in Charleston in July–August 1763, which did not occur in the comparable months in 1760–1762, see Hamer et al., eds., *Henry Laurens,* 3:19 n., price lists.

28. In the rice trade there was a fairly close coincidence between the shipowning and the trading groups, which means that the distribution by port-origin of the vessels used in the trade serves as a rough guide to the proportions of rice traded on the account of merchants in the various ports.

29. Clowse, *Measuring Charleston's Overseas Commerce, 1717–1767: Statistics from the Port's Naval Lists* (Washington, D.C.: University Press of America, 1981), 57, 125.

30. See Prankard to Jenys and Baker, 25 July 1732, 22 Aug. 1732; Prankard to Skinner, Smith and Co., 27 June 1733; Prankard to Watsone and Mckenzie, 19 Dec. 1738, DD/DN, 424, 427, Dickinson Papers; James Inglis, Edinburgh, business books, 1763–1780, letterbook, C.S. 96, 2250, Scottish RO; Edgar, ed., *Letterbook of Robert Pringle,* esp. 1:162–63, 356; 2:483, 576–77; for examples see Hamer et al., eds., *Henry Laurens,* 3:19–20, 23–24, 35, 58, 78.

31. For the early eighteenth century see, for example, Records of the Sec., 1675–1695, SCDAH, 128, 317, 417; Records of the Sec., 1694–1705, SCDAH, 113, 139–40, 203; Records of the Sec., 1711–1717, SCDAH, 34, 38. In the West Indies trade there was an almost total coincidence between the shipowning and the trading groups; see Edgar, ed., *Letterbook of Robert Pringle,* esp. 2:438, 476, 483, 823; Hamer et al., eds., *Henry Laurens,* 3:26, 54–55, 57; 4:181–82; 5:310; 7:367.

32. Assuming that all West Indies shipping departing from Charleston did so for the Caribbean, see Clowse, *Measuring Charleston's Overseas Commerce*, 103–4, 120, 139.

33. In the trade to southern Europe, Charleston shipping carried only 6 percent of rice exports in 1762–1763 and 1766; see ibid., 57, 125. However, Laurens and other Charleston merchants frequently exported to this market in non-Charleston shipping; for examples see Hamer et al., eds., *Henry Laurens*, 3:19–20, 23–24, 53, 438–39; Morgan, "The Organization of the Colonial American Rice Trade," 442–43, shows that a high proportion of the rice trade to Oporto, Portugal, was on Charleston account.

34. See, for example, Hamer et al., eds., *Henry Laurens*, 3:40–41.

35. In 1762–1766 and 1766, 74 percent of tar and pitch were exported in British-based ships and 7 percent in Charleston-based. See Clowse, *Measuring Charleston's Overseas Commerce*, 65, 125.

36. For examples see Records of the Sec., vol. E (1726–1727), SCDAH, 428; Judgment Rolls, 1722, SCDAH, 163A-2; Court of Chancery, bundle 1721–1735, SCDAH, 5–1, 5–4.

37. In the period 1733–1773, the average Charleston price for naval stores was £2.75 per ton of eight barrels, and for rice £6.83 per ton of 20 cwts; see Nash, "South Carolina and the Atlantic Economy in the Late Seventeenth and Eighteenth Centuries," *Economic History Review*, 2d ser., 45, no. 4 (1992): 699.

38. See Miscellaneous Records, vol. MM (1763–1767), SCDAH, 444; John Guerard to William Jolliffe, 13 Apr. 1754, Guerard letterbook, SCHS; Hamer et al., eds., *Henry Laurens*, esp. 3:127, 144–45, 484; 4:321, 322–23, 657–58.

39. See table 4.1, and Coclanis, *Shadow of a Dream*, 76.

40. For Charleston residents handling dry goods in the late seventeenth and early eighteenth centuries, see Records of the Sec., 1675–1695, SCDAH, 251; Records of the Sec., 1692–1700, SCDAH, 119–20; Records of the Sec., 1694–1705, SCDAH, 30, 110, 189, 219–20; Miscellaneous Records, vol. A (1682–1690), SCDAH, 53. For transient traders, see Records of the Sec., 1675–1695, SCDAH, 33–34, 51–52, 82; account book of Alexander Baily and Nathanial Lewis, 1711–1712, MS 11,096, Guildhall Library, London; and for imports from the West Indies, Records of the Sec., 1675–1695, SCDAH, 91; Records of the Sec., Miscellaneous Records, vol. A (1682–1690), SCDAH, 93–94; Records of the Sec., 1694–1695, SCDAH, 229–30; Records of the Sec., 1692–1700, SCDAH, 14–16; Records of the Sec., vol. D (1704–1709), SCDAH, 62; Judgment Rolls, 1703, 180–1–2; 1720, 51A-1–2, SCDAH.

41. The ranks of the Charleston dry goods dealers were increased by the junior partners and other salaried factors that some British firms sent to Charleston to handle their business interests over extended periods. For examples see Records of the Sec., 1711–1717, SCDAH, 10–12; Miscellaneous Records, vol. II, 1751–1754, SCDAH, 555–57; *Jolliffe v Olive*, Judgment Rolls, oversize, 1751, SCDAH, 15A; claim of John Davies, Loyalist Transcripts, vol. 52, New York Public Library, 81.

42. See Records of the Sec., 1709–1725, SCDAH, 116; Records of the Sec., vol. B (1722–1726), SCDAH, 163–71; Records of the Sec., vol. E (1726–1727), SCDAH, 492–98, 531–34; Records of the Sec., vol. F (1727–1729), SCDAH, 74–75; Court of Chancery, bundle 1721–1735, SCDAH, 7–1; Court of Chancery, oversize, 1736–1760, SCDAH, nos. 3, 5; Miscellaneous Records, vol. HH (1749–1751), SCDAH, 344–46; vol. LL (1758–1762), SCDAH, 157–62; Edgar, ed., *Letterbook of Robert Pringle*, esp. 2:827–28, 831; Hamer et al., eds., *Henry Laurens*, 1:16–22, 72–3, 79; 2:157–59; 3:98; Nash, "Trade and Business in Eighteenth-Century South Carolina: The Career of John Guerard, Merchant and Planter," *South Carolina Historical Magazine* 96 (1995): 15–18.

43. For examples of major independent importers from c. 1750 onwards see Miscellaneous Records, vol. MM (1763–1767), SCDAH, 201–4, 654–55; vol. NN (1765–1769), SCDAH, 1–5, 318; vol. OO (1766–1771), SCDAH, 493–505, 580–81; inventories of Benjamin Dart and Samuel Perroneau, Inventories, vol. R(2) (1753–1756), SCDAH, 300–307, 416–22; inventory of Samuel Winborn, Inventories, vol. V (1761–1763), SCDAH, 215–16; inventory of Samuel Perroneau, Inventories, vol. W (1763–1767), SCDAH, 81–82; inventory of John Jones, Inventories, vol. V (1761–1763), SCDAH, 422–30; Court of Chancery, bundle 1767–1769, SCDAH, no. 5. See also the references in n. 74, which document independent importing by a large number of major Charleston firms on the eve of the Revolution. For examples of minor importers see Miscellaneous Records, vol. FF (1743–1746), SCDAH, 413–14; vol. II (1751–1754), SCDAH, 296–97; vol. LL (1758–1763), SCDAH, 24–26, 79, 164, 169; vol. OO (1761–1771), SCDAH, 239; vol. RR (1774–1779), SCDAH, 16–29.

44. The country factors have usually been pictured as retailers who purchased their goods from Charleston wholesale factors and who only occasionally ventured into the transatlantic import trade from England; see Sellers, *Charleston Business,* 82–86. In fact, the evidence that we possess, fragmentary though it is, shows numerous country factors importing independently on a large scale from leading London merchants and tradesmen. For the imports of these factors, who have been identified from advertisements in the *South Carolina Gazette* and other sources, see Miscellaneous Records, vol. FF (1743–1746), SCDAH, 413–14; vol. HH (1749–1751), SCDAH, 344–46; vol. LL (1758–1762), SCDAH, 157–62; vol. NN (1765–1769), SCDAH, 49, 116, 158; Court of Chancery, bundle 1761–1762, SCDAH, no. 4; bundle 1763–1766, SCDAH, no. 5; Court of Chancery, oversize, 1763–1766, SCDAH, nos. 1–2; Judgment Rolls, 1753, SCDAH, 31A-2, 35A-1-5; Judgment Rolls, oversize, 1713–1767, SCDAH, 111A-1; inventory of William Ioor, Inventories, vol. X (1768–1769), SCDAH, 240–44; inventory of Thomas Gadsden, Inventories, vol. Y (1769–1771), SCDAH, 255–63; inventory of Newman Swallow, Inventories, vol. Z (1771–1774), SCDAH, 326–32; merchant's day-book [James Poyas], 1764–1766, SCHS, esp. 32, 45, 62, 68–69, 326–27, 470, 34–325; Treasury 79, Claims of British Subjects for Pre-1776 American Debts (hereafter cited as T 79), claim of Greenwood and Higginson, T 79, 225–26, 246–48, Public Record Office, London (hereafter cited as PRO), 15/69–70; claim of Davis, Strachan and Co., T 79, PRO, 36/237–38. See also Hamer et al., eds., *Henry Laurens,* 4:89–90.

45. For examples see Miscellaneous Records, vol. MM (1763–1767), SCDAH, 260, 289–90; Judgment Rolls, 1757, SCDAH, 93A-1, 93A-7, 105A-1, 105–A-3, 186A-1; Judgment Rolls, oversize, 1713–1767, SCDAH, 108–A-5, 243–A1–A13; and esp. merchant's daybook [James Poyas], 1761–1764, Charleston Museum Archives, Charleston; and merchant's daybook [James Poyas], 1764–1766, SCHS, 34–325.

46. For further details see below n. 78.

47. See claim of Greenwood and Higginson, T 79/15/117, 201, PRO; Miscellaneous Records, vol. NN (1765–1769), SCDAH, 318; vol. RR (1774–1779), pt. 1, SCDAH, 16–29; Judgment Rolls, oversize, 1713–1767, SCDAH, 111A-1; Court of Chancery, bundle 1761–1762, SCDAH, nos. 4–12.

48. Harrington, *New York Merchant,* 93, 100; Tyler, *Smugglers and Patriots,* 109–10, 180–81; Doerflinger, *Vigorous Spirit of Enterprise,* 138, 169.

49. Nash, "Trade and Business," 16–17; Edgar, ed., *Letterbook of Robert Pringle,* 1:10, 49–50; 2:578, 794; Hamer et al., eds., *Henry Laurens,* 1:148; 3:216, 494; 4:185, 233; 6:129–30, 220.

50. Hamer et al., eds., *Henry Laurens,* 6:129–30.

51. Calhoun, "Charleston's Merchant Community," 207–11. For imports see U.S. Bureau of the Census, *Historical Statistics,* 2:1176.

52. Peter H. Wood, "'More Like a Negro Country': Demographic Patterns in Colonial South Carolina, 1700–1740," in *Race and Slavery in the Western Hemisphere: Quantitative Studies,* ed. Stanley L. Engerman and Eugene D. Genovese (Princeton: Princeton University Press, 1975), 144; U.S. Bureau of the Census, *Historical Statistics,* 2:1173–74.

53. In the years 1758–1760 and 1762–1763, Charleston-based ships imported 2 percent or fewer of the slaves entering Charleston; see Clowse, *Measuring Charleston's Overseas Commerce,* 121–22.

54. W. Robert Higgins, "Charles Town Merchants and Factors Dealing in the External Slave Trade 1735–1775," *South Carolina Historical Magazine* 65 (1964): 205–17.

55. Nash, "Urbanization in the Colonial South," 15–16.

56. Higgins, "Charles Town Merchants." Of the 10 leading importers referred to above, 9 can be identified as export merchants and 1, Thomas Middleton, as a country factor. A number of country factors also had a more modest involvement in slave importing, although the great majority of the lesser mercantile importers of slaves can be identified as export merchants.

57. Hamer et al., eds., *Henry Laurens,* 1:258; Elizabeth Donnan, "The Slave Trade into South Carolina before the Revolution," *American Historical Review* 33 (1928): esp. 814–15.

58. However, from the 1730s some English merchants insisted that these remittances be made within a specified period.

59. Donnan, "The Slave Trade into South Carolina," 813–14; Hamer et al., eds., *Henry Laurens,* 4:400–402; 6:68; and esp. Price, "Credit in the Slave Trade," 310–14.

60. Hamer et al., eds., *Henry Laurens,* 5:293 n, 322–27, 696–97; claim of John Hopton, Loyalist Transcripts, vol. 54, New York Public Library, 509, 523–49.

61. These figures, however, slightly overstate the true decline in London's rice trade as after 1720 part of the London-owned fleet departing from South Carolina carried rice to ports on the south coast of England, trade which is categorized in the English customs records upon which table 4.2 is based, as *outport,* rather than London, imports. A more accurate picture of London's declining participation in the rice trade is given in the Charleston customs data, which provide information on shipping departing from Charleston for Britain, and which show that, of rice exports from Charleston carried in British-based ships, London vessels accounted for 67 percent of the total in 1717–1720, 48 percent in 1734–1738, and 38 percent in 1762–1763 and 1766. See Clowse, *Measuring Charleston's Overseas Commerce,* 57, 124–25. The original shipping records for Charleston after 1766 have been lost, although it is certain that London's share decreased in the following decade, in line with the trend, if not with the absolute figures, given in the English customs data.

62. The Navigation Acts decreed that "enumerated" commodities, such as rice, indigo, tobacco, sugar, etc., could only be shipped legally to another British colony or to Britain. From 1731 direct rice exports were permitted from the American colonies to ports south of Cape Finisterre, which is located in northwest Spain.

63. Nash, "South Carolina," 687–88.

64. John Guerard to Daniel Lesseur, 15 Nov. 1752, Guerard letterbook, SCHS. For data on the low costs of shipping rice through Cowes see George MacKenzie, Cowes, to Graffin Prankard, 17 Oct. 1737, trading accounts of Parham Pink, 1729–1746; Graffin Prankard's account with George Mackenzie (a leading agent at Cowes), 15 Sept. 1742, account books of Graffin Prankard, DD/DN 431–32, Dickinson Papers.

65. See, for example, James Inglis to Alex Ramage, Cowes, 29 Sept. 1772; James Inglis to James MacKenzie [at Cowes], 9 Oct. 1772; James Inglis, letterbook, C.S. 96, 2250, Scottish RO; Edgar, ed., *Letterbook of Robert Pringle,* esp. 1:162–63, 356; Morgan, "Colonial American Rice Trade," 450–51.

66. For the distribution of tobacco imports by port see Exchequer Port Books, E 190/834/9, PRO; Treasury Miscellaneous, T 64/276b/372, PRO; Price, *France and the Chesapeake: A History of the French Tobacco Monopoly, 1674–1791,* 2 vols. (Ann Arbor: University of Michigan Press, 1973), 1:589–90.

67. Clowse, *Measuring Charleston's Overseas Commerce,* 132, 134. For the use of south coast ports by a major Bristol merchant in the rice reexport trade, see Graffin Prankard letterbooks, 1728–1732, 1732–1734, 1734–1736, 1736–1738, DD/DN 424–27, Dickinson Papers. For a comment in 1756 on the inconvenient location of Bristol for the "reshipping of Rice," see Hamer et al., eds., *Henry Laurens,* 2:98.

68. See table 4.3; Hamer et al., eds., *Henry Laurens,* 1:51; Morgan, "Colonial American Rice Trade," 450–51.

69. So, in 1758–1760 Liverpool supplied 37 percent of enslaved Africans imported into Charleston, Bristol supplied 31 percent, and London supplied 10 percent, whereas in 1762–1763 the shares of the three ports in the trade were respectively 62 percent, 7 percent, and 5 percent. See Clowse, *Measuring Charleston's Overseas Commerce,* 31, 121–22; in these years average slave imports were 2,100.

70. Nash, "Trade and Credit," 26–27.

71. Hamer et al., eds., *Henry Laurens,* 2:295 (my italics). See table 4.2, (A) and (B), for the growing excess of the value of imports into the English outports over the value of exports from the outports; this had to be covered by bills of exchange drawn in Charleston on outport merchants.

72. For a discussion of the claims made by British merchants and for biographical details of the major claimants in the South Carolina trade, see Kellock, "London Merchants and the Pre-1776 American Debts."

73. For London firms see claim of John Nutt, T 79/5/3, 62, 64, 70, 75, PRO; T 79/42/part I, PRO; claim of John Wilson, T 79/11/407–09, PRO; claim of Greenwood and Higginson, T 79/15/69–70, 74, 89, 93, 105–18, 136, 160–63, 201, 205–12, 221–26, 246–48, PRO; claim of Harford and Powell, T 79/20/345, 351, PRO; claim of Davis, Strachan & Co., T 79/36/237–38, PRO; claim of John Nicholson, T 79/37/289, 295–96, 302–06, PRO; claim of William and James Carson, Loyalist Transcripts, vol. 53, New York Public Library, 85–89; claim of John Hopton, Loyalist Transcripts, vol. 54, New York Public Library, 509, 523–49; claim of Charles Atkins, Loyalist Transcripts, vol. 55, New York Public Library, 463, 474. A number of these claimants are referred to below. For the outports see claim of Wraxhall and Hall, Bristol, T 79/35/41, PRO; claim of Goodwin and Thomas, Chester, T 79/12/237–42, 292–94, 302, PRO; the latter accounts for all of Chester's claims.

74. See Miscellaneous Records, vol. FF (1743–1746), SCDAH, 413–14; vol. GG (1746–1749), SCDAH, 403–4; vol. HH (1749–1751), SCDAH, 344–46; vol. II (1751–1754), SCDAH, 296–97; vol. LL (1758–1763), SCDAH, 164; vol. MM (1763–1767), SCDAH, 201–4, 654–55; vol. NN (1765–1769), SCDAH, 116, 318; vol. OO (1767–1771), SCDAH, 493–505; vol. RR (1774–1779), SCDAH, 16–29, 604–06; Judgment Rolls, 1753, SCDAH, 31A-2, 35A-5; 1767, SCDAH, 276A-1, 394A-1; Judgment Rolls, oversize, 1713–1767, SCDAH, 111A-1; Court of Chancery, bundle 1721–1735, SCDAH, 7–1; Court of Chancery, oversize, 1763–1766, SCDAH, nos. 1–5; inventory of John Dart, Inventories, vol. R (2) (1753–1756), SCHS, 304; inventory of

Samuel Winborn, Inventories, vol. V (1761–1763), SCHS, 215–16 (on Winborn and his debts to London merchants see also Hamer et al., eds., *Henry Laurens*, 3:97–98, 165–66); inventory of Thomas Gadsden, Inventories, vol. Y (1769–1771), SCHS, 262–63; merchant's daybook [James Poyas], 1764–1766, SCHS, esp. 326–27, 470–71, 34–325.

75. Records of the Sec., 1675–1695, SCDAH, 51–52, 266; Records of the Sec., 1692–1700, SCDAH, 93–103; Records of the Sec., 1694–1705, SCDAH, 33–34, 146, 199–200, 253; Records of the Sec., 1714–1717, SCDAH, 65; Miscellaneous Records, vol. BB (1732–1733), SCDAH, 33–38; Stumpf, "Merchants of Colonial Charleston," 71–72; A. H. Hirsch, *The Huguenots of Colonial South Carolina* (Durham: Duke University Press, 1928), 145–46; M. Eugene Sirmans, *Colonial South Carolina: A Political History, 1663–1763* (Chapel Hill: University of North Carolina Press, 1966), 104.

76. Stumpf, "Merchants of Colonial Charleston," 42, 48–49; and esp. *Samuel Wragg v Joseph Wragg*, Court of Chancery, oversize, 1736–1760, SCDAH, no. 3."

77. Hamer et al., eds., *Henry Laurens*, 1:2 n; Rogers, *Evolution of a Federalist: William Loughton Smith of Charleston (1758–1812)* (Columbia: University of South Carolina Press, 1962), 9–10; Rogers, *Age of the Pinckneys*, 13–14.

78. Rogers, Age of the Pinckneys, 13–14; Hamer et al., eds., *Henry Laurens*, 1:96 n. Greenwood and Higginson claimed 34 percent of the 1775 debt owed by South Carolina to London merchants; see Chatham Papers, PRO 30/8/343/ PRO, 167–69 and the reference in n. 74 above.

79. See Chatham Papers, PRO 30/8/343/167–69, PRO. Other major London firms in the South Carolina trade after 1750 established by former merchants in Charleston include Neufville and Rolleston, Harford and Powell, Shubricks and Nickleson, and James Poyas.

80. John Nutt received a dowry of £6,000 from Crokatt's daughter; see Kellock, "London Merchants," 138; Rogers, *Age of the Pinckneys*, 14.

81. Jacob M. Price, *Capital and Credit in British Overseas Trade: The View From the Chesapeake, 1770–1776* (Cambridge, Mass.: Harvard University Press, 1980) 107–9, 111–12, 140–43.

82. Harrington, *New York Merchant*, 354–55; K. G. Davies, "The Origins of the Commission System in the West India Trade," *Transactions of the Royal Historical Society*, 5th ser., 2 (1952): 93–107; Pares, *Merchants and Planters*, 32–37, 47–50; Price, *Capital and Credit*, esp. 96–116; Price, "Buchanan and Simson," 35; R. B. Sheridan, *Sugar and Slavery: An Economic History of the British West Indies, 1623–1775* (Baltimore: Johns Hopkins University Press, 1973), 282–305; Doerflinger, *Vigorous Spirit of Enterprise*, 56, 86–88.

83. The outports, however, continued in part to depend on London particularly in the slave trade, where credit advances to planters in America were underpinned by London capital. See Ralph Davis, *The Rise of the English Shipping Industry in the Seventeenth and Eighteenth Centuries* (Newton Abbot: David and Charles, 1962), 26–43; Price, "The Rise of Glasgow in the Chesapeake Tobacco Trade, 1707–1775," *William and Mary Quarterly*, 3d ser, 11 (1954): 190–96; Price, "The Economic Growth of the Chesapeake and the European Market, 1697–1775," *Journal of Economic History* 24 (1964): 496–511; Sheridan, "The Commercial and Financial Organization of the British Slave Trade, 1750–1807," *Economic History Review* 11 (1958): 249–63; Nash, "Irish Atlantic Trade in the Seventeenth and Eighteenth Centuries," *William and Mary Quarterly*, 3d ser., 42 (1985): 344–49; Morgan, *Bristol and the Atlantic Trade in the Eighteenth Century* (Cambridge: Cambridge University Press, 1993).

84. First, because indigo was a nonbulk trade in which London's lack of competitiveness in comparison with the outports in the provision of low-cost shipping and port facilities did not apply; second, because London was the center of the commission trade, through which a proportion of Carolina indigo was marketed; finally, because London became a major European center for the distribution of dyestuffs during the eighteenth century.

85. Much of the late-colonial growth of the Chesapeake merchant class was associated with the rise of grain exports.

86. Menard, "Financing the Lowcountry Export Boom: Capital and Growth in Early South Carolina," *William and Mary Quarterly,* 3d ser., 51 (1994): 659–76. See also Elizabeth Pruden's essay in this volume.

87. The majority of Charleston merchants held one or more shares in ships, although these vessels were predominantly used in intercolonial rather than transatlantic trade; see Clowse, *Measuring Charleston's Overseas Commerce,* 137–39; Nash, "Urbanization in the Colonial South," 12.

88. Menard, "Financing the Lowcountry Export Boom," esp. 671–74.

89. See the inventories of Pepin and Osborn and that of John Vansusteren, Records of the Sec., 1675–1695, SCDAH, 133–35, 342–44; Records of the Sec., 1692–1700, SCDAH, 162–65. The largest inventories were held by Charleston agents who acted as the partners or salaried factors of English merchants. See, for example, inventory of Wilson Dunston, Records of the Sec., 1692–1700, SCDAH, 93–103. I would like to thank Dr. Charles Lesser for drawing this inventory to my attention and for his valuable advice on South Carolina sources.

90. Stumpf, "Merchants of Colonial Charleston," 75, lists 37 merchants, of whom 22 can be identified as landowners from, principally, Walter B. Edgar and N. Louise Bailey, eds., *Biographical Directory of the South Carolina House of Representatives,* vol. 2, *The Commons House of Assembly, 1692–1775* (Columbia: University of South Carolina Press, 1977); Records of the Sec., passim, SCDAH; Colonial Office, Original Correspondence, Register of Grants of Land, South Carolina, 1675–1665, CO 5/398, PRO.

91. Edgar and Bailey, eds., *Biographical Directory;* in a small number of cases I have altered the occupational designation of the representatives listed, where additional sources suggested that this was appropriate.

92. Lawrence S. Rowland, "Eighteenth-Century Beaufort: A Study of South Carolina's Southern Parishes to 1800"(Ph.D. diss., University of South Carolina, 1978), esp. 89–95, 173; Nash, "Trade and Business," 10–13.

93. Menard's important study, "Financing the Lowcountry Export Boom."

94. Inventories of John Guerard and of John McQueen, Inventories, vol. W (1763–1767), SCDAH, 109–17, 163–67; inventory of George Austin, Inventories, vol. AA (1774–1785), SCDAH, 42–51; Edgar and Bailey, eds., *Biographical Directory,* 2:282–83, 297–98, 428–31; Hamer et al., eds., *Henry Laurens,* passim.

95. Verner W. Crane, *The Southern Frontier, 1670–1732* (Durham, N.C.: Duke University Press, 1928), 108–36.

96. Menard, "Financing the Lowcountry Export Boom." For the structure of mercantile debt, see the following merchant inventories: inventory of John Jones, Inventories, vol. V (1761–1763), SCDAH, 430–34; inventory of John McQueen, Inventories, vol. W (1768–1769), SCDAH, 164–67; inventory of Francis Stuart, Inventories, vol. X (1768–1769), SCDAH, 107–14; inventories of George Seamen, Thomas Gadsden, David D'Oyley, Benjamin Smith, Inventories, vol. Y (1769–1771), SCDAH, 82–84, 256–63, 296–97, 373–76; inventory of Thomas Lind, Inventories, vol. & (1772–1776),

SCDAH, 97–99; inventory of Newman Swallow, Inventories, vol. Z (1771–1774), SCDAH, 326–32.

97. Steffen, "Baltimore County," the quotation is from p. 33; Steffen, "Gentry and Bourgeois: Patterns of Merchant Investment in Baltimore County, Maryland, 1658–1776," *Journal of Social History* 20 (1987): 531–48.

98. Doerflinger, *Vigorous Spirit of Enterprise*, 129–33, 283–334, 344–64, 375–78.

99. Unfortunately, the evidence does not allow us to assess precisely the profitability of trade or planting, let alone compare them. However, for the view that rice production was highly profitable, providing returns of between 12.5 and 33.5 percent in the colonial period, see Coclanis, *Shadow of a Dream*, 141.

100. Steffen, "Gentry and Bourgeois." This aspect of merchant behavior is not considered in this paper.

V

Colonial South Carolina's Rice Industry and the Atlantic Economy

Patterns of Trade, Shipping, and Growth, 1715–1775

STEPHEN G. HARDY

In 1980 the work of Alice Hanson Jones confirmed what every visitor to the American colonies had suspected: on the eve of the American Revolution, free white people in the colonies from Maryland to Georgia enjoyed far greater wealth, on average, than did their counterparts from Pennsylvania northward.[1] Slave-based plantation agriculture gave these southern colonies higher income and wealth per free white person than any other region of British North America, probably the result of a higher rate of overall economic growth. Differences even existed among the southern colonies. Recent work on the Lower Southern colonies, particularly South Carolina, suggested that they enjoyed a higher level of per capita wealth than the Chesapeake.[2] The estimated wealth per free person for South Carolina was six times that for all the southern colonies. Given that the Carolinas and Georgia were founded later than the colonies in the Chesapeake and yet achieved greater wealth, the economy of the Lower Southern colonies must have grown quite rapidly.

In general, economic historians have not systematically investigated the causes and rates of economic growth in the Lower Southern colonies responsible for the high level of wealth. While the question of overall regional economic growth falls beyond the scope of this essay, it will address the question of economic growth in relation to the production of rice, the leading staple of South Carolina. First, it will establish the levels and values of rice exports. Second, it will test the model of colonial economic growth advanced by James F. Shepherd and Gary M. Walton through the use of import and export data. And finally, it will offer alternative explanations in those areas where Shepherd and Walton's thesis does not adequately explain the data.

Shepherd and Walton in *Shipping, Maritime Trade, and the Economic Growth of Colonial North America* examined various possible causes of colonial economic growth and explicitly derived a model to explain it.[3] They theorized that colonial economic growth came from one of two sources—either lower production costs due to increased productivity or lower transaction costs due primarily to reduced shipping costs.[4]

Because agriculture in the British North American colonies generally did not experience rising productivity and because the economies of the colonies were largely based on staples produced for overseas markets, Shepherd and Walton focused on the cost of transport. Their model posited that increased efficiency and gains in productivity in distribution and shipping were primarily responsible for general colonial economic growth. Components of this increased efficiency included larger ships, smaller crews, shorter port times, and greater utilization of shuttle routes. As these factors changed relatively gradually, they concluded economic growth over the course of the eighteenth century was relatively slow and steady. Shepherd and Walton's primary purpose was to propose a model, not to thoroughly test it; most of their data and conclusions were limited to the period from 1768 to 1772 and did not apply specifically to South Carolina.

The work of those historians who have focused on South Carolina and its rice industry has tended to be primarily descriptive and qualitative.[5] They have been concerned with establishing the broad outlines of production, quantities, changes in production techniques, the activities of individual merchants, or the effects of particular events on trade.[6] More recently, however, three historians—Russell Menard, R. C. Nash, and Peter Coclanis—have used quantitative data to address the levels and causes of economic growth in colonial South Carolina.[7] Menard posited a three-stage model of economic growth, with rapid growth prior to 1740, stagnation during the 1740s, and slow expansion after 1750; he credited the end of King George's War and diversification into indigo production with stimulating economic growth after 1750.[8] Nash insisted that European demand played an important role in the growth of the South Carolina rice industry.[9] Coclanis, meanwhile, found evidence of a significant increase in mean wealth, and ascribed the growth of South Carolina's economy to a variety of causes: specialization in the integrated Atlantic economy, greater demands on slaves for labor, relative increase of factor inputs (land, labor, and capital), productivity gains from technological changes, institutional responsiveness (both public and private), the growth of domestic credit sources, and improving terms of trade.[10]

Of all the economic historians who have speculated on the nature and causes of growth in the colonial economy, only Shepherd and Walton have developed a testable, theoretical model. The efficiency factors in their model can be specifically calculated from extant trade records to see if there were indeed increasing productivity and efficiency in the shipping and distribution functions associated with South Carolina's rice trade. Menard and Coclanis are the only two historians to date who have attempted to quantitatively examine Shepherd and Walton's thesis for colonial South Carolina. However, Menard's work covered a far more extensive temporal and geographical span than simply colonial South Carolina. Likewise, Coclanis's discussion of the Shepherd and Walton thesis was only a small part of a much larger work covering 250 years of lowcountry economic history.

The preliminary data on rice trade freight rates, compiled by Menard, suggested that there was a decline in freight rates over the course of the eighteenth century, generally supporting Shepherd and Walton's thesis.[11] However, these data must be viewed with caution. First, many of the data were from war periods, which distorted rates from their secular peacetime trends. Second, rice freight rates were highly variable, even within the same year.[12] Therefore, if there were only a few quotes for a given year, the average was more likely to be skewed. And, finally, we do not know how, or if, the cargo ton of rice varied over the course of the eighteenth century. The cargo ton was often a customary number of containers, and if the container sizes changed over time—as rice barrels did—the actual weight in the cargo ton must have changed as well.[13] The freight rates would then need to be adjusted for this change.

Instead of using freight rates, Coclanis examined the various components of shipping costs, specified by Shepherd and Walton, to determine if efficiency increased. For average port times, Coclanis took only two limited periods—the first quarter of 1722 and the first quarter of 1763—and averaged port times for *all* vessels departing Charleston. He found that port times "apparently declined significantly."[14] Implicitly, he assumed that there was constant linear change in this measure and that the average port time for all vessels was the same as that for vessels trading overseas. However, by 1763, there were many more coasting vessels trading into Charlestown than in 1722, suggesting that following Shepherd and Walton's constraints and having additional quarters of data between 1722 and 1763 might lead to different conclusions.[15] Additionally, the trade to different overseas areas, such as Great Britain or the West Indies, might have had characteristics that did not change in tandem with the other overseas regions. Likewise, Coclanis's conclusions based on mean tonnage suffered because they included all vessels in Charlestown, not just those trading overseas.[16] Thus, his conclusions about the validity of Shepherd and Walton's thesis merit reexamination.

Existing trade records, known as the Naval Officer Shipping Lists (NOSLs), permit a more refined testing of the Shepherd and Walton thesis. Careful selection of time periods was necessary to ensure their suitability for a discussion of long-term economic trends. Wars, business cycles, and data availability all affected the selection process.

During times of war, trade routes were vulnerable to enemy attack, leading to higher freight rates and insurance costs. The increased shipping costs especially hurt commodities with relatively high bulk-to-value ratios, such as tobacco and rice. The loss of ships to enemy capture decreased the supply of shipping and drove freight rates even higher. Ships spent longer and therefore costlier periods in port while waiting for convoys or for intelligence of a safer sailing period. For these reasons, the periods selected excluded war years.

While less obvious, the effects of business cycles on trade and commerce were just as real as they are today.[17] Loosely, the business cycle can be defined as the periodic change from good economic times to bad economic times and back to good economic times. To ameliorate distortions caused by these stages of the business cycle, only periods in the same part of the business cycle were examined.

Data availability also limited period selection. The NOSLs, which provided the bulk of the data for this study, were lists of all ships entering and clearing from a particular colonial port.[18] Naval officers compiled these lists quarterly from 1697 until the end of the colonial period. Colonial governors transmitted these lists to the Board of Customs, Lords of Treasury, or the Board of Trade.[19] Unfortunately, no colony has a complete set of these records, but enough from South Carolina have survived to allow analysis of selected periods.

Given these criteria and constraints, five periods provide the data for this essay: 1717–1719, 1723–1725, 1732–1734, 1736–1738, and 1765–1767.[20] All of these periods were nonwar years, and all were on the upside of a business cycle, with the last year being the crest of the cycle (except for 1723–1725, when 1726 was the crest of the cycle). The use of three-year periods helped to further eliminate any unpredictable year-to-year variations within the periods. Ideally, the years from 1751 to 1753 should also have been included to serve as an interwar period and to break up the nearly thirty years between 1736–1738 and 1765–1767. However, data survived for only two of the twelve quarters, proving insufficient for analysis.[21]

To consistently apply the limitations imposed by Shepherd and Walton's model in relation to the rice trade, only those ships that were both trading to overseas areas and involved in the rice trade were analyzed. These overseas areas were primarily Great Britain (England and Scotland), the West Indies (all the British West Indies, the Mosquito Shore, Honduras, but not the Bahamas), and Southern Europe (areas of Europe south of Cape Finisterre, the Madeiras, the Azores, the Canary Islands, and the Cape Verde Islands). Not all ships that exported rice should be described as having been in the rice trade. For example, a ship exporting a few barrels of rice along with several hundred barrels of naval stores was clearly not involved in the rice trade; the rice exported was incidental to its primary trade in naval stores. Thus, the market forces that affected that ship's tonnage, port time, and shuttle pattern were those of the naval stores industry, not of the rice

FIGURE 5.1
VALUE OF SOUTH CAROLINA RICE EXPORTS
(Constant £ sterling, 1860=100)

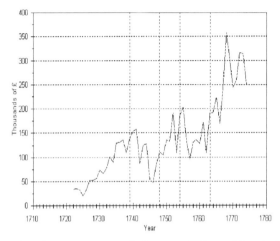

SOURCE: Table 5.1, Quantity and Constant Value of South Carolina
Rice Exports

industry, and the inclusion of that ship could distort the rice trade data. To
eliminate these sources of error from the calculations, only ships that carried
the top 95 percent of the total rice exported for each period to each overseas region were used.[22]

The overall growth of South Carolina's rice industry is presented in figure 5.1, which is a graph of the value of rice exports in constant pounds
sterling.

The figure indicates that the growth patterns of South Carolina's rice
industry can be divided into three distinct periods from 1722 to 1774.[23]
During the first period, from 1722 to 1738, the rice industry grew at a
steady, rapid rate, as the value of rice exports increased at an average rate of
£7,046 per year, a striking compound rate of growth of 13.9 percent per
year. In the second period, from 1739 to 1763, the value of rice exports
stagnated, most likely due to two periods of war sandwiching an uneasy
peace. In this turbulent period, the average growth fell to £1,719 per year,
or an annual compound rate of only about 1.3 percent. Finally, from 1764
to 1774, the value of rice exports expanded at a variable, but generally rapid
rate. In this third period, the average rate of growth in the value of rice
exported was £9,099 per year, a compound rate of growth of more than 3.6
percent per year.[24]

According to Shepherd and Walton's theory, there should be evidence that shipping productivity improved, especially in the periods of rapid growth in the colonial South Carolina rice industry. To determine how, and if, their theory is applicable in this case, each possible source of increased shipping productivity must be examined. Ideally, the data would have been mathematically analyzed using multiple regression analysis. Unfortunately, the spread of the periods of data precludes such a procedure, but a less rigorous, more general analysis is possible.

Shepherd and Walton postulated that average port times should have fallen and that average tonnage should have risen over the course of the eighteenth century. The fall in average port times held true for ships trading to Great Britain and the West Indies from 1717–1719 to 1736–1738; the declines were 16.7 percent and 36.3 percent, respectively.[25] By contrast, ships traveling to Southern Europe saw their average port times increase by 36.2 percent from 1732–1734 to 1736–1738. However, from 1736–1738 to 1765–1767 port times *increased* for ships trading to all of the overseas areas; average port times for ships trading to Great Britain increased an insignificant 3.1 percent, to the West Indies 24.4 percent, and to Southern Europe a remarkable 60.0 percent.[26]

Average tonnage, however, followed a pattern different than that for port times.[27] For ships clearing to Great Britain and the West Indies, average tonnages dipped slightly from 1717–1719 to 1723–1725, then increased from 1723–1725 to 1765–1767. Ship sizes increased relatively rapidly between 1732–1734 and 1736–1738, with the average tonnage of ships clearing to Great Britain growing at 2.03 tons per year and to Southern Europe at 1.75 tons per year. Both of these growth rates slowed considerably between 1736–1738 and 1765–1767; for ships clearing to Great Britain, the growth rate slowed to 1.21 tons per year while for Southern Europe, the growth rate fell to 1.02 tons per year.

The data for average port times and tonnages lead to conflicting conclusions regarding efficiency—increasing port times suggesting less efficiency and increasing tonnages indicating greater efficiency. Shepherd and Walton selected these measures because both were major parts of the operating costs for ships.[28] Idle port days meant higher capital and labor costs. The capital invested in a ship cost its owner the same per day whether that tonnage was sitting empty in port or earning revenue on a voyage. Sailors generally were paid and fed for the whole time they were away from their home ports, whether they were idle in port or sailing at sea.[29] One way to resolve this apparent conflict over efficiency is to compare actual cost factors: ton-port days and man-port days.[30] These data showed some improvements from 1717–1719 to 1736–1738, but both factors experienced large increases between 1736–1738 and 1765–1767 for ships trading to all overseas regions. Thus, reduced operating costs did not lead to improved efficiency; on the contrary, rising operating costs actually reduced shipping efficiency for this latter period. From 1736–1738 to 1765–1767, other efficiency factors in ship operations would have had to improve greatly to offset the growing inefficiency from ton-port days and man-port days if shipping costs were to have a net neutral effect on rice industry growth.[31]

Shepherd and Walton also posited that another area of change was the evolutionary "disarming" of trading ships. The need for self-defense, they believed, decreased due to the decline of piracy and privateering, which had especially plagued the Caribbean. A decrease in armament meant fewer men were needed on a particular voyage, since manning guns was no longer a concern. Thus, according to Shepherd and Walton, labor costs should have fallen, as tons per man rose, and the benefits of disarmament should have been particularly evident in the West Indies trade.[32]

Contrary to Shepherd and Walton's expectations, the West Indies trade experienced virtually no advantages from disarmament. The reason was simply that most ships clearing to the West Indies had sailed unarmed throughout the period under study. In 1723–1725, 21 of 26 ships were unarmed; in 1732–1734, that number was 24 of 53; and in 1736–1738, 19 of 26 ships carried no armaments.[33]

By comparison, ships clearing to Great Britain and Southern Europe were much more likely to be armed, especially in the years before 1740, and disarmament had uneven effects on efficiency. In 1732–1734, for example, there was virtually no difference in the tons-to-man ratio between armed and unarmed vessels in the most common categories of ships.[34] In any case, more than half the ships trading to Great Britain in these years were armed, as were more than two-thirds of the ships trading to Southern Europe.[35] Nor was there any decline in the number of guns armed ships carried; that number remained fairly constant.[36]

The movement to disarm virtually the entire commercial fleet led to more substantial gains in efficiency from 1736–1738 to 1765–1767. Smaller unarmed ships trading to Great Britain generally enjoyed a tons-to-man ratio around 14 percent higher than armed ships; for larger unarmed ships, the gain was more striking, with a tons-to-man ratio about a third higher.[37] For the trade to Southern Europe, gains from disarming were much less significant. In this period for the most common category of ships, the tons-to-man ratio increased less than 10 percent due to disarming.[38] The benefits of disarming for the West Indies trade was minimal.[39] While efficiency gains due to disarming ships trading to Great Britain and Southern Europe undoubtedly helped offset the large increases in ton-port days and man-port days, they were not large enough to result in any overall gains.

Shepherd and Walton additionally argued that manning requirements for ships dropped significantly, as demonstrated by higher tons-to-man ratios.[40] However, over the four decades from 1723–1725 to 1765–1767, tons-to-man ratios for unarmed ships trading to Britain increased slowly, if at all. And the same held true among armed ships. For Southern Europe, the averages for both categories of ships actually decreased over time while for the West Indies, the experience was mixed.[41] Thus, the only efficiency gains from changes in tons-to-man ratios came from a change from armed to unarmed.

The final area that Shepherd and Walton theorized would show noticeable efficiency gains was in the degree that ships followed a shuttle, or two-leg, voyage as opposed to a multi-leg voyage.[42] As trade became more organized and regularized, these routes should have become more common. Shuttle routes decreased costs because crews could be discharged in their home ports, they were not idle during calls at multiple ports, and they were not involved in long multi-leg voyages. For ships trading to Great Britain, the degree of shuttle voyages varied. The percentage of tons in the shuttle trade declined dramatically from 1723–1725 to 1736–1738, then rose to almost 60 percent in 1765–1767.[43] This decrease in shuttle routes was probably due to the rapid and chaotic nature of the reorganization of the rice trade in the decade after 1730, when a change in the Navigation Acts permitted the direct exportation of rice to Southern Europe. If, for the sake of argument, 1732–1734 and 1736–1738 were eliminated as aberrations, then during the period from 1717–1719 to 1765–1767, the percentage of tonnage employed in shuttle routes actually decreased slightly. For the West Indies, the story was much the same, with the percentage of shuttle voyages usually between 60 and 80 percent.[44] Over the entire period, then, the utilization of shuttle routes showed little overall increase.

Shuttle routes for ships trading to Southern Europe were problematic, as the Navigation Acts dictated that any European goods bound for the colonies had to be shipped first to Britain. The tonnage of ships making this three-legged voyage from South Carolina to Southern Europe to Great Britain and back to South Carolina apparently decreased from 1736–1738 to 1765–1767. While a direct South Carolina–Southern Europe route was possible, it required that the ship return to South Carolina without European goods, reducing returns for the shipowner. Thus, this direct shuttle route was never more than a minor factor in the rice trade.[45]

During the first major period of growth in South Carolina's rice industry, from 1722 to 1738, changes in the organization of trade and shipping appear to have played a significant part in that growth, supporting Shepherd and Walton's thesis. The 1730 exception to the Navigation Acts that allowed the direct export of rice south of Cape Finisterre undoubtedly led to shorter voyage times, since ships exporting rice no longer had to proceed to Great Britain first. During this period of reorganization in the rice trade, port times usually decreased and tonnages increased. Rice exports to other parts of North America, from which they were probably reexported, radically declined. Lowered transaction costs reduced prices to overseas consumers and increased profits for Carolina planters. There can be little doubt that the reduction of transaction costs in this period significantly contributed to growth in the rice industry before 1738.[46]

From 1764 to 1774, the other major period of growth in colonial South Carolina's rice industry, changes in transaction costs seem to have had little relationship to the growth experienced. Indeed, the shipping sector apparently became more inefficient—ton-port days and man-port days rose dramatically, and shuttle route utilization decreased. The only efficiency gain appeared to be in the almost complete conversion to unarmed vessels for commercial transportation. Thus, Shepherd and Walton's model does not explain the observed growth.

Significant gains in productivity in the rice industry itself partially accounted for the growth during the decade before the American Revolution. According to Nash, slave productivity, which had been flat from 1720 to 1750, grew by about 13 percent in the 1750s and 28 percent in the 1760s.[47] This productivity probably rested on the contributions slaves made themselves. Menard stated that rice "was widely grown in West Africa under a variety of conditions and by different techniques, while the lowcountry tasking system placed major responsibilities for the organization of work in the hands of the slaves and offered them incentives to work efficiently."[48] As David Coon argued, part of the improved productivity after 1763 likely resulted from the beginning of the shift in rice production from swamp to tidal culture.[49] According to Coclanis, this change, along with other technical improvements, increased output per hand about 50 percent in the late eighteenth century. This productivity increase seems to be supported by slave population figures for the lowcountry. For 1740 Coclanis estimated the black population of this region to have been 39,000, growing to 69,000 by 1770. More slaves presumably led to a more intensive agriculture, thus producing more rice.[50] The explanation for the economic growth from 1764 to 1774 seems to come largely from within South Carolina.

Increasing market demand in Europe and the West Indies also contributed to the rice industry's growth in this latter period, stimulating both production and efforts to improve productivity. Southern Europe greatly increased its imports from South Carolina.[51] Part of this increase came from a general rise in European demand for grain, but part also may have been due to the price advantage rice enjoyed over other small grains. For example, in Amsterdam from 1750 to 1770, rice became much cheaper relative to wheat and rye.[52] In the West Indies rice was used to feed slaves. In the decade before 1770, the West Indian slave population rose from 364,900 to 433,900, and it continued to grow until 1790, reaching 519,000.[53] This burgeoning slave population had to be fed; South Carolina rice readily filled the bill, especially as the real price of rice was less in 1765–1767 than it had been in 1736–1738.[54]

Along with the greatly increased amount of rice traded to the West Indies, shipping efficiency improved somewhat, but not enough to account for the observed growth. The average tonnage of ships trading to the West Indies rose only slightly between 1736–1738 and 1765–1767.[55] Ships trading to the West Indies probably did not increase much in tonnage because their average size was already the most efficient for the island trade. Larger ships with larger cargoes could have easily flooded a market on a small Caribbean island, causing prices to plummet. Also, smaller ships undoubtedly enjoyed better maneuverability in the dangerous waters around the islands. The West Indies trade was consistently one of the least armed over time. In 1736–1738, for example, of the twenty-one ships in the under 50 tons category, only four were armed.[56] Finally, the West Indies trade consistently employed the greatest degree of shuttle voyages.[57]

The great wealth possessed by white South Carolinians at the time of the Revolution came largely from the profitable rice trade. Shepherd and Walton's theory explains the initial rapid growth before 1738. However, their theory does not adequately explain the growth from 1764 to 1774, which did not result from changes in transportation and trade. Instead, internal factors in colonial South Carolina's economy and market changes, which increasingly demanded this cheap foodstuff for West Indian slaves and poor Europeans, apparently stimulated the latter period of growth. Understanding these internal changes will give us a better explanation of the growth of the rice industry in the late colonial period, and its ability to effectively supply the assorted markets that comprised the eighteenth-century Atlantic economy.

Appendix 1: Rice Barrel Sizes

The income calculations in this paper are based on the number of barrels of rice exported from South Carolina, multiplied by the size of those rice barrels in pounds, and then by the price per pound. However, the size of the average South Carolina rice barrel changed over the course of the eighteenth century. How this size changed is important.

Lewis C. Gray, in his classic study of Southern agriculture, cited numer-

FIGURE 5.2
AVERAGE RICE BARREL SIZE

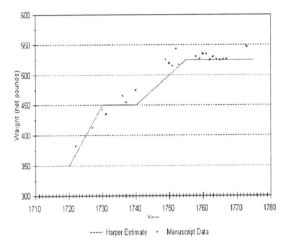

SOURCE: Table 5.13

ous pieces of eighteenth-century literary evidence on the weight of the rice barrel. However, he finally reported his findings in barrels instead of pounds because of the "discrepancies" in the sources.[58] Lawrence Harper, who compiled many of the colonial export statistics used in *Historical Statistics,* discussed the sources and the problems with trying to determine rice barrel weights in the eighteenth century.[59] Ultimately, Harper ventured a formula based on the limited data available to him. This formula, converting barrels into pounds, has been generally used since then. Converse Clowse's compilations of data from the Naval Officer Shipping Lists relied on it; as Clowse stated, "It should be pointed out that this formula is arbitrary."[60] David Coon reported his figures in barrels, again relying on Harper's estimates.[61]

At the conference, Russell Menard questioned the accuracy of Harper's formula, which he suggested might understate the actual size of the barrel, and thus the actual size of income from rice. Table 5.13 represents a preliminary effort to address this question by comparing Harper's formula estimates with data from surviving manuscript sources. Figure 5.2 presents both Harper's formula and the data in graph form.

For the data collected from manuscript sources, both the number of barrels and the number of observations are included. The number of barrels indicates sample size. Because barrel sizes could vary wildly, a smaller sample is more unreliable than a larger sample.[62] The number of observations is also included as an indicator of validity; a large number of barrels from the same source, such as a plantation record, is probably less representative than small numbers of barrels from a variety of sources.[63]

Before 1748, the data assembled here suggest that there was a steady, linear increase in average barrel size, and no level period from 1730 to 1740, as Harper suggested. However, these data before 1748 are so fragmentary that they do not permit any definite statements about growth. After 1748, it appears that there was either no growth or very slow growth in average barrel size. These data indicate that Harper's formulation may indeed underestimate the actual barrel size, but only by a very small margin. Therefore, the estimated value of rice exports in table 5.1 used the Harper formulation.

If the tentative trends in the barrel size data are borne out, the use of the Harper formula will have three effects on the estimated export values. First, it would tend to understate income growth from 1720 to 1725 and overstate income growth from 1725 to 1730. Second, the trends from 1735 to 1755 might be understated, as Harper's barrel sizes are consistently smaller than the manuscript data suggest. And finally, the overall growth from 1755 to 1775 might be slightly understated. None of these possible changes would adversely affect the arguments of this essay.

Notes

I would like to thank Beatriz Betancourt Hardy, John McCusker, Russell Menard, R. C. Nash, Roy Talbert, and Peter Coclanis for their valuable comments and helpful readings of this essay. Any errors of fact or interpretation remain mine alone.

1. Alice Hanson Jones, *Wealth of a Nation to Be: The American Colonies on the Eve of the Revolution* (New York: Columbia University Press, 1980). Jones made no distinction between the Chesapeake and Lower Southern colonies, combining them under the single designation "South." John McCusker and Russell Menard extended Jones's numbers to estimate that average wealth per free white person in 1774 increased as one moved southward, from £33 in New England to £51 in the Middle Colonies to £132 in the South. See John J. McCusker and Russell R. Menard, *The Economy of British America, 1607–1789* (Chapel Hill: University of North Carolina Press for the Institute of Early American History and Culture, 1985), 61. The average wealth per free white person in Jamaica of £1,200 was nine times greater than that of the southern colonies. All uses of £ in this essay refer to sterling, unless otherwise stated.

2. Menard calculated that in 1774 the mean value of moveable wealth per decedent in South Carolina was £1,955. While this figure was not directly comparable to those given above, some manipulation yields an approximate figure of £690 average wealth per free white person. See Russell R. Menard, "Slavery, Economic Growth, and Revolutionary Ideology in the South Carolina Lowcountry," in *The Economy of Early America: The Revolutionary Period, 1763–1790*, ed. Ronald Hoffman et al. (Charlottesville: University Press of Virginia, 1988), 266. A rough approximation for the mean wealth per free white person was obtained by using a ratio from tables 3–21 and 3–22 in Peter A. Coclanis, *The Shadow of a Dream: Economic Life and Death in the South Carolina Low Country, 1670–1920* (New York: Oxford University Press, 1989), 88–89. Table 3-21 contained an estimate of mean personal wealth of inventoried white decedents from 1757 to 1762:

£862.71. Table 3-22 contained an estimate of mean wealth per white inhabitant from 1757 to 1762: £303.62. The ratio of mean wealth per white inhabitant (£303.62) to the mean personal wealth of inventoried white decedents (£862.71) multiplied by Menard's figure for mean moveable [personal] wealth per decedent (£1,955) yielded a figure of £690. This figure was roughly comparable to Jones's. While there were a number of problems in the derivation of these figures, these problems do not affect the relationship between the magnitudes, which is important for this point.

3. James F. Shepherd and Gary M. Walton, *Shipping, Maritime Trade, and the Economic Growth of Colonial North America* (Cambridge: Cambridge University Press, 1972). They explained the derivation of their model in chap. 2 and discussed specific factors in chap. 5.

4. Lower transaction costs—essentially the cost of getting a product from producer to consumer—benefited both parties. Consumers enjoyed lower prices, enabling more consumers to buy more of the product. At the same time lower transaction costs raised the prices paid to producers, providing greater returns on investment and encouraging new production.

5. The historical literature dealing with various aspects of the history of rice in the Lower Southern colonies is voluminous; the best guides to this material are Coclanis, *Shadow of a Dream*, and Kenneth Morgan, "The Organization of the Colonial American Rice Trade," *William and Mary Quarterly*, 3d ser., 52 (1995): 433–52.

6. McCusker and Menard, *Economy of British America*, 261–62.

7. Menard, "Slavery, Economic Growth, and Revolutionary Ideology"; R. C. Nash, "South Carolina and the Atlantic Economy in the late Seventeenth and Eighteenth Centuries," *Economic History Review* 45 (1992): 677–702; Coclanis, *Shadow of a Dream*.

8. Menard, "Slavery, Economic Growth, and Revolutionary Ideology," 248–59. Recently, Menard has reinforced this interpretation in a more general essay. See Russell R. Menard, "Economic and Social Development of the South," in *The Cambridge Economic History of the United States*, vol. 1, *The Colonial Era*, ed. Stanley L. Engerman and Robert E. Gallman (New York: Cambridge University Press, 1996), 249–95, esp. 273–86.

9. Nash, "South Carolina and the Atlantic Economy," 687, 689.

10. Coclanis, *Shadow of a Dream*, chap. 3.

11. Russell R. Menard, "Transport Costs and Long-Range Trade, 1300–1800: Was There a European 'Transport Revolution' in the Early Modern Era?" in *The Political Economy of Merchant Empires*, ed. James D. Tracy (Cambridge: Cambridge University Press, 1991), 267–69. Menard called his data on freight rates "preliminary" in the notes to table 6.8, p. 269.

12. For example, during 1764, Henry Laurens quoted freight rates to London ranging from 27 shillings, 6 pence, to 55 shillings per ton. George C. Rogers et al., eds., *The Papers of Henry Laurens*, vol. 4 (Columbia: University of South Carolina Press, 1974); for rates specified, see 4:494 and 4:247, respectively. Unlike the relatively staid Chesapeake market where freight rates for tobacco were generally uniform in any particular year, the Charleston freight market seems to have been much more dynamic and volatile. Freight rates often varied according to the number of vessels in the harbor and the amount of rice available to ship. For Chesapeake freight rates, see John M. Hemphill II, "Freight Rates in the Maryland Tobacco Trade, 1705–1762," *Maryland Historical Magazine* 54 (1959): 36–58, 153–87.

13. This was true in the tobacco trade. The cargo ton was customarily four hogsheads of tobacco. Maryland tobacco hogsheads increased in weight from about 600 pounds in 1700 to almost 1100 pounds by the time of the Revolution; however, a cargo ton of

tobacco was always composed of four hogsheads. See Lorena S. Walsh, *To Labour for Profit: Plantation Management in the Chesapeake, 1620–1820* (forthcoming), for information on hogshead sizes.

14. Coclanis, *Shadow of a Dream,* 260 n. 148.

15. For the numbers of coasting vessels, see Converse D. Clowse, *Measuring Charleston's Overseas Commerce, 1717–1767: Statistics from the Port's Naval Lists* (Washington, D.C.: University Press of America, 1981), 97, 104.

16. Coclanis, *Shadow of a Dream,* 100.

17. Most of the literature of economic history about business cycles is concerned with trying to discover indicators to predict the occurrence and length of these cycles. See, for example, R. C. O. Matthews, *The Business Cycle* (New York: Cambridge University Press, 1967). For a nontechnical introduction to business cycles in colonial America, see McCusker and Menard, *Economy of British America,* 69–70. A table of British and colonial business cycles from 1614 to 1796 can be found on pp. 62–63. This is expanded and revised in John J. McCusker, *How Much Is That in Real Money? A Historical Price Index for Use As a Deflator of Money Values in the Economy of the United States* (Worcester, Mass.: American Antiquarian Society, 1992).

18. The originals are located in the Public Record Office, London, under the classification CO 5/508–511. Microfilm copies are readily available in two forms: *Naval Office Shipping Lists for South Carolina, 1716–1767,* British Records Relating to America in Microform, ed. Walter Minchinton (East Ardsley, Wakefield, Yorkshire, England: Micro Methods, Ltd., 1966), 2 reels; and Library of Congress and American Council of Learned Societies, *British Manuscripts Project* (Washington, D.C.: Library of Congress, 1941–1945), reels PRO 52 and PRO 53. The NOSLs generally contained the date of entry or clearance, name and type of ship, master's name, build of ship, tons, guns, men, cargo details, where cleared to or entered from, and where and when bond given (if required).

19. The quarters used were traditional English quarters: Ladyday (ending 25 Mar., O.S., or 5 Apr., N.S.), Midsummer (ending 24 June, O.S., or 5 July, N.S.), Michaelmas (ending 29 Sept., O.S., or 10 Oct., N.S.), and Christmas (ending 25 Dec., O.S., or 5 Jan., N.S.). For the transmittal requirement, see Leonard Woods Larabee, ed. and comp., *Royal Instructions to British Colonial Governors, 1670–1776,* 2 vols. (Washington, D.C.: American Historical Association, 1935; reprint, New York: Octagon Books, 1967), 2:775.

20. Not all quarters of NOSLs are extant for all the years in each period. Included are all quarters for 1717–1719; Michaelmas and Christmas quarters for 1723; all quarters for 1724; Ladyday quarter for 1725; all quarters for 1732; Ladyday quarter for 1733; all quarters for 1734; all quarters for 1736–1738; Michaelmas and Christmas quarters for 1765; all quarters for 1766; Ladyday, Midsummer, and Michaelmas quarters for 1767. Old Style dates falling between 1 January and 25 March have been designated as if 1 January began the new year. Otherwise, the dates have not been adjusted.

21. Data survived only for the Midsummer quarter of 1752 and the Ladyday quarter of 1753.

22. A factor of 90 percent of the total rice crop exported to a particular overseas area was also used to test the variance between the 95 percent and 90 percent figures. The difference was generally very small. Thus, the 95 percent figure was chosen.

23. While data on the quantity of rice exported are available before 1722, no price series is available to determine the value of the rice exported.

24. The compound growth rates are averages calculated from the regression data for the period specified.

25. See table 5.3.

26. The period 1765–1767 encompassed the nonimportation of British goods in reaction to the Stamp Act. See Merrill Jensen, *The Founding of a Nation: A History of the American Revolution, 1763–1776* (New York: Oxford University Press, 1968), 129–32. It is conceivable that nonimportation had some effect on the rice trade; however, nonimportation did not require nonexportation. The average port time for ships sailing to Great Britain was 65 days in 1766 and 48 days in 1767. This would seem to support the notion that nonimportation had some effect on port times. However, average port times for ships clearing in 1765–1767 to Southern Europe were 55, 89, and 49 days and to the West Indies 31, 47, and 30 days, respectively. So *all* shipping experienced longer port times in 1766. The dislocations due to nonimportation should have affected only British shipping; the best explanation for the longer port times for all shipping is that the rice crop for 1766 was very small. Compared to crops in the previous three years of over 100,000 barrels, the 1766 crop was about 78,000. The longer port time most likely arose from the difficulty of gathering a cargo of rice to ship. Even if 1766 were eliminated from the 1765–1767 period, average port times for ships trading to Great Britain would not have been better than those for 1732–1734, and average port times for ships trading to Southern Europe and the West Indies would have been about the same as in 1736–1738. The variance of average port times in 1765–1767 further demonstrates the importance of a multiple-year sampling to ameliorate any year-to-year variations.

27. See table 5.4. All references are to registered tonnage. For an excellent introduction to the various tonnages used in the eighteenth century, see John J. McCusker, "The Tonnage of Ships Engaged in British Colonial Trade during the Eighteenth Century," *Research in Economic History* 6 (1981): 73–105.

28. Shepherd and Walton, *Shipping*, 75–80.

29. Shepherd and Walton, *Shipping*, 74. Large numbers of ships based in Charlestown and participating in the rice trade might bias these figures, especially those for crew costs, since the Charlestown-based rice ships would have been able to discharge their crews. However, very few Charlestown-based ships participated in the trade, so the calculations are reasonable.

30. See table 5.5. Ton-port days are the number of days of a vessel in port multiplied by the number of tons of a vessel, and man-port days are the number of days of a vessel in port multiplied by the number of men on a vessel.

31. This would not be true if there were *significant* reductions in ship capital costs and sailors' wages. However, neither appears to have been the case in the eighteenth century.

32. Shepherd and Walton, *Shipping*, 80–85.

33. See table 5.7.

34. See tables 5.6–5.8. The most common size for ships trading to Great Britain and Southern Europe was 51–100 tons while the most common size for ships trading to the West Indies was 0–50 tons. In categories where the tons-to-man ratio between armed and unarmed vessels varied, the difference was usually less than one ton per man, on the order of 8 to 15 percent difference.

35. See tables 5.6 and 5.8.

36. See table 5.9. If shipowners had been reducing the number of guns while still keeping the ship armed, the tons-to-gun ratio should have risen. However, for armed ships of 51–100 tons trading to Great Britain, the average tons-to-guns ratio actually decreased from 27.70 for 1723–1725, to 22.79 for 1732–1734, to 17.85 for 1736–1738. This means that of those ships that were armed, the armament was increasing. A similar, but less clear pattern held for armed ships between 101–150 tons trading to Great Britain.

Likewise, in the most common category of ships trading to southern Europe, 51–100 tons, the armament grew heavier.

37. Ships from 51 to 100 tons form the "smaller" category, and those from 151 to 200 form the "larger" category.

38. Armed ships of 51–100 tons had an average tons-to-man ratio of 8.63 in 1736–1738; unarmed ships of the same size had a ratio of 9.30 in 1765–1767.

39. See table 5.7.

40. Shepherd and Walton, *Shipping*, 76.

41. See tables 5.6–5.8. For example, unarmed ships trading to Great Britain of 51–100 tons had a tons-to-man ratio of 10.04 in 1723–1725, and 10.08 in 1765–1767. In the category of 101–150 tons, there was a slight improvement from 11.40 to 12.21 for the same periods. For unarmed ships trading to southern Europe, there was an overall *decrease* in efficiency; in the 51–100 ton category, the tons-to-man ratio was 9.43 in 1732–1734, 9.85 in 1736–1738, and 9.30 in 1765–1767. Likewise in the 101–150 ton, unarmed category, the 1765–1767 ratio (11.6) was less than for the *armed* in 1732–1734 (13.85), and only slightly better than 1736–1738 (10.74). For the West Indies, the tons-to-man ratio of unarmed ships of 0–50 tons varied from 4.82 in 1723–1725, to 4.63 in 1732–1734, to 6.05 in 1736–1738, to 5.44 in 1765–1767.

42. The two legs of a shuttle voyage would have consisted of the first leg from home port to a trading port, and a second leg returning home. Multi-leg voyages would have involved two or more ports other than the home port.

43. See table 5.10.

44. See table 5.11.

45. See table 5.12.

46. One of the internal effects of this period of prosperity was the creation of a South Carolina–based capital market that helped fuel further growth. See Russell R. Menard, "Financing the Lowcountry Export Boom: Capital and Growth in Early South Carolina," *William and Mary Quarterly*, 3d ser., 51 (1994): 659–76.

47. Nash, "South Carolina and the Atlantic Economy," 682, 684, 689–99. According to Nash, "Rice . . . was an inferior good, a *substitute* for other small grains." Nash's figures for slave productivity must be used with caution, as they were based on price data, not labor requirements.

48. Menard, "Economic and Social Development of the South," 283.

49. David L. Coon, *The Development of Market Agriculture in South Carolina, 1670–1785* (New York: Garland Publishing, 1989), 182–84. Joyce Chaplin, in *An Anxious Pursuit: Agricultural Innovation and Modernity in the Lower South, 1730–1815* (Chapel Hill: University of North Carolina Press for the Institute of Early American History and Culture, 1993), 232, tended to see the transition to tidal cultivation more as a post-Revolutionary phenomenon because of the high capital and labor costs in building the necessary dams and works. However, Menard placed the beginning of these changes before the Revolution. See Menard, "Economic and Social Development of the South," 282–83.

50. Coclanis, *Shadow of a Dream*, 66–68, 96–97.

51. See table 5.2.

52. Nash, "South Carolina and the Atlantic Economy," 684, 692.

53. John J. McCusker, "Growth, Stagnation, or Decline? The Economy of the British West Indies, 1763–1790," in *The Economy of Early America*, ed. Hoffman et al., 279, 301.

54. See tables 5.1 and 5.2. Rice exports to the West Indies in 1765–1767 were over 15 times what they had been in 1736–1738 while exports to Britain were slightly less, and

those to Southern Europe about 2.5 times as great. Historians need to do much more work on why West Indian planters converted to rice to feed their slaves, what they converted from, and when the conversion took place. While this transition had obvious effects on South Carolina, it also had a significant impact on the Chesapeake colonies, which supplied large amounts of corn and pork to the sugar islands.

55. See table 5.4.

56. See table 5.7.

57. See table 5.11.

58. Lewis C. Gray, *History of Agriculture in the Southern United States to 1860*, 2 vols. (Washington, D.C.: Carnegie Institution of Washington, 1933; reprint, Clifton, N.J.: Augustus M. Kelley, 1973), 2:1020–23.

59. U.S. Bureau of the Census, *Historical Statistics of the United States: Colonial Times to 1970*, 2 vols. (Washington, D.C.: Government Printing Office, 1975), 2:1163–65.

60. Clowse, *Measuring Charleston's Overseas Commerce*, 58 n. a.

61. Coon, *The Development of Market Agriculture*, 349–51.

62. According to the introduction to the table on rice exports, "It must be remembered . . . that the weight of barrels might vary radically." See U.S. Bureau of the Census, *Historical Statistics*, 2:1164. For 1766, where there was information on over 30,000 barrels, the average net size of groups of rice barrels varied from 486 to 554 pounds. (See sources for table 5.13.) Because the information on small numbers of barrel sizes is not random, standard statistical techniques to determine validity and error range cannot be used.

63. The average barrel sizes for 1752 and 1773 both appear to be much greater than would be expected from the data in surrounding years. The data for these two years came from one and two sources, respectively, and appear to demonstrate the principle.

TABLE 5.1

QUANTITY AND CONSTANT VALUE OF SOUTH CAROLINA RICE EXPORTS, 1715–1774

Year	Barrels of Rice	Size of Barrel	Pounds of Rice	Price (s/cwt)	Colonial CPI (1860=100)	Deflated Price (s/cwt)	Constant Value of Rice Exports (,000s £)
1715	6,765	350	2,378,250		88		
1716	13,100	350	4,585,000		72		
1717	8,232	350	2,881,200		76		
1718	8,448	350	2,956,800		88		
1719	11,432	350	4,001,200		92		
1720	18,530	350	6,485,500		76		
1721	22,121	360	7,963,560		71		
1722	26,304	370	9,732,480	5.17	75	6.89	33.545
1723	23,151	380	8,797,380	6.01	76	7.91	34.784
1724	22,191	390	8,654,490	6.16	80	7.70	33.320
1725	17,734	400	7,093,600	5.62	95	5.92	20.982
1726	23,031	410	9,442,710	6.57	92	7.14	33.717
1727	26,884	420	11,291,280	8.03	86	9.34	52.715
1728	29,965	430	12,884,950	6.62	81	8.17	52.653
1729	32,384	440	14,248,960	6.38	80	7.98	56.818
1730	41,722	450	18,774,900	6.29	80	7.86	73.809
1731	39,487	450	17,769,150	5.32	71	7.49	66.572
1732	37,480	450	16,866,000	6.02	67	8.99	75.771
1733	51,656	450	23,245,200	5.72	66	8.67	100.729

1734	31,093	450	13,991,850	8.64	67	12.90	90.216
1735	47,244	450	21,259,800	8.26	68	12.15	129.122
1736	55,120	450	24,804,000	6.85	65	10.54	130.698
1737	44,892	450	20,201,400	8.89	66	13.47	136.053
1738	36,283	450	16,327,350	9.60	71	13.52	110.382
1739	71,484	450	32,167,800	5.47	63	8.68	139.649
1740	95,895	450	43,152,750	4.71	66	7.14	153.977
1741	85,153	455	38,744,615	7.45	91	8.19	158.597
1742	48,627	460	22,368,420	6.29	81	7.77	86.850
1743	77,280	465	35,925,900	4.91	71	6.92	124.255
1744	85,029	470	39,963,630	4.23	66	6.41	128.065
1745	62,765	475	29,813,375	2.29	64	3.58	53.338
1746	56,948	480	27,335,040	2.24	65	3.45	47.100
1747	56,996	485	27,643,060	4.43	71	6.24	86.239
1748	58,034	490	28,643,660	6.44	82	7.85	111.666
1749	43,194	495	21,381,030	8.28	84	9.86	105.378
1750	50,760	500	25,380,000	8.98	84	10.69	135.662
1751	68,846	505	34,767,230	6.53	85	7.68	133.547
1752	82,501	510	42,075,510	7.93	87	9.11	191.758
1753	37,393	515	19,257,395	9.55	84	7.80	109.469
1754	93,326	520	48,529,520	6.20	81	7.65	185.730
1755	104,682	525	54,958,050	5.82	79	7.37	202.440
1756	83,127	525	43,641,675	4.83	77	6.27	136.876
1757	61,731	525	32,408,775	4.82	81	5.95	96.426

Year	Barrels of Rice	Size of Barrel	Pounds of Rice	Price (s/cwt)	Colonial CPI	Deflated Price (s/cwt)	Constant Value of Rice Exports (,000 £)
1758	71,015	525	37,282,875	6.16	87	7.08	131.990
1759	54,440	525	28,581,000	9.40	99	9.49	135.688
1760	64,007	525	33,603,675	7.35	96	7.66	128.639
1761	106,725	525	56,030,625	5.51	90	6.12	171.516
1762	83,835	525	43,488,375	4.76	95	5.01	110.265
1763	110,335	525	57,925,875	6.31	95	6.64	192.375
1764	107,202	525	56,281,050	6.01	88	6.83	192.187
1765	119,887	525	62,940,675	6.35	89	7.13	224.536
1766	77,927	525	40,911,675	8.13	98	8.30	169.700
1767	109,605	525	57,542,625	8.01	95	8.43	242.588
1768	132,583	525	69,606,075	9.26	90	10.29	358.085
1769	122,482	525	64,303,050	8.62	93	9.27	298.007
1770	137,373	525	72,120,825	6.76	100	6.76	243.768
1771	130,360	525	68,439,000	7.28	96	7.58	259.498
1772	108,897	525	57,170,925	12.03	109	11.04	315.489
1773	133,621	525	70,151,025	9.04	101	8.95	313.943
1774	125,076	525	65,664,900	7.37	97	7.60	249.459

Sources: "Barrels of Rice": David L. Coon, *The Development of Market Agriculture in South Carolina, 1670–1785* (New York: Garland Publishing, 1989), 349–50. "Size of Barrel": Lawrence A. Harper, *Historical Statistics of the United States: Colonial Times to 1970* (Washington, D.C.: Government Printing Office, 1975), 2:1163–64. "Price (s/cwt)": Peter Coclanis, *The Shadow of a Dream: Economic Life and Death in the South Carolina Low Country, 1670–1920* (New York: Oxford University Press, 1989), 106–7. "Colonial CPI": John J. McCusker, *How Much Is That in Real Money? A Historical Price Index for Use As a Deflator of Money Values in the Economy of the United States* (Worcester, Mass.: American Antiquarian Society, 1992), 323–25. "Deflated Price (s/cwt)": "Price (s/cwt)" deflated using "Colonial CPI." "Constant Value of Rice Exports (,000 £)": "Pounds of Rice" multiplied by "Deflated Price (s/cwt)." Blanks indicate no data for that year.

TABLE 5.2
SOUTH CAROLINA RICE EXPORTS FOR SELECTED PERIODS (BARRELS)

Period	Great Britain	West Indies	North America	Southern Europe	Africa	TOTAL
1717–1719	22,586 (68.58%)	4,014 (12.19%)	6,333 (19.23%)			32,933
1723–1725	27,245 (82.36%)	1,969 (5.95%)	3,867 (11.69%)			33,081
1732–1734	71,693 (71.36%)	3,485 (3.47%)	2,974 (2.96%)	22,309 (22.21%)		100,461
1736–1738	96,037 (80.86%)	2,208 (1.86%)	1,804 (1.52%)	18,717 (15.76%)		118,766
1765–1767	92,183 (49.98%)	34,600 (18.76%)	9,427 (5.11%)	48,089 (26.07%)	145(0.08%)	184,442

SOURCE: CO 5/508–511. See text for discussion of source and quarters used. Percentages may not add up to 100 percent due to rounding. The totals for these periods vary from those given in table 5.1 as these data are compiled from NOSLs, some quarters of which are missing. See text for a discussion of the extant records used. Blanks indicate no rice exported to that area for that period.

TABLE 5.3
MEAN PORT TIMES OF SHIPS TRADING TO AN OVERSEAS AREA,
EXPORTING 95 PERCENT OF RICE FOR SELECTED PERIODS
(DAYS)

Period	Great Britain	West Indies	Southern Europe
1717–1719	66.3	48.2	
	(n=41 of 90)	(n=20 of 49)	
1723–1725	56.4	48.6	
	(n=69 of 72)	(n=20 of 20)	
1732–1734	44.9	43.6	34.0
	(n=119 of 136)	(n=31 of 42)	(n=35 of 42)
1736–1738	55.2	30.7	46.3
	(n=144 of 166)	(n=22 of 26)	(n=23 of 33)
1765–1767	56.9	38.2	74.1
	(n=107 of 126)	(n=127 of 159)	(n=61 of 67)

SOURCE: CO 5/508–511. For each overseas region, only the ships that carried the top 95 percent of the total amount of rice during the period are included. See the text for a discussion of the procedure. The letter "n" is the number of ships for which port times could be established, and are thus included in the mean; "of" is followed by the number of ships in the top 95 percent.

TABLE 5.4
MEAN TONNAGE OF SHIPS TRADING TO AN OVERSEAS AREA, EXPORTING 95 PERCENT OF RICE FOR SELECTED PERIODS (REGISTERED TONS)

Period	Great Britain	West Indies	Southern Europe
1717–1719	93.4	35.5	
	(n=90 of 90)	(n=49 of 49)	
1723–1725	89.9	31.5	
	(n=72 of 72)	(n=20 of 20)	
1732–1734	94.9	33.1	84.5
	(n=136 of 136)	(n=42 of 42)	(n=42 of 42)
1736–1738	103.0	42.5	91.5
	(n=166 of 166)	(n=26 of 26)	(n=33 of 33)
1765–1767	138.0	45.9	121.0
	(n=126 of 126)	(n=159 of 159)	(n=67 of 67)

SOURCE: CO 5/508–511. For each overseas region, only the ships that carried the top 95 percent of the total amount of rice during the period are included. See the text for a discussion of the procedure. The letter "n" is the number of ships for which port times could be established, and are thus included in the mean; "of" is followed by the number of ships in the top 95 percent.

TABLE 5.5
MEAN TON-PORT DAYS AND MAN-PORT DAYS OF SHIPS TRADING TO OVERSEAS AREAS, EXPORTING 95 PERCENT OF RICE FOR SELECTED PERIODS

Period	Great Britain		West Indies		Southern Europe	
	Ton-Port Days	Man-Port Days	Ton-Port Days	Man-Port Days	Ton-Port Days	Man-Port Days
1717–1719	6,072 (n=41)		2,154 (n=20)			
1723–1725	5,417 (n=69)	579 (n=69)	1,637 (n=20)	310 (n=20)		
1732–1734	4,391 (n=119)	450 (n=119)	1,577 (n=31)	280 (n=31)	2,921 (n=35)	305 (n=35)
1736–1738	5,965 (n=144)	605 (n=144)	1,572 (n=22)	199 (n=22)	4,129 (n=23)	413 (n=23)
1765–1767	7,909 (n=107)	626 (n=107)	2,079 (n=127)	270 (n=127)	8,917 (n=61)	843 (n=61)

SOURCE: CO 5/508–511. See the text for discussion of periods. For each overseas region, only the ships that carried the top 95 percent of the total amount of rice during the period are included. The letter "n" is the number of ships for which ton-port days and man-port days could be established.

TABLE 5.6
MEAN TONS-TO-MAN RATIO OF SHIPS TRADING TO GREAT BRITAIN, EXPORTING 95 PERCENT OF RICE FOR SELECTED PERIODS (REGISTERED TONS/MAN)

Tonnage Range	1723–1725 Unarmed	Armed	1732–1734 Unarmed	Armed	1736–1738 Unarmed	Armed	1765–1767 Unarmed	Armed
0–50	6.73 (n=12)	4.79 (n=3)	6.70 (n=6)	6.25 (n=5)	6.80 (n=7)	5.93 (n=4)	7.14 (n=1)	
51–100	10.04 (n=13)	8.42 (n=18)	8.94 (n=32)	8.89 (n=54)	9.95 (n=45)	8.86 (n=58)	10.08 (n=38)	
101–150	11.40 (n=8)	10.65 (n=11)	11.74 (n=8)	11.21 (n=29)	12.06 (n=14)	10.17 (n=23)	12.21 (n=46)	
151–200		10.67 (n=2)		17.27 (n=2)	12.30 (n=1)	12.63 (n=6)	16.77 (n=34)	
201–250						12.87 (n=4)	17.16 (n=6)	
251–300							21.67 (n=1)	
301-350					16.41 (n=3)			13.08 (n=1)

SOURCE: CO 5/509–511. Only the sips that carried the top 95 percent of the total amount of rice during the period are included. See the text for a discussion of the procedure. The letter "n" is the number of ships for which tons-to-man ratios could be established.

TABLE 5.7
MEAN TONS-TO-MAN RATIO OF SHIPS TRADING TO WEST INDIES, EXPORTING 95 PERCENT OF RICE FOR SELECTED PERIODS (REGISTERED TONS/MAN)

Tonnage Range	1723–1725		1732–1734		1736–1738		1765–1767	
	Unarmed	Armed	Unarmed	Armed	Unarmed	Armed	Unarmed	Armed
0–50	4.82	3.76	4.63	4.53	6.05	4.77	5.44	
	(n=20)	(n=4)	(n=22)	(n=26)	(n=17)	(n=4)	(n=120)	
51–100	14.55	7.00	10.29	10.36	10.00	9.29	9.48	
	(n=1)	(n=1)	(n=2)	(n=2)	(n=2)	(n=2)	(n=30)	
101–150				11.00		11.54	12.74	
				(n=1)		(n=1)	(n=5)	
151–200							13.75	
							(n=3)	
201–250							15.00	
							(n=1)	

SOURCE: CO 5/509–511. Only the ships that carried the top 95 percent of the total amount of rice during the period are included. See the text for a discussion of the procedure. The letter "n" is the number of ships for which tons-to-man ratios could be established.

TABLE 5.8
MEAN TONS-TO-MAN RATIO OF SHIPS TRADING TO SOUTHERN EUROPE,
EXPORTING 95 PERCENT OF RICE FOR SELECTED PERIODS (REGISTERED TONS/MAN)

Tonnage Range	1723–1725		1732–1734		1736–1738		1765–1767	
	Unarmed	Armed	Unarmed	Armed	Unarmed	Armed	Unarmed	Armed
0–50			8.33	6.98	8.33	8.33	9.30	
			(n=1)	(n=2)	(n=1)	(n=1)	(n=31)	
51–100			9.43	9.53	9.85	8.63	11.60	
			(n=4)	(n=26)	(n=7)	(n=14)	(n=22)	
101–150				13.85	8.75	10.74	15.00	
				(n=29)	(n=1)	(n=8)	(n=13)	
151–200					11.43		21.50	
					(n=1)		(n=1)	
201–250								

SOURCE: CO 5/509–511. Only the ships that carried the top 95 percent of the total amount of rice during the period are included. See the text for a discussion of the procedure. The letter "n" is the number of ships for which tons-to-man ratios could be established.

TABLE 5.9
MEAN TONS–TO–GUN RATIO OF SHIPS TRADING TO AN OVERSEAS AREA,
EXPORTING 95 PERCENT OF RICE FOR SELECTED PERIODS (REGISTERED TONS/GUN)

Tonnage Range	1723–1725		1732–1734			1736–1738			1765–1767		
	Great Britain	West Indies	Great Britain	West Indies	Southern Europe	Great Britain	West Indies	Southern Europe	Great Britain	West Indies	Southern Europe
0–50	8.47 (n=13)	10.00 (n=4)	21.67 (n=5)	7.22 (n=26)	9.79 (n=2)	10.21 (n=4)	8.54 (n=4)	12.50 (n=1)			
51–100	27.70 (n=18)	8.75 (n=1)	22.79 (n=54)	30.00 (n=2)	22.43 (n=26)	17.85 (n=58)	21.67 (n=2)	20.85 (n=14)			
101–150	30.90 (n=11)		38.80 (n=29)	27.50 (n=1)	18.83 (n=5)	22.47 (n=23)	18.75 (n=1)	26.15 (n=8)			
151–200	26.67 (n=2)		30.43 (n=2)			30.17 (n=6)					
201–250						28.69 (n=4)					
251–300											
301–350						42.50 (n=3)			52.33 (n=1)		

SOURCE: CO 5/509–511. For each overseas region, only the ships that carried the top 95 percent of the total amount of rice during the period are included. See the text for a discussion of the procedure. The letter "n" is the number of ships for which tons-to-guns ratios could be established.

TABLE 5.10
SHUTTLE FACTORS OF SHIPS TRADING TO GREAT BRITAIN, EXPORTING 95 PERCENT OF RICE FOR SELECTED PERIODS (REGISTERED TONS)

Tonnage of Ships Clearing to Great Britain

Where Ships Entered into South Carolina from	1717–1719	1723–1725	1732–1734	1736–1738	1765–1767
Africa	365 (5.26%)		400 (3.48%)	1630 (9.88%)	510 (3.46%)
Great Britain	4,353 (62.76%)	4,145 (67.07%)	5,297 (46.10%)	4,625 (28.02%)	8,655 (58.75%)
Northern Europe				170 (1.03%)	140 (0.95%)
Ireland	78 (1.12%)		130 (1.13%)	290 (1.76%)	290 (1.97%)
North America	725 (10.45%)	1,055 (17.07%)	2,278 (19.83%)	5,390 (32.65%)	2,215 (15.04%)
Southern Europe	375 (5.41%)	170 (2.75%)	1,125 (9.79%)	2,411 (14.61%)	1,752 (15.04%)
West Indies	1,040 (14.99%)	810 (13.11%)	2,260 (19.67%)	1,990 (12.06%)	1,170 (7.94%)

SOURCE: CO 5/508–511. Percentages may not add up to 100% due to rounding. Only the ships that carried the top 95% of the total amount of rice during the period are included (see text for a discussion of the procedure). The figures reflect only those ships for which a place of origin could be determined. For 1717–19, the total tonnage of the top 95% of rice-carrying ships clearing for Great Britain was 8,406 tons. The place of origin could not be determined for 17.49% of this tonnage. The same figures for 1723–25, 1732–34, 1736–38, and 1765–67 are 6,180 tons, 4.48%; 12,910 tons, 13.32%; 17,026 tons, 3.54%; and 17,375 tons, 15.21%, respectively. The regions are self-explanatory, except for Northern Europe (areas of Europe north of Cape Finisterre, except for Great Britain and Ireland), North America (which includes all of North America and Bermuda and the Bahamas), Southern Europe (which includes Europe south of Cape Finisterre, the Mediterranean, the Azores, the Madeiras, the Cape Verdes, and the Canaries), and West Indies (which includes all of the West Indian islands, Honduras, the Mosquito Shore, and South America). These definitions are consistent with those used in CUST 16/1, which is the basis for Shepherd and Walton's work. Blanks indicate no vessels in that category.

TABLE 5.11
SHUTTLE FACTORS OF SHIPS TRADING TO WEST INDIES,
EXPORTING 95 PERCENT OF RICE FOR SELECTED PERIODS (REGISTERED TONS)

Where Ships Entered into South Carolina from	Tonnage of Ships Clearing to the West Indies				
	1717–1719	1723–1725	1732–1734	1736–1738	1765–1767
Africa					60 (1.00%)
Great Britain	70 (6.44%)	20 (3.18%)	50 (4.48%)		517 (8.58%)
Ireland					50 (0.83%)
North America	192 (17.66%)	338 (53.74%)	360 (32.29%)	220 (21.07%)	810 (13.44%)
Southern Europe					190 (3.15%)
West Indies	825 (75.90%)	271 (43.08%)	705 (63.23%)	824 (78.93%)	4,401 (73.01%)

SOURCE: CO 5/508–511. Percentages may not add up to 100 percent due to rounding. Only the ships that carried the top 95 percent of the total amount of rice during the period are included. See the text for a discussion of the procedure. The above figures reflect only those ships trading to West Indies for which a place of origin could be determined. For 1717–1719, the total tonnage of the top 95 percent of rice-carrying ships clearing for the West Indies was 1,739 tons. The place of origin could not be determined for 37.49 percent of this tonnage. The same figures for 1723–1725, 1732–1734, 1736–1738, and 1765–1767 are 629 tons, 0 percent; 1,389 tons, 19.73 percent; 1,104 tons, 5.43 percent; and 7,300 tons, 17.42 percent, respectively. For an explanation of regions, see table 10. Blanks indicate no vessels in that category.

TABLE 5.12
SHUTTLE FACTORS OF SHIPS TRADING TO SOUTHERN
EUROPE, EXPORTING 95 PERCENT OF RICE FOR SELECTED
PERIODS (REGISTERED TONS)

Where Ships Entered into South Carolina from	Tonnage of Ships Clearing to the Southern Europe		
	1732–1734	1736–1738	1765–1767
Africa	120	100	200
	(4.14%)	(3.47%)	(2.71%)
Great Britain	1,218	2,015	4,123
	(42.03%)	(69.97%)	(55.87%)
Northern Europe			110
			(1.49%)
Ireland	60	80	100
	(2.07%)	(2.78%)	(1.36%)
North America	380	325	556
	(13.11%)	(11.28%)	(7.53%)
Southern Europe	650	270	1,140
	(22.43%)	(9.38%)	(15.45%)
West Indies	470	90	1,150
	(16.22%)	(3.13%)	(15.58%)

SOURCE: CO 5/509–511. Percentages may not add up to 100 percent due to rounding. Only the ships that carried the top 95 percent of the total amount of rice during the period are included. See the text for a discussion of the procedure. The above figures reflect only those ships trading to southern Europe for which a place of origin could be determined. For 1732–1734, the total tonnage of the top 95 percent of rice-carrying ships clearing for southern Europe was 3,548 tons. The place of origin could not be determined for 18.32 percent of this tonnage. The same figures for 1736–1738 and 1765–1767 are 3,020 tons, 4.64 percent; and 8,125 tons, 9.18 percent, respectively. For a description of the regions, see table 10. Blanks indicate no vessels in that category.

TABLE 5.13
AVERAGE NET SIZE OF SOUTH CAROLINA RICE BARRELS,
1715–1775
HARPER ESTIMATE AND MANUSCRIPT DATA AVERAGES

Year	Harper Estimate (pounds)	Manuscript Data Average Size (pounds)	Number of Barrels in Sample	Number of Observations in Sample
1715	350			
1716	350			
1717	350			
1718	350			
1719	350			
1720	350			
1721	360			
1722	370	383	99	2
1723	380			
1724	390			
1725	400			
1726	410			
1727	420	413	37	1
1728	430			
1729	440			
1730	450	442	95	3
1731	450	435	12	1
1732	450			
1733	450			
1734	450			
1735	450			
1736	450	465	1	1
1737	450	455	64	3
1738	450			
1739	450			
1740	450	475	22	1
1741	455			
1742	460			
1743	465			
1744	470			
1745	475			
1746	480			
1747	485			
1748	490			
1749	495	526	1,784	31
1750	500	519	5,046	97

1751	505	515	8,076	122
1752	510	543	8	1
1753	515	516	678	5
1754	520			
1755	525			
1756	525			
1757	525			
1758	525	530	10,261	20
1759	525	527	13,089	24
1760	525	535	19,102	49
1761	525	535	2,832	14
1762	525	525	11,089	22
1763	525	530	14,340	25
1764	525	527	11,910	18
1765	525	524	4,108	11
1766	525	527	30,131	54
1767	525	527	18,183	39
1768	525			
1769	525			
1770	525			
1771	525			
1772	525			
1773	525	547	152	2
1774	525			
1775	525			

SOURCES: "Harper Estimate": U.S. Bureau of the Census, *Historical Statistics of the United States: Colonial Times to 1970* (Washington, D.C.: Government Printing Office, 1975), 2:1164. "Manuscript Data": 1722: Ball Papers, 1631–1891, account and blanket book, 1720–1778, MS 11-515-5, South Carolina Historical Society. 1727: Richard Splatt Papers, South Caroliniana Library, University of South Carolina. 1730: Ball Papers. 1731: Ball Papers. 1737: Ball Papers. 1738: Ball Papers. 1740: Ball Papers. 1749: Henry Laurens Papers, 1747–1801, wastebook, 1749–1751, MS 37-53, South Carolina Historical Society. 1750: Laurens Papers, wastebook. 1751: Laurens Papers, wastebook. 1752: Laurens Papers, wastebook. 1752: Henry Ravenel Papers, 1716–1876, MS 11-331-1, South Carolina Historical Society. 1753: Henry Ravenel Papers; Naval Office Shipping Lists (NOSLs), CO 5/510. 1758: NOSLs, CO 5/510. 1759: NOSLs, CO 5/510; Henry Laurens Papers, 1747–1801, Austin, Laurens, and Appleby copy book of invoices outward, 1759–1763, MS 37-13, South Carolina Historical Society. 1760: NOSLs, CO 5/510; Laurens Papers, invoice copybook; Alexander Willock invoice, MS 43-591, South Carolina Historical Society. 1761: Laurens Papers, invoice copybook. 1762: NOSLs, CO 5/510; Laurens Papers, invoice copybook. 1763: NOSLs, CO 5/510. 1764: NOSLs, CO 5/511. 1765: NOSLs, CO 5/511. 1766: NOSLs, CO 5/511. 1767: NOSLs, CO 5/511. 1773: Baker-Grimké Papers, MS 11-338-39, South Carolina Historical Society.

VI

Indian Traders, Charles Town and London's Vital Link to the Interior of North America, 1717–1755

EIRLYS M. BARKER

Trade with the American Indians was one of the first and most important branches of commerce in the British colony of South Carolina, providing it with an economic justification for its existence. Important London merchants thus had a close interest in the well-being of the southern colonies, especially as some Charles Town merchants had relatives active in London. The increasing demand for quality, reasonably priced manufactured goods was often the deciding factor that kept an Indian nation within the British sphere of influence as the main European rivals, the French and Spanish, constantly failed to provide the quantity and quality of merchandise the Indians desired.[1]

This branch of imperial trade depended not only on the import-export merchants with money and prestige in cities such as London, Bristol, Charles Town, and later Savannah, but also on the people they hired to live and work for much of the year among the Indians. Many lowcountry folk actually spent about half of every year in what was then termed "Indian country," peddling manufactured goods to the Native Americans of South Carolina and after 1730 the colony of Georgia, in exchange for deerskins and other forest products. Agents ranged from respectable traders with their own plantations in the Carolina lowcountry, to a whole variety of helpers, some of whom were indentured servants or slaves. Whatever the status of these men, their fairness in dealing with the Indians was important in binding tribes to the British Empire, as trade connections enhanced diplomatic ties. Despite this significance, the southeastern Indian trade and its personnel have been neglected by most historians.[2]

The southeastern Indian nations trading with the British by 1715 included tribes such as the Yamasees, Cherokees, Creeks, Chickasaws, and Catawbas. These were not political units, and many were confederations of autonomous villages. Their age-old tribal rivalries made the Carolina frontier a dangerous place and the calamitous Yamasee War that began in 1715 showed the horrors that resulted when alien traders failed to respect native customers. The conflict had not only threatened the colony's very existence,

FIGURE 6.1
THE SOUTHEAST IN 1714

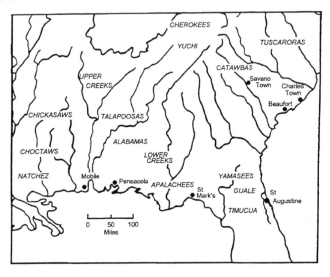

but had also ruined an established Indian trade. Over 200 traders were killed during the uprising. The recreated trade was first a government monopoly but after 1724 became a mix of private and public. The South Carolina Council acted as a board of Indian affairs, keeping separate journals in which to document those activities.[3] Merchants and traders were licensed by their colony and had to post bond for the good conduct of themselves and their servants. The trade was policed by colonial officials as lowcountry and London merchants heavily invested in the business demanded governmental control of traders in Indian country.[4]

Contemporaries by 1720 loosely used the phrase "Indian trader" to describe persons of any race engaged in trade with the Native Americans, especially in the Indian villages. The Anglo-American side of this business had its own hierarchy and terminology. The term "master trader" was current usage for a man with personal experience of living in "Indian country," that is, among the Native Americans and beyond the line of British settlement, and who had enough money or connections to acquire large quantities of the best trade goods. He often developed family ties among the allied Indian nations, which usually ensured respect for his goods, person, and servants. Below this strata were traders without those ties of influence or access to capital or quality goods. Most men engaged in the trade were such middling or lesser traders. They made a living as best they could, with little hope of making a fortune from the trade. Below this were the hundreds of servants, sometimes bound by indentures or enslaved. Other profiteers from the trade

FIGURE 6.2
CATEGORIES OF TRADERS

■ Master Trader—independent
■ "Middling" Trader—usually independent
■ "Lesser" Trader—usually an employee
■ Servants/"hirelings"
  • packhorsemen
  • storekeepers
  • indentured servants
■ Slaves
  • Indian
  • Black

included smaller storekeepers and tavern owners close to the chief trading paths, which led from Indian country to Charles Town or Savannah. Ceremonial visits of Indians to the cities to reaffirm their treaties with the colonies gave local craftsmen such as gunsmiths and tailors additional business.[5]

Master Traders

Carolinians and Georgians, whether engaged in the trade or not, recognized the importance of master traders to the colony's Indian relations. A master trader was in contact with influential persons in both cultures and was recognized in turn by both sides as "a most useful person."[6] Governors, the South Carolina Commons House of Assembly, and transatlantic merchants listened to the information that prominent traders such as Ludovic Grant and James Beamer sent down from their trading posts among the Indians. They trusted master traders' intimate knowledge of the peoples and diplomacy of the region and their understanding of any possible repercussions from dangerous incidents provoked by either Indians or whites. When an important meeting was imminent, the master traders were among the first summoned to help investigations, as in the September 1752 meeting of Upper Creek chiefs "and all the Master Traders" that could be summoned at short notice to deliberate on the purported crimes of a Creek chief named Acorn Whistler.[7]

Master traders surpassed the lesser traders in amassing and reinvesting money until, given luck, they could become lowcountry merchants or leading storekeepers themselves. Their probate inventories were among the most complex because they were involved in many economic ventures. They possessed luxuries such as mahogany furniture, books, fine clothing, and articles of silver.[8] When master trader John McQueen's estate was inventoried in 1764, he not only owned slaves, at least two plantations, and property at

both Charles Town and Savannah, but he was also partner in three companies.[9] Lachlan McGillivray's career indicated that a recent immigrant, even
an impoverished Highland Scot, could make a fortune in the Indian trade.
Aided by Scottish and Indian kin and connections, he rose through the ranks
from packhorse man to a place on the King's Council for Georgia.[10]

Many master traders went into the trade intending to make their fortunes quickly and then get out to invest their spoils in the more lucrative and
safer environments of Charles Town or Savannah. Such men, including
members of the Huguenot Roche family, soon became more involved in the
merchandising end of the trade, although Jordan Roche had spent part of
his youth as a factor (storekeeper) among the Chickasaws. He progressed to
master trader, with a special interest in seizing the Choctaw trade from the
French. He later became a merchant, slaveholder, and member of the Commons House of Assembly. He often served as a member of the Committee
for Indian Affairs.[11]

The master traders maintained a close correspondence with colonial
officials. Traders and officials realized that peace and tranquility on the frontier did not depend on one colony alone. Creek traders Lachlan McGillivray
and George Galphin maintained a long-lasting exchange of information with
Governor Glen of South Carolina, although they were licensed from and
traded mostly within Georgia. The environment was always dangerous and
even influential men lost their lives in pursuit of the trade. In 1748, George
Haig was a victim through no fault of his own, but was just in the wrong
place at the wrong time. He was killed by a roving war party of French-allied
Indians.[12]

One of the distinguishing characteristics of master traders was that they
did not function as lone individuals. The trade developed through individuals forming and recreating various companies for different ventures. This
trend evolved by the late 1740s into more long-lasting connections. Outsiders protested perceived favors these companies received from colonial
governments. James Adair's charge that Governor Glen was surreptitiously
involved in the "Sphinx Company," a secret partnership with other traders
aiming to seize the Choctaw trade in the 1740s, reflected the normal way
trade was conducted on the frontier.[13]

At times, the public suspected these larger companies of hindering
South Carolina and Georgia officials in the execution of their duties in the
nations in order to maintain their near monopoly. Thomas Bosomworth,
employed by South Carolina as agent to the Creeks in 1752, reported back
to the authorities that the dominant organization among the Creeks was
"the powerful Company at Augusta [which] seems to look upon the whole
Trade of the Creek nation as their undoubted Right." It was undermining

Bosomworth "as the greatest Part of the Traders in that Nation are under the [Company's] Influences and Authority and obliged implicitly to obey the Dictates of their Masters." He encountered widespread resistance whenever he tried to exercise his authority. The Augusta Company's leading figure, Patrick Brown, along with his associates "too often let their private Passions into their clandestine Information, and work their particular Spite and Malice against the Person they are sett to destroy."[14] Northern Irish immigrant Patrick Brown was the most important storekeeper and landowner at Augusta by 1743. Georgia's authorities approved his 1749 petition for land south of Augusta for he had already "acquired a handsome Fortune by the trade." He formed many partnerships with other master traders, Alexander Wood, John Rae, George Galphin, William Sludders, George Cussins, Jeremiah Knott, John Pettigrew, Isaac Barksdale, Daniel Clark, and Lachlan McGillivray. Outsiders labeled these men the "Augusta Company." Brown was the dominant member until his death in 1755, but each of these individuals was a master trader in his own right.[15]

Similar to the Augusta Company, leading Cherokee traders worked together as an informal network from the 1720s in such a way as to be called "the Cherokee Company." At several times a partnership existed under that very name. James Beamer was one of the leaders in this group of master traders among the Lower and Middle Cherokees, along with William Hatton, Gregory Haines, Cornelius Dougherty, and Lachlan McBean. The Cherokee Company was not as affluent or politically influential as the Augusta Company, nor did it manage to amass as much money. Partners were constantly sued for debts and could not go to Charles Town without immunity from arrest for debt. In July 1753, when Glen addressed Cherokee demands for better prices, he referred to their friend, James Beamer, as one who "went very young into your Country to settle as a Trader. Now he is grey headed and yet in Debt." It was Beamer's influence and knowledge more than his wealth that placed him among the ranks of the master traders. His Cherokee wife and offspring ensured that Beane was accepted as a reliable mediator by the Cherokees. Beamer relayed to the governor Cherokee complaints about traders such as Robert Gowdie, who only dealt with the Indians when they were bringing deerskins back from the hunt. Although Gowdie thus managed to acquire the best skins when they were desperate for manufactured items, ammunition, and cloth, he ignored their constant need for European goods the rest of the year.[16]

Cornelius Dougherty was another trader whose influence in two cultures, not wealth, made him a master trader. According to the lore of early frontier historians, he was around 120 years old when he died in 1788. He was certainly very old indeed, for he himself stated that he had been active in the Cherokee trade since 1719.[17] Cornelius became an important trader at Hiwassie where both cultures respected his opinions on Cherokee-Carolina relations. His Indian wife ensured him an esteemed niche in her society, and Governor Glen referred to him as "always a willing Composer of Differences." Although illiterate, he frequently acted as interpreter and often visited Charles Town as an official escort of bands of Cherokees. Unfortunately, prominence did not assure business success and by the 1750s, although he owned African slaves and some of his business ventures involved thousands of pounds in currency, he was often in debt.

Governors and other officials actively sought the advice of master traders about events in their parts of the world. In 1753 Beamer was summoned before Glen to inform him about the truth behind rumors of Cherokee "Dissatisfaction or Disorder." In this instance, Beamer was the spokesman for all the Cherokee traders. He reassured Glen that all was currently peaceful, despite Virginia's attempts to increase its trade with the Cherokees and despite the continued and increasing threat from the French and their allies. Beamer also petitioned for forts among both the Lower and Upper Cherokees, something headmen and traders alike believed would safeguard the trade by giving Indians and traders a secure place of refuge in times of trouble. Beamer warned Glen of the dangers inherent in letting too many unsupervised lesser traders among the Cherokees, especially the "white Men, who under the Notion of Traders, live a debauched and wicked Life, and have Nothing to do, and for Want of Subsistence become a Burthen to the Cherokee Indians."[18]

Middling and Lower Ranks of Traders

Most men in the profession did not become master traders, but struggled for a decent job with fair compensation for their efforts.[19] Cherokee trader James Adair was one of the men who failed to amass a fortune. He had been a Catawba and Chickasaw trader before venturing into the even riskier Choctaw trade, and he finally settled down among the Cherokees. When all these failed, he wrote his influential book, *The History of the American Indians*, published in 1775, partly to vindicate his past conduct, partly to castigate Governor Glen for his attempt to monopolize the Choctaw trade, and partly to make some money while presenting his firsthand evidence to support the theory that the Indians were the descendants of the lost tribes of Israel.[20]

Some middling traders combined settling on the frontier with trade, especially after the late 1730s. Herman Geiger, a recent German immigrant, and George Haig were two prominent men from the Congaree area. Geiger's inventory of goods reflected his combination of planting and trading. He owned cattle and horses, a grindstone, scales and weights, a fully

FIGURE 6.3
THE SOUTHEAST IN 1755

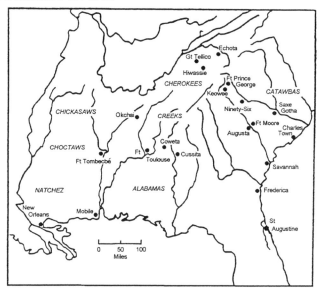

equipped trading boat, twenty-one wagons, and tackle for eight horses. He also owned slaves.[21] Haig's October 1749 probate inventory captured the possessions of a man killed in his prime, one combining the roles of trader and frontier planter. The trading paraphernalia included an old brass scale with lead weights and ten horses, fifteen packhorses, and forty-four mares and colts. Other items listed were sheep and hogs, five chamber pots, sixteen old law and history books, forty-two gallons of rum, and an old silver-hilted sword.[22]

It is impossible to evaluate the middle and lower ranks of traders categorically, for the evidence is too patchy. Economic success, social status, and respect were as important in delineating lesser traders from middling-ranked ones as it was for deliniating master traders. Respect and friendship between Indians and Europeans did not depend solely on wealth. Not every longtime trader amassed a fortune, but survival and contentment with the way of life required acceptance both by Indians and by colonial authorities. Some might progress from servant to middling trader. Loss of just one cargo, however, could mean ruin and a return to a lower rank.

Many of the lesser traders were almost indistinguishable from the traders' servants and slaves in the way of life they maintained in the nations. While there were huge profits to be made in the trade, many of the lesser traders died possessing little of real value. Alexander Long was well known for his many years among the Indians, language skills, and previous infamy.

Long had been a trader among the Indians since at least 1711, first among the Yuchis and later among the Cherokees. In 1712 he and Eleazer Wigan had manipulated the destruction of the Yuchi town of Chestowe. Long felt that he had been "abused" by the Yuchis about two years earlier when he had demanded payment of outstanding debts. Instead of receiving financial satisfaction, Long had been partially scalped. When Wigan and Long led a force of Cherokees against the Yuchis to enslave them as redemption of their debts and to satisfy Long's wish for revenge, the Yuchi men preferred to kill first their women and children, then commit suicide, rather than submit to capture and slavery.[23]

Long stayed a fugitive among the remoter Overhill Cherokees for many years while officials and planters in the lowcountry condemned this deed. During the 1720s Long wrote a journal and a "Small Postscript" that he believed would be of interest and value to the colonial government in understanding Native American customs, so he petitioned the assembly for funds to take it to London. This request was rejected, for although his knowledge of Cherokee life was acknowledged, the assembly decided that he had no new insights to offer "even if they could be depended on." His past history was the major stumbling block that prevented this literate trader from entering the ranks of the respected and wealthy. No doubt his years in exile among the Cherokees and later possibly among the "French Indians," pro-French Creeks, ensured that he had had little chance of amassing capital or regaining respectability. Few merchants would risk giving him their goods on credit. His will inventory, dated May 16, 1763, recorded few possessions, the most valuable of which were his five horses.[24]

Most of the 583 traders who can be traced as active from 1717 to 1755 were probably men like Long who straddled the lower levels of the trade. One hundred and ninety-one, or about 33 percent, of the participants warranted just one reference in the sources, as did Anthony Galloher and James McNally, mentioned in the *South Carolina Gazette* in 1735 as finding and burying the body of trader George Stevens after his violent death in Indian Country. James Ballensis escaped eternal anonymity when the *Gazette* reported that he had "drop'd from his Horse" and died suddenly in 1733. Another trader mentioned only once in the historic record was John Cameron, who broke out of Charles Town jail on January 5, 1752. He was there "on an action of debt, at the suit of messrs. Stuart and Reid."[25] Such individuals may have been small traders in their own right, or "licensed men," that is, added to a master trader's license as his employee.

The Indian trade was a family business for many a lower caste of trader, especially for mixed-blood offspring. William, Edward, and an unnamed Broadway (sometimes Broody), a father and two sons, worked for James

Francis and James Beamer as packhorse men and interpreters. Thomas Welch was a leading early trader in the Chickasaw trade and his half-Chickasaw offspring, James, Joseph, and Thomas, Jr., were all active in the trade.[26]

White "Hirelings"—Bound and Free Servants

Most of those who attempted to make a living for themselves began and ended their careers as "hirelings," usually functioning as packhorse men. Some could not even be counted as servants, either free or indentured, but were slaves—a term encompassing both blacks and Native Americans. Most of their names have not survived in the records. When officials and respectable traders wished to find scapegoats, they could always blame these powerless individuals. Some servants were hired to take care of specific functions, such as maintaining a store in an Indian village for a substantial trader. Jeremiah Swiney was employed as a storekeeper by William Clements in the Lower Creek town of Oconees until he was killed by Iroquois in 1750. The first rumors of his death were regarded as "Apocrypha" because the official reporting the incident did not trust Clements. It was later confirmed that Swiney and another servant, Jenks, as well as a leading Chickasaw, were dead and the store plundered and burned. Charles Jordan worked in the 1750s as a storekeeper in Coweta for Peter Randon, or Randall, a middling-ranked trader, who in his turn was employed by master trader John Pettigrew. While Jordan was literate and therefore perhaps of higher standing than most packhorse men, he behaved as generally expected of such a lowly servant by getting drunk with the Indians and running around Coweta naked. Many of these men found Indian society more accepting and charitable than their own, and chose a way of life that made them open to charges of being "white Indians."[27]

Some servants acted as unlicensed traders while employed by a licensed trader. This practice was constantly attacked because these men acted "with the same ffooting as the Principal" but usually without adequate supervision. Master traders and government officials criticized this practice, for respectable traders paid for licenses and bonds to "give security for behaviour" of their servants and there were no such guarantees in these cases.[28]

Many "hirelings" were indentured servants. Some of the lesser-to-middling-sized traders by the 1750s had entered the trade in that fashion. Bernard Hughes, active in the Cherokee trade in the 1750s, was probably the "Barnard Hughs," an Irish servant aged around twenty-five, whose master advertised for him as a runaway speaking "but indifferent English" in 1737. Trader and influential Creek Mary Musgrove's second European husband was her former indentured servant, Jacob Mathews.[29]

The Scottish Jacobite prisoners sent to frontier garrisons in 1716 as bound servant-soldiers often stayed to become traders when their sentences were over. They had acquired familiarity with the Indians and traders who visited the forts, and they could transfer the skills and knowledge of Indian ways and languages they acquired at their frontier garrisons into a future career. Creek master trader of the 1750s, Ludovic Grant, had arrived as prisoner on the *Susannah* in 1716. Many others on that ship and on its companion, the *Wakefield,* such as Lachlan McBean or McBain, many McGillivrays and McQueens, later became familiar names in the Indian trade network.[30]

Some servants who entered the trade in the aftermath of the 1715 Yamasee War did indeed find it an avenue to advancement. Menial employees of the colony of South Carolina in 1717 emerged as traders in their own right within a decade. The most notable of these, so probably the most exceptional, was the literate Scotsman David Dowey. He began as a packhorse man for the province in 1718 earning £160 currency per year while in charge of buying and then driving the horses to the Cherokee factor—the colonial official charged with overseeing the Cherokee trade. Dowey was suspected at that time of "Designs" of defecting to Virginia to evade his debts. He was, however, still involved in the South Carolina trade in 1751 and was proud of his thirty-two years among the Cherokees, stating that he had "always traded on his own account" in the remoter Overhill area.[31]

The other successful survivor was Thomas Devall. He, too, began as a packhorse man among the Catawbas but became an influential trader among the Upper Creeks. The natives must have respected him highly for one chief took the English name of "Devall's Landlord." Despite one rebuke for taking black slaves illegally to Indian country, he was generally commended by Carolina officials for his skill as an interpreter and for his hospitality. He rose from government-employed packhorse man in 1717 to independent trader within ten years and was active until his death in 1761. He was among the eleven of the sixty-two traceable packhorse men who were clearly literate, and one of only five known to have owned slaves, a symbol of social and material success in the colonial southeast.[32]

Probably more typical than these two were men such as William Mackrachun and Edward Carroll. Mackrachun warranted one reference in the few surviving Indian Books, the accounts kept by the colony of South Carolina to cover the meetings of the Indian Affairs Committee, when he, one of John Pettigrew's employees, was killed by a young Chickasaw in 1752. Carroll was shot in Cherokee country in February 1748 after incurring the wrath of an Indian, who had called him a "Devil & a Witch," although an English eyewitness did not believe he had done anything to provoke such an attack. The Indians did not want to avenge his death because he was "not a

Trader," maintaining that it was "hard to take the Life of one of their Warriors for what was as nothing." In this case, South Carolina's authorities finally managed to convince the Upper Cherokees that all British lives lost in the interior had to be avenged, however unimportant the victim had been, just as Indians avenged their dead and demanded similar justice from the colonial authorities.[33]

Black and Indian "Hirelings"

Blacks and Indians also participated directly in this Carolina trading network. Most were slaves, but there were exceptions. In 1711, two traders paid a bond to the colony pledging the good conduct of three "Indians that trade for them." In this instance, they were not regarded as slaves but as employees. After the Yamasee War and in the confusion of restructuring the trade, at least two Indians were active employees of the government's monopoly. Cherokee factor William Hatton received compensation in December 1717 for the interpreting services of his slave Indian Jack. Indian Sauhoe received £3 a month plus an allowance as packhorse man in the Creek trade. He was cheap labor compared to the £10 a month that John Carrell, Alexander Muckele, and Daniel Kennard received for the same job title and work.[34]

Several Indians worked as hired traders for prominent employers, according to the Cherokee chief called the Raven of Hiwassee in 1751. In suggesting a punishment for some Cherokee towns that had planned the murder of trader Daniel Murphy and the theft of goods from Bernard Hughes's store, the Raven suggested that those towns should not only have their traders removed, but also that "no Indian nor Half-breed should be Factor from any white Man among them, till [the towns] acknowledge their Faults, and see the Want of a white Man, and that they themselves, and their Women and Children should have weary Leggs to walk to Traders in other Towns to buy what they want." The Gun Merchant, a leading Creek chief, probably acquired his English name from acting in that capacity.[35]

Officials were terrified that blacks and Native Americans could find a common cause and foment an uprising against the white settlers. The trading regulations of 1751 declared that "it shall not be lawfull for any Indian Trader to employ any Negro or other Slave in the Indian Country," and set the fine at £100. The Indian nations were a "Natural Fortification" to the English colonies, barriers against runaway blacks as much as against other European powers. Still, traders ignored the law and increasingly used slaves in their businesses. In 1725 George Chicken complained to Arthur Middleton, the president of the council, that minor government officials John Sharp and Captain William Hatton were among the worst offenders, and he wished them to forfeit £100 of their bond for holding black slaves in Indian country. Interestingly enough, Chicken's major reason for making an example of these rather prominent men was that their slaves could speak Cherokee, and Chicken feared their ability to "tell falcities to the Indians." A house committee in May 1742 discouraged "Euchees or other Indians" from coming "into the Settlements," for it was especially important that the Indians should not "have any Intercourse with the Slaves at any Plantation." Indian agents and commissioners worried about allowing surveys of lands too close to Indian towns: "It is necessary to keep up [the Catawbas] as a distinct People to be a distinct Check upon the runaway Slaves who might otherwise get to a head in the Woods and prove as mischevious a thorn in our sides as the fugitive Slaves in Jamaica did in theirs." In May 1751 the dangers of allowing the races to mix in the backcountry were stressed, when six slaves were "seduced by the half breed with [trader James] Maxwell to run off to the Cherokees." Only three of these were ever recovered.[36]

Traders constantly brought blacks into the nations despite official concerns. One named Timboe was active in the Creek trade in 1718 for his master, Colonel Alexander Mackey. Mackey was awarded £2 a month for Timboe's five-month-long "extraordinary Service, and being Linguist." In 1752, trader Robert Steil outfitted one unnamed black, and according to a government-employed interpreter, the Catawbas complained, for they did not like having him among them.[37]

Most accounts of blacks in Indian country were official warrants against the owners, or documented the attempts of agents to seize or purchase runaways from the Indians. Tobias Fitch in 1725 had a frustrating time trying to recover a black slave from the Creeks at Apalachicola. The "Negro Sat in the Square in a Bould Manner" along with two Spaniards, and the local chief steadfastly refused to surrender him. Fitch also failed to recover four slaves belonging to trader John Sharp, as well as a white woman kept as a slave by the Creek chief known as the Dog King. In 1753 three Frenchmen and John Case a "Mallotta" born in Virginia, escaped their English trader escort while hunting for buffalo on their way down to Charles Town from Chickasaw country. Case was reckoned an "extraordinary woodsman," so not surprisingly, these men were never captured.[38]

Work Categories: Packhorse Men

Trade-related jobs and skills were not confined to the above status levels. Packhorse men were in charge of the horses and of all the equipment needed to get the long caravans of goods and hides safely to and from Indian country. By the 1740s, Archibald McGillivray and Company employed fifteen packhorse men to take charge of 103 horses working under one trader. The work of the hirelings and servants may have been menial, but it was not easy and often required a high degree of skill. Captains such as John Coleman possessed impressive logistical skills to direct horses and goods over flooded streams and through dense forests, which often harbored hostile Indians. All packhorse men needed the same basic hunting and survival skills as higher-ranked participants in the trade. They were, however, at the mercy of their employers and government officials, as well as of the Indians.[39]

In his 1755 survey of the Indian trade, its management, and its weaknesses, Edmond Atkin singled out the misbehavior of traders and their employees as the major evil. He especially blamed traders for "permitting and employing their Servants, even Pack horse Men, whom they have sent to and left in Towns alone, to trade with the Indians; whose Behaviour, being for the most part the most worthless of Men, is more easy to be conceived than described."[40] In the same fashion that Indian leaders blamed bloody incidents on the hot blood of their younger tribal members, so too did whites blame packhorse men for all kinds of misdemeanors, ranging from raping native women to cheating their native customers. The loquacious James Glen used this convention often. In June 1748 he mentioned the great expense and other impositions made on the government by "Obscure Indian Traders and Packhorsemen" through their "lying Letters and false Reports." In the particular incident that then incurred his wrath, persons "who could neither read nor write" had managed to spread rumors that were costly to South Carolina. The "panic of 1751" resulted in scores of Anglo-Americans leaving the backcountry believing that war was about to erupt between Cherokees and Carolinians. This was directly the result of rumors spread by the lower elements in both British and Cherokee trading circles.[41] Packhorse men, those on the bottom of the trading strata, were an easy group for their superiors to castigate, often in an attempt to deflect criticism away from their own activities.[42]

There were many more packhorse men engaged in the Indian trade than the handful whose names have survived. A 1735 petition of leading South Carolina merchants to lieutenant governor Thomas Broughton stressed the importance of the trade not only in terms of the "Seventy Six or Seventy Eight Thousand Deer Skins" exported yearly, but also because it helped "the poorer sort of People there being no less than Three hundred who find constant Employment therein." Of the traceable 583 participants in the Indian trade, sixty-two were referred to as packhorse men or some other kind of servant. Since nearly every trader of any substance needed help with the transportation of goods, the actual number must have approached at least 200 a year from the mid-1720s onward.[43]

Initially, the trade depended on Indian "burtheners" (burdeners), individuals who bore packs of skins on their backs along the well-worn Indian paths to the lowcountry. As far as European officials were concerned, these men were not always trustworthy. In 1716 twenty-one Indians arrived at Charles Town, each toting a pack of hides sent from the Cherokee factor; yet only fifteen packs had been packed and sent from the nation. An investigation showed that the bundles had been divided and repacked en route by these porters so that more tribal members would receive gifts for their services, an action that was profitable to their society.[44]

The Native Americans themselves were increasingly critical of this system. One reason for Cherokee receptivity to an increasing Virginia trade initiative in the early 1720s was that the Virginians did not treat Indians as beasts of burden but employed horses. George Chicken, former Indian trader, Yamassee War hero, negotiator, and Indian trade commissioner, had complained that Indian carriers would "not carry any burthens with out being first payed and as I am informed very often leave their burthens half way of the place they are designed to be Carried to, So that the Traders are Obliged to pay double burthenage for every Pack." Natives needed such strong incentives to act as porters for they realized that those who took goods to the European lowlands were increasingly likely to contract new and fatal diseases. No wonder, then, that by the mid-1720s, horses were increasingly familiar in the hinterland and were the preferred means of transportation, creating a demand for servants.[45]

By 1735 over 800 horses were involved in the trade. Will inventories of traders who died while still active in the trade showed that the most successful kept a stock of horses, both as packhorses and for their personal transportation. Upper Creek trader John Eycott, dead by 1751, possessed nineteen packhorses, nineteen packsaddles, and three "covering skins to each saddle," as well as fifteen other horses. When the half-Indian Thomas Brown, Jr., died in 1748, his horses were valued at £720.[46] References to the bells that traders attached to their horses when they left them while at camp emphasized the high value placed on horses, as did the energy that officials expended to retrieve strayed or stolen horses that had been acquired by Indians but claimed by traders as their property.[47] Horse stealing became so rampant that the *South-Carolina Gazette* ran a front-page story about it in July 1739, believing the problem was "occasioned . . . by Pack-horse-men and others picking up Horses in the Settlements and selling them in the Indian Countries." As late as 1752 Glen complained about the Creeks "carrying off great numbers of horses from our Traders among the Cherokees, and our Outsettlements . . . under pretense that they were Indian Horses."[48]

Packhorse men who can be traced over time were atypical either as constant troublemakers or for rising from lowly rank to later respectability. Many packhorse men seem to have been rovers by nature; indeed, they have been called the "true driftwood of Carolina society." John Carney, hired by the colonial administration as a packhorse man in 1717, was a former soldier. He was discharged, rehired, and then finally "deserted the Service," all in the space of a few months. In January 1724 a trader's request to employ another renegade Frenchman was rejected on the grounds that he might be a spy and so should not be allowed "into Indian Country." One of James Beamer's packhorse men in the late 1750s was a Frenchman who had deserted from the French in 1752.[49]

Interpreters

Interpreters might be traders and their servants, or Indians, Europeans, or Africans who were not otherwise directly involved in the trade. Some of the best interpreters were of low status, such as packhorse men or lesser traders. A few individuals were employed officially by the province of South Carolina as interpreters, but they were not educated, high-status men.[50] Many were unable to write their own names, something that was not crucial as most Europeans also functioned in a mostly oral culture. One of these was Stephen Forrest, employed in the 1740s as the official interpreter to the Lower Creek nation at a salary of £150 a year. As he was illiterate, he petitioned for a secretary to help with official communications. The assembly decided to increase his salary to £200 out of which Forrest himself could pay for an assistant. He was dismissed from his post in 1748 and took out a license to trade among the Creeks but was subsequently employed as an interpreter on an as-needed basis. He was, for example, hired to aid colonial envoy Thomas Bosomworth on his mission to the Creeks in 1752, but when Bosomworth met him, Forrest was "in Liquor" and the talks stalled until Forrest was sober.[51]

As the surviving records were written by officials and employers, they give the impression that trader-interpreters were not always responsible or respectable. Ambrose Davis, alias the Collier, was a lesser trader and interpreter to the Cherokees by the 1750s. Agent James May wrote to Governor Glen that Davis "abused the Prince & Head Men of Ioree" and had refused to aid him in arresting a troublemaker. Yet, Davis was continuously in demand as an interpreter, later employed by Colonel William Byrd of Virginia at the new Fort Prince George at Keowee for £1 a day and was commended for his "great Care and Diligence." He even rendered conspicuously valiant service during the 1760 Cherokee siege of that fort.[52]

Creek trader John Barton was another illiterate interpreter active by the 1730s. He was interpreter to Georgia's Indian agent, Patrick McKay, in 1735 although neither of them was happy in their relationship. McKay knew of Barton's reputation as "the boldest linguister in the Province of Carolina, Yet I shall keep him no longer then I've deliver'd the talk to the Indians." Barton had tried to avoid going with McKay. He only condescended when he got his allowance raised first to £35 a day plus two horses, and then finally, when McKay was in despair because others had also refused to work for him, to £40.[53]

When Native American leaders came to Charles Town or Savannah for treaty renewals and other formal ceremonies, interpreting was entrusted to leading traders such as Lachlan McGillivray, Eleazer Wigan, Robert Bunning, and James Beamer. They had long proven their reliability and skill in translating native customs and languages. Robert Bunning had lived and traded among the Lower Cherokees since before the Yamasee War. He had visited England as the official interpreter to leading Cherokee chiefs in 1730 and was still interpreting in 1758 for £20 currency a month. Acting as interpreter when needed was a sideline, for he remained a trader in his own right.[54]

The best "linguists" were often the Indian wives of traders or the offspring of such unions. When an interpreter was needed in 1717 to aid a garrison and trading factory, an agent reported that the colony had access to "an Indian Woman, for that Purpose." Another, only identified as "Bartlet's Wife," played a similar role in listening to and determining Creek grievances in 1735. James Beamer's Cherokee son, Thomas, was a man of some property who acted as a trader and interpreter and who was accepted in both white and Indian worlds.[55]

Some Indians who were not the products of mixed marriages were also interpreters. "Captain Caesar," an influential Cherokee chief in the 1750s, was often used as an interpreter. He was a leading influence on the person the English regarded as the head of the Cherokee nation, the Young Emperor, and he was a shrewd diplomat along with his other skills. He interpreted at Charles Town "for the Young King" in May 1751. In June 1749, a "Notchee interpreter" was used in talks with the Natchez Indians, and in 1763 a Catawba chief, referred to as Colonel Ayers, often interpreted for his nation.[56]

Illegal Traders

The colonies of South Carolina and Georgia spent much time and concern over the regulation of their respective Indian trades. Officials knew that the actions of a trader who cheated his clients could make a nation swing away from its reliance on the British trading system and respond positively to the overtures for trade and friendship that came from the Spanish in Florida and increasingly from the French, located at the mouth of the Mississippi. Many traders, however, wanted to work as unfettered by regulations as possible. There were always individuals who participated illegally in the trade, that is, without taking out licenses and posting bonds in South Carolina or Georgia. Others held licenses but broke some rules that hurt their profits, especially Georgia's total ban on selling rum within its boundaries or to its client Indians. There were more unlicensed traders among the Cherokees than other Indian nations because of their remoter location. Edmond Atkin in the 1750s stressed that these men "being the lowest People, having little thought of paying their Creditors for their goods, often greatly undersell the fair Licensed Traders, which makes the Indian very uneasy, suspecting therefrom that the latter wrong them." Some, like Samuel Elsenore, would "meet the Indians in the Woods" at the end of their winter hunts and get their skins before they returned to their towns. The traders who had outfitted them with guns and provisions on account were the losers.[57]

Protests against illegal traders came from the respectable participants in the trade. As Indian commissioner William Pinckney reported to the assembly in 1749, he "hath had frequent Application . . . by the licensed Traders for Redress against Interlopers and Persons visiting and trading with the Indian Nations without License . . . to the great Prejudice of the licensed Trader." Pinckney wanted more authority placed into the hands of officials to "enable him to support the honest and fair Traders." While a licensed trader's goods could be seized for breaking the law, there was no such provision against illegal traders. It was not surprising that legitimate traders complained of the actions of those who did not have the money or inclination to post bond and obey the law. Middling trader James Adair warned against the "Arab-like pedlars [who] skulk about" in the villages. These "lawless traders had furnished the Indians . . . with so great a quantity of prohibited liquors, [that it] might enable some of them to decoy the savages to squandering away thousands of drest deer-skins."[58]

Some of the traders who at one time or another had an acceptable role in the network traded illegally on other occasions without giving a bond at Charles Town or Savannah. It was sometimes hard to get to the cities to post bond and take out licenses at the correct time of year. Lachlan McGillivray explained in 1754 how he had lost his license for his usual Upper Creek towns the previous year because his duties to the colony had made it impossible for him to go down to Charles Town. Chickasaw and Choctaw traders were usually exempted from having to apply in person every year because of the great distances involved.

Lowcountry Storekeepers and the Trade

Other individuals outside the network of Indians, traders, and export-import merchants profited, if sporadically, from the trade. These included the men and women who received money for "entertaining" the Indians when they visited either Charles Town or Savannah for formal meetings with the authorities. Minor artisans, such as tailors, saddlers, and gunsmiths, who were not part of the direct exchange of goods and furs also furnished essential services that contributed to a successful trading experience for Indians and whites alike.

By the end of the 1730s, many of those who fed the Native Americans and otherwise aided them on their way down to the settlements were small planters and storekeepers, including many widows. Elizabeth Haig Mercier remarried twice but retained the store at the Congarees where she and George Haig had settled. She assumed Haig's role as storekeeper, catering to the needs of the growing white elements in that area. Her home remained a place where Indians stopped on their way from Cherokee country as it lay close to the major Indian trail to the lowcountry. She received money from the assembly in 1752 for entertaining sixty-six Cherokees on their way to Charles Town in 1751 and £18.17.6 for "dieting" seven Catawbas in August 1750.[59] Major Charles Russell, a former commander of the fort "at the Congarees," died in 1737. His widow, Mary, remained in the area (present day Columbia, S.C.) and provided for her children with a small plantation and store. She was regularly compensated by the Commons House of Assembly for her Indian expenses.[60]

Accounts for entertaining Indians in Charles Town showed that not only the most prosperous merchants dealing in imports benefitted from the Indian trade, but also many small traders and artisans. Every visit by a group of Indians was followed by a spate of bills for the assembly's consideration, ranging from pasturage and stabling for Indian horses to food and drink for the Indians themselves.[61] Silversmiths, such as Alexander Petrie in 1748, made "ear bobs" for the Indians, and saddlers such as John Laurens and Benjamin Addison repaired or made saddles. Tailors John Owen and Andrew Taylor submitted accounts for making "cloaths" for the Indians in the 1740s and 1750s. Gunsmiths repaired and cleaned Indian guns, since they did not have constant access to maintain their weapons in prime condition in their nations. Miscellaneous items bought as presents for the Indians included swan shot, rum, and sugar, as well as the usual cloth, flags, drums, and hats.[62] The local physicians also made money when the Indians were in town. In 1735 Nicholas Lynch and John Martini received payment for supplying "Physick and bleeding some Indians," and in February 1750 the assembly considered a bill from a carpenter for "Making Coffins for Indians."[63]

Not all accounts were paid. The assembly and its committee for petitions and accounts scrutinized every bill for additions, inflation, and unnecessary expenses. Susannah Brunett's account was rejected by the committee on petitions and accounts. She had asked for £26.5 "for keeping and maintaining Indians at Saludy old Town" but this was rejected as "being in the Out Settlements and in their hunting Ground." The Indians therefore should have taken care of their own provisions on their own land. One of Mary Russell's accounts in 1742 was reduced by £7.10, for there "is no Manner of necessity of giving the Indians Sugar, upon the Road." This was part of a general tirade against the current high cost of Indian accounts in general. In the old days, the visitors only needed "a little Corn, or Rice and Beef," which they could get at any plantation, and were "very well satisfied. . . . But of late the Traders, or Persons who come down with them, carry them to almost every Tavern on the Road, where they are supplied with Liquor; which tends greatly to augment the Article of Indian Expenses."[64]

By May 1748 the assembly challenged Governor Glen's assertion that Indian expenses were not unreasonable. The annual cost of South Carolina's Indian gifts and diplomacy was over £12,000. Glen countered that Indians expected presents and lavish entertainment as necessary preliminaries to the ritual of any formal negotiations. The assembly continued, indeed accelerated, its policy of paring Indian expenses as much as possible. Glen believed such actions would damage the whole structure of Indian diplomacy if people refused to feed the Indians on their way down unless the natives had "ready Money."[65]

Conclusion

By 1755 the Indian trade was no longer regarded as a business whose success or failure had repercussions for most Carolinians, and it had become increasingly difficult for Governor Glen and others to claim that hundreds of colonial lives and fortunes depended on costly protection for the trade and its personnel and on lavish gifts to leading chiefs. Few leading import-export merchants felt compelled to champion the profession. Not one was involved exclusively in the Indian trade, as they increasingly invested in other ventures. South Carolina's exports included more indigo and rice than skins or Indian slaves while African slaves supplanted Indian trade goods among the leading imports. The future seemed to lie with developing plantation agriculture, and the Indians were increasingly regarded as a barrier to that system's expansion.

The Indian trade and its hierarchy crumbled even further with the advent of the Cherokee and Seven Years' Wars. Traders who were already prosperous by 1750 managed to weather those storms, but it was no longer a venture that attracted ambitious Carolinians and Georgians. The already well-established Augusta Company's partners might prosper and grow in the Creek trade, but the middle and lower "hirelings" found it increasingly dif-

FIGURE 6.4
A CHEROKEE NETWORK, C. 1755

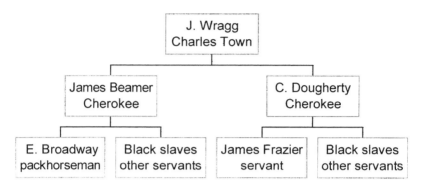

ficult to acquire a fortune in the trade, although those content to remain employees of a company could at least find employment. Many traders gave up on the Indian side of business, remaining in their old frontier homes to sell goods and equipment to the white settlers and their African slaves who swarmed into the backcountry as the Native Americans and their trade increasingly retreated to the west.

Notes

1. For statistics relating to Charles Town's overseas trade, see Converse D. Clowse, *Measuring Charleston's Overseas Commerce, 1717–1767: Statistics from the Port's Naval Lists* (Washington, D.C.: University Press of America, 1981). Charleston was officially "Charles Town" until 1784.

2. In the past, the trade has been regarded as part of Indian history more than as a part of the development of South Carolina and Georgia's diplomatic and economic history. One notable exception is Edward G. Cashin, *Lachlan McGillivray, Indian Trader: The Shaping of the Southern Indian Frontier* (Athens: University of Georgia Press, 1992).

3. Unfortunately, most of the "Indian books," separate recording of council meetings dealing with Indian affairs, have been lost. Some are still included within the journals of the meetings of South Carolina's Council (hereafter cited as SC-CJ).

4. Eirlys M. Barker, "Much Blood and Treasure: South Carolina's Indian Traders, 1670–1755" (Ph.D. diss., College of William and Mary, 1993), chap. 6, concerning the trade's regulation after 1717. For maps of "Indian country," see David H. Corkran, *The Creek Frontier, 1540–1783* (Norman: University of Oklahoma Press, 1967), 50; Charles Hudson, *The Southeastern Indians* (Knoxville: University of Tennessee Press, 1976), 430–31; Theda Purdue, *Slavery and the Evolution of Cherokee Society, 1540–1866* (Knoxville: University of Tennessee Press, 1979), 27.

5. I have tracked the 1670–1755 participants on a database compiled from official records, wills, probate records, court records, *South Carolina Gazette*, etc. The statistics for this article concentrate on those active in the trade in the Indian towns between 1717 and 1755, not on the import-export merchants. The surviving records are not complete enough to give a definitive quantified result but do give one a feel for the kinds of persons who entered the trade and were prominent in it.

6. An example is Governor James Glen's description of Cherokee trader Robert Kelly on hearing of his 1749 death at the hands of French-allied Indians. South Carolina Department of History and Archives (hereafter cited as SCDAH), W. Noel Sainsbury, comp., Records in the British Public Record Office Relating to South Carolina (hereafter cited as BPRO-SCDAH), 23:451.

7. W. L. McDowell, *Colonial Records of South Carolina: Documents Relating to Indian Affairs, 1750–1754* (hereafter cited as *Indian Affairs, 1750–1754*) (Columbia: South Carolina Archives Dept., 1958), Thomas Bosomworth's journal, 21 Sept. 1752, 289–90.

8. Charles Town Wills and Inventories (hereafter cited as CT Wills), bk. X (1765–1769), 250–52, SCDAH Francis Roche's estate totaled £18,220.9.6 South Carolina currency in January 1768, including all of the above as well as a backgammon table.

9. Ibid., bk. W (1763–1737), 159–67. He held five bonds or notes that were used as the exchange media since specie was scarce in the colony. By this time, the exchange rate was around £1.00 sterling to £7.00 South Carolina currency. See "Colonial Currency," *South Carolina Genealogical and Historical Magazine* 28 (1927): 138–39.

10. For McGillivray's extraordinary career, see Cashin, *Lachlan McGillivray*. Cashin's book is refreshing in its examination of both the Scottish and American roots of this extraordinary person.

11. Verner W. Crane, *The Southern Frontier: 1670–1732* (1928; reprint, New York: W. W. Norton, 1981), 274; SCDAH, Judgment Rolls, Court of Common Pleas, 1752, box 33A, no. 62A. His widow, Rebecca, was a member of the influential Brewton merchant family.

12. McDowell, *Indian Affairs, 1750–1754;* McGillivray to Glen, 14 Apr. 1754, 501–2. He was updating Glen about "the present State of the Nation," even when there was no real news. Barker "Much Blood and Treasure," chap. 7.

13. Baker, "Much Blood," 78, 323.

14. McDowell, *Indian Affairs, 1750–1754,* appendix to Bosomworth's journal, Nov. 1752, 329–30. Agents acted as policemen and magistrates, checking licenses and listening to trader and Indian disputes.

15. Kathryn E. Holland Braund, "Mutual Convenience—Mutual Dependence: the Creeks, Augusta, and the Deerskin Trade, 1733–1783" (Ph.D. diss., Florida State University, 1986), 37–38, 43–46; Kathryn E. Holland Braund, *Deerskin and Duffels: The Creek Indian Trade with Anglo-America, 1685–1815* (Lincoln: University of Nebraska Press, 1993), 42–43; Robert L. Meriwether, *The Expansion of South Carolina: 1729–1765* (Kingsport, Tenn.: Southern Publishers, 1940), 53, 191; Oct. 1749, Allen D. Candler, *Colonial Records of Georgia* (hereafter cited as *CRG*), 32 vols. (Atlanta: Franklin Publishing Co., 1906), 6:225.

16. W. L. McDowell, *Colonial Records of South Carolina: Documents Relating to Indian Affairs, 1754–65* (hereafter cited as *Indian Affairs, 1754–65*) (Columbia: South Carolina Archives Dept., 1970), xiii; Beamer to Glen, 22 Sept. 1754, 8–9. SCDAH, Records of the Secretary of the Province, Works Progress Administration Transcripts, vol. 64 (1731–1733), 253, 262; J. H. Easterby, ed., *Journal of the Commons House of Assembly, Jan. 19–June 29, 1748* (Columbia: SC Archives Dept., 1961), 327; Glen to Upper and Lower Cherokees, 5 July 1753, McDowell, *Indian Affairs, 1750–1754,* 442.

17. J. G. M. Ramsey, *Annals of Tennessee* (Charleston: John Russell, 1853), 63; McDowell, *Indian Affairs, 1750–1754,* 112, 115, 449. No doubt Cornelius's illiteracy was a contributing factor to the various spellings of his name: Douty, D'Hartie, Docherty, Doharty, Dogherty, Dorothy, etc. Perhaps the "Dohery" in the trade from Virginia in 1690 was his father.

18. In November 1751 he was to interpret and assist ninety Indians. Terry W. Lipscomb and R. Nicholas Olsberg, eds., *Journal of the Commons House of Assembly* (hereafter cited as *JCHA*) Nov. 1751 to Oct. 1752 (Columbia: University of South Carolina Press, 1977), 119. McDowell, *Indian Affairs, 1754–65,* 330, 446–47; in May 1758 another Cherokee trader, Robert Gowdie sued him for repayment of a debt of £10,407.18.2; see SCDAH, Judgment Rolls, Court of Common Pleas, 1758, box 45B, no. 56A. Gowdie received £100 damages.

19. It is almost impossible to quantify the different ranks in the trade; not only are the financial records incomplete, but status also depended on intangible factors such as respect. The personnel also slipped in and out of these blanket categories, but there were probably about twenty master traders among the Creeks and Cherokees at one time.

20. For his impact on the Choctaw trade and revolt, see Barker, "Much Blood and Treasure," 319–20; James Adair, *History of the American Indians* (1775), ed. Samuel Cole Williams (New York: Promontory Press, 1986).

21. CT Will Inventories, bk. R (1) (1751–1753): 107–9. One slave, William Smith, was valued at £380.

22. Ibid., bk. B (1748–1751): 174–76, dated 30 Oct. 1749. See Barker, "Much Blood and Treasure," 333–35, for his death.

23. *JCHA,* 13 Apr. 1725; William Sumner Jenkins, comp. Records of the States of the United States of America (microfilms, Washington, DC, 1949), South Carolina A1a/1/3, 299, 300, 304 (hereafter abbreviated as RSUS, with references to category/reel/unit, page number); W. L. McDowell, *Journals of the Commissioners of the Indian Trade, 1710–18* (hereafter cited as *JCIT*) (Columbia: SC Archives Dept., 1955), 55.

24. A. Long, "A Small Postscript 1725," ed., David Corkran, *Southern Indian Studies* 21 (1969): n.p.; 14 Apr. 1725, JCHA, RUSUS A1a/1/2/p. 304; CT Will Inventories, bk. V (1761–1763), 441.

25. *South Carolina Gazette,* 5 Apr. 1735, 25 Aug. 1733, 8 Jan. 1752.

26. SC–CJ, RSUS E1p/5/2, 62, 76; McDowell, *Indian Affairs, 1750–1754,* 51; CT wills, vol. 62A (1729–1731), 199; SCDAH, Records of the Public Treasurers of South Carolina, 1725–1776, SCDAH microfilms M/3, reel 1, 1727; *South Carolina Gazette,* 30 Dec. 1732, account of "half-breed" Thomas's death at the hands of Choctaws; 21 May 1765, McDowell, *Indian Affairs, 1754–65,* 548.

27. McDowell, *Indian Affairs, 1750–1754,* 19, 22 Mar. 1750, 11–13, 59, 303, for later similar complaints of his drunkenness and abuse of the Indians. See James Axtell, "The White Indians of Colonial America," *The European and the Indian: Essays in the Ethnohistory of Colonial North America* (Oxford: Oxford University Press, 1981), 168–206.

28. Newton D. Mereness, *Travels in the American Colonies: 1690–1783* (New York: Macmillan Company, 1910), 136, 167.

29. *South Carolina Gazette,* 5 Mar. 1737.

30. John Donald Duncan, "Servitude and Slavery in Colonial South Carolina, 1670–1776" (Ph.D. diss., Emory University, 1971), 57–61. The Jacobite Rebellion in Britain in 1715 had seen many Scotsmen fight for the "Old Pretender," whom they regarded as the true Stuart successor to James II.

31. His name is also spelled Dowie, Dawie, David. McDowell, *JCIT,* 265, 271, 300–301; CJ, RSUS E1p/5/2/, 105; McDowell, *Indian Affairs, 1750–1754,* 57.

32. McDowell, *Indian Affairs, 1754–1765,* 375; Hasting's journal, 1723, BPRO, 10:186; McDowell, *JCIT,* 176, 283. His name is also spelled Duval, Duvall, Dual, Da

Vall, De Vall, etc.; *Abstracts of Colonial Wills of the State of Georgia, 1733–1777* (Atlanta: Department of Archives and History, 1962), 40.

33. Easterby, ed., *JCHA, 1748,* 7 Apr. 1748, 171; 20 June 1748, 355; CJ, 10 Apr. 1748, RSUS E1p/3/4, 191, 214

34. McDowell, *JCIT,* Mar. 1711, 11 June 1718, 7, 286–88.

35. McDowell, *Indian Affairs 1750–1754,* Talk of the Raven, 14 May 1751, 75; Cashin, *Lachlan McGillivray,* 60.

36. "Chicken's Journal, 1725, " in Mereness, *Travels in the American Colonies,* 138–39; BPRO, 24:303; J. H. Easterby, ed., *JCHA, May 18, 1741–July 10, 1742* (Columbia: Historical Commission of South Carolina, 1953), 26 May 1742, 536–37; Commissioner William Pinckney's representation, 29 June 1754, BPRO, 26:78; CJ, May 1751, RSUS E1p/5/2, 121.

37. For blacks in Creek country, see Kathryn E. Holland Braund, "The Creek Indians, Blacks, and Slavery," *Journal of Southern History* 57 (1991): 601–36; McDowell, *JCIT,* 287; Matthew Toole to Glen, 13 Jan. 1752, McDowell, *Indian Affairs, 1750–1754,* 201. His name is also given as Steel.

38. McDowell, *Indian Affairs,* 1750-1754, 31 Aug. 1751, 136, John Buckles' journal, 20 Jan. 1753, 38; "Fitch's Journal, 1725," Mereness, *Travels in the American Colonies,* 184–85, 210–11.

39. According to William Byrd, it took fifteen or more persons to look after a hundred horses; Crane, *Southern Frontier,* 126; 11 June 1718, McDowell, *JCIT,* 291.

40. Wilbur R. Jacobs, *Indians of the Southern Colonial Frontier: The Edmond Atkin Report and Plan of 1755* (Columbia: University of South Carolina Press, 1954), 22.

41. Gregory E. Dowd, "The Panic of 1751: The Significance of Rumors on the South Carolina–Cherokee Frontier," *William and Mary Quarterly,* 3d ser., 53 (1996): 527–60.

42. CJ, 29 June 1748, RSUS E1p/3/4, 345.

43. Charles Town merchants' petition to Broughton, July 1735, BPRO, 17:413; The journals of the Commissioners of the Indian Trade for the period of the government monopoly between 1716 and 1718 are the only detailed records of the names and payments of these lowly persons over a period of time. McDowell, *JCIT,* 69–321.

44. McDowell, *JCIT,* 14–24 July 1716, 79–84. This was a way of gaining extra needed and scarce trading goods.

45. "Chicken's Journal, 1725" in Mereness, *Travels in the American Colonies,* 128.

46. Petition of merchants to Broughton, July 1735. BPRO, 17:413; CT Will Inventories, vol. R (2), 1753-1756, 173, dated 7 Aug. 1751; *JCHA, 1748,* 385; ibid., *JCHA,* 1751–1752, 36, 45. Such saddles had been made for fifty shillings apiece in 1716, McDowell, *JCIT,* 77; and in 1767, a packsaddle was inventoried as worth £3. CT Will Inventories, vol. V, 123; vol. B, 12. Tom Hatley, *The Dividing Paths, Cherokees and South Carolinians through the Era of Revolution* (New York: Oxford University Press, 1993), 39, shows how the Cherokees had become "suppliers of horses to the colonial trade" as early as 1730.

47. Ian K. Brown, "Historic Trade Bells," *1975 Conference on Historical Sites Archaeology Papers,* vol. 10 (Columbia: University of South Carolina Press, 1977), 69–82; William Bartram, *Travels of William Bartram through North & South Carolina, East & West Florida* (1791), ed. Mark Van Doren (New York; Dover Publications, 1928), 350–51; McDowell, *Indian Affairs, 1750–1754,* 244, 247–48, 527.

48. *South Carolina Gazette,* 14 July 1739; 16 Dec. 1752, BPRO, 25:132.

49. John Phillip Reid, *A Better Kind of Hatchet: Law, Trade, and Diplomacy in the*

Cherokee Nation during the Early Years of European Contact (University Park: Pennsylvania State University Press, 1976), 155; McDowell, *JCIT,* Nov. 1717–June 1718, 226, 265–66, 284; *South Carolina Gazette,* 22 Sept. 1759. The Frenchman's name was Peter Arnaud; *JCHA,* 23 Jan. 1724, RSUS A1b/2/3, 381, 393.

50. This is in contrast to the situation among the Iroquois, where the English tended to educate and then employ the same individuals who made a profession from this skill. Nancy Hagendorn, "'At Home in Their Manners and Modes of Expression': The Education and Training of Interpreters" (paper presented at the Institute of Early American History at Williamsburg, 15 Feb. 1993).

51. *JCHA, 1741–42,* 24 Feb. 1742, 412–15; 21 May 1742, 512; 22 May 1742, 517; *JCHA, 1748,* 18 June 1748, 326–27; 22 June 1748, 342; 25 June 1748, 359; McDowell, *Indian Affairs 1750–1754,* 24–25 Aug. 1752, 283–84. He also worked to undermine Bosomworth, telling the Indians that it was he, Forrest, who had news for them from the governor. He was still a Creek trader in 1772; see "Taitt's Journal, 1772," Mereness, *Travels in the American Colonies,* 538.

52. McDowell, *Indian Affairs 1754–65,* 80, 83, 472, 500.

53. 10 Aug., 20 Nov. 1735, *Colonial Records of Georgia 1732–35,* ed. Kenneth Coleman and Milton Ready (Athens: University of Georgia Press, 1982), 20:69, 72, 111–12.

54. South Carolina Upper House Journal (hereafter cited as UHJ), June 1731, RSUS A1a/2/1, 95; McDowell, *Indian Affairs, 1750–1754,* 74; Samuel Cole Williams, *Dawn of the Tennessee Valley and Tennessee History* (Johnson City, Tenn.: Watauga Press, 1937), 216. His name is often reproduced as "Bunyan." He received £20 currency a month in 1758.

55. McDowell, *JCIT,* 22 Nov. 1716, 127; *CRG,* 20:185. Beamer's nuncupative will, proven Feb. 1761, *Abstracts of the Wills of the State of South Carolina, 1760–84,* ed. Carolyn T. Moore (Columbia: R. L. Bryan Co., 1969), 3:5–6.

56. McDowell, *Indian Affairs, 1750–1754,* 72; S C-CJ, June 1749, RSUS E1p/4, 526. 5 Nov. 1763, BPRO, 30:63. He may have been a descendant of Thomas Ayres, a turn-of-the-century trader. See James H. Merrell, *The Indians' New World: Catawbas and Their Neighbors from European Contact through the Age of Removal* (Chapel Hill: University of North Carolina Press, 1989), 235, for a different explanation of the name.

57. Petition of Lachlan McGillivery (*sic*), McDowell, *Indian Affairs, 1750–1754,* 518. He was given satisfaction; *South Carolina Gazette,* 14 July 1733. The Chickasaw and Natchez Indians then in town had traveled over 900 miles to get there; Jacobs, *Atkin Report and Plan,* 34; McDowell, *Indian Affairs, 1754–65,* 325, 355, name also spelled Elsinor, Alshenor.

58. J. H. Easterby, ed., JCHA March 8, 1749–March 19, 1750 (Columbia: Archives Dept., 1962), 17 May 1749, 126–27; Adair, *History of the Indians,* 394, 396.

59. She petitioned the Commons House in January 1752 to establish a ferry over the Congaree River. 23 Jan. 1752, 93; 5 Mar. 1752, *JCHA, 1751–52,* 119.

60. This was the location of the township of Saxe Gotha. Meriwether, *Expansion of South Carolina,* 52; *JCHA, 1749–50,* 9 Feb. 1750, 402; *JCHA, 1751–52,* 11 Jan. 1752, 45; Terry Lipscomb, ed., *JCHA, November 12, 1752–September 6, 1754* (Columbia: University of South Carolina Press, 1983), 27 Apr. 1754, 458.

61. M. O'Neale submitted accounts 1749–1754, e.g., *JCHA* 20 Feb. 1753, 94–95.

62. *JCHA, 1741–42,* 19 Jan. 1742, 318; 24 Jan. 1742, 353; 27 Jan. 1742, 412; *JCHA, 1748,* 62; *JCHA, 1749–50,* 26 Jan. 1750, 356; 9 Feb. 1750, 402; *JCHA, 1751–52,* 20 Mar. 1752, 176; 24 Apr. 1752, 176, 244; *JCHA, 1752–54,* 11 Jan. 1754, 310.

63. *JCHA,* 1752–54, 5 Feb. 1735, RSUS A/1b/5/1, 61, 69; 27 Jan. 1750; 9 Feb. 1750; 14 Mar. 1750, *JCHA, 1749–50,* 360, 402, 462.

64. *JCHA, 1741–42,* 16 Feb. 1742, 37; *JCHA, 1752–54,* 5 Feb. 1754, 353.

65. *JCHA, 1748,* 8 June 1748, 292.

VII

"All & Singular the Slaves"

A Demographic Profile of Indian Slavery in
Colonial South Carolina

WILLIAM L. RAMSEY

When the first Carolina settlers arrived on the banks of the Ashley River in
March 1670, they carried with them a number of assumptions about the
nature of the colony they sought to establish. One such assumption, confirmed by the Fundamental Constitutions of Carolina and encouraged by
the headright system of land grants, was that slavery would be allowed and
protected in the new province. Since many of the colony's first settlers and
most of its leaders came from Barbados, where slavery had been a profitable
fixture for several decades, this was not unusual. Yet, convinced as they were
about the importance of slave labor, Carolinians still harbored some uncer-
tainty about the relationship of race to slavery.

Winthrop D. Jordan, in *White over Black*, concluded that the fundamental features of "chattel racial slavery" had taken shape in all British plantation colonies by the end of the seventeenth-century.[1] In South Carolina,
however, the evolution of race-based slavery in its familiar, nineteenth-century form was complicated by a slave system that included from the outset
significant numbers of individuals from two distinct racial groups, Indian[2]
and African.[3] There, white planters forced a more diverse array of peoples
into slavery over a longer period and in larger numbers than had been
attempted anywhere in the British empire. The number of enslaved Indians
working on South Carolina plantations ultimately rose as high as 1,400 in
1708, roughly 25 percent of the enslaved labor force,[4] and South Carolina
whites had exported many thousands more to other British colonies on the
mainland or in the West Indies.[5] Yet by the early 1730s the slave trade that
once brought thousands of captive Indians into the colony had all but van-
ished, and the number still working on lowcountry plantations had fallen to
less than 3 percent of the enslaved labor force.[6] In the interim, African slaves
became increasingly vital, and they continued to serve as the foundation of
Carolina's plantation economy through the middle of the nineteenth century.

Whereas in the last few decades scholars have produced several excellent
studies of African slavery in colonial South Carolina, the history of Indian
slavery remains, for a variety of reasons, relatively unexplored.[7] The present
study seeks to redress this imbalance by, first, providing some insight into the

TABLE 7.1
RATE OF HOUSEHOLD OWNERSHIP OF SLAVES, 1690–1739

Years	Number of Wills	Households with Slaves		
		Indians	Africans	Mustees
1690–1694	30	2=6%	4=13%	0
1695–1699	23	1=4%	6=26%	0
1700–1704	14	2=14%	5=36%	0
1705–1709*	14	6=43%	8=57%	0
1710–1714	46	12=26%	15=32%	0
1715–1719	43	9=21%	15=35%	2=4%
1720–1724	133	15=11%	61=46%	5=4%
1725–1729	122	9=7%	47=38%	7=5.7%
1730–1734	167	3=1.8%	63=38%	4=2.4%
1735–1739	185	6=3%	77=41%	6=3%

SOURCE: South Carolina Will Transcripts, Wills of Charleston County, vols. 1-4, microfilm, South Carolina Department of Archives and History.

*There is good reason to believe that a larger sample of wills would produce a more moderate result.

demographic structures that shaped the experience of slavery for Native Americans and, second, assessing when, how, and why South Carolina moved from a multiracial slave labor force to a monoracial population of largely African descent.

Despite a paucity of archival records, it is possible to make a few, general observations about the composition of the enslaved population during the last decade of the seventeenth century. A survey of South Carolina wills indicates that between 1690 and 1694 about 13 percent of all households owned some number of African slaves. The number of households owning African slaves increased significantly between 1695 and 1699, however, to about 26 percent. On the other hand, the number of households owning Indian slaves fluctuated uncertainly between 4 and 6 percent over the same period, suggesting that Indian slavery served only as an ancillary form of labor during Carolina's earliest years.[8]

These figures indicate that ownership of slaves was not as widespread during the 1690s as it would soon become. It should be stressed as well that the rates of household ownership of African and Indian slaves are not mutually exclusive figures. Most households that owned Indian slaves also owned African slaves.

The twenty-seven surviving postmortem inventories from this decade tell a story similar to that in the wills. Although there is a significant wealth bias in this record series, as only those estates valuable enough to require systematic appraisal are included,[9] Indian slavery still appears to have been a minor component of the enslaved labor force prior to the turn of the century. Of the sixty-five total slaves who appeared in these inventories, only 6 percent were identified as Indians.[10]

As these numbers indicate, the trade in Native American slaves was still gaining momentum during the 1680s and 1690s. The Yamasee Indians, who migrated to the Port Royal area of South Carolina in the mid-1680s, became early leaders in the trade. They scoured the Spanish province of Guale, which lay along the coast of present-day Georgia, in search of Timuccuan and Gualean victims and effectively forced the evacuation of the Georgia tidewater by the turn of the century. Successful warriors could typically expect compensation well in excess of the usual profit from the deerskin trade, a single slave sometimes bringing the same price as 200 deerskins. This amounted to a good deal more than most warriors could gather in an entire hunting season, so it is not surprising that many warriors from powerful tribes spent much of their time making "war" on weaker tribes, particularly those outside the Carolina trade system who had not yet acquired firearms.[11] Of course, white Carolinians participated in the trade primarily for profit, but many also harbored more sinister motives. Thomas Nairne, for instance, the Indian agent for South Carolina, expressed hopes that the slave trade would "in som few years . . . reduce these barbarians to a farr less number."[12]

The first decade of the eighteenth century saw by far the greatest influx of Indian slaves, due in large part to the expeditions of Governor James Moore against St. Augustine in 1702 and the Apalachee missions in 1704. A census recorded by the governor and council indicated that the number of Indian slaves had risen to 350, or 10 percent of the enslaved labor force by 1703. It then exploded to 1,400 over the next five years, thus comprising slightly over 25 percent of the slave population by the end of the decade.[13]

Probate records are almost nonexistent between 1700 and 1709, but the few wills available nevertheless suggest that the number of households owning Indian slaves rose dramatically.[14] A more abundant supply of wills for the five-year period 1710–1714 indicates that about 26 percent of all households owned some Indian slaves.[15] These years, just prior to the outbreak of the Yamasee War in 1715, clearly represented the high-water mark of the Indian slave trade and of Indian slavery in South Carolina.[16]

Most enslaved Indians, both men and women, probably worked as field hands on plantations.[17] A promotional tract by John Norris, published in 1712, suggested that a profitable plantation could be established with "fifteen Indian women to work in the field" and "three Indian women as cooks

TABLE 7.2
POPULATION STATISTICS FOR INDIAN SLAVES

Years	Total Population Of Indian Slaves	Age and Gender Information		
		Women	Men	Children
1703	350	43%	29%	29%
1708	1,400	43%	36%	21%
1722–1727	1,100–1,280	37%	31%	32%

SOURCE: Population figures for 1722–1727 are derived from a survey of post-mortem inventories. Based on 169 inventories, Indian slaves represented either 7 percent or 8 percent (depending on how slaves not identified by race are apportioned) of the entire slave labor force, which stood somewhere between 12,000 in 1720 and 20,000 in 1730. I have taken 16,000 as a mean figure for 1722–1727. See Wills, Inventories, and Miscellaneous Records, 1722–1724, vol. 58; 1722–1726, vol. 59; 1724–1725, vol. 60; 1726–1727, vols. 61A and 61B (hereafter cited as WIMR). Figures for the years 1703 and 1708 are based on information in a report of the "Governor and Councill," 17 Sept. 1708, in *Records in the British Public Record Office Relating to South Carolina, 1701–1710*, ed. A. S. Salley (Columbia: Historical Commission of South Carolina, 1947), 5:203–10 (hereafter cited as *RBPRO*).

for the slaves, and other household business."[18] Yet Indian slaves worked at specialized occupations as well. "Lawrence" and "Toney," for instance, sold by Peter Royere to William Rhett in 1716, worked as a cooper and a shoemaker respectively.[19] Others, primarily women and children, appear to have worked as household servants. Judging from the prevalence of the name "Nanny" among Indian women bequeathed in wills by male testators to their wives and daughters, child rearing and care may have been one important function performed by Indian females.[20]

As with "Nanny," slaves' names reveal a great deal about the world in which they lived. Although first generation slaves were generally assigned names by their new masters, slave mothers exercised considerable liberty in naming their own offspring. As a result, African slaves in South Carolina succeeded over several generations in selecting a culturally distinctive set of names from the arbitrary collection originally assigned to the first generation. They even managed to retain a number of African names and many African traditions, such as naming a child for the day of the week on which it was born.[21]

First-generation Indian slaves undoubtedly valued their own traditional names and naming practices as well. Yet they appear to have been far less successful in retaining those names than their African coworkers.[22] Of the 68 Indian slaves whose names are given in colonial South Carolina wills between 1690 and 1740, only one, a girl named "Inotly," possessed a recognizably Indian name. The remainder were given common European names such as Lucy, Jack, and Hannah, or names from classical antiquity such as Nero or Pompey.[23] Postmortem inventories from the 1720s reveal a similarly low rate of traditional Indian name retention. Only two of the 103 names listed for Indian slaves, or about 2 percent, appear to be of Indian origin: Tipa and Meggilla.[24]

Indian slaves of this first generation clearly encountered intense pressure to relinquish the old trappings of their free lives in favor of new ones provided by their masters. African slaves endured similar pressures but nevertheless managed to retain African names at a rate of about 15 to 20 percent.[25] The corresponding rate of only 1 to 2 percent for Indian slaves suggests that the two groups either responded differently to the experience of slavery or experienced slightly different forms of oppression. It may indicate, for instance, that white Carolinians considered Indian identity a greater potential threat than African identity, perhaps due to the large number of armed, independent nations poised just across the frontier. It is also possible, however, that radically different gender compositions within the African and Indian slave populations, the former predominantly male and the latter female, may also have conditioned their respective strategies for coping with the hardships of slavery.

Finally, pressures acting to discourage the retention of Indian names may simply have arisen from the general demographic context within which Indian slavery existed. Many plantations prior to the Yamasee War possessed African laborers exclusively, but relatively few utilized Indian labor alone. Wherever Indian slaves worked in lowcountry Carolina, they generally worked amid mixed African-Indian populations, with Africans predominating. In 1720, for example, Robert Seabrooke's plantation in Colleton County listed a total of 20 slaves, 50 percent of whom were African, 35 percent Indian, and 15 percent mustee,[26] the term for mixed Indian-African or Indian-European offspring.[27] Meanwhile, John Goodby's plantation, probated the same year as Seabrooke's, was staffed by a labor force in which Africans comprised 79 percent and Indians 21 percent of the workers.[28] Such cases, however, probably represented the upper ranges of the native American presence. At the opposite extreme were plantations such as William Skipper's, where a single "Indian woman named Phebe" worked alongside sixteen African slaves in the mid-1720s. Similarly, John Whitmarsh recorded forty-eight slaves who worked on his plantation in 1718, one of whom was named "Indian Rose."[29]

It is not surprising that Indians, working alone or, at best, as part of a minority contingent within the "black majority," found it difficult to maintain overt vestiges of their heritage. Perhaps more curious is why more

Indian appellations do not appear among second-generation offspring. Second-generation Indian mothers, like African mothers, probably exercised the liberty to choose the names of their own children. Yet Indian and mustee infants born into slavery continued to bear the names given by European masters to their parents' generation. The only movements away from this pattern were movements not toward a resumption of traditional Indian names but toward African names. An "Indian boy" slave, for instance, owned by John Royer in the early 1720s, bore the distinctly African name "Cuffey."[30] The tendency toward Africanization may have been especially strong among mustee children who had no personal memories of their Indian heritage, as suggested by the decision of a "mustee woman Phillis" to name her son "Quacoo."[31] Similarly, a mustee man owned by James Stanyarne in 1723 was named "Sambo," while Nancy Gflbertson owned "a mustee boy" named "Mingo."[32] Such examples suggest that native American slaves experienced a double-edged process of acculturation, requiring the accommodation of two foreign cultures which, in that particular demographic setting, possessed more currency on a daily basis than their own.[33]

Despite overwhelming pressures, however, certain aboriginal traditions did persist on lowcountry plantations, primarily through the efforts of Indian women. Throughout the colonial period, free Indian women appear to have clung more effectively to old customs and folkways than their male partners, serving as "guardians of tradition" during an era of chaotic change.[34] Archaeologically, their influence manifests itself in ceramic traditions, controlled exclusively by women, which remained vigorous and consistent even in direct competition with European trade goods.[35] Native American women appear to have taken these skills with them to a number of South Carolina plantations, where they continued to make pottery characterized by recognizably Indian vessel types and decorative motifs.[36] At Newington plantation near Charleston, for instance, excavations uncovered a fragment from an Indian-style earthenware vessel in the kitchen fireplace of the main house, suggesting that Indian slaves may have prepared foods with aboriginal utensils of their own making.[37]

The presence of mustee slaves on many plantations testifies to the interrelation of Africans, Indians, and Europeans, but the extent of interethnic unions is difficult to quantify. The first reference to a mixed-race slave dates only to 1716, when James Lawson bequeathed "a mastee girle called Dina" to his wife.[38] By that time, the two groups had been working together for nearly two decades, and it is reasonable to assume that some degree of mixing had gone unrecorded prior to Dina's appearance. Women outnumbered men among Indian slaves during the first decade of the eighteenth century, the only decade for which there is reliable census information. Meanwhile, among African slaves during the same period, men outnumbered women by between 600 and 900.[39] For many Indian women and African men, therefore, it may have been easier to find suitable partners among members of the other race than among their own.[40] This may also explain why slaves classified as mustees were the most common product of interethnic unions for most of the eighteenth century, outnumbering mulattos by a considerable margin.[41] The greatest number of mustees, most of them children, appeared in South Carolina wills during the 1720s. Between 1725 and 1729, approximately 6 percent of all households owned at least one mustee slave. Thereafter, the number declined to about 3 percent, roughly the same number of households that owned Indian slaves.[42]

It is likely, however, that this decline represents changing habits of classification and, hence, changing ideas about race rather than actual population trends. An act drafted by the Commons House of Assembly in 1716 essentially attempted to legislate the category of "mustee" out of existence altogether. In order to avoid "all doubts and scruples that may arise" about the definition and valuation of mustee slaves, the act ordered that "all and every such slave who is not entirely Indian, shall be accounted and deemed as negro."[43] The importance of this first, public effort to eradicate the connecting link, or middle ground, between Indian and African slaves cannot be overemphasized, and it was no coincidence that it materialized immediately after the Yamasee War. While the language of the law cited practical, monetary concerns over the appraisal of different types of slaves, the very nature of the act revealed a much more ambitious agenda. It sought for the first time to create a clear and legal demarcation, however arbitrary, between Africans and Indians. Moreover, by declaring that all mixed-race slaves be "deemed as negro," it effectively maneuvered the gravitational pull of slavery to that side of the line, with grave implications for the subsequent development of white racial ideology. From a demographic standpoint, it meant that mustees became increasingly invisible on paper and may well have comprised a much larger percentage of the work force than records indicate.

Evidence of miscegenation involved Europeans as well. On several occasions plantation owners granted freedom to Indian women and acknowledged paternity of mixed-race children. In 1707, for instance, Richard Prize granted freedom to "an Indian woman of mine by whom I have two children Elizabeth and Sarah Prize."[44] He went on to bequeath to his "Indian woman" two other Indian women, who unfortunately remained slaves. Prize may have feared, however, that the mother once free might attempt to raise his daughters as Indians, for he instructed his executors to "take my two said children and bring them up in ye fear of God."[45] The eldest son of Governor Robert Johnson, named after his father, also developed strong feelings for his "Indian woman named Catharina, whom I design to marry.[46] Robert accordingly made arrangements to "manumett and set free" his bride to be and since Catharina was "with child" at the time, stipulated in the same legal instrument that the baby once born should be entitled to a share of his estate equal to those of his other four children.[47] It is unknown whether his "design" ever came to fruition.

Given the range of possible categories under which the offspring of Indian parents might be classified, it is difficult to gauge reproductive rates. It stands to reason, however, that scattered settlement patterns acted to diminish both social cohesion and at least within their own racial group, reproductive opportunities for Native Americans. In fact, based on post-mortem inventories between 1722 and 1727, the trend toward dispersion and isolation, evident even during the earliest periods, appears to have increased dramatically following the Yamasee War, when the influx of new Indian slaves ended.[48] Of the fifty inventoried estates that indicated ownership of Indian slaves during this period, Africans outnumbered Indians by seven to one, with the number of Indians ranging from a minimum of one to a maximum of ten and appearing at an average rate of about 2.4 slaves per estate. Most ominous of all from a reproductive standpoint, only 24 percent of these estates owned both male and female slaves. It thus appears that fully three-quarters of the enslaved Indian population had no access whatsoever to partners from their own race.[49]

It is unlikely that a population dispersed in this manner could produce a second generation recognizable as purely Indian. Nevertheless, the problem was masked by new slave imports prior to the Yamasee War. Even as late as the mid-1720s, the age and gender distribution of Indian slaves included a sizable proportion of children, as much as 32 percent. This represented about the same percentage of African children to African adults during the same decade.[50] By the 1730s, however, the situation seems to have altered. For the ten-year period between 1730 and 1740, a survey of 352 wills yielded ten mustee children but only a single Indian child, named Prince.[51] Significantly, perhaps, Prince's three brothers and sisters were classified as mustees.[52]

With the outbreak of the Yamasee Indian War in 1715, the Indian slave trade was essentially wiped out. As a result, few new slaves came into the system thereafter and natural demographic factors came to the forefront. As might be expected of a population largely isolated from itself, Indian slaves began declining in number immediately. The rate of household ownership of Indian slaves, derived from a survey of South Carolina will transcripts, fell from a prewar level of 26 percent between 1710 and 1714 to about 21 percent for the five-year period following the war, 1715 to 1719.[53] Between

1720 and 1724, moreover, the rate of ownership dropped drastically to about 11 percent. Thereafter the decline continued at a more moderate rate throughout the 1720s, falling to about 7 percent for the five-year period between 1725 and 1729. Ultimately, the percentage of households owning Indian slaves leveled out during the 1730s at about 2 to 3 percent.[54]

Planters who owned multiracial labor forces often resorted to unwieldy terminologies to express the composition of their holdings. Christopher Smyth, for instance, bequeathed to his grandson "all & singular the negroe & Indian slaves," while Robert Daniell left his wife Martha "all my slaves, whether negroes, Indians, mustees, or molattoes, both male & female."[55] Where slaves were identified by name and bequeathed to particular relatives, however, it is likely that they held special value for the family and may have been intended for use within the household as personal servants. Such was the case when Henry Bower drafted his will in 1724. He stipulated that his wife be allowed to select from his slave holdings "a young negro or Indian woman which of them she will (such as understands house business)."[56] Similarly, Robert Stevens in 1720 left his wife "a negroe girl . . . to be solly att her comand."[57] Indian and African children were often given to children or grandchildren of similar ages and genders, perhaps in an effort to foster personal attachments. Mary Crosse thus bequeathed her "Indian girle slave, named reigner," to her daughter in 1699 while ten years later Thomas Dalton gave "an Indian boy called Thomasse" to his son.[58]

The percentage of Indian slaves identified in this manner, relative to Africans, offers yet another perspective on the demographics of Indian slavery. During the five-year period preceding the Yamasee War, 1710 to 1714, Indians comprised approximately 34 percent of slaves bequeathed to family members. That figure dropped to 22 percent, however, in the five years following the war, 1715 to 1719, and fell further to 10 percent between 1720 and 1724. By the second half of the decade, between 1725 and 1729, the number of Indian slaves likely to have been working within the household had fallen to only 3 percent.[59]

These numbers suggest two possible interpretations. First, the declining Native American presence within the household may simply reflect an overall decline in the enslaved Indian population. Postmortem inventories are not available for the first and final years of the 1720s, but a survey of 169 inventories from 1722 to 1727 indicates that Indian slaves comprised only 7 to 8 percent of the total labor force.[60]

Even adjusting for the rapid influx of African slaves during these years, that figure suggests that the enslaved Indian population had begun to decline by the mid-1720s.[61] It is conceivable, therefore, that the declining importance of Indian slaves as domestic servants simply mirrored demographic trends prevailing outside the household.

TABLE 7.3
SURVEY OF SOUTH CAROLINA POSTMORTEM INVENTORIES

Years	Estates	Estates with Slaves			Number of Slaves			
		Indian	African	Mustee	Indian	African	Mustee	Unknown
1722	12	5	8	2	8	51	2	
1723	40	11	34	5	21	231	5	62
1724	32	5	22	2	14	369	5	88
1725	39	14	32	4	34	284	7	6
1726	35	11	25	3	28	241	10	102
1727	11	4	10	2	16	96	2	14

Slaves listed as "unknown" in this table were not identified by race in the inventories. Since Indian and African slaves carried very different values, however, appraisers were very careful to distinguish between them. Large numbers of slaves, valued collectively without reference to race, were very probably African. Source: WIMR, SCDAH.

It is also possible, however, that new social dynamics between Indians and white Carolinians forced Indian slaves out of the household and into the fields after 1715. Although inventories reveal a moribund population of enslaved Indians during the 1720s, they do not indicate a rate of decline as pronounced as the disappearance of domestic servants in the will transcripts. They suggest, instead, stagnation and moderate decline.[62] It is clear, moreover, from the relative monetary values assigned to Indian and African slaves in postmortem inventories from the 1720s that Indians were considered much less desirable.[63]

The reasons for this price differential are unclear, but they may have been related to white anxieties about the use of Indian slaves. One of the glaring differences between the will transcripts and other records, even prior to the Yamasee War, is the lack of male Indians in the wills and their relative abundance in postmortem inventories and census records.[64] Since the wills were heavily biased toward domestic servants, the relative absence of male Indian slaves in this record series may indicate that Indian men were never widely trusted to work closely with the planter's family. If so, the outbreak of the Yamasee War must surely have strengthened existing prejudices. The rapid disappearance of all Indians from the immediate domicile after 1715 may therefore be viewed in part as a defensive measure, perhaps intended to preserve not only the safety of the planter's family but also their peace of mind.

Did white Carolinians intentionally distance themselves from their Indian slaves by relegating them to the fields? Unfortunately, the evidence does not conclusively answer this question. According to Winthrop Jordan, English colonists used "the separate meanings of *Indian* and *negro*" to "triangulate their own position in America."[65] Before they could do this, however, they first had to separate the "meanings of Indian and negro," and evidence suggests that many white South Carolinians were in the process of doing just this after the Yamasee War. As slave names suggest, lowcountry planters tried mightily to draw Indians into the category of *slave* by divorcing the individual's identity from that of his free brethren on the far side of the frontier. Nevertheless, the connection must have remained vividly apparent to all concerned. In 1700, for instance, white Carolinians were alarmed to discover that two Indian slaves had attempted to incite a neighboring Indian nation to attack the colony. They apparently told their free Indian acquaintances that "a great many nations of Indians had already agreed & confederated to make war & cutt off all the white men."[66] Concerns over this sort of collusion between free and unfree Indians must from the outset have driven English efforts to deny Indian slaves those vestiges of their former lives deemed threatening. After the horrors of the Yamasee War, however, white conceptions of the Indian as *enemy* may have grown too persuasive to allow even guarded confidence any longer in the Indian as "Nanny."

Although a conceptual, social shift such as the one hypothesized above may have contributed indirectly to the decline of Indian slavery by depressing the value of Indian slaves and, hence, the profitability of the slave trade, many Carolinians were by all indications just as eager to acquire Indian slaves after the war as they had been before. Even while hostilities continued with many tribes, the Commissioners for the Indian Trade authorized traders doing business with the Cherokees to accept "all such manner of truck, as skins, furrs, *slaves* or other vendible commodities, as is customary to receive from Indians" (italics mine)[67] They initially felt it might be prudent to restrict the trade in male Indians to boys under the age of fourteen years but perhaps unsatisfied with the number of slaves brought in, quickly amended that instruction in late 1716 to allow traders the "liberty" to buy male slaves "at any age not exceeding thirty years."[68] For a number of reasons, however, their efforts failed to secure captives at a rate sufficient to replenish the declining population of Indian slaves.

Slave traders may in fact have begun to experience difficulties prior to the Yamasee War. The principle slaving regions of Apalachee and Guale in Spanish Florida had probably been denuded of victims well before 1715.[69] As early as 1708, Thomas Nairne observed that English-allied Indians endeavoring to capture slaves "are now obliged to goe down as farr on the point of Florida as the firm land will permitt," having "drove the Floridians to the islands of the cape. . . ."[70] The Indians of Spanish Florida appear to have suffered more than any other group, and archaeological work indicates that the overwhelming majority of Indian artifacts found on South Carolina plantations derive from Floridian traditions.[71] One scholar has even suggested that the depopulation of Spanish Guale and Apalachee contributed to the economic hardships of some tribes, such as the Yamasees,[72] who were heavily involved in the slave trade, and made war the only real solution to their growing indebtedness to English traders.[73]

Nairne also noted that Carolina's western Indian allies, particularly the Tallapoosas (later known as Upper Creeks) and the Chickasaws, had been active "in making slaves of such Indians about the lower Mississippi as are now subject to the French."[74] In all probability, the majority of these captives were Choctaw Indians. By 1702, the French estimated that about 500 Choctaws had already been enslaved by Chickasaw raiding parties in league with the English.[75] Had the French followed the Spanish policy prohibiting the distribution of firearms to Indians, the Choctaws might well have suffered a fate similar to that of the Timucuans and Apalachees of Florida. Instead, French muskets began appearing in Choctaw villages soon after the arrival of the French in 1699. By 1715, the Choctaws may have been sufficiently armed to face down the Chickasaws and Tallapoosas, making slave raids far more costly and the prospect of retribution proportionately greater.[76]

Compounding these problems, South Carolina lost many of its external markets for slave exports between 1712 and 1715. Alarmed at reports of Indian atrocities during the Tuscarora War, which erupted in 1711, as well as by the behavior of its own Indian slaves, Massachusetts passed an act in 1712 to prohibit further Indian slave imports: "Whereas divers conspiracies, outrages, barbarities, murders, burglaries, thefts, and other notorious crimes, at sundry times, and especially of late, have been perpetrated by Indians and other slaves, within several of his Majesties plantations in America, being of a malitious and revengeful spirit, rude and insolent in their behaviour, and very ungovernable; the over-great number of which, considering the different circumstances of this colony from the plantations in the islands, and our having considerable numbers of the Indians of the country within and about us, may be of pernicious consequence to his Majesties subjects and interests here, unless speedily remedied."[77] Pennsylvania and Rhode Island followed suit the same year by enacting prohibitive import duties on "Carolina Indians," as they were known in the northern colonies.[78] In 1713 and 1714 respectively, New Jersey and New Hampshire also took measures to curtail Indian slave imports by levying a duty of £10 on every slave brought into port.[79]

The outbreak of the Yamasee War in the spring of 1715 provided additional confirmation for many northern colonists that the risks attending the use of Indian slaves were unacceptably high. Only three months after the outbreak of hostilities in South Carolina, Connecticut officials expressed concern over the "considerable number of Carolina Indians" coming into the colony. Above all, they feared that rebellion might prove infectious among Connecticut's free Indian population and that "our Indians may be tempted to draw off to those enemies." The governor and council accordingly agreed to a complete prohibition against any further importation of "Carolina Indians" and made additional arrangements for any slaves that happened to arrive in port thereafter to be "put into the strictest custody . . . to prevent their communication with any Indians in this his Majesties colony."[80]

In addition to reducing South Carolina's already dwindling export market among other mainland colonies, the Yamasee War struck a more direct blow at the slave trade by destroying the primary means by which it was conducted: the traders. These individuals functioned as intermediaries between Indian groups wishing to sell war captives on the one hand and the merchants and planters of Carolina who sought to buy them on the other. In many cases, traders lived in Indian villages and possessed extensive ties to local communities. They encouraged slave raids and extended credit and supplies to outfit the raiding parties. One trader, Anthony Probert, even had his own raiding party and apparently sent "his slaves to war" to capture new slaves.[81] In the first week of the Yamasee War, the vast majority of English traders died, perhaps as many as ninety men.[82] Their loss deprived South Carolina of practical knowledge, experience, personal networks, and paraphernalia, without which the slave trade could not function.

Few, if any, serious attempts were made to repair and resume the Indian slave trade after 1715. By contrast, the African slave trade, functioning independently of South Carolina, remained undamaged by the war and proved more than capable of servicing the labor needs of the colony's expanding economy. In the three years between 1717 and 1719 alone, over fifty ships transported 1,519 African slaves to Charleston, a figure that may approach or even exceed the total population of Indian slaves prior to the Yamasee War.[83]

The Indian slave trade, therefore, with its machinery and personnel wiped out, its principal slaving regions either depopulated or dangerously well armed, and its export markets rapidly evaporating, offered little real competition to the trade in African slaves. It failed even to maintain the enslaved Indian population at its prewar level. With few new slaves coming in after 1715, natural demographic forces and attrition steadily reduced the number of Indian slaves already working on Carolina plantations until, by the 1730s, they had become a rarity, appearing in only 2 to 3 percent of all households.

It is reasonable to assume that economic forces and demographic realities might ultimately have ended or curtailed the Indian slave trade and the use of Indian slaves in South Carolina had the Yamasee War never occurred. Yet the abruptness of the decline in the war's aftermath tends to suggest that it served greatly to accelerate the process and may even have initiated it. If left intact, the machinery of the slave trade would certainly have continued to function for many years beyond 1715, though perhaps with diminishing effectiveness. It is even possible that a naturally sustainable, enslaved Indian or mustee population might have developed as a permanent adjunct to African slavery. That the Indian slave trade ended as it did, and that Indian slavery ended with it, resulted both from natural demographic forces at work within the colony and the intervention of historical forces in the form of the Yamasee War.

The decline of Indian slavery after 1715 effectively ended South Carolina's experimentation with a multiracial labor force and committed white planters thereafter to an increasing reliance on African slaves. It seems clear that this transition had an enormous impact not only on the subsequent evolution and character of the plantation regime but also on the formation of white concepts of ethnicity, race, and "place," possibly facilitating a greater degree of precision in the differentiation between Indians and Africans. As suggested by efforts to establish a legal distinction between African and

Indian slaves and the possible expulsion of Indians from the immediate household following the Yamasee War, white Carolinians may have been struggling with conceptual and social developments that paralleled the changing demographics of the enslaved labor force. The extrication of Native Americans from involvement in slavery, both physically and conceptually, represented an essential step in the process of triangulation Winthrop Jordan has proposed. From 1715 onward, Carolinians gradually stopped trying to bring Africans and Indians together under the unified mantle of slavery and began instead a prolonged effort to keep the two groups apart and, equally important, opposed to each other.

Notes

1. Winthrop D. Jordan, *White over Black: American Attitudes toward the Negro, 1550–1812* (Baltimore: Penguin Books, 1969), 98.

2. It is regrettable that broad, generic terms such as "Indian," "Native American," or "native" must be used to refer to a diverse population of aboriginal peoples who would certainly not have recognized the validity of such categories themselves. Unfortunately, Apalachees, Timuccuans, Gualeans, Tuscororas, and Choctaws who were forced into slavery became, at least in the documentary records produced by white colonists, simply "Indian slaves." Since these records represent the only available source from which to draw evidence, efforts to quantify the demographics of enslaved, aboriginal peoples while acknowledging the underlying reality of diversity, must of necessity be studies of "Indian slaves." In deference to prevailing scholarly trends, the current study has utilized the terms "Indian," "Native American," and "native." The author proffers the same apology, for similar reasons, for the use of the term "African."

3. As a result of miscegenation, moreover, these racial types were further complicated in succeeding generations by a proliferation of slaves that manifested a mixture of Indian, European, and African ancestry.

4. The remaining 75 percent were overwhelmingly African but also included mustee and mulatto slaves.

5. Alexander S. Salley, ed., *Records in the British Public Records Office Relating to South Carolina,* 5 vols. (Columbia: The Historical Commission of South Carolina, 1946), 5:203–10.

6. Peter H. Wood, *Black Majority: Negroes in Colonial South Carolina from 1670 through the Stono Rebellion* (New York and London: W. W. Norton, 1974), 155.

7. William R. Snell attempted such a study in the early 1970s, but his dissertation was flawed by faulty methodologies and ethnographic inaccuracies. See William R. Snell, "Indian Slavery in Colonial South Carolina, 1671–1795" (Ph.D. diss., University of Alabama, 1972). The present study was complicated by the scarcity of archival resources from Carolina's early years. Probate records from the proprietary period are too scanty to reconstruct a complete and precise portrait of the rise of Indian or even African slavery. Those records that do exist fall into two categories that may be used to supplement each other: wills and postmortem inventories. The most numerous records for the years 1690–1720 are the wills, which number about 170. By contrast, there are only about sixty postmortem inventories for the entire proprietary period. See the South Carolina Will Transcripts, Wills of Charleston County, vol. 1 (1671–1724), microfilm, in the South Carolina Department of Archives and History (SCDAH). This record series contains only

seven surviving wills from the two decades following the colony's establishment. Records for the 1690s are more copious but still fall well short of being a reliable sample. As such, they should be regarded only as a rough index to general demographic trends. For a discussion of probate records in successive decades, see below.

8. The percent figures derived from my analysis of probate records indicate the percentage of households owning slaves of a particular type, either "Indian," "Negro," or "mustee." The record series utilized in the study, the Will Transcripts in SCDAH, vols. 1–4, primarily offers insight into the prevalence of each type of slave within the colony as a whole and is therefore only indirectly useful in determining exact population statistics. The figures were obtained by dividing the number of estates listing each type of slave by the total number of estates probated per five year period.

9. Approximately 52 percent of all inventoried estates reported owning some number of African slaves while only 11 percent reported Indian slaves. Records of the Secretary of the Province, 1692–1700, Inventories, SCDAH. These numbers suggest that prior to 1700 South Carolina was a "society of slaves" rather than a "slave society."

10. Records of the Secretary of the Province, 1692–1700, SCDAH.

11. William L. McDowell, Jr., ed., *Journals of the Commissioners of the Indian Trade, September 20, 1710–August 29, 1718* (Columbia: SCDAH, 1992), 53 (hereafter cited as McDowell, *JCIT*); Kathryn E. Holland Braund, *Deerskins and Duffels: The Creek Indian Trade with Anglo-America, 1685–1815* (Lincoln and London: University of Nebraska Press, 1993), 70–71.

12. Thomas Nairne's memorial to the Earl of Sunderland, 10 July 1708, in *Nairne's Muskhogean Journals: The 1708 Expedition to the Mississippi River*, ed. Alexander Moore (Jackson and London: University Press of Mississippi, 1988), 75 (hereafter cited as *Nairne's Muskhogean Journals.*)

13. Salley, ed., *RBPRO*, 5:203–10.

14. Only twenty-eight wills survive for the years 1700–1710. For the five-year period 1700–1704, available records suggest that the number of households owning Indian slaves increased to 14 percent. For the five-year period 1705–1709, however, the figures are clearly an aberration, indicating a rate of ownership in excess of 40 percent. Will Transcripts, vol. 1, SCDAH.

15. There are forty-six wills for the period 1710–1714. Will Transcripts, vol. 1, SCDAH.

16. The precise peak of Indian slavery cannot be determined. It occurred at some point between 1705 and 1715, probably between 1708 and 1713. The trend may have crested before 1715, in 1711 or 1712, perhaps as a result of an influx of slaves taken during the Tuscarora War. The forces led by John Barnwell against the Tuscaroras were primarily comprised of South Carolina's Indian allies, who hoped to profit from the venture by taking as many slaves as possible. Probate records place the crest of the curve around 1708, but there are only fourteen wills between 1705 and 1709. With such a small number of documents, a single household could skew the figure as much as 7 percent upward or downward, resulting in a 14 percent aberration.

17. Almon Wheeler Lauber, "Indian Slavery in Colonial Times within the Present Limits of the United States," *Studies in History, Economics, and Public Law* (New York: Columbia University, 1913), v. 54, part 3, pp. 244–45.

18. Jack P. Greene, ed., *Selling a New World: Two Colonial South Carolina Promotional Pamphlets* (Columbia: University of South Carolina Press, 1989), 132.

19. Miscellaneous Records, Charleston County, 1714–1717, SCDAH, 269–71, cited in Snell, *Indian Slavery*, 155. One "Mahaw boy slave" (possibly an abbreviation of

Altamaha, a Yamasee Town), owned by Joseph Atwell, may have taken his name, "Boatswain," from his occupation. See the will of Joseph Atwell, 13 Jan. 1722/3, Will Transcripts, vol. 1 (1722–1724), SCDAH, 26.

20. Of the slave names listed in the will transcripts for Indian women between 1690 and 1740, "Nanny" occurs more often than any other name. Approximately 11 percent of female Indian slaves referred to by name in South Carolina wills, most of whom probably worked within the household, were named Nanny. Will Transcripts, vols. 1–4, SCDAH.

21. Between about 15 and 20 percent of Carolina slave names were of African origin during the colonial period, but these became less common over time. By contrast, the use of Biblical names increased steadily during the course of the nineteenth century. See John C. Inscoe, "Carolina Slave Names: An Index to Acculturation," *Journal of Southern History* 49 (Nov. 1983): 532, 535, 542, 527–54. Other discussions of African names may be found in Newbell N. Puckett, *Black Names in America: Origins and Usage* (Boston: G.K. Hall, 1975), and Lorenzo D. Turner, *Africanisms in the Gullah Dialect* (Chicago; University of Chicago Press, 1949). Also see Peter H. Wood's discussion of African slave names and naming practices in *Black Majority*, 181–86, and David DeCamp, "African Day-Names in Jamaica," *Language* 63 (Mar. 1967): 139–49.

22. Differences between Native American and African naming practices make a direct comparison between the two groups problematic. Among free Indian males, for example, birth names held little importance. Although Indian women generally possessed a single name throughout their lives, the typical warrior held a sequence of names, commemorating notable events, such as military achievements. See J. Leitch Wright, Jr., *Creeks and Seminoles: The Destruction and Regeneration of the Muscogulge People* (Lincoln and London: University of Nebraska Press, 1986), 29–30; Charles Hudson, *The Southeastern Indians* (n.p.: University of Tennessee Press, 1976), 325; also see John R. Swanton, "Social Organization and Social Usages of the Indians of the Creek Confederacy," *Forty-Second Annual Report of the Bureau of American Ethnology* (Washington, D.C.: U.S. Government Printing Office, 1928), 276–307.

23. About 16 percent of Indian slave names derived from classical sources, South Carolina Will Transcripts, vols. 1–4. SCDAH. By comparison, John Inscoe arrived at a figure of about 21 percent for African slaves during roughly the same period, "Carolina Slave Names," 542.

24. Wills, Inventories, and Miscellaneous Records (hereafter cited as WIMR), vols. 58–61B, SCDAH.

25. Inscoe, "Carolina Slave Names," 532.

26. Although the term "mustee" carried different meanings in different parts of the empire, it was used in South Carolina to refer to either Indian-African or Indian-European offspring. The former, however, were probably much more common. See Wood, *Black Majority*, 99; Daniel C. Littlefield, *Rice and Slaves: Ethnicity and the Slave Trade in Colonial South Carolina* (Baton Rouge and London: Louisiana State University Press, 1981), 171.

27. Will of Robert Seabrooke, 22 Sept. 1720, Will Transcripts, vol. 1, will book, 1720–1721, SCDAH, 44–47. Seabrooke's plantation is also revealing where questions of gender are concerned. Although Indian slaves comprised 35 percent of the enslaved labor force there, Indian women outnumbered men by five to one. Meanwhile, African men outnumbered African women by seven to three. As a result, Indian and African responses to slavery on the Seabrooke plantation, considered separately, may have been very strongly influenced by gender differences.

28. Will of John Goodby, 18 Oct. 1720, ibid., 39. On Goodby's plantation, there were two Indian women and two Indian men, but once again African men outnumbered African women by nine to four.

29. Will of William Skipper, 2 Jan. 1724/5, Will Transcripts, vol. 2, will book, 1724–1725, SCDAH, 79; will of John Whitmarsh, 1 June 1718, ibid., vol. 1, will book, 1720–1721, SCDAH, 12–13; and will of John Whitmarsh, 20 May 1723, ibid., vol. 2, will book, 1722–1724, SCDAH, 40–41.

30. Will of John Royer, 13 Dec. 1721, Will Transcripts, vol. 1, will book, 1721–1722, SCDAH, 32–33.

31. Will of Charles Colleton, 27 Oct. 1727, Will Transcripts, vol. 2, will book, 1727–1729, SCDAH, 15–20.

32. Inventory of the estate of James Stanyarne, 1723, WIMR, 1722–1724, vol. 58, SCDAH; and inventory of the estate of Nancy Gilbertson, Aug. 1726, ibid., 1726–1727, vol. 61A, SCDAH.

33. I am indebted to Alan Gallay for his insightful comments on the process of acculturation at work here.

34. The quote is taken from the title of Kathryn Holland Braund's article "Guardians of Tradition and Handmaidens to Change: Women's Roles in Creek Economic and Social Life during the Eighteenth-Century," *American Indian Quarterly* 14 (Summer 1990): 239–58; also see Braund, *Deerskins and Duffels*, 130–32.

35. Carol I. Maston, "Eighteenth-Century Culture Change among the Lower Creeks," *Florida Anthropologist* 16 (Sept. 1963): 68–69, 73–74; also see Charles Fairbanks, "Excavations at Horseshoe Bend, Alabama," *Florida Anthropologist* 25 (1962): 41–56.

36. Leland Ferguson, *Uncommon Ground: Archaeology and Early African America, 1650–1800* (Washington and London: Smithsonian Institution Press, 1992), 82–84.

37. Ferguson, *Uncommon Ground*, 83; given the prevalence of ceramic artifacts, it is possible that other native crafts performed traditionally by women, such as the dressing of deerskins, which were less likely to be preserved in the archaeological records, may also have found expression at some plantations.

38. Will of James Lawson, 4 Feb. 1715/6, Will Transcripts, vol. 1, will book, 1711–1718, SCDAH, 82–83.

39. These figures are based on the census recorded in 1708, *RBPRO*, 5:203–10.

40. The majority of recorded instances of mothers fostering mustee children involved native women. There is only one clear instance in which a mustee child belonged to an African mother, see the will of Thomas Ellis, 27 Dec. 1722, Will Transcripts, vol. 2, will book, 1722–1724, SCDAH, 23.

41. Littlefield, *Rice and Slaves*, 144, 169–71.

42. Will Transcripts, vols. 1–4, SCDAH.

43. Thomas Cooper, ed., *The Statutes at Large of South Carolina*, 22 (Columbia, S.C.: A. S. Johnston, 1837), 2:671.

44. Will of Richard Prize, 19 May 1707, Will Transcripts, vol. 1, will book, 1687–1710, SCDAH, 52.

45. Ibid.

46. Will of Robert Johnson, 5 Apr. 1725, ibid., vol. 3, will book, 1732–1737, SCDAH, 249; Governor Robert Johnson mentioned his eldest son Robert in his own will ten years later but made no reference to his wife; see will of Robert Johnson, governor, 21 Dec. 1734, ibid., vol. 3, will book, 1732–1737, SCDAH, 191; the man who designed to marry Catherina in 1725 is probably the son rather than the governor himself, since

the elder Johnson was, by all accounts, resident in England between 1723 and 1730, when he returned to South Carolina as its first royal governor; see Richard P. Sherman, *Robert Johnson: Proprietary and Royal Governor of South Carolina* (Columbia: University of South Carolina Press, 1966), 59, 74.

47. Will of Robert Johnson, 5 April 1725, Will Transcripts, vol. 3, 1732–1737, SCDAH, 249.

48. WIMR, vols. 58–61A, SCDAH.

49. Ibid.

50. Russell R. Menard, "Slave Demography in the Lowcountry, 1670–1740: From Frontier Society to Plantation Regime," *South Carolina Historical Magazine* 96 (Oct. 1995): 293.

51. Will Transcripts, vols. 2–4, SCDAH.

52. Will of Hannah Guerard, 15 May 1735, Will Transcripts, vol. 3, will book, 1732–1737, SCDAH, 266–68.

53. The real significance of this decline naturally depends on the total number of households that existed in each period. Peter Wood found that the free white population increased from about 4,200 in 1710 to 6,525 in 1720. The resulting increase in households may thus make decline appear more exaggerated than it actually was. But I consider it unlikely. There was after all no such effect on the rate of household ownership of African slaves during the same period. See figure 1, Wood, *Black Majority*, 152.

54. In order to arrive at a figure for the percentage of households that owned Indian slaves during any five-year period between 1690 and 1740, the number of estates that indicated ownership of Indians (regardless of how many individuals were listed for any particular estate) was divided by the total number of estates probated during that five-year period. For instance, between 1735 and 1739, 185 wills were recorded, out of which only seven indicated possession of Indian slaves, indicating that only about 3 percent of all households owned such slaves during the late 1730s. Estates owning slaves of African descent were recorded as a control. For the same period, 1735–1739, about 41 percent of all households owned African slaves. Mustee slaves were recorded separately in order to provide an index to miscegenation. It should be noted that the percentage of households owning Indian or any other type of slaves should not be confused with the percentage of Indian slaves in the total slave population. Many estates, for instance, owned substantially more than one Indian slave, especially in earlier and peak periods. The relationship between the number of households owning Indian slaves and the actual number of Indian slaves held in South Carolina is discussed more fully below.

55. Will of Christopher Smyth, 9 July 1706, Will Transcripts, vol. 1, Will Book, 1687–1710, SCDAH pp. 38-51; Will of Robert Daniell, 1 May 1719, Will Transcripts, vol. 1, 1711–1718, SCDAH, pp. 94-97.

56. Will of Henry Bower, 26 July 1724, Will Transcripts, vol. 2, Will Book, 1720-1726, SCDAH, pp. 5-8.

57. Will of Robert Stevens, 8 Sept. 1720, Will Transcripts, vol. 2, Will Book, 1720-1721, SCDAH, p. 37. Gift patterns in the will transcripts clearly suggest that slaves identified by name were intended for use as personal servants. Between 1690 and 1725, all native female slaves identified as "girls" were bequeathed to a female relative, usually a daughter or granddaughter. The same was true of "Mustee girl" slaves. There was simply no clear instance in which an Indian or Mustee "girl" passed to a male recipient. Adult Indian women slaves appear to have been distributed with less discrimination, but the majority, 60 percent, were also bequeathed to female relatives. Meanwhile, 67 percent of all Indian "boy" slaves passed to male relatives, usually sons or grandsons. Decedents

almost never bequeathed adult Indian men by name. 58. Will of Mary Crosse, 6 Mar. 1699/1700, Will Transcripts, vol. 1, will book, 1687–1710, SCDAH, pp. 2–4; will of Thomas Dalton, 3 Oct. 1709, Will Transcripts, vol. 1, will book, 1711–1718, SCDAH, pp. 12–13. Likewise, in 1709 Thomas Hubbard gave his "two Indian girles Inotly and Nanny" to his two grandchildren, Ann and Dorothe. See the will of Thomas Hubbard, 26 Aug. 1709, ibid., vol. 1, will book, 1687–1710, SCDAH, pp. 51ff.

59. Will Transcripts, vols. 1–2, SCDAH.

60. Between 1722 and 1727, Indian slaves numbered 121 out of a total number of 1,696 slaves listed in postmortem inventories, WIMR, vols. 58–61A, SCDAH.

61. I have assumed a rough population figure of 16,000 for the total number of slaves at work in South Carolina during the mid-1720s, based on population estimates in Peter Wood, *Black Majority*, 146–50.

62. Postmortem inventories between 1722 and 1727 indicated that the population of native slaves had declined in absolute terms by about 300 persons from its prewar level of 1,400. Yet it seems to have reached a plateau by the middle of the decade. The ratio of Indians to Africans remained fairly constant, as did the rate of household ownership. WIMR, vols. 58–61A, SCDAH.

63. Between 1722 and 1726 African men were worth on average about £80 more per person than Indian men, and African women about £60 more than Indian women. Indeed, African women were on average appraised at about £30 more than Indian men. Unfortunately, there are not enough inventories from the first and second decades of the eighteenth century to make a reliable comparison with slave prices prior to the Yamasee War. WIMR, 6 vols. 58–61B, SCDAH.

64. Will Transcripts, vols. 1–2, SCDAH. No adult Indian men at all appear in this record series prior to 1715. Nevertheless, a 1708 census indicated that males comprised fully 33 percent of the total population of enslaved Indians, and they appear at a rate of 31 percent in postmortem inventories between 1722 and 1727. See table 7.2.

65. Jordan, *White over Black*, 90.

66. A. S. Salley, ed., *Commissions and Instructions from the Lords Proprietors of South Carolina to the Public Officials of South Carolina, 1685–1715* (Columbia: Historical Commission of South Carolina, 1916), 144.

67. McDowell, *JCIT*, 86.

68. Ibid., 138.

69. The Spanish province of Apalachee was located in northern central Florida, centering on present-day Tallahassee while Guale was located along the coast of Georgia.

70. Moore, *Nairne's Muskhogean Journals*, 75.

71. Ferguson, *Uncommon Ground*, 84.

72. From about 1684 to 1715, the Yamasee Indians lived in the vicinity of Port Royal, S.C., and made frequent slaving expeditions into the Spanish province of Guale, which lay directly to the southward.

73. Richard L. Haan, "The 'Trade Do's Not Flourish As Formerly': The Ecological Origins of the Yamasee War of 1715," *Ethnohistory* 28 (Summer 1981): 341–58.

74. Moore, *Nairne's Muskhogean Journals*, 75.

75. Journal Du Sieur D'Iberville, *Decouvertes et Etablissements Des Francais Dans L'Quest et Dans le Sud de L'Amerique Septentrionale*, ed. Pierre Margry, 6 vols. (Paris: Maisonneuve et c'ie, 1881), 4:517.

76. Richard White, *The Roots of Dependency: Subsistence, Environment, and Social Change among the Choctaws, Pawnees, and Navajos* (Lincoln and London: University of Nebraska Press, 1988), 47.

77. "An Act Prohibiting the Importation or Bringing into this Colony any Indian Servants or Slaves," in *The Public Records off the Colony of Connecticut,* ed. Charles J. Hoadly, 15 vols. (1850; reprint, New York: AMS Press, 1968), 5:534; the Connecticut act, passed in 1715, was a transcript of the 1712 Massachusetts act.

78. *The Statutes at Large of Pennsylvania* (Philadelphia, 1896), 2:433; *Records of the Colony of Rhode Island and Providence Plantations in New England* (Providence, 1856–1865), 4:134, cited in Lauber, "Indian Slavery," 235–36.

79. Albert Stillman Batchellor, ed., *Laws of New Hampshire* (Manchester, N.H., 1904), 53; Samuel Allinson, ed., *Acts of the General Assembly of the Province of New Jersey* (Burlington, N.J., 1776), 31, cited in Lauber, "Indian Slavery," 236.

80. Hoadly, *Public Records,* 5:516.

81. McDowell, *JCIT,* 57.

82. *Boston News Letter,* 13 June 1715.

83. Daniel C. Littlefield, "The Slave Trade to Colonial South Carolina: A Profile," *South Carolina Historical Magazine* 91 (Apr. 1990): 71.

VIII

This is "Mines"

Slavery and Reproduction in Colonial Barbados and South Carolina

JENNIFER LYLE MORGAN

African women enslaved in the Americas found their productive and reproductive labors exploited by English slave owners. Both the unfolding ideological mechanism that deemed Africans as usable chattel and the day-to-day world of late-seventeenth- and early-eighteenth-century American slave societies depended on ideas about women's reproductive capacity. As European settlers developed colonial slave societies, ideologies of African women's reproductive potential became central to both the individual experience of enslavement and the larger institution of racial slavery. For slave owners, black women's ability to bear children became imbedded in the ideological framework of race, justifying racial slavery and providing a secondary source of plantation produce. Moreover, for enslaved African women the ability and inability to bear and rear children became inextricable from the material realities of forced labor in the Americas.

African women, transported to the Americas at ages at which their fertility had already been both biologically and socially inscribed, found their reproductive experiences and expectations violently disrupted by slavery. New landscapes transformed both the physicality of childbirth and its cultural meanings. As those responsible for the agricultural labor in most West African societies, these first generations of enslaved women were likely accustomed to demands on their physical labors—but unprepared for their new biological identities as the very "conduits of slavery."[1] Across the colonial frontier English slave owners cobbled together legal codes and definitions of perpetual racial slavery based precisely on black women's reproductive identities, effectively inscribing childbirth at the heart of that which made Africans enslavable.[2] Slaveholding legislators defined perpetual racial slavery through the wombs of enslaved women, thus ushering childbirth into the economy. But regardless of its new economic dimensions, childbirth remained a contradictory for the enslaved woman, one in which expectations of the past clashed with the reality of the present. Thus, enslaved women and men found themselves faced with the monumental task of assigning new meaning to birth, struggling to disassociate childbirth from the violence of the labor regime and the violation of its economic value in the American colonies.

For those men and women involved in the seventeenth-century slave trade, the connection between slavery and reproductive ideologies was not new. Well before the arrival of English men and women to the Americas, English travelers had articulated a foundational relationship between reproduction and racial hierarchy. As they wrote on slavery and their travels to West Africa and the West Indies, early modern authors created naturalized images of African women's "propensity" to work based on their equally naturalized predilection for uneventful childbirth.[3] Travelers described these women as apathetic mothers who reproduced without pain and nursed their children with breasts slung indifferently over their shoulders. For early modern English and European writers, the connection between production and reproduction formed a crucial buttress to racialist ideology—beliefs in African inferiority found roots in the reproductive labors of African *women*.[4]

While images of African women's reproductive reality played an essential role in constructing racial difference, the establishment of English slave societies in North America and the Caribbean initiated other relationships between race, slavery, and the black female body. Faced with the fears generated by being in the minority, slave owners conferred to female slaves a pacifying influence on the colonies while simultaneously denying African women the protective status of "femaleness" that their reproductive properties ought to have conferred.[5] Childbearing did not insulate women from forced labor, for as white settlers transferred their demands for skilled labor from white indentured male servants to enslaved African men, slave owners forced women to shoulder the bulk of field work throughout the English colonies.[6] Finally, as English settlers' sense of security and long-term colonial success grew, so did their reach into African women's reproductive futures. When slave owners imagined the wealth and stability of their own progeny's economic prospects, they looked to the reproductive potential of enslaved women with increasing frequency. For the British colonies of Barbados and South Carolina, probate records allow a partial exploration of the consequences wrought by slave owners' expectations upon the working and reproductive lives of the women they enslaved.

Reproduction occupies a central position in scholarship on slavery. Few historians of American slavery have failed to develop conceptual frameworks organized around questions of biological and cultural reproduction. Studies of early slave societies and comparative slavery undertaken over the past twenty years concern themselves with the achievement of sexual parity, the interplay between reproduction and the development of a Creole or African-American culture, and the demographically distinct example of natural increase in North American slave societies. Historians are well aware that disease, malnutrition, and overwork suppressed birthrates for all Africans, particularly those enslaved in the British West Indies, and thus few have explored the experience of reproduction in the West Indies beyond explanations of the absence of natural increase.[7] Historians of mainland American slave societies, on the other hand, faced with the anomaly of an enslaved population that reproduced itself naturally by the mid-eighteenth century, have focused attention upon the cultural implications of natural increase rather than upon more immediate questions about how childbirth under slavery affected both slave owners and the enslaved.[8] In effect, however, these studies reify the connections between sex, reproduction, and viable childbirth and thus oversimplify reproduction under slavery. The very mortality and infertility rates that depressed childbirth among Africans throughout the Americas, changed the reality of birth and childhood for surviving children. Overly determined attention to natural increase, in contrast to a view that includes reproduction that did not effect a positive rate of growth, overlooks a crucial developmental dimension of American racial slavery, one that has been less frequently explored.

Because historians understand that reproduction rates were very low in the Caribbean, it has been assumed that throughout the region men always outnumbered women. While it is true that male majorities categorized the eighteenth- and nineteenth-century black Caribbean populations, sex ratio changed dramatically over time and space. Throughout the seventeenth century the slave trade brought similar numbers of men and women to the English-occupied Caribbean, and thus the first generations of slave owners and enslaved persons experienced racial slavery as a phenomenon that involved equal numbers of women and men.[9] By the century's end, sex ratios either approached balance or favored women on the British Leeward Islands, Jamaica, Bermuda, and Barbados.[10] Only in Barbados, however, did the balanced sex ratio of the seventeenth century remain constant until after emancipation. Partially as a result of this long-term balance in Barbados, mortality and birth rates were such that the black population sustained its numbers naturally by the closing decades of the eighteenth century.[11]

When Barbadian slave owners involved themselves in the settlement of the new mainland colony of South Carolina, they set in motion a transfer of slave owning practices whose consequences on South Carolina have been well documented.[12] Many scholars have noted the connection between the two colonies and have speculated on the long-term political and economic consequences of a South Carolina elite with Barbadian origins. Questions remain, however, about the material effects of the Barbadian experience on Carolina's evolution, both for slave owners and for the enslaved. In the decades following the 1670 settlement of Carolina, slave owners from Barbados constituted the core settler population in the mainland colony and transferred their assumptions and behaviors about many aspects of colonial slave ownership—including those regarding reproducing women—to Carolina. Prior to the 1720s, balanced sex ratios led to a period of natural increase in Carolina, but with the onset of rice production, malaria-ridden rice fields replaced the healthier (albeit more isolated) cattle stations and foresting sites of the first decades of settlement and brought rising rates of mortality, a male-dominated slave trade, and a decline in birth rates. Not until the 1760s did birthrates rise again such that the population attained consistent natural increase.[13]

The important demographic difference between rates of natural increase in the two colonies does not negate an essential similarity in slave owners' attitudes toward laboring women or in the extent to which enslaved women in Barbados and Carolina experienced their reproductive identities as enmeshed in the fabric of forced labor. Slave owners in both Barbados and South Carolina worked to capture women's reproductive capacity, link it to the growth and development of their individual estates, and thus bolster their entire colonial ventures. While demographic realities remained outside their control, slave owners' wills, inventories, and purchasing patterns in Carolina suggest that planters followed a Barbadian model of slave ownership when they saw women's reproductive potential as an essential element of their socioeconomic success and one that they attempted to shape to their own advantage.

The Englishmen who first settled the uninhabited island of Barbados in 1627 understood that they could not survive alone. Weeks after arrival, a delegate from the island persuaded thirty-two Arawak Indians on the South American mainland to accompany him back to Barbados where the Arawaks' agricultural expertise safely brought English setters through their initial perilous attempts at subsistence.[14] As the settlers began to clear the wooded island, allocate land, and turn their agricultural efforts toward export crops, they looked to English indentured servants for exploitable labor and utilized them until the middle of the seventeenth century. In the 1640s, when Dutch planters from Brazil brought sugar-cultivating technologies to the small island, Barbadian landowners began to systematically turn their attention toward Africans to labor in the island's sugar fields.

As early as the 1640s the presence of African women on Barbados seemed to demand multilayered attention. Planters appear always aware that the presence of women on their plantations brought both social and demographic changes. In 1647 Richard Ligon (an English traveler to and temporary planter in Barbados) advised all those Englishmen interested in establishing a plantation on Barbados to enslave equal numbers of African men and women. (The demographics of the seventeenth-century slave trade colluded with Ligon by creating a market in which his advice could, in fact, be followed.) Ligon framed his advice in the need for social control, not for work or reproduction. By enslaving sufficient numbers of women, he suggested, the planter would avoid a siege of African men claiming to be unable to "live without Wives."[15] Ligon's approach to the question of sex ratios among the enslaved highlights a specific facet of the black female presence in Barbados: when Ligon used the term "Wives" to refer to enslaved African women, he rallied images of family, children, and the tranquillity of the conjugal unit. Because he had detailed planters' fear of revolt earlier in his manuscript, Ligon had already provided ample evidence to his readers regarding the subliminal benefits of a labor force depicted in terms of connubial domesticity. The previous decades had shown "servants" and "slaves" to be quite capable of revolt; perhaps "husbands" and "wives" would be less so.[16]

It is hardly surprising that Ligon failed to describe the difficulties experienced by "husbands" and "wives" who tried to establish and maintain conjugal ties in the face of enslavement. Women's presence on the plantation, even at this early date, brought about the demographic transformations that caused slave owners to identify enslaved women as "wives" in the first place and further to watch, enumerate, and define the sexual unions of the women and men they enslaved. The degree to which the women and men identified as "husband" and "wife" actually experienced intimacy in their designated roles is, of course, unknowable. No matter how balanced sex ratio were, they could neither insure stability nor marriage partners for the enslaved.[17]

The African woman Bessie, enslaved on the island sometime in the late 1640s or early 1650s, certainly understood the insecurities of "marital" unions. When her owner died in 1654, Bessie, her children, and the other men and women with whom she lived were at the mercy of his beneficiaries. In the fragmentary piece of evidence in which Bessie is mentioned, she is listed in the inventory taken of her deceased owner's property: "Negro man named Sam and his wife and piqueninies, Peter and wife and three piqueninies, Bessie and her piqueninies, Dick and his wife and two piqueninies, Adam his wife and two piqueninies, one Negro by name Abala."[18] In the absence of a spouse her presence is made manifest because, unlike the other women enslaved on this plantation, Bessie was named. The others were recorded only as anonymous and presumably pacifying "wives." The absence of a named spouse may indicate that Bessie had a "visiting" marriage, that her spouse had succumbed to the violence of slave labor, or that the vagaries of the slave market had forcibly removed him from her proximity. While his absence inscribes Bessie's presence, it also speaks to the insecurity of conjugality even on a plantation "stable" enough to produce four couples and more than seven children in the insecure decade of the

1650s. The sale of the plantation on which Bessie lived would cause tremendous anxiety. After all, nothing could assure her that she would keep her children or that they would even survive. The only certainty had already occurred at the point of their birth—at which time her status of "slave" was joined by that of "parent," irrevocably changing the terms under which she endured her enslavement. For despite Richard Ligon's language, slave owners purchased African women for their capacity to work. And thus coupling, parenting, *and* forced labor shaped Bessie's life in colonial Barbados.

In the twenty-year period between 1650 and 1670 there are seventy-four extant estate inventories in which enslaved persons were named and enumerated.[19] Between 1650 and 1659 (or the first decade during which Barbados was clearly on its way toward becoming a full-fledged slave society) women were enslaved in equal or greater numbers than men in 62 percent of the extant twenty-nine inventories. On none of the remaining 38 percent did women comprise less than 40 percent of the total enslaved adult population of the estate. And thus it would appear that the first generations of Barbadian slave owners enslaved a proportionally substantial number of African women.[20] The inventories provide, at best, spotty evidence concerning the actual value that slave owners conferred upon the women they enslaved. However, when augmented by another set of sources, it becomes more clear that Ligon correctly identified a primary concern of Barbadian slave owners—that their female chattel not only worked, but that they "pacified."

Between 1662 and 1664 some 206 slave owners purchased enslaved Africans from the Company of Royal Adventurers.[21] Of these 200 purchases, 60 percent (125) purchased groups of slaves that included both women and men. Of these, only 17 percent (22) involved groups in which the ratio of men to women was 2:1 or higher. Twelve percent (16) purchased more women than men; 27 percent (34) purchased equal numbers of women and men; and 56 percent (70) purchased groups that approximated sex balance, such as one in which there were eight men and six women. Forty percent of all transactions involved bondspersons of a single sex. Of that group 62 percent (49) purchased only men while 38 percent (30) purchased only women.[22]

These purchasing patterns suggest that most Barbadian slave owners, faced with a cargo of men and women, did not rush to purchase men, leaving women behind for the latecomers. Rather, by the 1660s they saw women as valuable laborers whom they easily integrated into their work force—albeit in proportions designed to enact an additional kind of valuable labor. For reasons entirely separate from those that caused slave owners to modify the sex ratios of their labor force, enslaved women and men did have

FIGURE 8.1
NUMBER OF PERSONS ENSLAVED ON EACH INVENTORIED PLANTATION

NOTE: In the years for which the table is blank, the numbers of women and men could not be determined.
SOURCE: Deed Books, Series RB1, Barbados Archives, Cave Hill, St. Michael's Barbados.

children. On fully a third of the inventoried plantations "children" are named, while on a quarter of these estates "boys" and "girls" are distinguished from "men" and "women," at a time in which the slave trade brought negligible numbers of children to the Americas.[23]

The presence of children on midcentury Barbadian plantations should not overshadow the fact that many women transported to Barbados, like their counterparts throughout the Americas, had difficulty bearing children.[24] Inadequate diets lowered fertility, and the labor regime of a Barbados sugar plantation rendered many women unable to conceive or to carry fetuses to term. For those pregnancies carried full term, infant mortality rates stood at least at 50 percent.[25] Childbirth under slavery thus occurred in an environment more marked by death than birth, and those who gave birth to surviving children could not fail to understand that. To unravel the tangle of violence created by the interplay between coerced labor and the attempt to create and maintain relationships with children is impossible. However, while Bessie and the women who shared her dual identity of producer and reproducer were in a unique position from which to appreciate the violence that resulted from their multiple roles, they were not the only persons cognizant of their reproductive capacities.

At midcentury Henry Whistler, a visitor to the island, commented upon the practice of slave owners' raising slave children: "thes Negors they doue alow as many wifes as they will have, sume will have 3 or 4 according as they find thayer bodie abell: our english heare doth think a negor child the first day it is born to be worth 05 l., they cost them noething the bringing up, they goe all ways naked: Some planters will have 30 more or les about 4 or

5 years ould: they sete them from one to other as we doue shepe."[26] While plantations with thirty or more infants seem to have existed only in this writer's imagination, planters did anticipate and obtained wealth in the form of slave children, and they utilized that wealth as they saw fit. Slave owners' wills illuminate the human dimensions of this particular form of plantation "produce," as women found their tenuous hold on the children they bore tested by the economic and social agendas of Barbadian slave owners.

In 1654, for example, John James bequeathed two-thirds of his property—eight acres of land, "nine negroes young and ould, with one cow with certain stock of Hoggs [and] dunghill Fowles"—to his daughter. He reserved the remaining third of his property for the use of his wife during her lifetime. After her mother's death, the daughter would inherit the "said land negroes stock of hoggs fowles and cowes *[and] what they shall produce by their increase.*"[27] James imagined that along with chicks, foals, and calves, enslaved children might also come to buttress the economic position of his wife and daughter.[28] When planters looked to "increase," they crafted real and imagined legacies. In the absence of slave children, their heirs still inherited the promise of future wealth. In this act of laying claim to an African woman's unborn child, the slaveholder reinforced his belief in the longevity of his enterprises and the certainty of a future in and for the colony, thus cementing the relationship between his colonial future and her progeny.

While Barbadian planters saw the reproductive potential of the enslaved as a matter of the white community's own stability and wealth, they also recognized the inherent instability of their position in a colony in which they were outnumbered by persons whom they had already experienced as capable of revolt.[29] Slave owners, as Ligon suggested, who encouraged the conjugal unit and reproduction transformed the uneasy reality of a black majority into mothers, wives, husbands, and hopefully, children. Particularly in the context of the tremendous socioeconomic change wrought by the introduction of sugar to the island's economy, black women's bodies became vessels into which slave owners poured their hopes for the future—icons for the stability and wealth of the white community.

Throughout the next decade Barbadian slave owners continued to leave evidence of this proclivity for a sex-balanced labor force in their probate records. While some wills say little other than that the testator owned property (and therefore they cannot be relied upon as a source for demographic data), there is a very particular assumption evidenced by the wills concerning the legacy that slave owners believed enslaved women to embody. As they dispersed their human property, slave owners revealed their reliance upon enslaved women's labor and divulged their assumption that reproductive potential comprised an important part of women's productive value.

Between 1660 and 1669, 138 slave owners mentioned enslaved persons in their wills. Those wills which itemized women jumped from 37 percent (18) the previous decade to 59 percent (82) in the 1660s; female laborers were everywhere on the island's plantations. Indeed, in the 1660s more planters neglected to mention adult men than adult women (twenty-six and ten respectively). On the forty-five estates inventoried during this decade, 60 percent were home to more women then men, and on 13 percent equal numbers of women and men worked.

On none of the remaining 27 percent (with three exceptions) do women comprise less than 30 percent of the work force. As Barbadian slave owners increasingly relied upon enslaved women as laborers, they also valued them more systematically as potential reproducers, and subsequently they began to act explicitly upon women's reproductive value in their wills, shaping bequests along the lines of black women's fertility. In the 1660s, 9 percent (13) of slave owners who mentioned women in their wills used the term "increase" to pass down future unborn children while another 11 percent (15) explicitly paired individual men and women in their bequests. These paired couples emerge from the documents as evidence that some planters had begun to organize their labor around notions of conjugality and fertility. And of course many more slave owners may have had reproduction in mind as they bequeathed a woman with many men, or many women alongside few men.[30] In identifying women's reproductive potential in this way, planters responded to enslaved men and women's own desire to create intimate spaces in their lives, for by the second decade of Barbadian planters' full-scale importation of slave labor, such intimacies resulted in the increased need to balance the demands of labor with those of child rearing.

Planters manifested their assumptions about women's reproductive roles in various ways. For example, in an act that aligned the consumable bodies of cattle with the producing bodies of black women and men, William Browne carefully listed the names of his cattle along with the list of men and women: "Bessie" under "Women" and "Bessy" under "Cows."[31] Other planters evoked the value of "breeding" property more subtly. In 1660 John Redway bequeathed his two adult slaves, both women, to his children. He bequeathed Besse to his daughter. His son obtained Sibb, whose fertility made her more valuable, along with her two children. Having already borne two children, Redway still garnered Sibb's reproductive potential. He stipulated that "all [other] such children as she shall hereafter bring into this world" should also go to John Redway II.[32] The use of Besse and Sibb for their productive labor inscribed a new linkage between race and femaleness while Redway's division of Besse and Sibb along the lines of their fertility-based value simultaneously reinscribed old patriarchal patterns of inheritance. It was, after all, Redway's son who inherits the more valuable property that Sibb embodied; Redway's daughter was left with the, perhaps

TABLE 8.1
BARBADOS WILLS, 1650–1669

	1650-59	1660-69
Total Number of Wills Itemizing Enslaved Persons	48	138
Number of Wills Identifying Women	18 (37%)	82 (59%)
Number of Wills Identifyig Children	3 (6%)	26 (19%)
Number of Wills using the term "Increase"	4 (8%)	13 (9%)
Number of Wills Identifying a Parent	1(2%)	12(9%)
Number of Wills in which slaves are "Coupled"	2 (4%)	15 (11%)
Number of Wills Identifying a Spouse	0	2(1%)

Percentages are of the total number of documents containing slaves; all percentages have been rounded off.
SOURCE: Recopied Will Books, Series RB/6, Barbados Department of Archives and History, Cave Hill, Barbados.

FIGURE 8.2
NUMBER OF PERSONS ENSLAVED ON EACH INVENTORIED PLANTATION

NOTE: In the years for which the table is blank, the numbers of women and men could not be determined.
SOURCE: Deed Books, Series RB1, Barbados Archives, Cave Hill, St. Michael's, Barbados.

disappointingly, less valuable Besse. In this area in which slave owners could most severely undermine the lives of the enslaved, Redway found a space in which to reinforce old notions about the transfer of personal wealth and to bolster the assumption that their economic and social investment in the island colony would be a long-term success.

In the 1660s, far more than in the previous decade, probate officials inventoried children along with adult men and women. Thirty-one percent (twenty-six) of the wills that mentioned women also mentioned children, children whose presence on plantations required parenting and forced labor to coexist. In the 1650s ten out of thirty-three plantations with adult men and women contained children. In the 1660s twenty-two out of forty-eight (or 45 percent) plantations enumerated in planters' wills contained children. Moreover, if we return to the inventoried estates, 49 percent of the forty-five estates inventoried in the 1660s contained children. As the plantation became the dominant unit of production for slave owners, the presence of children (even for those who did not give birth) meant that for the enslaved it functioned as an equally important unit of attempted autonomy and cultural reproduction. Time and again, those deemed the least fertile and the least likely to reproduce, became parents in an environment where slave owners reduced the relationship between mother and child to the economics of legacies, and basic assumptions about parenting could not be guaranteed.

In 1678, eight years after the settlement of the mainland colony, actions set in motion hundreds of miles away shaped Jack and Aram's lives in Carolina. Back in Barbados, Willoughby Yeamans wanted to help secure the future for his kinsman in Carolina. He ordered his attorney, Christopher Barrow, to "give my Cozen Mr. John Yeamans a Negro man and a Negro woman."[33] Barrow immediately procured Jack and Aram in Carolina with "their profitts and increase" for John Yeamans. Barrow did not take Aram's fertility for granted. He purchased Aram and Jack along with their two children, Jack and Namy, ages three and one, providing John Yeamans with a woman whose reproductive capacity was assured. Furthermore, Aram and Jack's identity as parents meant that their desire to maintain and protect the integrity of their family unit made them appear to be both a stable and productive source of wealth for the Carolina "cozen." From the moment of their arrival in the mainland colony, Barbadian slave owners put their assumptions that slavery involved both production and reproduction into practice through their purchasing, transporting, and bequeathing patterns.

Since a tangible link existed between the two colonies, Jack and Aram probably came to Carolina from Barbados. Barbadian planters worked to ensure that the settlement of Carolina would profit them. In 1665, for example, the proprietors of the new colony wrote that land would be granted in parcels of up to 150 acres per settler, his dependents, and his servants. The Barbadian Adventurers, investors in the Carolina colony, sought to clarify the proprietors' meaning by stipulating that "Man-servant" and "Woman-servant" be augmented to include "Negro-man or slave" and "Woman Negro or slave." Barbadian planters knew their interest lay in a land-grant system that equally rewarded the introduction of slaves and servants. The proprietors also came to understand this. In a 1670 letter they clarified their language by claiming that "man-servant" always "mean[t] negroes as well as Christians."[34] Thus, planters who journeyed from Barbados brought enslaved men and women with them secure in the knowledge that their wealth in the new settlement would be produced by unfree black labor.

As a result of the Adventurers' intervention, those with the means to do so transported both black and white laborers to the new colony, knowing that their status as slave owners there would not be undermined. White settlers from the island where black labor had long since displaced white servitude were the obvious beneficiaries of the new land-grant system. The Adventurers thus inextricably linked the future of Carolina to enslavement, assuring white Barbadian settlers that land entitlements would be based on generous headright. When the land-grant system worked in tandem with ideologies of labor contingent upon women's reproductive capacities, such as those enacted by Willoughby Yeamans, the fight to ensure privilege for wealthy settlers in the new colony illustrates two implicit assumptions, namely that black laborers would both constitute and produce wealth on the mainland.

Transplanted Barbadian slave owners, known as the "Goose Creek Men" for the community they settled, dominated the first generation of political actors in the mainland colony. These legislators passed the first Carolina slave law in 1690. In crafting the "Act for the Better Ordering of Slaves," they borrowed extensively from Barbados's 1688 slave code.[35] As in Barbados, lawmakers in Carolina defined slaves as all those who had been "to all Intents and Purposes" slaves.[36] Their legislative language located the defining condition of enslavement in circular logic: one is a slave because one has been a slave. Thus legislators rooted customary slavery, simply, in the bodies of women. If one is a slave because one has been a slave, then the act of *becoming* took place through the act of birth. The need to define those whom they enslaved only arose when Africans in the Americas began to have children. For the men and women transported to the colony as slaves, status had been fixed by their capture and transport. The language of customary slavery became important only with the birth of children whose status needed to be codified and articulated and thus only through the bodies of women. In Carolina, as in Barbados, no explicit law existed stating that the child of a slave should be a slave. Virginian legislators enacted that statute in 1662: "children got by an Englishman upon a Negro woman shall be bond or free according to the condition of the mother."[37] But Carolinian slave owners left things less clear. From the perspective of an enslaved childbearing woman, however, the reality was certain. For her there was no question but that her child would also be enslaved. In fact the slave owners' legal chimera actually resonated clearly. Slave owners developed the definition of slavery upon her body. Their linguistic pretense of "customary" slavery in the seventeenth century carried little meaning for the enslaved black woman who knew precisely how systematic racial "custom" could be.[38] Alone among the mainland colonies in their replication of a custom-based slavery system,[39] Barbadian settlers in Carolina reinforced their ideological and economic ties to the island colony through a legal definition of enslavement, dependent upon enslaved women, rapidly transplanted to the mainland.[40]

The majority of the first black arrivals to Carolina from Barbados and elsewhere in the West Indies came in pairs of men and women.[41] While settlers received equal amounts of land for white or black laborers, allocations favored males over females.[42] Such inequities did not deter early slave-owning settlers from bringing familial, or at least sex-balanced, groupings of black women and men to the new colony. White emigrants from Barbados, accustomed to balanced sex ratio among the enslaved on the small island, took for granted their replication as they established a new slave society on the mainland. Unsure of their ability to survive in the new settlement, slave-owning settlers brought couples. They were unwilling to risk large-scale transportation of enslaved property but they knew that in transporting a couple they simultaneously transported the possibility of future increase.

As rice cultivation developed and the colony expanded in the early eighteenth century, the numbers of enslaved persons brought directly from Africa to Carolina rapidly rose. In 1706 only twenty-four Africans entered the colony by ship. Just three years later slave traders transported 107 enslaved Africans from the African coast. By 1726 that number approached 2,000 per annum.[43] Carolinian planters quickly grasped the significance and scope of their society's changing demography. In a letter to English officials in 1699, Edward Randolph accurately assessed the number of white inhabitants of the colony, but put the black population at four times the white, at least twice their actual numbers.[44]

With the growth in the numbers of transported Africans, the Barbadian roots of South Carolina's black population grew increasingly tenuous. Over the course of the eighteenth century, enslaved persons from Barbados, and the West Indies in general, fell from more than half the total enslaved population in Carolina to as little as 15 to 20 percent. Nonetheless, despite falling numbers and in contrast to the Chesapeake region to the north, more enslaved Africans from the West Indies than from any other North American port of embarkation continued to arrive in Carolina throughout the colonial period.[45]

Unlike men and women from West Africa, those from Barbados came in small cargoes. Between 1717 and 1719 the average ship from the African coast arrived in Charleston with seventy-two men and women, while ships from the West Indies averaged only fourteen passengers of African descent.[46] The passage from Barbados did not replicate the physical dangers and high mortality rates of long, crowded, disease-infested journeys with inadequate food and water from the West African coast.[47] Enslaved Barbadians did not experience the sheer terror of the unknown to the same degree as their African counterparts. Even as the decades passed and the numbers of enslaved Barbadians in Carolina fell, the terms of passage for enslaved Barbadians would connect them to those first men and women transported in the 1670s and 1680s. They came along with slave owners, sharing with them an awareness of their mutual past, an anticipation of their future, and an understanding of the owner-slave relationship as it had already developed. Once in Carolina, those who had experienced enslavement in Barbados would find much that was familiar.

Elite society in Carolina echoed that of Barbados in many ways. Indeed, for some contemporary observers, the two occupied the same space. In 1682 Thomas Ashe wrote that "the Discourses of many Ingenious Travellers (who have lately seen *this part of the West Indies*) . . . justly render Carolina Famous."[48] The association with the West Indies resonated for black and white Carolinians in infamous ways as well. White death rates in Bridgetown and Charleston (the capitals of Barbados and South Carolina respectively) at comparable periods of each colony's development are striking in their similarity. In both towns the ratio of burials to baptisms approached four to one.[49] In the face of such high mortality rates, enslaved women from Barbados embodied Carolina planters' hopes for wealth. Newly arrived slave owners in Carolina groped about for agricultural successes, experimenting with cattle and corn, olives and silkworms, and finally rice. But throughout, they assumed that African women and men would continually provide secure, stable, and ongoing labor.

Sex-balanced groups of slaves appear in records from the first decades of settlement. White settlers' earliest economic successes came in the form of cattle raising.[50] The Africans minding cattle in the upcountry were often a man and a woman, perhaps accompanied by a child. Jack and Jugg, for example, tended seventeen head of cattle on Francis Jones's bleak settlement. Jones's entire estate, aside from cattle and slaves, consisted of some old pots and "one old beadstead, three old chests, two old chaires, one fourme, two stools, and one table top."[51] Likewise, in 1696 Mingo and Mall and a boy named Cudgeon tended thirty head of cattle and fifty-five pigs somewhere in the outer reaches of Carolina. When their owner died toward the end of the century, he did not own even a single piece of furniture.[52] Mall and Jugg lived their lives among men and boys in poverty and rural isolation on the colony's frontier, and evidence simply does not exist as to how they experienced that isolation. However, the presence of these women did, of course, change the landscape in which they lived. Stagnant demographic patterns carried real emotional and social consequences. From the first years of settlement, men like Jack and Mingo saw their futures linked to these women who symbolized a future in which their sociosexual lives might possibly be complete. Birthrates remained low, but at the beginning of the eighteenth century, and again well before its end, enslaved Carolinians experienced natural growth rates.[53]

In Carolina, as in Barbados, slave owners responded to black women's multiple roles. For the slave owners who brought Mall and Jugg to Carolina from Barbados these women were passive manifestations of assumptions about wealth in the Americas, although both slave owners and enslaved women recognized childbirth as central to the slave society. Like their Barbadian predecessors, Carolinian planters and writers recognized the multiple value of enslaved women, identifying in them the capacity to pacify the unruly, augment slaveholdings, and work in the fields.

By 1715 enslaved women occupied an essential position in the colony, both in regards to their sexuality and their labor. In the context of the Yamasee War, Carolina legislators looked to Virginia for military assistance. Virginia legislators demanded that Carolina pay 30 shillings per month and "a Negro woman to be sent to Virginia in lieu of each Man Sent to Carolina to Work till their Returne." Virginia's slave-owning legislators clearly saw the laboring bodies of black women as proper recompense for the fighting bodies of white men. But South Carolina slave owners deemed it "impracticable to Send Negro women . . . by reason of the discontent such Usage would have given their husbands to have their Wifes taken from them w ch might have occasioned a Revolt also of the Slaves."[54] After deliberation they rejected Virginia's terms; ultimately Virginia officials had to be content with mere monetary remuneration for the "poor Ragged Fellows" they shipped to Carolina.[55] Ostensibly, Virginian legislators couched the terms of their request in the need for labor not sex, but both colonies' legislators linked sex to labor. The request for women did not surprise Carolina's legislators, who seemingly understood that their military vulnerability necessitated a valuable exchange. Carolina legislators did not question the legitimacy of the request. They recognized the inherent value enslaved women embodied and saw the stability of the colony as linked to a female presence. White Carolinians and Virginians valued enslaved laborers whose bodies promised to combine plantation labor with sexual and reproductive gratification, and who could thus be utilized as laborers, peacekeepers, and "increasers."

Carolinian planters' reliance upon women as field laborers did not grow exclusively from the Barbadian past. By 1712 when John Norris wrote his promotional tract for the colony, an exclusive use of women as field workers was entirely normative. In his projected inventories he advised both wealthy and middling settlers to utilize only Indian women as field workers, the work of animal husbandry and artisanal jobs fell to African men. Norris advised the poor settler to purchase "two slaves; a good Negro Man and a good Indian Woman," while he told the wealthier settler to obtain "fifteen good Negro Men . . . [and] fifteen Indian Women to work in the Field."[56] The degree to which plantations with these demographics actually existed is unclear. By the end of the first decade of the eighteenth century, at the peak of Carolinians use of Indian slave labor, Native Americans comprised 25 percent of the total enslaved labor force. But that percentage rapidly declined in the aftermath of the Yamasee War.[57] Norris's recommendation certainly reflects both the assumption that women and men should be enslaved in equal numbers (a mathematics grounded in hopes of coupling and reproduction) and that field work was the province of women.

Carolinian slave owners did demand that their fields be worked by women—whether they were of Indian or African descent. Both African women and their children comprised an essential and visible source of labor in the colony. An observer wrote of the process of clearing the forested lands to make way for rice plantations and described male workers laboring after dark "lopping and firing," while women and children cut down shrubs and brushes.[58] Only a few years later, John Archdale remarked that "little negro Children" performed valuable complementary labor on plantations. Their work, essential but small, freed adults for larger more physically strenuous jobs.[59] Surrounded by enslaved laborers—men, women, and children who built roads, maintained houses and stores, worked crops, minded cattle, or fed silkworms—South Carolina whites recognized the inherent and explicit value of enslaved female labor, and relied upon women's bodies for more than work.

In 1706 the Society for the Propagation of the Gospel in Foreign Parts (SPG) sent Francis LeJau to Carolina. He critiqued black and white

Carolinians in his correspondence home.[60] LeJau's distress—and that of many missionaries sent by the society to Carolina—over his ongoing difficulties in reaching the colony's black population is palpable. In September 1708 LeJau wrote that "the evil I complain of is the constant and promiscuous cohabitating of slaves of different sexes and nations together. When a man or a woman's fancy dos alter about his party they throw up one another and take others which they also change when they please—this is a general sin for the exceptions are so few they are hardly worth mentioning."[61] LeJau's other letters reflect his ongoing concern with the "promiscuous disorder" of the enslaved. He wrote that "one of the most scandalous and common crimes of our Slaves is their perpetual changeing of Wives and Husbands which occasions great disorders." He "proposed . . . that none of [the Negroes] that are not yet Marry'd pressume to do it without his masters consent and likewise those that are now marry'd do not part without the like consent."[62] Much to his frustration, through their refusal to "better order" their marriage choices, enslaved women and men protected their ability to impose internally derived order on their most intimate decisions. LeJau's religious imperative made him unable to see anything but "chaos" in the personal lives of the enslaved, when in fact autonomous emotional choices may represent hard-won freedom from interference and Christianity. He felt the few men and women among the black population in Carolina who incorporated Christian notions of nuptial morality were "hardly worth mentioning." He therefore spoke to the already naturalized assumption that women comprised a significant portion of the enslaved labor force when he similarly considered the very presence of enough enslaved women to make this "chaotic" behavior possible equally unworthy of comment.[63]

As they worried over the behavior of black couples, SPG ministers turned a more hopeful eye toward black children, seeing them as targets for proselytizing throughout the first decade of the eighteenth century. In 1707 Reverend William Dunn of Charlestown complained to the SPG of his "extreme difficult[y]" in persuading slave owners to allow him to give religious instructions to the enslaved: "However I have persuaded some of them to let their slaves come at last to hear Sermon every Sunday, and likewise to cause the Children of their slaves to be taught to read."[64] Dunn correctly perceived that enough children existed to make the likelihood of instructing them a significant inroad to Christianizing the black community. In 1708, Governor Johnson estimated the colony's population for the Lords Proprietors. The population of enslaved men and women had grown since his last report; there were 300 more men and 200 more women than there had been in 1703. He reported that enslaved men outnumbered enslaved women (1,800 men to 1,100 women in 1708), but since 1703 the number of "Negro children slaves" had doubled (from 600 to 1,200). This represented a higher rate of increase than that for white children (who rose in number from 1,200 to 1,700) during a period in which the proportion of children in the transatlantic slave trade was negligible.[65]

This period of natural increase among the enslaved came to an end with the development of an export economy based primarily on rice production. The demands of rice cultivation worsened working conditions for the enslaved, and childbirth rates dropped. Moreover, ratios of women to men fell as the ethnic composition of the enslaved population shifted. Slave owners continued to import black women, and the amount of land apportioned by the Crown to newly arrived settlers with "households" of black and white laborers became the same for men and women, fifty acres.[66] But ships bringing enslaved men and women to Carolina from Angola and Senegambia in the 1720s carried different proportions of men and women than those that left the Bights of Benin and Biafra for Barbados more than fifty years earlier. As Carolina slave owners' demands for labor grew, slave traders transported an African population that radically changed the cultural landscape of the mainland colony. Ethnic African laborers rapidly outnumbered "acculturated" persons of African descent, and females found themselves in a diminishing minority.

For their part, prior to the 1720s, Carolina slave owners lived surrounded by the effect of relatively equitable sex ratios in the black children that populated the colony. In his examination of gender ratios and birth rates among blacks and whites in St. George's Parish in 1726, Peter Wood contrasts low birthrates among enslaved women with the higher rates among free white women to indicate the terrible conditions of the rice fields and the toll that work took on the bodies of women who might otherwise have been mothers.[67] I would argue, however, that the comparison of black to white women, while essential to our understanding of the ways that slavery mutated black women's reproductive rates in contrast to those not enslaved, draws attention away from the essential fact that despite the worsening conditions of enslavement, black women continued to bring children into the world. Wood's research shows that the average white woman in 1726 had more than two children (2.24) while the average black woman had just over one child (1.17), evidence that highlights the physical trauma of dislocation and the intense labor regime in the colony. But it also indicates that through the 1720s children, even only 1.17 of them, had become a ubiquitous part of enslaved women's response to and experience of enslavement.

Searching for valuable staple crops, South Carolina's slave owners employed the small bodies of enslaved children. In their wills and sales they organized for and anticipated the birth of these children. They not only rec-

TABLE 8.2
WILLS AND INVENTORIES, SOUTH CAROLINA, 1711–1729

	1711-1729
Total Documents Identifying Enslaved Persons	114
Number of Documents Identifying Women	82 (72%)
Number of Documents Identifying children	50 (43%)
Number of Documents using the term "Increase"	37 (32%)
Number of Documents Identifying Parents	19 (17%)

Percentages are of the total number of documents containing slaves; all percentages have been rounded off.
SOURCE: Secretary of the Province Records, 1711–1719; 1711–1717; 1714–1717; 1709–1725; 1714–1719; 1719–1721; 1721–1722; 1722–1726; and Will Book 1732–1737. South Carolina Department of Archives and History, Columbia.

ognized the social and economic value of slave women's reproductive capacity, but they acted upon it. When Richard Harris wrote his will in 1711 he parceled out the "increase" of both mares and women to his children.[68] In a 1704 lease of the Thorowgood plantation, William Hawlett promised John and Elizabeth Lancaster half of all the plantation's profits accrued in a seven-year period. That included "halfe the Rice halfe the pease halfe the Corne halfe the Butter halfe the Cheese ye Calves halfe the Hoggs halfe the Lams and the halfe parte of all the Negro Children that shall be borne."[69] Few probate records exist for the proprietary period (there are, for example, only twenty-eight extant wills recorded in the first decade of the eighteenth century), but those that do reflect the centrality of enslaved women's presence in early Carolina. In the first decade of the eighteenth century, twenty-one documents identify enslaved persons (two wills and nineteen inventories); only six are all-male transactions. By the turn of the eighteenth century, slave owners in Carolina responded to laborers in much the same way that Barbadian planters had fifty years earlier.

Robert Daniel transferred the men and women he enslaved as a group to his son in 1709.[70] From Daniel's perspective, the six women and eight men he owned all provided valuable labor on his Berkeley County plantation. They also had forged relationships with one another that may have led him to assume that the women he enslaved would soon provide him, or his son, with additional valuable laborers. "Paw Paw Tom and his wife Nancy [and] Tom Godfrey and his wife Hagar" no doubt felt pleased that they would not be separated from one another in the foreseeable future. The potential that other men and women on Daniel's plantation had for meaningful partnerships among themselves must have equally shaped the ways in which they conceived of their futures. In all but six of the documents in which women were mentioned—or in 65 percent of them—young children accompanied enslaved women.[71] Daniel thus behaved rationally when he assumed that by carefully balancing the men and women he purchased to cultivate his land he would also expand his slaveholdings. Through careful patterns of purchases, he constructed a group of men and women whose sexual composition was central to his sense of his economic future.

The opportunities to forge a future that included a semblance of family must have appeared boundless for the thirty enslaved men and twenty-nine women on David Davis's plantation, not to mention the thirteen boys and fourteen girls, as they did to Davis himself who saw the purchase of these forty-three black female workers as a profitable investment.[72] That his dreams had not quite come to fruition at the point of his estate's sale (only three of the twenty-nine adult women are listed with children) may reflect many factors. No evidence indicates the duration of time men and women on Davis's land lived together, or whether Davis's treatment of them precluded either the development of intimacies or the physical capacity to reproduce.

Women like those on Davis's plantation, who had no children, were not alone. The definition of their "increase" as property alone provided ample reason for enslaved women to want to forego childbirth. Only a year after the death of their owner in 1710, for example, three of ten women and men on Dorothy Daniell's plantation had died. Surrounded by death, on a struggling colonial frontier, Mary, Flora, Betty Comber, and Susanna, not surprisingly, remained childless. Nor was it likely that they would have children in the future. Alongside Panto, Joe, and Bransoe, the women would spend the next three years working for various landowners in order to pay off their owner's debt before being put to the "use and benefitt" of a minor grandson.[73] Although the very terms of the next three years of enslavement provided them with opportunities to forge connections with other enslaved women and men on plantations around the area, they could hardly feel secure about their future. On the Boowatt plantation George Dearsley enslaved sixteen persons, including seven women. Dearsley bequeathed them, in male-female pairings, to his children. In doing so he signaled hope more than surety. As a mother, Nancy was alone among the seven, the other women remaining childless.[74] For reasons as simple and as complex as the effects of forced labor on their bodies and their souls, though their owner carefully and intentionally provided the opportunity for his slaves to reproduce, these men and women did not do so.

Other enslaved women, however, did locate hopes in the bodies of children and subsequently understood the violence that slavery did to parenthood. Abinibah, for example, was sold in 1705 with her son Cuffee to a merchant in Charleston. Five years later, ill health forced the family which then owned her to move back to Barbados. Thus, in 1710 Abinibah, in the company of a woman named Cornelia and "one Negro boy named Morat," left for Barbados. Apparently without all her children, she left family and friends to endure a sea voyage to a place that may or may not have been familiar to her and her small child.[75] On their journey to Barbados, a larger group of enslaved women and men from Carolina joined Abinibah and Morat. To clear his debt, Stephen Gibbs of Charleston sent eight enslaved men and women to a Barbadian planter. Old Abigail and her adult daughter Bess traveled with Old Jack Smith and Young Jack, and Jupiter and the boy Little Jupiter. The man Lowrus and the girl Nancy are the only two of the eight not clearly related to one another by name or implication.[76] Spanning as it does three generations, the rarity of this particular community of enslaved men and women draws attention to the more common kin ties developing between parents and children throughout the new colony. Moreover, the group's forced migration highlights the potential for pain that kin ties embodied, for while these eight traveled together, there is no telling how many other family members their owner's financial distress forced them to leave behind.

In 1713 Arrabell illustrated, with clarity and heartbreak, that which was at stake for enslaved women who could and did have children throughout the Diaspora. Arrabell lived with seven women and nine men in Berkeley County. Three of the women had single children, and a fourth two-year-old was cared for on the plantation in the absence of a named parent. In a few years, the population of enslaved Africans would eclipse that of white settlers, and Arrabell and the women around her may have begun to feel portents of the changing tide about to engulf the colony. They witnessed the trauma of familial separation in the aftermath of many slave owners' deaths, and searched for a way to shield themselves and their children from separation and distribution among slave owners' heirs and creditors. For some women perhaps the birth of children offered a means to reappropriate that which should have been theirs all along. Arrabell's child's name poignantly symbolizes the struggle inherent in reproduction in this most unstable moment in the development of a slave society. Arrabell called her child "Mines"—as she could little else.[77]

The migration of slave owners from Barbados to Carolina led to a planter population singularly poised to act on reproductive potential. Moreover, the initial transportation of sex-balanced groups of men and women from Barbados made Carolina slave owners predisposed to regard female laborers, and the dual potential they embodied, as valuable. Thus the Bar-bados-Carolina connection illustrates the centrality of reproduction, both as an ideology and a reality, in these two colonial slave societies' formative years. The rhythms of sex ratio, fertility, and mortality among the enslaved occurred outside the control of slave owners in both Carolina and Barbados. Enslaved women's experience of childbirth intersected with planter ideology only insofar as those ideas did violence to women's ability and desire to bear and raise children. Nonetheless, the example of slave owners' ideological and material relationship to the bodies of black women in the two colonies illus-trates the centrality of reproduction in the formation of the African Dias-pora. Linked to profit and progeny, reproductive potential was embedded in the language of slave ownership and racial domination and in the day-to-day lives of both slave owners and enslaved women.

Notes

1. Hilary Beckles, "Sex and Gender in the Historiography of Caribbean Slavery," in *Engendering History: Caribbean Women in Historical Perspective,* ed. Verene Shepard, et al. (New York: St. Martin's Press, 1995), 125–40; the quotation is from p. 129.

2. For discussions of the link between black female reproduction and the develop-ment of legal definitions of racial slavery see, for example, A. Leon Higgenbotham, Jr., *In the Matter of Color: Race and the American Legal Process: The Colonial Period* (Oxford and New York: Oxford University Press, 1978), 43; Joan Dayan, "Codes of Law and Bodies of Color," *New Literary History* 26 (Spring 1995): 283–308; Kathleen Brown, *Good Wives, Nasty Wenches, Anxious Patriarchs: Gender, Race, and Power in Colonial Virginia* (Chapel Hill: University of North Carolina Press, 1996).

3. Jennifer L. Morgan, "Some Could Suckle over Their Shoulder: Male Travelers, Female Bodies and the Gendering of Racial Ideology, 1500–1770," *William and Mary Quarterly,* 3d ser., 54 (Jan. 1997): 167–92.

4. Scholars such as Kim Hall, Peter Erickson, and Lynda Boose have examined Eng-lish literary and artistic imagery for evidence of early modern racial ideology. See Kim F. Hall, *Things of Darkness: Economies of Race and Gender in Early Modern England* (Ithaca, N.Y.: Cornell University Press, 1995); Peter Erickson, "Representations of Blacks and Blackness in the Renaissance," *Criticism* 35 (Fall 1993): 514–15; Lynda Boose, "'The Getting of a Lawful Race': Racial Discourse in Early Modern England and the Unrepre-sentable Black Woman," in *Women, "Race," and Writing in the Early Modern Period,* ed. Margo Hendricks and Patricia Parker (London and New York: Routledge Press, 1994), 35–54, esp. 49.

5. This gendered notion of passivity also had a cultural component. Slave owners con-ferred values such as tractability on the "country born" or Creole men and women they enslaved and rebelliousness on "New Negroes" directly imported from West or West Cen-tral Africa. As the plantation complex expanded in most of the southern and Caribbean colonies, complicated cultural overlays developed as the descendants of Africans sup-planted and then, in turn, were supplanted by newly imported ethnic Africans. As slave owners faced the realities of black majorities, their need to obtain profit sometimes flew in the face of their need to maintain control. Their impulses to create stable "familial"

labor units, to encourage women's reproduction, borne of humanitarianism or of profit motives, conflicted with the drive to extract the maximum amount of production from men and women's labor in the fields; and indeed the conflict rarely resolved.

6. In many of those colonies, more women than men performed field work. Marietta Morrissey, *Slave Women in the New World: Gender Stratification in the Caribbean* (Lawrence: University of Kansas Press, 1989), 67–68; Ira Berlin and Philip D. Morgan, "Labor and the Shaping of Slave Life in the Americas," in *Cultivation and Culture: Labor and the Shaping of Slave Life in the Americas,* ed. Berlin and Morgan (Charlottesville: University Press of Virginia, 1993), 1–48, esp. 19. The exception occurred in slave societies in which men constituted a considerable majority of the black population.

7. For an example, see Kenneth Kiple, *The Caribbean Slave: A Biological History* (Cambridge: Cambridge University Press, 1984), 107–34. For a discussion of African women's infertility see Allan Kulikoff, "A 'Prolific People': Black Population Growth in the Chesapeake Colonies, 1700–1790," *Southern Studies* (Winter 1977): 398–403; Herbert S. Klein and Stanley L. Engerman, "Fertility Differentials between Slaves in the United States and the British West Indies: A Note on Lactation Practices and Their Possible Implications," *William and Mary Quarterly,* 3d ser., 35 (1978): 357–74; Ward, *British West Indian Slavery,* 136.

8. For examples see Charles Joyner, *Down by the Riverside* (Urbana and Chicago: University of Illinois Press, 1984); Herbert Gutman, *The Black Family in Slavery and Freedom, 1750–1925* (New York: Vintage Press, 1976); Allan Kulikoff, *Tobacco and Slaves: The Development of Southern Cultures in the Chesapeake, 1680–1800* (Chapel Hill: University of North Carolina Press, 1986); Michael Mullin, *Africa in America: Slave Acculturation and Resistance in the American South and the British Caribbean, 1736–1831* (Urbana and Chicago: University of Illinois Press, 1992).

9. For a statistical analysis of sex ratio in the early transatlantic slave trade see David Eltis and Stanley L. Engerman, "Was the Slave Trade Dominated by Men?" *Journal of Interdisciplinary History* 23 (Autumn 1992): 237–57.

10. Richard S. Dunn, *Sugar and Slaves: The Rise of the Planter Class in the English West Indies, 1624–1713* (Chapel Hill: University of North Carolina Press, 1972), 127, 181; Jerome Handler and Frederick Lange, *Plantation Slavery in Barbados: An Archaeological and Historical Investigation* (Cambridge and London: Harvard University Press, 1978), 67–72; Cyril Outerbridge Packwood, *Chained on the Rock: Slavery in Bermuda* (New York: Eliseo Torres & Sons, 1975), 73–76.

11. Slave owners in Barbados stopped relying upon the African slave trade in the 1760s when the population came to sustain itself. In the aftermath of the American War of Independence slave imports fell from 3,755 per annum to 300 per annum. They never again rose above 398. These figures are a compilation of Philip Curtin and Richard Sheridan's demographic work by Handler and Lange, *Plantation Slavery,* 20–23, table 8.1. See also Michael Craton, *Testing the Chains: Resistance to Slavery in the British West Indies* (Ithaca, N.Y., and London: Cornell University Press, 1982), 257; and Barry Higman, *Slave Populations of the British Caribbean, 1807–1834* (Baltimore: Johns Hopkins University Press, 1984), 314.

12. Peter H. Wood's chapter "The Colony of a Colony" provides a full discussion of the political and social origins behind white Barbadians' relocation to and influence in Carolina; *Black Majority: Negroes in Colonial South Carolina from 1670 through the Stono Rebellion* (New York and London: W. W. Norton, 1974), 13–34. See also Richard B. Dunn, "The English Sugar Islands and the Founding of South Carolina," *South Carolina*

Historical Magazine 72 (Summer 1971): 81–93; Jack P. Greene, "Colonial South Carolina and the Caribbean Connection," *South Carolina Historical Magazine* 88 (Winter 1987): 192–210; Eugene Sirmans, "The Legal Status of the Slave in South Carolina, 1670–1740," *Journal of Southern History* 28 (Nov. 1962): 462–73.

13. Using figures from Wood and Kulikoff, Russell Menard estimates that positive growth rates among enslaved South Carolinians occurred beginning in 1750. See "Slave Demography in the Lowcountry, 1670–1740: From Frontier Society to Plantation Regime," *South Carolina Historical Magazine* 96 (Oct. 1995): 298, table 8.10.

14. David Watts, *The West Indies: Patterns of Development, Culture and Environmental Change since 1492* (Cambridge: Cambridge University Press, 1987): 156–57.

15. Richard Ligon, *A True and Exact History of the Island of Barbados* (London: 1647), 47.

16. For discussion of cooperative resistance between white servants and black slaves see Hilary Beckles, *Black Rebellion in Barbados: The Struggle against Slavery 1627–1838* (Bridgetown, Barbados: Antilles Publications, 1984), 25–51.

17. As Brenda Stevenson has shown for a later period, age differentials, the effect of sales, and "the complex rules of exogamy which slaves exercised," all disrupted the formation of stable marital unions even under circumstances in which men and women were enslaved in equal numbers. Brenda E. Stevenson, "Gender Convention, Ideals, and Identity among Antebellum Virginia Slave Women," in *More than Chattel: Black Women and Slavery in the Americas, pp. 169–190*, ed. David Barry Gaspar and Darlene Clark Hine (Bloomington: Indiana University Press, 1996), 178.

18. An unattributed manuscript from 1654, Davis MSS, box 7, envelope 15, Royal Commonwealth Society, London, England.

19. These inventories are found in recopied deeds, record book 3, vols. 2–7, Barbados Archives, Cave Hill, St. Michael's, Barbados. There are other deeds in which "negroes" are mentioned but are not distinguished by number, sex, or name, and thus they are not included in the tabulations that follow.

20. During this period, Barbados was shaped by large-scale dependence upon the Bights of Benin and Biafra for the supply of slave labor—regions that exported large numbers of women. David Richardson, "Slave Exports from West and West-Central Africa, 1700–1810: New Estimates of Volume and Distribution," *Journal of African History* (1989): vol. 30, 1–22, esp. 11–20; Eltis and Engerman, "Dominated by Men?" 256. Will of John May, 24 July 1659, record book 6, vol. 14, Barbados Archives, 445 (hereafter cited as RB 6/14, BA, 445); will of Thomas Kennett, 5 Nov. 1659, RB 6/14, BA, 438; inventory of John Lewis, 26 Nov. 1661, RB 3/3, BA, 428; inventory of Judith Powery, 19 Mar. 1662, RB 3/2, BA, 554; inventory of Philip Banfield, 11 May 1662, RB 3/2, BA, 564. Individual plantation holdings with relatively balanced sex ratio mirrored the larger social reality of the island. In 1673, Peter Colleton of the Barbados Council reported that the black population was comprised of 10,236 men, 5,827 boys, 11,914 women, and 5,207 girls. Sir Peter Colleton, president of the Council of Barbados to "[the Council for Trade]", 28 May 1673, *Calendar of State Papers, Colonial Series* (1669–1674), vol. 7, ed. W. Noel Sainsbury (London, 1889), 497, entry 1101. Slight fluctuations in the population ratio would occur throughout the remainder of the seventeenth century, but by the eighteenth century the sex ratio settled into approximately 48 percent male and 52 percent female. It remained at that level until emancipation. See Hilary McD. Beckles, *Natural Rebels: A Social History of Enslaved Black Women in Barbados* (New Brunswick, N.J.: Rutgers University Press, 1989), 7–22; Handler and Lange, *Plantation Slavery in Barbados*, 67–72, table 8.6; see also Jerome Handler, *The Unap-*

propriated People: Freedmen in the Slave Society of Barbados (Baltimore and London: Johns Hopkins University Press, 1974), 24–25, table 8.4.

21. The restoration of the Stuart monarchy in England in 1660 reinvigorated English trade with Africa. That same year the Crown granted a charter to the Royal Adventurers for trade of all sorts, including slaves. From August 1663 through March 1664 the company delivered at least 3,075 slaves to Barbados. The initial company dissolved in 1667 to be replaced in 1672 by the Royal African Company. See K. G. Davies, *The Royal African Company* (London and New York: Longmans Green & Co., 1957), 40–44. The record of Barbados purchases covers 2,020 enslaved Africans sold to 206 slave owners between 1662 and 1664. David Galenson, using a far more complete set of purchasing patterns initiated in 1678, draws a different conclusion regarding the desirability of female laborers than I do. Using records that not only indicate who is sold and for how much, but also the point at which the purchase took place during the duration of the sale, his evidence shows that the most healthy African men comprised the first group of persons purchased, with the most healthy African women alongside "second best" men being purchased next. The 1662–1664 ledger does not allow the kind of specificity that the later records do. Barbados ledger, 1662–1664, Company of Royall Adventurers, T 70/646, Public Record Office, London (hereafter cited as PRO). David W. Galenson, *Traders, Planters, and Slaves: Market Behavior in Early English America* (Cambridge: Cambridge University Press, 1986), 71–92.

22. Two purchases did not identify the gender of the enslaved. Barbados ledger, T 70/646, PRO, 29.

23. Children comprised only eleven out of one hundred persons in the middle passage in the period prior to 1700. See Eltis and Engerman, "Dominated by Men?" 243, table 8.2.

24. It is also conceivable that, through access to fertility control, African women actively lowered birthrates as a means of resistance to the slave society. See Barbara Bush, *Slave Women in Caribbean Society: 1650–1838* (Bloomington and Indianapolis: Indiana University Press, 1990), 120–50.

25. Kiple, *The Caribbean Slave*, 76–134, 114, 149; for a discussion of African cultural responses to child mortality rates see Bush, *Slave Women in Caribbean Society*, 146–47.

26. "Extracts from Henry Whistler's Journal of the West India Expedition, 1654," in *The Narrative of General Venables*, ed. C. H. Firth (New York and London: Longmans Green & Co., 1900), 146. The wills of planters in the 1650s do not bear out Henry Whistler's observations on children, but as we shall see, plantation inventories in the next decade do.

27. Will of John James, 24 Jan. 1654, RB 6/14, BA, 432; emphasis mine. English common law stipulated that widows be left at least a third of their husband's property.

28. In acknowledging this possibility, he became the first of many Barbadian planters to use the term "increase" to represent potential reproduction among enslaved women. In her critique of Allan Kulikoff's assumptions concerning family formation in the Chesapeake, Jean Butenhoff Lee notes that in Virginia "masters planned to dispose of children still in the womb [or] . . . deliberated what to do with a woman's future increase." Thus, Barbadian planters' language is not unique but rather belongs on a continuum in American slave societies. Jean Butenhoff Lee, "The Problem of Slave Community in the Eighteenth-Century Chesapeake," *William and Mary Quarterly*, 3d ser., 43 (July 1986): 359.

29. For an overview of early revolts in Barbados see Beckles, *Black Rebellion in Barbados*.

30. It is only in the cases where couples are clearly delineated that I counted them as

"seed" couples. Will of Nicholas Cowell, 23 Oct. 1667, RB6/9, BA, 321; will of Thomas Morris, 7 Aug. 1666, RB6/8, BA, 132; will of Judith Mossier, 14 June 1668, RB6/10, BA, 130. Slave owners' recognition of reproducing enslaved women's value may seem unremarkable, but the fact that they did so as early as the mid-seventeenth century warrants attention. In other Caribbean slave societies it was not until Britain's amelioration policy of the late eighteenth century that slave owners encouraged reproduction among the enslaved. J. R. Ward, *British West Indian Slavery, 1750–1834: The Process of Amelioration* (Oxford: Clarendon Press, 1988), 120–89.

31. Inventory of William Browne, 17 Mar. 1662, RB3/3, BA, 276. Carol Barash, noting a similar proximity between the enslaved and cattle in Jamaica, maintains that by listing slaves and cattle together on inventories both are "consumed if not literally eaten," the slave owner anxious to emphasize the commodification of both bodies in his possession. Carol Barash, "The Character of Difference: The Creole Woman as Cultural Mediator in Narratives about Jamaica," *Eighteenth Century Studies* 23 (Summer 1990): 413.

32. Will of John Redway, 11 Jan. 1660, RB6/14, BA, 503.

33. Willoughby Yeamans to Christopher Barrow, 7 Apr. 1678, Records of the Register of the Secretary of the Province, 1675–1695 and 1703–1709, Secretary of State Miscellaneous, vol. 2, South Carolina Department of Archives and History, Columbia, 58 (hereafter cited as Records of the Register of the Secretary of the Province, Miscellaneous, vol. 2, SCDAH, 58). John Yeamans was the son of Sir John Yeamans (d. 1674), first governor of the colony.

34. In a final collusion with the desires and powers of Barbadian slave owners, John Locke and the Earl of Shaftesbury's *Fundamental Constitutions* for the new colony codified both the power of whites over blacks and the fixity of a slave's status, even in the face of Christian conversion. Locke carefully defined the servile status of Africans in the context of a Christian colony. He paraphrased Paul (1 Cor. 7:20–24) thus: "Christianity gives not any one any new privilege to change the state, or put off the obligations of civil life, which he was in before. Wert thou called, being a slave? Think thyself not the less a Christian, for being a slave." Locke's title as Landgrave, with its accompanying 48,000 acres of land in Carolina, not to mention his investments in the Bahamas, situates his interest in securing the institution of African slavery in the Americas. *The Works of John Locke*, 10 vols. (London: 1823; reprint, Darmstadt, Germany: Scientia Verlag Aulen, 1963), 8:116–17; also quoted in Wayne Glausser, "Three Approaches to Locke and the Slave Trade," *Journal of the History of Ideas* 51 (Apr.–June 1990): 199–218.

35. During the proprietary period (pre-1719) while the largest number of assemblymen and deputies always came from England, Barbadian settlers consistently and closely made up the second largest group. Planters maintained professional ascendancy in the ranks of legislators throughout the period, comprising 60 to 70 percent of assemblymen. For tabulations on the high proportion both of Barbadians and of slave-owning planters among South Carolina legislators see Richard Waterhouse, *A New World Gentry: The Making of a Merchant and Planter Class in South Carolina, 1670–1770* (New York and London: Garland Publishers, 1989), 37–42. Speaking solely in terms of social conventions, Eugene Sirmans notes that as late as 1750 "there were still traces of a Barbadian influence in South Carolina as the [white] people retained some West Indian customs." M. Eugene Sirmans, *Colonial South Carolina: A Political History, 1663–1763* (Chapel Hill: University of North Carolina Press, 1966), 229. For analysis of the two colonies' slave codes see Dunn, "English Sugar Islands," 81–82; and Sirmans, "Legal Status of the Slave," 464.

36. "An Act for the Better Ordering and Governing of Negroes and Slaves" (1696), in *Statutes at Large of South Carolina*, ed. Thomas Cooper and David J. McCord, 10 vols. (Columbia, S.C.: A. S. Johnston, 1836–1841), 7:352–65.

37. Act XII, 1662, in *Statutes at Large of Virginia*, ed. William W. Hening, 2 vols. (Richmond: Franklin Press, 1819–1820), 2:170, cited in A. Leon Higginbotham, Jr., *In the Matter of Color: Race and the American Legal Process: The Colonial Period* (Oxford and New York: Oxford University Press, 1978), 43.

38. Slave owners in Barbados and South Carolina customarily treated the enslaved as chattel. Planters in Barbados listed slaves alongside moveable property in their inventories and freely appropriated all aspects of black women's productive and reproductive capacity in their wills. They did this despite early laws that defined the enslaved as real estate, tied to land, and not moveable. As early as 1682, planters in Carolina would do the same. "An Act declaring the Negro Slaves of this Island to be Real Estate" (1668), in *Acts Passed in the Island of Barbados from 1643–1762*, ed. Richard Hall (London, 1844), 64. Inventory of John Smyth, 13 Feb. 1683, Records of the Register of the Secretary of the Province, Miscellaneous, vol. 1, SCDAH, 21. For more on the question of slaves as chattel see Sirmans, "Legal Status," 464–68.

39. Greene, "Colonial South Carolina," 198.

40. Comparative studies of enslavement have, for many years, been concerned with legal definitions of enslavement. Scholars contrasted "chattel" slavery in British colonies with the almost contractual form of slavery in Latin America. They have suggested that the law reflected experience and therefore that legal definitions translated into more benign enslavement in Latin America. Elsa Goveia's seminal work remains a touchstone in these debates. See Elsa Goveia, *Slave Society in the British Leeward Islands at the End of the Eighteenth Century* (New Haven: Yale University Press, 1965), 155–202, and "The West Indian Slave Laws of the Eighteenth Century," in *Slavery in the New World: A Reader in Comparative History*, ed. Laura Foner and Eugene Genovese (Engelwood Cliffs, N.J.: Prentice-Hall, 1969), 113–37. For a recent refutation of the claims that legal recognition of a slave's humanity equaled better treatment see Alan Watson, *Slave Law in the Americas* (Athens and London: University of Georgia Press, 1989), 115–24.

41. See Wood, *Black Majority*, 21.

42. McCrady, *History of South Carolina*, 118; Wood, *Black Majority*, 15–20; and Robert M. Weir, *Colonial South Carolina: A History* (New York: KTO Press, 1983), 51–54.

43. Wood, "'More like a Negro Country': Demographic Patterns in Colonial South Carolina, 1700–1740," in *Race and Slavery in the Western Hemisphere: Quantitative Studies*, 131–72, ed. Stanley Engerman and Eugene Genovese (Princeton: Princeton University Press, 1975), 144.

44. "Letter of Edward Randolph to the Board of Trade, 1699," in *Narratives of Early Carolina*, ed. Alexander Salley (New York: Charles Scribner's Sons, 1911), 204.

45. Daniel Littlefield, "The Slave Trade to Colonial South Carolina: A Profile," *South Carolina Historical Magazine* 9 (Apr. 1990): 69.

46. Littlefield, "Slave Trade," 74.

47. For discussions of the precise rate and causes of death during the middle passage see, for example, Joseph C. Miller, "Mortality in the Atlantic Slave Trade: Statistical Evidence on Causality," *Journal of Interdisciplinary History* 11 (Autumn 1991): 317–29; Richard Steckel and Richard Jensen, "New Evidence on the Causes of Slave and Crew Mortality in the Atlantic Slave Trade," *Journal of Economic History* 46 (Mar. 1986):

57–77; Charles Garland and Herbert Klein, "The Allotment of Space for Slaves aboard Eighteenth-Century British Slave Ships," *William and Mary Quarterly*, 3d ser., 42 (Apr. 1985): 238–48; and David Eltis, "Mortality and Voyage Length in the Middle Passage: New Evidence from the Nineteenth Century," *Journal of Economic History*, 44 (June 1984): 301–8.

48. Thomas Ashe, *Carolina, or a Description of the Present State of That Country . . . 1682* (London: 1682), printed in Salley, ed., *Narratives of Early Carolina*, 139. Emphasis mine.

49. While no such records exist for the enslaved, black mortality rates in both colonies were also exceedingly high. Peter Coclanis, *The Shadow of a Dream: Economic Life and Death in the South Carolina Low Country, 1670–1920* (New York and Oxford: Oxford University Press, 1989), 43. For more on the connections between the colonies see Greene, "Caribbean Connection," 192–210; Dunn, "The English Sugar Islands," 81–93; and Dunn, *Sugar and Slaves*, 116.

50. For a discussion of the African origins of Carolina animal husbandry see Wood, *Black Majority*, 28–32; see also Walter Rodney, *A History of the Upper Guinea Coast, 1545–1800* (London: Oxford University Press, 1970), 24–25; for a discussion of the origins of cattle grazing in Carolina and its implications for the Caribbean connection see John Otto and Nain Anderson, "The Origins of Southern Cattle-Grazing: A Problem in West Indian History," *Journal of Caribbean History* 21 (1988): 138–53.

51. Inventory of Francis Jones, 20 Sept. 1693, Records of the Register of the Secretary of the Province, 1692–1700, SCDAH, 89.

52. Inventory, 2 Mar. 1696, Records of the Secretary of the Province, 1692–1700, SCDAH, 237.

53. Wood, *Black Majority*, 142–66. Russell R. Menard has critiqued Wood's figures, and posited less increase and more slave imports for this period in his recent. "Slave Demography in the Lowcountry, 1670–1740: From Frontier Society to Plantation Regime," *South Carolina Historical Magazine* 96 (Oct. 1995): 280–303.

54. Joseph Boone and Richard Beresford, agents for the Commons House of Assembly in South Carolina, to the Council of Trade and Plantations, 5 Dec. 1716, *Calendar of State Papers, Colonial Series* (Jan. 1716–July 1717), vol. 29 (London, 1930), 216. See also Wood, *Black Majority*, 128–29.

55. Wood, *Black Majority*, p. 129 n. 132.

56. John Norris, *Profitable Advice for Rich and Poor,* in *Selling a New World: Two Colonial South Carolina Promotional Pamphlets*, ed. Jack P. Greene (Columbia: University of South Carolina Press, 1989), 77–147; the quotations are from pp. 128, 132.

57. William L. Ramsey, "The Yamasee War and the Decline of Indian Slavery in Colonial South Carolina: A Demographic Profile" (paper presented at the third annual Omohundru Institute of Early American History and Culture meeting, Winston-Salem, N.C., June 1997). I am grateful to William Ramsey for drawing my attention to the preponderance of women among enslaved Indians held in Carolina.

58. Timothy Silver, *A New Face on the Countryside: Indians, Colonists, and Slaves in South Atlantic Forests, 1500–1800* (Cambridge and New York: Cambridge University Press, 1990), 106–7.

59. Archdale, in *Early Carolina*, 310. He particularly discussed enslaved children's suitability for feeding silkworms. Experiments in silk production were abandoned in the face of the successful introduction of rice to the colony. Silver, *New Face*, 147.

60. See the introduction to *The Carolina Chronicle of Dr. Francis LeJau, 1706–1717,* ed. Frank J. Klingberg (Berkeley and Los Angeles: University of California Press, 1956), 1–14.

61. Francis LeJau to the Society for the Propagation of the Gospel, 15 Sept. 1708, Charles Town. Society for the Propagation of the Gospel Papers, South Carolina, 1702–1710, vol. 16, Lambeth Palace Library, London, 224 (hereafter cited as SPG, South Carolina, vol. 16, LP, 224).

62. LeJau to SPG, 20 Oct. 1709, SPG, South Carolina, vol. 16, LP, 237.

63. The next year he wrote to the SPG that he "has refused to baptise and marry several sober slaves (their masters being unwilling)," LeJau to SPG, 17 Oct. 1709, SPG, South Carolina, vol. 2, LP, 65.

64. William Dunn to the SPG, 21 Apr. 1707, SPG, South Carolina, vol. 16, LP, 153. For discussions of the impact of Society for the Propagation of the Gospel ministers among enslaved Africans in South Carolina see Wood, *Black Majority*, 132–42; and Margaret Washington Creel, *"A Peculiar People": Slave Religion and Community-Culture among the Gullahs* (New York and London: New York University Press, 1988), 67–80. For an earlier discussion of the religious experiences brought by enslaved Africans to the Americas see John Thornton, *African and Africans in the Making of the Atlantic World, 1400–1680* (Cambridge and New York: Cambridge University Press, 1992), 254–62.

65. While imports contributed to some of the population growth, Peter Wood has documented natural increase among the enslaved prior to 1720. Governor Johnson to the Lords Proprietors, 17 Sept. 1708, Transcripts of Records in the British Public Record Office Relating to South Carolina, 1701–1710, SCDAH, 203–10; see also Wood, *Black Majority*, 143–45, esp. table I; and n. 23 above.

66. Report of council meeting, 19 Oct. 1731, Board of Trade Correspondence, 1730–1733, Colonial Series 5/362, Public Record Office, 65 (hereafter cited as CO 5/362, PRO, 65).

67. Wood, *Black Majority*, 162.

68. Will of Richard Harris, Records of the Secretary of the Province, 1711–1719, SCDAH, 17.

69. Sale of William Hewlett, 23 Aug. 1704, Records of the Secretary of the Province, 1714–1715, SCDAH, 125.

70. Sale of Robert Daniel, 17 Oct. 1709, Records of the Secretary of the Province, 1709–1725, SCDAH, 43.

71. Of those six, two women were actually accompanied by "boys" or "girls." Such language evokes a pubescent or adolescent child who may well have come to the colony via the middle passage. Three of the remaining group of women were accompanied by "increase."

72. Sale of David Davis, 30 May 1710, Records of the Secretary of the Province, 1709–1725, SCDAH, 136.

73. Will of Dorothy Daniell, 15 Oct. 1711, Records of the Secretary of the Province, 1714–1717, SCDAH, 44.

74. Will of George Dearsley, 20 June 1702, Records of the Secretary of the Province, 1711–1719, SCDAH, 33.

75. Sale of Timothy Corbrow, 13 Oct. 1705, Records of the Secretary of the Province 1709–1725, SCDAH, 69; and transport application of Michael Mahon, 9 Nov. 1710, Records of the Secretary of the Province, 1709–1725, SCADH, 98.

76. Sale of Stephen Gibbs, 7 Nov. 1710, Records of the Secretary of the Province, 1709–1725, SCDAH, 96.

77. Sale of John and Elizabeth Gibbes, 7 May 1713, Records of the Secretary of the Province, 1711–1717, SCDAH, 47. In her discussion of the meanings of mothering under slavery, Deborah Gray White states: "It was, ironically, an act of defiance, a signal

to the slaveowner that no matter how cruel and inhumane his actions, African-Americans would not be utterly subjugated or destroyed. Slave mothers gave African-Americans the right to say collectively what one slave woman once said of her offspring: 'My child him is mine.'" *Ar'n't I a Woman: Female Slaves in the Plantation South* (New York: W. W. Norton, 1985): 110.

IX

Affiliation without Affinity

Skilled Slaves in Eighteenth-Century South Carolina

S. MAX EDELSON

South Carolina masters, writing in eighteenth-century runaway advertisements, often characterized their skilled slaves as "sensible," a term they seldom used to describe field hands.[1] The word carried a complex of meanings;
it denoted qualities of awareness, capability, and rationality as well as a willingness on the part of slaves to employ these attributes as contributors to
plantation production.[2] Sensible slaves broke through a barrier that prevented other slaves from appearing to their owners as distinct and compe-
tent individuals. Unlike most field workers, who could be ranked as "prime
hands" or "half hands" expected to produce a certain quantity of rice, skilled
slaves presided over significant aspects of production by virtue of their special capabilities. They worked independently, traveled extensively, and
learned to gauge social situations, making the personal quality "sensibility"
a synonym for cultural fluency. As slave owners embraced the advantages of
gaining greater control over the exercise of specialized skill, they recognized
individual ability and encouraged slaves to participate in production as semi-
autonomous agents within larger plantation enterprises. But masters also
described these slaves as "cunning" and "artful," associating valuable craft-
like skills with a craftiness they could not always channel reliably toward productive endeavors.

This essay attempts to portray enslaved specialists as a distinct group by
exploring the cultural consequences of their economic experiences. It argues
that skilled slaves affiliated themselves with plantation enterprises in ways
that furthered their pursuits of individual autonomy. These affiliations
allowed slaves and planters to follow otherwise antagonistic courses within
highly individualized labor arrangements that created a unique space for
compromise. The planters' aggressive quest for economic mastery, however,
frequently came into conflict with the slaves' defensive attempts to preserve
and enlarge autonomy. The ways in which working arrangements dissolved
when slaves rejected the sacrifices that affiliation imposed reveals their fundamental character as strategic connections.

This essay considers the economic context for the growth and elabora-
tion of a skilled slave sector of the labor force, the role of these slaves versus
that of white artisans as planters sought to diversify and improve their plantations, the ways enslaved specialists managed contrary commitments in a

plantation setting, and the cultural position and behavior of skilled run-aways. These disparate views of skilled slave life present a consistent pattern of economic experience. Both planters and slaves availed themselves of the opportunity to create specialized roles for slave workers, but with strikingly different agendas. Along with various types of skilled work came material benefits, opportunities to obtain cash, and work agreements that featured a comparatively high degree of mobility and individual autonomy. Arrangements employed to manage these relationships tended to be individually tailored to specific work situations rather than customary systems that applied to all enslaved specialists. Skilled slaves committed themselves to the economic enterprises to which they contributed their labor and for which they were compensated, more than they identified with their owners or exhibited signs of selfless personal loyalty.

Slaves in British North America typically responded to the harsh labor regimes that came with an increased focus on commodities produced for export by building a defensive community life focused on family and religion.[3] Skilled slaves, on the other hand, often left such cultural enclaves to work and live in economic settings featuring frequent contact and communication with whites. They obtained a degree of conditional autonomy, not by taking shelter in a black sphere that might withstand a white hegemonic assault, but by actively contributing expertise to plantation enterprises and becoming versed in the cultural terms that governed white society. While most slaves reacted to an emerging plantation system by making the most of opportunities that attended a calculated retreat into community, skilled slaves strategically engaged in this economy in often individualistic, almost entrepreneurial, ways.

By affiliating with their masters' plantation enterprises, skilled slaves attempted to build a material foundation for greater individual autonomy. The planters' desire to control a flexible, trained, and mobile corps of workers encouraged them to substitute incentives and reciprocation in place of routinized accountability and coercive force. Affiliation, as a concept, implies a bond, but one that bears lines of separation inscribed from the outset: slaves figured in such relationships as subordinate, self-interested participants but rarely as ideologically committed subalterns. As plantations grew from crude settlements into large, diverse businesses as the century progressed, skilled slaves made commitments, as economic agents, to plantation enterprises. They avoided enmeshing themselves psychologically into a paternalistic or adversarial relationship with an individual slave owner, as long as arrangements designed to make specialized work possible took the character of a binding agreement rather than a tenuous privilege. When the compromises that permitted both slaves and master to simultaneously pursue autonomy and mastery collapsed, slaves often severed pledges of affiliation and withdrew from their roles by running away and working clandestinely. Slaves and masters eyed one another with cold calculation as they carved niches within an expanding lowcountry plantation economy. The range of experiences that occurred within these relationships reveals a world of strategic maneuver, in which interests came into alignment to support a stable labor system and clashed in confrontations marked by varying degrees of dissonance.

Relationships of affiliation between slave specialists and their owners figured as one of several developments that distinguished the plantation economy after 1720 from the frontier conditions that had prevailed before the rise of rice as South Carolina's most important export.[4] From the colony's founding in 1670 through the first two decades of the eighteenth century, slaves and masters commonly worked in small, familial groups and met the challenges of production in the expanding lowcountry plantation economy with ad hoc solutions. They felled trees, cleared land, planted crops, tended livestock, packed preserved meat, and rendered naval stores from the surrounding pine forests. In this small-scale extractive economy geared toward establishing viable and profitable settlements, an equality of material conditions and the exigencies of frontier life modulated the power disparities between owners and those they claimed to own. Masters expected slaves to work with a high degree of flexibility, as "jacks-of-all-trades," at tasks both menial and requiring special skills.[5]

This settlement phase of production witnessed the training of enslaved sawyers and coopers, who turned forest cover into arable land and salable produce, and a class of black cowboys and livestock workers.[6] By the first decade of the eighteenth century plantations hired slave labor, sought slaves with special training to saw wood and fashion lumber as new land was cleared for agriculture, and made special compensatory arrangements with slaves who worked at specialized tasks.[7] Once rice production transformed the South Carolina plantation economy in the 1720s and the advent of a local indigo culture after 1745 deepened planters' commitment to commodity production geared for European markets, the improvisational character of master-slave relations changed. After 1720 planters shifted their expectations for slave labor, valuing disciplined and rigorous work in the rice fields over the ability to work independently and adapt to a variety of tasks. The size of plantation communities increased during this period, straining further the informal character of master-slave relations. As planters presided over labor camps consisting of scores of individuals rather than the ten to twenty common before 1720, they hired overseers to manage slave workers and could rarely be found working with their slaves.[8]

While the majority of slaves under the new regime saw former privileges eroding, the new commitment to export-oriented production increased the need for specialized, nonagricultural slave work. The demands of large-scale plantation commodity production promoted the articulation of the slave labor force into a majority of agricultural workers, who chiefly cultivated and processed rice, and a specialist minority that labored at a broader range of tasks. These skilled slaves built the plantations' structures, prepared commodities for market and transported them, managed other slaves in increasingly hierarchical labor arrangements, and became the flexible, versatile workers who adapted their abilities to the novel opportunities and pressing needs of plantation enterprises. The versatility that once characterized the enslaved labor force as a whole came to be limited to this skilled minority.

This economic transition from an extractive, settlement phase to one dominated by the imperatives of transatlantic trade left firmly in place a degree of slave autonomy preserved by the terms of the task labor system. Planters assigned most rice workers a daily task that they could complete at their own pace with limited supervisory control. The task system allowed many slaves the opportunity to cultivate their own produce after completing a partial day's work for the plantation. A mutual adherence to past practice sustained the system as a viable means for masters to obtain a degree of slave compliance with the objectives of plantation agriculture and for slaves to reserve time and labor for themselves.[9] For agricultural workers, the task system retained avenues toward autonomy under assault in an emerging plantation system that permitted far less individual freedom of economic activity than had previously prevailed.

Slave specialists retained more directly the flexible labor arrangements of the early settlement stage of the colony's development, in part because of the nature of specialized labor. Rice tasks divided work into units of readily measurable quantity: acres of land hoed and weeded, bushels of rough rice pounded, and yards of ditch dug. But much skilled work could only be evaluated in terms of the quality of a final product. Enslaved drivers presided over a seasonal crop, land in good or bad "order," and a slave community that might be quiet or discontented. One driver discussed with his master the course of summer planting around a map of the plantation "chalked out" on the floor of a Charles Town residence "for the driver's study and understanding." On one of the Ball family plantations, three traveling craftsmen departed for months at a time during the 1740s to work in town and build indigo vats on other plantations, probably bringing wages they had earned on their return.[10] While agricultural workers salvaged a degree of customary autonomy through a commitment to tasked labor, skilled slaves in the new economy affiliated themselves with plantation enterprises in order to retain and enlarge their scope for independent action.

The emergence of a customary task system for agricultural workers, however, influenced all slaves who sought to defend and enlarge spheres of autonomy against encroachments by slave owners. The principle of receiving privileges that ran counter to the masters' idealized vision of slave dependence was taken from the rice fields and adapted to the specialized job. The task system's articulation of the terms of master-slave exchange as a clear, contractual agreement influenced other labor arrangements, even those not involving daily tasks.[11] The logic a labor system endorsed by the vast majority of enslaved workers in South Carolina, with its appeal to the legitimacy of precedent and an implicit assertion that a master's power was constrained by custom, informed the way skilled slaves evaluated, affirmed, and terminated their affiliations to larger plantation enterprises.

The rice and indigo plantation economy supported a wide range of specialized slave work, claiming 15 to 20 percent of the slave population during the colonial period and more than a quarter of all slaves after the Revolutionary War.[12] Yet the increasing size and variety of positions within this economy did not guarantee all enslaved specialists a chance to barter a commitment of affiliation into real advantage. A skilled slave's ability to pursue autonomy through affiliation varied especially in terms of gender, the locus of employment, and the degree of independence or managerial authority allotted to different occupations. Some sense of the range and distribution of specialized slave occupations can be gleaned from table 9.1.[13]

Six hundred and two distinct slave runaway advertisements published in South Carolina newspapers from 1732 to 1790 mention enslaved specialists. Construction, plantation, and transport trades dominate the list of primary occupations and account for over half of all slaves in the sample. Most of these workers possessed abilities that suggest an orientation toward work on plantations or in handling plantation produce. Those whose primary occupation was that of carpenter, cooper, or sawyer totaled 159, or just over one-fourth all advertised skilled runaways. The numbers of urban and service workers and those in miscellaneous occupations show a strong secondary concentration of skilled slaves in Charles Town, by far South Carolina's largest and most important port city.

Women made up just over 10 percent of the sample, and were employed in textiles crafts, marketing, and washing almost exclusively.[14] Gender divisions in skilled work followed contemporary European conventions, drawing men toward work in crafts, transportation, and managerial positions on plantations while women worked in urban marketing and occupied domestic positions as house servants, washerwomen, and seamstresses.[15] Perhaps no longer able to work in the fields, older women occasionally tended cattle while planters hired out others as wet nurses and midwives.[16] Not only were approximately nine out of ten skilled workers men and boys, but slave owners hired out male workers for temporary labor at rates that were almost

Table 9.1

SOUTH CAROLINA SKILLED RUNAWAYS, 1732–1790

	Primary Occupation	Secondary Occupation
Construction and Plantation	203 (34%)	
Carpenter	73	11
Cooper	50	5
Sawyer	36	7
Bricklayer	23	
Blacksmith	8	
Painter	6	
Wheelwright	5	2
Brickmaker	1	
Saw Mill Worker	1	
Transportation	125 (21%)	
Sailor	58	7
Boatman	35	16
Patroon	13	1
Porter	7	
Indian Trader	4	
Carter	3	
Ferryman	3	
Wagoner	2	1
Pilot		1
Textiles and Leather	62 (10%)	
Shoemaker	28	3
Seamstress	18	
Tanner	8	3
Textile Producer	6	1
Saddler	2	1
Currier		1
Miscellaneous	55 (9%)	
Hired or Laborer	20	2
Musician	18	
Doctor	4	
Public Works Laborer	4	
Apprentice	2	
Distiller	2	
Bell Ringer	1	
Chimney Sweep	1	
Dancing Master	1	
Lamp Lighter	1	
Newspaper Boy	1	

Urban and Service Trades	100 (17%)	
Market Slave	21	4
Washerwoman	20	2
Taylor	15	3
Barber	12	2
Butcher	9	2
Cabinetmaker	7	
Hostler	5	2
Shoptender	5	
Baker	2	
Jeweler	2	
Coachman	1	
Nurse	1	
House Slave		14
Cook	7	

Agriculture and Fishing	35 (6%)	
Fisherman	17	6
Cattle worker	6	
Gardener	6	
Ploughman	4	1
Driver	2	1
Net Maker		3
Farmer		1
Mower		1
Shipbuilding	22 (4%)	
Shipwright	12	1
Caulker	4	2
Sailmaker	3	
Ship Yard Worker	3	
Total	602	114

SOURCE: Lathan A. Windley, comp., *Runaway Slave Advertisements: A Documentary History from the 1730s to 1790*, vol. 3: South Carolina (Westport, Conn. and London: Greenwood Press, 1983).

twice that charged for female workers.[17] Planters, and the social conventions that they upheld, largely confined slave women and girls to the fields and to jobs in what might be called a domestic sphere within the plantation economy. Female house servants and field workers often spent at least some time in a plantation kitchen or at the spinning wheel, just as men occasionally left the fields to work as sawyers or wagoners.[18] Women sometimes worked as indigo makers, strategically important positions on plantations devoted to production of the dye, perhaps drawing on a familiarity with indigo in West Africa, where home textiles production typically fell under the purview of women.[19] During the Revolutionary War, when plantations increased production of home-produced textiles to clothe slaves in a process of import substitution, female seamstresses, spinners, and carders probably rose in importance in plantation hierarchies.[20]

In the plantation countryside, slave drivers assumed managerial responsibilities as plantations grew in size, and planters became seasonal absentees and multiple plantation owners based in Charles Town. In addition, by mid-century, plantations contained a customary complement of specialized workers, almost always including a carpenter, cooper, at least one sawyer, and at times seamstresses, gardeners, and livestock workers. By the 1780s, a planter could write that he sought "a proportion of such Tradesmen, as are commonly among Gangs of Plantation Slaves" for a new settlement, and expect his correspondent to know precisely what he meant.[21] Clearing land, building fences, erecting houses and outbuildings, making barrels and casks in which commodities could be packed for market, maintaining a more or less self-sufficient white residence, and making slave clothing occupied a core group of skilled plantation slaves during the eighteenth century.

In Charles Town, white artisans presided over the building trades, shipping services, the production of luxury goods such as jewelry and furniture, and processing and manufacturing industries such as leather tanning, shoemaking, and brick making. Enslaved workers composed urban entourages maintained by wealthier planters and merchants, often moving between residences and market stalls or counting houses and traveling with masters from countryside to town. By the 1770s, slaves dominated produce markets and controlled butchering in Charles Town.[22] As commodities converged on the port from throughout the province, slaves traveled with them, carting, loading, and ferrying barrels of rice and naval stores, and casks of indigo.

Occupational position determined the degree to which slaves might affiliate with plantation enterprises by working as subordinate economic agents. Drivers, "patroons" or boat captains, experienced artisans, and indigo makers, for example, managed important units within larger plantation enterprises, interacting frequently with slave owners and exercising direct authority over enslaved subordinates. Those who labored in teams under the command of slave managers often alternated between the rice and indigo fields and more specialized work. Their labor was often tasked, just as rice work was tasked, and members of such working gangs found themselves in the middle rungs of a plantation labor hierarchy, a position that limited their mobility and access to master-bestowed privileges. Some workers left the fields only to saw wood, process indigo, or man the oxcarts that carried produce a few miles to the nearest landing, entering nonagricultural work on a seasonal basis.[23] But "jobbing" artisans and laborers temporarily hired away from a plantation, by contrast, participated in a labor system that departed furthest from the core task traditions of agricultural production that came to characterize supervised and temporary skilled work on plantations. When work featured a high degree of individual mobility and isolation, even slaves with skills requiring limited training, such as washerwomen, found new abilities to pursue autonomy through wage earning and participation in exchange and by moving between sites at which masters, overseers, and slave managers monitored labor most rigorously.

As skilled slaves claimed an increasing proportion of the labor force during the eighteenth century, their labor became a central component of the plantation economy rather than merely a complement to commodity production. Planters hired out skilled slaves to generate substantial income. While slave owners and those who hired slaves kept accounts and often recorded when slaves came and went, transient slave workers sought employers on their own and negotiated the terms of their tenures, often returning an agreed-upon portion of earnings to their masters.[24] Hiring out slaves offered a means of generating cash, investing income, and managing the assets of estates in transition after the death of an owner. A visitor to South Carolina in the 1780s reported that hired-out slaves generated a return on investment in the range of 15 to 20 percent per year and that slave owners could "place their capital in negroes" for hire and live off their wages. When a planter died, his executors might manage a plantation for years until heirs came of age, and hiring out slaves could serve as a first stage before all of the estate's assets, including slaves, were sold.[25]

Wealthier planters living abroad depended on wages from slave hire in addition to rental income as a convenient way of purchasing bills of exchange, which they converted into sterling currency in England. Before settling in England in 1753, Charles Pinckney evaluated the income-generating potential of his Carolina estate. After renting Charles Town and plantation properties, he expected that ten skilled slaves could generate annually the substantial sum of £868. On J. C. Ball's Back River Plantation, a team of six "Valuable Carpenters" brought in almost a third as much as the entire crop produced by a slave community of eighty individuals. Payments for slave hire were invariably made in specie or provincial cash, making them especially important in an economy in which exchanged goods, book and bonded debts, and bills of exchange served as less than liquid surrogates for currency. Once planters exploited the financial utility of detaching skilled slaves from plantation communities and applying their labor most profitably, these workers gained, to varying degrees, the chance to operate as economic agents less restrained by daily supervision or imposed routines. Slaves who could be reliably moved out of primary master-slave relationships and placed under the command of temporary masters or on their own accountability and whose mobility marked their labor became quasi-autonomous affiliates of plantation enterprise.[26]

The character and evolution of eighteenth-century South Carolina's skilled slave labor force depended largely on changes in lowcountry plantations. Planters strengthened the economic foundation for the expansion of the skilled slave sector as they promulgated schemes for plantation diversification and agricultural improvement, and encouraged the transfer of economic agency from free white artisans to dependent black slaves. Planters sponsored greater slave specialization in part to widen the scope of their already formidable economic mastery. The relations of affiliation that supported the rise of skilled slave labor in the lowcountry can be seen in part as a planter-sponsored innovation in slave management.

The position of labor in the eighteenth-century lowcountry changed around midcentury when planters realigned the mission of their plantation enterprises in response to economic crises, market opportunities, and an evolving commitment to agricultural "improvement" through innovation. During King George's War (1739–1748), Atlantic privateering increased freight and insurance costs to such a degree that proceeds from rice "would barely pay the Outgoings [expenses] of a plantation." Even some of the colony's "most careful Planters" were "reduced to the greatest Distress," during this period of economic crisis, and many fled with their mortgaged slaves, leaving dishonored bonds behind them.[27] If this global, imperial confrontation flared more violently elsewhere, it also brought tangible economic trauma to South Carolina and altered the course of the colony's plantation agriculture. The war diverted planters from intensive monocultural rice production and toward the twin goals of self-sufficiency and diversification, measures designed to keep plantation enterprises from hemorrhaging resources, preserve planter creditworthiness, and reorient production so that future crises might be better weathered. Wartime experience committed planters to investing in significant secondary income-generating activities and increasing the training of skilled slave specialists.

The war years encouraged planters to strive toward greater plantation self-sufficiency after declining incomes during the 1740s exposed their dependence on outside food and skilled labor. They increasingly assigned slaves tasks in the corn and sweet potato fields and made the home production of slave provisions a priority.[28] By 1768 enough slaves had entered into craft trades that James Grant observed that on "established Plantations . . . the Planter has Tradesmen of all kinds in his Gang of Slaves, and 'tis a Rule with them, never to pay Money for what can be made upon their Estates, not a Lock, a Hing[e] or a Nail if they can avoid it."[29] Planters sought to maintain commodity production despite disruptions in Atlantic trade and create autarkic plantations capable of producing goods for local consumption. Always essential to the basic functioning of South Carolina's plantation economy, slave specialists increased in importance after midcentury as planters broadened their productive repertoire and conscripted slave workers into a correspondingly broad range of activities.

Planters employed carpenters and other skilled workers to construct plantation buildings, disseminate indigo making techniques, and build and maintain rice processing machinery after midcentury. Such an emphasis on improved production encouraged the rise and articulation of a skilled slave labor force to supplement a scarce pool of free white artisans, complement the demands of plantation agriculture, and keep in check the expenses of plantation agriculture. In the 1730s free, white artisans commanded what one observer thought were exorbitant prices, ranging from 20 to 30 shillings per day. By the 1760s a Georgia planter reduced the expenses of building a house, barn, stable, and other buildings by hiring free artisans for a short time and informally apprenticing two of his own slaves to learn some basic carpentry skills. After a month or two, these slaves "learnt so much of the art in that time, that by working since with them occasionally, they are become good carpenters enough to raise a shed, or build any plain outhouse, such as you see common in England in little farmyards." Substituting an irregularly trained force of slave workers for their expensive white counterparts could generate substantial savings to planters concerned enough with costs to forgo craftsmanship associated with an ideal estate in favor of buildings one might find on the "little farmyards" of English yeomen.[30]

Members of the Lucas and Pinckney families, elite proponents of crop diversification, experimented with indigo production in the mid-1740s, as King George's War depressed rice prices and made otherwise conservative planters eager to attempt new ventures. Initial attempts to purchase West Indian slaves skilled in the cultivation and manufacture of the dye failed, and the white workers hired to train slaves and spread indigo culture proved reluctant to part with their knowledge. Instead, these white specialists hoped to enhance the value of their skills by restricting their dissemination.[31]

After early frustrations with white workers, the Lucas family succeeded in establishing indigo as a lucrative secondary commodity to rice, in part, by relying on enslaved specialists to disseminate indigo skills. When locally made brick vats tainted the dye, Quashy, a slave carpenter, built the first wooden indigo works at the Lucases' Garden Hill plantation. This adaptation from the traditional West Indian stone or brick structures soon became the South Carolina standard.[32] Once knowledge passed out of the hands of expensive and reluctant white tutors and was learned by slaves, the techniques of indigo production could circulate through a hiring-out system already in place to exchange specialized labor. In the early 1780s, a visitor to South Carolina noted that "the headmen" in charge of indigo making were "commonly negroes."[33]

Planters trained and employed skilled slaves to construct and maintain the processing equipment for the new indigo industry, a move that reduced costs, kept vital machinery in repair, led to important local innovations in production, and disseminated skills necessary for the industry's acceptance in South Carolina. The wages of hired free laborers needed to build vats, drainers, and drying sheds accounted for most of the costs of setting up an indigo works. Wooden vats and outbuildings warped and deteriorated, creating a permanent demand for carpentry work. Indigo planters relied on the training of slave craftsmen to replace or supplement the labor of their expensive white counterparts, a move that could yield substantial savings. During the Revolutionary War, when "proper workmen were not to be hir'd" to repair indigo vats, planters hired slave carpenters in preparation for the harvest.[34] As white workers attempted to engross specialized knowledge, skilled slaves proved able and willing affiliates who, in the process of acquiring and exchanging indigo skills, helped create a range of new positions for skilled slave workers.

Throughout the eighteenth century, South Carolina rice planters sought to increase productivity and lessen the onerous labor of rice processing with the traditional West African mortar and pestle by developing mechanized devices to pound rice.[35] A contributor to the *South-Carolina Gazette* offered a skeptical evaluation of why such potentially useful innovations had not taken hold by the 1730s: "though we could have the best Mills in the Universe, and not a Number of Artificers to keep them in order, our Work must be at a stand." Just as a shortage of willing white artisans impeded the development of a viable indigo culture in South Carolina until planters invested in the training of slave specialists, improvements in rice processing depended on a combination of free and unfree skilled labor. When fire destroyed a rice processing machine built by a white artisan on George Austin's Pee Dee River plantation, the plantation's team of slave carpenters erected another. The machine "was not so well put together as a regular bred tradesman could have done it, and being thus clumsily jointed, twas continually calling for repair." What the general run of slave carpenters seem to have lacked in precision inculcated by traditional training, they made up for in the ability to adapt their skills to the diverse construction needs of plantations.[36]

The demands of the agricultural calendar and the constant need for building and machine maintenance favored the relatively inexpensive, on-site labor of slaves that the small supply of itinerant white artisans could not provide. Another lowcountry planter, whose rice machine was in need of extensive repairs, hired a white carpenter at four shillings six pence per day and a "Negro Fellow" whose labor was assessed at three shillings five pence per day.[37] As planters invested in the improvement of rice processing through mechanization they drew on both enslaved and free skilled workers to restrain expenses and meet ongoing needs for specialized work. Highly skilled white artisans, hired slave specialists, and resident slave workers with an ability to engage in a range of carpentry tasks on an ad hoc basis comprised a flexible corps of skilled workers tailored to meet plantation needs.[38]

Despite the gains in flexibility, diversification, and improvement that enslaved specialists made possible, some in the colony registered their ambivalence over the social consequences that might attend the transfer of economic agency from comparatively poor whites to black slaves. Merchants importing European immigrants into South Carolina were "very Sensible of the Want of more White People" in this black-majority province, especially as replacements for slave tradesmen. Christopher Gadsden articulated such concerns in 1778 when he noted that skilled slave hiring ("which I have ever though excessively impolite") would drive the transient poor populations of the Lower South into the arms of the British, due to "want of work, the negroes eating them out of that." Some South Carolinians wondered whether enslaved specialists, "who discover great capacities, and an amazing aptness for learning trades, where dangerous tools are used," posed a greater internal threat than the majority of field slaves and condemned planters for putting "motives of profit and advantage" over a concern for the public good.[39]

Some white artisans viewed the planters' reliance on an increasingly unfree source of skilled labor as an assault on their social position as well as their economic well-being. The Negro Act of 1740 sought to restrict slave movement and prohibit unsupervised work, but increasing numbers of skilled slaves traveled as hired-out, itinerant "jobbers" or commanded schooners and plantations without white oversight.[40] Such a disquieting trend mobilized political support for white artisans seeking to secure legislation to curb the growth of the skilled slave sector. Throughout the eighteenth century, the colonial assembly, state house of representatives, and other bodies attempted to limit slave training, restrict slave hiring, mandate white supervision of skilled slave labor, and stipulate that white workers be hired in place of slaves.[41]

Despite ominous references in petitions of complaint and legal preambles to slaves working without supervision, traveling at their pleasure, and stealing to pay wages to their masters, slave owners had good reason to see hiring out as a relatively stable system rather than as a threat to white security. If whites as a group continued to fear slaves in general as a potentially violent internal enemy, individual masters entrusted individual slaves with the freedom to work independently. If some took the opportunity to run away, most others returned their wages diligently enough to sustain the system. Slave owners could appreciate the logic of the white artisans' self-interested appeal to public safety, but their own valuable skilled slaves seemed exempt from such comprehensive criticism. The appearance of similar laws throughout the century and the lack of any available evidence that might indicate that these laws were ever enforced suggests that planters' view of the place of enslaved specialists in South Carolina society prevailed.

Too many white artisans profited from the training and sale of slaves to unify South Carolina's tradesmen behind measures to check the growth of the skilled slave labor force. When a group of shipwrights petitioned to bar slave artisans from the trade, their more prosperous slave-owning competitors opposed the proposal: they expected to retire owning enslaved artisans capable of supporting them.[42] For many white artisans, training slave apprentices opened the possibility of accumulating savings and labor forces capable of working new plantations.[43] A friend of a Philadelphia weaver cautioned the tradesman about a prospective move to South Carolina in 1747, predicting that "his service in Carolina will last probably no longer than until two negro slaves shall have learned the weaver's trade from him and can weave themselves. So it goes through all Carolina; the negroes are made to learn all the trades and are used for all kinds of business. For this reason white people have difficulty in earning their bread there, unless they become overseers or provide themselves with slaves."[44]

Demand for skilled white overseers drew artisans away from Charles Town and into the countryside where they might eventually settle on inexpensive land.[45] So frequently did white artisans purchase marginal lowcountry lands with the intention of setting up plantations that one plantation agent referred to a tract as "only suitable for a tradesman."[46] White artisans embraced the financial opportunities offered by training slaves as a means of trading the limited rewards of craftsmanship for the possibility of becoming planters.[47]

Planters complained vehemently regarding shoddy workmanship, insufferable delays, and the high costs of white craftsmanship, revealing a drive toward mastery that conflated rational, capitalistic calculation with a firm attachment to hierarchical social order. John Lewis Gervais's strained forbearance finally collapsed into indignation when a white carpenter not only delayed repairs on a vital flat boat but returned it with a rotten plank that gave way, damaging twenty-nine barrels of rice. "Mr[.] Stone has triffled with us indeed," he fumed, adding that "it is the same with all Workmen, it is very difficult to get any thing out of their hands." Gervais then sent the boat to a slave carpenter who promptly effected the necessary repairs.[48] Although planters continued to import skilled indentured servants throughout the eighteenth century, fraudulent claims of skilled work experience and a tendency to run away soured most planters on unfree white tradesmen.[49] For planters who expected to patronize laborers, the market power white artisans possessed galled elite sensibilities and at the same time interfered with the proper functioning of increasingly complex productive enterprises.[50]

By investing in the human capital represented by their slaves, planters consciously curtailed the market authority of white artisans and sought to exercise it for themselves. As skilled slaves entered a niche once reserved for individualistic white tradesmen, some of the assumptions of autonomy and work-related latitude that social convention employed to define the colonial artisan clung to the slaves who labored in a gray area between contradictorily defined social roles: agency-less dependents and independent entrepreneurs. The tension between these incompatible roles did not, however, threaten to shake the foundations of slave society by catching it in an abstract contradiction. Rather, the mechanisms by which South Carolina society managed this tension revealed its enormous capacity to meet the exigencies of planter interest with social innovations.

Overall, the transition from free to slave skilled labor involved a clear net gain of economic authority to the planter elite. Over the course of the eighteenth century planters sought to ease the chronic shortage of artisans in their quest to make plantations more self-sufficient and less tied to rice monoculture. They took control of the costs and dissemination of specialized labor by creating a mobile force of skilled slave plantation workers and wage earners. In doing so, they exempted skilled slaves from the ideal of a stationary and supervised slave population and the traditional labor relations that pertained to field hands. Affiliation with skilled slaves remained a planter-sanctioned innovation in labor management. It was a means to secure economic objectives, and planters never meant to relinquish control of the concessions it implied.

Oriented around the tasks of plantation production, relations of affiliation were conditioned by the mobility of various specialized occupations and the degree to which work brought individual skilled slaves into the orbit of plantation communities. Two kinds of forces operated to limit the autonomy of enslaved specialists who lived and worked continuously on a single plantation. Like all who commanded plantation slaves, specialists with power over labor were pressured to negotiate to maintain their authority while kinship obligations drew them into alliances subversive to strong master-slave affiliations. Planters, however, imposed labor hierarchies on their plantations and monitored slave accountability more rigorously than they possibly could for mobile wage earners and more transient workers. Such countervailing pressures created recognizable occupational personalities among slave laborers with close ties to plantation communities. The slave drivers, who often ran plantations with little or no white supervision, responded to material incentives as they mediated between the demands of subordinate slaves and their masters and defended their masters' interests against the depredations of white overseers. Other skilled workers, such as sawyers, coopers, shoemakers, seamstresses, and indigo workers, remained enmeshed in a plantation labor hierarchy that planters used to reward and punish behavior. Finally, a group of especially transient enslaved specialists, such as itinerant craftsmen, transport workers, and elderly urban-based servants acted as more detached entrepreneurs who enforced their masters' standards on plantation slaves while making the most of their own abilities to transgress them.

By the last quarter of the eighteenth century, planter absenteeism and multiple plantation ownership gave slave drivers increasing command of lowcountry plantations. One planter entered in his register the names of drivers and the dates when they took charge in precisely the same way that he noted the employment of white overseers.[51] Planters rewarded drivers and other skilled slaves with material goods, which served the dual purpose of creating incentives for performance and using distinctive clothing to shore up a plantation labor hierarchy. English absentee John Channing gave hats to all male slaves and handkerchiefs to all female slaves. One driver, Saby, received a great coat with brass buttons and cloth with which to make up winter clothes. Another driver named Roger received a great coat with plain buttons and the promise of special winter clothes "if he behaves well & makes me a good Crop," for he "is too apt to be careless and easy, & to want a little spurring." Sixteen years earlier Saby seems to have been in Roger's position, as a junior driver forced to earn gifts by making large rice crops.[52] By carefully granting and withholding status-conveying clothing to his drivers, Channing adopted a common management strategy based on incentives aimed at encouraging the jealousy of skilled slave workers as they competed for goods.[53] Items given to specific slaves from 1766 to 1773 by Henry Laurens, a planter who owned five lowcountry plantations in this period, show a preponderance of special clothing items, including great coats, special caps and hats, bolts of cloth finer in quality that the coarse "oznabrigs" rationed to field hand, more expensive shoes, and the "fearnaught" jackets of sailors (table 9.2).[54]

Over the course of several years Old Cuffee and one Gambell, a white overseer, struggled for power on Laurens's Altamaha Plantation in Georgia. In August 1772 Gambell punished and demoted Old Cuffee to "hard Labour & disgrace," but Laurens took his slave's side in the dispute. By March of the following year, Laurens intended to find "some method for getting rid of Gambell" and to appoint a new overseer who was to learn the management of the plantation with "the assistance of Old Cuffee." This experienced plantation driver appears to have endured under Gambell's harsh command until a new overseer took charge at Altamaha in 1774. In 1777 Laurens's agent was to order shoes for Old Cuffee "when he wants."[55]

The actual value of these incentives paled in comparison with goods and commodities imported into and produced by lowcountry plantations, and drivers took advantage of their control of plantation resources to supplement such meager income illicitly. On Channing's plantation, Saby convinced white agents that he was allowed to bring livestock to market for sale as a "perquisite," while Channing himself sought only to allow his drivers a single hog each for consumption and a few items of clothing. On George Austin's Pee Dee River plantation, Quackow "has lately fallen under a heavy Censure for dishonesty," that inclined the plantation's agent to "degrade him from his present office of Driver, into that of a common Field hand." A black driver alone presided over one of absentee Ralph Izard's plantations where the embezzlement of plantation produce had become an endemic problem.[56]

Henry Laurens regarded March, his driver at Wright's Savannah Plantation as a "Man of a placid & obliging disposition & always as far as I knew a good & faithful Servant." When the plantation's overseer, Casper Springer, discovered that March had been "stealing rice out of the Machine house" he confronted the slave and attempted to grab him "but the Negro proved to be the Strongest & threw him, & upon his ordering the negroes to Seize him, they would not do it." When Springer tried again to capture the slave, March maimed his own hand with a knife and moved to attack the overseer before the other slaves separated them.[57] Mepkin Plantation runaways in 1777 included "Doctor Cuffee" who "served five Years to the Shoemakers Trade & could & no doubt can now make a very good Shoe, he is a good water Man a Sawyer & has abilities for every kind of Plantation work." Laurens blamed Mary, March's wife and Doctor Cuffee's mother, for the "cor-

Table 9.2
HENRY LAURENS ACCOUNT BOOK EXPENDITURES TO NAMED SLAVES, 1766–1773

Slave Name, Occupation	Types of Goods Given to Slaves	Cost of Goods (£S.C. converted to decimal values)
Tom Peace, patroon	greatcoat, handkerchief, jacket, hose, trousers, cap, shoes	27.09
Sam, bricklayer	felt hat, cloth, greatcoat, hose, thread	17.01
Grant	jacket, yarn hose, milled cap, woolen trousers, shoes	16.14
Pompey	jacket, yarn hose, milled cap, woolen trousers, shoes	16.14
Bill-Isle	jacket, yarn hose, milled cap, woolen trousers, shoes	15.14
Prince, driver	cloth	12.38
Tom	steel spring tress	10.00
Schooner Wambaw Boatmen	shirts, hats, handkerchiefs	7.75
Æra	bound hat, blanket, greatcoat	6.63
Topaz, boatman	clothing	5.75
Friday	blanket, greatcoat	5.63
Sambo	shirts, jacket	5.13
Schooner Baker Boatmen	shirts, trousers	5.00
Nat	greatcoat	4.50
Old Cuffee, driver	shoes	2.50
Jack	shirt, trousers, shoes	2.25

Shrewsberry	shoes	1.22
Othello	shoes	1.22
Mercutio, bricklayer	shoes	1.00
Quebec	bound hat	1.00
Cæser	felt hat	0.75
Peter	milled cap	0.32
	Total:	164.55

SOURCE: Henry Laurens Account Book, Robert Scott Small Library, Special Collections, College of Charleston.

ruption" of his skilled slaves. He derided this kinship network, which proved strong and subversive to his own links to individual slaves, as the "Noble family." Laurens sold Mary and others in the group, hoping that "the removal of Such leaven may Stop a contagion."[58]

If material incentives failed to achieve a degree of personal loyalty that drivers never unconditionally offered, demotion from a plantation's most senior to its most demeaning position under the authority of others served as a threat to ensure "honesty." Enslaved specialists in the middle rungs of plantation hierarchies suffered more frequent demotions and received fewer material rewards. Henry Laurens removed Amy from her duties as an indigo maker in 1766 and ordered "that impudent gipsey into the field" where she would be forced to "perform a task every day to keep her cool & avoid such trouble as she had lately occasioned upon the plantation." He replaced her with a "Negro Woman named Hagar, strongly recommended for her honesty, care of Negroes, & her great care of [the] Indigo." To Laurens and his recalcitrant slave the move from skilled indigo management to task work in the rice fields was a punishment, a degrading descent in rank that substituted hard labor for technical and supervisory expertise. Jack, George Austin's boatman and a "professd Drunkard," was sent to labor at Austin's Shifnal settlement.[59] Some workers, such as sawyers and wagoners, doubled as field hands and moved between specialized and agricultural labor seasonally. If many others lived apart from the slave quarter,[60] their position as affiliates expected to contribute their abilities to the larger plantation enterprise was weakened by the imposition of punitive scrutiny by their superiors.

Those skilled slaves most detached from plantation communities exploited the benefits of affiliation most fully. In one of Henry Laurens's surviving account books, the heading "Handicraft Slaves" records transactions relating to traveling craftsmen, sailors and boatmen, and hired-out slaves whose transience made them difficult to categorize under the common entries relating to specific plantations and schooners.[61] When Laurens returned to his Charleston residence from an extended trip to England he "found nobody here but three of our old Domestics Stepny Exeter & big Hagar, these drew tears from me by their humble & affectionate Salutes & congratulations my Knees were Clasped, my hands kissed my very feet embraced. . . ."[62] This display of subservience and affection evokes a kind of textbook paternalism, which fractured intraslave "solidarity among the oppressed by linking them as individuals to their oppressors" and confirmed Laurens's self-image as a benevolent patriarch.[63] But for Stepney and Exeter, working as gardeners at Laurens's principal Charleston residence in 1774 was a kind of earned retirement after long careers undertaking skilled tasks at several other plantations.[64] Although these slaves offered such fealty freely in this instance, their past work experience revealed the conditional nature of strong affiliations. Skilled slaves received material benefits from Laurens and found themselves entangled in plantation affairs that set them in opposition to white overseers, artisans, and other slaves. These conflicts linked them to Laurens's interests and necessitated Laurens's protection.

A decade before Stepney greeted his master so effusively, Laurens sent him to Mepkin Plantation, ostensibly "to s[t]ay three or four Weeks & assist in turning & watching the new Indigo." But his primary task seems to have been guarding against slave theft. "He is very honest & if you will speak to him he will not allow anybody within his sight to rob you," Laurens wrote to his overseer. Before his visit, Abraham, perhaps a slave cooper or sawyer, sold 22 cords of wood without permission. Laurens suspected other slaves, most notably "George & his associates," with large-scale plantation theft. Not only did Laurens rely on Stepney to exert influence over the slave community to prevent stealing when he could and to report slaves who made away with plantation resources when he could not, but he permitted Stepney, who was not "very willing to be from home," to return to town.[65] Stepney's special relationship with Laurens earned him the power to make choices over where he lived and what work he would perform. In return, he sacrificed close associations with other slaves, remaining aloof as a representative of his owner's interests.

Sam, Laurens's chief carpenter, undertook projects as a versatile craftsman who traveled between Charleston and many of his master's lowcountry plantations. During the winter of 1773–1774, he built an efficient rice pounding machine near Savannah, moved to Mepkin in South Carolina to repair the plantation's rice irrigation system, and came to town to work on Laurens's tenements. Laurens often addressed instructions to Sam, whose literacy allowed for direct written communication between master and slave. When a white shipwright delayed the repairs on a needed boat, Sam readied the wood-carrying "pettiagua" for service in a matter of days.[66] In 1772 Sam reported the extensive theft of Wright's Savannah Plantation goods by one Godfrey, the white overseer, and stood his ground when interrogated by him. Godfrey also measured smaller rice tasks for Wright's Savannah field hands, possibly attempting to "make Friends with the Negroes" and purchase their complicity with lighter work loads. In contrast, Sam sometimes "carried a high hand with his Boys," the team of workers who labored under him, exercising his authority with such severity, Laurens suspected, that his junior carpenters were on the verge of running away.[67] Staunch in his commitments to Laurens's plantation enterprise, Sam faced the potential violence of a white overseer and enforced a rigid and alienating discipline upon the slaves he controlled.

Stepney, Sam, and Old Cuffee maintained their tenuous positions through direct relationships with Laurens, a connection that tended to isolate them from other slaves and set them at odds with white plantation employees. Laurens strengthened such links through special gifts. He instructed Gervais to give "twenty five pounds to Sam's wife. [I]f he has behaved well I would wish him to add Some indulgencies to bare necessities for him[s]elf." Prince, the driver at New Hope Plantation, received four yards of calico, among other goods.[68]

Perhaps the most common privilege granted to slave artisans was a regular supply of alcohol. But alcohol meant more than merely another luxury: it distinguished skilled slaves as artisans in traditional terms and signaled a special level of trust accorded to slaves by masters. The right of the English artisan to consume alcohol on the job survived in places in the colonies.[69] Laurens earmarked "a Bottle or two" of rum "for old Cuffee" and instructed an overseer to "pay him in due time . . . what further will be due to him," indicating a regular allowance. Stepney received "half a dram & a Little Toddy every day but not too much" while participating in indigo production at Mepkin and "a Drink of Grog as from me, upon the Occasion" from James Laurens while Henry Laurens toured England. When Sam worked at Wambaw Plantation in 1766 he received "8 bottles sweet Rum." Laurens hired a white artisan and a team of skilled slaves to work at Mepkin, but he denied them an expected rum allowance as a means of expressing his displeasure with the work of "Russel's Lazy Boys." On another occasion, he paid slaves hired to construct new indigo vats £3 "for their Sunday," as well as 40 shillings and four bottles of rum as a gratuity.[70]

If, ideally, masters permitted their skilled slaves such allowances as a material recognition of trust, they also sanctioned the transgression of normal rules of slave conduct that could attend alcohol consumption. Laurens reported in 1768, with more bemusement than anger, that "Old Stepney the Drunken honest Old Fellow is still alive. Tho too often he gets dead drunk." At times, Sam's drunkenness seemed excessive enough to Laurens that he threatened his chief carpenter with confinement in the work house and considered sending him away from Charles Town ("where otherwise it would best suit his Interest & convenience to be") to the more isolated Altamaha Plantation in Georgia.[71] If less important slaves could be sold when the trouble they caused exceeded their value to production, these slaves enjoyed the freedom to cross the lines that defined proper slave behavior and escape punishment. If every drink comprised a little ceremony in which masters affirmed slave privileges and engendered (sometimes literal) dependence, drinking to excess reversed the message, affirming the importance of some skilled slaves and the measure of permissiveness allowed them.

As long as Laurens's skilled slaves looked after their master's interests and proved their loyalty by taking his side in conflicts with whites and other slaves, they could expect alcohol, cash, small gifts, the power to command other slaves, and the freedom to travel and work without supervision.

Abundant documentary evidence exists to suggest how and why South Carolina slave owners learned to value enslaved specialists as affiliates to plantation enterprise. Comparatively little remains in the historical record to illustrate the slaves' perspective in these relationships. Hundreds of slave runaway advertisements published in South Carolina newspapers from 1732 to 1790, however, feature skilled slaves who left in these documents a faint impression of behavior and identity at the moment when relations of affiliation collapsed. The advertisements emphasize mobility as perhaps the most important distinguishing feature of skilled slave labor. As slaves undertook skilled tasks demanded by an expanding plantation economy, they acquired cultural as well as technical abilities. Working in close contact with whites and traveling far beyond the boundaries of a single plantation, enslaved specialists learned to speak "proper" English. They developed a cosmopolitan sense of the way white society operated as well as a more comprehensive understanding of the slave system and their own places within it.

But these narratives of working relationships suddenly severed reveal most of all how relationships of affiliation temporarily reconciled the antagonistic pursuits of mastery and autonomy instead of cementing the emotional and psychological bonds of paternalism. Despite occasional slave pledges of personal commitment to masters and encomiums offered in tribute by appreciative masters of their most valued slaves, both groups saw such labor arrangements as means to divergent ends.

According to the suspicions of their masters, slave runaways chose Charles Town as their single most popular initial destination. Here master craftsmen (by 1790 there were at least 429 of them) taught slave apprentices and plied their trades with the aid of slave workers.[72] Boatmen and sailors from throughout the province and beyond converged at the city's wharves. Women runaways and wage earners found concealment and employment at "negro washing-houses" and the public markets.[73] Charles Town, the focalpoint of the plantation economy, became a center for impermanent communities composed of skilled slaves and a forum for their education in the economic and social systems affecting their interests.

Skilled slaves with less access to town still roamed farther afield than most ordinary hands. As neighboring planters exchanged skilled laborers, a cooper, blacksmith, or sawyer born and raised in the plantation countryside built neighborhood and regional networks of friends and relatives. Runaway advertisements alerted whites to slaves such as Tom, a carpenter, who was "well known on St. Helena [Island], Edisto-Island, and at Ponpon."[74] Multiple plantation owners transferred skilled slaves between settlements throughout the province. Transport workers, by the very nature of their jobs, gained access to a wide range of experiences in the world beyond the plantations. Shadwell, a schooner "patroon" or captain, was "well acquainted with all the rivers and inlets to the southward of Charlestown."[75]

Skilled slave work and mobility in both urban and rural milieus fostered a comprehensive sense of both black and white worlds. Charles Ball, a slave working in the Lower South during the first decade of the nineteenth century, drove a wagon for his master throughout the Georgia lowcountry: "As I traveled through the country with my team, my chief employment, beyond my duty of a teamster, was to observe the condition of the slaves on the various plantation by which we passed on our journey, and to compare things in Georgia . . . with similar things in Carolina." Ball typically retired to plantation kitchens in the evenings to "pass some time in conversation with the black people I might chance to find there," conversations that usually turned toward work, food, punishment and privilege, and the varying customs regarding these fundamental aspects of slave life.[76] Such knowledge helped slaves shape identities as members of an emerging culture that stretched far beyond the confines of a single plantation and, in more tangible terms, provided points of comparison as they evaluated their own treatment and opportunities with specific masters and working situations. Their experiences made them consummate creoles, deeply aware of the commonalities and divergencies of enslavement in a variety of locales.

Skilled slaves also participated in production as partial insiders. They entered into direct relationships with masters and overseers as supervisors, wage earners, and workers who performed a flexible range of tasks that served the changing labor needs of plantations. As they engaged in their trades they traveled among whites and worked with them, improving their proficiency with standard English speech, learning the intricacies of social exchange, and marking the limits that defined appropriate slave behavior, whether or not they chose to risk transgression.[77]

Demographic developments around midcentury contributed to a growing cultural division between creoles and recently imported slaves. After the 1739 Stono Rebellion the provincial assembly mandated prohibitive taxes on new slaves, and during the war years of the 1740s economic factors likewise limited the growth of the "new Negro" population.[78] Meanwhile, African-born slaves already in South Carolina became increasingly acclimated to life in lowcountry society after weathering a cultural "seasoning" that mirrored their survival in a new disease environment. When the war ended and the taxes were repealed after 1748, the surge in slave imports seemed to condemn the African-born to the fields while "country" slaves filled the ranks of a skilled elite. Governor James Glen commented on this division in 1751, noting that the creation of a creolized class of skilled workers posed no threat to the internal security of the colony despite a rising slave population. Skilled workers, he argued, not only contributed to the strength of the economy but also accepted their enslavement in the process of acculturating. As "Natives of Carolina who have no notion of Liberty," they

> have been brought up among White People, and by White People have been made at least many of them, useful Mechanicks, as Coopers, Carpenters, Masons, Smiths, Wheelwrights, and other Trades, and that the rest can all speak our Language, for we imported none during the War, I say when it is Considered that these are pleased with their Masters, contented with their Condition, reconciled to Servitude, seasoned to the Country, and expert at the different kinds of Labour in which they are employed, it must appear difficult if not impracticable to ascertain their intrinsick Value.

As Glen saw it, two distinct peoples who filled different economic roles composed the colony's slave population at midcentury: "weak Raw New Negroes" and "strong seasoned handy Slaves."[79]

The behavior of skilled runaways suggests that many slaves rejected this trajectory of acculturation, one that pushed skilled slaves away from connections to the plantation community and propelled them toward a subordinate position in white society.[80] For many skilled fugitives, the decision to abscond with themselves proved to be a calculated move to continue as mobile wage earners unbound by slavery's enforced obligations. Those who escaped slavery revealed the depths of their capacities to manipulate the systems employed to regulate slave work and alter their own identities to conform to white expectations. As the owners who advertised in the hope of recapturing them recognized, these were "plausible" slaves in the eighteenth-century sense of the word.[81] Skilled runaways consciously exercised their cultural knowledge as a means of surviving independently within South Carolina society. The deceptions of identity slave specialists employed as runaways speak to the tentative and multiple orientations of African American acculturation. The runaway advertisements alluded to the cultural poses slave specialists assumed as they negotiated the hidden and explicit hazards of exercising mobility and independent work in a slave society. What allegiances existed behind these often effective masks remains mysterious, but slave affiliation seems to have qualified slave acculturation in important ways. To pursue and preserve autonomy, enslaved specialists made strategic commitments to their masters' culture, one that never appeared to endorse it without reservations.

When slave owners indicated the language abilities of their skilled runaways, most spoke "good" or "very good" English, descriptions that seem to have been more an indicator of accent or dialect (the degree to which white ears heard speech that was "plain and tolerable free from the common negro dialect") than a measure of the slaves' facility with the vernacular English variants common to the slave quarter.[82] A small proportion, including Mick, a sailmaker who "talks English as well as negroes generally do," fell into a category of "tolerable" or "indifferent" speech. Several sailors, West Indians, and Louisianans spoke more than one language while others earned the compliment of "remarkable" spoken English skills. For whatever reason, Joe "sometimes affects to speak broad Scotch or Northumberland dialect," a talent that betrayed an extraordinary grasp of the subtleties of European-American speech.[83]

Despite the limitations of runaway advertisements as a representative sample of all enslaved specialists, the high proportion of skilled runaways who could speak English well enough to be understood easily by whites lends credence to the assertion that skilled slaves attained a better than average level of proficiency. Speech skills underwrote the effective performance of specialized work that was dependent on communicating directly with slave owners and other whites. But for fugitive slaves, the stakes were much higher. Evading capture often depended on convincing whites that they were merely going about sanctioned business. Quamino and Quacco, two sawyers who spoke "very well," were "so crafty, that they would almost deceive any Body, and if taken, will frame a very plausible Story that they are not runaways." Those who might encounter Pompey, an escaped shipwright, were warned by his master that he was "very cunning, and can tell a fine story; he is country born, and speaks good English."[84] Slave owners indicated the birthplace or ethnicity of their skilled runaways in fewer than half of all advertisements, but the backgrounds of those described in greater detail generally confirm Glen's assertion that skilled slaves were a class of creoles. South Carolina "country born" slaves composed the largest group, and others, including most West Indians, slaves from "northward," and mulattos and mustees,[85] also had most likely grown up in British America.

African-born slaves, however, made up approximately a quarter of runaways identified by birthplace or ethnicity and just under a tenth of all slave specialists advertised.[86] Artisans and planters often purchased "new Negro" boys as the most economical means to build a team of skilled slaves. After working for a few years with whites and country-born slaves, improving English, technical abilities, and cultural sensibilities put them on an accelerated path toward cultural fluency and high market value. On one of Henry Smith's plantations, a single country-born sawyer worked and then absconded with five "able young" Angolans.[87] Jamie ("a mulatto"), Peter ("of the Guinea country"), and York ("of the Ebo country") were "all bred to the cabinet making business" and worked together before running away as a group from John Fisher's workshop. Peter, an "active and artful" crafts-man in his early thirties, spoke "very bad English," which had not improved noticeably since his previous escape more than four years before.[88] If some older Africans had difficulty learning English and appearing as acculturated, younger slaves seemed to have been transformed quickly from "weak Raw New Negros" to "strong seasoned handy Slaves" by engaging in their trades. Eighteen-year-old Sambo, a "Guinea"-born wagoner, spoke "good English," as did nineteen-year-old London, an Angolan butcher. Prince, at twenty-one, had experience as a hired carpenter in the Santee River planta-tion region and working in Charles Town where his master lived. His "very good English" as well as the "country marks on his face" (the product of African ritual scarification) revealed the rapid pace at which specialized work encouraged cultural acquisitions.[89]

South Carolina slaves often ran away with canoes, hoes, axes, and pots to facilitate a long and arduous journey to Amerindian territory or Spanish Florida. Sometimes they waited until the corn ripened to ensure a source of food along a northern escape route.[90] But skilled slaves tended to carry off their tools, work at their trades within the province, and "pass for free." By disguising their fugitive status and pretending to be free blacks or legitimate wage earners looking for employment, skilled runaways molded the way their identities were perceived to the exigencies of the moment and sus-tained a more genuine, if sometimes unrecognized and always tenuous, free-dom. Simon and Ned "carried their carpenters tools with them, in order to deceive people who may meet them." Frank took "his shoemaking tools, and is thought will make for the back parts of this province and pass for a free man." Barber, named for his trade, "carried with him several razors and dressing implements." Sam "took with him some workman's tools," and his owner "supposed he will pass for a free negro, as he has formerly done." When another Sam "carried with him a Hand-Saw, A Square, and Blacking-Line," he asserted a clear intention to work independently. Whites in need of workers aided such deceptions and asked few questions, especially ship captains pressed to assemble outbound crews.[91]

The loose arrangements that allowed slaves to seek income on their own terms sometimes confused masters who wondered whether their slaves had broken off ties completely or merely taken temporary excursions as unsanc-tioned wage earners. Job Colcock advertised for Leonard, a Charleston porter, who "has absented himself from time to time from me" but deter-mined to offer a reward for his capture because his most recent absence "looks so much like running away." Young Domina had made a habit of tak-ing off "sometimes for three or four days at a time" when the schooner on which he worked docked in the city. All slaves who worked for wages were ostensibly required to submit a written permit in their master's hand setting out the terms for their employment, but a "plausible" slave could often make do with the appearance that all was in order to generate independent income. In their frustration, masters sometimes advertised to publicly deny their permission for slaves to work independently. James St. John accused his slave Limas, a carpenter who "wrought clandestinely about Town," of defrauding him of unreported wages; Rawlins Lowndes threatened to prosecute anyone who hired Tom, a bricklayer who "has undertaken Jobs in the Way of his Business, without Comptroll" and lacking a proper permit. Elizabeth Smith complained bitterly of the failures of a ticketing system that allowed her slave Lancaster, a white-washer who "constantly earns Money," to evade repeated attempts to control his labor for her own profit.[92]

Jack, a mulatto tanner, possessed the ultimate permit: his light brown hair and pale skin allowed him to "pass for a white man." Other skilled slaves, however, had to create more malleable tokens of identity in order to feign legitimacy. Scipio, a shoemaker, "writes a pretty good Hand, of which he may probably avail himself, by furnishing himself with a Ticket in his Master's Name." But illiterate slaves managed to obtain forged passes or simply used out-of-date permits for their own ends. A handwritten letter served as one element in a larger ruse that involved constructing false life histories, changing names, and presenting a plausible outward appearance with clothing and demeanor combined to deflect scrutiny and facilitate employment. Less experienced slaves might have had less success with a questionable ticket than did Bob, a "remarkable artful and ingenious" tanner, shoemaker, saddler, carpenter, and wheelwright who "has Money and Cloaths sufficient to make his Appearance suitable to his Intention" of leaving the province as a free man or earning wages at one of his many trades. Sam "pretends he was born free in Virginia." Others assumed a new first name to conceal their fugitive status.[93]

For some runaways, forging a new identity contained a deeply personal dimension rather than merely serving as a strategy for independent survival. For Hannah, who sold cakes in a Charleston market for more than fifteen years, the decision to take her former mistress's name and make her way as the free "Hannah Bullock" declared a new identity but at the same time threatened to identify her as a fugitive.[94] Because a few skilled slaves actually obtained their freedom, "passing for free" became a tactical option for runaways as well as an objective they might secure by changing locales and persisting in the disguise long enough.[95] Other free, skilled blacks were not so fortunate. Joe, a carpenter who "used to work about the town," "was formerly a free man" and continued to work in the city after his subsequent enslavement and escape. His master's condemnation of Joe's "bad and deceitful behaviour" and characterization of him as "the greatest liar and most artful negro in the province" indicated Joe's long history of living by his wits at the margins of the slave system.[96]

Enslaved specialists often ran away to avoid being sold, an event that could break up families and compromise individualized work arrangements negotiated between masters and slaves. A slave owner's death risked the dissolution of slave communities as executors divided estates among heirs and sold real, personal and human property to settle debts. But masters also calculated the value of their skilled slaves in purely economic terms. They appraised their value versus that of other slaves, featured them in slave sales to attract buyers, and sold them south to Georgia and East Florida where new planters paid premium prices for skilled workers.[97] Skilled slaves distinguished themselves as economic actors integral to profitable production, but financial instability or opportunity could transform seemingly irreplaceable workers into a source of income.

The runaway advertisements indicate a heavy traffic in the buying and selling of enslaved specialists. In approximately one-third of the advertisements relating to skilled runaways, masters mentioned the names and locations of former owners or gave some indication that their slaves had been recently sold or purchased. Although these advertisements offer only a rough account of the recent sale experience of the young males who dominated the group, they not uncommonly mentioned two or three former owners.[98] Older slaves had often lived under twice as many owners, and their relatives were dispersed throughout the region. Ned, a market slave in his forties, ran away from his fourth owner in 1778, and Cyrus, a 36-year-old cooper, probably headed to one of three separate plantations on which family members lived.[99] For the youngest and most mobile skilled slaves, apprenticeships marked a separation from parents, and subsequent sales separated husbands and wives. The dissolution of estates because of death or bankruptcy threatened the wholesale auctioning off of slaves and some skilled workers escaped along with entire families.[100] Slaves ran away when forced to move from the rich social life of Charles Town to the comparative isolation of the countryside. Whatever package of rewards planters might offer to their skilled slaves in the short term to maintain relations of affiliation, their inability to guarantee family integrity or the persistence of expected benefits rendered such bonds particularly tenuous.

Slave artisans recognized that, by teaching their skills to others, they might diminish the uniqueness of those skills. In 1775 James Habersham supplied the Countess of Huntingdon's new Georgia plantation, temporarily, with a cooper "to make Rice Barrels and teach two of your People that Business," and another experienced driver to "instruct and direct your Negroes how to plant." The latter accused Habersham of trying to "*sell him softly,* that is without his Consent and Knowledge."[101] Hiring slaves to other planters, particularly new planters lacking a force of skilled workers, often served as a pretext for selling them. The practice, common enough to give rise to a slave idiom, inspired more than fear: skilled slaves realized that if they could be spared from plantations as hired workers, the flexible character of their role in production combined with skill-enhanced market value to make them prime candidates for sale, "softly" or otherwise.

Although this driver suspected that his temporary assignment might end up as a permanent sale, his owner had already refused an offer of 200 guineas for him. Governor James Glen reported a remarkable instance of "a Gentleman who refused five Hundred Guineas for three of his [skilled] Slaves." When "two of the most valuable fellows" on a Pee Dee River plantation were inherited by a nonresident heir, the plantation manager determined to buy back this driver and cooper, "whom the Plantation cannot well spare," at approximately £700 each, although they had been purchased as boys for a fraction of that price more than thirty years before.[102] Technical skills combined with cultural abilities to render a few skilled slaves more valuable than their selling price, but even when slave owners boasted of the amounts they would refuse for their most important specialists, they rarely neglected to quantify their appreciation in South Carolina currency.

The work histories and runaway experiences of skilled slaves reveal the degree to which the terms of specialized work sponsored a tentative brand of acculturation, one that involved the calculated use of cultural skills rather than a decisive shift in cultural allegiance. The runaway advertisements offer a diverse sample of experience at charged moments in master-slave relationships. Through them we can glimpse the uniqueness of skilled workers in the eyes of their masters and measure in a rough way the cultural residue of equally distinctive working relationships in the language abilities, mobility, and social confidence that slave fugitives' behaviors exhibited. Yet the most obvious interpretation of the advertisements reveals skilled slave affiliation as a labor system chronically lacking in stability, as each traumatic vignette narrates the breakdown of a relationship once marked by interdependence and affirmed by special privileges. Admiration for the courage and ingenuity of fugitive specialists, however, should be contextualized by an appreciation of the uncertain labor positions that drove many to extreme measures. Slave owners believed they could open and close the narrow aperture that separated slave specialists from the opportunities they desired to exploit, proffering a work regime structured around the model of free white artisans and yet exercising their power as masters to alter work arrangements and sell their human property when they chose. These actions precipitated flight and probably appeared as unjustified reneging to slave workers conditioned by the logic of the task system to regard privileges once grated as permanent rights.

Skilled slave specialists comprised a category of individuals with varying experiences, one that must be configured openly so as to avoid homogenizing a remarkably diverse group within eighteenth-century South Carolina society. What linked the experiences of slave goldsmiths and hired washerwomen, indigo makers and boatmen, was not necessarily the level of expertise demanded by their jobs, but rather the labor arrangements employed to balance work that required an active engagement in production within a slave system characterized by coercion. The conceptual zero-sum game that portrays slave life in terms of either "resistance" or "accommodation" leaves little room for the depiction of slave experience beyond the norm. Considering enslaved specialists outside of this dichotomy, as affiliated participants in plantation enterprises, draws attention to the diversity of economic ventures employing slave labor in the early plantation South.

Skilled slaves responded to labor arrangements featuring incentives to contribute their expertise and took advantage of noncoercive systems designed to ensure their accountability as partially independent workers. Understanding such behaviors within relationships of affiliation suggest how some specialists could figure prominently in revolutionary conspiracies while others turned down offers of manumission.[103] Enslaved specialists pursued autonomy by engaging in work for their masters while most other slaves sought to limit the encroachments of plantation demands on their time. This difference made skilled slaves anomalous, but the ways in which they sought to enlarge their limited economic agency bespoke strong continuities among all South Carolina slaves. Affiliations were tenuous arrangements that allowed slaves and masters to traverse the standards that regulated slave roles without sacrificing core commitments. Working as affiliates of plantation enterprises made enslaved specialists culturally capable of turning privileges encumbered with sacrifices within slavery into a foretaste of freedom when they worked as independent fugitives.

Notes

1. The author wishes to thank Michael P. Johnson, Jack P. Greene, and members of the Johns Hopkins University Seminar in Early American History for their critiques of an earlier draft of this essay. The terms "skilled slaves" and "enslaved specialists" are used here interchangeably to designate slave workers employed at specialized tasks, excluding domestic servants. The terms allude to commonalities in labor arrangements rather than disparities in training, ability, or the difficulty of certain types of work. While many workers considered in this light were artisans, some included as "skilled" might in other contexts be considered "unskilled" workers, among them boatmen, washerwomen, and market slaves. My understanding of enslaved specialists draws on Ira Berlin's characterizations in "Time, Space, and the Evolution of Afro-American Society on British Mainland North America," *American Historical Review* 85 (1980): 54–8, 62–7.

2. Samuel Johnson defines "sensible" as "Convinced; persuaded. . . . In low conversation it has sometimes the sense of reasonable; judicious; wise." Samuel Johnson, *Johnson's Dictionary: A Modern Selection,* comp. E. L. McAdam, Jr., and George Milne (New York: Pantheon, 1963), 366.

3. Herbert G. Gutman, *The Black Family in Slavery and Freedom, 1750–1925* (New York: Vintage Books, 1976), and Margaret Washington Creel, *"A Peculiar People": Slave Religion and Community-Culture among the Gullahs* (New York and London: New York University Press, 1988).

4. Peter A. Coclanis, *The Shadow of a Dream: Economic Life and Death in the South Carolina Low Country* (New York and Oxford: Oxford University Press, 1989), 72–85.

5. Peter H. Wood, *Black Majority: Negroes in Colonial South Carolina from 1670 through the Stono Rebellion* (New York and London: W. W. Norton & Company, 1974), 95–130.

6. John Solomon Otto, "Livestock-Raising in Early South Carolina, 1670–1700: Prelude to the Rice Plantation Economy," *Agricultural History* 64 (1987): 23; Wood, *Black Majority*, 28–33.

7. Alexander Moore, "Daniel Axtell's Account Book and the Economy of Early South Carolina," *South Carolina Historical Magazine* 95 (1994): 285–90; [Elizabeth Hyrne] to [Burrell Massingberd], c. 1701–1702, "Hyrne Family Letters, 1701–10," in *The Colonial South Carolina Scene: Contemporary Views, 1697–1774*, ed. H. Roy Merrens (Columbia, S.C.: University of South Carolina Press, 1977), 18–19.

8. William George Bently, "Wealth Distribution in Colonial South Carolina" (Ph.D. diss., Georgia State University, 1977), 86; Russell R. Menard, "Slave Demography in the Lowcountry, 1670–1740: From Frontier Society to Plantation Regime," *South Carolina Historical Magazine* 96 (1995): 303; Philip D. Morgan, "The Development of Slave Culture in Eighteenth Century Plantation America" (Ph.D. diss., University of London, 1977), 1, 4; Morgan, "Black Society in the Lowcountry 1760–1810," in *Slavery and Freedom in the Age of the American Revolution*, ed. Ira Berlin and Ronald Hoffman (Charlottesville: University Press of Virginia, 1983), 93, 95.

9. On the task system see Lewis C. Gray, *History of Agriculture in the Southern United States to 1860*, 2 vols. (1933; reprint, Gloucester, Mass.: Peter Smith, 1958), 2:548–57; Philip D. Morgan, "Work and Culture: The Task System and the World of Lowcountry Blacks, 1700–1880," *William and Mary Quarterly*, 3d ser., 39 (1982): 563–99; Morgan, "Task and Gang Systems: The Organization of Labor on New World Plantations," in *Work and Labor in Early America,* ed. Stephen Innes (Chapel Hill, NC: University of North Carolina Press, 1988), 189–220.

10. Samuel Dubose, "Address Delivered at the Seventeenth Anniversary of the Black Oak Agricultural Society" (1887), in *A Contribution to the History of the Huguenots of South Carolina,* ed. T. G. Thomas (Columbia, S.C.: R. L. Bryan, 1972), 9–10; account and blanket book, 1720–1778, 11/515/5, Elias Ball XIV Family Papers, South Carolina Historical Society, Charleston (hereafter cited as SCHS).

11. In nineteenth-century Virginia, ironworkers employed tasked labor and offered incentives to sustain similar affiliations with skilled slave iron workers. See Charles B. Dew, *Bond of Iron: Master and Slave at Buffalo Forge* (New York: W.W. Norton & Company, 1994), 109–15, 150–63.

12. Morgan, "Black Society in the Lowcountry," 97–99. These figures revise earlier statistics included in Morgan, "Development of Slave Culture," 101–2, 106–7.

13. This sample was complied from advertisements published in Lathan A. Windley, comp., *Runaway Slave Advertisements: A Documentary History from the 1730s to 1790,* vol. 3, *South Carolina* (Westport, Conn., and London: Greenwood Press, 1983). Advertisements that repeated previously published information were not included. Similar tables appear in Morgan, "Black Society in the Lowcountry," 99–104; Daniel C. Littlefield, *Rice and Slaves: Ethnicity and the Slave Trade in Colonial South Carolina* (Baton Rouge:

Louisiana State University Press, 1981), 136–37. The tables differ as to newspaper sources, time periods, and types of workers included.

14. See n. 80 below.

15. A similar gendering of skilled work occurred in the Caribbean and Chesapeake as well. See Robert W. Fogel, *Without Consent or Contract: The Rise and Fall of American Slavery* (New York and London: W. W. Norton & Company, 1989), 50–52; Richard Dunn, "Sugar Production and Slave Women in Jamaica," in *Cultivation and Culture: Labor and the Shaping of Slave Life in the Americas*, ed. Ira Berlin and Philip D. Morgan (Charlottesville and London: University Press of Virginia, 1993), 61; David P. Geggus, "Sugar and Coffee Cultivation in Saint Domingue and the Shaping of the Slave Labor Force," in ibid., 84, 86; David B. Gaspar, "Sugar Cultivation and Slave Life in Antigua before 1800," in ibid., 100; Lorena S. Walsh, "Slave Life, Slave Society, and Tobacco Production in the Tidewater Chesapeake, 1620–1820," in ibid., 186.

16. Sam[u]el Stiles to William Telfair, 21 Feb. 1779, Edward Telfair Papers, Special Collections, Duke University, Durham; Noble Wimberly Jones to ?, 13 Feb. 1780, Noble Wimberly Jones Papers, Special Collections, Duke University; Mepkin Plantation to Abraham Schad, 19 Apr. 1770, Henry Laurens account book, Special Collections, College of Charleston, Charleston (hereafter cited as Laurens account book).

17. In 1795 in South Carolina, George Wagner hired slaves from Alex Inglis, paying £20 per year for the men and £12 per year for the women, Alexander Inglis Papers, 28/678/6, SCHS.

18. See, for example, the advertisement of James Robert in the *South Carolina Gazette*, 22 Dec. 1737.

19. See Creel, *"A Peculiar People,"* 36; Brigitte Menzel, *Textilien Aus Westafrika* (Berlin, Museum für Völkerkunde, 1972), passim. See n. 59 below.

20. "Copy of James Bailey's Letter," 2 June 1778, box 140 (no. 9), letters 1777–1785, Henry Laurens Papers, SCHS.

21. [Joseph Clay?] to ?, 6 Dec. 178[5?], Edward Telfair Papers. Special Collections, Duke University. For examples of the proportion and type of skilled slave common to plantation work forces, see C[harles] W[oodmason], "The Art of Manufacturing Indigo in Carolina," *Gentleman's Magazine* 25 (1755): 258; Philip Hamer, et al., eds., *The Papers of Henry Laurens* (Columbia; University of South Carolina Press, 1968–), 4:584 (hereafter cited as Hamer et al., eds., *Henry Laurens*); Thomas Middleton Plantation book, Southern Historical Collection, University of North Carolina, Chapel Hill (hereafter cited as SHC), 11.

22. Henry Laurens to John Knight, 20 Jan. 1764, Hamer et al., eds., *Henry Laurens*, 4:138; *South Carolina Gazette*, 24 Sept. 1772.

23. William Gerhard De Brahm, "Philosophico-Historico-Hydrogeography of South Carolina, Georgia, and East Florida," in *Documents Connected with the History of South Carolina*, ed. P. C. J. Weston (London, printed for private distribution, 1856), 199; Morgan, "Development of Slave Culture," 127; John Drayton, *A View of South Carolina As Respects her Natural and Civil Concerns* (Charleston, 1802), 141–42.

24. Richard Hutson to John Drayton, 14 July 1776, Richard Hutson letterbook, SCHS; *South Carolina Gazette*, 30 Mar. 1734; account of Peter Porcher to estate of Philip Williams, Jan. 1778–Apr. 1779, box 1 (letter), folder 5; account of the estate of Philip Williams, Apr. 1786, box 3 (legal), folder 28, Palmer Family Papers, South Caroliniana Library, University of South Carolina, Columbia (hereafter cited as SCL); Leila Sellers, *Charleston Business on the Eve of the American Revolution* (Chapel Hill: University of North Carolina Press, 1934), 99–100; Joyce E. Chaplin, *An Anxious Pursuit: Agricul-*

tural Innovation and Modernity in the Lower South, 1730–1815 (Chapel Hill and London: University of North Carolina Press, 1993), 86.

25. Johann David Shoepf, *Travels in the Confederation, 1783–84,* ed. and trans., Alfred J. Morrison, (Philadelphia: W.J. Campbell, 1911), 2:201–2. Charles Town widows especially relied on skilled slave wages for income; see Cara Anzilotti, "'In the Affairs of the World': Women and Plantation Ownership in the Eighteenth Century South Carolina Lowcountry" (Ph.D. diss., University of California, Santa Barbara, 1994), 220. The work of hired slaves sometimes earned planters credits in interplantation exchanges that could be cashed in for needed goods, such as corn provisions; see misc. expense journal, box 1728–1771, folder 1769–1771, William Gibbons, Jr., Papers, Special Collections, Duke University; account of the estate of Philip Williams, box 3 (legal), folder 28, Palmer Family Papers, SCL.

26. John Lewis Gervais to Henry Laurens, 15 Apr. 1784, Henry Laurens, ALS, SCL; "A Rent Roll of the Estate of Charles Pinckney" (1753), 11/383/21, Benjamin Rutledge Huger Family Papers, SCHS; "Estimate of J. C. Property" (c. 1791), 11/515/23, Ball Papers, SCHS; Robert Raper to R[obert] Swainston, 5 Nov. 1762, Robert Raper letterbook (photocopy), SCHS.

27. See Chaplin, *An Anxious Pursuit,* passim; Henry Laurens to Richard Oswald, 26 May 1757, Hamer et al., eds., *Henry Laurens,* 2:203; [Great Britain], *Journals of the House of Commons,* 56 vols. (printed by order of the House of Commons: 1803–1813), 25:619–25, 635; Henry Laurens to Devonsheir, Reeve, & Lloyd, 4 July 1757, Hamer et al., eds., *Henry Laurens,* 1:286.

28. George D. Terry, "'Champaign Country': A Social History of an Eighteenth Century Lowcountry Parish in South Carolina, St. Johns Berkeley County" (Ph.D. diss., University of South Carolina, 1981), 256; see, for example, Henry Laurens to Lachlan McIntosh, Dec. 20, 1771, Hamer et al., eds., *Henry Laurens,* 8:109.

29. Quoted in Littlefield, *Rice and Slaves,* 135.

30. Jean Pierre Purry, "Memorial of . . . Carolina," in *Tracts and Other Papers, Relating Principally to the Origin, Settlement, and Progress of the Colonies in North America,* comp. Peter Force (Washington, D.C., 1836): vol. 1, 11:7; *American Husbandry* (1775; reprint, New York: Columbia University Press, 1939), 343–44. For an example of the greater expenses of using white labor for construction see Josiah Smith, Jr., to George Austin, 17 June 1771, Josiah Smith, Jr., letterbook, SHC.

31. George Lucas to Charles Pinckney, 25 July 1745, ser. 1, box 3, Charles Cotesworth Pinckney and Family Papers, Library of Congress, Manuscript Division; Eliza Pinckney to C. C. Pinckney, 10 Sept. 1785, Charles Cotesworth Pinckney Papers, SCHS; see also the advertisement of Capt. De La Chapelle, *South Carolina Gazette,* 11 Nov. 1745; Henry Laurens to Richard Oswald & Co., 26 May 1756, Hamer et al., eds., *Henry Laurens,* 2:203.

32. See Chaplin, *Anxious Pursuit,* 134; George Lucas to Charles Pinckney, Dec. 174[5?], ser. 1, box 3, Pinckney Papers, Library of Congress.

33. Schoepf, *Travels in the Confederation,* 159.

34. Henry Laurens to Joseph Brown, 10 May 1766, Hamer et al., eds., *Henry Laurens,* 5:126–27; ibid., 5:624 n; on reported costs of slave-built indigo vats, see box 1 (legal), folder 2, and box 1 (letter), folder 13, Palmer Family Papers, SCL; letter of William Allston to Plowden Weston, 29 June 1779, SCL; see also account and blanket book, 1720–1778, 4 Mar. 1746, 11/515/5, Ball Papers, SCHS.

35. David L. Coon, *The Development of Market Agriculture in South Carolina, 1670–1785* (1972; reprint, New York and London: Garland Publishing, Inc., 1989), 119,

173–74, 186; Peter Manigault to Ralph Izard, 18 June 1764, Peter Manigault letterbook, 11/277/8, Manigault Family Papers, SCHS; see also Judith Carney, "Rice Milling, Gender and Slave Labour in Colonial South Carolina," *Past and Present* 153 (1996): passim.

36. *South Carolina Gazette*, 3 Feb. 1773; Josiah Smith, Jr., to George Austin, 25 Feb. 1772, Smith letterbook, SHC.

37. Misc. expense journal, 1771–ca. 1790?, box 1728–71, folder 1769–71, Gibbons Papers, Special Collections, Duke University.

38. Charles Town building practices followed this pattern of mixed free and slave skilled employment from the first decade of the eighteenth century, Elizabeth Sindry estate account book, 1705–1721, SCHS; Johann Martin Bolzius, "Johan Martin Bolzius Answers and Questionnaire on Carolina and Georgia," ed. and trans. Klaus G. Loewald et al., *William and Mary Quarterly*, 3d ser., 14 (1957): 247.

39. Robert Pringle to Andrew Pringle, 5 Feb. 1743, *The Letterbook of Robert Pringle*, ed. Walter B. Edgar, 2 vols. (Columbia: University of South Carolina Press, 1972), 2:498; C[hristopher] G[adsden] to [William Henry?] Drayton, 1 June 1778, copies of correspondence relating to the eighteenth-century history of Charleston, Porcher Family Papers, College of Charleston, Special Collections; [Alexander] Hewit, "An Historical Account of the Rise and Progress of the Colonies of South Carolina and Georgia" (1778), in *Historical Collections of South Carolina*, ed. B. R. Carroll, 2 vols. (Charleston, 1836), 1:351. On reactions to skilled slave labor in early Georgia see Mart A. Stewart, *"What Nature Suffers to Groe": Life, Labor, and Landscape on the Georgia Coast, 1680–1920* (Athens and London: University of Georgia Press, 1996), 55; Bolzius, "Questionnaire on Carolina and Georgia," 227, 242.

40. See Robert Olwell, "Authority and Resistance: Social Order in a Colonial Society, the South Carolina Lowcountry, 1739–1782" (Ph.D. diss., Johns Hopkins University, 1991), 19.

41. On these bills, laws, and ordinances, and the petitions and jury presentments that relate to skilled slaves, see Marcus W. Jernegan, *Laboring and Dependent Classes in Colonial America, 1607–1783* (1931; reprint, New York: Frederick Ungar Publishing Co., 1960), 20–21; Sellers, *Charleston Business*, 99–101, 105; Loren Schweninger, "Slave Independence and Enterprise in South Carolina, 1780–1865," *South Carolina Historical Magazine* 93 (1992): 144; Richard Walsh, *Charleston's Sons of Liberty: A Study of the Artisans, 1763–1789* (Columbia: University of South Carolina Press, 1959), 126; [South Carolina Colonial Assembly], *The Journal of the Commons House of Assembly, September 14, 1742–January 27, 1744*, ed. J. H. Easterby (Columbia, S.C., 1954), 556.; [South Carolina Colonial Assembly], *Journal of the Commons* [1744–1745], ed. J. H. Easterby (Columbia, S.C., 1955), 46, 56; [South Carolina House of Representatives], *Journals of the House of Representatives, 1783–84* ed. Theodora J. Thompson (Columbia, S.C., 1977), 237; *South Carolina Gazette*, 30 Mar. 1734, 3 Apr. 1742, 27 Apr. 1752, 8 Nov. 1742.

42. [South Carolina Colonial Assembly], *Journal of the Commons* [1742–1743], 547.

43. Walsh, *Charleston's Sons of Liberty*, 18, 24; Sellers, *Charleston Business*, 102–4; Philip S. Foner and Ronald L. Lewis, eds., *The Black Worker: A Documentary History from Colonial Times to the Present*, 4 vols. (Philadelphia: Temple University Press, 1978), 1:10; Leonard Stavisky, "Negro Craftsmanship in Early America," in *The Other Slaves: Mechanics, Artisans and Craftsmen*, ed. James E. Newton and Ronald L. Lewis (Boston: G.K. Hall, 1978), 195; Carl Bridenbaugh, *Cities in Revolt: Urban Life in America, 1743–1776* (New York: Knopf, 1968), 274.

44. Quoted in Bridenbaugh, *The Colonial Craftsman* (New York: New York University Press, 1950), 15–16.

45. Artisan investment and slave ownership: Hewit, "An Historical Account," 1:419, Jackson Turner Main, *The Social Structure of Revolutionary America* (Princeton: Princeton University Press, 1965), 59; advertisements for artisan-overseers: *South Carolina Gazette*, 15 Mar. 1735, 14 Aug. 1736, 4 Dec. 1740, 9 May 1743, 8 Sept. 1744, 15 Feb. 1752; see also misc. expense journal, 1771–ca. 1790?, box 1728–71, folder 1769–71, Gibbons Papers, Special Collections, Duke University; Josiah Smith, Jr., to George Austin, 30 Jan. 1773, Smith letterbook, SHC.

46. Robert Raper to William Vanderspeigel, 16 July 1760, Raper letterbook, SHCS.

47. John Norris, "An Interview with James Freeman, 1712," in *Colonial South Carolina Scene*, 51–52; Hewit, "An Historical Account," 1:377; Bolzius, "Questionnaire on Carolina and Georgia," 237; Peter Manigault to [William Blake], 10 May 1771, Manigault letterbook, SHCS. See also will of James Withers, 17 Feb. 1756, Wills of Charleston County, 7 (1752–1756), South Carolina Department of Archives and History, Columbia, 537–39; Michele K. Gillespie, "Planters in the Making: Artisanal Opportunity in Georgia, 1790–1830," in *American Artisans: Crafting Social Identity, 1750–1850*, ed. Howard B. Rock et al. (Baltimore: Johns Hopkins University Press, 1995), 33–47.

48. John Lewis Gervais to Henry Laurens, 26 Nov. 1777, Hamer et al., eds., *Henry Laurens*, 12:85, 87–88.

49. *South Carolina Gazette*, 30 July 1732; Joseph [Butler?] to William and Edward Telfair, 12–24 May 1774, Telfair Papers, special collectios, Duke University; Henry Laurens to Samuel Wainwright, 16 Feb. 1763, Hamer et al., eds., *Henry Laurens*, 3:262.

50. On artisans' social status see Main, *Social Structure*, 199. On attempts in seventeenth-century Massachusetts to restrict consumption among artisans see Stephen Innes, *Creating the Commonwealth: The Economic Culture of Puritan New England* (New York, 1995), 169–81. For a nineteenth-century example of the economic decision making involved in employing skilled slaves over free white workers see Dew, *Bond of Iron*, 66–67, 100.

51. Morgan, "Black Society in the Lowcountry," 118–20; Isaac Hayne register, SCHS.

52. J[ohn] Channing to [Edward Telfair], 10 Aug. 1786, Telfair Papers; John Channing to William Gibbons, 26 June 1770, Gibbons Papers.

53. Morgan, "Development of Slave Culture," 122–23.

54. Laurens account book, passim. During this period Henry Laurens owned Mepkin, Broughton Island, New Hope, Altamaha, and Wright's Savannah plantations and a half interest in Wambaw plantation.

55. Henry Laurens to James Laurens, 6 Aug. 1772, Hamer et al., eds., *Henry Laurens*, 8:399; Henry Laurens to John Lewis Gervais, 22 Mar. 1773, ibid., 8:635; Henry Laurens to James Baillie, 23 Sept. 1774, ibid., 9:262–63; Henry Laurens to John Loveday, 14 June 1777, ibid., 11:367. See table 9.2: Old Cuffee received two pair of shoes, one black and one white, valued at £2.50 when he worked at Laurens's Broughton Island Plantation in 1769, Broughton Island Plantation to General Merchandise, 4 Nov. 1769, Laurens account book.

56. John Channing to [Edward Telfair], 3 Oct. 1787, Telfair Papers; Josiah Smith, Jr., to George Austin, 14 June 1775, Smith letterbook; Morgan, "Development of Slave Culture," 191.

57. Henry Laurens to John Lewis Gervais, 5 Sept. 1777, Hamer et al., eds., *Henry Laurens*, 11:486–87; John Lewis Gervais to Henry Laurens, 25 July 1777, ibid., 11:407–8.

58. Henry Laurens to William Brisbane, 17 Oct. 1777, ibid., 11:562; Henry Laurens

to John Lewis Gervais, 5 Sept. 1777, ibid., 11:492; Henry Laurens to John Lewis Gervais, 18 Oct. 1777, ibid., 11:565.

59. Henry Laurens to John Smith, 9 May 1766, ibid., 5:125; see also the case of "Sampson," Henry Laurens to Joseph Brown, 28 June 1765, ibid., 4:645; Josiah Smith, Jr., to George Austin, 17 June 1771, Smith letterbook.

60. Kenneth E. Lewis, "Plantation Layout and Function in the South Carolina Lowcountry," in *The Archaeology of Slavery and Plantation Life*, ed. Theresa A. Singleton (Orlando: Academic Press, 1985), 55.

61. Handicraft Slaves to Stock, 1 Oct. 1766; Peter and John Horlbeck to Handicraft Slaves, 13 Nov. 1766; Front Marsh Land to Handicraft Slaves, 4 May 1767; Captain Thomas Courtin to Handicraft Slaves, 8 May 1767; Captain Henry Todd to Handicraft Slaves, 30 Aug. 1768; Handicraft Slaves to Captain Henry Todd, 30 Aug. 1768, Laurens account book.

62. Henry Laurens to John Laurens, 12 Dec. 1774, Hamer et al., eds., *Henry Laurens*, 10:2–3.

63. Eugene D. Genovese, *Roll, Jordan, Roll: The World the Slaves Made* (New York: Pantheon, 1974), 5.

64. Henry Laurens to Martha Laurens, 17 Aug. 1777, Hamer et al., eds., *Henry Laurens*, 11:254.

65. Henry Laurens to John Smith, 15 Aug. 1765, ibid., 4:661.

66. James Laurens to Henry Laurens, 22 Dec. 1773, ibid., 9:269; James Laurens to Henry Laurens, 3 Mar. 1774, ibid., 9:334; Henry Laurens to James Laurens, 5 Feb. 1774, ibid., 9:269; John Lewis Gervais to Henry Laurens, 26 Nov. 1777, ibid., 12:85, 87–88.

67. John Lewis Gervais to Henry Laurens, 5–10 May 1772, ibid., 8:287–91; Henry Laurens to William Brisbane, 8 Sept. 1772, ibid., 11:265.

68. Henry Laurens to John Lewis Gervais, 5 Sept. 1777, ibid., 11:491–92; ibid., 8:111 n.

69. See Benjamin Franklin, *The Autobiography and Other Writings* (New York: Penguin, 1986), 50; Gaspar, "Sugar Cultivation," 108; account of Margaret Colleton to Robert Raper, c. 1778, Margaret Colleton MSS, SCL.

70. Henry Laurens to Christopher Zahn, 20 June 1777, Hamer et al., eds., *Henry Laurens*, 11:375; Henry Laurens to John Smith, 15 Aug. 1765, ibid., 4:661; Henry Laurens to James Laurens, 5 Dec. 1771, ibid., 8:68; Henry Laurens to Abraham Schad, 6 Apr. 1766, ibid., 5:101; Henry Laurens to John Smith, 23 Dec. 1765, ibid., 5:46–47; Henry Laurens to Nathaniel Savineau, 15 Aug. 1765, ibid., 4:660.

71. Henry Laurens to Benjamin Addison, 26 May 1768, ibid., 5:702; see also Henry Laurens to Martha Laurens, 17 Aug. 1777, ibid., 11:254, Henry Laurens to John Laurens, 4 Jan. 1775, ibid., 10:17 Henry Laurens to James Laurens, 5 Dec. 1771, ibid., 8:66–67; Henry Laurens to Felix Wharley, 5 Dec. 1771, ibid., 8:73; Henry Laurens to John Lewis Gervais, 16 Apr. 1774, ibid., 9:414.

72. Walsh, *Charleston's Sons of Liberty*, ix.

73. "Kate" (1757), in Windley, *Runaway Slave Advertisements*, vol. 3, *South Carolina*, 158–59.

74. "Tom" (1756), in ibid., 149.

75. "Shadwell" (1775), in ibid., 477.

76. [Charles Ball], *Fifty Years in Chains; Or, The Life of An American Slave* (1858; reprint, Indianapolis: Mnemosyne Publishing Co., 1969), 282–83.

77. See Gerald W. Mullin, *Flight and Rebellion: Slave Resistance in Eighteenth-Century Virginia* (New York, 1972), 90–91.

78. See Wood, *Black Majority*, 325.

79. Quoted in Jernegan, *Laboring and Dependent Classes*, 19–20. On demographic developments see Morgan, "Development of Slave Culture," 310; Coclanis, *Shadow of a Dream*, 42–46, 66–67.

80. For an exception to this generalization, see Berlin, "Time, Space, and the Evolution of Afro-American Society,": 63, 67. As a representative sample, the advertisements possess some inherent flaws. Certain groups, such as sailors, boatmen, and hired slaves, are overrepresented: these slaves could escape their servitude more easily than others, especially those who worked primarily on plantations, and probably did so more often. Advertisements analyzed here span the period 1732–1790, but over half are concentrated around the period 1770–1785, when there were more skilled slaves in general and more opportunities for running away afforded by social and political instability during the Revolutionary War. Planters advertised most often for men between the ages of 15 and 30, who might have been less constrained by obligations toward families than other slaves, especially women. See Philip D. Morgan, "Colonial South Carolina Runaways: Their Significance for Slave Culture," *Slavery and Abolition* 6 (1985): 57-78.

81. As Samuel Johnson defines the term, "plausible" meant "such as gains approbation; superficially pleasing or taking; specious; popular; right in appearance." Johnson, *Dictionary*, 297.

82. Advertisers indicated language ability in reference to 136 out of 602 slaves in this sample (23 percent). In this group 12 (9 percent) spoke "bad" or "thick" English; 9 (7 percent), "tolerable" or "indifferent"; 69 (51 percent), "good"; 23 (17 percent), "very good" or "proper"; 5 (4 percent), "remarkable"; 6 (4 percent) indicated some degree of literacy.

83. "Ben" (1790), in Windley, *Runaway Slave Advertisements*, 3:410; "Mick" (1782), in ibid., 3:598–99; see also ibid., 3:231, 719; "Joe" (1786), in ibid., 3:424–25.

84. "Quamino and Quacco" (1733), in ibid., 3:7; "Pompey" (1776), in ibid., 3:482.

85. "Mustee," a term derived from the Spanish "Mestizo," typically referred to the children of black slaves and American Indians, although in some few cases it was used to describe skin color alone as in John Simmons's description of Primus as "a little inclined to the mustee." "Primus" (1777), in ibid., 3:513; see Wood, *Black Majority*, 99.

86. Advertisers indicated birthplace and ethnicity in reference to 219 out of 602 slaves in this sample (36 percent). In this group, 72 (33 percent) were born in the Lower South; 66 (30 percent) were born in the Chesapeake, Middle Colonies, or were of mixed race; 24 (11 percent) were born in the West Indies; 57 (26 percent) were African-born or bore "country marks."

87. "Samson" and five others (unnamed) (1763), in Windley, *Runaway Slave Advertisements*, 3:239.

88. "Jamie, Peter, and York" (1777), in ibid., 3:506–7; "Peter" (1773), in ibid., 3:320.

89. "Sambo" (1784), in ibid., 3:734; "London" (1746), in ibid., 3:68; "Prince" (1781), in ibid., 3:578–79.

90. Michael Mullin, *Africa in America: Slave Acculturation and Resistance in the American South and the British Caribbean, 1736–1831* (Urbana and Chicago: University of Illinois Press, 1992), 38; [Ball], *Fifty Years in Chains*, 308–9, 392, 399.

91. "Simon and Ned" (1773), in Windley, *Runaway Slave Advertisements*, 3:685; "Frank" (1772), in ibid., 3:446; "Barber" (1767), in ibid., 3:419; "Sam" (1770), in ibid., 3:654; "Sam" (1771), in ibid., 3:295.

92. "Leonard" (1781), in ibid., 3:584; "Young Domina" (1765), in ibid., 3:247; for other examples see *South Carolina Gazette,* 31 July 1736, 3 Sept. 1737; "Limas" (1741), in Windley, *Runaway Slave Advertisements,* 3:48; "Tom" (1766), in ibid., 3:606; "Lancaster" (1740), in *The Black Worker,* ed. Foner and Lewis, 1:9.

93. "Jack" (1772), in Windley, *Runaway Slave Advertisements,* 3:311; "Scipio" (1769, 1778), in ibid., 3:281, 524; see "Cuffie" (1775), in ibid., 3:470; "Harry" (1778), in ibid., 3:357; "Jemmy" (1771), in ibid., 3:196; "Sandy" (1774), in ibid., 3:333; "Sukey" (1781), in ibid., 3:589; "Bob" (1774), in ibid., 3:334; see also Frederick Douglass, *My Bondage and My Freedom,* ed. Philip S. Foner (New York, 1969), 286–87; "Sam" (1741), in Windley, *Runaway Slave Advertisements,* 3:49.

94. "Hannah" (1751, 1766), in Windley, *Runaway Slave Advertisements,* 3:110, 608.

95. On free black artisans see Larry Koger, *Black Slaveowners: Free Black Slave Masters in South Carolina, 1790–1860* (Jefferson, N.C., and London: McFarland, 1985), 141–42; Michael P. Johnson and James L. Roark, *Black Masters: A Free Family of Color in the Old South* (New York; W.W. Norton & Company, 1984); see also Alexander Garden to [Richard Bohun Baker] [c. 1761], 11/536/23, Alexander Garden, medical, botanical letters, SCHS; *South Carolina Gazette,* 13 Nov. 1736; on examples of manumissions for black artisans see Allison Carll-White, "South Carolina's Forgotten Craftsmen," *South Carolina Historical Magazine* 86 (January 1985): 34–36; will of James Aiken 19 (1780–1783), 140, wills of Charleston County, South Carolina Department of Archives and History; memorandum, 7 July 1790, Henry Laurens Papers, SCHS.

96. "Joe" (1781) in Windley, *Runaway Slave Advertisements,* 3:583; see also "Saul and Jack" (1773), in ibid., 3:327.

97. Appraising slave value: Schoepf, *Travels in the Confederation,* 159; R. F. W. Allston Papers, 23, SCHS; Josiah Smith, Jr., to George Austin, 14 June 1775, Smith letterbook, SHC; "Rent Roll of the Estate of Charles Pinckney," 11/383/21, SCHS. Slave sales: Richard Hutson to Isaac Hayne, 21 Jan. 1766, Charles Woodward Hutson Papers, SHC; *South Carolina Gazette,* 9 Mar. 1738. Sale to Georgia and Florida: *South Carolina Gazette,* 21 Apr. 1733; Littlefield, *Rice and Slaves,* 141–42.

98. This was true for slaves in Virginia as well, see Mullin, *Flight and Rebellion,* 89.

99. "Ned" (1778), in Windley, *Runaway Slave Advertisements,* 3:521; "Cyrus" (1769), in ibid., 3:645.

100. See, for example, "Baccus" (1781), in ibid., 3:585; "Saul" (1775), in ibid., 3:302.

101. James Habersham to the Countess of Huntingdon, 19 Apr. 1775, in *A Documentary History of American Industrial Society: Plantation and Frontier,* ed. Ulrich B. Phillips, 2 vols. (1910; reprinted New York: Russell & Russell, 1958), 1:2 (my emphasis).

102. Jernegan, *Laboring and Dependent Classes,* 20; Josiah Smith, Jr., to George Appleby, 22 Sept. 1774, Smith letterbook, SHC.

103. Mullin argues in *Africa in America,* 216–35, that artisans and other "assimilateds" formed a revolutionary core of activists in the post–Revolutionary War era, including those involved in the Denmark Vesey conspiracy of 1822; Henry Laurens wrote that his slave carpenter, George, had refused offers of manumission, Henry Laurens MSS, 7 July 1790, SCL.

X

"Practical Justice"

The Justice of the Peace, the Slave Court, and Local Authority in Mid-Eighteenth-Century South Carolina

ROBERT OLWELL

The justice of the peace (J.P.) was by far the most common representative of government in colonial South Carolina. In the two decades before the outbreak of the Revolution, the number of J.P.'s appointed at any moment exceeded the number of positions available as councilors, assemblymen, or militia officers combined. Before 1775, many of South Carolina's future revolutionary leaders served their local communities as J.P.'s.[1] Yet despite its numerical significance, little is known and even less has been written about the place and function of the J.P. in the colonial regime.[2]

In the eighteenth century, the office of J.P. carried a great deal of responsibility. In the absence of regular police forces, the local J.P. was the equivalent of the "cop on the beat" whose charge it was to keep the peace and to uphold law and order in his own neighborhood. An individual J.P. could impose a host of small fines for such minor offenses as neglecting to attend militia muster or using false weights and scales. To prevent trouble, a J.P. could swear prospective offenders to keep the peace in the parish. When faced with more serious offenses, a single J.P. could issue warrants, levy bail, and remand accused criminals to trial. Acting alone, a J.P.'s responsibilities were accurately reflected by his other title: parish officer.[3]

When two or more J.P.'s assembled, they could assume a judicial authority. Magistrates' courts, or "petty sessions" as they were also known, had evolved in England as a way of clearing the court docket of minor offenses. By the eighteenth century magistrates' courts determined cases of petty theft or other "small and mean causes" for which the penalties did not exceed fines, a few days in the stocks, or a dose of corporal punishment. Petty sessions dispensed a rough-and-ready justice without recourse to lawyers or juries.[4] In South Carolina, J.P.'s exercised a similar authority and acted in a similar manner as parish officers. Petty sessions, or magistrates' courts, were convened on occasion but appear to have been less active and important than was the case in the metropolis.

Soon after the founding of the colony, however, South Carolina J.P.'s were given a new field upon which to exercise their judicial ambitions. Beginning in 1686, the colony's slave codes gave J.P.'s the task of convening slave courts consisting of two justices and three freeholders and determining the guilt or innocence of all slaves charged with crimes. After sitting upon the case, the justices and freeholders could impose any punishment, including death, upon convicted slaves.[5] Evidence suggests that J.P.'s did not hesitate to use these vast new powers. In the thirty-five years between 1740 and the outbreak of the Revolution, the colony's assembly compensated the masters of almost 200 slaves who were executed at law.[6]

Therefore, for a majority of colonial South Carolina's inhabitants, the slave population, the powers of the J.P. were literally those of life and death. But the colonial J.P. was an important figure in other several respects. Besides policing the boundary that divided white from black and free from slave, J.P.'s also occupied a middle ground that lay between the colonial and imperial authority and the local community and elites of each parish and neighborhood. Moreover, in their actions and in their office, J.P.'s mitigated the conflicts and contradictions that arose when the white colonists' desire to act in "English ways" and their wish to replicate the institutions and ideologies of the eighteenth-century English establishment met the practical necessity of adapting themselves and their society to suit harsh New World realities and conditions, like slavery.[7]

Because maintaining control over the colony's black majority was always the colonial slave society's most important concern, it can fairly be argued that the J.P. was in fact colonial South Carolina's most important law officer and the slave court its most significant judicial arena. Consequently, understanding who colonial South Carolina's justices were, how they perceived themselves and their role, and how this perception may have influenced the operations of the slave court, can shed light upon a vital, yet hitherto largely neglected, facet of colonial South Carolina society. It can also illuminate how authority was constructed and power exercised in one corner of the eighteenth century Anglo-American world.

To begin, consider two contrasting portraits of the J.P. in colonial South Carolina. First, the proceedings at a magistrate's court in 1771 as described by Charles Woodmason, an itinerant Anglican minister: "Here have I seen, the Bible, the Cards—the Brutes and the Laws, on one Stool—the Magistrate sitting in his Chair, and administering Oaths—rabbling over the Form, so as none to understand his Speech—many in the Crowd, at the instant Cursing and Swearing—While others intoxicated with Liquor, were calling for 'tother 1/2 Pint. . . .[8]" Second, a funeral reported in the Charleston newspaper of 1768: "On Saturday, the 21st instant, was buried, at St. George's, Dorchester, John Skene [Skeene], Esq; Colonel of the Regiment of Horse, in this Province. His Funeral was attended by the Parishioners, whose weeping Eyes testified their Sorrow of Heart for the great Loss they looked upon themselves to have sustained; for he was a Magistrate of strict Integrity and Impartiality, a sincere Friend, hospitable, humane, and, according to his Abilities, charitable to the Poor."[9]

At first glance, the vast difference in these two depictions might be explained as evidence of the gulf that separated the rude reality of colonial practice from the ideal of the gentleman magistrate. Upon further reflection however, both portraits are easily recognizable as caricatures. As described in his obituary, Colonel Skeene closely resembles the fictitious Squire Allworthy, portrayed by Henry Fielding in *Tom Jones* as "a most patient magistrate" who "entertained his neighbours with a hearty welcome to his table, and was charitable to the poor."[10] Similarly, Charles Woodmason's chaotic courtroom scene echoes the farcical magisterial proceedings that can be found in the pages of many eighteenth-century novels.[11]

The close facsimile between English fiction and colonial fact is no accident. Fielding's droll depiction of Squire Allworthy's virtues mocked the same notions of gentility that Colonel Skeene's eulogizers more soberly evoked. Parson Woodmason's imitation may have been even more calculated. Like Fielding, who was a London J.P. as well as a novelist, Woodmason had personal knowledge of the bench. Prior to his ordination in 1765, Woodmason had been for a time "the principle acting magistrate" in Charleston. English born and educated, well traveled and well read (in 1758, he offered "100 Vol. of Books" as security for a loan), Woodmason's use of satire in his journal and other writings has led one scholar to compare him to a more famous eighteenth-century Anglican clergyman, Jonathan Swift.[12]

Thus, our two dominant impressions of the eighteenth-century South Carolina J.P.—a venal, drunken, ignoramus, or a paragon of patriarchal virtues—are in fact two opposing, and exaggerated, stereotypes. As such, they reveal more about eighteenth-century expectations concerning justices' character and conduct than of the justices themselves. These two starkly contrasting portraits represent on the one hand, society's hope and ideal of who the J.P. would or should be, and on the other hand, its fear of what he in fact was or might become.

To get beyond these caricatures and determine to what extent colonial South Carolina's J.P.'s lived up or down to these expectations is not easy. The documents with which to reconstruct the actions of most J.P.'s most of the time simply do not exist. In one sense, South Carolina's J.P.'s have remained hidden in plain sight and have been obscured by their very ordinariness. Throughout the colonial era, for example, the records of the J.P.'s were not regarded as public documents. Given the combined ravages of nature and history over the past two centuries, the result of this policy of deliberate neglect has meant that evidence of the proceedings of colonial J.P.'s are extremely rare. Statutes and handbooks offer evidence of how good J.P.'s were supposed to behave, and complaints to the council, assembly, or newspaper can illuminate the actions of the bad J.P.'s, but neither of these sources can tell us much about the actions of the everyday, "ordinary," J.P. quietly doing his job in his local parish.[13]

We do know who the J.P.'s were. Every decade or so through the mid-eighteenth century, the *South Carolina Gazette* published the roster of the colony's J.P.'s. From these printed rosters it can be seen that the number of J.P.'s in the colony increased rapidly, almost doubling in twenty years. In 1756, there were 199 J.P.'s in the colony. Eleven years later, this number had grown to 264. By 1775, the final roster of the colony's J.P.'s contained nearly 400 names.[14]

Part of this expansion in the number of J.P.'s can be explained by the creation of circuit courts in the backcountry after 1772. Nonetheless, the rise in the number of J.P.'s did not entirely correspond with a rise in the number of courts or people in the colony. For example, the number of J.P.'s grew significantly between 1756 and 1767, although no new courts were as yet established. Moreover, the majority of both the old and the newly created J.P.'s continued to reside in the lowcountry where the white population remained almost stagnant throughout this period.[15] Forty-two percent of the J.P.'s enrolled in 1775 lived either in Charles Town or within a thirty-mile radius of the city.[16]

By the late colonial era, South Carolina threatened to become a society of magistrates. Dividing the colony's burgeoning number of J.P.'s into its small white population, reveals that from 1740 to 1775, about one in twenty-five of the lowcountry's adult white males were serving as J.P.'s at any given moment. In Charles Town and its immediate vicinity, where the ratio of justices to citizens was as low as one in fifteen, it may have seemed that white men had taken the law into their own hands in an almost literal sense.[17]

However, that one could not swing a cat without hitting a J.P. does not mean that they comprised a representative cross section of the colony's population. Leaving aside the obvious fact that the exclusion of blacks and women from all political privileges rendered four-fifths of the colony's adults ineligible for the office, J.P.'s also stood out among South Carolina's white, male minority. According to Chief Justice William Simpson, colonial South Carolina's J.P.'s were to be chosen from "the most sufficient persons dwelling in . . . [each] county. . . ."[18] Evidence suggests that this was indeed the case. David Morton Knepper discovered that all of the 1756 J.P.'s whose estates were assessed after their death possessed above average wealth and were, without exception, slaveholders. The richest of them was Edward Fenwicke, who at the time of his death in 1775 owned 470 slaves and 8,500 acres of land.[19] Fenwicke's total estate was appraised at over £30,000 sterling. Five years earlier, and at the other end of the spectrum, Dougal Campbell died possessed of only seven slaves, a few bank notes, and a large library of law books.[20] Nonetheless, even Campbell's relatively modest estate easily surpassed the mean value of all probate inventories, a category that itself does not include those at the very bottom of the economic ladder whose estates were unlikely to be appraised at all.[21]

To obtain a glimpse of how individual J.P.'s' wealth and slaveholding may have compared to that of their neighbors on any given day, rather than at the end of their lives, one can look at an annual record of all adult male slaves kept by the road commissioners in St. Johns Berkeley from 1760 to 1798.[22] On August 3, 1767, for example, the commissioners counted 1,032 adult male slaves in the parish. These 1,000 slave men were distributed among eighty-seven estates. Thus, the *average* planter in the parish owned twelve adult male slaves, a figure that offers vivid corroboration of St. Johns Berkeley reputation in this era as the "Champaign Country."[23] Moreover, as adult males comprised no more than 40 percent of the slave population at this time, the actual number of all slaves (men, women, and children) on a typical St. Johns Berkeley plantation was probably closer to thirty.[24] Yet even amid such large slave holdings, the parish's J.P.'s stood out as the richest of the rich. St. Johns Berkeley's seven justices in this period possessed an average of twenty-one slave men each, suggesting an average total slaveholding among this group of approximately fifty, men, women, and children.[25]

Correlating the roster of J.P.'s with membership in the colonial assembly reveals that not only were J.P.'s drawn from the same wealthy, slaveholding, social strata as were members of the legislature, but the two groups were considerably intertwined. When Knepper traced office holding among the 199 J.P.'s in the 1756 cohort, he discovered that 27 of them were concurrently seated in the 1756 assembly while a further 71 J.P.'s either formerly had been or would in the future become legislators.[26] Thus, fully half of the J.P.'s of 1756 either were, had been, or would be in the legislature. Likewise, J.P.'s formed a majority among the forty-seven members of the 1756 assembly. A similar study of the 108 J.P.'s in Berkeley county in 1767, reveals that 58 (or 54 percent) of them served in the assembly at some time in their public careers.[27]

In 1761 South Carolina's royal governor, James Glen, described the position of J.P. as an office "of no Profit and some Trouble," and wrote that people would consent to serve as J.P.'s only if they were "much courted."[28] But given the sheer number and prominence of the men who accepted the office, his complaint must be questioned. In fact, the inclusion of so many of the colony's elite in the roster of J.P.'s raises several questions. First, what was the purpose that lay behind the appointment of so many J.P.'s, far more than the ordinary operations of the law would seem to require? Second, what induced so many men to accept the "Trouble" that the position entailed? In seeking answers to these queries we might also find clues to the illusive questions concerning J.P.'s' conduct and the nature and logic of their proceedings, including the slave court.

The office of the J.P. was one of the few posts in colonial South Carolina that lay entirely at the discretion of the colony's royal governor. The law did not specify a fixed number of J.P.'s, and each royal governor could create as many new J.P.'s as he wished. Colonial governors had none of the patronage plums that were liberally distributed to grease the gears of state in eighteenth-century England. Control over the appointment of J.P.'s was the one meager carrot with which governors could seek to win friends and gain influence among the members of the assembly.[29] Such political aims probably account for the presence of so many J.P.'s in the colonial assembly.

To avoid an embarrassing rebuff, governors probably first "courted" (in Glen's phrase) prospective recipients to ascertain if the appointment would be acceptable. Once appointed, however a J.P. was under no further obligation to the governor. A J.P. would continue to hold the office until he died or until the death of the reigning monarch (when most J.P.'s were reappointed automatically upon their taking an oath to the new king).

Wealthy planters found the office of J.P. an attractive prize for several reasons. First, the office conveyed a degree of social prestige and honor. In eighteenth-century England, the office was valued because it bestowed "credit and title in the county"[30] In both England and the colonies, a J.P. was entitled to carry the distinguishing title of esquire. In a very real sense, being appointed a J.P. confirmed (or conferred) membership in an exclusive club: the eighteenth-century Anglo-American ruling class.

The office of the J.P. may have been a mark of political as well as of social distinction. Studies of colonial South Carolina politics have illustrated how Carolinians' consumed and imitated the ideas of the English Parliamentary opposition or "country" party.[31] The eagerness with which these same men accepted the offer of a J.P.'s commission suggests that the "court" may also have had a powerful allure. Through his office, the J.P. was, as one Carolinian put it, "serving . . . King & Country."[32] Similarly, a popular handbook for South Carolina J.P.'s claimed that because "the power of constituting J.P.'s . . . [resided] only in the King," the governor, in appointing magistrates, was merely the conduit of the royal prerogative. Thus, the colonial J.P. could claim to wield a tiny share of the king's vast powers.[33]

The procedure for appointing J.P.'s emphasized the ties that bound the South Carolina J.P. to the distant monarch. Each J.P.'s commission came in the king's name. Before taking office, the appointee swore five separate oaths. Along with his oath to execute the office "well and truly," the candidate swore allegiance to the king, denounced the "impious and heretical" doctrine that subjects might justly depose or murder "princes excommunicated . . . by the pope," took the "Oath of Abjuration" against the pretender and in support of the Hanoverian succession, and finally, affirmed "The Declaration against Popery."[34]

There were also other, less symbolic reasons that a J.P.'s commission might be coveted. South Carolina's militia did not muster often enough to cause much inconvenience, but its mere existence created something of an "crisis" of honor.[35] In a slave society that deemed subordination of any sort deeply humiliating, many slaveholders were galled at the prospect of being "out- ranked" by their neighbors in the local militia. Other British slave societies addressed this problem in different ways. In Jamaica, the number of officers in the militia was allowed to expand, so that anyone could buy themselves a rank befitting their wealth.[36] In Virginia, wealthy men could escape militia service by agreeing to furnish a specified number of common soldiers.[37] In the South Carolina militia, however, the number of officers remained small. Outside of Charles Town, few parishes were allowed more than five commissioned militia officers.[38] By law, however, a J.P. was exempted from militia service. A prominent slaveholder who was not a member of the assembly, council, or Anglican clergy (all of which also conferred exemptions) might be very grateful to a governor who, through the timely offer of a J.P.'s commission, spared him from being publicly ranked beneath the more prominent (or more fortunate) residents in his parish who held militia commissions.[39]

Although matters of rank and status were doubtless important, South Carolina slaveholders well knew that the ultimate measure of social status was the possession of wealth in the form of land and slaves. Consequently, men might have hesitated to accept a J.P.'s commission if it weighed them down with onerous duties and interfered with their private business. Such was not the case. While enjoying the social benefits of his commission, a J.P. was under no obligation actually to perform his office. Such laxity was very common in England where one observer thought most men who accepted a J.P.'s commission did so only to gain "credit and title in their county without giving themselves the trouble of doing the Duty. . . ."[40]

Several studies of English J.P.'s in the eighteenth century have shown that the majority of those who held the office seldom or never exercised it. In Kent County in 1758–1759, for instance, only 40 percent of the J.P.'s commissioned in the county ever engaged in any judicial business whatsoever.[41] Even among the minority who practiced at all, a very few men were responsible for undertaking the vast bulk of the duty. In Surrey County between 1751 and 1752, three J.P.'s (out of twenty-six) carried more than 70 percent of the magisterial work load.[42]

The custom in colonial South Carolina appears to have been very much the same. Although routine records of J.P.'s proceedings are lacking, a crude measure of activity (or inactivity) can be obtained by examining the records entered into the colony's miscellaneous record books. In these instances, the J.P. acted more in the capacity of a notary, transcribing, witnessing, and validating a private deed or contract. Although there were 264 J.P.'s enrolled in the colony's commission of the peace in 1767, only 74 individual J.P.'s (or 28 percent) signed even one of the miscellaneous records that were compiled between 1765 and 1769. A mere thirty-five men (or 13 percent) signed more than a single deed. Of these few, nine J.P.'s (or 3 percent) accounted for over half of the signatures. Two J.P.'s, John Bull and George Murray, together were responsible for nearly a third of all of the deeds recorded in these years.[43]

More subjective evidence also supports the notion that many J.P.'s did not actively exercise their office. In 1770, for example, the Charles Town Grand Jury complained of "a general supineness and inactivity in Magistrates."[44] Two years later, an anonymous observer reported that the colony "had many Magistrates who were contented with the bare *Name*—others, who had solicited the Insertion of *their's,* from the *patriotic Motive* of being excused from Musters of the Militia—and some, merely to obtain, and be addressed, in *such Cases,* with the *paltry* Title of *Esquire.* . . ."[45]

It is perhaps not surprising that passive J.P.'s, who took their commission for granted and treated the office merely as a well-deserved badge of social distinction, opened themselves up to criticism. What is more remarkable is the fact that the small minority of active J.P.'s, those men who carried on most of the work, were even more vociferously condemned. Rather than earning praise for their dedication and public spirit, such men were suspected of exercising their office in the interest of their private financial gain. In 1771, for example, Charles Woodmason preached against "the Practice of some Magistrates, who instead of being backward in administering Oaths, multiply them as much as possible, for the sake of the paultry fee annex'd to the Administration."[46]

In England, J.P.'s suspected of seeking to make a living from their judicial practice were scornfully termed "trading justices."[47] In 1773, the Charles Town Grand Jury complained in similar language "that among the great Number of *nominal,* the few *acting,* Justices of the Peace, are not Gentlemen of such independent Fortunes, as to render them above making a Trade of the Office. . . ."[48]

That some justices were criticized for their "supineness and inactivity," while others were simultaneously attacked for being *too* active, illustrates the contrary impulses and imperatives that lay at the heart of eighteenth-century Anglo-American attitudes regarding power, authority, and the law. Colonial Americans deeply distrusted power. As Bernard Bailyn has noted, "power meant the dominion of some men over others . . . ultimately force [and] compulsion."[49] Authority, on the other hand, denoted "trust and opinion" and was based on "the willing obedience of the people."[50] The day-to-day operation of the law, or the state, required both qualities. While power gave the state energy, authority provided it with legitimacy. If power was the might to rule, authority was the right to rule.

However, although power and authority were intertwined in an almost symbiotic way, the relationship was not a stable one. Authority, was thought to be personal, inherent, and self-evident, an ideal embodied in the concept that the common people should defer to their "betters." Authority, in this sense, was synonymous with prestige and was largely passive; it could be lost but could not easily be earned or captured. Power, on the other hand, was thought to be restless, acquisitive, and dangerous. The corrupting influence and boundless appetite of power was eighteenth-century political dogma. Like a snake swallowing its tail, the state's need to exercise power in order to govern always threatened to consume its authority or legitimacy to rule.[51]

Seen in this context, the apparent contradiction of the public's denunciation of J.P.'s both for being *too* passive and *too* active can be explained. The concern was not that too few of the J.P.'s practiced their office (there is no evidence that people could not find a justice when they needed one) as it was a fear that the wrong sort of men were practicing as J.P.'s and for the wrong reasons. Ideally, a J.P. should imbue his office with his own personal authority and prestige. The guiding principle for magisterial conduct, according to Charles Woodmason, was that "Gentlemen serve the Public for Honour and not for Profit."[52] By "making a Trade of the Office," over zealous justices cast their social identity into doubt. In eighteenth-century eyes, the term "trading justice" smacked of fraud, and of a world turned upside down. By definition, a tradesman was not a gentleman. Because "trading justices" could not hold true authority, they were seen as the corrupt servants of power.

The surest way to escape the accusation of being a "trading justice," and to demonstrate that one did not need either the income or power that the post offered, was to deliberately decline to exercise the office. "Gentlemen" J.P.'s, who may already have been inclined to take their office for granted, therefore had another reason to refrain from actually fulfilling the duties of the job. Moreover, far from invoking criticism, this inactivity may actually have increased the passive justices' prestige. Few actions better enhanced a person's credit than to publicly refuse the temptations of power.[53] Colonel Skeene's reputation as a "magistrate of strict impartiality and integrity" may in part be explained by the fact that, at least according to the miscellaneous record books, he never acted as a J.P. at all.

With their more wealthy and prominent colleagues exercising a calculated detachment, most of the actual magisterial workload fell upon the shoulders of the poorer and less prestigious J.P.'s. For example, although approximately half of all J.P.'s served in the assembly at some time in their lives, only eight of the thirty-five J.P.'s who signed more than one of the miscellaneous records compiled between 1765 and 1769 were ever assemblymen. Among the nine J.P.'s who created a majority of the records, only two, James Parsons and Thomas Skottowe, were ever chosen to represent their parish in the Commons House of Assembly.[54]

There were several reasons why the lesser men among the J.P.'s stepped forward to undertake the work neglected by their betters. First, the less wealthy J.P.'s may indeed have placed a higher value on the money that could be derived from cultivating their office. There may have been some men for whom the term "trading justice" was not entirely unwarranted. Yet the fees secured by even the most zealous J.P. could not have provided more than a meager income, and practice as a magistrate was most likely a supplement to other, more lucrative activities.[55] But money was not the active J.P.'s sole, or even primary, object. For example, most J.P.'s apparently declined to collect fees in cases, such as slave trials, where the money would have come from the public purse.[56] The acting J.P.'s, although well above average in wealth, stood upon the lowest rung of the colonial ruling class. Seldom prominent enough to be selected to serve as representatives to the assembly or even as churchwardens in their local parishes, the post of J.P. offered these men a rare opportunity to wield authority and gain public recognition of their status.[57]

Viewed from this perspective, the two opposing popular stereotypes images of the J.P., each contained a measure of truth. Justices of the peace could, in fact, be divided into two camps. On one side, lay the passive majority of J.P.'s. Drawn from among the most socially and politically prominent of the J.P.'s, these "Squire Allworthys," such as Colonel Skeene, made an important contribution to the operation of the law. Their passive inclusion in the roster of J.P.'s enhanced the prestige (and authority) of the office. It was this reflected prestige that the minority of acting J.P.'s, men from the lower ranks of the ruling class, could draw upon and make the basis of their authority when they took on the duties of the job.

Colonial South Carolina's J.P.'s undertook tasks that while necessary, were not destined to be universally popular. In rendering judgements, imposing fines, administering punishments, and sentencing convicted slaves to death, J.P.'s intruded upon the authority and property rights of individual freeholders and slave masters. In many ways, the divide between passive and acting justices was both practical and useful, for it separated the law's need to cultivate authority (and legitimacy) from the antagonisms and resentments that its everyday operation would inevitably engender.

The dynamic that existed between the passive and acting justices, between authority and power, had a powerful impact upon the operation of the J.P.'s' most important responsibility: the slave court. Between the slave code and the slave stood the J.P.'s who transformed the letter of the law into practice. The ordinary operation of the law in the eighteenth-century Anglo-American world deliberately gave magistrates a great deal of discretion in rendering their verdicts. Like the bewigged judges who presided at an English assize, colonial South Carolina's J.P.'s, as they sat in judgment of slaves, were able to decide, through their interpretation of loosely constructed rules of evidence and proof, when to be harsh and when to be firm, and whether to make any particular criminal slave an example of the slave society's "justice" or of its "mercy."[58]

Justices of the peace sought to cloak themselves and their decisions in the authority of the law. In 1749 an anonymous contributor to the *South Carolina Gazette* offered the colony's justices, "to be continually had in Remembrance," a set of "Rules, which the great Judge [Sir Matthew] Hale prescribed to himself in the Execution of his Office."[59] The first rule was "that in the administration of Justice, I am intrusted for God, the King and Country." Most of the remaining rules concerned the importance of impartiality, objectivity, and careful deliberation. In rendering judgment, he told justices, "it be a measuring Cast to incline to Mercy" but also conversely "that in Business Capital, though my Nature prompt me to Pity; yet to consider, that there is also a Pity due to the Country. . . ."[60]

Like any eighteenth-century Anglo-American gentleman, J.P.'s were very protective of their dignity and acutely sensitive to any infringement upon it. For example, a letter from John Mulryne, a Port Royal J.P., to Governor James Glen in 1749 complaining about his interference in the verdict of a slave trial was full of injured pride. "I will not suppose," Mulryne began, "that your Excellency is any ways deficient in the knowledge of all persons acting by the King's authority in any office under your government or that you would take the least step to degrade or lessen that authority." For this reason, Mulryne could not "believe this letter came from your Excellency or the management of it (supposing by any mistake it did) can be agreeable to you." Consequently, the J.P. boldly concluded, "Your Excellency will I hope for these reasons excuse my not answering it."[61]

At the same time, given their insecure status and the suspicion with which they were regarded, acting J.P.'s possessed neither the will nor the prestige necessary to render decisions that defied the wishes of the locality (or more precisely that of the local elite). Each J.P. was imbedded in local communities where legal knowledge (or at least judicial authority) was a very common possession. In each local parish, and in Charles Town in particular, J.P.'s presiding at slave courts lived in close proximity to more prominent J.P.'s, who although they did not practice, might be expected to sit in judgment of their lesser, more active peers. It was not a situation in which independence or innovation was either likely to occur or likely to be highly prized.

The belief that the judicial process should not be separated from the neighborhood in which both accuser and accused were well known was a basic principle in this system of law.[62] The court in which slave crimes were tried was deliberately constructed as a form of neighborhood justice. The places in which slave courts were convened indicates their impromptu and local character. Some J.P.'s convened courts in taverns.[63] In England, where this practice was common, some tavern owners even maintained a special "justice's room."[64] Although few Carolina taverns could have afforded such a facility, their well-known and central location, relatively large rooms, and ample refreshments for the court and the assembled spectators made them popular sites for trials.[65] Other slave courts were conducted in country stores. Some Carolina J.P.'s, more in keeping with the ideal of the gentleman magistrate, convened slave courts in their own homes.[66] The home of Richard Richardson, who held multiple offices as a J.P., militia officer, and assemblyman, was said to have "the appearance of the assizes" to the inhabitants of his Pee Dee River neighborhood.[67] In fair weather, J.P.'s might convene a slave court out-of-doors. The record of a slave trial in October 1783, for example, notes that the proceeding was held "at the French Quarter Musterfield in St. Thomas Parish."[68]

The convening of a slave court was an important local event. Charles Woodmason wrote that the inhabitants of the neighborhood treated the meeting of a magistrate's court as "a Sort of *Fair*."[69] The drama of watching a slave being tried for his life probably drew the idle and curious (including presumably slaves) whenever a slave court was convened in their vicinity. Justices of the peace probably welcomed the opportunity to exhibit their authority before an audience and, like one South Carolina judge, may have hoped that "the solemnities attendant upon a court, . . . [would] awe the people into respect. . . ."[70] Given the ready presence of drink and the constant murmuring and mixing of the crowd, however, the atmosphere that prevailed at a magistrate's court was likely less sober and attentive than the presiding J.P.'s may have desired.

Later critics of the slave court decried the ability of the attending audience to influence the decisions of the presiding J.P.'s and freeholders. In the nineteenth century, when some South Carolina judges were attempting to establish a more professional judiciary, Judge John Belton O'Neall attacked "the tribunal for the trial of slaves . . . [as] the worst system which could be devised. . . . the passions and prejudices of the neighborhood," he wrote, "arising from a recent offence, enter into the trial and often lead to the condemnation of the innocent."[71] To the slave court's supporters, however, it was only right that "the prejudices of the neighborhood" play an important role in the judicial process. In the eighteenth-century understanding, the law was supposed to take local opinion into account when rendering a verdict.

A 1791 record of a slave trial in Georgia suggests how public opinion could help to dictate the verdict of the slave court. In this case Billy had been convicted of burglary and sentenced to death. As this was Billy's first offence, his owner, Thomas Stone, petitioned the governor complaining that the sentence was uncommonly harsh. In reply, the J.P.'s who presided at Billy's trial described the accused as "a notorious thief" and "a felon daring in principle and perverse in all his conduct." They defended their conduct not by citing the facts of the case but by arguing that "it is the general voice of the people he should be executed." The Georgia J.P.'s claimed that the governor's grant of a stay of execution to allow an inquiry into the verdict had "very much incurred the displeasure of nineteen twentieths of the vicinity. . . ."[72]

Public participation in the operation of the slave court was more than informal. The inclusion of three freeholders on the panel alongside the two J.P.'s put the will of the neighborhood in the judges' chambers as well as in the spectators' gallery and the jury box. All verdicts and sentences the slave court produced had to be agreed upon between the J.P.'s, representing the law, and the freeholders representing local opinion. Before any decision could be pronounced at least one of the J.P.'s and one of the freeholders had to support it.

Such a subjective system of justice could not, of course, be "blind," in the sense of being detached from personalities. Nor was it supposed to be. For eighteenth-century Anglo-Americans the personal nature of the law was one of its greatest virtues. As one of the system's defenders explained, a legal system based upon local feelings and personal ties "knew how to discriminate between a friend and an enemy" and had "room for favour and for kindness."[73] In a similar vein, one of South Carolina's royal governors celebrated "the happy temperament of justice and mercy in our Negro Acts."[74]

The slave court was very much a slaveholders' court. Not only were J.P.'s all slaveholders, but the plaintiffs could choose which of the J.P.'s in the parish would hear their case. Although J.P.'s were forbidden to judge their own causes or to give counsel to either party, they were not barred from presiding over cases in which one or more of the principals were close friends or relations. In the close knit and intermarried planter communities of the rural lowcountry, such "incestuous" proceedings may well have been the rule rather than the exception.

Justices of the peace were reluctant to intrude themselves unwanted into private plantation affairs. Thus, the majority of cases that appeared before the slave court involved crimes that transgressed plantation boundaries.[75] The law was a convenient arena in which to arbitrate disputes between slaveholders concerning the trespasses of their slave property. Although J.P.'s were charged to "inquire . . . [into] all manner of felonies . . . and offenses whatsoever committed by negroes," in most cases they waited passively for a charge to be brought to the court by someone willing to undertake the costs and trouble of prosecution.[76]

Even when slave trespasses occurred, the parties involved on each side often settled the matter privately "out-of-court." One lowcountry account book, for example, noted a payment of £5 to "the Dutch Servant for smart and hush money on being wounded by Negro Billy."[77] Similarly, when in 1771 two of James Grant's Florida slaves "were detected in a robbery" and the stolen goods found in their homes, Grant's overseer wrote that he agreed "to make it up" with the victim of the theft. After he paid damages of £9 sterling, the charges were dismissed.[78] The extent of such arrangements can only be surmised, but as the compensation for an executed slave was barely half the cost of a prime field hand, the owner of the accused had a strong incentive to buy off the prosecution.

Masters not only had a great deal of say as to when a criminal slave would be brought to the bar, they also wielded a great deal of influence in the courtroom itself. A newspaper exchange in 1762 illustrated the central role that a master could play in the trial of his slaves. The dispute began when Thomas Wright published an open letter in the *South Carolina Gazette* addressed to John Remington, a Charles Town J.P. Wright complained, "My slave [Caesar] was punished agreeable to your award of justice; he was whipped round the town, when no offence criminal was really committed" and "tho' his crime could only be grounded on suspicion."[79]

In this contest, Thomas Wright held far better cards than his opponent. Wright was also a J.P. (albeit an inactive one), but he was also a member of the assembly and the owner of three ships, two plantations, a Charles Town house, and nearly 100 slaves.[80] Remington, on the other hand, was one of the small minority of "acting justices" and never served in the assembly.[81]

Remington undertook to defend his conduct in the paper's next issue.

"Your negro Caesar," the magistrate replied, "was . . . charg'd by Mr. Thomas Smith, Jun., of Charles-Town . . . with having . . . feloniously entered the dwelling-house of the said Mr. Smith, and hid or secreted himself in the garret, with intention to commit some felony; he was try'd and convicted agreeable to the negro act, and sentenced to be whipp'd at [the] four corners in the town. . . ."[82] By citing the name and testimony of Thomas Smith, Jr., who was an assemblyman and officer in the militia, Remington may have hoped to counter Wright's superior prestige.

But in the remainder of his reply, the J.P. did not seek to defend his legal prerogative. Instead, Remington wrote that before the trial he had sent a message to Wright's house asking "if any person there wou'd appear on his [the accused's] behalf . . . but was told, they wou'd have nothing to do with him. . . ." Remington asserted that "had the freeholders been acquainted" with Caesar's "distinguishing qualifications," from his master's own testimony, he was "pretty confident" the outcome of the trial would have been quite different. In short, the offended J.P. implied that if Wright did not like the verdict, he had only himself to blame for not appearing to point the court in the proper direction.[83]

There were many ways in which masters could seek to place their thumb upon the scales of justice. They could, for example, alter their description of a slave's character according to their desire to increase or decrease the punishment accorded. Thomas Broughton, a J.P. in St. Johns Berkeley Parish complained in 1749, that "Mr. Akin's Character of [his slave] Robin at the Time that Joe [another of Akin's slaves] was condemned was very black but that Mr. Akin had given the same fellow Robin a different character now . . . to wit that he is a good clever fellow."[84] Although in this instance Akin may have gone too far in proclaiming the virtues of a notorious offender, slave courts probably accepted such a change of heart on the part of masters more often than not.

Certainly, the presence and support of their master or mistress at the trial could greatly strengthen an accused slave's defense. Eliza Pinckney described an incident in 1742 in which her slave "Mull[att]o Quash" was charged with plotting to escape to St. Augustine. "I was at his tryal," she wrote, "when he proved him self quite innocent."[85] Similarly, when Peter Manigault attended at the trial of Polydor, a slave in his charge who was accused of robbery, Manigault's description of the principal witness for the prosecution (and Polydor's wife) as "a lying Jude" probably indicates which side he was on. Not surprisingly, Polydor was also acquitted.[86]

The influence that masters exercised at the slave court by their testimony or mere appearance beside the accused served to reinforce their role as the benevolent patriarchs of their plantations. An extreme example of the way masters could use the law to suit their own ends is provided by a Virginia slaveholder who, after discovering one of his slaves in the act of robbery in 1770, "prosecuted him and got him pardoned with a halter round his neck. . . ."[87]

Slaves who hoped to survive the slave court had to throw themselves not only upon the mercy of the court but first, and more importantly, upon the mercy of their master. On the day of their trial, slaves like Caesar who disobeyed or rejected their master's rule might find that their master wanted "nothing to do with them." In this way, the J.P.'s in the slave court both recognized and fortified slaveholders' personal authority. As Douglas Hay argues was the case for the criminal courts of eighteenth-century England, where the opinions of the "rich and great" also held enormous sway, the proceedings in the slave court were "part of the tissue of paternalism"[88]

For the J.P.'s who sat in judgment in the slave court, as well as for the masters who stood behind their slaves as they testified, the day-to-day operation of the law served to reinforce and reenact social hierarchies. The most important of these, of course, was the dominance of whites over blacks and masters over slaves. But the verdicts of the slave court also weighed the influence of local planters against the will of the parish and against each other. In this way, the bodies of accused slaves served as surrogates for white struggles over status. When slaves lost the case (and not uncommonly their life), the verdict was also a triumph for the white plaintiff (who often collected damages) over the owner of the executed slave.

South Carolina's J.P.'s filled many roles. As parish officers it was their responsibility to regulate the markets held in their parishes and to "try all weights and measures, beams and scales" to discover if they were "unjust or false."[89] The slave court was a market of another kind. In the slave court J.P.'s and freeholders also were called upon to "try" what was brought before them and to decide upon its truth. But the task of the slave court, was not to merely weigh the facts of the case but to measure the seriousness of the crime against the character of the defendant. In the "scales of justice" as tried in the slave court, the heaviest weight was not given to evidence of guilt or innocence but rather to considerations of deference and pity, opinion and authority. When the balance weighed against the accused, South Carolina's J.P.'s sent slaves to the gallows or the whipping post to redress the scales of the colony's very "practical" system of "justice." In doing so, the J.P.'s also asserted the authority and power both of the law and of themselves as its representatives.

Notes

1. For example, William Henry Drayton, Rawlins Lowndes, Thomas Lynch, Arthur Middleton, William Moultrie, Charles Pinckney, and John Rutledge all served as J.P.s at one time or another in the period 1756–1775. See Walter B. Edgar and N. Louise Bai-

ley, eds., *Biographical Directory of the South Carolina House of Representatives*, vol. 2 [the Commons House of Assembly, 1692–1775] (Columbia: University of South Carolina Press, 1977).

2. An exception is David Morton Knepper, "The Political Structure of Colonial South Carolina, 1743–1776" (Ph.D. diss., University of Virginia, 1971).

3. Norma Landau, *The Justices of the Peace, 1679–1760* (Berkeley: University of California Press, 1984), 173–208.

4. Ibid., 209–39; see also J. M. Beattie, *Crime and the Courts in England, 1660–1800* (Princeton: Princeton University Press, 1986), 269–70. Peter Hoffer describes a very similar informal justices' court, termed a "called court," that existed in colonial Virginia; Peter Charles Hoffer and William B. Scott, eds., *Criminal Proceedings in Colonial Virginia; [Fines], Examinations of Criminals, Trials of Slaves, etc., from March 1710 [1711] to [1754] [Richmond County, Virginia]* (Athens: University of Georgia Press, 1984), xxxv–xliv.

5. The text of South Carolina's slave codes can be found in Thomas Cooper and David J. McCord, eds., *The Statutes at Large of South Carolina*, 10 vols. (Columbia, S.C., 1836–1841), vol. 8.

6. The number of slaves executed each year at law can be found in the colony's annual budget because masters of such slaves were able to claim recompense from the colony of two hundred pounds currency.

7. A more detailed examination of the slave code and slave court proceedings is contained in Robert Olwell, *Masters, Slaves, and Subjects: The Culture of Power in a Colonial Slave Society: The South Carolina Lowcountry, 1740–1782* (Ithaca, N.Y., 1998). An examination of slave courts in nineteenth-century South Carolina can be found in Michael S. Hindus, "Black Justice under White Law: Criminal Prosecutions of Blacks in Antebellum South Carolina," *Journal of American History* 63 (Dec. 1976) 575-599; and also in Hindus, *Prison and Plantation: Crime, Justice, and Authority in Massachusetts and South Carolina, 1767–1878* (Chapel Hill, University of North Carolina Press, 1980).

8. Charles Woodmason, *The Carolina Backcountry on the Eve of the Revolution: The Journal and Other Writings of Charles Woodmason, Anglican Itinerant*, ed. Richard J. Hooker (Chapel Hill, N.C.: University of North Carolina Press, 1953), 127.

9. *South Carolina Gazette*, 23 May 1768.

10. Henry Fielding, *The History of Tom Jones: A Foundling*, bk. 2, chap. 6, and bk. 1, chap. 3.

11. See for example, *Tom Jones*, bk. 2, chap. 6; and also Fielding, *The Adventures of Joseph Andrews*, bk. 1, chap. 3, and bk. 4, chap. 5.

12. For information on Woodmason's life and writings, see Richard Hooker's introduction to *The Carolina Backcountry on the Eve of the Revolution*, xi–xxxvi.

13. This documentary silence regarding the eighteenth-century South Carolina J.P is echoed on the other side of the Atlantic and is in itself reflective of the local character of the office. As Norma Landau, a historian of English justices notes, because magistrates "were not required to explain themselves to any higher authority, official archives contain few accounts of . . . [their] operation." See Landau, *The Justices of the Peace*, 209–10.

14. *South Carolina Gazette*, 4 Nov. 1756, 19 Oct. 1767, and 23 Jan. 1775.

15. For estimates of the lowcountry's white population between 1740 and 1775, see Peter A. Coclanis, *The Shadow of a Dream: Economic Life and Death in the South Carolina Lowcountry, 1670–1920* (New York; Oxford University Press, 1989), 67.

16. The figure was 166 of 384; Knepper, "The Political Structure of Colonial South Carolina," 139.

17. According to Coclanis, the colony's white population was approximately 25,000 in 1750; 37,000 in 1760; and 49,000 in 1770. If (as is customary) adult men are estimated as comprising one-fifth of the entire population, the ratio of justices to white, adult men was 1 in 25 in 1750; 1 in 28 in 1760; and 1 in 25 in 1770. Coclanis also estimates the "free" (white) population of Charles Town "district" in 1775 as 12,500. Thus the number of J.P.s to white men in this region was 166 to 2,500, or about 1 in 15; Coclanis, *Shadow of a Dream*, 64, 273. My use of "citizen," is admittedly anachronistic. In this context I use the word as a shorthand for the politically enabled proportion of the population (i.e., adult white men). Nor was this plague of justices a purely provincial phenomenon. For example, the number of justices commissioned in the county of Surrey, just south of London, expanded from 150 in 1710, to 345 in 1742, to nearly 500 by 1760; see Beattie, *Crime and the Courts in England*, 60, 28.

18. William Simpson, *The Practical Justice of the Peace and Parish Officer in His Majesty's Province of South-Carolina* (Charleston, 1761), 1.

19. Knepper, "The Political Structure of South Carolina," 140.

20. Campbell's large library might be explained by the fact that he was the clerk of the court of common pleas as well as a J.P.; ibid., 141.

21. Campbell's estate was appraised at £14,500 "current money," the equivalent of about £2,000 sterling; ibid. According to Peter Coclanis, the mean total wealth of white inventoried decedents in 1757–1762 was £1,293 sterling; Coclanis, *Shadow of a Dream*, 88, table 3-21. For information on the biases inherent in probate inventories, see Carole Shammas, *The Pre-Industrial Consumer in England and America* (Oxford: Oxford University Press, 1990), 18–20.

22. St. Johns Berkeley Parish Commissioners of the Roads, Minutes, 1760–1798, South Carolina Department of Archives and History, Columbia (hereafter cited as SCDAH).

23. Ibid., 30–31; see George D. Terry, "Champaign Country: A Social History of an Eighteenth Century Lowcountry Parish in South Carolina, St. John's Berkeley County" (Ph.D. diss., University of South Carolina, 1981).

24. This calculation is extrapolated from a table on male-female and adult-child ratios among South Carolina slaves in this period contained in Philip D. Morgan, "The Development of Slave Culture in Eighteenth Century Plantation America" (Ph.D. diss., University of London, 1977), 293.

25. The seven J.P.s in St. Johns Berkeley Parish, and the number of adult male slaves at their estates were Nathaniel Broughton, 22; Nicholas Harleston, 45; William Moultrie, 21; Benjamin Marion, 2; Peter Porcher, 17; Henry Ravenel, 20; and John Rutledge, 19; ibid., and *South Carolina Gazette*, 19 Oct. 1767.

26. Knepper, "The Political Structure of Colonial South Carolina," 141.

27. *South Carolina Gazette*, 19 Oct. 1767; and Edgar and Bailey, eds., *Biographical Directory of the South Carolina House of Representatives*, vol. 2.

28. James Glen, "A Description of South Carolina" (London, 1761), reprinted in *Colonial South Carolina: Two Contemporary Descriptions*, ed. Chapman J. Milling (Columbia: University of South Carolina Press, 1951), 42.

29. Jack P. Greene, *The Quest for Power: The Lower Houses of Assembly in the Southern Royal Colonies, 1689–1776* (Chapel Hill: University of North Carolina Press, 1963), 223–33.

30. Quoted in Beattie, *Crime and the Courts in England*, 59.

31. Robert M. Weir, "'The Harmony We Were Famous For': An Interpretation of Pre-Revolutionary South Carolina Politics," *William and Mary Quarterly*, 3d ser., 26 (Oct. 1969): 473–501.

32. William Henry Drayton to Peter Manigault, 21 Dec. 1754, Manigault Papers, South Caroliniana Library, University of South Carolina, Columbia.

33. Simpson, *The Practical Justice of the Peace*, 1.

34. Ibid., 1-6.

35. In 1767, for example, the grand jury complained of "the neglect of the militia law, many parishes not mustering . . . for many years past," *South Carolina Gazette*, 9 Nov. 1767. This was a recurring theme of presentments throughout the period.

36. Edward Brathwaite, *The Development of Creole Society in Jamaica, 1770–1820* (New York: Oxford University Press, 1971), 27–28. Brathwaite describes the Jamaican militia as "an army of officers," ibid., 27.

37. Rhys Isaac, *The Transformation of Virginia, 1740–1790* (Chapel Hill: University of North Carolina Press, 1982), 105.

38. There were only 204 militia officers in total in 1756; "Return of the Militia," in Journal of the Council, 4 Mar. 1757, SCDAH, 80–101.

39. On those exempt from militia duty, see Simpson, *The Practical Justice of the Peace*, 142.

40. Quoted in Beattie, *Crime and the Courts in England*, 59.

41. Landau, *The Justices of the Peace*, 323.

42. Beattie, *Crime and the Courts in England*, table 2.3, "Recognizances Returned to the Surrey Quarter Sessions," 61.

43. *South Carolina Gazette*, 19 Oct. 1767; Miscellaneous Records, vol. NN (1765–1769), SCDAH..

44. Presentments of the Grand Jury of Charles Town, 15 Jan. 1770, Journal of the Court of General Sessions, 1769–1776, SCDAH, 43.

45. *South Carolina Gazette*, 27 Aug. 1772. Compare this with the following comment from England in 1754: "Gentlemen are apt to be very pressing to get into the Commission of the Peace, and when they are appointed, to be very backward in acting. 'Tis a common complaint in many counties, that tho' great numbers are in the Commission, yet there are not acting justices enough to do the ordinary business of the country." Quoted in Beattie, *Crime in the Courts in England*, 59–60 n. 64.

46. Woodmason, *The Carolina Backcountry on the Eve of the Revolution*, 123.

47. Landau, *The Justices of the Peace*, 184–85.

48. *South Carolina Gazette*, 24 May 1773.

49. Quoted in Bernard Bailyn, *The Ideological Origins of the American Revolution* (Cambridge: Harvard University Press, 1967), 56.

50. Quoted in Jack P. Greene, *Imperatives, Behaviors and Identities: Essays in Early American Cultural History* (Charlottesville: University of Virginia Press, 1992), 195–96.

51. The argument outlined in this paragraph was influenced by Jack Greene's provocative discussion of these issues in his *Imperatives, Behaviors and Identities*, 195–202; by Bailyn, *Ideological Origins of the American Revolution*, 55–93; and by Weir, "The Harmony We Were Famous For," passim.

52. Woodmason, *The Carolina Backcountry on the Eve of the Revolution*, 124.

53. For a fascinating discussion of the eighteenth-century game of politics and a master player of it see Garry Wills, *Cincinnatus: George Washington and the Enlightenment* (New York: Doubleday, 1984), 3–16.

54. The roster of justices was published in the *South Carolina Gazette* on 19 Oct. 1767; Miscellaneous Records, vol. NN, SCDAH. Details on service in the assembly are taken from Edgar and Bailey, eds., *Biographical Directory of the South Carolina Commons House of Representatives*, vol. 2. Although Edgar and Bailey list two John Bulls as having

served in the assembly, neither seems a likely candidate for the man who signed thirty-four deeds in the miscellaneous records between 1765 and 1769. The elder John Bull was seventy-two years old in 1765, was dead by 1767, and was never a magistrate at all. The younger John Bull—while of a more appropriate age (twenty-five in 1765), and a justice—is an unlikely match due to his residence far from Charles Town (in St. Peters Parish on the Savannah) and his late entry into the commission of the peace (in 1768). Norma Landau found that the most active justices in Kent in the eighteenth century were less wealthy than was the average for all the commissioned justices in the county; Landau, *The Justices of the Peace*, 184–90.

55. For instance, the thirty-four acts that George Murray signed in the miscellaneous records from 1765 to 1769 would have provided him with an income of less than £2 sterling per year. While admittedly this is only a tiny sample of an active J.P.'s business, it may indicate how hard a justice would have to work to earn a living from the post, let alone live in the style that the status of a "gentleman" demanded.

56. The only record I have found of fees charged by a J.P. upon the trial of slaves in the assembly budget accounts of this period is contained in the journal of the assembly of 25 May 1764, which recorded a payment of three pounds ten shillings currency (approximately ten shillings sterling) to Moses Thompson "for fees as a magistrate on the tryal of a criminal slave"; Journal of the Commons House of Assembly, SCDAH. As the law directed that the colony pay all costs when slaves were convicted and the accounts are very extensive with regard to paying the expenses of constables concerned in slave trials and punishments, it seems reasonable to assume that most J.P.s must have waived the fees due them from slave trials.

57. In a similar vein, Bertram Wyatt-Brown has written of courts in the antebellum South: "The more cases that a court tried, the better served were its practitioners, struggling for place, profit, or higher professional standards," Bertram Wyatt-Brown, *Southern Honor: Ethics and Behavior in the Old South* (New York: Oxford University Press, 1982), 387.

58. Douglas Hay, "Property, Authority, and the Criminal Law," in Hay et al., *Albion's Fatal Tree: Crime and Society in Eighteenth Century England* (New York: Pantheon, 1975), 17–63; for a similar process of mitigation at work in eighteenth-century North Carolina see Donna J. Spindel, *Crime and Society in North Carolina, 1663–1776* (Baton Rouge: Louisiana State University Press, 1989), 116–25.

59. *South Carolina Gazette*, 9 Oct. 1749.

60. Ibid.

61. John Mulryne to Governor James Glen, 5 Feb. 1749, Journal of the Council, 10 Feb. 1749, SCDAH.

62. Describing justice in the nineteenth-century South, Bertram Wyatt-Brown noted that "law is a cultural artifact; the more personal, oral, and small-scale the community in which it is administered, the more certain it is that the law will reflect the neighborhood will." See Wyatt-Brown, *Southern Honor*, 364.

63. For example, Charles Woodmason complained to a gathering of backcountry magistrates of "Their holding of Courts at Taverns," in Woodmason, *The Carolina Backcountry on the Eve of the Revolution*, 128.

64. Landau, *The Justices of the Peace*, 231.

65. Two accounts survive of tavern owners who sought recompense from the assembly for "provisions supplied at the tryal" of slaves. In one instance, from 1754, the bill was over £23 currency. In the other, from 1767, it was 30. These relatively large sums of money may indicate both the duration and degree of public interest in what were both

celebrated cases. The first involved slaves suspected of fatally poisoning their master, a militia colonel; the second required "sundry meetings . . . on the examination and trial of slaves suspected of a conspiracy." J. H. Easterby et al., eds., *The Journal of the Commons House of Assembly,* 14 vols. to date (Columbia, S.C., 1951–), 13 Mar. 1754; and journal of the Commons House of Assembly, 27 Jan. 1767, SCDAH. In more ordinary cases justices probably paid for their refreshment out of their own pocket. For example, Henry Ravenel noted in his daybook on 12 May 1764, one pound fifteen shillings "paid Mary Jane for two Dinners on the tryal of slaves," daybook of Henry Ravenel [1744–1785], South Carolina Historical Society, Charleston (hereafter cited as SCHS).

66. The prevailing atmosphere, however, may still have been rather like a tavern. For example, Woodmason also complained of justices who took the opportunity presented by the court day crowd to engage in the "retailing of Liquors in their own Houses (most of them without Licence)," Woodmason, *The Carolina Backcountry on the Eve of the Revolution,* 128.

67. Joseph Johnson, *Traditions and Reminiscences Chiefly of the American Revolution in the South* (Charleston, 1851), 158–59. For the black population of the area, for whom Richardson's powers really did extend to life and death, the resemblance to the assize was more than symbolic.

68. The case, "The State against a Negro Man named Charloe & a Negroe Woman Named Bess," was held on 3 Oct. 1783, and a copy of the sentence was included in a petition from their owner to the assembly seeking recompense (they were both executed for poisoning). General Assembly Papers, petitions 1785–05–03, SCDAH.

69. Woodmason, *The Carolina Backcountry on the Eve of the Revolution,* 127.

70. *South Carolina Gazette,* 15 June 1765.

71. John Belton O'Neall, *The Negro Law of South Carolina* (Columbia, S.C., 1848), 35.

72. Details of this case are drawn from Betty Wood, "'Until He Shall be Dead, Dead, Dead': The Judicial Treatment of Slaves in Eighteenth-Century Georgia," *Georgia Historical Quarterly* 71 (Fall 1987): 393.

73. Quoted in Hay, "Property, Authority, and the Criminal Law," 58.

74. "Governor William Bull's Representation of the Colony, 1770," in *The Colonial South Carolina Scene: Contemporary Views, 1697–1774,* ed. H. Roy Merrens (Columbia: University of South Carolina Press, 1977), 260.

75. Michael Hindus, for example, argues that the law acted as an arbiter of interplantation crime in nineteenth-century backcountry South Carolina. Hindus, "Black Justice under White Law," 582–83.

76. Simpson, *The Practical Justice of the Peace,* 2. Similarly, in eighteenth-century England the cost of bringing charges, summoning witnesses, etc., was to be borne by the plaintiff, even in criminal cases. See Beattie, *Crime and the Courts in England,* 35. Evidence that this was also the case in South Carolina slave courts can be found in the Journal of the Commons House of Assembly, 11 Feb. 1756, SCDAH, 90.

77. Quoted in Morgan, "The Development of Slave Culture in Eighteenth Century Plantation America," 171.

78. David Yeats to James Grant, 31 Aug. 1771, Ballindalloch Castle Muniments, Ballindalloch, Scotland, O771–250.

79. *South Carolina Gazette,* 30 Oct. 1762.

80. Wright signed none of the deeds recorded in the miscellaneous records between 1765 and 1769. Edgar and Bailey, eds., *Biographical Directory of the South Carolina House of Representatives,* 2:736–38.

81. Remington was one of only 17 of the 264 justices enrolled in the 1767 commission of the peace who signed four or more of the miscellaneous deeds recorded between 1765 and 1769.

82. *South Carolina Gazette,* 6 Nov. 1762.

83. Ibid.

84. Journal of the Council, 6 Feb. 1749, SCDAH, 146.

85. Journal entry of 7 Jan. 1742, *The Letterbook of Eliza Lucas Pinckney, 1739–1762,* ed. Elise Pinckney (Chapel Hill: University of North Carolina Press, 1972), 57–58. "The ring leader [of the slaves] is to be hanged and one [other] Whyped," Pinckney concluded.

86. Peter Manigault to Daniel Blake, 10 Mar. 1771, Peter Manigault Letterbook, SCHS.

87. Jack P. Greene, ed., *The Diary of Colonel Landon Carter, of Sabine Hall, 1752–1778,* 2 vols. (Charlottesville: University of Virginia Press, 1965), 1:397.

88. Hay, "Property, Authority, and the Criminal law," 47.

89. Simpson, *The Practical Justice of the Peace,* 135.

XI

"Melancholy and Fatal Calamities"
Disaster and Society in Eighteenth-Century South Carolina
MATTHEW MULCAHY

"Please excuse my incorrect Confused Scrawl," wrote Robert Pringle, a prominent Charleston merchant to his brother Andrew in London. It was late, Pringle explained, and his poor penmanship resulted from a lack of sleep over the previous several days and nights. Four nights earlier, on November 18, 1740, a "great fire" had raged through Charleston, consuming much of the southern port city. "The fire came so suddenly upon us," Pringle wrote, that he and others were forced to patrol the streets day and night because of "the great Risque we run from an Insurrection of our Negroes."[1] Pringle suffered heavy personal losses from the fire, but his immediate concern, and the concern of a great many whites in Charleston, was about the actions of the city's large enslaved population. Although we have no written reports of what slaves were thinking or doing during the fire, there is evidence that Robert Pringle had reason to worry. Accounts indicate that slaves took advantage of the fire to loot stores and homes in the city, and that some attempted to escape.

Twelve years later, in September 1752, "a most violent and terrible HURRICANE" swept along the South Carolina coast.[2] Once again, Charleston suffered great physical destruction. However, unlike the fire, in the aftermath of the hurricane there were neither reports of added patrols nor expressed fears that slaves would rebel. There were no letters to London complaining about lack of sleep. Despite the similarly chaotic conditions, no slaves appear to have challenged white authority. Indeed, in the following months, whites in the colony pushed their slaves to incredible lengths to hasten a speedy recovery from the economic devastation wrought by the storms. Why did such similar conditions, both resulting from large-scale disasters, produce such different results?

Throughout the eighteenth century, disasters wrought havoc in all the British colonies, and particularly in the port cities along the Atlantic coast. Fires, earthquakes, epidemics, and hurricanes repeatedly struck the colonies, claiming large numbers of lives, disrupting trade and commerce, and plunging society into general disarray.[3] These "stupendous" and "dreadful" events were the source of fascination and alarm, and provided endless material for sermons, pamphlets, and broadsides.[4] Most contemporaries interpreted disasters as acts of God, and thus outside the purview of human affairs.

"Whereas it has pleased Almighty God to afflict Charlestown" was the standard opening to government announcements in eighteenth-century South Carolina. But disasters are never completely exogenous acts of God or nature. They are instead intimately linked to human actions and social organization. Thus, regardless of their cause, disasters are defined to a great extent by their social consequences.[5] As the historian Stuart Schwartz has argued, catastrophes "only become disasters because of the vulnerability of specific social and economic structures and because of political decisions and a variety of human actions before and after their impact."[6] Disasters thereby provide an opportunity to examine society at moments of extreme stress, when established social and economic structures are disrupted, and perhaps transformed, by the force and scale of a given catastrophe.[7]

In South Carolina, the impact of disasters was measured first and foremost by one social institution in particular: African slavery. More than any other factor, slavery conditioned responses to catastrophes for both masters and slaves. South Carolina, of course, was not the only mainland colony with slaves, but its experiences were unique because of the scale of slavery there. By 1740 the colony's black population numbered over 39,000 compared to 20,000 whites, and one Swiss traveler to the region commented that "Carolina looks more like a Negro country than a country settled by whites."[8] Only the Caribbean islands offered a similar social system and therefore similar experiences with disasters.

Disasters created particular conditions in slave societies and presented both opportunities and burdens for masters and slaves. On the one hand, the disruption to the established order allowed slaves to challenge authority by theft, flight, or even outright rebellion. These same circumstances were terrifying for whites, who often were forced to take extreme actions to maintain control. On the other hand, disasters were usually felt most severely by those at the bottom of society, and slaves suffered disproportionately from the loss of housing or food supplies. For whites, slavery provided a "disciplined" and skilled labor force that enabled them to begin the process of rebuilding with relative speed and efficiency.

In South Carolina, the fire and hurricane were followed by such different responses (the former by slave assertiveness and white fear, the latter by relative stability and quick rebuilding) because the conditions in which they struck were vastly different. The institution of slavery especially underwent important transformations between 1740 and 1752. Prior to 1740, the number of slaves in South Carolina grew dramatically as rice production expanded. As more Africans were forcibly brought to the colony, "rising tensions" marked the relationship between slaves and their masters, tensions that culminated in the fear surrounding the Stono Rebellion and the 1740 fire. By the time the hurricane struck, however, slave imports were curtailed dramatically, laws aimed at controlling the slave population were passed, and a new "social equilibrium" characterized, according to the historian Peter Wood, by "a heightened degree of white repression and a decreased amount of black autonomy" governed social relations.[9] Exploring the effects of the fire and the hurricane thus highlights the shifting nature of master-slave relations in mid-eighteenth-century South Carolina, and more importantly, illustrates the extent to which the impact of disasters and responses to them were defined by larger social processes and relations.

The years preceding the fire of 1740 were ones of tremendous economic expansion in South Carolina. The colony exported large quantities of cattle and timber to the West Indies, and its major staple crop, rice, was in high demand in Europe.[10] If the fortunes that made the lowcountry (in)famous had not yet been accumulated, several individuals and families were well on their way. To meet the labor demands for this export boom, planters and merchants imported large numbers of enslaved Africans. Slave imports averaged over 2,100 a year during the 1730s, and by 1740 the colony's black majority outnumbered the white population by almost two to one.[11] Although the demographic imbalance was less pronounced in Charleston, the city still had a black majority as early as 1720.[12]

Slave labor was not only a source of great wealth, but also of great fear. South Carolina was a "very weak Province," explained one resident, "and [the] great part of our weakness (though at the same time is part of our riches) consists in having such a number of slaves amongst us."[13] The threat posed by their enslaved laborers meant that white Carolinians placed great emphasis on social control and order. Any breakdown in the "normal" functioning of society and in the established system of social control, was, in their eyes, an opportunity for slaves to gain a degree of freedom, either temporarily or permanently.[14]

Although order and control were of paramount importance to whites, both were being undermined by a variety of forces at the end of the decade. The years 1738 to 1740 were turbulent ones in South Carolina. A number of events combined to shake the confidence of the colony's leaders. First, the leaders themselves were divided in a fractious dispute over a number of legislative issues that brought a virtual halt to government business in 1739. Questions concerning the authority of the Governor's Council to amend financial bills dissolved into a name-calling match between the upper and lower houses that one historian has labeled "childish."[15] Although a settlement was eventually brokered, doubts emerged about elite ability to govern the colony, leading one member of the assembly to plea for greater harmony. "It is well known to us," John Fenwicke warned his Assembly colleagues, "that many of our Inhabitants are determined, if the present session of the

Assembly is determined with the same unhappy Conclusion as the last, to remove themselves and their Effects out of this Province."[16]

Internal political squabbling was a serious matter, but far more serious was the threat posed by nearby Spanish Florida. The colorfully named War for Jenkins' Ear between England and Spain began in 1739, and for the next several years South Carolinians scrambled to build up their defenses and to raise a small army in preparation for what many believed would be an inevitable invasion. None came, but the Spanish threat remained. Moreover, the presence of the Spanish in Florida created concern among Carolina whites about their slave population. The governor of Florida declared that all slaves making their way to St. Augustine would be granted freedom, and several slaves attempted to escape. Although some were successful, those caught paid a heavy price. Before he was hanged in a public square as an example, authorities forced one slave to make a speech urging slaves to be content with their masters and their conditions in South Carolina.[17]

Outbreaks of smallpox and yellow fever in 1738 and 1739 respectively compounded anxieties among white colonists.[18] The diseases ravaged Charleston, killing hundreds between them, and officials worried that the Spanish, or their own slaves, or worse yet both, would take advantage of the weakened position of the colony. "The speediest Methods should now be concerted for stopping the Progress of the small-pox," urged the speaker of the lower house, Charles Pinckney, "whereby the whole Province will be better enabled to join in exerting with Vigour these necessary Means of Defense."[19]

Although the Spanish did not take advantage of the colony's "weakened position," enslaved Africans did. On September 20, 1739, about twenty slaves gathered at the Stono River and began a march to Florida and freedom. They were eventually defeated, but not before they had killed twenty-five whites and struck fear into the hearts of countless others.[20] There is no direct proof that the timing of the rebellion was linked to the outbreak of yellow fever, but it may have played a role.[21] Regardless, it is clear that slaves were well attuned to the social and political climate in South Carolina and that they were indeed likely to take advantage of any disorder to challenge white authority. Not all challenges were as dramatic as Stono, but as the 1730s came to a close, John Fenwicke and others had good reason to worry about resistance, large and small, from South Carolina's enslaved population.

It was into this already tense environment that the largest and most destructive fire of the eighteenth century struck Charleston. The fire broke out at about two o'clock in the afternoon on November 18, 1740. An accident in a hatter's shop appears to have caused the blaze, although that was not known immediately.[22] From that small beginning, flames spread rapidly across the city. It had been hot and dry along the southern coast for several weeks, and the fire found ready fuel among Charleston's wooden buildings, leaping from one to another "with an astonishing violence and fierceness," according to the newspaper account.[23]

The fire was fanned by strong winds as day turned into evening and the blaze continued to intensify, impervious to the attempts by some city residents to douse the flames with buckets of water. It was only after British troops stationed in the city tore down several houses, thereby impeding the flame's progress, that the fire was brought under control. By that time the damage was done. Most of Charleston, including over 300 homes and the central part of the city, "the most valuable part of the town on account of the Buildings and Trade," lay in ruins.[24] One resident described the fire as "a most melancholly and fatal Calamity," but it was decidedly more melancholy than fatal; miraculously, only one person died.[25] The physical damage to the city, however, was extensive. Along with burning of homes and other buildings, the fire destroyed thousands of pounds worth of goods. A report published in London stated that the entire rice crop stored in city warehouses burned, along with "all the rum and wine and other goods in cellars . . . 7 or 8,000 deerskins, above 200 tons of Braziletto wood, in general all sorts of Goods on the wharfs." The total damage was estimated at £250,000. "From one of the most flourishing towns in America," one observer wrote, "Charlestown is at once, in five hours time, reduced to ashes."[26]

Fires had raged in Charleston before 1740, often with terrible results. The city was plagued by fires every year between 1698 and 1701, and in 1734, a major blaze "gutted the town."[27] Experience taught some lessons, and over the years colonial officials took steps to limit fires in the growing city. As early as 1699 they created a board of five fire commissioners and endowed them with taxing power to purchase several ladders and leather buckets. In 1713, special funds were raised to purchase a fire engine from England, making Charleston the second city in the colonies to have such fire-fighting apparatus.[28] Finally, and ironically, just six months before the "great fire," the town fire marshals surveyed the city to determine how well Charleston residents were provided with buckets and ladders to fight any blazes that did erupt.[29]

Despite such plans, the response to the fire in November 1740 was neither organized nor effective. The suddenness with which the blaze struck and the rapid movement of flames across the city created a general panic among residents and hindered efforts to fight the fire and control the damage. The *Gazette* reported that "inhabitants of all ranks" worked together "with Care and Diligence" to fight the fire, but other accounts painted a more chaotic picture. In the early hours of the blaze, individual residents tried to rescue personal belongings rather than control the flames, and there was no coordinated effort to form a fire-fighting force. According to one account, "admidst the cries and shrieks of women and children . . . the men were put into confusion, and so anxious were they about the safety of their families that they could not be prevailed upon to unite their efforts for extinguishing the blaze." Only with the arrival of disciplined British troops was the city saved from even greater damage.[30]

The fire left hundreds of people homeless, forcing two and often three families to crowd into a single dwelling. A petition to the king seeking assistance was drawn up, emphasizing the "distressed situation of this Province" and the "misfortunes of the unhappy sufferers," beleaguered by a series of catastrophes. Lieutenant Governor Bull likewise drafted letters to his counterparts in the northern colonies and the West Indies asking that they "[recommend] their distressed condition to the many wealthy inhabitants in your Province."[31] Although it took time, relief did eventually arrive: Parliament sent £20,000 (an unprecedented action) and other colonies sent food and money.[32]

For some in the city, the fire was a clear sign of God's wrath. The year 1740 marked the beginning of the Great Awakening in South Carolina, and many converts were sure that the fire, coming as it did on the heels of a major epidemic and the Stono Rebellion, was not an isolated incident. Hugh Bryan, a lowcountry planter converted to evangelical Christianity by George Whitefield, interpreted the disaster as retribution for the sinful excess of lowcountry society in general and Charleston in particular. "Surely God's Judgments are upon us," wrote Bryan in a letter that was reprinted in the *South Carolina Gazette* in January 1741.[33] Cataloging the misfortunes that plagued the colony, Bryan questioned, "Is there an evil befallen to a city and the Lord hath not done it? . . . O! that this fiery dispensation may now lead us, and that we may not be utterly consumed." Bryan went on to urge leaders (including to the King) to "humble themselves."[34]

Bryan hoped to use the fire to muster support for the teachings of Whitefield, but instead his letter provoked the wrath of his fellow citizens, and he was jailed in early 1741. His charges against local officials were seen as further challenges to order in the city, and most Carolinians were more immediately concerned with the hands of slaves than they were with the hand of God, particularly in the wake of a major fire.[35] Large-scale fires raised the immediate possibility of slave arson among whites in the city. Despite their frequency, and the accidental nature of most of them, fires were one disaster where human agency was a possible cause. It is no surprise then that immediate suspicion for the fire fell on slaves. The first account of the blaze to appear in the *Boston News-Letter* reported that "in the time of the fire the Negroes rose upon the whites; which made it believed they set the town on fire to further their designs against the people."[36]

It quickly became clear in Charleston that the tragedy was not arson and that slaves had not conspired to set the town ablaze. The fire was simply an accident or an act of God (although not an act of retribution, as Bryan thought). But regardless of its origin, whites remained concerned about the actions of enslaved Africans. Slaves were quite capable of taking advantage of the chaos created by the fire, even if they were not responsible for starting it, and that possibility panicked whites. The author of a letter to the *Gentlemen's Magazine* in London was apprehensive in the days after the blaze, not knowing "how far this accident may encourage our Negroes and other enemies to form dangerous schemes."[37] Other residents, like Pringle, openly expressed their concern about an "Insurrection of our Negroes." In an effort to restore order and maintain confidence, Lieutenant Governor William Bull called out the local militia to patrol Charleston's streets. They were joined by city residents like Pringle, and by British troops from the ship *Tartar* stationed in the harbor. The ship's commander, Charles Fanshawe, ordered his men to stay ashore after extinguishing the fire in a show of force designed to serve as a "Cheque on the Negroes, Least they should make any Attempts in this time of Hurry and Confusion."[38]

Slaves did not rise up in a rebellion, but despite the best efforts of Bull, Pringle, and Fanshawe, they did take advantage of the fire to further their own ends. Some sought to profit at their masters' expense, taking whatever goods they could from harried and confused whites in the city. Widespread looting occurred during and after the blaze, and slaves were certainly among the "wick'd and ill-disposed persons" involved.[39] Pringle complained that he could not "be certain what is lost and what not, there being . . . a great many Embezlements and Goods Stole & Conceal'd which are not yet found."[40] Like others in the city, Pringle rushed to save as many of his possessions as possible, throwing them into the street and returning to burning buildings for more. This made them easy targets for thieves. Slaves likewise made use of their familiarity with the rivers and waterfront in the city, loading small boats with goods awaiting shipment, and then stealing off into the dark harbor with their booty.[41]

There is also some evidence that slaves sought to use the cover of fire as a means of escape. The *South Carolina Gazette* reported that one "Negro girl, with her Face and Arms very much scorched . . . by the Late fire" was captured three weeks after the fire and dragged to the workhouse.[42] It is unclear exactly how far she managed to flee, but that the newspaper did not note where she was captured may indicate she did not get too far. Others who either escaped or were captured may not have made the pages of the *Gazette*, but it seems certain that at least some other slaves took advantage of the confusion around the fire to seek freedom.

Finally, whites worried that even if slaves did not set Charleston ablaze, the destruction caused by the fire might inspire more "dangerous schemes" in the near future. Their concerns were well founded: in ten months following the 1740 blaze, slaves twice set fires designed to destroy Charleston. Neither attempt was successful, but together they were enough to throw the city into "much Confusion."[43] In the tense atmosphere of 1740 to 1741, slaves were well aware of the fear they inspired in their masters, and the fear created by fires in particular.

White fears carried over and influenced rebuilding efforts in Charleston following the conflagration. The fire physically devastated the city, but in doing so, it presented an opportunity for Charleston to improve itself. The city had been built haphazardly over the years as it expanded beyond the walls of its original settlement plan, and officials now hoped to design the city in a more orderly fashion and to strengthen its defenses.[44] In a sense, the fire allowed leaders to plan their city anew. But while the fire provided such an opportunity, conflict and tension within the colony influenced the extent to which those plans could be implemented. In particular, elite concerns about the slave population, exacerbated by the increasing threats from Spain, worked against reconstruction efforts and limited the success of officials' vision for an improved city.[45]

The immediate task facing the city was to clean up and rebuild. Such rebuilding was particularly urgent as the fire had burned many of the city's key fortifications and assembly members worried that Spain would exploit Charleston's weakened position. Slaves constituted an important source of labor that could be used to speed up the rebuilding process, and shortly after the fire a bill was introduced in the assembly requiring slaveholders in the city and the surrounding parishes to supply every fifth male slave for one week to repair the fortifications and "[entrench] the said town."[46] Fearful of too many slaves converging on the city at one time, a limit of 100 from each parish was established. Even with these restrictions, officials worried about their ability to control the slaves, and the bill was rejected. Likewise, political leaders rejected a provision requiring all male slaves in Charleston to work for one week cleaning up the city. Again, the fear of bringing large numbers of slaves together outweighed other factors.[47] Despite the external threat from Spain, local officials apparently feared the internal threat from slaves even more.

African Americans did contribute to the rebuilding of the city. The assembly hired several slaves from local residents to complete a variety of tasks. Mrs. Mary Blare, for example, was paid £5 for her slave's help in "pulling down the ruins of Charlestown," and other slaves were used to cart away the rubble of chimneys and buildings.[48] Likewise, the assembly records indicate that some slaves were hired to work on rebuilding projects: in setting price controls on what merchants and craftsmen could charge for the services, the assembly set rates for "Negro men carpenters" at £1 a day (a pound lower than the rate for white carpenters) and "Apprentices" at seven shillings, six pence a day (for both white and black apprentices).[49] But these were individual cases. Overall, local officials rejected the idea of mobilizing the largest (and most skilled) workers in the city and more importantly, drawing upon hundreds of workers from the surrounding lowcountry to speed up the cleaning and rebuilding process. Officials were not willing to use large numbers of slaves to rebuild fortifications, or on any other public works projects in the city.

The destruction wrought by the fire and the resulting anxiety within the city's white population also pushed colonial officials to enact a series of measures designed to prevent fires from breaking out, and to limit the impact of those that did. The assembly passed extensive codes regulating the distance that buildings could be constructed from the street and from one another. They also instituted a form of zoning that moved high-risk businesses, such as candle makers, to less densely populated areas of the city. A new fire commission was charged with ensuring that such changes were enforced. Finally, the assembly enacted a law that required all buildings be constructed of brick or stone.[50] While this latter provision was nothing new, it appears to have been enforced to some degree in the years following the 1740 fire.[51] The local brick making industry was given a boost by the law, and several travelers to the city in the next decade were struck by its transformation.[52] According to one, "most of the places, where the terrible fire of the year 1740 raged, have been covered with handsome houses and other buildings built more beautifully than before."[53]

Colonial leaders hoped these new regulations would make the city "more safe against future perils of fire." In the context of 1740 the "perils of fire" included not only the physical destruction from flames, but also the resulting social disruption.[54] Officials hoped to lessen the physical damage caused by fires and by extension, to diminish the inevitable social confusion and disorder that rebellious slaves could exploit. Fires were all-too-vivid demonstrations of the vulnerability of white "control" of slaves and the social order, and elites in Charleston were anxious to minimize that vulnerability as quickly as possible. Their very insecurity, however, ensured that efforts to rebuild the city and its defenses and to control the specter of fires would be rushed and limited. The nature of those limitations would become clear when the next large-scale disaster struck the city in the following decade.

According to one historian, "Hurricanes and the Spaniards were the twin scourges of South Carolina . . . during the colonial period."[55] Hurricanes regularly struck the South Carolina coast, beginning with a major storm in 1690, after which, in the words of one survivor, "the whole country seems to be one entire map of devastation." Charleston and the lowcountry again suffered major hurricanes in 1700, 1713, and 1728.[56] The storms were frequent enough that residents anticipated the annual hurricane season and adjusted their activities to accommodate the potential threat from Mother Nature. Merchants, for example, warned their business partners to wait until the hurricane season was over before shipping slaves or merchandise to the colony. Captains of ships already in port often sailed upriver to avoid becoming caught in a violent storm.[57] Likewise, lowcountry planters tried to protect their workforce by building round wooden and brick storm towers in which slaves could seek shelter if they were caught in the fields when a hurricane struck.[58]

Despite their experience with the storms, few colonists could imagine the level of devastation that followed the "Great Hurricane" of September 15, 1752, "the most violent and terrible Hurricane that was ever felt in this Province."[59] The storm began in the early morning hours of the fifteenth. Strong winds, torrential rains, and rising tides all battered the city over the course of the next five hours, destroying homes and property. Panicked citizens rushed to get themselves and their families to the highest ground possible. Some "already up to their necks in water," resigned themselves to their fate and according to one account, "began to think of nothing but certain death."[60] Others were not so lucky as to have time to contemplate their end: one family was unable to evacuate its dwelling, and ten members of the household perished in the floodwaters. Only the father and one female slave survived, the latter by "clinging to a tree" after having been swept down the street by the wind.[61] As the storm continued through the morning, residents prepared for the high tides that were certain to add to the already floodlike conditions in the city. But suddenly the winds shifted to the east-southeast, and then to the southwest (indicating that the eye of the storm had passed over the city), and the waters began to recede, "falling five feet in the space of ten minutes." According to the *South Carolina Gazette*, it was "as signal an instance of the immediate interposition of Divine Providence as ever appeared," without which "every house and inhabitant in this town, must, in all probability, have perished."[62]

However melodramatic the newspaper and other accounts may have been in describing the hurricane, the impact of the storm was indeed catastrophic. Damage assessments that appeared in the following days were somewhat more sober, although equally disheartening. It is not known how many lives were claimed by the storm; estimates varied from 20 to 95, and the *Gazette* simply noted that "many people were drowned and others much hurt by the fall of houses."[63] There was no general estimate of the total value of losses in the city or the surrounding region. One plantation owner reported damage on his estate at £50,000.[64] While there is no specific financial figure to compare to the fire, the destruction was nevertheless overwhelming. People emerged from their hiding places to find the streets of Charleston littered with the rubble of chimneys, buildings, and boats. The storm was so violent that many ships in the harbor were driven ashore, the smaller ones so thoroughly destroyed that their remains were "crushed and blended with the materials of the wharves and warehouses so hardly to be discriminated."[65] Even larger vessels were not immune; several had their masts blown away and onto shore, one of which rammed through Charles Pinckney's balcony door. And just as residents were coming to grips with the impact of the hurricane, another one hit two weeks later. Although not as ferocious as the first, the storm contributed more misery to an already devastated city.[66]

The hurricane created chaos in Charleston similar to that of the fire twelve years earlier. A good portion of the city was destroyed or greatly damaged, and the streets were filled with people trying to salvage what they could, some at the expense of their neighbors or masters. Governor James Glen issued a proclamation, based on several reports of looting, declaring that anyone caught with goods would be sent to the jail or the workhouse.[67] The looting was extensive enough to warrant the attention of the governor, but it was not comparable to that which occurred twelve years earlier. Indeed, the governor and other officials were decidedly unconcerned about any breakdown of order in the streets. Glen did not feel the need to call out the militia or even to call upon regular citizens to patrol the streets, as Bull had after the fire. Officials were ordered to arrest anyone accused of absconding with stolen goods, but that was the only official response to the breakdown of order.

Local elites seemed particularly nonplussed about the actions of slaves, especially compared to the fear following the fire of 1740. Hurricanes, unlike fires, had decidedly divine origins in the minds of South Carolinians, but it is worth noting again that it was not the origins of disasters that created opportunities for slaves and instilled fear in their masters. It was instead the breakdown of social order following the disaster that created such conditions, and the general chaos after the hurricane was similar to that of the fire. But slaves do not appear to have taken advantage of the confusion to free themselves or to engage in widespread looting or other forms of low-level resistance, and there were no reports of captured runaways in the *Gazette* or expressed fears of slaves uprisings from individuals or local officials.

Why was there so little concern among whites about the breakdown of order after this disaster? Why were there no fears of rebellion? The lack of concern about slaves was linked to a number of factors. First, elite reactions to the hurricane were based to a certain extent on their past experience with disasters. The fire and epidemics that plagued the colony the previous decade had raised serious doubts about the future of South Carolina and the position of elites atop the social hierarchy, doubts expressed in the comments of John Fenwicke and others. But the colony survived the difficult period of 1738 to 1740, and having overcome those challenges, elites gained confidence in their ability to manage trying situations. They had little reason to question their capacity to respond to the current crisis in 1752.

Disasters were not the only obstacle surmounted, however, and elite confidence also reflected changes that occurred in Charleston and Carolina society during the 1740s.[68] The hurricane struck a society vastly different from the one in which the fire had raised the specter of slave rebellion. As Glen announced to the assembly, 1752 was a "period of profound peace."[69] Colonists had weathered the decade-long economic depression—caused by the war with Spain and France—and emerged from the 1740s with a new crop, indigo, and great hopes for economic prosperity in the future.[70] Furthermore, local officials had settled most of the internal disputes that so worried Fenwicke, including dismissing the challenges to social order brought about by the Great Awakening. Their ability to do so ushered in a long period of political stability, characterized by an "unprecedented willingness by local leaders to compromise and cooperate with each other."[71]

Finally, opportunities for slaves to run away or rebel were diminished by two factors. First, the settlement of neighboring Georgia meant that Spanish Florida was not so readily accessible, and the defeat of Spain lessened fears of foreign subterfuge. Second, slave imports were dramatically curtailed in the years following the Stono Rebellion. A prohibitive tariff passed in 1740 reduced slave imports from 2,017 in 1739 to one in 1741. Imports would not return to pre-Stono levels until the mid-1750s.[72] A reduction of imports created a more "creolized" slave population, which, at least in the minds of many whites, was important in reducing the threat of revolts. As Governor Glen explained, many slaves were now "natives of Carolina, who have no notion of liberty nor no longing after any other country."[73]

The hurricane created difficult times for planters and merchants in the colony, but its impact was felt most severely among South Carolina's slave population. The hurricane not only caused extensive damage to the physical infrastructure of the region, it also destroyed the lowcountry's food supply. The storm wiped out numerous plantation provision fields, and many "suffered greatly in the loss of cattle, sheep and hogs."[74] According to one resident, "the Crops have suffered Extremely and we fear a great Scarcity of Provisions."[75] A bill was immediately introduced and passed in the assembly prohibiting the export of corn, peas, and other food stuffs. Leaders were convinced that "there [wa]s great reason to fear that the corn, Pease, and small rice made in this province will not be sufficient for the Support of the Inhabitants thereof," and throughout the next year officials worked to secure corn imports from northern colonies.[76] If food was in short supply, slaves were likely to suffer the most. Glen noted that without assistance from the North, the colony would be "wholly destitute of provisions in the month of July and August," not counting the "betwixt forty and fifty thousand Negroes to be fed."[77] In Glen's mind, at least, feeding slaves was of secondary importance to maintaining a food supply for the nonslave population. There is no direct evidence that the storms created faminelike conditions for the slaves, but it is probable. Major hurricanes in the Caribbean damaged or destroyed food supplies and often led to what one historian has labeled a "crisis in slave subsistence," and it is likely similar conditions prevailed in Carolina.[78] Regardless, it seems certain that meager slave diets were cut further as food became scarce in the wake of the hurricane.

Slaves were not only fed worse, but they were driven to work harder and under worse conditions. The hurricane destroyed the rice crop for 1752 and greatly damaged much of the complex infrastructure used in growing the staple. According to one account, many lowcountry plantations were "completely overflowed [*sic*]" and several others "had their negro houses and many of their outhouses blown down."[79] The extent of the economic damage is revealed in export figures: rice exports from South Carolina plummeted from over 82,000 barrels in 1752 to just over 37,000 barrels in 1753. What is even more startling, however, is the rapid recovery from the hurricane. By 1754 rice exports substantially surpassed 1752 levels, reaching over 93,000 barrels. In little more than a year, the colony managed to rebuild its rice plantations and dramatically increase production of the staple. That productivity is indirect evidence of the ferocious working conditions under which lowcountry slaves labored to rebuild planter profits. Needing to recover from a terrible year, planters pushed their enslaved workers to record levels of output.[80]

Slaves were likewise put to work rebuilding Charleston. The hurricane caused widespread damage to the city and its fortifications, and once again colonists were presented with an opportunity to replan and rebuild their capital city. But whereas in the aftermath of the fire reconstruction was compromised by an unwillingness to use a large segment of the labor force, Charleston elites in 1752 did not hesitate to use slave labor. The destruction caused by the storms exposed the weaknesses of the earlier rebuilding efforts. Surveying the (once again) damaged fortifications surrounding the city and making a plea to the assembly to hire an engineer, Governor Glen stated that Charleston's defenses "may be said to have been ruined before they were fully raised. . . . They were built piece-meal, carried on at divers time and under the directions of different persons."[81] Those "divers times" of the past included most notably the period of rebuilding after the fire. The need to rebuild the forts had been an issue of paramount importance in 1740, but combined threats from the Spanish and the colony's slave population limited the success of those efforts. The governor argued that since the threat from the slaves was diminished and the Spanish gone, Charleston now had the luxury of time and that designs for the city's fortifications should be carefully considered. If poor planning "has been formerly our Error," Glen stressed to the assembly, "let us not now persist in it."[82]

Construction of the new forts was delayed for several years as the governor and assembly argued about designs and who should control the process. There was, however, no debate about whether slave labor should be used for rebuilding. Indeed, it appears slaves were used despite a law forbidding such practices. A clause in an older act regulated the number of slaves that could be in the streets of Charleston at a given time, but in 1756 the assembly stated that enforcement of the clause "will be an obstruction to the carrying out of the work of the fortifications, as we have reason to believe that many slaves are employed there who are not within the exception."[83] Moreover, later in that session, an assembly committee noted that several slaves hired to work on the forts had not been paid.[84] Fortifications were not the only public works in need of repair, and slaves were used on these projects as well. Several streets and moats in the city were filled in or extended with slave labor. The assembly also paid out nearly £500 pounds to an overseer and an unspecified number of slaves for one year's labor in "clearing the moat before the Bay of Charlestown."[85]

Slaves were used on massive projects that required backbreaking labor, such as clearing moats, but they also formed an important part of the city's skilled workforce and were employed in rebuilding the city's homes and public structures. Slaves had long been trained as carpenters, bricklayers and the like, but the number of skilled slaves increased after midcentury. The difficult economic climate created by the war during the 1740s and the virtual halt of slave imports pushed planters to diversify their operations and to look for ways to save money. The result of this was an upsurge in the number of skilled slaves in Charleston and the surrounding plantation districts.[86] In the same report in which he stated that Carolina slaves had no notions of liberty, Governor Glen added that many "have been made . . . useful [as] Mechaniks, as Coopers, Carpenters, Masons, Smiths, Wheelwrights, and other trades . . . and [are] expert at the different kinds of Labour in which they are employed."[87] While we can only guess how many were involved, a number of skilled slaves were employed on rebuilding projects following the hurricane.

The hurricane provided Charleston elites with an opportunity to improve their city, and they took full advantage of it.[88] With an eye toward aesthetic qualities that mirrored their sense of power and self-importance, and employing slave labor, the results of elite reconstruction plans would be evident in the following years. An elaborate new statehouse, whose cornerstone was laid on grounds filled in after the hurricane, was finished in the early 1760s, symbolizing the government's stability and security. The increasing wealth of the city's merchants and planters manifested itself in the form of elegant townhouses and gardens that were built throughout Charleston. The remaining streams and creeks that ran through Charleston were filled in, and city streets were extended fully between the Ashley and Cooper rivers. Finally, a seawall of palmetto logs was constructed along the Ashley River, forming the foundations of the modern Battery.[89] Several historians have argued that the fire transformed Charleston's physical appearance, but the hurricane also played a key role in shaping the city's layout and appearance. One commentator writing in the early twentieth century noted that "the outlines of the lower part of the present city may be said to have been traced then [1752]. Especially does the Battery, the pride of Charleston, owe its existence to this great gale."[90] Contemporaries likewise noted the changes that took place in the city. Indeed, because of the repeated destruction of the fire and hurricane, Charleston gave the appearance of being something of a "modern" city.[91] One northerner arriving several years after the hurricane marveled that the city was filled "with sumptuous brick houses in very great number. One cannot go anywhere where one does not see new buildings and large and small houses. . . . To me who comes from poor humble Rhode Island, it seems to me a new world."[92]

Disasters are themselves agents of historical change, and analyzing the destruction wrought by the fire and hurricane is important to any examination of Charleston's development. However, disasters also provide a window onto larger social processes. An eighteenth-century Charlestonian's varied responses to the fire of 1740 and the hurricane of 1752 underscored the extent to which disasters were linked to human actions and decisions. Both calamities caused extensive damage to the city and led to a temporary breakdown in existing social relations, but the two had vastly different legacies because colonial society had undergone important changes in the intervening years. The fire raged through a city and society on the defensive, haunted by a major slave rebellion and posed for war with neighboring Spanish

Florida. The hurricane, by contrast, struck a society at peace—internally and externally—and one in the middle of an economic boom. These larger economic and political conditions in South Carolina shaped master-slave relations, which in turn determined responses to the calamities. Slave assertiveness and, more notably, white fears, were at their peak following the fire, but both had diminished greatly by the time the hurricane swept through the city. And it was after the hurricane, rather than the fire, that more substantial and lasting changes were made to Charleston's physical layout as elites confidently constructed their vision for the city.

The political, economic, and social relationships that characterized eighteenth-century Charleston were pivotal in determining both the initial responses to disasters and their long-term impact. Charleston would not be immune to disasters after 1752, and the effects of these disasters would likewise be defined by particular social and economic structures. Such calamities were "extraordinary" events in Charleston's history, but it was "ordinary" human actions and institutions that defined their social importance and legacy.

Notes

1. Robert Pringle to Andrew Pringle, 22 Nov. 1740, in *The Letterbook of Robert Pringle*, ed. Walter B. Edgar, 2 vols. (Columbia: University of South Carolina Press, 1972), 1:273. Hereafter cited as *Letterbook*.

2. *South Carolina Gazette*, 19 Sept. and 10 Oct. 1752.

3. Carl Bridenbaugh, *Cities in the Wilderness: The First Century of Urban Life in America, 1625–1742* (New York: Knopf, 1938) and *Cities in Revolt: Urban Life in America, 1743–1776* (New York: Knopf, 1955), details the disasters that struck towns and cities. For more specific accounts of certain disasters, see David Ludlum, *Early American Hurricanes, 1492–1870* (Boston: American Meteorological Society, 1963).

4. Some of these are compiled in Ola Winslow, *American Broadside Verse from Imprints of the 17th and 18th Centuries* (New Haven: Yale University Press, 1930).

5. Historians tend to distinguish between disasters with some degree of human agency (like fires) and those that have no human connections. Sociologists tend not to make these distinctions and "lump all disasters together." While important differences do exist between disaster types, I have followed the sociology model in this essay because I want to emphasize the impact of disasters. Their causes are of less importance, even, as I argue, in the case of the fire. See John Burnham, "A Neglected Field: The History of Natural Disasters," *Perspectives Newsletter of the American Historical Association* 26 (Apr. 1988): 22–24.

6. Stuart Schwartz, "The Hurricane of San Ciriaco: Disaster, Politics and Society in Puerto Rico, 1899–1901," *Hispanic American Historical Review* 72 (Aug. 1992): 303–33.

7. The literature on disasters crosses many disciplinary boundaries. The most helpful in formulating the above were Eric Jones, *The European Miracle: Environments, Economies and Geopolitics in the History of Europe and Asia* (Cambridge: Cambridge University Press, 1981); Burnham, "A Neglected Field: The History of Natural Disasters,"

22–24; and Dennis Wegner, "Community Response to Disaster: Functional and Structural Alterations," in *Disasters: Theory and Research,* ed. E. L. Quarantelli (London: Sage Publications, 1978), 18–44. Schwartz's case study of the San Ciriaco hurricane in Puerto Rico provided a helpful model for a social history of a disaster. Schwartz, "The Hurricane of San Ciriaco," 303–33.

8. Samuel Dyssli, quoted in Peter Wood, *Black Majority: Negroes in Colonial South Carolina from 1670 through the Stono Rebellion* (New York: W. W. Norton, 1972), 132.

9. Wood, *Black Majority,* 326. Wood discusses "rising tensions" on pp. 193–268.

10. John McCusker and Russell Menard, *The Economy of British America, 1607–1787* (Chapel Hill: University of North Carolina Press, 1985), 169–88; Peter Coclanis, *The Shadow of a Dream: Economic Life and Death in the South Carolina Lowcountry, 1670–1920* (New York: Oxford University Press, 1989); R. C. Nash, "South Carolina and the Atlantic Economy in the Late Seventeenth and Eighteenth Centuries," *Economic History Review* 45 (Nov. 1992): 677–702.

11. *Historical Statistics of the United States, Colonial Times to 1970,* 2 vols. (Washington, D.C.: Government Printing Office, 1975), 2:1174. For an argument on why South Carolinians embraced African slavery, see Russell Menard, "The Africanization of the Lowcountry Labor Force, 1670–1740," in *Race and Family in the Colonial South,* ed. Winthrop Jordan and Sheila Skemp (Jackson: University of Mississippi Press, 1987), 81–109.

12. Philip D. Morgan, "Black Life in 18th Century Charlestown," *Perspectives in American History* 1 (1984): 187–232.

13. Christopher Gadsen to William Johnson, 16 Apr. 1766, in *The Writings of Christopher Gadsen, 1746–1805,* ed. Richard Walsh (Columbia: University of South Carolina Press, 1966), 72.

14. Robert Olwell, "'Domestick Enemies': Slavery and Political Independence in South Carolina, May 1775–March 1776," *Journal of Southern History* 55 (Feb. 1989): 21–48. For a discussion of opportunities for rebellion during periods of social tension (although concerned primarily with the revolutionary period), see Peter Wood, "Liberty Is Sweet: African-American Freedom Struggles in the Years before White Independence," in *Beyond the American Revolution: Explorations in the History of American Radicalism,* ed. Alfred Young (Dekalb: Northern Illinois University Press, 1993), 151–84.

15. M. Eugene Sirmans, *Colonial South Carolina: A Political History, 1663–1763* (Chapel Hill: University of North Carolina Press, 1966), 203. For a useful, but shorter, discussion of politics in this period, see Robert Weir, *Colonial South Carolina: A History* (Millwood, N.Y.: KTO Press, 1983), 105–40.

16. John Fenwicke, quoted in *Journal of the Commons House of Assembly, 1739–1741,* ed. J. H. Easterby, vol. 2 (Columbia: Historical Commission of South Carolina, 1951–1989), 98.

17. Sirmans, *Colonial South Carolina,* 210–16; Wood, *Black Majority,* 282–84 and 313.

18. Disease epidemics can also be classified as disasters, and often are by historians. Although the outbreaks of yellow fever and smallpox did create chaotic conditions, as I argue in the following paragraph, I have not focused on them. My rationale is that diseases differ fundamentally from hurricanes and fires in that they strike living things and have no impact on infrastructure. Since an important part of my argument concerns how societies respond to the actual physical destruction wrought by disasters, I ignore epidemics as disasters, although they did play a large role in furthering the tensions of the period 1738–1740.

19. *Journal of the Commons House of Assembly, 1736–1739,* vol. 1, 576. On smallpox,

see *South Carolina Gazette*, 11 May and 5 Oct. 1738. For general information on both diseases, see John Duffy, *Epidemics in Colonial America* (Baton Rouge: Louisiana State University Press, 1953), 17–112.

20. The best history of the rebellion is Wood, *Black Majority*, 308–26.

21. Wood makes this suggestion in ibid., 313.

22. *Pennsylvania Gazette*, 29 Jan. 1741.

23. *South Carolina Gazette*, 20 Nov. 1740. Accounts of the fire are also found in *The Gentleman's Magazine*, vol. 11 (Jan. 1741): 55; Alexander Hewatt, *An Historical Account of the Rise and Progress of the Colonies of South Carolina and Georgia*, 2 vols. (London: A. Donaldson, 1779), 2:83–84; Kenneth Scott, "Sufferers in the Charleston Fire of 1740," *South Carolina Historical Magazine* 64 (1940): 203–11; George Rogers, *Charleston in the Age of the Pinckneys* (Columbia: University of South Carolina Press, 1980), 27–28; Walter Fraser, *Charleston! Charleston! The History of a Southern City* (Columbia: University of South Carolina Press, 1989), 67–68.

24. *South Carolina Gazette*, 20 Nov. 1740.

25. Pringle to John Erving, 29 Nov. 1740, in *Letterbook*, 1:274–75.

26. *Gentleman's Magazine*, Jan. 1741.

27. Bridenbaugh, *Cities in the Wilderness*, 212, 371.

28. Boston was the first city with an engine. See Bridenbaugh, *Cities in the Wilderness*, 209–12.

29. *South Carolina Gazette*, 10 May 1740. Charleston residents also took steps to lessen the economic devastation resulting from fires and formed a "friendly society" to insure property and possessions. Subscriptions were sold for £100, with small annual payments thereafter, and the money was lent out as short term bonds to gather interest. The destruction caused by the 1740 blaze, however, was too great for the society to meet its obligations, and it was forced out of business. See *South Carolina Gazette*, 15 Nov. 1735; 13, 20, and 27 Dec. 1735; Bridenbaugh, *Cities in the Wilderness*, 372.

30. *South Carolina Gazette*, 20 Nov. 1740; Hewatt, *An Historical Account of the Rise and Progress of the Colonies of South Carolina and Georgia*, 83–84.

31. One of Bull's requests for aid—to Thomas Penn of Pennsylvania, dated 29 Nov. 1740—can be found in the Chester County Historical Society, MS 266. Thanks to Lucy Simler for bringing this document to my attention.

32. *Journal of the Commons House of Assembly, 1739–41*, 408–9; *Journal of the Commons House of Assembly, 1741–42*, 3, 544; Scott, "Sufferers in the Charleston Fire of 1740," 203–11.

33. *South Carolina Gazette*, 1 Jan. 1741.

34. For a discussion of Hugh Bryan and the fire, see Harvey Jackson, "Hugh Bryan and the Evangelical Movement in Colonial South Carolina," *William and Mary Quarterly* 43 (Oct. 1986): 519–41; Leigh Schmidt, "'The Grand Prophet' Hugh Bryan: Early Evangelicalism's Challenge to the Establishment and Slavery in the Colonial South," *South Carolina Historical Magazine* 87 (1986): 238–50.

35. Jackson, "Hugh Bryan and the Evangelical Movement in Colonial South Carolina," 603.

36. *Boston Weekly News-Letter*, 8 Jan. 1741. The next week the paper printed a revised report, noting the accidental nature of the fire. Ibid., 15 Jan. 1741.

37. *Gentleman's Magazine*, Jan. 1741.

38. Pringle to Andrew Pringle, 22 Nov. 1740, in *Letterbook*, 1:273. Charles Fanshawe to the Admiralty Office, 22 Nov. 1740, quoted in John Duncan, "Servitude and Slavery in Colonial South Carolina, 1670–1776" (Ph.D. diss., Emory University, 1971), 740.

39. *South Carolina Gazette,* 27 Nov. 1740.

40. Pringle to John Erving, 29 Nov. 1740, in *Letterbook,* 1:275.

41. Ibid., 275; *South Carolina Gazette,* 27 Nov. 1740; Fraser, *Charleston! Charleston!* 68.

42. *South Carolina Gazette,* 1 Jan. 1741.

43. *Boston Weekly News-Letter,* 24 Sept. 1741.

44. A good discussion of Charleston's physical growth can be found in the introduction to Peter Coclanis's economic study of the region. See "The Sociology of Architecture in Colonial Charlestown," in *Shadow of a Dream,* 3–11.

45. For a discussion of fire as an instrument of urban planning and the limitations of enacting effective plans in general, see Christine Rosen, *The Limits of Power: Great Fires and the Process of City Growth in America* (Cambridge: Cambridge University Press, 1986). Also see Karen Sawislak, *Smoldering City: Chicagoans and the Great Fire, 1871–74* (Chicago: University of Chicago Press, 1985).

46. *Journal of the Commons House of Assembly, 1739–41,* 420–21.

47. Ibid., 420, 426–27.

48. Ibid., 486.

49. These rates were published in the *South Carolina Gazette* on 18 Dec. 1740.

50. Ibid. For the debate in the assembly on those measures, see *Journal of the Commons House of Assembly, 1739–41,* 416–54.

51. Similar laws were passed after earlier fires. See Bridenbaugh, *Cities in the Wilderness,* 207–9.

52. Walter Robbins, ed., "John Tobler's Description of South Carolina (1753)," in *South Carolina Historical Magazine* 71 (1970): 144–45.

53. Pringle, in the weeks following the fire, wrote to Boston merchants advising them to "make their bricks larger and the same size of old England Bricks or this Province [since] a Very great Quantity might be vended" in Charleston. Pringle to John Erving, 12 Mar. 1741, in *Letterbook,* 1:300. Evidence for this also comes from Lucy Wayne, "Burning Brick: A Study of a Lowcountry Industry" (Ph.D. diss., University of Florida, 1992), xiv.

54. *South Carolina Gazette,* 18 Dec. 1740.

55. Ludlum, *Early American Hurricanes,* 41.

56. Paper to the Lords Proprietors, c. 1686, quoted in ibid., 41–42. Also see Jeanne Calhoun, *The Scouring Wrath of God: Early Hurricanes in Charleston, 1700–1804,* Charleston Museum Leaflet 29 (Apr. 1983), 2–12.

57. Pringle reports that one of his ships was moved "40 miles up Cooper River where she lies with a good many other vessels," because it was hurricane season. Robert Pringle to Andrew Pringle, 7 Sept. 1742, in *Letterbook,* 1:407. Likewise, Henry Laurens regularly warned his correspondents of the seasonal danger of storms. On 17 July 1755, for example, he wrote that he "would not choose [slaves] sent in the Hurricane season" because the risk was too great. Laurens to Smith and Clifton, in *The Papers of Henry Laurens,* ed. Philip Hamer et al., 14 vols. (Columbia: University of South Carolina Press, 1968), 1:295.

58. Elias Bull, "Storm Towers of the Santee Delta," *South Carolina Historical Magazine* 81 (1980): 95–101. It is not known when these towers first came into use in the lowcountry, but Bull found evidence of their existence during a hurricane in 1822, and it seems likely they were used in the eighteenth century as well.

59. *South Carolina Gazette,* 19 Sept. 1752. In addition to the *Gazette,* the following description of the hurricane came from Hewatt, *An Historical Account of the Rise and*

Progress of the Colonies of South Carolina and Georgia, 2:181; Fraser, *Charleston! Charleston!*, 84–89; Harriott Horry Ravenel, *Eliza Pinckney* (New York: Scribner's, 1896), 138–40; Ludlum, *Early American Hurricanes*, 44–47; David Ramsay, *History of South Carolina from Its First Settlements in 1670 to the Year 1808*, 2 vols. (1808), 2:179–181 An account also appeared in the *Gentleman's Magazine*, December 1752, but it was essentially a reprint of the *Gazette* reports.

60. *South Carolina Gazette*, 19 Sept. 1752.

61. Ramsay, *History of South Carolina*, 2:179–81.

62. *South Carolina Gazette*, 19 Sept. 1752; Fraser, *Charleston! Charleston!*, 84.

63. *South Carolina Gazette*, 19 Sept. 1752; Ludlum, *Early American Hurricanes*, 46.

64. *South Carolina Gazette*, 10 Oct. 1752.

65. Ramsay, *History of South Carolina*, 2:180 n.

66. *South Carolina Gazette*, 3 Oct. 1752. The second hurricane certainly contributed to the disorder, but the storm did more damage in Winyaw than anywhere else, and its impact on Charleston was minimal, in part because so much of the city was already devastated.

67. *South Carolina Gazette*, 19 Sept. 1752.

68. My argument here was based on the position put forward by Philip Morgan and George Terry in "Slavery in Microcosm: A Conspiracy Scare in Colonial South Carolina," *Southern Studies* 21 (1982): 121–45. For a different interpretation of how elites responded to crises during this period, see Winthrop Jordan, *White over Black: American Attitudes towards the Negro, 1550–1812* (Chapel Hill: University of North Carolina Press, 1968), 110–22.

69. *Journal of the Commons House of Assembly, 1751–52*, ed. Terry Lipscomb and R. Nicholas Olsberg (Columbia: University of South Carolina Press, 1977), 395.

70. For a discussion of the changing economic circumstances in South Carolina, and the impact of indigo on the economy, see Russell Menard, "Slavery, Economic Growth and Revolutionary Ideology in the South Carolina Lowcountry," in *The Economy of Early America*, ed. Ronald Hoffman et al. (Charlottesville: University Press of Virginia, 1988): 244–74. On the introduction of indigo, see Joyce Chaplin, *An Anxious Pursuit: Agricultural Innovation and Modernity in the Lower South, 1730–1815* (Chapel Hill: University of North Carolina Press, 1993), 188–95.

71. Robert Weir, "'The Harmony We Were Famous For': An Interpretation of Pre-Revolutionary South Carolina Politics," *William and Mary Quarterly*, 3d ser., 26 (Oct. 1969): 473–501.

72. *Historical Statistics of the United States*, 2:1174–75.

73. Glen to the Lords Commissioners for Trade and Plantations, Mar. 1752, in *The Colonial South Carolina Scene: Contemporary Views, 1697–1774*, ed. H. Roy Merrens (Columbia: University of South Carolina Press, 1977), 182–83.

74. *South Carolina Gazette*, 19 Sept. 1752.

75. John Guerard to William Jolliffe, 20 Sept. 1752, in John Guerard letterbook, South Carolina Historical Society, Charleston.

76. *South Carolina Gazette*, 9 Oct. 1752.

77. *Journal of the Commons House of Assembly, 1752–54*, ed. Terry Lipscomb, vol. 12 (Columbia: University of South Carolina Press, 1983), 125.

78. Richard Sheridan, "The Crisis of Slave Subsistence in the British West Indies during and after the American Revolution," *William and Mary Quarterly* 3d series, 33 (Oct. 1976): 615–41. For a more contemporary account of food shortages created by hurricanes (the 1675 hurricane in Barbados in particular), see John Oldmixon, *The British Empire in America*, 2 vols. (London: J. Nicholson, et al., 1708), 1:36–37.

79. Ramsay, *History of South Carolina*, 182 n.

80. R. C. Nash, "Trade and Business in Eighteenth-Century South Carolina: The Career of John Guerard, Merchant and Planter," *South Carolina Historical Magazine* 96 (1995): 6–29. Thanks to Professor Nash for pointing out his figures and suggesting their relevance to slaves' working conditions.

81. *Journal of the Commons House of Assembly, 1751–52,* 395.

82. Ibid., 395.

83. *Journal of the Commons House of Assembly, 1755–57,* vol. 14, 137. Slaves were not the only laborers used on these projects. A group of Acadian refugees were also put to work on the fortifications. See Fraser, *Charleston! Charleston!,* 88.

84. Ibid., 143–44.

85. Ibid., 402. The process of rebuilding after the hurricane is also discussed in Harriott Horry Ravenel, *Charleston: The Place and Its People* (New York: Macmillan, 1906), 134–36.

86. Philip Morgan found that the number of skilled slaves in runaway ads and inventories increased in both actual numbers and percentages in the 1740s, from a low of 8.5 percent to a high of 12.9 percent. Philip D. Morgan, "Colonial South Carolina Runaways: Their Significance for Slave Culture," *Slavery and Abolition* 6 (Dec. 1985): 57–78. For the economic difficulties of the 1740s and planters' responses to them see Menard, "Slavery, Economic Growth and Revolutionary Ideology in the South Carolina Lowcountry." For skilled slaves, see Marcus Jernegan, *Laboring and Dependent Classes in Colonial America, 1607–1783* (1931; reprint, Westport, Conn.: Greenwood Press, 1980): 14–21; S. Max Edelson, "The Terms of Affiliation: Skilled Slaves in 18th Century South Carolina" (paper presented at "New Directions in the Study of the Lowcountry and the Atlantic World," Charleston, S.C., May 1995).

87. Glen to the Board of Trade, in *The Colonial South Carolina Scene,* 182–83.

88. Efforts at "improvement" were also happening in other cities (although not always after disasters) in British America. The process is described in Richard Bushman, *The Refinement of America: Persons, Houses, Cities* (New York: Knopf, 1992), 139–68.

89. Ravenel, *Charleston: The Place and Its People,* 135–36.

90. Ibid., 136. David Ramsay also argues that "the city was very much changed since the year 1752." Ramsay, *The History of South Carolina,* 2:179 n.

91. Rogers, *Charleston in the Age of the Pinckneys,* 27.

92. Moses Lopez to Aaron Lopez, 3 May 1764 in "Charlestown in 1764," ed. Thomas Tobias, *South Carolina Historical Magazine* 67 (1966): 67–68.

XII

"Planters Full of Money"

The Self-Fashioning of the Eighteenth-Century
South Carolina Elite

EDWARD PEARSON

All the World cries, There goes a Gentleman, And when you have said
Gentleman, you have said Everything.

South Carolina Gazette, January 8, 1737

In early February 1773, Josiah Quincy sailed from his native city of Boston
to the southern colonies, intent on learning about the most prosperous
region of British North America and on improving his poor health.[1] Landing in Charleston several weeks later, Quincy immersed himself in a society
where dinner parties and card evenings, racing and hunting, concerts and
balls formed the fabric of daily life for the families who constituted the ruling class of lowcountry South Carolina. Throughout March, the height of
the city's social season, the Bostonian navigated through the world of "opulent and lordly planters," rubbing shoulders with members of the wealthiest
and most politically stable elite on the mainland, enjoying their lavish hospitality as he moved between drawing rooms, dining tables, and concert parties with great skill.[2] Between these engagements, Quincy traveled into the
countryside, observing as legions of enslaved Africans and Afro-Carolinians
cultivated the plantation staples that had transformed the small city of
Charleston into the Lower South's leading political, commercial, and social
center, and its rural hinterlands into a region that possessed "more value
than mines of gold and silver."[3]

For the visitor from Boston, Joseph Allston was among the men who
personified the lowcountry elite. A rice planter who owned extensive estates
along the Waccamaw River near the coastal settlement of Georgetown, Allston had risen through the ranks of the lowcountry's yeomanry to acquire
"an immense income . . . [with] five plantations with an hundred slaves on
each" by the age of forty.[4] Besides these extensive holdings of land and
slaves, Allston exercised political influence at both local and provincial levels,
serving as a commissioner of roads and as a justice of the peace, as well as
sitting in the Commons House of Assembly as a representative for All Saints'
Parish and Prince George Winyah.[5] But Allston did not symbolize the elite
solely because of his economic power or public position; he also embodied
the ruling class due to the elegant taste that he displayed as he entertained

guests at his country seat. After dining with Allston and his family at the Oaks, his Waccamaw River estate, Quincy regarded his host and hostess "with more warmth of affection and hearty benizons than I have ever toasted King or Queen, Saint or Hero."[6]

Drawing on Quincy's journal, in addition to other accounts of polite society of the eighteenth-century lowcountry, this essay examines the social and cultural milieu in which "planters full of money," to borrow a phrase from slave trader and plantation owner Henry Laurens, worked and played.[7] Building on scholarship by historians including Carl Bridenbaugh, Peter Coclanis, and Jack P. Greene, this article explores the ways in which this elite articulated its power in cultural terms on a daily basis, and the ways in which it fashioned a distinct identity through the deployment of taste and genteel behavior.[8] Traveling through North America about a century after Quincy's visit to Charleston, Alexis de Tocqueville noted how "nothing, at first sight, seems less important than the external formalities of human behavior, yet there is nothing to which men attach more importance."[9] The elite's hold over the lowcountry's social order rested as much on their economic strength as it did on their ability to project power through their public performance of refinement and gentility.

Recent works by Richard Bushman and French sociologist Pierre Bourdieu have given historians several important empirical and theoretical insights into the construction of elite life and style. In *The Refinement of America*, Bushman skillfully excavates the gentry's mental world in the colonial and early national periods by closely reading everything from clothes to conversation to courtesy books, suggesting that "gentility bestowed concrete social power on its practitioners . . . a resource for impressing and influencing powerful people."[10] Bourdieu, concerned with modern France, explores the symbolic role played by goods and services, theorizing how consumption and the use of cultural capital, defined as the practices and accouterments that constitute elite life, communicate social power, and status.[11]

Elaborating on these ideas, several historians are currently reexamining the Anglo-American past through the lens of consumption, persuasively arguing that it entails more than just buying things. A complex cultural activity, consumption involves the creation and maintenance of a social identity through the acquisition of items that radiate symbolic meaning.[12] Clothes and chairs are, as cultural theorist John Fiske observes, "not just objects of economic exchange; they are goods to think with, goods to speak with."[13] Looking at the colonial past, Timothy Breen notes how the world of goods that Anglo-Americans inhabited communicated "perceptions of status and politics to other people through items of everyday material culture."[14] Creating distinctions between various people, goods also delineated boundaries that served to distinguish "lordly and opulent planters" from the "poor and spiritless peasants and vile slaves" who inhabited the lowcountry.[15] Then as now, material goods and manners served as modes of social classification.

Buying and displaying the trappings of fine living served a number of purposes for the elite. The manners and furnishings that denoted gentility functioned as "representations of power in action."[16] The artifacts of everyday elite life provided the backdrop in front of which ladies and gentleman engaged in the presentation of self before their peers. In this sense, the gentry's houses, carriages, furniture, and other possessions functioned as "props" (itself the diminutive of the word "property") in the theatrical sense of the word, serving as integral elements of the stage on which they performed. Likewise, the manner in which they conducted themselves can also be viewed in theatrical terms.[17] Commenting on the "studied and elaborate hegemonic style" of the gentry in eighteenth-century England, E. P. Thompson has argued that their "continuing theatrical style" provided a firm basis for the articulation of their power.[18] The discourses of refinement and taste—gesture, speech, behavior, and consumption—played an integral role in the construction of cultural authority among lowcountry patricians as they eagerly converted the cash from their silk-lined purses and pockets into practices that articulated their social power and class distinctiveness.

Presiding over a society built upon slavery, the lowcountry patriciate used the luxuries with which they surrounded themselves to define themselves as rulers over their own dominion. In his reflections on the contours of slaveholders' power, Laurens spoke about himself as "an absolute Monarch" who governed "his subjects" with an iron fist hidden in a velvet glove.[19] Designating himself as a king, Laurens felt obliged to behave accordingly, fashioning his conduct in a style befitting such an exalted position. Although other planters appear not to have been as reflective as Laurens, they nonetheless attempted to fashion themselves as patriarchal rulers over both their legally recognized families and the "fictive" families that labored on their plantations.[20] Behind the language of patriarchy, however, lay the brute force and coercion that were integral to slavery. Even as they affected gentility and noblesse toward their peers, gentlemen planters remained capable of terrorizing their slaves through whipping and other forms of punishment. Perhaps it was no coincidence that those whose power depended on the barbarities of slavery took the performance of gentility so seriously.

Despite wielding significant economic and political power, elite South Carolinians never enjoyed absolute hegemony over the people they gov-

erned. Regarded by Lieutenant Governor William Bull as "domestic enemies," the thousands of enslaved Africans, who lived "thickly sown in Our
Plantations," presented a constant threat to the stability of the lowcountry's
social order.[21] Although most slaves who resisted their enslavement often
engaged in acts of petty insubordination or vandalism rather than rebellion,
the events of early September 1739, when a band of enslaved Angolan men
who lived along the Stono River rose up against the plantation order and
killed a number of planters, served as a powerful reminder of the inability of
slaveholders to control and govern their slaves.[22]

Furthermore, although elite men rarely met with open insubordination
from family members, they found their public behavior questioned by lowcountry women from time to time. Elite women played a major role in setting the standards for refined behavior and organizing the dinner parties and
dances that were integral to the articulation of gentility among the elite, yet
several women spoke disapprovingly of wealthy planters who spent too many
hours "racking their brains, in contriving how to dissipate their time and
money, in what they call Parties of Pleasure."[23] Although elite men continued to hold the reins of power throughout the eighteenth century, maintaining some degree of control over their wives and their enslaved workers,
they were, perhaps to a lesser degree than their counterparts in the Chesapeake, "anxious patriarchs," beset by challenges from restive slaves and from
their wives who, on occasion, looked askance at their "intemperate" behavior.[24] In short, the power of elite men in the lowcountry was neither as seam-
less as they might have wished nor as invulnerable to challenge as their
confident performances of gentility suggested.

The rise of large-scale rice cultivation across the lowcountry in the early
decades of the eighteenth century laid the economic foundations for the
emergence of the elite. Benefitting from the steady supply of enslaved
African laborers skilled in tropical agriculture, an abundance of fertile land
and the presence of two profitable staples in rice and indigo, lowcountry
planters had "vastly superior opportunities of making a fortune than a British
farmer can ever enjoy."[25] Beyond bringing vast numbers of African slaves to
the coastal plain, the "rice revolution" greatly accelerated the expansion of
Charleston's economy. A modest trading post at the end of the seventeenth
century, the rapid growth of commercial agriculture, and a boom in the slave
trade transformed a town denigrated as "miserably thin and disconsolate" by
Gideon Johnston in 1710 into the fourth largest city in British North America, inhabited by 5,200 whites and 6,275 enslaved Africans and Afro-Carolinians by the eve of the American revolution.[26] Eagerly embracing this new
prosperity, a large number of enterprising men established themselves as
merchants, lawyers, and factors, offering their commercial and legal services

to planters "full of Spirits for purchasing Slaves" as well as consumer goods.[27] As these merchants and lawyers grew wealthy, they purchased their own slaves and plantations and joined the ranks of the landed gentry.[28]

The career trajectory of Joseph Wragg illustrates the path of many elite men who rose from the ranks of traders, artisans, and storekeepers to become plantation owners. Initially involved in the provisions trade to the English West Indies at the turn of the century, Wragg soon emerged as a major importer of slaves, shipping about 4,000 Africans into the colony between 1735 and 1740. The fortune that Wragg amassed from these transactions enabled him to purchase more than 14,000 acres throughout the colony beyond the four plantations on which more than 200 enslaved laborers worked. Philadelphian William Logan noted that Wragg "Very Genteely and handsomely Entertained" guests in the well-appointed library of his substantial brick house in Charleston's Wraggsborough neighborhood where thirty slaves waited on him.[29] Additionally, this patrician also managed his considerable commercial and agricultural empire and attended to the business of colonial government while serving as a member of the Governor's Council.[30]

To retain their hold on lowcountry society, Wragg and his peers followed the time-honored practice of striking advantageous marriage alliances with other elite families. The men and women with whom Quincy shared "company, elegant tables and the best provisions" came from a handful of families whose members were related either by blood or marriage. These social events, moreover, provided the settings in which the children of the elite courted and took the first steps toward matrimony. As Scottish immigrant Alexander Cumine prepared to celebrate the wedding of a friend to a woman with a "Handsome Fortune of 3,000 pounds," he commented how "fine marriages" were commonplace among the elite, expressing the hope that he too might find "matrimonial happiness" that entailed both romantic and financial security.[31] For Laurens, the institution of marriage proved essential to his own rise to social prominence. Only after he married Eleanor Ball in 1756 did this former clerk and trader secure his place among the landed gentry. A daughter of Elias and Mary Ball, Eleanor provided her new husband a place at the table of a family who owned 12,000 acres and 200 slaves. Laurens further advanced the fortunes of his family when daughter Mary married into the Pinckney family. Wragg had similarly consolidated the position of his family when his daughters, Ann and Elizabeth, married Christopher Gadsden and Peter Manigault, respectively, who were both lawyers and planters.

The elite accordingly created dense layers of interlocking kin networks through intermarriage, cementing familial loyalties, reciprocal obligations and political allegiances. These family alliances also sustained the ruling class in other ways. As these dynasties began monopolizing political life, this extended cousinage played a part in fostering consensus in the Commons House of Assembly that remained remarkably solid even as the clouds of revolution gathered on the horizon. Watching the representatives meet during these years of crisis in the early 1770s, Quincy observed the equanimity that prevailed among members as they "conversed, lolled, and chatted much like a friendly jovial society."[32] Moreover, by shrewdly overseeing the marriage settlements of their children, elite families kept a firm grasp over the land and slaves that served as the foundation for planter power.

To maintain their position at the apex of the colony's social order, the elite not only had to attend to the material bases of their prosperity, but to demonstrate their centrality to the colony's economic, political, and social life. Although the ownership of land and slaves stood as major qualifications to enter government, they did not alone justify the elite's right to rule. To exercise effective authority, the patrician class had to fabricate an identity as a distinct group imbued with certain qualities that announced their claim to power as legitimate rulers. To turn themselves into men whose right to govern appeared natural, lowcountry planters looked to the modes and manners of refinement and gentility as a way to bolster their claims to leadership. Attempting to express this sensibility, the elite inaugurated a variety of formal and informal institutions and several recreational events that enabled them to display the accouterments of gentility and conduct themselves in refined ways, further distancing themselves from the ordinary men and women of the lowcountry.

Unlike English gentlemen who relied primarily on the dubious distinction of birth as an index of status, the Carolina gentry had no such guide. The lowcountry elite was composed of parvenus, who had swiftly risen to economic preeminence primarily due to their hardheaded business practices in the trade in slaves, rice, indigo, and commercial agriculture. Capital rather than blood enabled these men to affect a refined sensibility, allowing them to ground their claims to authority. Money, and what it purchased, dictated social and cultural authority. In a society in which "everybody is flying from his inferiors in Pursuit of Superiors [where] every Tradesman is a Merchant, every Merchant a Gentleman, and every Gentleman is one of the Noblesse," the ability to define one's self and perform according to that definition rose to paramount importance.[33]

For Humphrey Sommers, the act of self-definition apparently proved to be easily negotiated. Initially listing himself as a "bricklayer" in 1749, this tradesman began identifying himself as a "gentleman" four years later, as he began to purchase land and slaves in the lowcountry parishes of St. George and St. Paul as well as Colleton County. In accordance with his new, albeit self-proclaimed position, Sommers commissioned Jeremiah Theus to paint his and his wife's portrait. How other gentleman regarded Sommers's self-presentation as a gentleman is not recorded, but he no doubt knew that to be acknowledged as genteel depended not just on his skills as an actor, but also on the receptivity of the audience to his performance.[34]

Without the genealogies that the English gentry found so useful as a register of status, the lowcountry elite looked to other measures to assess social position. Devoting many columns to explicating the elements that constituted elite style, the *South Carolina Gazette* provided a useful guide to the art of refinement and gentility. One writer, with the intriguing pen name of "Black Amore," noted how people from humble backgrounds who became wealthy were seized by "an Ambition . . . to become *Gentlefolks*."[35] It was no easy task, he continued, for "a Clown or a Laborer" to affect "the natural and easy manner of those who have been genteely educated."[36] Despite wealth or distance traveled from pedestrian origins, the man who lacked a cultivated sensibility might find himself regarded as an ersatz gentleman. One contemporary epithet caught this notion well. Without the requisite "Judgement, Wit, Vivacity . . . and Knowledge of Books," a man might be dismissed as a "Molatto Gentleman" by his peers.[37] The languages of race and rank collided as the author of this remark used an explicitly racial characteristic to classify a person hoping to traverse the cultural distance that existed between the world of the commoner and the world of the gentleman. The language of racial impurity here connoted class impurity.

Anxious to avoid such criticisms that might undermine their cultural authority, the elite looked to formal schooling, itself an important marker of social distinction, to provide their sons and daughters with the manners and refinement, as well as the practical knowledge, necessary to fulfill their respective roles as plantation owners and household managers. Running a school that prepared "men for the busy world and ladies for the domestic and social duties of life," Rebecca Woodin trained her pupils in the "different branches of polite education . . . reading, writing, English, French, arithmetick, and music, and dancing taught by proper masters."[38] For young women who had to navigate the socially treacherous waters of the elegant drawing rooms in which mothers and fathers regularly brokered marriages, the ability to make "judicious remarks on Opera Airs and Stage Plays . . . Romances, and Other Books" became a requisite conversational skill.[39] In contrast, young men not only had to acquire manners and bearing, but also had to become proficient in utilitarian subjects such as surveying, navigation, arithmetic, Greek, and Latin that would provide the grounding for careers in planting, trading, or law.

Elite planters did not simply rely on local resources or dame schools like that of Rebecca Woodin to educate their children. Private tutors schooled a large number of young pupils while adolescent boys often traveled to England to complete their studies, such as Charles Cotesworth Pinckney and Thomas Pinckney who attended Westminster School before moving to Oxford University, or serving an apprenticeship as Henry Laurens did at a London merchant house. A number of elite men completed their education in England, studying at Oxford or Cambridge University or completing a legal training, such as did Peter Manigault and John Rutledge, at the Inns of Court in London. That the only Anglo-Americans at Cambridge between 1764 and 1769 came from the lowcountry, and that South Carolinians outnumbered students from other colonies two to one at Oxford from 1761 to 1776 suggests the value elite parents placed on an English education. Although many elite men educated in England would become leading figures in the struggle for independence, their schooling at the crossroads of the Anglo-American world allowed them to establish connections that improved their status and commercial prospects within the imperial system.[40]

This combination of formal education and finishing school paid handsome dividends for the Pinckney family. After attending Westminster School in London and Christ College at Oxford, Charles and Thomas completed their education among the lawyers of the Middle Temple. This classical training not only enabled Charles to become a prominent lawyer and planter in Charleston, but also equipped him with the skills and confidence to emerge as a leading political figure during the American Revolution. At the Constitutional Convention in Philadelphia in 1787, he conducted a spirited defense of slavery that drew on his talents as an orator and classical scholar. His brother's education also served him well; besides his distinguished service in the Continental Army, his peers regarded him as "the best Hellenist we ever had in America."[41]

Education also served to distinguish Anglo-Carolinians from the alien peoples who surrounded them on plantations and in the forests of the backcountry. Determined to prevent their heirs from falling prey to "the savage dispositions" that allegedly characterized both indigenous peoples and enslaved Africans, the Charles Town Library Society, established in 1748, aimed "to take every step . . . to prevent our descendants from sinking into a similar situation" by "handing down European arts and manners" to their patrons' children.[42] To encourage this "civilizing" project in "the finer as well as in the inferior arts," the society lined its shelves with books on subjects including political theory, history, mathematics, and geography.[43] As its members browsed through the latest London periodicals and embraced a culture of gentility, the Library Society became associated with the refined tastes and sensibilities of the metropole rather than with the "wolfish and brutish" nature that many elite Carolinians believed signified the New World.

The city's social season provided several occasions at which the elite might exhibit both the genteel sensibilities and sense of self instilled by an exclusive education at schools either in Charles Town or in England. During the autumn and winter months, the elite established themselves in Charles Town, participating in a number of social events that ranged from concerts performed by the St. Cecilia Society, to plays and operas held in the city's theater, to a series of horse races that concluded the "season" in March. Within the elegant setting of the concert hall, the elite could not only deploy conversational skills gained in their years at school, but also display their "riches and luxuries" to other members of the audience.[44] Attending a post-concert supper at which "noise and flirtations" prevailed, Quincy observed women "in richness of dress" and men clad in a "richness and elegance" that far surpassed the sartorial styles of his hometown.[45]

Held at the Newmarket track just outside Charleston, the races acted as the culmination of the social season, providing elite men and women with a final opportunity to exhibit their wealth. Unlike the theater or concert hall that was primarily the preserve of the well-to-do, the races forced members of the elite to rub shoulders with stable lads, vendors, blacksmiths as well as petty criminals who, on at least one occasion, lifted "several Pocket Books out of Gentlemen's Pockets."[46] In such a setting, the performance of consumption to establish the elite's cultural authority became a central element of these events. It entailed considerable expense to enter a mount in the races, requiring the purchase of a suitable animal, in addition to fees and equipping the jockey in "waistcoat, Leather Breeches, Leather Boots . . . and a Cap of Silk or Velvet."[47] The races themselves could also prove costly as men displayed their knowledge about "the singular art of the Turf" by wagering on the horses.[48] With defeat came a loss of money and reputation while victory brought status as well as trophies such as the Charleston Plate. "He who won the . . . last horse-race," noted Quincy, "assumed the airs of a hero or German potentate."[49] Staking their reputations by placing large bets on the various horses and wearing the latest fashions were critical signifiers for the elite's social identity in this public setting.

In addition to the races, large and formal dinner parties also characterized the season, serving as a counterpoint to the public character of the track. During his sojourn in the city, Quincy spent many evenings at tables laden with fine food and wine and furnished with elegant plate and glass.[50] As an event at which authority and power manifested themselves through a number of cultural forms, the dinner party functioned as a significant moment in the construction of an elite sensibility. From the ornamentation of the dining room itself, to the elegance of the table decorations and the quality of the courses consumed, to the artistry of the toasts and the wit of the conversation, power and authority were embedded in the words spoken and the food consumed. Dining with Miles Brewton, his family, and his other guests, Quincy was greeted by his host in "the grandest hall" decorated with "azure blue satin window curtains, rich blue paper . . . elegant pictures, excessive grand and costly looking glasses, etc."[51] Seated around the elegant mahogany table set with "very magnificent plate [and] large exquisitely wrought Goblet," the diners then consumed several courses that they washed down with "the richest wine I have ever tasted."[52] During dinner "a very fine bird" (presumably a parrot) flew about the room, "picking up the crumbs . . . and perching on the windows and chairs."[53]

An ornate setting, a table laden with oranges and other tropical fruits, and an exotic bird signaled Brewton as a man of unparalleled quality.[54] The success of this occasion not only depended on the elegant surroundings in which Brewton and his guests dined, but also on the artistry of the table talk. Keen to display their knowledge and offer their opinions on a range of subjects, the diners spent much time discussing relations between England and the colonies. Regarded as a critical sign of refinement, elegant discourse stood at the center of such social events. Quincy, in his role of ethnographer of the elite, often commented on "the drift of . . . discourse" as he socialized, even forcing Charles Pinckney to repeat a particularly amusing story so that he would be "better able to relate it" on other occasions.[55] Designed "to promote good Humour and good manners; to increase in Knowledge and Virtue; and to tie the Knot of Friendship closer and stronger," polite conversation let people display their wit, sensitivity, and erudition as they exchanged news, gossip, and opinions.[56] The demands of gentility thus highlighted the educational attainments of elite men and women, who brought knowledge deemed either "most useful" or "most fashionable" to the gathering.[57]

Silence also played a role in conversation. If conversation enabled people to display "Judgement, Wit, Vivacity, Humor [and] Good Nature," it might also cause them to fall into "saying what they will [with] no Shame nor Sense of Decency."[58] To prevent any conflicts that might develop in such situations, the *South Carolina Gazette* instructed that people should redirect the conversation onto "more manly and becoming Topicks," or display their discomfort through silence.[59] Such strategies enabled the guest who was "wise in one Thing and a Blockhead in everything else" to withdraw from the conversational fray gracefully.[60]

These grand affairs also served as a stage on which elite women might display their genteel sensibilities. The conversational skills that Eliza Pinckney brought to the dinner table paralleled the brightest female characters in Jane Austen's novels. Thanks to Pinckney's "uncommon strength of memory . . . so highly cultivated by travel and extensive reading," she enjoyed a reputation as a talented and enlightening conversationalist.[61]

In addition to table talk, the act of toasting also gave women a forum to affirm widely held sentiments as well as to acknowledge the host's hospitality. The heterosocial conviviality that accompanied the meal itself underwent a shift as guests began to offer toasts to the table. After being toasted by a male diner, a female guest would then rise, offering such thoughts as "when passions rise may reason be the guide" to the table.[62] These rituals could thus provide the skillful woman with an opportunity gently and playfully to undermine the sentiments of male guests or perhaps even those of the host. After completing their toasts, the women would adjourn to needlework and conversation, perhaps talking about the crisis in imperial relations that proved to be an absorbing topic at Charles Town's dinner tables, leaving the men to their own discussions and drinking. The men would join the women later and conclude the evening by consuming coffee, playing cards, or engaging in some other form of entertainment.

From planning to execution, dinner parties were the province of women. Using their power as consumers, elite women purchased both the food and accouterments for these occasions, and using their authority within the household, they fulfilled the role of hostess, organizing and overseeing every aspect of the event. At the dinner itself, they actively participated at its most ritualistic and public moment as they offered toasts to the guests that not only demonstrated their feminine sensibilities, but may have also expressed their own opinions about the state of imperial affairs.

Such elegantly staged dinner parties were not the only venue for elite women to exhibit refined sensibilities and influence polite behavior. The various social occasions that constituted Charleston's season provided the wives and daughters of prominent lowcountry planters, merchants, and lawyers with another stage on which to demonstrate their conversational abilities and dancing skills as well as an opportunity to display the latest fashions. Balls and dances thus served a particularly useful role in the definition and articulation of female refinement. For Eliza Wilkinson, a ball held in Charleston's Assembly Rooms provided an ideal occasion to spend "some agreeable happy hours" in the company of friends, swapping gossip, and spinning about the dance floor. After a hectic afternoon spent "powdering! and frizzing! Curling! and dressing," Wilkinson along with her female companions set off to hear "Musick play'd sweetly" and pass an enjoyable evening engaged in genteel pursuits.[63] Although Wilkinson and her friends managed to converse with several "powder'd Beaus," the outbreak of a fire in a neighboring room thwarted her "Strong inclination for dancing." Within moments, the mask of propriety slipped as the revelers "scamper'd away" to escape flames that soon reduced the "Elegant Rooms" to "dust and ashes." Had fire not disrupted this event, Wilkinson likely would have demonstrated her abilities as a dancer ("I cou'd not," she later wrote, "keep my feet still" as the small band played), chatted, and compared notes on the styles of hair that had so occupied her and her friends earlier in the day.

At a dance held at Miss Phoebe Fletcher's Pinckney Street residence in late 1785, elite women had yet another opportunity to display their genteel sensibilities among members of their own class. Decorating her home with "festoons of myrtle and gold leaf . . . natural and artificial flowers" and lighting them, using blazing wax tapers reflected in a series of "rich mirrors," Fletcher endeavored to transform a set of ordinary rooms into an exotic setting designed, as the *Evening Gazette* surmised, to transport "the imagination to the paradise of Mahomet."[64] Having set the stage, Fletcher brought the scene to life with "an Ethiopian band [who] lulled the soul to peace and soft delight" with their playing. The evening's highlights included dancing, a performance by Fletcher, who sang "several songs clear as a bell," as well as a supper table laden with "cold tongues, oisters, hams [and] salt herrings," which her male guests consumed with considerable relish, "diluting their food with bumpers of generous wine." In contrast, the women at the party did not "swallow a morsel" of this lavish spread, perhaps out of concern for the smooth fit of their gowns or to avoid public displays of appetite.

These events shed some further light on the contours of female refinement. The "cotillions [and] rigadoons" that proved to be a highlight of Fletcher's soiree enabled her female guests to demonstrate their skills in executing a series of movements in an orderly, but graceful fashion. Moreover, the posture and gestures integral to these dances also required that the dancers exhibit control and discipline over their bodies as they moved through the sequence of steps. Several young women at Fletcher's gathering apparently had not fully mastered these skills, prompting one observer to note how these "nymphs were a little at a loss in crossing over," resulting in "contortions, animated gestures" that disturbed the flow of the dance.[65] The successful exhibition of the refined body did not just depend on elegant apparel and well-coifed hair, but also on proper movement and posture. That Fletcher's female guests decline to join the men at the supper table to eat and drink may also indicate their heightened awareness of the role of their bodies in conveying feminine grace and delicacy.

Elite women also sought to influence refinement and gentility in less public ways. As mothers, they might exert significant influence over their children, schooling them in the manners and morals of the lowcountry patriciate. For Eliza Pinckney, rearing her daughter Harriott formed "one of the greatest Businesses of my life" as she sought "to cultivate the tender mind."[66] Stored among her private papers, Pinckney kept a list on which she enumerated her moral duties as a wife and mother. Resolved "to be a good Mother," Pinckney reminded herself "to carefully root out the first appearings and budings of vice . . . and never omit to encourage every Virtue I may see Dawning in them."[67] Apart from calibrating the moral compasses of her children, Pinckney also introduced her boys to the polite arts, including writing and reading. An elegant letter writer and tireless correspondent, Pinckney conveyed her thoughts and experiences with as much skill and sensitivity on paper as she did before guests at a dinner party. Trying to pass on this art to her children, she often noted the arrival of their letters with great enthusiasm, chastising her son Thomas on one occasion for his failure to write from England more frequently and telling him that "one scrip of a penn from his hand would have given his mama more joy than all the pleasures of Bath could him."[68] Along with school teachers and tutors, the mothers of elite children could, to a significant degree, pass on the foundations of refined behavior from one generation to the next.

Away from the domestic concerns of the household and dinner table and the public world of the theater and the race track, customs house and assembly, private clubs enjoyed much popularity with lowcountry gentlemen. Informal forums in which they gathered over "solid, plentiful, good tables, and very good wines," these homosocial enclaves, with colorful titles like the Society of Brooms (a social club for unmarried men) and the Convention of Ubiquarians (a Mason-like organization), provided congenial settings in which men could engage conversation.[69] These institutions enabled men to discuss politics and other matters deemed outside the realm of women's interests that might have been regarded as offensive to female sensibilities. Although women were not privy to such conversations, the slaves who waited on gentlemen as they freely exchanged opinions on such topics as "negroes, rice and the necessity for British Regular troops to be quartered in Charlestown," as did the members of the Friday Night Club when Quincy attended one of their gatherings, could learn much about the current crisis in Anglo-American relations.[70]

While these exclusive establishments bestowed a sense of distinction on their members, they also demanded a degree of conformity imposed through the various rules that governed their operations. In this sense, club constitutions defined the limits of male gentility as any transgression of the rules constituted conduct unworthy of a gentleman. Although some visitors who spent an evening in the company of the Segoon-Pop Club or the Smoaking Club discovered that their hosts often showed more interest in "cards, dice, the bottle and horses" than in addressing the momentous issues of the time, these institutions generated a sense of fraternity among men who shared similar values and modes of living and served as a counterweight to the heterogeneity that prevailed outside the club room.[71]

Although Charleston never rivaled Boston or Philadelphia as a center of learning and scholarship, a number of elite men did pursue the life of the mind. The city's library allowed members to style themselves as men interested in matters of moral philosophy or literature as well as to acquire the accessories of refined living as they read about the latest fashions of London's polite society in publications, including the aptly titled *Gentleman's Magazine*. The library was not only for the consumption of knowledge. It also served as a focal point around which Charleston's small community of amateur scientists and other intellectuals could gather. Men like Lionel Chalmers, a physician and meteorologist, published several essays on the relationship between disease and the lowcountry's climate while Alexander Garden, a doctor and amateur botanist, corresponded with Linnaeus and the Royal Society about the various plants, including the gardenia, that he came across during his travels.[72] Bringing the methods of empirical science to the lowcountry's ecology, these men began to classify and describe an environment that remained profoundly strange and exotic.

Beyond the social events and formal institutions that catered specifically to elite tastes, the city itself became a stage on which they sought to dramatize their authority. By midcentury, Charles Town had grown into a substantial town. Visiting after a twenty-year absence in 1764, a Newport merchant claimed that the city had doubled in size, with its "sumptuous houses . . . new buildings and large and small houses" creating an impression of "a new world."[73] The fires that periodically razed sections of the town accounted in part for its new appearance, but the desire to create a built environment that matched the affluence and elegance of the elite also resulted in "handsome houses and other buildings [being] built much more beautifully than before."[74]

Articulating the elite's civic pride, aesthetic sensibility and cultural authority, these buildings spoke directly to the political and economic concerns of the men who ruled the lowcountry's social order. More imposing than any private residence, edifices such as the Customs House that Quincy noted as a "most noble" structure, and the Assembly, described by another visitor as a "large, handsome, substantial" building, eloquently symbolized elite power as well as their dedication to economic development and political stability.[75] While these public buildings highlighted the material bases of elite power, the modest structures that stood along Broad and Meeting Streets sold the accouterments of fine living from the "laces of Flanders and French Cambricks" to "Hyson Tea and other East India Goods."[76] As places of cultural interaction, the city's grand public structures enabled elite men to broker commercial and political deals while its thoroughfares gave the prosperous an opportunity to display their refinement through their clothing and consumption habits. Sedan chairs and cambric silk shaped and communicated social identity within this public sphere.

No public space was the exclusive preserve of the elite, however. The city's slave population challenged the elite's control over these sites of display, consumption and authority. As elite men and women stepped from the elegant porticoes of their houses, they confronted a street culture that they deemed unruly and disorderly and in which African and Afro-Carolinians played a leading role. Dramshops, tippling houses, and street corners all provided venues for enslaved Charlestonians to drink, dance, gamble, and socialize. To one visitor, the enslaved people who worked on Charleston's streets, in its shops, and its markets seemed "abandonedly rude, unmannerly, insolent, and shameless."[77] In its grievances to the Assembly, the city's grand jury frequently complained about "unmannerly, rude, and insolent slaves" milling about the streets, passing time by playing dice, smoking pipes, and "profanely swearing, cursing, and talking obscenely."[78] Jurors also objected to those female slaves who refused "to restrain themselves in their clothing . . . but dress in Apparel quite gay" that included colorful head scarves, aprons, and skirts.[79] Although elite men regularly engaged in the practices enumerated in the grand jury's first complaint, they did so in the confines of their own houses and clubs rather than in a public setting. Such daily encounters with enslaved people in Charleston's bustling thoroughfares doubtless imparted an added urgency to "the civilizing project" among the families of the elite, contributing to the widespread use of carriages and sedan chairs as they sought to distance themselves physically from the city's streets and its culture.

Surrounding the city's public buildings, retail establishments, taverns, and markets—the places where planters most formally displayed their authority, but where they were most vulnerable to challenges from enslaved people—stood the houses in which the patrician class lived. Like the public structures in which elite men gathered, these dwellings further reinforced the claims of this class to social and political leadership. Although more substantial and elegant than the modest houses in which most Charlestonians lived, many of the dwellings of the elite did not possess the formal, neoclassical grandeur of the city's public buildings. Rather than lavish money on exterior ornamentation, it appears that the elite spent money decorating the interiors of their houses, furnishing them with elegant tables, chairs, mirrors, longcase clocks, fireplaces, and the other items of domestic life. Faced with the potentially undermining disorder of the city's streets, elite people brought some of their most lavish performances of gentility indoors, where they might exhibit their refined manners and engage in polite conversation to a more attentive audience. Both the houses and the well-turned cabriole legs of finely crafted walnut tables bespoke economic power, but they also articulated the presence of refinement and taste. To meet the standards of taste in furniture as in other things, the lowcountry looked to London's polite society for guidance, devouring the latest reports on English styles so that Charleston's artisans might replicate them.

Composed of Anglo-Americans and Scots as well as Huguenots and Anglo-Barbadians, the lowcountry elite may have been among the most cosmopolitan in British North America. Apart from the small community of French Huguenots, the common denominator for these people was England. Besides the commercial, political, and educational links between Charleston and London, fashion and taste also drew the two locales together. "As they thrive," noted Governor James Glen in 1751, "they delight to have good things from England."[80] The "Anglicization" of the lowcountry took place on several levels, ranging from furniture built on designs printed in volumes such as Thomas Chippendale's *Gentleman's and Cabinet-Makers Directory* and other imported goods to the rituals that celebrated the monarch's birthday. Whether purchasing superb pieces of furniture in walnut and mahogany for the bed chambers and dining rooms, donning the latest clothes from London, or offering a patriotic toast at some imperial occasion or victory that punctuated the calendar, elite Charlestonians inhabited an environment in which the presence of English modes and manners remained palpable.[81]

The genteel way of life that the elite pursued with such vigor thus served a particularly important purpose in the lowcountry. Deportment and dress, conversation and concerts all served as the vehicles by which the elite fabricated a sense of distinction that set them apart from others. Just as refinement distanced elite men and women from the "rude woodsman" of coastal Carolina, it simultaneously drew them closer to the manners of the metropole. Even Eliza Lucas Pinckney, the upper-class woman who successfully experimented with indigo cultivation in the 1730s and was responsible for adding this crop to the lowcountry's list of export commodities, considered herself to be "an old woman in the Wilds of America." She fretted about living in "a remote Corner of the Globe," but drew the codes of conduct that structured the everyday life of her household directly from the modes of polite society in England.[82] The replication of English manners was not simply rooted in the idle desire to hold tea parties, don the latest London fashions, or engage in trivial gossip. It was no laughing matter to maintain "gentility" amid the "savagery" that people like Pinckney saw when they looked out of their windows onto Charles Town's streets where enslaved Africans and Afro-Carolinians went about their owner's business and the occasional Cherokee or Catawba Indian from the backcountry came to trade.

To maintain social distance from the ordinary people in their midst demanded that both elite men and women play their respective roles with great dedication, incorporating the qualities needed for success into their very identities. For gentlemen, the pursuit of gaming became one important way of expressing masculinity. Gambling appeared to accompany virtually every activity on which wagers could conceivably be laid, including cock-fighting, card playing, and the prospective yield of the annual rice harvest.[83] Noting that elite Charlestonians devoted "prodigious amounts of time and attention" to betting, Quincy observed that "the ingenuity of a Locke or the discoveries of a Newton" stood as minor accomplishments against an ability to know "when to shoulder a blind cock or start a fleet horse."[84] These pas-times allowed elite men to demonstrate their cavalier attitude toward money before their peers as they bet on various contests, and it established them as men willing to take risks, backing their opinions with cash.

Just as gambling and manhood became intertwined, the enormous consumption of vintage wines and spirits also played a part in defining masculinity.[85] David Ramsay, the first historian of South Carolina, believed intoxication to be "an endemic vice of Carolina," and Pennsylvania artist Benjamin West, visiting in the 1770s, observed how decanters filled with "arrack, brandy, Madeira wine [and] rum" lubricated most elite gatherings.[86] A "Drinker's Dictionary," that appeared in May 1737, made the link between manhood and drinking clear. Offering readers a series of colloquial epithets drawn primarily from the masculine culture of mariners, such as "he's got his gallant Top Sails out" and "he's been seafaring," to describe drunkenness, the language of this list has a distinctly male flavor.[87] Even remarks alluding to the effect that alcohol had on male sexual performance, such as "he's a Dead Man" and "his Flag is Down" (both reminiscent of the porter's comments in William Shakespeare's *Macbeth*) appear in this cata-logue designed to "surprize and divert the sober Reader."[88] Although a significant number of free and enslaved men gambled and drank to some extent, their pursuit by elite men distinguished them from the rest of lowcountry society as well as establishing boundaries between elite men and women.

Although the consumption of fine wines may have signaled distinction and intoxication signified masculinity, this conduct perhaps indicated some sense of apprehension among the elite. Excessive drinking possibly arrested feelings of insecurity and vulnerability that may have nagged at elite men as they grappled with the social and cultural implications of being a wealthy gentry class in a colonial setting and of maintaining an enslaved labor force through coercion even as they strove to make their authority appear natural and effortless. The presence of a sizable and potentially rebellious slave population, combined with the need to maintain their position and authority through an endless series of social encounters, doubtless contributed to elite men's taking "one cup too many."[89] The toasts that lauded the durability and enterprise of their society may have, in fact, disguised the apprehension of those who made them.

A study of the "civilizing process," to borrow a phrase from Norbert Elias, that unfolded in the eighteenth-century South Carolina lowcountry discloses the ways in which members of a colonial elite sought to fashion an identity and embody authority through modes of behavior that distinguished them from the men and women, both free and enslaved, they governed. The patterns of conduct and consumption that loudly broadcast this sense of distinction endured into the nineteenth century. Visiting the lowcountry after the Revolutionary War, Johann Schoepf observed that "luxury in Carolina has made the greatest advance, and their manner of life, dress and equipages, furniture denotes a higher degree of taste and love of show" than elsewhere in a new nation that ostensibly embraced republican simplicity. Yet elite style was not simply about the ostentation and the display of refinement; it was also about power that retained its authority only by being continually exercised. The elite accordingly strove to incorporate and insinuate itself into the practices of everyday life to ensure its effectiveness. Power, observed Michel Foucault, "exists only when it is put into action."[90] Unlike the candles that illuminated their dinner parties and card evenings, elite power could not be extinguished and relit at will. Rather, it was a form of social energy that constantly circulated around the lowcountry. In a society where the strange and the alien threatened the known and familiar, elite power required constant upkeep lest its carefully fashioned sense of self evaporate.

Notes

The phrase in the subtitle is from Henry Laurens, cited in David D. Wallace, *The Life of Henry Laurens* (New York: Russell and Russell, 1915), 21. The term "self-fashioning" is borrowed from Renaissance literary scholar Stephen Greenblatt. In his introduction to *Renaissance Self-Fashioning: From More to Shakespeare* (Chicago: University of Chicago Press, 1980), 3–4, he defines the concept thus: "Self-fashioning is in effect the Renaissance version of these control mechanisms [plans, recipes, rules, instructions for the governing of behavior], the cultural system of meanings that creates specific individuals by governing the passage from abstract potential to concrete historical embodiment."

1. Mark De Wolfe Howe, ed., "The Journal of Josiah Quincy, Jr.," *Proceedings of the Massachusetts Historical Society* 49 (June 1916): 424–67.

2. Howe, ed., "Journal of Josiah Quincy, Jr.," 454.

3. David Ramsay, *History of South Carolina, from Its First Settlement in 1670 to the Year 1808*, 2 vols. (Charleston, S.C., 1809), 2:202; for another analogy to mineral wealth, see George Milligen-Johnson, "A Short Description of the Province of South Carolina," in *Colonial South Carolina: Two Contemporary Descriptions,* ed. Chapman J. Milling (Columbia: University of South Carolina Press, 1951), 119.

4. Howe, ed., "Journal of Josiah Quincy, Jr.," 453.

5. On the Allston family, see Walter B. Edgar and N. Louise Bailey, eds., *Biographi-*

cal Directory of the South Carolina House of Representatives: The Commons House of Assembly, 1692–1775, 4 vols. (Columbia: University of South Carolina Press, 1977), 2:35.

6. Howe, ed., "Journal of Josiah Quincy, Jr.," 453.

7. Laurens, cited in Wallace, Life of Henry Laurens, 21.

8. Peter A. Coclanis, The Shadow of a Dream: Economic Life and Death in the South Carolina Lowcountry, 1670–1920 (New York: Oxford University Press, 1989); Jack P. Greene, The Quest for Power: The Lower Houses of Assembly in the Southern Royal Colonies, 1689–1776 (Chapel Hill: University of North Carolina Press, 1963); Carl Bridenbaugh, Myths and Realities: Societies of the Colonial South (New York: Atheneum, 1963); Richard Waterhouse, "The Responsible Gentry of Colonial South Carolina: A Study in Local Government, 1670–1770," in Town and Country: Essays on the Structure of Local Government in the American Colonies, ed. Bruce Daniels (Middletown, Conn.: Wesleyan University Press, 1978), 160–85; Waterhouse, A New World Gentry: The Making of a Planter and Merchant Class in South Carolina, 1670–1770 (New York: Garland Publishing, 1989).

9. Alexis de Tocqueville, Democracy in America, ed. J. P. Mayer (New York: Doubleday Books, 1966), 605.

10. Richard L. Bushman, The Refinement of America: Persons, Houses, and Cities (New York: Vintage Books, 1992), xix; Bushman, "American High-Style and Vernacular Cultures," in Colonial British America: Essays in the New History of the Early Modern Era, ed. Jack P. Greene and J. R. Pole (Baltimore: The Johns Hopkins University Press, 1984), 345–83. On elite style, see also Rhys Isaac, The Transformation of Virginia, 1740–1790 (Chapel Hill: University of North Carolina Press, 1982), esp. 34–42, 70–78, 88–114.

11. Pierre Bourdieu, Distinction: A Social Critique of the Judgement of Taste (Cambridge, Mass.: Harvard University Press, 1984), 11–96. For analyses of this and other works by Bourdieu, see Richard Jenkins, Pierre Bourdieu (London: Routledge Press, 1992), 128–51; Bryan S. Turner, Status (Minneapolis: University of Minnesota Press, 1988), 65–78.

12. The historiography on this activity is vast. See John Brewer and Roy Porter, introduction to Consumption and the World of Goods, ed. Brewer and Porter (London: Routledge Press, 1993), 1–18; see also Cary Carson, Ronald Hoffman, and Peter J. Albert, eds., Of Consuming Interest: The Style of Life in the Eighteenth Century (Charlottesville: University Press of Virginia, 1994).

13. John Fiske, Reading the Popular (Boston: Beacon Press, 1989), 31. Works that bring the insights of cultural studies to consumer behavior continue to multiply. See Consumption and the World of Goods, ed. John Brewer and Roy Porter; Robert Bocock, Consumption (London: Routledge Press, 1993); Martyn Lee, Consumer Culture Reborn: The Cultural Politics of Consumption (London: Routledge Press, 1993); Carson et. al., eds., Of Consuming Interests; and Barbara G. Carson, Ambitious Appetites: Dining, Behavior and Patterns of Consumption in Federal Washington (Washington, D.C.: Smithsonian Institute Press, 1990).

14. T. H. Breen, "'Baubles of Britain': The American and Consumer Revolutions of the Eighteenth Century," Past and Present 119 (May 1988): 75; see also Breen, "An Empire of Goods: The Anglicization of Colonial America, 1690–1776," Journal of British Studies 25 (Oct. 1986): 467–99.

15. Howe, ed., "Journal of Josiah Quincy, Jr.," 454.

16. Rhys Isaac, "On Explanation, Text and the Terrifying Power in Ethnographic History," Yale Journal of Criticism 6 (Spring 1993): 228; for a discussion of the creation of "spaces of power," see Greg Dening, Mr. Bligh's Bad Language: Passion, Power, and Theatre on the Bounty (New York: Cambridge University Press, 1992). The questions of power and its discourses are central to Michel Foucault's work. Foucault, History of Sex-

uality: An Introduction (New York: Vintage Books, 1980); Paul Rabinow, ed., *The Foucault Reader* (New York: Pantheon Books, 1984), 51–75, 239–56; Colin Gordon, ed., *Power/Knowledge: Selected Interviews and Other Writings by Michel Foucault, 1972–1977* (New York: Pantheon Books, 1980), 55–62, 109–45.

17. Erving Goffman, *The Presentation of Self in Everyday Life* (New York: Anchor Books, 1959); for able discussions on gentility and refinement in another setting, see Peter Burke, *The Historical Anthropology of Early Modern Italy: Essays on Perception and Communication* (New York: Cambridge University Press, 1982), 3–14; Ronald F. E. Weismann, "The Importance of Being Ambiguous: Social Relations, Individualism, and Identity in Renaissance Florence," in *Urban Life in the Renaissance*, ed. Weisman and Susan Zimmerman (Newark: University of Delaware Press, 1989), 269–80.

18. E. P. Thompson, "Patrician Society, Plebeian Culture," *Journal of Social History* 7 (Summer 1974): 389; "Eighteenth-Century English Society: Class Struggle without Class," *Social History* 3 (May 1978): 133–65; *Customs in Common: Studies in Traditional Popular Culture* (New York: W. W. Norton, 1991), esp. 16–96.

19. Henry Laurens to Alexander Hamilton, 19 Apr. 1785, in *The Papers of Alexander Hamilton*, ed. Harold C. Syrett et al., 27 vols. (New York: Columbia University Press, 1961–1987), 3:605–8. For an incisive discussion of this topic, see Olwell in this volume.

20. On the question of patriarchy, see Kathleen M. Brown, *Good Wives, Nasty Wenches, and Anxious Patriarchs: Gender, Race, and Power in Colonial Virginia* (Chapel Hill: University of North Carolina Press, 1996), 319–66; Philip D. Morgan, "Three Planters and Their Slaves: Perspectives on Slavery in Virginia, South Carolina and Jamaica, 1750–1790," in *Race and Family in the Colonial South*, ed. Winthrop D. Jordan and Sheila L. Skemp (Jackson: University Press of Mississippi, 1987), 37–80.

21. Lieutenant Governor William Bull to the Earl of Hillsborough, 10 Sept. 1768, Original Correspondence, Secretary of State, CO 5/391, Public Record Office, London.

22. On this rebellion, see Peter Wood, *Black Majority: Negroes in South Carolina from 1670 through the Stono Rebellion* (New York: W. W. Norton, 1974), 308–30; Edward A. Pearson, "'A Countryside Full of Flames': A Reconsideration of the Stono Rebellion and Slave Rebelliousness in the Early 18th Century South Carolina Lowcountry," *Slavery and Abolition* 17 (Aug. 1996): 22–51.

23. *South Carolina Gazette*, 5 Oct. 1769.

24. Ibid.; Brown, *Good Wives, Nasty Wenches, and Anxious Patriarchs*, 319.

25. Harry Carmen, ed., *American Husbandry* (London, 1775; reprint, New York: Columbia University Press, 1939), 303.

26. Gideon Johnson, cited in *Carolina Chronicle: The Papers of Commissary Gideon Johnson, 1707–1716*, ed. Frank J. Klingberg (Berkeley: University of California Press, 1946), 99; on the city's population, see Coclanis, *Shadow of A Dream*, 115; Philip D. Morgan, "Black Life in Eighteenth-Century Charleston," *Perspectives in American History*, n.s., 1 (1984): 190.

27. Henry Laurens to Charles Gywnn, 12 June 1755, in *The Papers of Henry Laurens*, ed. Philip Hamer et al., 10 vols. (Columbia: University of South Carolina Press, 1968–1985), 1:263.

28. R. C. Nash notes that "it was merchants who became planters rather than the other way around . . . it was trade that lent assistance to planting rather than planting which financed trade." See Nash in this volume.

29. William Logan, "Journal," *Pennsylvania Magazine of History and Biography* 36 (1912): 162.

30. On Wragg, see Edgar and Bailey, eds., *Biographical Directory,* 2:727; for a detailed analysis of government, see Greene, *Quest for Power;* M. Eugene Sirmans, *Colonial South Carolina: A Political History, 1663–1763* (Chapel Hill: University of North Carolina Press, 1966).

31. Alexander Cumine to Alexander Ogilivie, 17 June 1763, in "Discoveries of America: Letters of British Emigrants to America on the Eve of Revolution," ed. Barbara DeWolfe, *Perspectives in American History,* n.s., 3 (1986): 65.

32. Howe, ed., "Journal of Josiah Quincy, Jr.," 452.

33. *South Carolina Gazette,* 1 Mar. 1773.

34. On Sommers, see John Bivins, Jr., "Charleston Rococo Interiors, 1765–1775," *Journal of Early Southern Decorative Arts* 12 (Nov. 1986). p. 1–129

35. *South Carolina Gazette,* 22 Mar. 1735.

36. Ibid.

37. Ibid.

38. Ibid., 29 June 1767; see also Frederick P. Bowes, *The Culture of Early Charleston* (Chapel Hill.: University of North Carolina Press, 1942), 34–53; Walter J. Fraser, Jr., *Charleston! Charleston! A History of a Southern City* (Columbia: University of South Carolina Press, 1989), 103–4; Julia Cherry Spruill, *Women's Life and Work in the Southern Colonies* (Chapel Hill: University of North Carolina Press, 1938), 197–99.

39. Sophia Hume, *An Exhortation to the Inhabitants of the Province of South Carolina* (Bristol, 1750), n.p.; see also Bowes, *Culture in Early Charleston,* 34–54.

40. Richard Beale Davis, *Intellectual Life in the Colonial South, 1585–1763,* 3 vols. (Knoxville: University of Tennessee Press, 1978).

41. Marvin Zahniser, *Charles Cotesworth Pinckney: Founding Father* (Chapel Hill: University of North Carolina Press, 1967), 9–21; Harriot H. Ravenel, *Eliza Pinckney* (New York: Scribners' Books, 1896), 134–66; Paul Finkelman, "Slavery and the Constitutional Convention: Making a Covenant with Death," in *Beyond Confederation: Origins of the Constitution and American National Identity,* ed. Richard Beeman et al. (Chapel Hill: University of North Carolina Press, 1987), 216–17; Charles Cotesworth Pinckney, *Life of General Thomas Pinckney* (Boston: Houghton Mifflin, 1895), 12.

42. *A Short Description of the Province of South Carolina* [London, 1763], in B. R. Carroll, ed., *Historical Collections of South Carolina,* 2 vols. (New York, 1836), 2:489–90; "Original Rules and Members of the Charleston Library Society," *South Carolina Historical Magazine* 23 (Oct. 1922): 163–70; Joseph Ewan, "The Growth of Learned and Scientific Societies in the Southeastern United States to 1860," in *The Pursuit of Knowledge in the Early American Republic: American Scientific and Learned Societies from Colonial Times to the Civil War,* ed. Alexandra Oleson and Sanborn C. Brown (Baltimore: The Johns Hopkins University Press, 1976), 208–18. See also Joyce Chaplin, *An Anxious Pursuit: Agricultural Innovation and Modernity in the Lower South, 1730–1815* (Chapel Hill: University of North Carolina Press, 1993), 49.

43. Richard Beale Davis, *A Colonial Southern Bookshelf: Reading in the Eighteenth Century* (Athens: University of Georgia Press, 1979); Bridenbaugh, *Myths and Realities,* 104; Bowes, *Culture of Early Charleston,* 61–64.

44. Hector St. Jean Crevecoeur, *Letters from an American Farmer,* ed. Albert Stone (New York: Penguin Books, 1981), 166.

45. Howe, ed., "Journal of Josiah Quincy, Jr.," 442.

46. *South Carolina Gazette,* 4 Mar. 1756.

47. "The St. George's Club," *South Carolina Historical Magazine* 8 (Apr. 1907): 89.

48. Howe, ed., "Journal of Josiah Quincy, Jr.," 451.

49. Ibid., 467.

50. On dinner parties, see Barbara G. Carson, *Ambitious Appetites*.

51. Howe, ed., "Journal of Josiah Quincy, Jr.," 444–45; on elite furnishings, see Harriet P. Simons and Albert Simons, "The William Burrows House of Charleston," *Winterthur Portfolio* 3 (1967): 172–204; M. Allison Carll, "An Assessment of English Furniture Imports into Charleston, 1760–1800," *Journal of Early Southern Decorative Arts* 11 (Nov. 1985): 10–25; John Bivens, Jr., "The Charleston Rococo Interiors, 1765–1775: The 'Sommers' Carver," *Journal of Early Southern Decorative Arts* 12 (Nov. 1986): 45–72.

52. Howe, ed., "Journal of Josiah Quincy, Jr.," 446.

53. Ibid.

54. Ibid.

55. Ibid., 445, 447.

56. *South Carolina Gazette,* 15 Aug. 1743.

57. Ibid.

58. Ibid., 15 Aug. 1743; 10 June 1732.

59. Ibid., 10 June 1732.

60. Ibid., 15 Aug. 1743.

61. *City Gazette* (Charleston), 17 July 1793.

62. Howe, ed., "Journal of Josiah Quincy, Jr.," 448.

63. Eliza Wilkinson to Miss Porcher, 6 Mar. 1783 in George Armstrong Wauchope, *The Writers of South Carolina* (Columbia, S.C.: The State Company, 1910), 408–9.

64. *Charleston Evening Gazette,* 20 Oct. 1785.

65. Ibid.

66. Mary Beth Norton, "'What an Alarming Crisis Is This': Southern Women and the American Revolution," in *The Southern Experience in the American Revolution,* ed. Jeffrey J. Crow and Larry E. Tise (Chapel Hill: University of North Carolina Press, 1978), 208.

67. Eliza Pinckney, "To Improve in Every Virtue," in *Early American Women: A Documentary History, 1600–1900,* ed. Nancy Woloch (New York: McGraw Hill, 1992), 49–50.

68. Eliza Pinckney to Mrs. Evance, 16 July 1759, in *The Letterbook of Eliza Lucas Pinckney,* ed. Elise Pinckney (Chapel Hill: University of North Carolina Press, 1972), 121; see also Bushman, *Refinement of America,* 90–92.

69. Howe, ed., "Journal of Josiah Quincy, Jr.," 450; see also Peter Burke, *The Art of Conversation* (Ithaca, N.Y.: Cornell University Press, 1993); Bushman, *Refinement of America,* 83–90.

70. Howe, ed., "Journal of Josiah Quincy," 450.

71. James E. Smith, ed., *A Selection of the Correspondence of Linneaus,* 2 vols. (London, 1821), 1:477; see also Mark C. Carnes, *Secret Ritual and Manhood in Victorian America* (New Haven, Conn.: Yale University Press, 1989); Howe, ed., "Journal of Josiah Quincy," 455.

72. Lionel Chalmers, *An Account of the Weather and Diseases of South Carolina* (London, 1776); Joseph I. Waring, ed., "Correspondence between Alexander Garden, M.D., and the Royal Society of Arts," *South Carolina Historical Magazine* 63 (Jan. 1964): 16. See Bowes, *Culture of Early Charleston,* 75–91.

73. Thomas J. Tobias, ed., "Charles Town in 1764," *South Carolina Historical Magazine* 67 (Apr. 1966): 67.

74. Walter L. Robbins, ed., "John Tobler's Description of South Carolina (1753)," *South Carolina Historical Magazine* 71 (July 1970): 144–45. On fires in the city, see Kenneth Scott, "Sufferers in the Charleston Fire of 1740," *South Carolina Historical Magazine* 64 (Oct. 1963), 203–11; Samuel G. Stoney, ed., "The Great Fire of 1778 Seen

through Contemporary Letters," *South Carolina Historical Magazine* 64 (Jan. 1963), 23–27; Fraser, *Charleston! Charleston!* 67–69, passim.

75. "Charleston at the End of the Colonial Era, 1774," in *The Colonial South Carolina Scene: Contemporary Views, 1697–1774,* ed. H. Roy Merrens (Columbia, S.C.: University of South Carolina Press, 1977), 283; Howe, ed., "Journal of Josiah Quincy," 441.

76. P. C. Weston, ed., *Documents Concerned with the History of South Carolina* (London, 1856), 84–85.

77. *South Carolina Gazette,* 27 Aug. 1772.

78. Ibid., 6 Aug. 1741; on enslaved Charlestonians, see also Morgan, "Black Life in Eighteenth-Century Charleston."

79. *South Carolina Gazette,* 27 Aug. 1772; see also Grand Jury Presentments, Charleston District, *South Carolina Gazette,* 5 Nov. 1744.

80. James Glen, "Governor James Glen's Valuation," in *The Colonial South Carolina Scene,* ed. Merrens, 180.

81. Carll, "An Assessment of English Furniture Imports into Charleston, 1760–1800."

82. Eliza Pinckney to Mr. Keate, Feb. 1762, in *Letterbook of Eliza Lucas Pinckney,* ed. Pinckney, 181–82.

83. Peter Manigualt to Benjamin Stead, 6 Sept. 1771, Peter Manigault letterbook, South Carolina Historical Society, cited in Chaplin, *An Anxious Pursuit,* 81. On elite gambling, see Timothy H. Breen, "Horses and Gentlemen: The Cultural Significance of Gambling among the Gentry of Virginia," *William and Mary Quarterly,* 3d ser., 24 (Apr. 1977), 239-257; Isaac, *The Transformation of Virginia, 1740–1790.* See Randy J. Sparks, "Gentleman's Sport: Horse Racing in Antebellum Charleston," *South Carolina Historical Magazine,* vol. 93 (Jan. 1992): 15–30; Bertram Wyatt-Brown, *Southern Honor: Ethics and Behavior in the Old South* (New York: Oxford University Press, 1982), 341–45. For an anthropological discussion on gambling, see Clifford Geertz's classic article on Balinese cockfighting in his *The Interpretation of Cultures: Selected Essays* (New York: Basic Books, 1973), 412–53.

84. Howe, ed., "Journal of Josiah Quincy, Jr.," 467.

85. G. J. Barker-Benfield, *The Culture of Sensibility: Sex and Society in Eighteenth-Century Britain* (Chicago: University of Chicago Press, 1992), 91–93; Colin Campbell, "Understanding Traditional and Modern Patterns of Consumption in Eighteenth-Century England: A Character-Action Approach," in *Consumption and the World of Goods,* ed. Brewer and Porter, 50.

86. Ramsey, *History of South Carolina,* 2:391; Benjamin West to Samuel West, 25 Feb. 1778, in *Life in the South: Letters of Benjamin West, 1778–1779,* ed. James Schoff (Ann Arbor: University of Michigan Press, 1963), 33; see also James Glen, "Governor James Glen's Valuation," in *The Colonial South Carolina Scene,* ed. Merrens, 183; on West, see Kenneth Silverman, *A Cultural History of the American Revolution: Painting, Music, Literature, and the Theatre in the Colonies and the United States from the Treaty of Paris to the Inauguration of George Washington, 1763–1789* (New York: Columbia University Press, 1976), 124–30.

87. *South Carolina Gazette,* 7 May 1737.

88. Ibid.

89. Ibid.

90. Nobert Elias, *The Civilizing Process: A History of Manners* (Oxford: Blackwell, 1939); Michel Foucault, "Afterword: The Subject and Power," in *Michel Foucault: Beyond Structuralism and Hermeneutics,* ed. Herbert Dreyfus and Paul Rainbow (Chicago: University of Chicago Press, 1982), 219.

XIII

Economic Power among Eighteenth-Century Women of the Carolina Lowcountry

Four Generations of Middleton Women, 1678–1800

G. WINSTON LANE JR.

Historians have long debated the role of women in colonial America. Most agree that where women held financial power, economic independence had been achieved. A study of the Middleton family of colonial South Carolina provides a case study to determine whether women actually achieved economic power and, perhaps more significantly, whether doing so was an important objective for them.[1] Because of the demographics of the historical period, the examination is largely restricted to Middleton wives, most particularly widows. An evaluation of Middleton daughters does not appear until late in the story, for daughters did not survive childhood until the fourth generation.[2] Questions addressed include: Did women have economic power? If so, was it continuous throughout the period or did it change? Were these changes for better or for worse? Did Middleton women actively pursue economic power and, if so, were they successful? And finally, was the experience of Middleton wives, widows and daughters unique, or was it typical for elite women in eighteenth-century South Carolina?

Data for this study are drawn almost entirely from legal documents, particularly wills. In spite of evidence that all Middleton women of the first four generations were literate, if not widely read, only five letters they wrote have survived. Three of these are business letters by Sara [?] Morton Middleton/Mrs. Arthur Middleton (2) and are located in an archive in Bristol, England.[3] The two remaining are by Mary Izard Middleton/Mrs. Arthur Middleton (4): a personal letter in the Historical Society of Pennsylvania and a business letter in the North Carolina State Archives.

Middleton women occupied an enviable position among their contemporaries, for they were members of one of the wealthiest and most influential of all English colonial families. The four generations of Carolina Middletons included three members of the Proprietary Council, three members of the Royal Council, five members of the Commons House of Assembly, one acting governor, one elected governor (the position was declined), three members of the revolutionary Provincial Congress, two members of the Continental Congress, and a signer of the Declaration of Independence. Family wealth paralleled their political prominence. While information on total wealth has not survived for the first generation, Arthur Middleton (2) died possessed of 10,987 acres and 115 slaves; Henry Middleton (3) died possessed of 26,263 acres and 199 slaves; and Arthur Middleton (4) died possessed of still more acreage and 745 slaves. These figures actually underestimate the wealth of Middleton fathers, for they do not include Charleston properties, and before their deaths all but Arthur (4) had transferred both lands and slaves to their sons. In short, the Middletons were at the apex of South Carolina's colonial elite.

First Generation

Edward Middleton emigrated from Barbados to South Carolina in 1678, and Arthur followed him a year later. Both brothers waited several years before taking marriage vows, and both married widows of relatively successful men. By July 19, 1679, Mrs. Sara [?] Fowell had become Mrs. Edward Middleton, for on that date Edward Middleton and John Fowell, her former brother-in-law, signed a contract leasing the *Mary of Carolina*, a thirty-ton bark, to Maurice Matthews and James Moore.[4] As there is no evidence of any children being born to Sara and Richard Fowell, by English common law Sara Fowell was entitled to one-half of her late husband's estate.[5] Edward Middleton had to know of Sara's inheritance, for he had served as one of the executors of Richard Fowell's estate. (The other executors were Sara herself and John Fowell.) In addition to inheriting half interest in the vessel, Sara Fowell also inherited half of Fowell's personal estate, valued at £332.[6] Sara acquired additional property during her marriage to Edward Middleton, for his next land acquisition, dated June 1680, was issued jointly to Edward Middleton and his wife, Sara.[7] This would bear major ramifications for the family's future.

In 1685 Edward Middleton died without leaving a will. As Sara had borne him a son, English common law entitled her to a life estate in one-third of the real property owned by Edward at any time during their marriage. In addition, as Edward had died intestate, by common law Sara was also entitled to one-third of his personal property.[8] Instead of the traditional "widow's thirds," however, Sara actually inherited the bulk of Edward's estate. Most significantly, she received absolute title to the home plantation—The Oaks—which by the time of Edward's death constituted his only substantial property. This outcome, so favorable to Sara, was perhaps due in part to the fact that she had once again been appointed executor of a deceased husband's estate.

Was Sara Fowell Middleton deliberately acting so as to acquire economic independence? Her joint land grant with Edward Middleton suggests that she was. Was she successful at acquiring it? Once again, the land grant and subsequent complete ownership of the home plantation indicate so. Did she enjoy her independence? It seems that she did. Her inherited assets from two husbands made her quite a marital catch, yet apparently she felt no need for male protection and chose to remain single. Following the precedent of her Carolina contemporaries—Lady Margaret Yeamans, Mrs. Affra Coming, and Lady Rebecca Blake—she chose to live alone on her plantation several hours' distance from Charleston. In a time of severe shortage of marriageable women, Sara Middleton remained single for at least another ten years, choosing to raise her son and manage her plantation without a husband.[9]

In December 1682, Mary [?] Smith, widow of the late John Smith, a proprietary deputy, became Mrs. Arthur Middleton (1). Arthur Middleton, like his brother Edward, had established himself in the new colony before turning his sights toward marriage. Mary Smith was well aware of both the scarcity of women and the fact that, unless modified by prenuptial agreement, the entire estate from her late marriage would come under Arthur Middleton's control. Shortly before the couple wed such an agreement was recorded in the colonial secretary's office:

> 7 December 1682 between Arthur Middleton of Carolina, Esquire and Maurice Matthews, James Moore and Robert Gibbes in consideration of marriage by God's Grace to be solemnized between the said Arthur Middleton and Mrs. Mary Smith, . . . and for jointure, plantation on which the said Arthur Middleton now lives nigh Goose Creek in the province of said [Carolina] called Yeshoe 1780 acres with ten Negroes.[10]

While confirming the continuation of marriage as an economic institution, the indenture suggests that Mary Smith did not trust Arthur Middleton to manage her dowry. This would not have been an unreasonable suspicion, for many contemporaries remarried only to have their husbands squander their estates and die, leaving them once again widowed but this time impoverished as well.

Mary Smith Middleton's marriage negotiation aptly represents what colonial historian Edmund Morgan has described in seventeenth-century Virginia as a "widowarchy."[11] Enjoying longer life spans than men, women typically remarried several times. The death of each husband brought an additional inheritance. After several such cycles, some women found themselves quite economically powerful and independent. Not only did property from former husbands enhance their future marriage choices, it gave these widows greater leverage when negotiating prenuptial agreements.[12] Mary Smith Middleton's marriage indenture provides an excellent example. She, however, had to agree to provide for Arthur Middleton in the event that she predeceased him. She contracted that if that were to occur Arthur would receive one hundred pounds from her estate, free from any outstanding debts.[13]

Mary Middleton's marriage was short-lived, for Arthur Middleton died in 1685. Tradition maintains that, unlike his brother, he left a will bequeathing his entire estate to his widow.[14] That bequest was a drastic deviation from the norm of the time and suggests that Mary Smith Middleton had a very strong influence upon Arthur Middleton's decision.[15] At any rate, she maintained her economic independence for two years after Arthur's death. Mary then wed Ralph Izard, a wealthy proprietary councillor and Goose Creek planter. Her third husband was as politically powerful as her Middleton spouse, but more reckless. In November 1685 Governor Morton and five others issued a warrant for Izard's arrest following Izard's theft of a black box containing government records.[16] (This incident may explain the disappearance of Arthur Middleton's will.) As the wife of another of its leading politicians, Mary Smith Middleton Izard remained in the center of the colony's political scene until her death in 1693.[17] She had successfully accumulated fortunes from two previous husbands, only to bestow them posthumously upon her third. In this particular case it proved to be the widower, not the widow, who took all.

Though Mary Smith Middleton Izard had passed away, Sara Fowell Middleton remained alive and quite well. Sometime after 1697 she married Job Howe. One of her closest neighbors, Howe was also one of the most powerful members of the Commons House of Assembly. Sara was forced to bury a third husband, for Howe died from "distemper" in the fall of 1706. Though records are sketchy, it appears that one child may have been born to the Howes. Job Howe's intestate death plus the existence of issue provided Sara Howe with one-third of Howe's estate by English common law.

Sara Fowell Middleton Howe subsequently appears as a power to be reckoned with. In February 1704 her only child, Arthur Middleton, returned from an apprenticeship with English cousins. He was now prepared to establish himself as a planter. Sara, however, owned the Middleton home plantation and had no intention of relinquishing the degree of financial security it brought—at least not without compensation. In July 1706 she sold the property to her son for one hundred pounds. Nor was this the end of her financial transactions.[18]

Three years later Sara Fowell Middleton Howe challenged the parish rector. The parish glebe consisted of two properties separated by a 250-acre triangular-shaped property that had belonged to Job Howe. According to the rector, Francis Le Jau, Captain Howe had long made it known that he intended to give this property to the church in order to connect the parsonage to the glebe. Howe apparently was caught unprepared by the distemper and died intestate, leaving nothing in writing to verify such noble intent. According to Le Jau, Captain Howe's heirs had a different view regarding dispersal of the property: they had no intention of giving it to the church.[19] From surviving records, the heir most opposed was none other than Sara Fowell Middleton Howe. By December 1706, only months following Job Howe's death, Sara Howe had already ordered a plat drawn. It was signed by Lieutenant Governor Thomas Broughton, a family friend and political ally. The plat gave Sara 540 acres, including the entire disputed tract.[20] Eventually she relented somewhat: the church would receive connecting property along Goose Creek, but only 150 acres.[21]

Sometime after 1709 Sara Fowell Middleton Howe died. The few legal documents she left behind, especially her appointment as coexecutor of the estates of her first two husbands, suffice to reveal an independent woman of shrewd business acumen. It is also clear that Sara allowed neither maternal nor ecclesaisatical love to stand between her and economic security. Of more importance for the future of the Middleton family, however, is the joint land grant to Sara Fowell Middleton and her second husband. Having been widowed once, Sara appears determined that in the case of a second widowhood her interests would be protected. That protection included coverage against any possible claims of English relatives and most particularly Edward Middleton's son Henry.[22]

Regarding the first generation, it is evident that both Middleton wives recognized that economic power was crucial if they were to be among the few women who enjoyed security and independence. Whether through a marriage indenture, a land grant, or a land sale, these women actively sought and maintained such power with remarkable success. Both women served as executors of their husbands' estates, and both derived unusual economic advantages from those estates. It seems clear that both women knew exactly what they were doing.

Second Generation

The second generation of Middletons in South Carolina was represented solely by Sara Fowell Middleton's son, Arthur Middleton. In 1706, the year in which he purchased The Oaks from his mother, Arthur was twenty-two. That year he married fifteen-year old Sara Amory, daughter of the late colonial receiver. As is repeated throughout the Middleton narrative of the eighteenth century, the bride was an heiress. Sara Amory's dowry included two very sizable and valuable Charleston lots and more than 500 pounds.[23] In contrast to marriages of the first generation, however, there is no evidence of a prenuptial agreement, nor is there any evidence that Sara strove for economic independence.[24] Her role, like that of all Middleton first wives, was that of mother and companion. She fulfilled her maternal role admirably, giving birth to six sons and a daughter. Of these, only three sons would reach adulthood. Unfortunately, Sara seriously weakened her health in the process, for she died in 1722.

On August 23, 1723, Sara [?] Morton, a forty-year-old widow, became the second Mrs. Arthur Middleton (2). This marriage marks a return to the matrimonial economics of the first generation. Sara Morton Middleton's previous husband, Landgrave Joseph Morton, had been one of the colony's most politically influential and wealthy men. Subsequent records suggest that she was left in comfortable circumstances and retained control of at least a portion of her Morton properties.[25] Her business sense was recognized outside the family as well as within, for not only was she an executor of her husband's will, she (along with Arthur Middleton) was also named a coexecutor for the estate of their neighbor Samuel Brialsford. A wealthy Charleston merchant with a country seat near the Middletons' plantation, Brailsford would not have suffered fools to administer his estate.

Having been married to one of the colony's wealthiest and most enterprising planters and now married to another, Sara Morton Middleton apparently learned a few lessons from the successes of her husbands. In 1736, while still married to Arthur Middleton, she received a land grant of 3,500 acres in Granville County, in her name alone.[26] This grant strongly suggests that Sara not only retained control of her properties from her previous marriage, she also made sizable investments completely independent of her husband.

In 1737 Arthur Middleton died at the age of fifty-six. After fifteen years of a seemingly happy marriage, Sara Morton Middleton found herself once more a widow and an executor. Unlike his father, Arthur Middleton had written a will. Sara Morton Middleton received a life estate in the following: Arthur Middleton's real estate in Great Britain (properties reportedly producing an annual income of 300 to 400 pounds sterling); in his plate, linen, furniture, and coach; and in one-third of his personal estate in Great Britain. She inherited in fee simple his Broad Street townhouse and the lot upon which it stood. Though she was left quite comfortably, especially considering that she had retained properties from her previous marriage, only the Broad Street townhouse—which was relatively small—became hers in fee simple. Everything else was restricted to a life estate, meaning that Sara Morton Middleton could enjoy its income but was barred from selling any of it.[27]

One might suppose this restraint on his widow was Arthur Middleton's reaction to having had to purchase the Middleton home plantation from his own mother. Perhaps, but this appears to have been a growing trend among South Carolina planters as a whole as well as for male colonists in other regions.[28] As lands were increasingly claimed, real estate became a male domain. Although wealthy husbands usually provided amply for their widows in their wills, most were also careful to prevent them from liquidating their inheritance. This strategy guaranteed the widow a continuation of her accustomed lifestyle, but it sacrificed her economic independence for that of the testator's sons by any wife.

In fact, Arthur Middleton's restrictive will did not undermine his widow's independence, for at his death Sara Morton Middleton was already a wealthy woman in her own right. By 1745 Arthur Middleton's estate had been settled. That same year, when the colony was facing one of its most serious economic recessions (one result of King George's War), the most financially secure of the entire Middleton clan was Sara Morton Middleton.[29] In 1745 she owned 215 slaves, all residing on her properties in St. James Parish, where she owned 2,041 acres. In addition, she owned 1,160 acres on Wadmalaw Island and the Edisto River, and 2,350 acres in Granville County (apparently Sara had liquidated 1,150 acres in Granville, for her grant had been for 3,500 acres). She also drew interest from £56,348 that she had loaned at six percent interest. Judging from Sara Morton Middleton's case, the economics of widowarchy were little affected by world markets.

Nor did she relinquish control of properties before her death. In 1765 she died at age eighty-two. She left an estate estimated at £50,000 sterling, which warranted note not only in the *South Carolina Gazette* but in the *Gentlemen's Magazine* of London as well.[30] Though she retained her properties to the end, Sara's bequests were more than generous. She bequeathed Henry Middleton and each of his children £6,000 currency, in addition to valuable personal items. Other Middletons received similarly ample inheritances.

Sara Morton Middleton's death marked the end of the second generation of Middletons in South Carolina. Her story well illustrates that it was the widows fortunate enough to survive several husbands who were the most likely to achieve economic independence. Success in this sphere, however, required more than mere demographic good fortune. It also required a certain degree of shrewdness and intelligence. Sara Morton Middleton had both. She was an executor not only for her husband's estate, but that of a successful Charleston merchant. Consequently, she not only maintained the economic status of the previous generation of Middleton widows, she made a very significant stride forward. Her acquisition of a 3,500-acre land grant in her name alone, independent of her then-living husband, represents a extraordinary accomplishment for an eighteenth-century woman.[31]

Historian Allan Kulikoff has sought to explain the emergence of a widowarchy as the result of frontier conditions. He suggests that fervor for profit among first-generation Virginia men left them little time to impose social control upon women and servants.[32] This is a perfectly reasonable explanation for the emergence of widowarchy in both Virginia and South Carolina during the seventeenth century. Sara Morton Middleton's achievements are all the more remarkable in that they came during the second generation rather than the first. By her day South Carolina had long been settled and long enjoyed prosperity, leaving ample time for its men to handle the "widow problem."

The economic advances made by first-generation Carolina women were temporary. As seen, husbands increasingly restricted their widows' inheritances to life estate. The ample income for life that Arthur Middleton bequeathed Sara Morton Middleton guaranteed her economic security but provided very little actual economic power. It was Arthur, not Sara, who made all major decisions about the future disposition of his estate. If her earlier husband had similarly restricted her inheritance to a life estate, her story would have been quite different.

Third Generation

The third generation of South Carolina Middletons was composed of Arthur and Sara Amory Middleton's three sons and their families. All three sons married heiresses and did so several times, repeating the pattern already observed in their late father's marriages. First wives tended to marry young, bring considerable wealth to their husbands, spend the majority of their married life in pregnancies, and ultimately die before seeing their children reach adulthood. Second wives more often than not reared the children of the first. Though first wives were likely to die young, later wives usually survived their husbands.

William Middleton, the late Arthur Middleton's oldest son, returned from an English education at twenty-one, was immediately established by his father as a planter, and soon married Elizabeth Izard, the heiress next door. Within four years he buried two wives (Elizabeth Izard Middleton and Mary Morton Middleton), four children, and his father. William and his third wife, Mary Wilkinson Middleton, spent most of their married life in England, where they lived from 1754 until their deaths, hers in 1772 and his three years later. Details involving their lives have not survived.

Thomas Middleton (3), Arthur's youngest son, married twice, both times to heiresses. His first bride was Mary Bull, the daughter of John Bull of Bull's Island, a wealthy planter and brother to the lieutenant governor. Mary Bull brought Thomas an enviable dowry, which appears to have consisted of approximately three plantations, totalling 2,477 acres. As with most first marriages, there are no surviving marriage indentures nor any signs of economic independence on the part of Mary Bull Middleton. After bearing at least three children, she died in 1760. An odd occurrence took place, however, which would later become more frequent among lowcountry planters.

By the mid-eighteenth century, Carolina fathers of brides had discovered equity law as a means to protect the economic interests of their daughters. There were two main dangers which fathers sought to avoid. One was the misfortune of a spendthrift son-in-law who would squander the daughter's dowry. The second was legal action by a son-in-law's creditors which threatened the dowry. The latter was a permanent threat, for even the most financially astute son-in-law could not escape the local recessions which occurred regularly due to European wars. Once transatlantic trade lanes were closed, rice crops sat in warehouses; no profits came forth while debts mounted and creditors clamored.

Provided they had at least one surviving child, by common law a husband would immediately inherit the entire estate of his deceased wife. Equity courts allowed the creation of a trust protecting the wife's interest and that of her children. While a son-in-law had varying degrees of control over his wife's property by equity settlement, upon her death he became a mere trustee. Her dowry devolved not to the widowed husband, but to the children of the couple. If the children were of legal age, they assumed immediate ownership; if the children were minors, husbands became trustees of the property for their children until they attained legal age.[33] Only if there were no children could a wife's property devolve to her surviving husband. In the event the wife/mother died intestate, the property descended directly to her issue.[34]

Throughout his marriage to Mary Bull Middleton, Thomas Middleton (3) described himself as of True Blue Plantation, Sheldon Parish. Yet following Mary Bull Middleton's death and immediately upon his son William's (4) attaining adulthood, William became master of True Blue as well as two other plantations that had originally belonged to his grandfather, John Bull. The fact that these properties passed to Mary's son rather than her husband almost certainly indicates that they had been part of her dowry.

Thomas Middleton's second marriage to seventeen-year-old Anne Barnwell Middleton luckily involved a similar arrangement. Thomas Middleton died in 1766 utterly bankrupt owing to poor business decisions by his mercantile firm. His personal estate was valued at £22,522, while his outstanding debts totalled £45,000.[35] One might expect that Middleton's widow and children would have been left destitute. John Bull, however, had not been the only one of Thomas Middleton's fathers-in-law to decide that his daughter needed economic protection, for John Barnwell apparently reached the same conclusion. Though its furnishings were publicly auctioned, Thomas and Anne Barnwell Middleton's magnificent country seat Laurel Bay remained in Anne Middleton's possession, having been part of her marriage dowry to Thomas Middleton.[36] If one overlooks the embarrassment of the publicity surrounding her late husband's financial disaster, as a widow Anne Barnwell Middleton fared quite well.[37]

Middleton marital information is most plentiful for Henry Middleton (3), the second son of Arthur and Sara Amory Middleton. In 1741 Henry Middleton was married to Mary Williams, the only child and heiress of John Williams of neighboring St. George Parish. Henry was twenty-four years old; Mary was twenty-six. The ages of the two partners, especially Mary's, suggest that this was not primarily an economically arranged marriage but rather one of emotional attachment. (Brides of arranged marriages tended to be very young.) Mary Williams Middleton's (3) dowry included her father's home plantation and seven other properties along the Ashley River, a total of 2,458 acres. When added to the 4,838 acres inherited from his father, Mary Williams's dowry brought Henry Middleton's total holdings to 7,296 acres.[38] These properties were especially valuable because they were to a large extent already under cultivation. Though Mary Williams brought great economic benefit to the union, no marriage indenture has survived, nor any evidence that she sought to safeguard her economic independence. Predictably, Mary Williams Middleton (3) spent nine of her remaining twenty years pregnant; she died on January 9, 1761, from malaria.[39]

The second Mrs. Henry Middleton was Maria Henrietta Bull, daughter of the former lieutenant governor and sister to the current one. The marriage occurred in 1762, when Henry was forty-five and Maria Henrietta Bull thirty-nine. Once again a marriage indenture has not survived, but it is known that Maria Henrietta Bull brought several plantations on St. Helena's Island to the marriage in addition to her late father's three-story townhouse on lower Meeting Street in Charleston. No details of the marriage survive other than Maria Henrietta Middleton's endearment to her stepdaughters. Ten years later Maria Henrietta Middleton was dead. Since there had been no issue, all of her marriage properties became the absolute property of Henry Middleton, a reversal of the usual tendency.

Henry Middleton was not ready to be single. In 1776, at age fifty-nine, he married Lady Mary McKenzie Drayton Ainslie, a well-known member of the Middletons' social circle.[40] Henry Middleton was Lady Mary's third husband. Both of her earlier South Carolina husbands had been financially successful planters; thus her accumulation of dowry properties should have been substantial.[41] A marriage settlement to Henry Middleton has not survived, but based on later family documents, Henry Middleton agreed that Lady Mary Middleton's slaves were separate from his own. Unfortunately for the historian, he did not indicate the number of slaves. As illustrated by the will of Arthur Middleton (2), restricting widows' inheritance of land to life estates had become common practice among lowcountry husbands. Consequently, women's inheritances in fee simple were restricted to personalty (that is, slaves or movable property). Henry Middleton was careful to ensure that his heirs would not confuse his and Lady Mary's slaveholdings.

Eight long years later, years that included the ravages of the Revolutionary War, Lady Mary Middleton found herself widowed once again. Henry Middleton had provided for Lady Mary's maintenance in the same comfortable style to which she was accustomed during their marriage. She received an annual income of £400 sterling, basically interest from a principal sum that Henry Middleton had ordered his executors to invest. Henry bequeathed her the continued use of his Charleston mansion, furnishings, house linens, silver, and pew in St. Michael's—but only for life. She received absolute title to his carriages and carriage horses. Lady Mary was left with no disposable income other than her annuity. Henry Middleton left a hint that Lady Mary might not be altogether pleased with his will, for he wrote that he hoped she would accept his bequests rather than demand her dowry rights.[42]

There are no surviving letters to indicate Lady Mary Middleton's reactions to her bequests. Actions, however, are louder than words. In 1786 Lady Mary Middleton sailed for Scotland. British authorities had finally released the Scottish estate of Lady Mary Middleton's late father from confiscation, and Lady Mary journeyed there to secure her portion. She died on the return voyage in 1788. Records have not survived to indicate whether her mission was successful. The conspicuous fact, however, is that Lady Mary, at what must have been a fairly old age, chose a transatlantic voyage in order to acquire disposable properties.[43] Then as now convertible assets were the best guarantee of real economic independence. Lady Mary undertook this trip in spite of the ample provisions Henry Middleton had provided for her, not to mention her slaves from her previous marriages. Apparently, economic independence was as important to Lady Mary as to earlier Middleton widows.

Lady Mary had written a will before embarking that eliminates any possible doubt on that score. Among its provisions are a bequest to Harriot Pinckney Horry/Mrs. Daniel Horry, the daughter of her best friend, Eliza Lucas Pinckney. In it Lady Mary left £150 to Mary Horry, expressly providing that it could not be touched by Daniel Horry. No clearer evidence that Carolina women recognized their need for economic independence can be found.[44]

The third generation of Middleton women generally mirrored the patterns established by the second. First wives brought plantations and children to their husbands before dying, and surviving widows enjoyed the greatest chance of achieving economic power. Increasingly, however, this outcome was thwarted by the growing custom of leaving widows only life estates. Though Lady Mary Middleton (3) enjoyed some economic independence, it was far less than that achieved by Sara Morton Middleton (2). The difference is very largely due to the growing utilization of life estates.

It must be noted, however, that another important factor was operating to undermine the economic position of women during this era, namely the American Revolution. The destruction of lowcountry plantations by two British invasions disproportionately damaged the economic power of women, for the property damage was inflicted mainly on moveables. Women suffered relatively greater losses than men because male financial resources were in both land and slaves, while a woman's economic resources had been increasingly restricted to moveable property, especially slaves. During this tumultuous period slaves were quite likely either to escape to the British in hopes of freedom or to be captured by the British for resale in the Indies.[45] Furthermore, cattle and other moveables were commandeered by both armies as they plundered the landscape.

The economic recession following the Revolutionary War also prompted encroachments on women's property rights that would not necessarily have occurred during peacetime. When Lady Mary finally relented and married Henry Middleton in 1776, he could have no reasonable motive to interfere with her properties. Rebuilding devastated plantations during the postwar depression, however, often required desperate measures. Thus, faced with urgent financial needs, Henry Middleton sold Lady Mary's slaves.[46] This action was the reason for his carefully adding a codicil to his will explaining the circumstances to both his and her executors. Lady Mary's reaction was probably one of unhappy resignation. While widows emerged once again with varying degrees of economic power, they did so during a period of continuing and even accelerating erosion of their interests.

Fourth Generation: Middleton Daughters

It was not until the fourth generation that any Middleton daughters survived to adulthood. While among the most interesting, their experiences were so varied as to confound any attempt at sharp generalization.

Colonel Thomas Middleton (3) was survived by a son and three daughters. A fourth daughter would be born the day after his death. In spite of their father's bankruptcy, his daughters by Mary Bull fared very well. Sara married future governor Benjamin Guerard in 1766, while Mary wed Major Pierce Butler in 1771. Both grooms were widely rumored to be little more than fortune hunters, suggesting that these young women somehow retained economic assets. As noted earlier, their brother William had inherited their mother's dowry properties in real estate. Though evidence is lacking, Sara and Mary undoubtedly inherited slaves from their mother's estate. So where was the allure to attract these young fortune hunters?

As should be suspected by this point, Middleton widows were not the only Middleton women who accumulated economic assets. In 1765 all three of Thomas Middleton's daughters received inheritances of £2000 from Sara Morton Middleton. In addition to their inheritance from their paternal stepgrandmother, Thomas's two younger daughters by Anne Barnwell benefited from their uncle Henry Middleton's (3) sympathy and affection, for he left £300 to both girls. For Mary Middleton Bull's daughters, however, it was their maternal grandmother, Mrs. John Bull, who proved the saving grace. In her 1771 will, Mrs. John Bull ordered her vast estate of numerous plantations in St. Helena's Parish to be divided equally among her four granddaughters: Mary Middleton Butler/Mrs. Pierce Butler, Sara Middleton Guerard/Mrs. Benjamin Guerard, and their two first cousins Mary Izard Brewton/Mrs. Miles Brewton and Elizabeth Izard Blake/Mrs. Daniel Blake. Though apparently fooled about Pierce Butler's intentions, Mrs. Bull did not trust Sara's husband, Benjamin Guerard.[47] In her will she specified that Sara Middleton Guerard's share was "independent and free from the intermeddling of her husband." This seems to mark a major step in the evolution of the economic independence of Middleton women. For the first time, so far as we know, a Middleton widow attempted to ensure the economic independence of a Middleton daughter—specifically from her non-Middleton husband.[48]

Major Pierce Butler would earn the distrust of Sara Middleton Guerard's cousin, Elizabeth Izard Blake. Mrs. Blake's will, dated 22 February 1791, left considerable property to her first cousin Mary Middleton Butler, much of which was Mrs. Blake's share of their grandmother Bull's estate. She did so only after establishing a trust that completely removed the property from the control of Mary's husband, Pierce Butler. Elizabeth Blake went so far as to specify, probably unnecessarily, that following Mary Middleton Butler's death, the properties would go to Mary's children. If the children were minors at the time, a trusteeship was established and trustees were named, Pierce Butler not among them. In Mrs. Blake's bequest to Mary Middleton Butler, Mary's husband was carefully and completely bypassed. (Upon the reading of the will Butler abruptly ended his mourning in a fit of rage.)[49] In the wills of both Mrs. John Bull and Mrs. Daniel Blake, Middleton women and their mothers, grandmothers, and other female forebears clearly articulated their recognition of a woman's need for economic independence from a husband's meddling.

Henry Middleton's (3) daughters offer a complete contrast to those of Colonel Thomas Middleton (3). Although their father remained a successful planter until his death, except for the inheritance they received from their paternal step-grandmother Sara Morton Middleton (2), there is no evidence that these girls brought large dowries to their marriages. On the contrary, in a letter to their brother, Arthur Middleton, in 1768, Henry Middleton (3) wrote: "I have it not in my power to make them [his daughters] great fortunes, for it is seldom of any advantage to a young lady, and too often proves a snare to them."[50]

Nor does Henry Middleton appear to be joking. Though he was possessed of thousands of acres of prime rice plantations and thousands more of undeveloped property, his daughters would receive only the customary share of his slaveholdings at the time of his death.[51] Those lands Henry Middleton considered unimportant—the ones not bequeathed to his sons—were to be sold and the proceeds divided among his daughters. Land remained a male domain. Oddly enough, while Middleton men married women possessed of vast landed estates, Middleton daughters were not provided with similar assets at their own marriage table. In spite of Henry Middleton's defensive comment, however, all his daughters did marry, indicating that their share of their father's slaves and proceeds from land sales were sufficient to attract acceptable suitors. In fact, his daughters married some of the most prominent young men in the colony, suggesting that the Middleton girls may have possessed larger dowries than their father was willing to admit.

Fourth Generation: Middleton Wives

It was not until the fourth generation that a Middleton's first wife outlived her husband.[52] As information regarding most of the Middleton wives is very limited, the main focus here is on Mary Izard Middleton/Mrs. Arthur Middleton (4). Early in 1764 Arthur returned to the colony after nine years abroad. On August 19, 1764, he and Mary Izard became man and wife. Mary Izard's home plantation, Cedar Grove, lay directly across the Ashley River from Middleton Place.[53] Arthur was twenty-two; Mary, known to the family as "Polly," was seventeen. Her father, the late Walter Izard, had been an extremely wealthy planter of St. George Parish.[54] Upon his death his personal property, including 278 slaves, was valued at £110,383.[55] The proximity of the families' plantations, along with the youth of the couple, strongly suggests that their marriage was a planned, economic arrangement.

Though a marriage indenture has not survived, Mary Izard more than likely brought a sizable dowry to the marriage, possibly including several plantations in St. Helena's Parish.[56] She played the typical role of a first wife: bearing children, managing the household, and traveling with her husband. There is no evidence that she exercised or attempted to exercise economic power. She was, however, a remarkably well-read woman, garnering several compliments from male contemporaries regarding her intelligence. She traveled with her husband to the Continental Congress in Philadelphia, where at least one of her husband's colleagues sent copies of pamphlets and addresses not to Arthur Middleton but to Mary Izard Middleton. Though Mary did not pursue independent economic interests, she was clearly an independent thinker. Even so, her foremost interest was and would always prove to be her family.

After twenty-three years of marriage, in 1787 Mary Izard Middleton found herself a widow at the age of thirty-nine. Though she was left with nine children, eight of whom would survive to adulthood, the fact that both Mary Izard Middleton and her husband had been heirs to large estates prevented any possibility of economic difficulties.[57] Arthur Middleton had died intestate, and as South Carolina inheritance laws remained based on English common law, Mary Izard Middleton inherited a third of her husband's estate by dowry rights. Through this inheritance, and evidently also as the sole heir of her late brother, Mary Izard Middleton accumulated a vast estate. According to her will, her landed properties totalled approximately seven thousand acres, including Cedar Grove, her childhood plantation.[58]

Like earlier Middleton widows, Mary Izard Middleton chose not to remarry, remaining single and managing her plantations until her sons reached legal age. She was an heir to the previous generations of Middletons widows in other ways as well. In October of 1799, shortly before their nuptials, Mary Izard Middleton attempted to establish her favorite daughter, Septima Sexta Middleton Rutledge/Mrs. Henry Middleton Rutledge, and her husband by presenting them with Jenys, a 942-acre plantation adjacent to Cedar Grove.[59] Perhaps it would be more accurate to say she attempted to established her daughter. Following a now familiar pattern, Mary Izard Middleton placed the property in a trust from which her son-in-law, Henry Rutledge, was more or less excluded. Even if the plantation were to be sold, Mary Izard Middleton specified that the proceeds were to become part of a trust governed by the same trustees as the plantation. Once again, a wife's property was placed completely out of the reach of her husband.[60]

Such efforts did not end with the eighteenth century but extended into the early nineteenth century, as already exemplified by Mary Izard Middleton's establishment of Septima Sexta Middleton Rutledge at Jenys. Another example from the early nineteenth century is Harriott Pinckney Horry/Mrs. Daniel Horry, the previously mentioned legatee of Lady Mary Middleton and a lifelong friend of Mary Izard Middleton. Unlike Mary Izard Middleton, who appears to have arranged the marriages of all five of her daughters, Harriott Pinckney Horry had given up on on her daughter Harriot's ever marrying. In order to ensure her daughter's independence as a single woman, around 1800 Harriott Pinckney Horry began construction of an elegant country seat near her own home plantation and named it Harriott's Villa. Harriott Horry was to be guaranteed a comfortable home and a certain degree of economic independence by virtue of this plantation.[61]

On the surface these acts by both Harriott Horry and Mary Izard Middleton appear merely generous gestures. Both women, however, had not far to look to see the consequences when such provisions were not made. Henrietta Drayton was the niece of Mary Izard Middleton and an intimate member of the Horry-Middleton circle. Her late father, Charles Drayton, had been part of the wealthy lowcountry elite, having inherited from his father the palatial Drayton Hall on the Ashley. Henrietta Drayton had never married, and her father, apparently suspecting she never would, provided in his 1820 will that she would always have the use of two rooms at Drayton Hall. Shortly afterward a visitor to Drayton Hall left a depressing account of the spinster alone in a dark and shuttered house that seemed more a deserted castle than a residence. Drayton Hall at that time belonged to Henrietta Drayton's only brother, the youngest of Charles Drayton's four children. Both Mary Izard Middleton and Harriott Pinckney Horry seemed to realize that, unless their daughters had independent economic means, they might share the dismal fate of Henrietta Drayton. Both mothers acted decisively to provide those means.

Did the Middleton women possess economic power? Excluding the late-seventeenth-century generation, a definite pattern emerges regarding a Middleton male's first wife, a pattern which extends from the second generation through the fourth. For all three generations, a Middleton's first bride demonstrated no interest whatsoever in acquiring economic power following marriage. These women tended to be very young, previously unmarried, and preoccupied with bearing and rearing children. Though certain third-generation brides appear to have enjoyed marriage settlements established by their fathers, none aggressively sought economic independence like the first-generation brides, Sara Fowell Middleton and Sara Morton Middleton. After the exceptional first generation, Middleton first wives spent the vast majority of their lives being mothers to their children and companions to their husbands. Though not appearing until the fourth generation, Middleton daughters reflect the same pattern.

Middleton widows, however, are a completely different matter. From the first generation through the fourth, Middleton widows enjoyed economic power, though to varying degrees. As the eighteenth century progressed, these widows sought not only to ensure their own economic independence, but to establish that of females of the next generation as well. Their tools were bequests, often containing clauses specifically prohibiting the beneficiary's husbands from having any control over the bequest.

Though still possessed of economic power, widows beginning with the third generation experienced a slow erosion of their financial security. The source of this erosion was the growing practice of husbands leaving their widows ample resources, but resources restricted to life estates. This is well illustrated by the contrast between Lady Mary Middleton/Mrs. Henry Middleton (3) and Sara Morton Middleton/Mrs. Arthur Middleton (2). Though left with ample means to provide economic comfort, in no way did Lady Mary Middleton enjoy the economic power of Sara Morton Middleton, for Sara possessed economic assets that she could liquidate and invest at her discretion. Lady Mary's bequests, though ample, were restricted to a life estate. While a life estate undoubtedly brought a widow economic comfort, it brought little if any economic independence and no economic power.

Did Middleton women actively pursue economic power and, if so, were they successful? It seems clear that second- and third-generation Middleton widows sought and acquired economic power. Though possessing economic independence, the fourth generation of Middleton widows shows few signs of further pursuit of economic goals. This group includes Mary Izard Middleton/Mrs. Arthur Middleton (4) and Frances Motte Middleton/Mrs. John Middleton (4).[62] This relative passivity is of particular note since these women represented the Revolutionary War generation and, according to some historians, should consequently have been more aggressive in seeking independence than preceding generations. Their indifference may be explained in part by the fact that these Middleton widows were first-time widows. All Middleton widows of the previous generations had experienced widowhood at least once prior to their Middleton husband's death. Prior widowhoods apparently had provided them with greater opportunities to enjoy economic independence as single females. Another significant factor may be that their husbands left estates vastly larger than those of any preceding Middletons in South Carolina. Consequently, the widows of the fourth generation were left quite comfortable and perhaps felt no need to seek additional economic power. Their handsome inheritances surely go far to explain why, like earlier Middleton widows, neither Mary Izard Middleton nor Frances Motte Middleton rushed into marriage following the deaths of their husbands. Mary Izard Middleton never remarried. Frances Motte Middleton waited thirteen years, refusing at least one proposal in the interval.[63]

Were the actions of Middleton women unique, or were they representative of their contemporaries? The traditional stereotype of the helpless female left alone on the plantation finds little or no support among Middleton women or their counterparts in other elite families. As noted, a number of wealthy widows of the seventeenth and early eighteenth centuries saw no need to remarry for economic or physical protection but chose instead to remain single and manage their estates. Undoubtedly, research into early legal records will reveal additional members of this group. Nor did the low-country widowarchy disappear after frontier conditions had been eliminated, as Allen Kulikoff has suggested for Virginia. Rather, there continued to be a number of economically powerful widows, such as Mary Brandford Bull/Mrs. John Bull and Elizabeth Izard Blake/Mrs. Daniel Blake, who sought to protect the economic interests of female relatives.

In spite of the economic successes of the Middleton women and their socio-economic circle, one fact must never be forgotten. These women, while sharing economic goals with their lowcountry contemporaries, remained a universe apart from the typical woman of their day. They had been born into an incredibly small minority of elites and blessed not only with intelligence but the opportunity to demonstrate it. Their successes went beyond the wildest dreams of the average colonial daughter or wife.

Notes

1. This study is based on the late author's doctoral dissertation, "The Middletons of Eighteenth-Century South Carolina: A Colonial Dynasty, 1678–1787" (Emory University, 1990). It has been edited for publication by John T. Juricek and Rosemary Brana-Shute.

2. Only one daughter is known to have been born within the first two generations in South Carolina: Arthur and Sara Amory Middleton had a daughter, Hester, who died in infancy around 1711.

3. In an effort to avoid confusion regarding different Middletons sharing the same name, the generation to which a particular Middleton belonged is indicated by a numeral in parentheses. A "[?]" following a first reference to a Middleton wife's given name indicates that her maiden name is unknown. The virgule (/) separates a woman's succession of names from her correct married name, indicated by Mrs.

4. This vessel had been jointly owned by Sara Fowell Middleton's late husband Richard Fowell and his brother John. Upon Richard Fowell's death, his interest descended to Sara; upon her marriage it devolved to Edward Middleton.

5. Marylynn Salmon, *Women and the Law of Property in Early America* (Chapel Hill: University of North Carolina Press, 1986), 141.

6. Inventory of Richard Fowell, Secretary's Office Records, 1678–1682, p. 332, South Carolina Department of Archives and History (hereafter SCDAH).

7. Alexander S. Salley, Jr. and R. Nicholas Olsberg, eds., *Warrants for Land in South Carolina, 1672–1711* (Columbia: University of South Carolina Press, 1973), 227.

8. Salmon, *Women and the Law of Property*, pp. 141–43.

9. Tindall estimates the ratio between single men and marriageable women as being seven to one (George Tindall, *America, A Narrative History*, 2 vols. [New York: W. W. Norton & Co., 1984], 1:80).

10. Secretary's Office Records, 1696–1704, p. 92, hereafter Middleton/Smith Marriage Jointure, SCDAH.

11. Edmund S. Morgan, *American Slavery, American Freedom* (New York: W. W. Norton & Co., 1975), 165–68.

12. In Virginia the foremost example is Lady Berkeley. In South Carolina the foremost example for the seventeenth century would be Lady Margaret Yeamans, although we have already seen how both Middleton widows reaped benefits from a widowarchy as well.

13. Middleton/Smith Marriage Jointure, SCDAH.

14. This is borne out by peripheral legal documents such as the sale by Mary and Ralph Izard of Charleston Lot 65, which had belonged to Arthur Middleton and descended to Mary following his death. Charleston County, Record Mesne Conveyance Office, Book BB, p. 213 (hereafter RMCO).

15. ". . . to Arthur Middleton Esq: who in his life time, viz: ye 27 April 1684 did make his last will &c and give unto his dearly beloved wife Mary Middleton all his estate real and personal &c. . . ." Secretary's Office Records, 1696–1704, p. 92, SCDAH.

16. Article 42, 17 November 1685 [warrant] in Bartholemew Rivers Carroll, ed., "Lists and Abstracts of Papers in the State Paper Office, London Relating to South Carolina, Done under Authority for the Historical Society of South Carolina in 1857," in South Carolina Historical Society, *Collections of the South Carolina Historical Society*, 5 vols. (Charleston: S. G. Courtney & Co., 1857–97), 1:94.

17. John Stewart to William Dunlop, 20 October 1693, in Mabel L. Webber, ed., "Letters from James Stewart to William Dunlop," *South Carolina Historical Genealogical Magazine* (hereafter *SCHM*) 32 (1931): 171; Langdon Cheves, "Izard of South Carolina," ibid., 2 (1901): 207–8.

18. Secretary's Office Records, 1704–1709, pp. 119–21, SCDAH.

19. Le Jau to SPG Secretary, 1 February 1709, in *The Carolina Chronicle of Dr. Francis Le Jau, 1706–1717*, ed. Frank J. Klingberg (Berkeley: University of California Press, 1956), 66.

20. Plat for "540 acres laid out to Madame Sara Howe, widow of Job Howe . . . 10 December 1706 by Thomas Broughton, Lieutenant Governor." (A legend on the plat establishes that the grant was made 15 December 1706 by Governor Nathaniel Johnson.) McCrady Plats, 8:4233/C/142, RMCO.

21. Le Jau to SPG Secretary, 13 June 1710, in Le Jau, *Carolina Chronicle*, 78.

22. According to family tradition and the documentation of an older son, Edward had been previously married. This wife apparently remained in England while Edward sailed the Atlantic between London and Barbados, since no entries of family births or deaths appear in Barbadian parish records or South Carolina legal records for this period. Edward Middleton's previous marriage is corroborated by the 1703 appearance of Henry Middleton, Edward's son. This Henry Middleton is described in legal documents as Edward's son, an assertion reinforced by his inheritance of a portion of Edward Middleton's estate. BB:212 and T:602, RMCO; Henry Middleton's kinship is indisputably established by a Release and Quitclaim, 3 June 1703, in Miscellaneous Records, 1682–1692, pp. 132–33, SCDAH.

23. Sara Amory Middleton's inheritance of Barbadian properties seems likely because of her father's Barbadian residency prior to his arrival in South Carolina and by the appointment of Othniel Haggatt with power of attorney for Sara Middleton in 1707 in regard to Barbadian properties. Interestingly enough, on the same date Arthur Middleton appointed Richard Middleton as having Sara's power of attorney. Arthur's appointment may have related to properties that he had inherited from his Aunt Hester Browning. Gertrude E. Meredith, *The Descendants of Hugh Amory, 1605–1806* (London: privately printed for author by Chiswick Press, 1901), 28; power of attorney for Sara Mid-

dleton, Power of Attorney [Barbadian Records] 29:115, cited in Beth Bland Engel, *The Middleton Family: Records from Wales, England, Barbados and the Southern States* (Jesup, Ga.: Jesup Sentinel Press, 1972), 232 (hereafter Engel, *Records*).

24. It was not until 1836 that South Carolina statutes required that marriage indentures be recorded. Salmon, *Women and the Law of Property*, 94.

25. This is inferred from a 1736 land grant made solely to Sara Morton Middleton while Arthur Middleton was still alive. Since she was not in a position to bring new settlers to the colony, she evidently spent her own money for the land grant. If so, the only likely source for such an amount would have been her inheritance from John Morton. Marriage settlements for the period have been discovered by Marylynn Salmon in which women were specifically allowed to retain control of specific properties or even entire estates (Salmon, "Women and Property in South Carolina: The Evidence from Marriage Settlements, 1730–1830," *William and Mary Quarterly*, 3rd series, 39 [1982]: 668; hereafter Salmon, "S. C. Women").

26. Royal Grants, 2:430; Colonial Plats, 2:504, SCDAH.

27. Charleston Wills, LL: 626–32, SCDAH.

28. For similar patterns in colonial New York see David E. Narrett, "Men's Wills and Women's Property Rights in Colonial New York," in Ronald Hoffman and Peter J. Albert, eds., *Women in the Age of the American Revolution* (Charlottesville: University of Virginia Press for the U.S. Capitol Historical Society, 1990), 123.

29. In 1745 the Middleton clan consisted of Sara Morton Middleton, her three stepsons—William, Henry, and Thomas—and their emerging families.

30. "Relict of the Hon. Arthur Middleton, Esquire, formerly President of the South Carolina Council in South Carolina, aged 82, worth 50,000 [pounds]," *Gentlemen's Magazine* 35 (1765): 590; *South Carolina Gazette*, 28 September 1765 (hereafter *SCG*).

31. While Sara Fowell Middleton had obtained land grants in her own name (St. James glebe), she did so as a widow rather than a wife.

32. Allen Kulikoff, *Tobacco and Slaves: The Development of Southern Cultures in the Chesapeake, 1680–1800* (Chapel Hill: University of North Carolina Press, 1986), 167.

33. The terms of marriage settlements varied. See Salmon, "S. C. Women," p. 677.

34. Ibid. In the case of the Middletons, there appears to have been a provision specifically naming the oldest son as the heir of any properties.

35. Henry Laurens to William Reeves, 2 October 1768, Henry Laurens Papers, South Carolina Historical Society, Charleston.

36. Though they had at least two daughters, no son was born to the couple.

37. In 1774 Anne Barnwell Middleton would marry Stephen Bull, an established planter but unfortunately as much as a spendthrift as Thomas Middleton.

38. Memorial Books, 7:426 (doc. no. 0030 002 0007 00426 03), SCDAH.

39. Mary W. Middleton epitaph, tomb at Middleton Place, Ashley River Road.

40. Lady Mary, born Mary McKenzie, was the third daughter of the Earl of Cromartie, a prominent Jacobite. She had come to South Carolina in the 1760s as the wife of Thomas Drayton, proprietor of what is now known as Magnolia Gardens.

41. In 1774 John Ainslie's estate was valued at £74,895, of which £65,230 was invested in slaves. Unfortunately for the Middletons, Ainslie's daughter Hanna received the bulk of her father's estate.

42. Charleston District Wills/Ordinary, A (1783–1788), 345–47, SCDAH.

43. Lady Mary Middleton never told her age, even to her closest friends. As she had been born in Scotland apparently no one in South Carolina ever knew.

44. Lady Mary Middleton's will is attached to a petition by Henry Middleton Rutledge to the Charleston County Court dated 4 November 1803, presently located in the SCDAH.

45. See Sylvia R. Frey, *Water from the Rock: Black Resistance in a Revolutionary Age* (Princeton: Princeton University Press, 1991), 107–42.

46. He may well have sold his own as well, but the scarcity of surviving documentation leaves it all a mystery.

47. In 1768, Pierce Butler had planned to elope with young South Carolina heiress Betsy Izard, only to have Miss Izard's trustees discover the plot and send her from Charleston to an isolated plantation. Malcolm Bell, Jr. *Major Butler's Legacy: Five Generations of a Slaveholding Family* (Athens: University of Georgia Press, 1987), 6, 55–58.

48. Mrs. John Bull's bequests predate by fifteen years the previously mentioned bequests by Lady Mary Middleton. Also, the former was a female version of keeping money within the family, whereas Lady Mary's bequest was not to a blood relative but a close friend.

49. Ibid., 55. (Ed.: Perhaps relying on an additional source, Lane's exact words here are that Butler "ripped off his mourning [gloves?] in a fit of rage.")

50. Ibid.

51. Their brothers had both received large slaveholdings from their father in order to become established as planters.

52. The four Middleton males of the fourth generation had a total of five wives, only one of whom predeceased her husband. Thomas Middleton, son of William Middleton married twice: Mary Gibbes, 17 November 1774–December 1775, and Elizabeth Deas, 22 December 1778, who survived him; John Middleton, son of William Middleton, married Frances Motte, 31 July 1783, who survived him; Arthur Middleton married Mary Izard, 19 August 1764, who survived him; Thomas Middleton (4), son of Henry Middleton (3), married Anne Manigault, 1 April 1783, who survived him. The Middleton-Manigault nuptials included a marriage indenture, which probably reflects the insecurity of the times more than personal concerns.

53. *SCG*, 9 September 1764.

54. Cheves, "Izard of South Carolina," 231–32.

55. Charleston Inventories, 1758–1761, 139–51, SCDAH.

56. Although no deeds have survived, Arthur's election to the Commons House of Assembly from these two parishes documents his ownership of property within their boundaries.

57. In 1780, Mary Izard Middleton's brother John Izard apparently foresaw his imminent death. He and his wife having produced no children, Izard left his entire estate to his widow Isabella Hume Izard, but only for life. It was then to pass to Mary Izard Middleton. This inheritance probably constituted the bulk of their late father's estate. Charleston Wills, 1780, Charleston County Courthouse.

58. Charleston County Wills, 32 (1807–1818): 442–50, SCDAH.

59. Marriage Settlements, 3: 425–27, SCDAH.

60. There is some evidence that Mary Izard Middleton attempted to do the same for her daughter Anna Louisa. This daughter married Daniel Blake in what was probably a marriage arranged by her mother. In a deed dated 1797, Mary Izard Middddleton purchased the plantation adjacent to Middleton Place. Though the couple had been long betrothed, the deed stated that the property was acquired "unto said Mary Middleton in trust and to and for the use and behoof of Ann Middleton, the daughter of said Mary Middleton." No mention is made of Daniel Blake, suggesting that the marriage indenture

would place the property out of his control. No additional documents establishing the trust, however, have been located, and by 1785 marriage settlements had to be registered. It seems likely that Mary Izard Middleton also sought to establish her daughter Isabella Johannes Middleton Blake ("Bell," Mrs. Daniel Blake) in a similar fashion: ". . . unto said Mary Middleton in trust and to and for the use and behoof of Ann Middleton, the daughter of said Mary Middleton. . . ." Charleston Deeds, T-6:87, Charleston Mesne Conveyance Office, Charleston County Courthouse.

61. Fate decreed otherwise, for to everyone's surprise Harriott Horry married her cousin Frederick Rutledge. Harriott Horry's brother had married the Marquis de Lafayette's niece and eventually relinquished his title to the plantation, choosing to remain in France for the rest of his life. This allowed Harriott Horry Rutledge and her husband to inherit the home plantation.

62. Frances Motte Middleton (Mrs. John Middleton) was not included within the text due to scarcity of information. The daughter of colonial treasurer Jacob Motte, she had married John Middleton, son of William Middleton.

63. Pierce Butler, the widower of her late husband's first cousin Mary Middleton Butler, proposed, but Frances Motte Middleton declined. Bell, *Major Butler*, 54.

XIV

Investing Widows

Autonomy in a Nascent Capitalist Society

Elizabeth M. Pruden

Women in colonial British America had limited opportunities for economic self-support. Law and tradition circumscribed their choices and limited their options to activities that were extensions of housekeeping skills or artisan responsibilities that women shared with fathers and husbands. Women could ply their domestic skills in the public marketplace as cooks, laundresses, seamstresses, tavern keepers, nurses, and midwives. Other women continued already established family businesses as silversmiths, blacksmiths, coopers, tanners, and newspaper editors. Southern staple crop production required the maintenance and improvement of plantations, an option some women chose as a way to provide for their families.[1]

An examination of the lives of women in colonial South Carolina reveals a heretofore unexamined opportunity that women, primarily widows, utilized to distinct advantage. Earlier studies have examined the occupations that women pursued in order to support themselves and their families, but nothing has been written about the role of women in the profitable mortgage market of the colonies, particularly the substantial mortgage market of South Carolina.[2] Women in South Carolina invested small and large sums of capital that provided a relatively secure and profitable source of income that, in turn, contributed to the burgeoning plantation economy. Who were these women? To whom did they provide capital? What portion of their capital resources did they invest in this way? How did these women employ this system of capital investment to their own benefit?[3]

The accumulation of capital was fundamental to the growth of the South Carolina lowcountry, as well as to individual wealth.[4] Capital was necessary for the accumulation of land and slaves, which were the core of South Carolina's prosperity, a prosperity far exceeding that of the colonies to the north.[5] Settlers striving to succeed as merchants and determined to prosper as planters needed capital to purchase parcels of land and gangs of slaves. This need became particularly evident by the beginning of the eighteenth century when the rice market boomed and planters required more slaves to plant and harvest this staple crop. In addition to borrowing money from England, the people of South Carolina turned to each other. The local economy generated significant amounts of surplus capital for reinvestment in the subsequent development of the region.[6] Although there were mortgage markets in the northern colonies, the small farms to the north demanded far less investment capital than did the plantation economy of South Carolina.

The two primary instruments of capital formation in British North America were bonds and mortgages. Bonds were a formal, legally recorded loan agreement between lender and borrower that involved a general obligation with no collateral put forth by the borrower. The person taking out the loan was obliged to continue payment for the full term of the bond, commonly six months or one year. Under South Carolina law, the penalty for nonpayment of interest or principal was twice the value of the original bond.

A mortgage was also a formal, legally recorded agreement but carried a specific obligation on the part of the borrower to provide collateral worth twice the value of the mortgage. Slaves and personal goods were the most familiar forms of guarantee put up for such loans. The mortgage also had a limited term and carried a penalty for nonpayment of twice the value of the original mortgage.[7]

Women, predominantly widows, in the South Carolina lowcountry lent money, lived off the interest, and participated in the growth of a nascent capital market between 1700 and 1770, a market that was increasingly stable and profitable after the depression of the 1740's. Whereas some of these widows were extremely wealthy, widows and other women with only meager holdings also invested money, at times in nothing more substantial than a single bond extended to a neighbor. Along with the income women earned by their own efforts from the wages of their enslaved laborers, these investments afforded women in South Carolina a degree of economic freedom and autonomy. For some women that meant substantial legacies for children and extended kin. For other women, it meant a choice of whether or not to remarry. For all women, investment in mortgages and bonds meant personal income secured from the public marketplace. Women in South Carolina used these instruments of capital investment within eighteenth-century restrictions. South Carolina embraced English common law, which made clear distinctions between single or widowed and married women. Single and widowed women retained legal property rights similar to men, but once a woman married, her legal identity became one with her husband. *Feme covert* status consigned women to the legal restrictions and protection of marriage.[8] A married woman's legal identity was subsumed by her husband in part so that he could protect his wife from legal suit. But that status also meant women could not sue, own property, or convey property. Wives could legally claim *feme sole* status, with the permission of their husbands, if they wished to function as traders "to recover debts—sell and deliver to any person" goods and merchandise just as if they were sole.[9]

Women did function as merchants in South Carolina, and a recent study indicates that they "operated *de facto* as *feme sole* traders until 1823 when the state's notification requirements were tightened."[10] A *feme sole* could claim the right to convey property and collect debts but she exposed herself to legal suits. Extant records indicate that it was more common for widows than *feme soles* to invest money and manage estates, a reflection of these legal limitations. It was also more common for widows who were facing remarriage than young unmarried women to stipulate premarital agreements to legally protect inheritances, property, wages, and the right to convey property. Women in South Carolina, more than women in any other British mainland colony, entered marriages with antenuptial agreements that protected their property rights.[11]

Women who traveled to or grew up in South Carolina shared some characteristics with their sisters in the northern colonies. Some, arriving as indentured servants or members of extended families, married aspiring planters and fit the profile of "planter's wife." Other women accompanied their merchant, artisan, and seafaring husbands and worked alongside and in the place of absent spouses as "deputy husbands."[12] It was as widows that the women of South Carolina diverged from the experience of women in northern colonies.[13] Whereas widows in other colonies were typically dependent on familial support, widows in South Carolina were less reliant on their sons' mandated provisions and protection. Fathers rarely tied sons' legacies to a widow's support by requiring their sons to support their mothers. It was far more common for men in South Carolina to bequeath "slaves and money . . . more valuable than the dower right to use one-third of the real estate" directly to their widows as a means of "adequate maintenance rather than the entitlement to a particular proportion of the family's property."[14]

This study draws from ongoing research on 327 women who wrote wills in South Carolina between 1670 and 1770.[15] Four hundred and seventeen probate inventories of women's estates during the same period provide evidence for an analysis of investment activity.[16] Due to some overlap of wills and inventories, there are a total of 532 women in this study. Twenty-one percent of these 532 women were involved to some degree in the mortgage and bond markets of South Carolina, a significant percentage when one considers the limited economic opportunities generally available to women in the American colonies.

This essay does not analyze the capital market of colonial South Carolina, but rather how women invested in the market. Although it is yet unclear what percentage of the total capital market women provided, it is unlikely that it was a substantial portion when the entire capital market is assessed. Rather than analyze the aggregate value of women's contributions to the formation of the capital market and plantation economy, an examination of their participation reveals noteworthy facets of colonial society. First, women made available a range of funds to people in their communities, particularly men, who needed limited funds to meet debts or purchase merchandise, slaves, and land. Family members and neighbors could seek financial assistance from women who had ready cash and were interested in investment income. Second, one can ascertain the security of bonds and mortgages in light of the number of women who invested children's legacies in the capital market. Even women who had not invested money on their own behalf trusted the stability of the mortgage market for their children's welfare. Third, the bond and mortgage market was clearly significant in the lives of the women in South Carolina.

Mrs. Elizabeth Buretel, a Charleston widow who died in 1727, made substantial investments in the lowcountry community, illustrating the early participation of women in the capital market of South Carolina.[17] A postmortem inventory of her estate provides the most explicit detail in this study of one woman's investment history. The record begins in 1703, the year after her husband, Pierre, died. Over the next twenty-four years the Widow Buretel lent capital to 110 South Carolina settlers, presumably for the purchase of land and slaves or for mercantile ventures. Mrs. Buretel died intestate, and the only record that remains of her activity is a single probate inventory of investments.[18] It is probable that her executors compiled another inventory of the rest of what must have been a considerable estate, but it no longer exists.

Elizabeth Chintrier Buretel was a Huguenot refugee who arrived in South Carolina sometime between 1684, when she buried a child in La Rochelle, France, and 1687, when her husband became a naturalized citizen of the British colony. Following the Revocation of the Edict of Nantes in 1685, the Buretels fled with their daughter, the sole survivor of several children. Years before his death in 1702, Pierre Buretel was a successful merchant in Charleston and an elder in the Huguenot Church. In 1708 Widow Buretel buried her only daughter, Elizabeth Chastaigner, the mother of three children under the age of twenty-one years. It was the spouses of those three grandchildren who prepared the inventory of Elizabeth Buretel's outstanding bonds in 1727.[19]

The grandchildren of Widow Buretel all married French Huguenots, just as their mother had married A. T. Chastaigner.[20] Shared ethnicity appears to have been an influential factor in the people Widow Buretel chose for investments, for over half of the individuals to whom Widow Buretel loaned money were of French Huguenot extraction. It is possible that the ethnic connections were even more extensive than the records first indicate.[21] Some of these families shared a heritage from France while others had struggled together in Holland and England as refugees. The Atlantic voyage and initial settlement as French-speaking people who created a new identity in an English colony sealed their bond. Elizabeth Buretel's confidence in fellow Huguenots revealed her shrewdness in anticipating the success of those people, many of whom became financial and political leaders in South Carolina.

Widow Buretel was an astute business person who charged interest on her loans and expected regular payments.[22] With the exception of two bonds carrying terms payable in six months, all the rest of the seventy-four bonds in her inventory were to be paid at the end of one year. The short term of the bonds made it possible for Elizabeth Buretel to call bonds for full payment at any time after the term was completed and allowed her to manage her investments carefully. The liquidity of such loans was a particularly attractive feature, yet Widow Buretel kept the seventy-six bonds outstanding; the debtors paid ongoing annual interest rather than meet the final obligation. Leaving them out at interest may have been a matter of convenience that simplified the collection of principal. Perhaps an empathic response to the struggles of fellow refugees predisposed her to leave the loans uncollected. Another scenario could have been her inability to collect the payment of principal because of a bondholder's incapacity to pay. However, if that were frequently the case, one might safely assume that she would have called the loan in and ceased to make similar loans. Instead, Widow Buretel apparently trusted the individuals with whom she contracted, and accepted the bonds as good long-term risks that provided reasonably stable annual income. In that respect, she observed the standard practice of the lowcountry of leaving loans out past the short term of the bond.[23] Almost two-thirds (65 percent) of the bonds she held in 1727 were older than five years. It would appear then that she developed a strategy to ensure a form of annuities over a twenty-year period.

Her investments increased in number over the years, which suggests her growing confidence and ability as a capital investor. She advanced 12 percent of the bonds during the first ten years of her investment experience (1703–1737), 58 percent of the bonds during the next ten years, and 30 percent of the bonds in the last four years of her life. The value of the individual bond obligations over the total span of years ranged from £6.45 to £693.[24] At an interest rate of 10 percent, the legal rate in South Carolina, Widow Buretel drew an income of £1,771.8 a year by 1727.[25] This income is a conservative estimate because it accounts for only outstanding bonds, not additional investments that she may have liquidated before her death. The value of outstanding bonds, including both principal and interest, at the time of her death was £19,330. Her estate included an additional £1,151 in cash.

The absence of any other Buretel records makes it impossible to analyze her shifting investment strategies closely. Local events surely influenced the bond market during the period Buretel provided capital. The most significant event was the Yamassee War. Expansion by settlers in South Carolina halted when various Indian tribes led by the Yamassee Indians attacked colonists in 1715. Before the war, Mrs. Buretel extended eleven loans (15 percent) but that involvement dropped to four loans (5 percent) between 1715 and 1717, the years of the conflict with the Yamassee Indians. Following the treaty and in response to the accelerated growth of South Carolina, Mrs. Buretel made the majority of her loans (61 or 89 percent). In the early years the bonds were infrequent, with some years totally devoid of any bonds. In the period after 1718, she offered bonds annually, with the fewest bonds in any one year numbering four. The average value of the bonds climbed steadily after 1718, from £164 to £404, until two years before her death in 1727, when the average dropped to £233. Again, this is probably an underrepresentation of the actual investment activity. The significant shift in proportions does suggest firmly a notable increase in investment activity after the Yamassee War.

Elizabeth Buretel was not the only woman to participate in the capital market of South Carolina. At least eighty women left probate inventories, dated between 1720 and 1770, that include references to outstanding bonds and mortgages, and an additional five women, from the sample described at the beginning of this essay, appear in South Carolina mortgage records.[26] Russell Menard provides a context for comparison with his analysis of a sample of 305 mortgages from the 1720s to the 1740s in which he identified widows as one occupation or status of mortgagees and mortgagors.

His figures reveal greater activity for secured loans by women at the beginning of the century, which suggests women had greater need for cash funds during early settlement.[27] Single women who traveled to the colony would have been in need of capital for both farming and shopkeeping. A more likely reason for mortgaging property would have been the sudden and critical need for cash because of the death of a husband who left a widow liable for estate debts. The high mortality rates and limited availability of kin at the beginning of the century would have made women more economically vulnerable. Menard's findings do not include women who held bonds, a transaction that was not recorded in the manner of mortgages. The inclusion of bonds would not only alter his figures, but would show a steady involvement of women in the 1740s and 1750s. By this time, women were more inclined to earn money through investments than to purchase land and slaves themselves. Changes in social expectations may have fostered this shift in financial strategy.

Although the wills and probate inventories provide no evidence of

TABLE 14.1

	1710s	1720s	1730s	1740s
Widows as mortgagees	18.2%	8.2%	3.7%	5.3%
Widows as mortgagors	9.1%	2.8%	6.5%	0.0%
	n=33	n=71	n=107	n=94

women who might have mortgaged their property, they do provide revealing information about the women who lent cash for immediate consumption or capital for the development of a plantation culture. They were women of sufficient means that members of their family and community deemed it worthwhile to inventory their possessions.[28] Approximately one-third (31.5 percent) of the women had estates valued near the mean and appear to have been of a "middle wealth" status.[29] One might expect to find a strong representation of widows from the preeminent planter families in this group of capital investors, but that was not the case. Sarah Middleton was by far the wealthiest woman in this company, wealthier than most men in South Carolina. Her inventory, valued at £195,858, placed her among the 23.3 percent of the women classified here as rich.[30] It is important to note that 77 percent of the women who invested capital were not of the elite and wealthy population. The growing if erratic economy of South Carolina ensured an increasingly safe return even for women with little cash to spare. Almost half (45.2 percent) of the women had estates whose value was less than half the mean value of general probated inventories. These conditions suggest meager lives for some women and poverty for others.

As might be expected, women with meager estates owned few or no slaves. Although slaves were the most common investment of the period, these women were inclined to tie up what little capital they had in bonds. Five of the women had possessions in their estates worth less than £500 but invested an average of 46 percent of that value to bonds. Of these five women, only two owned slaves, and each of them owned only one slave. The opportunity to provide cash for varying bond amounts meant women could invest smaller sums than were required for the purchase of a slave. Thus, small amounts they had saved or earned could be invested to earn interest. The speed and ease of liquidity of the smaller loans were an additionally attractive factor. Also, bonds could not run away, become ill and die, or resist supervision.

Wills left by women provide additional evidence of ethnicity, religion, and age that further elucidates the identity and common characteristics of these women. Sixty of the women, or 78 percent, left wills for examination in this study.[31] A surprising 36 percent of the women were affiliated with the

French Huguenot community, which made up only 10 to 15 percent of the general population.[32] This overrepresentation corresponds to the number of Huguenot clients in Elizabeth Buretel's accounts as well. Historian Jon Butler believes that they made up a larger portion of the population of means. Whether as merchants or planters, the Huguenots assimilated quickly and prosperously.[33] Evidently, Huguenot women were more financially enterprising than the English women.

Age is a problematic consideration in a number of ways. Date of birth, age at marriage, or age at childbirth are not available for these women because of the paucity of records for residents of South Carolina. One must infer age based on references the women make in their wills to life cycle events or familiar relationships. At least 96 percent of the women appear to have been widows, but widowhood was not necessarily an indicator of advanced age. Bequests to grandchildren and great-nieces and -nephews are better indicators of age. Fifty-five percent of the women mention such relationships or refer to themselves as advanced in years. To cite one example, Lois Mathews, widowed only three years, made bequests to her daughter, two sons, six grandchildren, and one great-grandson.[34] Less than one-quarter (22.5 percent) of the women refer to minor children, younger children, or unmarried daughters, suggesting they were at an earlier stage of the life cycle. This is still a problematic interpretation because some of the grandmothers were young enough to still bear children while women with young adult children could have been members of the oldest cohort. The remaining 21.5 percent of the wills provide only obscure clues, insufficient for any kind of reliable interpretation.

One additional dilemma remains concerning the age of the women who invested capital. The inventories reveal investment activity at the time of death, but offer no clues about how long the women invested in the bond market or how young they were when they initiated their investments. The evidence suggests that the majority of the women with bonds were widows of advanced years who controlled their own funds and needed to augment their incomes.

Religious affiliation also suggests a community or network in which women found models or precedents of investment activity, as well as individuals seeking investors. Sixteen of the women revealed religious affiliation when they bequeathed property to their churches. Of particular interest are the conditions of the bequests. The majority of the bequests were ongoing investments for the benefit of the churches, a demonstration of the women's patronage for further development of institutionalized religion in their growing communities. The women bequeathed money or profits of property sales to be "put to interest" for the benefit of their ministers or the poor members of their church. Nine of the women were members of the Church of England, six women identified themselves as Dissenters, and one women was Jewish. Martha d'Harriette, Providence Hutchinson, and Ann Peacock all included Anabaptist Minister Oliver Hart in their wills. Both d'Harriette and Hutchinson stipulated that their bequests be "put out . . . to Interest on good Security" so Reverend Hart or his replacement could benefit from the yearly interest in the years to come. Martha d'Harriette made additional bequests of slaves, money, and land to a total of six ministers and the mother of one of the ministers, Dissenters all. Anne Peacock designated her "true and Trusty Friend" Reverend Hart her sole executor.[35] The nine members of the Church of England named four Anglican parishes, one in Charleston and the remaining three in surrounding Berkeley County. Margaret Child left £100 to the Vestry of St. John's to build a new chapel, but if the money was available before construction began, Widow Child stipulated that the money be put out to interest until it was needed. Rather than let the money lie dormant, she intended for it to increase until it was necessary to liquidate the funds.[36] Ann Livingston belonged to St. John's at the same time as Margaret Child, but she stipulated that the interest from her bequest of £200 go to the poor.[37] Charlotte La Tour and Henrietta Jenys belonged to the same church twenty years later. Both left money for the poor but whereas Henrietta put hers out to interest, Charlotte provided funds only if her cousin's family were not in greater need. All these women viewed their investments as instruments of benevolence that supported both church and community into the future.

The wills reveal where 81 percent of the women lived, making it possible to distinguish between town and country residences.[38] Charleston, the largest metropolitan center south of Philadelphia, was home to 42 percent of the women who cited their place of residence in their wills.[39] The close proximity of residences and businesses within an urban setting facilitated investing, as these women regularly encountered neighbors who solicited capital funds for themselves or served as intermediaries for other acquaintances who needed loans.

However, an examination of the women's residential patterns runs contrary to the expected flow of lowcountry capital investments "from the city and mercantile fortunes toward the country and plantation development."[40] Menard's study shows that from one-third to just under one-half of the general investors identified the hinterland as home. The distance from plantations does not seem to have obstructed the investment strategy of women outside Charleston who made up the majority of the women who provided funds. Three-quarters of the rural residences were in Berkeley County, the county that surrounded Charleston, and the remaining one-quarter of the women lived further out in Colleton and Craven counties. Rural residence as a planter or planter's widow probably familiarized women with the need for capital funds for development and expansion.

Among the women with identifiable residential locations, more women with estates below the mean value of probated estates lived away from Charleston. What is not clear is if they lived on land they owned or if they resided on family estates. In either case, small bonds provided some cash in the form of accrued interest.

The wills and inventories provide no information about how often rural women visited friends and family in Charleston, but rural women of wealth customarily visited and even spent part of the year in Charleston. Traveling between town and country may have promoted connections with people who needed capital or provided models who practiced that investment strategy. By the 1750s and 1760s, more of the women with identified residences lived in Charleston than in the earlier period. Impressionistic evidence suggests that widows sold land to move to town or retained family property in Charleston where they lived with fewer slaves and had more options for income than the plantation culture. Whether they lived in town or country, some of the women in this study were personally associated with each other and moved within a close circle.[41]

Whether or not the women had personal relationships with each other, they shared the practice of exercising legal control over their estates. A comparison of inventories of women who wrote wills with women's estate inventories in general reveals a greater activity in the bond market among the women who wrote wills.[42] The higher ratio of involvement for women with wills suggests either that women who wrote wills were more inclined to exercise control over the management of their lives and thus invested capital or that women who invested capital were more inclined to exercise their legal right to write a will so they could control the dissemination of their estates. In either case, women who invested capital in the local economy maintained a degree of legal control in their lives and in the lives of their families and friends. That is not to say that poorer women did not act to control their lives within their limited circumstances. The point is that women, with some resources to invest, frequently relied on legal protocol to protect their investments and family estates.

The women who provided capital could also turn to the court for legal recourse to liquidate loans if borrowers proved too risky. South Carolina Court of Common Pleas judgment rolls for 1703 to 1770 show very little activity on the part of women seeking legal help to recover their investments, although male and female executors alike went to court to settle estates. Gender does not seem to have been a factor that limited access to the courts for this purpose.[43] The investments were secure, and legal action was not necessary to collect interest or principal. When payment of bonds was not forthcoming, women did go into court for settlement.

Elizabeth White, a *feme sole* trader who married Michael Hackett, exercised her legal rights in this manner. It was the standard practice for merchants to extend bonds for promise of payment by planters who needed to borrow against a future harvest. Once the planters gathered and harvested their crops, the merchants could collect on debts. For the three years of 1765 to 1767, Elizabeth White Hackett went into court with her husband to sue for the payment of nine outstanding bonds ranging from £68 to £1,150, the average amount being £374.[44] Mrs. Hackett received additional damages in at least two of the cases, although judgment on the remaining bonds is unclear.

Elizabeth White chose to remarry but many women remained widows, and their investments should be considered as factors that might have influenced their decisions regarding remarriage. Widows who remarried often relinquished their first husband's legacies, an incentive to eschew remarriage for some widows. Women who invested capital in the bond-mortgage market had two considerations to contemplate. Interest from investments might have allowed women a real choice in what otherwise might have been a decision driven by financial needs. Fiscal independence accorded widows a choice to avoid remarriage that was prompted solely by the economic need for food, clothing, and shelter. Second, it would have been necessary to arrange an antenuptial agreement to protect those assets from the *feme covert* status that marriage imposed. For the widows for whom there is detailed information, the average length of widowhood was eight and one-half years, ranging from Mary Dutarque who remained a widow only three-quarters of one year, to Sarah Middleton who was widowed for twenty-eight years.[45] One-quarter of the women were widows for thirteen to fifteen years. Whereas regular interest payments provided supplemental income for some women, these payments constituted the sole income for others, the difference between financial dependence on family members and some degree of autonomy.

Just as widows in South Carolina with ample investments could support themselves by living on earned interest, widows could rely on the labor that slaves provided or the wages that slaves earned. An analysis of the estate inventories reveals an intriguing imbalance between slave ownership and capital investment. Only a small minority of the women (18 percent) owned no slaves yet had an average of 66 percent of their estates dedicated to bond investments. Significantly, all of these women left estates that fell well below the mean value of estates in the general population. In other words, a woman with limited funds could provide capital for small bonds or bonds worth less than the average cost of a slave. The same woman, however, might not be able to afford a slave who would earn income, but she could invest capital that would earn interest.

The absence of slaves in women's wills and inventories raises several questions. Were there other slaves in their homes belonging to someone else? Did they turn to investments because they did not have slaves to provide wages? Were bonds a safer, less risky form of investment? Did the women own slaves at one time and sell them to obtain capital for investment purposes? These questions of motivation cannot be answered because personal memoirs do not exist, but one can speculate about the rationale that prompted the women to turn to capital investments. For some women who eschewed human bondage, capital investments might have posed less of a moral dilemma.

Capital investment was a secure venture, but most of the women with money to invest still relied on slave ownership as their primary source of wealth, and thus relied on the conventional lowcountry form of economic security. The majority of women who did own slaves (82 percent), allotted only an average of 39 percent of their estates to bonds, a striking difference of 27 percent less than nonslaveholding women.

As reflected in table 14.2, the number of bonds and mortgages held by women increased significantly in the 1730s.[46] Multiple small bonds that could be called in quickly during economically strained times, such as the depression of the 1740s, could have been more attractive than ownership of slaves. The increase of the proportion of bonds in estates in the 1750s reflects the participation of women's investments in the growth and gentrification of Charleston and the plantation economy.

Whereas the majority of women who provided capital for bonds were widows, wives provided capital for investment as well. Providence Dennis was a widow who married Ribton Hutchinson in 1733 and predeceased him twenty-three years later.[47] Their antenuptial agreement settled her real property in joint tenancy and allowed Providence the right to manage her own money and to write a will. At one point in their marriage, she even extended capital in the form of a bond to her husband. At the time of her death, she held an estate worth £13,739, 11 percent of which was invested in bonds and 74 percent in slaves.[48] She left little of her estate to her husband and stipulated that he could have the use of her twelve slaves as long as he lived, but could neither sell nor remove them from the province. She legally restricted his control of her slaves, similar to the condition that husbands often placed on their wives. In her will, she bequeathed some of her money directly to various extended kin (as she and Ribton had no children), and directed that

TABLE 14.2
PERCENTAGE OF INVENTORIED ESTATE VALUE
SOUTH CAROLINA WOMEN, 1720–1770
n=30   n=23   n=146   n=153

other funds be invested so that nieces, nephews, and her Anabaptist minister could benefit from the accrued interest.

Women who successfully increased their estates through savvy investments provided that portions of their estates be reinvested for the welfare of their heirs. Other women who themselves did not participate in the capital market recognized the security and success of such a venture. These women often stipulated in their wills that their estates were to be sold and invested, with the interest to go to named heirs and the principal to be available later. Rather than leave an estate in the hands of a guardian, widows with minor children often instructed their executors to invest the estate, using the interest to support their children until they reached the age of majority when the heirs could access the principal. This active management of estates moved women into a public exchange that they believed would sustain their families. Their persistent participation in the capital market strongly suggests that it was profitable and that it enabled women to leave larger estates to their kin, thus strengthening their positions in kin networks.[49]

This public exchange of capital reached beyond kin networks. Elizabeth Buretel's detailed accounts weaves an intricate web that spanned at least sixty years. Benjamin d'Harriette provided £10,000 for his widow, Martha d'Harriette to "put to interest" when he died in 1756 after only two years of marriage.[50] This same Benjamin d'Harriette took a bond worth £550 from Elizabeth Buretel thirty years before, when he first embarked on his career as a merchant in Charleston. He took that loan with Lawrence Dennis, the first husband of Providence Hutchinson who protected her inheritance when she married Ribton Hutchinson. Marianne Godin invested inheritances from her husband, Benjamin Godin, and her father, Isaac Mazcyk, both of whom borrowed capital from Elizabeth Buretel.[51] Sarah Middleton used 19 percent of her sizable estate of £195,858 as investment capital, an estate that she inherited from her husband, Arthur, another recipient of Elizabeth Buretel's investments.

Even though some of these financial relationships were sanguineous or conjugal, it was still incumbent on women to know the financial reputation of the people to whom they made loans. Women relied on these exchanges for income, so it was imperative that they be familiar with the business acumen and reliability of their borrowers. Networks helped protect women by screening potential clients and by helping to collect interest payments. There were no public institutions that organized or regulated the bond market, and most bonds were arranged directly between lender and borrower and rarely through brokers. Some women did rely on brothers and sons to arrange investment while other women made the arrangements themselves. Although the transactions may have been of a private nature they played out in a public arena. Women who decided to parlay their capital in the mortgage market needed to know the other players.

Men understood that market as well, but the evidence indicates that women dedicated larger portions of their estates to capital investments than men. From 1722 to 1762, men invested an average of 16 percent of their estates in capital markets whereas women invested twice as much during the same period.[52] The difference is even more staggering when one looks at the period 1741 to 1762 when men dedicated only 15 percent of their estates while women invested an average of 45 percent of their estates. Women did not participate in the slave and land market as much as they did the investment capital market. Men, who were more involved in developing a plantation economy, borrowed more than they lent and held the balance of their estates in slaves, livestock, and farm equipment. On the other hand, women tended to sell plantations, move into Charleston, and lend capital at 8 to 10 percent. For them, liquidity of assets was an attractive feature of bonds and mortgages. This market had become such a viable alternative that Margaret Adamson, who died in 1742 with an estate valued at only £75, had put out five small bonds worth a total of £31.[53] Martha d'Harriette died in 1760 with an estate valued at £24,621, of which £18,778 or 76 percent of her estate was invested. Each of these women turned to the bond market to invest capital and to secure an annual interest payment. However circumscribed the traditional possibilities for income were, these women recognized and utilized an opportunity developed by the men of Charleston to ensure the expansion of the South Carolina lowcountry.

Who were the people who borrowed capital? Gender was the primary distinction, as many more men than women borrowed money. Mrs. Buretel provided funds to four women and 106 six men. Women appear as borrowers in only 7 percent of the transactions in the larger study of inventories.[54] Planters used the majority of bonds and mortgages to procure or replace the "additional labor, livestock, or tools and machinery absolutely necessary" for daily operations or expansion of plantations.[55] Planters, some of whom were women, required large sums to purchase groups of slaves for plantation labor. Most women tended to buy slaves individually or in pairs rather than in large numbers. Women were more inclined to sell land than to buy it, and so had less need for slave gangs. Most likely those women who borrowed capital did so to buy a single slave, to set up a commercial venture, or to cover debts.

Although there is little information about the women who borrowed funds, Mrs. Buretel's inventory suggests a profile of the men who did so. Thirty-eight percent of these men for whom there is information were planters, merchants, or Indian traders who served at least one term in the general assembly. They were men of means, planters who owned land ranging from 934 to 29,085 acres and who owned from 22 to 2344 slaves.[56] Women loaned money to increasingly prosperous men who became leaders of South Carolina society.

Questions remain. The probate inventories capture one moment in the lives of the women and disclose the number and value of bonds at the time of their deaths. As a result, the inventories reveal the minimum activity of women in the South Carolina capital market. How many women participated in the bond market as a strategy of survival before they wrote a will? How many women intended to increase their own holdings as bequests to their heirs? What does one make of women providing capital for a plantation aristocracy that evolved into an oppressive patriarchy?

The women of South Carolina took advantage of the mortgage and bond market to assure themselves an alternative means of income and to provide annuities in their widowhood. They then converted the additional earnings into legacies for their families and community. A network of women modeled for each other an investment strategy that profited from their encounters in urban Charleston and throughout the plantation low-country. They achieved a level of participation in the economic arena heretofore unexamined and unexpected. These women reached beyond traditional opportunities for income with an innovative spirit and business savvy. In this unique Carolina commercial center, women pursued capital investments more vigorously than men as a strategy of survival and as a method of increasing the property they would bequeath to their heirs. Whether they were women of means or women of only meager estates, they provided the capital that men sought in order to develop a plantation economy.

Notes

1. Julie Matthai, *An Economic History of Women in America: Women's Work, the Sexual Division of Labor, and the Development of Capitalism* (New York: Schocken Books, 1982); Jeanne Boydston, *Home and Work: Housework, Wages, and the Ideology of Labor in the Early Republic* (New York: Oxford University Press, 1990); Julia Cherry Spruill, *Women's Life and Work in the Southern Colonies* (Chapel Hill: University of North Carolina Press, 1938).

2. Laurel Thatcher Ulrich, *Good Wives: Images and Reality in the Lives of Women in Northern New England, 1650–1750* (New York: Alfred A. Knopf, 1982); Ulrich, *A Midwife's Tale: The Life of Martha Ballard, Based on Her Diary* (New York: Vintage Press,

1990); Mary Beth Norton, "The Evolution of White Women's Experience in Early America," *American Historical Review* 89 (1984): 593–616; Spruill, *Women's Life and Work,* passim.

3. The endeavor to research the experience of white women in South Carolina is complicated by the paucity of resources pertaining to women and the absence of studies of probate records of the larger population in general and of men in particular.

4. No one has undertaken an extensive study of the role of capital formation in the expansion of the plantation economy of South Carolina. Clearer information about who invested, how much was invested, and how the loans were used would provide a larger historical context for women's investments. For the purpose of this essay, I borrow William Bentley's definition of capital as that portion of personal wealth "clearly used for business purposes and not for household consumption." William George Bentley, "Wealth and Distribution in Colonial South Carolina" (Ph.D. diss., Georgia State University, 1977), 93.

5. Peter Coclanis states, "For nowhere else in British North America or perhaps in the world for that matter did so sizable a population live so well." Peter Coclanis, *The Shadow of a Dream: Economic Life and Death in the South Carolina Low Country, 1670–1920* (New York: Oxford University Press, 1989), 90. Alice Hanson Jones states that over half of the aggregate private physical wealth of all the colonies on the eve of the Revolution was in the South and that the South was the richest region whether or not slaves or servants were included. This is abundantly evident in Jones's list of the ten wealthiest individuals in the thirteen colonies in 1774 in that nine of those people were from South Carolina. Alice Hanson Jones, *Wealth of a Nation to Be: The American Colonies on the Eve of the Revolution* (New York: Columbia University Press, 1980), 51, 59, 171.

6. Russell R. Menard, "Financing the Lowcountry Export Boom: Capital and Growth in Early South Carolina," *William and Mary Quarterly,* 3d ser., 51 (Oct. 1994): 659–76.

7. Notes, a third type of lending transaction, were short-term agreements for face value, which tended to be informal and were more difficult to enforce. Notes appeared infrequently in the inventories and were for negligible amounts, so are not included in this analysis.

8. William Blackstone, *Commentaries of the Laws of England, 1765,* facsimile of first edition, vol. 1 (Chicago: University of Chicago Press, 1979), 430–33.

9. David McCord, ed., *The Statutes at Large of South Carolina,* vol. 7, *Containing the Acts Relating to Charleston, Courts, Slaves, and Rivers* (Columbia, S.C.: A. S. Johnston, 1840), 187.

10. Mary Parramore, "For Her Sole and Separate Use: *Feme Sole* Trader Status in Early South Carolina" (master's thesis, University of South Carolina, 1991), 5.

11. Marylynn Salmon, *Women and Property in Early America* (Chapel Hill: University of North Carolina Press, 1986), 184; Nancy Cott, "Eighteenth-Century Family and Social Life Revealed in Massachusetts Divorce Records," in *A Heritage of Her Own: Toward a New Social History of American Women,* ed. Cott and Elizabeth H. Pleck (New York: Simon & Schuster, 1979), 124.

12. Lois Carr and Lorena Walsh, "The Planter's Wife: The Experience of White Women in Seventeenth Century Maryland," *William and Mary Quarterly,* 3d ser., 34 (Oct. 1977): 542–71; Ulrich, *Good Wives,* 6–10.

13. Further research may show that widows of South Carolina more closely resemble or portend the widows of Pennsylvania, or "men of business." Lisa Wilson, *Life after*

Death: Widows in Pennsylvania, 1750–1850 (Philadelphia: Temple University Press, 1992), chap. 4.

14. Crowley states, "Fewer than ten percent of the widows in South Carolina were in the passive situation of having maintenance (food, lodging, clothing) provided them, the usual arrangement for widows in rural New England and Pennsylvania." John Crowley, "Family Relations and Inheritance in Early South Carolina," *Histoire Sociale—Social History* 17, no. 33 (May 1984): 44–45n. 50.

15. All of the women testators were white. Nearly 83 percent of the women were widows, 3 percent were unmarried, and 9 percent mentioned their living husbands in their wills. The marital status of the remaining women is unclear. Seventy-three percent of the women mentioned children and 30 percent mentioned grandchildren. Ten percent of the grandmothers designated guardians for their own minor children, an indication of women's generationally extended responsibilities.

16. The 417 inventories represent all of the inventories of women's estates between 1670 and 1767 and a sample of inventories for the final two years of the study, 1768–1770, in South Carolina. The shift from all inclusive to sample reflects a shift in the availability of data. The final years of the study have a more intact set of inventories, so this sample includes only those inventories of women's estates for which there are accompanying wills. These inventories are located in the public records of the South Carolina Department of Archives and History (SCDAH).

17. Inventory of Mrs. Elizabeth Buretel, Records of the Secretary of the Province, vol. F (1727–1729), SCDAH, 94–95.

18. Wills and Miscellaneous Probate Records, vol. 61B, SCDAH, 688.

19. Virginia Gourdin, "Madeleine Chardon, of Tours, Touraine and Her Family," *Transactions of the Huguenot Society of South Carolina* 91 (1986): 102; Gourdin, "Huguenot Genealogy," *Transactions of the Huguenot Society of South Carolina* 93 (1988): 15–17.

20. Gourdin, "Huguenot Genealogy," 16–17.

21. The number may have been even larger than appears, as often French and English immigrants intermarried, so Englishmen may very well have been married to women from the French community.

22. In 1716, she accepted 400 acres and twelve slaves as security for a mortgage that she extended to Peter Robert. Records of the Secretary of the Province, 1714–1717, SCDAH, 328.

23. Russell Menard's analysis of 305 mortgages reveals that, among those mortgages that reveal the arrangements for payment, the average length of time was four and one-half years. Menard, "Financing the Lowcountry Export Boom," 669. Peter Coclanis notes, "It became increasingly common in South Carolina for loans to be carried beyond their due dates so long as the interest was paid." Coclanis, *Shadow of a Dream*, 104.

24. Unless otherwise noted, all monetary values cited here refer to South Carolina currency.

25. The legal interest rate dropped to 8 percent in 1748, where it remained until 1777, Coclanis, *Shadow of a Dream*, 105; John McCusker, *Money and Exchange in Europe and America, 1600–1775: A Handbook* (Chapel Hill: University of North Carolina Press, 1978), 220.

26. The significance of these numbers is still difficult to ascertain. Peter Coclanis's examination of Court of Common Pleas judgment rolls in South Carolina between 1720 and 1737 uncovers a total of 140 bonds, meaning women provided capital for 6.5 percent of the bonds during that period. Coclanis, *Shadow of a Dream*, 105.

27. Menard, "Financing the Lowcountry Export Boom," 670–71.

28. Inventories in South Carolina did not include land, so women who invested bonds and mortgages may well have owned land as well. The absence of land from inventoried property obscures the real value of all estates.

29. William Bentley has calculated the mean estate for the inventories of 2,209 inhabitants of colonial South Carolina between 1722 and 1762. Between 1722 and 1731, 75 percent of the women holding bonds did not achieve the mean value of £681; between 1731 and 1741, 67 percent of the women did not achieve the mean value of £3,164; between 1742 and 1751; 65 percent did not achieve the mean value of £4,608; and between 1752 and 1762, 58 percent did not achieve the mean value of £5,722. Bentley, "Wealth and Distribution in Colonial South Carolina," 104.

30. Seven of the women held bonds or mortgages for whom there are no inventories, so the final value of their estate is not known. To determine the socioeconomic status of these women, I used a mean estate value calculated by William Bentley for the middle wealth, half the mean value for an indication of privation, and twice the mean value for an indication of wealth. Alice Jones suggests a gauge with fixed amounts but those figures do not follow this period and do not allow for inflation during the seventy-year period. I do borrow her terms "middle wealth" and "rich." Jones, *Wealth of a Nation to Be,* 196.

31. Wills were the legal instruments by which wives with antenuptial agreements or widows could exercise control over their estates following their deaths. Within a few days or weeks of death, an interested party, usually the designated executor or primary creditor, could approach the court to file the will or proclaim the death in the event that the individual died intestate. At that time, the court appointed an administrator and charged three individuals to make a "true and perfect inventory of all the 'goods, and chattels, rights and credits' of the deceased." It would appear the intent of the inventories was to protect creditors and family members before claims were settled. Jones, *Wealth of a Nation to Be,* 4–5.

32. Jon Butler, *The Huguenots in America: A Refugee People in New World Society* (Cambridge: Harvard University Press, 1983), 102. The determination of French Huguenot affiliation is based on names and a preponderance of French Huguenot representatives as witnesses, executors, and appraisers of estates. The inclusion of only one such representative was not sufficient to designate a woman as French Huguenot. The selection of numerous witnesses and executors by the testator and the appointment of appraisers by the court reflects women embedded in their ethnic community.

33. Conversation with Jon Butler, 25 Aug. 1994, University of Minnesota.

34. Will of Lois Mathews, 1752, *Wills and Miscellaneous Probate Records, 1671–1868,* vol. 7 (Salt Lake City: Genealogical Society of Utah, 1952), 54–56 (hereafter cited as *WMPR* and GSU, respectively).

35. Will of Providence Hutchinson, 1755, *WMPR,* 7:468–74; will of Martha d'Harriette, 1760, *WMPR,* vol. 8 (GSU), 453–67; will of Ann Peacock, 1768, *WMPR,* vol. 12 (GSU), 472–72.

36. Will of Margaret Child, 1738, *WMPR,* vol. 4 (GSU), 124–25.

37. Will of Ann Livingston, 1732, *WMPR,* vol. 3 (GSU), 43–44.

38. Although 72 percent of the women cite the parish or town in which they resided, the breakdown of numbers provides samples too small for comparison. For that reason, I have used the more collective legal demarcation of county.

39. That means that at least 34 percent of the entire population of female investors lived in an urban setting.

40. Menard, "Financing the Lowcountry Export Boom," 670.

41. For example, Elizabeth Perronneau left £100 for mourning clothes for friend and successful investor Catherine Moody. Elizabeth McGrigor named the husband of investor Elizabeth Harleston the trustee of her daughter's estate. Margaret Child provided funds for Elizabeth Doggett as an investment. Eight other women associated with men listed in Elizabeth Buretel's extensive inventory suggests an intimate awareness of the practice of capital investment. Marianne Godin was married to one recipient of a Buretel bond while Catherine de St. Julian de Malacare and Henrietta Jenys were related to other recipients. Henrietta Jenys and Charlotte La Tour named Henrietta's two brothers as executors of their individual wills, men who had earlier paid interest to Elizabeth Buretel for capital they had borrowed from her. Will of Elizabeth Perroneau, 1767, *WMPR*, vol. 11 (GSU), 166–67; will of Martha McGrigor, 1746, *WMPR*, vol. 6 (GSU), 372–73; inventory of Margaret Child, *Miscellaneous Records of the Secretary of the Province*, vol. 11, SCDAH, 337.

42. The first stage of this study examined all inventories from 1670 to 1767. From 1768 to 1770, only those inventories for which there were accompanying wills were included. That analysis reveals that 21 percent of the women were involved in the bond market. An examination of the remaining women's inventories, from 1768 to 1770, discloses that only 11 percent of the women were involved in the bond market.

43. South Carolina Court of Common Pleas Judgment Rolls, 1703–1790, record group 0151, series 0002, SCDAH.

44. "South Carolina Court of Common Pleas Judgment Rolls." Box 61a, file 54a; box 631, file 274a; box 64a, file 324a; box 65a, files 38a and 45a; box 66a, file 180a; box 67a, file 203a; box 68a, file 308a; box 68b, file 29a; box 71a, file 271a., SCDAH.

45. Will of Mary Dutarque, 1767, *WMPR*, vol. 11 (GSU), 189–90; will of Sarah Middleton, 1765, *WMPR*, vol. 10 (GSU), 740–48.

46. Menard, "Financing the Lowcountry Export Boom," 672.

47. Will of Providence Hutchinson, 1755, *WMPR*, vol. 7 (GSU), 468–76; Walter B. Edgar and N. Louise Bailey, eds., *Biographical Directory of the South Carolina House of Representatives*, vol. 2, *The Commons House of Assembly, 1692–1775* (Columbia: University of South Carolina Press, 1977), 349.

48. Inventory of Providence Hutchinson, 1756, *Miscellaneous Records of the Secretary of the Province*, vol. RR, SCDAH, 443.

49. Further research may reveal the value of estates when the women became widows and began to manage their own legacy, which could then be compared to the value of the estates they bequeathed.

50. Edgar and Bailey, eds., *Biographical Directory*, 193; will of Martha d'Harriette, 1760, *WMPR*, vol. 8 (GSU), 453–67.

51. Will of Marianne Godin, 1752, *WMPR*, vol. 7 (GSU), 357–62.

52. Bentley, "Wealth and Distribution in Colonial South Carolina," 113.

53. Inventory of Margaret Adamson, 1742, *Miscellaneous Records of the Secretary of the Province*, vol. QQ, SCDAH, 229.

54. This number is a minimum indicator at best because so few of the inventories identify the parties who borrowed capital. Only 23.3 percent of the inventories provide names of individuals who borrowed capital, which helps to determine gender.

55. Menard, "Financing the Lowcountry Export Boom," 675.

56. Edgar and Bailey, eds., *Biographical Directory*, passim.

XV

"Adding to the Church Such As Shall Be Saved"

The Growth in Influence of Evangelicalism in Colonial South Carolina, 1740–1775

THOMAS J. LITTLE

Although the high-profile religious controversy in South Carolina between George Whitefield and Alexander Garden has received much attention from historians, the spiritual awakenings that occurred during the middle decades of the eighteenth century have never been explored in any detail, not to mention the impact of vital ideas associated with evangelical religion.[1] This neglect is partly due to the conviction among many historians that, as Samuel S. Hill once put it, "religion in the South before it was the South— rather only a geographical territory of colonies and people until the Revolutionary era—is, in all candor, not very impressive."[2] Probably no less important to this continuing scholarly neglect, however, is the strong reaction that has been mounting against the oversimplified view of the First Great Awakening as a unifying event that swept through the colonies.[3]

If the midcentury evangelical movement in South Carolina did not comprise part of a generalized "great awakening," it is significant nonetheless. For as this essay makes abundantly clear, close examination reveals that it raised a corps of zealous ministers and produced a complex network of churches in the colony from the 1740s through the 1770s, a synergistic process that laid the foundation for a resounding series of revivals in subsequent years. Indeed, on the eve of the American Revolution an alternative religious belief system, subsumed here under the rubric of evangelicalism, was firmly in place, with thousands of converts confessing a vital religious experience.

To many South Carolina promoters of that experience, the interdenominational revival that George Whitefield's ministry precipitated in the early 1740s seemed to portend a new age for the Christian church. Josiah Smith, pastor of the Independent Church in Charleston, for example, wrote, "And now behold! God seems to have revived the ancient Spirit and Doctrines. He is raising up . . . our young men with zeal and courage to stem the Torrent. They have been in *labours more abundant.* They have preached with such *Fire, Assiduity,* and *success;* such a solemn awe have they struck upon their hearers; so unaccountably have they conquered the prejudices of many persons; such deep convictions have their sermons produced; so much have they roused and kindled the zeal of *ministers* and *people; so intrepidly* do they push through all opposition, that my soul overflows with Joy, and my heart is too full to express my Hopes. It looks as if some happy period were opening, to bless the world with another Reformation."[4] Unfortunately for Smith and others who shared his sentiments, there was no new Reformation in South Carolina—at least not immediately—because the thunder of revivalism and the religious fervor that accompanied it subsided after Whitefield departed the colony in 1741. Nevertheless, a number of warmhearted evangelicals of Whitefield's "stamp" sought, as Smith put it, to "clinch the nails" that the "*great master of assemblies* has already fastened."[5]

Many Congregationalists and Presbyterians, both with long histories in the colony, profoundly influenced by Whitefield and inextricably linked to one another, were at the forefront of the effort to carry on the spirit of revivalism. In contrast to the situation in many congregations in the northern colonies, however, there was not an easily discernable split between "Old Light" and "New Light" Congregationalists and "Old Side" and "New Side" Presbyterians in South Carolina, making it rather difficult to distinguish those who stood aloof from the revivalist impulse from those who embraced it.[6] Notwithstanding this fact, the extant data make it possible to identify clearly some individuals who kept evangelicalism pulsating in the colony.

Josiah Smith serves as a case in point. He was born in Charleston in 1704 into one of the most wealthy and influential families in the colony. After matriculating at Harvard, he was ordained in the Congregational ministry in 1726. Subsequently he set out for Bermuda, but after only two years on the island he accepted a pastoral invitation from the members of a Presbyterian church, Cainhoy, located on the Wando River. Smith spent six years there and then became minister of the "White Meeting House" or Independent Church in Charleston in 1734.[7]

For reasons that are not altogether clear—but certainly including his "generous" and widely noted "catholick and Christian Spirit," a metaphor used by contemporaries to connote a capacity for the toleration and acceptance of religious diversity—Smith welcomed Whitefield with open arms and became one of the key players in the South Carolina revival of the early 1740s. He was the first to write in defense of Whitefield in the heated newspaper controversy, traveled with him during his tour of the colony, and was an outspoken advocate of slave proselytization. What is more, in the years following the revival, Smith played an active role in organizing congregations that had been awakened and was himself responsible for several conversions.[8] John Newton (1725–1807), a former slave trader turned prominent British abolitionist and author of the hymn "Amazing Grace," for instance, attributed his eventual conversion to the "excellent and powerful" preaching of Smith, whom he encountered while in Charleston in 1748.[9]

In 1749 Smith suffered a stroke that left him partially paralyzed. Although the affliction prevented him from carrying out his regular ministerial responsibilities, he continued to do what he could to facilitate the spread of experiential religion. Not only did he write and publish numerous "gospel sermons" with the aid of an assistant; he helped to secure an evangelical Presbyterian, James Edmonds, as his successor at the Independent Church in Charleston.[10]

Apparently Edmonds had some initial reservations about ministering to a congregation that was composed mainly of Congregationalists, but George Whitefield, after having "some close talk with Mr. L——, and several of Mr. S[mith]'s congregation," assured him that "all seemed unanimous to give you a call." "I need only observe," Whitefield added, "in the congregation there are many dear children of God. . . . And . . . I hope you will be an happy instrument of . . . adding to the church such as shall be saved." Equally attractive in Whitefield's mind was the fact that there were "several pious ministers of other denominations, who will be glad to keep up a Christian correspondence with you, and strengthen your hands." Ultimately Edmonds accepted the call to minister at the Independent Church, and his initial reservations proved to be unwarranted. He was in fact so successful that the church had to be enlarged.[11]

Other Congregational and Presbyterian ministers, such as John Hutson, were equally successful. Hutson was converted by Whitefield in 1740 and afterwards began to preach on the Bryan family estate where he was employed as a tutor. In 1742 the zealous youth moved to Georgia and became a licentiate at the Bethesda Orphanage; a year later he accepted a call from members of the soon-to-be-formed Stoney Creek Independent Presbyterian Church. Located on a tributary of the Pocataligo River in an area of Prince Williams Parish referred to by contemporaries as "the Indian Land," the Stoney Creek church was founded in June 1743 by Hutson, the Bryans, and other disaffected Anglicans who had been profoundly influenced by Whitefield's evangelical message. After Hutson was ordained by Josiah Smith and John Osgood, another evangelical Independent minister operating in the South Carolina lowcountry, "a day was set apart by the church for fasting and prayer, to settle matters about and to organize the church."[12]

William Hutson remained at the Stoney Creek church until 1756, but then he removed to Charleston, where he died five years later. Before his death, however, Hutson did much to advance experiential religion in the South Carolina lowcountry. Following the example of Whitefield, he visited and preached at numerous Congregational and Presbyterian churches south of Charleston, including Wando Neck, Dorchester, Pon Pon, Beaufort, James Island, and Beech Hill. In addition, he frequented many Baptist congregations in the region.[13]

Hutson's successor at Stoney Creek, Archibald Simpson, also went far in spreading the evangelical ethos in the colony. Simpson was born in Glasgow, Scotland, in 1734. At the age of fourteen and shortly after the death of his brother, the young Scot's "religious impressions deepened." Accordingly he traveled around Glasgow in search of "relief," but the sermons he heard and the services he attended were, in his words, "Christless." Then Simpson came into contact with George Whitefield, who preached "a most beautiful gospel sermon." Afterwards, Simpson spent several days "in the field, in prayer, praise, and reading God's word." It was during this spiritual journey, according to Simpson, that the Holy Spirit descended upon him, filling his heart with "love and joy."[14]

Following this experience, Simpson was admitted to Glasgow College. Upon graduating in 1752 he accepted an invitation from Whitefield to manage the Bethesda Orphanage. Simpson did not remain in Georgia very long, however, for in 1754, less than six months after his arrival in the colony, he moved to South Carolina and was employed as a probationer at the Wilton Presbyterian Church in Colleton County. While here, Whitefield came to see him and demanded to know why he had not fulfilled the terms of their contract. Simpson replied that there were many "hungry souls" in South Carolina and that his "labours" would go far in providing them with spiritual food. Apparently, the explanation did not satisfy Whitefield, because he demanded that Simpson refund the money he had advanced him for his passage, which Simpson did.[15]

This head butting weighed heavily on Simpson's mind, but it did not dampen his enthusiasm for spreading gospel religion. Nor did it permanently fracture his relationship with Whitefield. Indeed, ten years after the incident, during Whitefield's next visit to South Carolina, the two evangelicals smoothed over any differences that might have existed between them. Moreover, Simpson still defended Whitefield, his method of preaching, and his evangelical thrust. While visiting with two Presbyterian ministers in Charleston, both of whom had recently arrived in the colony, for example, Simpson wrote in 1768 that he was "not greatly pleased nor edified with this night's conversation, it being mostly against Mr. Whitefield and ministers of his stamp." "As I felt myself pointed at," he continued, "I thought it my duty to speak freely, and stand up for the preaching warmly and zealously the doctrines of grace, the necessity of regeneration, the Catholic practice of preaching in all pulpits, employing pious ministers of every denomination, and holding occasional communion with all sound Protestants, with all Christians who held of the glorious Head, and both lay and ministerial communion."[16] Attacks on Whitefield, in other words, were attacks on Simpson and the increasing number of other evangelical ministers.

In fact, by the time Simpson penned these remarks, he, like many other ministers of Whitefield's "stamp," had become a fixture in the South Carolina landscape. Originally licensed as a probationer at the Wilton church in 1753, he was ordained two years later as a Presbyterian minister of the Stoney Creek Independent Church, where he remained until his departure from the colony in 1772. Judging from the references in his journal and by the number of families said to have been connected with the church, Simpson had considerable success. In addition to his work at the Stoney Creek church, Simpson traveled throughout the colony to preach. Between 1753 and 1772, in fact, he delivered at least one sermon in every formally organized Presbyterian and Congregational church in the South Carolina lowcountry; he also preached in Georgia and to some backcountry congregations. What is more, Simpson mentioned visiting Baptist, Lutheran, and Anglican churches on several occasions.[17]

For the most part, Simpson seems to have focused his efforts on organized churches that were "vacant" (i.e., without a regular minister), but he also helped to organize a number of incipient congregations. In 1765 and 1766, for instance, he made several trips to Salt Ketcher Creek in Colleton County. "The people of the neighborhood," he wrote, "were originally of the church of England, and had no desire for the preaching of the gospel till two families of the name of Dunham, from the Bethel [Presbyterian] Church, Pon Pon, and another from the same, by the name of Hamilton, moved among them." Afterwards, they "resolved on establishing gospel worship among them, and I commenced to assist them."[18]

As in the lowcountry, vital ministerial activity was increasing in the backcountry in the second half of the eighteenth century, and more than a few Presbyterian ministers, such as William Richardson, eventually decided to locate there. Richardson was born in Egremont, England, in 1729, the youngest son of a comfortable middling family. After attending the University of Glasgow, where he met and became a close associate of Archibald Simpson, Richardson emigrated to Philadelphia in 1750. Traveling south, he was befriended and taken in by the fabled Samuel Davies, a New Light Presbyterian who, according to Donald G. Mathews, "brought the first impulse of Evangelicalism to maturity" in Virginia.[19]

Although little is known about his activities, it is clear that Richardson was a product of that maturation process. In 1759 he informed Simpson that he had been ordained by the Hanover Presbytery as "a missionary to the Cherokee Upper Towns" but had "laid down his mission and accepted an invitation from a people at the Waxhaws, about two hundred miles beyond Charlestown." "The support is indeed less," Simpson remarked, "but the opportunity of usefulness is greater."[20]

Indeed, there were great opportunities in the rapidly expanding South Carolina backcountry, especially in the Waxhaw region below Pinetree Hill where Richardson settled in 1759. By that time, as Robert L. Meriwether has shown, "over a hundred and fifty South Carolina warrants and surveys amounting to thirty thousand acres had been recorded in the Wateree-Catawba valley." Roughly 60 percent of the land had been secured by settlers who identified themselves as coming from Virginia while about 30 percent had been granted to colonists who said they came from Pennsylvania. The remaining 10 percent was occupied by petitioners from Maryland, the Jerseys, North Carolina, and the South Carolina lowcountry. The majority of the 1,200 whites in the region were Scotch-Irish Presbyterians who traveled down the Great Wagon Road. Most blacks, numbering from 200 to 250 in 1760, were country born or Creole slaves.[21]

Thus when Richardson arrived on the scene there was a ready field of action, and it did not take him long to get down to the business at hand. Shortly after settling at the recently formed Waxhaw church, he began to itinerate within a seventy-mile radius, preaching regularly at and helping to organize at least five other Presbyterian churches before 1763—Fairforest, Fishing Creek, Catholic, Purity, and Union. Soon Richardson extended his efforts to the southwest, and by the end of the decade he was laboring as far away as Long Canes, located in present-day Abbeville County. Of course Richardson did not labor alone. Other Presbyterian ministers from the lowcountry frequented the backcountry, and Presbyteries to the north continued to send representatives to "labor among the vacancies in the back parts." Following Richardson's lead they even began to locate in churches above the fall line.[22]

As a result of the efforts of Richardson, Simpson, and other ministers operating in South Carolina, the number of Presbyterian churches rose steadily in the colony between 1740 and 1775, increasing from eight to forty-eight. Elam Potter, a New Englander who visited South Carolina in 1767 and compiled a report on each Presbyterian congregation in the colony, estimated that there were 1,940 families connected with those churches. How many Congregationalists there were in the colony at this time is not clear, but only one Congregational church was established after 1740. However, it seems that all the Congregational and a majority of the

Presbyterian churches in South Carolina had, as Archibald Simpson put it, "gospel religion among them."[23]

Many German and German-Swiss colonists who settled in Amelia, Orangeburg, Purrysburg, Saxe Gotha, and near the confluence of the Saluda and Broad rivers during the middle decades of the eighteenth century also had among them, as one observer in Halle commonly referred to it, *seligmachenden Bible Glauben*, or living Bible faith. About one-quarter to one-third of South Carolina's German-speaking settlers, numbering more than 3,500 in 1760 and constituting roughly 10 percent of the colony's white population, were Reformed (Calvinists), and roughly two-thirds to three-quarters were Lutherans. Most were evangelical pietists who emphasized *Erleuchtung* (illumination or enlightenment of the Holy Spirit), *Empfindung* (feeling or sensation of faith), *Gnadendurchbruch* (piercing through of grace), *Wiedergeburt* (new birth), and *Frommigkeit* (piety). Samuel Urlsperger noted in 1750 for instance that there were "280 souls of Evangelical Lutheran people" living near Congarees while only a handful were *rechtglaubig*, or "orthodox." This was due to the fact that considerably more than one-half of all the German speakers who migrated to the colony came either from the Rhineland, Baden, or Wurtemberg.[24]

The major problem that confronted Reformed and Lutheran settlers in colonial South Carolina was their continued use of the German language. Not only did it prevent them from becoming a major evangelizing force, it also made it extraordinarily difficult to sustain the churches they established formally, for it was nearly impossible to secure a regular supply of German-speaking ministers.[25] But the number of Lutheran and Reformed churches did grow nevertheless, rising from four in 1740 to twenty-one in 1775, as did the influence of evangelicalism, partly due to continuing immigration and partly to lay participation and the establishment of conventicles—what evangelical Lutherans called *collegia pietatis*—for Bible study and prayer.[26]

John Ulrich Giessendanner's life serves as a case in point. Born in Lichtensteig, Switzerland, in 1660 Giessendanner, a goldsmith who sat on the city council, converted to evangelicalism during the pietistic awakenings brought about by Philipp Jakob Spener (1635–1705). In fact, he taught at the Orphan House in Halle and later became an "illuminist," claiming special revelations from God. At age seventy-six he migrated to South Carolina and, after spending some time in Charleston, settled in Orangeburg.[27] Though he was never formally ordained, he became a spiritual leader and unofficial minister.

The old illuminist died in 1738, yet he and other laypersons helped to preserve and encourage the growth of evangelicalism among the German-speaking settlers of South Carolina. Indeed, as W. Richard Fritz has correctly pointed out, "if there was a common denominator" among the German and German-Swiss in the colony, "it was . . . the pervasive pietism of the mass of the settlers as the real expression of their Christianity," an expression that placed "emphasis on the individual and [her or] his inner life," and "supported a voluntaristic approach to religion."[28]

Scores of Baptists shared with a growing number of Lutherans, Reformed, Congregationalists, and Presbyterians a commitment to experiential faith in the decades following 1740. For the first half century of settlement, most Baptists in the colony were Particulars (Calvinistic) who held to the idea of election and closed communion, but in the late 1720s and early 1730s an Arminian or free will General Baptist faction emerged. Over the next few years many Particulars gravitated toward General Baptist sentiments. Yet, in the words of one contemporary, "Mr. Whitefield's coming caused a revival, and many soon joined [the Particulars]." Isaac Chandler, minister of the Ashley River Baptist Church, was the leader of this group and a strong supporter of Whitefield. He worked diligently to keep the revival spirit alive in and around Charleston.[29]

Chandler also did much to spread the evangelical ethos among a group of Welsh Baptists from Newcastle County, Pennsylvania, who had recently secured and settled a large tract in Queensborough Township on the Big Peedee River. In 1743 after several visits to the so-called Welsh Neck settlement, Chandler ordained Philip James, a member of the group and a man of "great spirituality." There was something of a mini-awakening among the Welsh Neck Baptists in the mid-1740s as a result of Chandler's efforts and the subsequent preaching of James. While some of the religious excitement quickly died down, the Peedee area in general and the Welsh Neck church in particular became an important center of Baptist activity in the colony.[30]

Meanwhile, Chandler continued to labor in Charleston and its environs, and gradually he brought many of the General Baptists back into the Particular fold. But he became ill and died in 1749. Many evangelical Baptists believed that after the death of this "worthy gospel minister" there would be a "famine of hearing the word of the Lord." On the same day Chandler was buried, however, Oliver Hart, who proved to be one of the most successful Baptist preachers in the colony, arrived in Charleston to assume the pastorship of that city's First Baptist Church, an event that "was believed to have been directed by a special providence in their favour."[31]

Hart (1723–1795), a native of Pennsylvania, had been reborn in the Baptist faith in 1741 shortly after hearing Whitefield and New Light leaders William and Gilbert Tennent preach. Five years later he was "called by the [Southampton, Pennsylvania,] Church to the Exercise of my Gifts," and "put on trial for the work of the ministry at meetings of preparation or in private meetings that might for that purpose be appointed." After hearing of the "great work to be done in South Carolina," he desired "to go and visit this field." Thus, once officially ordained he sailed south, endeavoring to promote the "salvation of sinners."[32]

With this overall goal in mind Hart established the Charleston Baptist Association in 1751, the second such organization in British America. Initially three churches—Charleston, Ashley River, and Welsh Neck—joined the association with an expressed desire to help bring about "harmony and peaceful progress." It was clearly understood, however, that the "said [Charleston] Baptist Association arrogates no higher title than that of advisory council," and that membership in the organization would by no means undermine the "independence of the constituent congregations."[33]

Delegates to the association met annually, and after two full days of public worship proceeded "to business," which included ordaining ministerial candidates, appointing preachers to fill vacancies, issuing replies to queries received from congregations, and forming committees to aid in settling difficulties within or friction between churches. The association also provided funds for ministerial training—raising £133 for assisting "pious young men" almost immediately—and assumed responsibility for missionary activity.[34] In 1755, to take one example, they employed John Gano to itinerate in the backcountry. Gano, a minister in the Philadelphia Association, wrote in his journal that he endeavored to "proclaim free grace wherever I went."[35]

After its founding in 1751, the Charleston Baptist Association increased in both size and influence, and in general the organization achieved the goals laid down by the founders, namely "harmony and peaceful progress." In several important respects, the success of the association was due to the leadership of Oliver Hart, the motivating force behind it. Indeed, Hart gave direction to the association and set an example that others sought to emulate. As the various entries in his diary make clear, he worked tirelessly to advance evangelicalism in South Carolina, establishing conventicles in Charleston to supplement regular services, traveling throughout the colony to preach, and assisting in the constitution of a number of new churches. Ministers of various persuasions often preached at the First Baptist Church of Charleston, and Hart frequently spoke to Anglican, Presbyterian, and Independent congregations. In 1754, for instance, Richard Clarke, who succeeded Alexander Garden as the rector of St. Philip's Church in Charleston, gave him "free Liberty to speak in my Own way; which Discovered an Catholick Spirit."[36]

In the same year that Hart was first given "free Liberty" to preach at St. Philip's, there was a brief religious awakening in Charleston and surrounding areas. Very little is known about this sudden flurry of enthusiasm, but on one visit to James Island in October Hart recorded in his journal that he baptized ten individuals. He also noted that "several young people" in Charleston "cried out under a sense of sin" and that "many came to consult me with regard to their spiritual state."[37]

One of the apparently numerous individuals converted during the localized but effusive 1754 revival was the celebrated Samuel Stillman (1738–1807), who later became the pastor of the First Baptist Church in Boston. After hearing Hart preach a sermon based on Matthew 1:21, "Thou shalt call his name Jesus, for he shall save his people from their sins," the sixteen-year-old Philadelphian experienced a new birth and was baptized. With the assistance of "a few serious, and well disposed persons" (a group that possessed "a sincere view to promote the interest of vital Religion in their own souls, and, as far as their influence might extend, amongst their fellow creatures in general") Stillman received ministerial training and in 1758 was licensed to preach to the recently awakened on James Island. A year later he was ordained and organized a church there, but before long he was afflicted with a "pulmonary disorder" and was forced to leave the lowcountry, an area notorious for its appallingly unhealthful conditions and high mortality.[38]

Although Stillman abandoned the malignant disease environment of the colony, an increasing number of other evangelicals remained. Called to the Baptist ministry during the middle decades of the eighteenth century, they fanned out in all directions and gradually helped to create a network of evangelical churches. Before 1760 most of those churches were located in a broad arch stretching from the upper reaches of the Peedee River through the lowcountry to Savannah, because Charleston and the Welsh Neck were the two primary centers of Baptist activity. Afterwards, however, new nuclei emerged in the backcountry.

In contrast to most of the Baptist churches below the fall line, where South Carolina's numerous rivers descend from the upland to the lowland, all but a few of those established in the backcountry during the colonial era were Separate Baptist churches. Originally, the Separate Baptist movement erupted out of a rift within the Congregational church in New England during the 1740s. Separate Baptists were rigidly biblicistic, insisting on complete adherence to the plainest sense of the Word of God. They were also spiritual individualists, believing, as one convert wrote, that it was "an absolute Necessity for every Person to act singly, as in the Sight of God only: and this is the Way, under God, to bring the Saints all to worship God sociably, and yet have no Dependence upon one another." This egocentric type of individualism made even the church itself secondary in importance. However, it was by no means unique. In fact, a central European Pietist, not unlike John Giessendanner and those thousands of other German-speaking settlers who were pouring into South Carolina, reported in his autobiography that his father bluntly told him that "whoever wants to get to Heaven, must act as if he were alone."[39] In addition to their strict biblicism and their insistence that religion was fundamentally a personal relationship with God, Separate Baptists, like other evangelicals, felt that all true Christians were responsible for spreading the Word. It was precisely this evangelical zeal that motivated two ardent Separate Baptist brothers-in-law, Shubal Stearns and Daniel Marshall, to carry the Separate Baptist message to the rapidly expanding southern colonial frontier.[40]

Sterns and Marshall first established themselves at Opequon Creek in Berkeley County, Virginia, in 1754, but warfare broke out after a British expeditionary force under General Edward Braddock was almost annihilated by a small French and Indian force a few miles from Ft. Duquesne. Faced with the possibility of attack, many settlers in Berkeley and other frontier counties retreated eastward across the Blue Ridge. Stearns and his party decided to head further south after learning that the Carolina backcountry offered unlimited opportunities for missionary work. They established themselves at Sandy Creek in Orange County, North Carolina, and immediately formed a church in November 1755.[41]

Stearns's "zealous, animating manner" of preaching at Sandy Creek quickly attracted attention, and before long word of the Separate Baptist meetings reached neighboring settlements. In 1756 Stearns, Marshall, and a host of itinerants embarked on an ambitious preaching tour from Sandy Creak all the way to the coast. In their wake, one contemporary noted that "there was no little enthusiasm among their converts." Many soon-to-be-prominent Separate Baptist preachers were converted during or as a result of this tour, including Philip Mulkey, who founded the first Baptist church in the South Carolina upcountry.[42]

Within three years of the Separates' settlement at Sandy Creek at least six churches had been established—Sandy Creek, Abbotts Creek, Deep River, Grassy Creek, New River, and Black River. Reportedly, they had a combined membership of over 900. In 1758 these six churches, despite a jealous regard for local church autonomy and a thinly veiled suspicion of "ecclesiasticism" in denominational organization, voluntarily formed the Sandy Creek Baptist Association. This organization was similar to its counterpart in Charleston and had similar objectives.

Ministerial representatives present at the first Sandy Creek Association meeting devised a plan to spread the revivalistic impulse to surrounding regions, with each preacher apparently having designated areas of responsibility. The strategy worked, for in the late 1750s and early 1760s Separate preachers moved out in all directions. In the process, they established a far-ranging network of regionwide Baptist churches throughout North Carolina, Virginia, South Carolina, and Georgia in the years prior to the American Revolution.[43]

Philip Mulkey (1732–1795) was the first Separate Baptist minister to settle in South Carolina. A native of Halifax County, North Carolina, Mulkey had an transforming religious experience in 1756 that "turned [his] thoughts to Christ, and salvation by him." He was subsequently baptized by Stearns and ordained as a minister to the Deep River Separate Baptist Church. According to one contemporary who heard him preach, Mulkey had "a very sweet voice and a smiling aspect; that voice he manages in such a manner as to make soft impressions on the heart and fetch down tears from the eyes in a mechanical way."[44]

Shortly after the first meeting of the Sandy Creek Association, Mulkey and thirteen other members of the Deep River congregation moved to South Carolina and in 1760 established a church on the Little River, a tributary of the Broad. Membership soon increased, but Mulkey, the thirteen original constituents, and a handful of others relocated in 1762 to an area situated about thirty-five miles northwest, just below the Tyger River. Here the Separates founded the Fairforest Baptist Church, the first of four important Separate nuclei in the South Carolina backcountry that contemporaries referred to as "mother churches." The expansiveness associated with these four "mother churches" was remarkable. Within a decade, for instance, Fairforest had four branches or "daughter churches" in addition to the central congregation.[45]

Less than a year after Philip Mulkey and his group left Deep River, Daniel Marshall and some members of the Abbots Creek church moved into western South Carolina. Eventually, they settled in 1762 near Stephens Creek, a small river running into the Savannah, about ten miles above Augusta, Georgia, establishing a second nucleus or "mother church." With the help of his son Abraham and several associates, Marshall spread the Separate Baptist ethos far and wide. At least six new congregations sprang up, two of which were formally constituted into churches prior to the Revolution.[46]

In addition to those at Fairforest and Stephens Creek, a third Separate Baptist nucleus was established in the fork between the Congaree and Wateree rivers. Both Mulkey and Marshall preached in the region with good results and in 1766 a church was constituted. Among the early converts and constituent members was Joseph Reese, an energetic Baptist "whose natural eloquence, and command of the passions of his hearers was extraordinary." He was ordained as minister of the Congaree church in 1768 by Oliver Hart and Evan Pugh, lowcountry Regulars who, it will be remembered, were quite active proselytizers, just as the Separates were.[47] No less than their counterparts, Reese and his licentiates sought to extend the revivalistic impulse to the inhabitants of the surrounding countryside. Already by 1772 they had succeeded in establishing five branches that were "ripening fast toward churches."[48]

Of course there was a strong tendency over time for these so-called daughter churches to become "mother churches" with branches of their own. But during the period under consideration it appears that only High Hills of Santee, a branch of the Congaree Church, did so, primarily because of spatial and temporal phenomena and the sheer force of one individual personality—Richard Furman (1755–1825). Converted and baptized in 1769, Furman began exhorting, and in almost no time he was ordained as minister of High Hills by Joseph Reese and Evan Pugh. Largely through his efforts, High Hills became an important center of activity; within five years of its constitution the church had established four branches. In contrast to Fairforest, Stephens Creek, and to a considerably lesser extent, Congaree, however, the region in and around High Hills of Santee was more settled and had better transportation facilities. Too, many of the inhabitants had been influenced by the Regular Baptists of the Peedee. These factors certainly contributed to Furman's success and probably help to explain why High Hills was transformed into a "mother church" in such short order.[49]

Three other Baptist churches in the backcountry were organized under the aegis of the Separates but had no clear relationship to the four above-mentioned nuclei. The first, Little River of Broad Church, was established in 1770 where Mulkey and his Deep River followers originally settled while the second, Little River of Saluda, and third, Mine Creek, were established by immigrants from the Upper South, many of whom apparently had been converted by Colonel Samuel Harris, the so-called Apostle of Virginia.[50]

The establishment of Little River of Broad, Little River of Saluda, and Mine Creek, like the four nuclei and their daughter churches, contributed significantly to the growth of the Separate Baptist movement. By 1772 the Separates had a total of 9 churches and 17 branches, according to Morgan Edwards, a representative of the Philadelphia Association who visited the Lower South. As well, roughly 2,250 adults were Separate Baptist adherents, 627 (28 percent) of whom were formal members, representing around 900 families.[51]

While the Separate Baptists were busy establishing themselves in the backcountry, the Particulars, who began calling themselves Regular Baptists with the arrival of the Separates, were proceeding apace in the lowcountry.[52] Oliver Hart, pastor of the First Baptist Church of Charleston, continued to play an important role in the history of the this group during the years preceding the American Revolution. After the 1754 revival, Hart surrounded himself with a host of zealous young licentiates and with their help won scores of converts. They established a number of new Baptist churches and branches throughout the lowcountry as a result.

One branch at Euhaw, located about 50 miles south of the mother church on the road from Charleston to Savannah, emerged as an dynamic center of activity during the late 1750s and early 1760s under the leadership of Francis Pelot. Originally a licentiate of Isaac Chandler, Pelot was ordained by Hart and John Stephens, minister of the gradually expanding Ashley River Baptist Church, in 1752. Although the Euhaw church was technically constituted six years earlier, it was not dismissed from the First Baptist Church of Charleston until Pelot's ordination. At that time a church was constructed and appropriately "it so happened that as soon as the place of worship was finished, Mr. Whitefield came this way, and, as it were, consecrated it by celebrating divine service in it for the first time, Mar. 5, 1751–2."[53]

According to Oliver Hart, Pelot was "a serious, lively Baptist minister and a pious and useful man." Soon after the Euhaw church was established, he set about exhorting in the surrounding area. With the help of Edmund Matthews, who had been converted by Philip Mulkey, Pelot had considerable success, eventually helping to organize three "daughter churches."[54]

Just as Euhaw's influence was spreading, a group of Baptists migrated en masse from Lynches Creek in the Peedee to Coosawhatchie, the region just north of Pelot's church. Several of these Peedee Regulars, together with some members of the Euhaw congregation, began holding biweekly meetings. In 1759 a formal church was constituted by Hart, Pelot, and James Smart, a Virginian who had only recently arrived in the colony. Under the leadership of Smart, the Coosawhatchie church grew steadily. Only four or five years after its initial founding in fact, a daughter congregation emerged on Pipe Creek.[55]

Like High Hills on the Santee, the Separate nucleus discussed above, Coosawhatchie's establishment testifies to the powerful influence exerted by the Welsh Neck church and its numerous branches in the Peedee River Basin. Originally founded by Welsh Baptists from Pennsylvania in 1738, the mother church grew steadily during the middle decades of the eighteenth century, giving rise to at least six daughter congregations. Three of these became important nuclei with established branches of their own.[56]

The growth of these Peedee congregations added greatly to the strength of Regular Baptists in colonial South Carolina. Indeed, both the number of formally constituted Regular churches and the number of arms or branches in the Charleston Association rose steadily between 1750 and 1772. The number of churches more than doubled, increasing from four to ten, and the number of branches jumped from two to sixteen. As the number of churches and branches increased, of course, the number of families connected to and membership in them rose proportionally.[57] In 1772 Morgan Edwards estimated that together, churches in the Charleston Association had some 581 families in connection; therefore, about 1,453 adults were Regular adherents. Almost one-third (423, or 29 percent) of these adults were communicants.[58]

The meaning of these figures for understanding the growth in influence of evangelicalism during the middle decades of the eighteenth century becomes especially salient when considered together with other estimates of congregation formation and church adherence discussed previously. Between 1740 and 1775, the number of established congregations in the denominations considered here (Baptist, Congregational, Lutheran, Presbyterian, and Reformed) multiplied by more than a factor of five, rising from 24 to 134; and Presbyterians and Baptists claimed over 17,000 adherents on the eve of the American Revolution, roughly 14 percent of the white and 35 percent of the total population in 1770.[59] Thus evangelicals emerged as a significant minority, with their churches dotting every settled region of South Carolina.

Even outside observers were impressed with the mounting spiritual energy in the province. Joseph Philmoor, a Wesleyan Methodist, for instance, wrote during his visit to the colony in 1773 that "the Lord is opening my way before me, and will, I trust, give me his blessing." In his journal he mentioned meeting numerous "pious" individuals who were "friendly to the people of God and spiritual religion" as well as zealous preachers, such as "the Rev. Mr. Hart, the Baptist minister, who is not only *sensible*, but truly evangelical, and very devout." The churches in the colony were "wonderfully crowded," teeming with people who were ready "to receive the word with gladness." On one occasion, Philmoor preached in Charleston "to the largest congregation I have seen since I left Virginia." Indeed, "the house was so full it was with the utmost difficulty I could get to the pulpit, and there were hundreds at the outside that could not get in at all." "Greatly comforted by the work of the Lord" and the prevailing "catholik spirit" among all denominations, the young clergyman felt "such freedom of mind in preaching . . . free salvation to sinners, and calling them to Christ just as they are, that they might be saved by grace." His experience led him to the same conclusion drawn by many Carolina commentators: that the "word of the Lord" was being "made effectual for the conversion of sinners and building up the children of Zion."[60]

Joseph Philmoor's perception was not inaccurate, for the picture that emerges from a close examination of the extant data strongly supports the thesis that "gospel religion" became a pervasive and powerful force in colonial South Carolina between 1740 and 1775. Though no paradigmatic "great awakening" set the colony ablaze, thousands were brought into formed congregations, churches were built at a prolific pace, and a growing cadre of committed ministers found their calling in the province. This cumulative expansion opened up the prospect of ever greater religious prosperity in the years ahead, laying the foundation for the subsequent spreading of a vital form of religious belief that gave individuals a new sense of themselves and a new purpose. Despite dislocations during the revolutionary era, the result was such that evangelicalism won almost complete dominance in South Carolina at the turn of the century, when the so-called Great Revival of the early 1800s erupted throughout much of the South.[61] Hence, evangelicals set under way a process in the three and a half decades after 1740 that fundamentally transformed the history of southern religion, "adding to the church such as shall be saved."

Notes

1. Whitefield's visits to Charleston have been the focus of several studies. See, for example, William H. Kenny III, "Alexander Garden and George Whitefield: The Significance of Revivalism in South Carolina, 1738–1741," *South Carolina Historical Magazine* 71 (1970): 1–16; David T. Morgan, Jr., "George Whitefield and the Great Awakening in the Carolinas and Georgia, 1739–1740," *Georgia Historical Quarterly* 54 (1970): 517–39; Morgan, "The Consequences of George Whitefield's Ministry in Georgia and the Carolinas, 1739–1740," *Georgia Historical Quarterly* 55 (1971): 62–82; and Morgan, "The Great Awakening in South Carolina, 1740–1775," *South Atlantic Quarterly* 80 (1971): 595–606. S. Charles Bolton also gives the controversy between Whitefield and Garden considerable attention in his *Southern Anglicanism: The Church of England in Colonial South Carolina* (Westport, Conn., and London: Greenwood Press, 1982), 50–56.

As the editors of a recent book on the subject have correctly stated in their introduction, evangelicalism can be associated with "*biblicism* (a reliance on the Bible as ultimate religious authority), *conversionism* (a stress on the New Birth), *activism* (an energetic, individualistic approach to religious duties and social involvement), and *crucicentrism* (a focus on Christ's redeeming work as the heart of essential Christianity)." See Mark A. Noll, David W. Bebbington, and George A. Rawlyk, eds., *Evangelicalism: Comparative Studies of Popular Protestantism in North America, the British Isles, and Beyond, 1700–1990* (New York and Oxford: Oxford University Press, 1994), 6 (emphasis added).

2. Samuel S. Hill, "A Survey of Southern Religious History," in *Religion in the Southern States: A Historical Study*, ed. Hill (Macon, Ga.: Mercer University Press, 1983), 385.

3. Jon Butler's work precipitated the reaction against earlier interpretations of the Great Awakening. See his "Enthusiasm Described and Decried: The Great Awakening as Interpretive Fiction," *Journal of American History* 69 (1979): 305–25, and *Awash in a Sea of Faith: Christianizing the American People* (Cambridge, Mass., and London: Harvard University Press, 1990), 164–65.

4. Josiah Smith, *The Character, Preaching, &c., of Rev. George Whitefield* (Boston, 1740), 7–8.

5. Importantly, Smith conceived of these nails as vital ideas, "the doctrines [Whitefield] insisted upon and so well established amongst us," made sharp by "the *Pauline* one of justification by faith alone." Ibid., 9.

6. For the Congregationalists in New England, see C. C. Goen, *Revivalism and Separatism in New England, 1740–1800* (New Haven: Yale University Press, 1962), and Edwin Scott Gaustad, *The Great Awakening in New England* (New York: Harper Publishers, 1957). The split within the Presbyterian church may be followed in Leonard J. Trinterud, *The Forming of an American Tradition: A Re-examination of Colonial Presbyterianism* (Philadelphia: Westminster Press, 1949), and Martin E. Lodge, "The Crisis of the Churches in the Middle Colonies, 1720–1750," *Pennsylvania Magazine of History and Biography* 45 (1971): 195–220. George Howe's *History of the Presbyterian Church in South Carolina*, 2 vols. (Columbia, S.C.: Duffie & Chapman, 1870), is still the best denominational history.

7. Howe, *History of the Presbyterian Church*, 1:185, 205.

8. William V. Davis, ed., *George Whitefield's Journals* (Gainesville: Scholar's Facsimilies and Reprints, 1969), 381–83, 397–400, 438–46, 505–9 (hereafter cited as *Whitefield's Journals*); Morgan, "The Consequences of George Whitefield's Ministry in the Carolinas and Georgia"; *South Carolina Gazette*, 26 Jan. 1740 (quotation).

9. John Newton, *An Authentic Narrative of some Particulars in the Life of John Newton* (London, 1764); R. Cecil, *Memoirs of the Rev. John Newton* (London, 1826); and Newton's letters in *The Correspondence of William Cowper*, ed. Thomas Wright, 4 vols. (Oxford, 1904).

10. Several of these sermons were advertised in the *South Carolina Gazette* but apparently none have survived.

11. Howe, *History of the Presbyterian Church*, 1:264.

12. Ibid., 248 (quotations); Alan Gallay, *The Formation of a Planter Elite: Jonathan Bryan and the Southern Colonial Frontier* (Athens: University of Georgia Press, 1989), 8–9 (map), 47.

13. Howe, *History of the Presbyterian Church*, 1:310.

14. Ibid., 1:273–74; Reverend Archibald Simpson, Journals and Sermons, 1748–1784 (South Carolina Historical Society Publications [Microfiche], 51–155–A/B), fiche no. 1 (1748), frames 3, 5–10 (quotations). Hereafter cited as Simpson, *Journals and Sermons*. Simpson's original journal and sermons are in the collections of the Charleston Library Society, Charleston, S.C.

15. Henry Alexander White, *Southern Presbyterian Leaders* (New York, 1911), 86–89; Simpson, *Journals and Sermons*, fiche no. 27 (1754–1756), frames 12–27 (quotations).

16. Quoted in Howe, *History of the Presbyterian Church*, 1:319.

17. Ibid., 273–389; Simpson, *Journals and Sermons*, fiche nos. 27–38 (1754–1772).

18. Simpson, *Journals and Sermons*, fiche nos. 27–9 (1755–1756), frames 45–60, 1–60, 1–29; no. 28 (1755), frame 38–40 (quotations).

19. White, *Southern Presbyterian Leaders*, 90–94; Donald G. Mathews, *Religion in the Old South* (Chicago and London: University of Chicago Press, 1977), 17.

20. Simpson, *Journals and Sermons*, fiche no. 3 (1759), frame 23.

21. Robert L. Meriwether, *The Expansion of South Carolina, 1729–1765* (Kingsport, Tenn.: Southern Publishers Inc., 1940), 136–46, 141 (quotation).

22. Howe, *History of the Presbyterian Church*, 1:285–300, 329–44; "Proceedings of Hanover Presbytery, 1755–1786," typescript, Presbyterian Historical Foundation, Montreat, N.C.

23. Frederick Lewis Weis, *The Colonial Churches and the Colonial Clergy of the Middle and Southern Colonies, 1607–1776* (Lancaster, Mass.: Society of the Descendants of the

Colonial Clergy, 1938); Howe, *History of the Presbyterian Church*, 1:363; Simpson, *Journals and Sermons*, fiche no. 37 (1772), frame 34.

24. The South Carolina Synod of the Lutheran Church in America, *History of the Lutheran Church in South Carolina* (Columbia: The R.L. Bryan Company, 1971), 2–93; Gilbert P. Voigt, "German and German-Swiss Element in South Carolina, 1732–1752," *Bulletin of the University of South Carolina*, no. 133 (1922), 8–33; William J. Hinke, "The Origin of the Reformed Church in South Carolina," *Journal of the Presbyterian Historical Society* 3 (1906), 367–371; Gottfried Dellman Bernheim, *History of the German Settlements and of the Lutheran Church in North and South Carolina* (Philadelphia, 1872), 81–171; Meriwether, *Expansion of South Carolina*, 42–65; Theodore G. Tappert, "The Influence of Pietism in Colonial American Lutheranism," in *Continental Pietism and Early American Christianity*, ed. Ernest Stoeffler (Grand Rapids, Mich.: William B. Eerdmas Publishing Company, 1976), 13–33; James Tanis, "Reformed Pietism in Colonial America," in ibid., 34–73; *Der Ausfuhrlichen Nachrichten von den Saltzburgischen Emigranten, herausgegeben von Samuel Urlsperger* (Halle, 1734–1752) (quotation); and *Amerikanische Ackerwerke Gottes; oder zuverlaessige Nachrichten den Zustand der americanisch englischen und von Salzburgischen Emigranten . . .* (Augsburg, 1754).

25. Samuel Urlsperger reported that Henri Chiffele, a pastor in Purrysburg who was French Swiss, attempted "to speak German occasionally, as best he could." *Ausfuhrlichen Nachrichten*, 1:277.

26. The figures in Weis, *The Colonial Churches and the Colonial Clergy of the Middle and Southern Colonies, 1607–1776*, have been revised upward based on information presented in the South Carolina Synod's *History of the Lutheran Church*, 4–93.

27. William J. Hinke, *Minsters of the German Reformed Congregations in Pennsylvania and Other Colonies in the 18th Century* (n.p.: Historical Commission of the Evangelical and Reformed Church, 1951), 328.

28. South Carolina Synod, *History of the Lutheran Church*, 39.

29. Leah Townsend, *South Carolina Baptists, 1607–1805* (Florence, S.C.: Florence Printing Company, 1935), 1–20; Morgan Edwards, *Materials towards a History of the Baptists, 1772*, prepared for publication by Eve B. Weeks and Mary B. Warren, 2 vols. (Danielsville, Ga.: Heritage Papers, 1984), 2:122 (quotation).

30. Edwards, *Materials*, 2:126–28; Townsend, *South Carolina Baptists*, 61–77, 63n. (quotation).

31. Edwards, *Materials*, 2:125–26; Townsend, *South Carolina Baptists*, 20; Basil Manly, "History of the First Baptist Church from 1683 to 1825," in *Two Centuries of the First Baptist Church of South Carolina, 1683–1883*, ed. H. A. Tupper (Baltimore: R. H. Woodward, 1889), 101–2 (quotations).

32. William G. Whilden, ed., "Extracts from the Diary of Rev. Oliver Hart from a.d.1740 to a.d. 1780," in *Year Book City of Charleston* (1896), 378 (hereafter cited as Hart, "Diary").

33. Wood Furman, *A History of the Charleston Association of Baptist Churches in the State of South-Carolina, with an Appendix containing the Principal Circular Letters to the Churches* (Charleston, 1811), 8–9 (quotations).

34. Ibid., 10–13.

35. Quoted in "Biography of John Gano," in *Southern Light* (Edgefield, S.C.) 1 (Sept. 1856): 323.

36. Townsend, *South Carolina Baptists*, 21–23; Hart, "Diary," 378–401. The quotation is drawn from six unpaginated sheets located at Furman University that are apparently fragments of Hart's original diary (hereafter cited as Hart, "Fragments"). For information on Richard Clarke, see Bolton, *Southern Anglicanism*, 76–77, 95, 118.

37. Hart, "Fragments" (Oct. 1754).

38. Manly, "History of First Baptist Church," 105–6.

39. Ebenezer Frothingham, as quoted by Alan Heimert, *Religion and the American Mind from the Great Awakening to the Revolution* (Cambridge, Mass.: Harvard University Press, 1966), 129; Hemme Hayen, "The Autobiography of a Seventeenth-Century Pietist," trans. and ed. D. E. Bowan and G. M. Burnett, *Downside Review* 87 (1969): 28.

40. Goen, *Revivalism and Separatism in New England*, 296–99; William L. Lumpkin, *Baptist Foundations in the South: Tracing through the Separates the Influence of the Great Awakening, 1754–1787* (Nashville: Broadman Press, 1961), 1–23.

41. Lumpkin, *Baptist Foundations in the South*, 24–32.

42. Ibid., 33–45, 40 (first quotation), 41 (second quotation).

43. Ibid., 46–59.

44. Edwards, *Materials*, 2:140–43 (quotations); J. D. Bailey, *Reverends Philip Mulkey and James Fowler: The Story of the First Baptist Church Planted in Upper South Carolina* (Cowpens, S.C.: Band and White Printers, 1924), 1–16.

45. Vera Smith Spears, *The Fairforest Story: History of the Fairforest (Lower) Baptist Church and Community* (Charlotte, N.C.: Crabtree Press, Inc., 1974), 14–52; Townsend, *South Carolina Baptists*, 125–41; Edwards, *Materials*, 2:139–40. According to a sociologist who has looked closely at the organizational dynamic of the Separate Baptist movement in Virginia, "a mother church can be understood as an organized group whose collective energy was not only directed inward to meet the needs of its own constituency but also outward in an effort to transmit the revival culture." See J. Stephen Kroll-Smith, "Transmitting a Revival Culture: The Organizational Dynamic of the Baptist Movement in Colonial Virginia, 1760–1777," *Journal of Southern History* 50 (1984), 551–68, 560 (quotation).

46. Edwards, *Materials*, 2:143–44, 148–49; Townsend, *South Carolina Baptists*, 158–67.

47. Edwards, *Materials*, 2:145.

48. Ibid., 2:144 (quotation), 149; Townsend, *South Carolina Baptists*, 142–50.

49. Edwards, *Materials*, 2:149–50; Townsend, *South Carolina Baptists*, 150–58.

50. Edwards, *Materials*, 2:147–48; Townsend, *South Carolina Baptists*, 136–39, 148–49.

51. Edwards, *Materials*, 2:119–61.

52. Initially Particular Baptists viewed Separate Baptists as "irreglar," but the two groups quickly worked out a reapproachment.

53. Edwards, *Materials*, 2:130.

54. Ibid., 2:130; Hart, "*Diary*," 380.

55. Edwards, *Materials*, 2:138.

56. Townsend, *South Carolina Baptists*, 61–110.

57. Ibid., 120–21, 124–27, 130–38, 146, 156; Furman, *History of the Charleston Association*, 14–16; Townsend, *South Carolina Baptists*, 20–110.

58. Edwards, *Materials*, 2:120–61.

59. See nn. 23, 26, 51, and 58. A standard multiplier of five was used to calculate church adherence among Baptists and Presbyterians, the only groups for which colonial estimates are available. For population statistics, consult U.S. Bureau of the Census, *Historical Statistics of the United States, Colonial Times to 1970*, 2 vols. (Washington, D.C.: U.S. Government Printing Office, 1975), 2:1168; and John J. McCusker and Russell R. Menard, *The Economy of British America, 1607–1789* (Chapel Hill and London: University of North Carolina Press, 1985), 172.

60. Extensive extracts from Philmoor's journal can be found in Albert M. Shipp, *The*

History of Methodism in South Carolina (Nashville, Tenn.: Southern Methodist Publishing House, 1884), 125–35.

61. John B. Boles interprets the eighteenth-century revivals in Virginia similarly. See his article, "Evangelical Protestantism in the Old South: From Religious Dissent to Cultural Dominance," in *Religion in the South,* ed. Charles Reagan Wilson (Jackson: University of Mississippi Press, 1985), 13–34.

Contributors

Eirlys M. Barker received her initial honors degree in history from the University of Wales, Cardiff, and her M.A. from the University of South Florida, Tampa. She received her Ph.D. in American history from the College of William and Mary in Virginia. Her areas of interest are southern history, ethnohistory, and women in the colonial South. She is currently professor of history at Thomas Nelson Community College, Hampton, Virginia, secretary-treasurer of the North American Association for the Study of Welsh Culture and History, and director of the honors studies program at TNCC.

Meaghan N. Duff is assistant professor of history at Western Kentucky University and adjunct assistant professor of history at Vanderbilt University. Her research interests include Atlantic colonization, New World cartography, and ethnohistory. She is currently revising a manuscript on the social and geographical settlement of colonial South Carolina for publication as a monograph.

S. Max Edelson is assistant professor of history and assistant director of the Program in Carolina Lowcountry and the Atlantic World at the College of Charleston. He has attended Deep Springs College, Cornell University, the University of Oxford, and the Johns Hopkins University. His dissertation, "Planting the Lowcountry: Agricultural Enterprise and Economic Experience in the Lower South, 1695–1785" (1998), examines plantership in colonial South Carolina and Georgia.

Stephen G. Hardy is deputy director for administration at the Maryland Humanities Council in Baltimore, Maryland. His research focuses on the Atlantic economy of the seventeenth and eighteenth centuries, examining how changes in technology, trade, and legal and financial structures influenced the economies of various regions in colonial America. He is currently completing his dissertation on trade and economic growth in the eighteenth-century Chesapeake at the University of Maryland, College Park.

Gary L. Hewitt's scholarly interests focus on comparative colonial experiences and slavery in the Atlantic world. He is presently completing his book "Origins of the Old South," a study of expansion, politics, and ideology in South Carolina and Georgia from 1663–1763. His recent publications include "New Worlds, 1450–1750: An Historian's Perspective on Colonial

History" in *Teaching the Literatures of Early America*, edited by Carla Mulford, and "Virtue and Vegetables: Eliza Lucas Pinckney," in *The Human Tradition in Revolutionary America*, edited by Ian K. Steele and Nancy Rhoden. He teaches at Grinnell College.

G. Winston Lane Jr., received his doctorate in American history from Emory University in 1990. The late author's essay is based on his dissertation, "The Middletons of Eighteenth-Century South Carolina: A Colonial Dynasty, 1678–1787," and was edited for publication by John T. Juricek of Emory University and Rosemary Brana-Shute of the College of Charleston.

Thomas J. Little is assistant professor of history at Emory & Henry College in Virginia. He received his Ph.D. from Rice University in 1995, and is the author of several articles. Currently he is completing a book on the eighteenth-century origins of the Great Revival in South Carolina.

Jennifer Lyle Morgan is assistant professor of history and women's studies at Rutgers University, New Brunswick, New Jersey. She received her Ph.D. in history from Duke University and is currently at work in completing a manuscript on enslaved women in colonial Barbados and South Carolina.

Matthew Mulcahy is assistant professor of history at Loyola College in Baltimore. He received his Ph.D. from the University of Minnesota in 1999. This essay is part of a larger project examining the impact of natural disasters on colonial society in South Carolina, Jamaica, and Barbados from the 1620s to the 1780s.

R. C. Nash has a B.A. from the University of East Anglia, Norwich, England (1972), and a Ph.D. from the University of Cambridge on English eighteenth-century transatlantic trade. He has been a lecturer in economic history at the University of Manchester, England, since 1975. He has published a number of articles in British and American journals on the economic history of South Carolina and Charleston, and other papers on the British Atlantic and European economies in the colonial period.

Robert Olwell received his Ph.D. from Johns Hopkins University in 1991. His first book, *Masters, Slaves, and Subjects: The Culture of Power in the South Carolina Low Country, 1740–1790*, was published by Cornell University Press in 1998. Currently, he is associate professor of history at the University of Texas at Austin.

Edward Pearson is currently assistant professor of history at Franklin and Marshall College in Lancaster, Pennsylvania. He is the author of *Designs against Charleston: The Trial Record of the Denmark Vesey Slave Conspiracy of 1822,* published by the University of North Carolina Press, Chapel Hill, in 1999. He received his Ph.D. from the University of Wisconsin and is currently completing a manuscript tentatively titled "Slaves and Slave Holders in Town and Country: Rural and Urban Culture and Society in Early South Carolina, 1670–1822."

Elizabeth M. Pruden is the associate dean for academic affairs at Wilmington College, in Wilmington, Ohio. She received her B.A. at the College of Mt. St. Joseph and her M.A. and Ph.D. in history at the University of Minnesota. Her research focuses on the multifaceted experiences of white women during settlement and assimilation in the Carolina lowcountry from 1670 to 1770.

William L. Ramsey received his M.A. from Valdosta State University in 1992 and his Ph.D. from Tulane University in 1998. He has published articles in the *Georgia Historical Quarterly,* and his poems have appeared in periodicals such as *Poetry, Poetry Northwest,* and *Hellas.* He is currently an adjunct professor at Tulane University.

Bertrand Van Ruymbeke is associate professor at the University of Toulouse, France. A graduate from the Sorbonne-Nouvelle, he has written extensively on various aspects of the Huguenot diaspora and the Huguenot emigration to colonial South Carolina. He is currently working on a monograph on the Huguenots in Proprietary South Carolina.

Index